Wexford: History and Society

Interdisciplinary Essays
on the History of an Irish County

EDITOR:
Kevin Whelan

ASSOCIATE EDITOR:
William Nolan

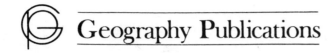

Published in Ireland by
Geography Publications
Kennington Road
Templeogue, Dublin 12

Copyright © 1987

ISBN 0 906602 0 68

First Printing

Design and Typesetting by Graphic Plan, 52 Blackhall Place, Dublin 7.
Printed by Genprint Ltd., Newtown Industrial Estate, Clonshaugh, Dublin 17.
Bound by Museum Bookbindings, Dublin 2

Contents

Preface

This volume on Wexford is the second in the Irish County History series, initiated by the publication of a similar work on Tipperary in 1985. This series utilises a multidisciplinary approach to explore at the county level the dynamics of economic, cultural and social change. By using the county unit (a reasonably small and, in the case of Wexford, homogeneous area), sterile generalisation can be avoided while the integrity and diversity of a living local history can be preserved. The Irish County History series blends the work of local and national scholars: while using the county as a convenient (if arbitrary) frame of reference, the series aims to establish wider regional and national patterns.

Wexford is one of the more comfortable of Irish counties, where the 'doom and gloom' scenarios which dominate many perceptions of the Irish past are not much in evidence, and the theme of stability is a noteworthy one. The county embraces a wealth of diverse cultures, whose interplay has created a trifold division within the county — a Gaelic (later planted) north, a Normanised south and a hybrid middle ground. These internal divisions offer a superb laboratory for indepth analysis of national issues. County Wexford is also heir to a rich historiography and the county is amongst the best documented in the country. For these reasons, this volume of Wexford studies presents a challenging perspective on Ireland.

As a 'Yellowbelly', the production of this volume gives me great pleasure. I have always received encouragement and support in my native county. I have over the years appreciated the many distinctive pleasures of Wexford life — from the wooded Derry valley in my native Johnstown to the sea-girt splendour of Hook Head, from the purple and gold of a Blackstairs sunset to the condensed gloom of the Tomhaggard masshouse, from the decorous clash of the mummer's sticks to the elegant passion of the hurling field, from the age-old discipline of the fields to the hustle and bustle of a Wexford harvest. I have been especially fortunate in being a member of a large family with diverse interests. I would like to thank my mother and father for their constant support over the years. I would also like to thank my brothers (Liam, Patrick, Tom, James and Eamonn) and my sisters (Essie, Eileen, Kathleen, Frances and Rita) for their assistance. In particular, I owe my sister Rita a debt of gratitude for her longstanding stint as chauffeur to an unpredictably mobile brother.

I have also incurred many other debts during the completion of this book. I am grateful to the Wexford Historical Society, the Ui Cinnsealaigh and the New Ross Historical Society for their patronage of my efforts. Tony and Jane O'Malley were warm and kind in providing an evocative painting. Fintan MacPhillips was a tower of strength in the earlier, more tedious aspects of book production. I am also grateful to my colleagues in the National Library, especially Mairín Curran, Eugene Hogan, Gerry Long, Gerry Lyne and Brian MacKenna. Vincent Butler and Conchubhair Ó Fearghail lavished love and affection on their work for the book. Graphic Plan provided painstaking professional and personal commitment to the book, for which I am grateful to Paddy Doyle, Pat Brennan, Bernard Flood, Joe Healy, Paddy Kane, Frank Kearney and Brendan Quigley. I would also like to thank Genprint (especially Charlie O'Reilly) and Museum Bookbindings (especially Colm Moore, Paddy Kavanagh and Gerry Hurley).

In my many forays into Wexford, I have been lucky to meet a plethora of generous hosts. Billy and Noreen Colfer have been constant and gracious hosts and friends and I would like to thank also the following families — Berrys of Drinagh, Brownes of Bigbarn and Millquarter, Cadogans of Newbawn, Doyles of Newbawn and Ardross, Dowlings of Glenmore, Flynns of Drealiestown and Aclare, Foleys of Courthoyle, Hennessys of Wilton, Kanes of Courthoyle, Kehoes of Tenacre, MacDonalds of Newcastle, Mullallys of Glenmore, Murphys of Sweetmount, Mythens of Ballingowan and Coolgreaney, O'Hanrahans of Kilkenny, O'Mahonys of Rathmacknee, Rackards of Killann and Sweetmans of Carrig-on-Bannow. I would also like to thank the following individuals for their help. John Andrews, Jonathan Bell, Paddy Berry, Bernard Browne, Ed Buckmaster, Jack Burtchaell, Jim Byrne, Tom Carroll, Brendan Comiskey, Patrick J. Corish, Bill Crawford, Louis Cullen, Danny Dowling. Benedict Doyle, Jim Doyle, Patricia Fagan, Sheila Foley, Joan Foley, Nicholas Furlong, Michael Gibbons, Jarlath Glynn, Fr Matt Glynn, Tomás Hayes, T. Jones Hughes, Kathleen Keane, Fr Lory Kehoe, Michael Ledwith, Fidelma Maddock, John and Maura Mannion, Jimmy MacDonald, Tom McGrath, Carmel Meehan, Andy Minihan, Seamus Molloy, Grace Mulchrone, Celestine Murphy, Hilary Murphy, Teresa Nolan, Aly O'Brien, Brendán Ó Cíobháin, Tom Power, Dick Roche, Anngret Simms, John Small, Willie Smyth, Geraldine and Mathew Stout, Jim Sutton, Andy Tobin, Brian Trainor, Julian Walton.

Finally, in the world beyond books, I would like to thank the following for their friendship: the two Angelas, the two Annes, Assumpta, Billy, Brian, Cathy, Con, Deirdre, Denis, Éilis, Fidelma, Finbar, Fintan, Geraldine, Grace, Hank, Ita, Jim, Jimmy, John, Johnny, Kate, the three Marys, Mathew, the three Micks, Noreen, Niall, Patricia, the two Peters, Petra, Rose, Shiner, Siobhán, Una, Victor, Vinnie and especially Carmel, Jack and Willie — my longest standing companions. The dedication of the book reflects a wish for the future.

My best thanks must also go to Willie Nolan, an indefatigable publisher and associate editor, whose unremitting attention and concern for quality are evident everywhere in this book. Teresa Nolan handled the administrative details with her usual efficiency, good humour and patience.

List of Abbreviations

Acts privy council, Ire., 1550-71	'Acts of the privy council in Ireland, 1556-1571', ed. J. T. Gilbert, in *H.M.C. rep. 15*, app III (London, 1897)
A.F.M.	*Annala rioghachta Eireann: Annals of the kingdom of Ireland by the Four Masters from the earliest period to the year 1616*, ed. and trans. John O'Donovan (7 vols, Dublin, 1851; reprint, New York, 1966)
Alen's reg.	*Calendar of Archbishop Alen's register, c. 1172-1534; prepared and edited from the original in the united dioceses of Dublin and Glendalough and Kildare,* ed. Charles MacNeill; index by Liam Price (Dublin, 1950)
Anal. Hib.	*Analecta Hibernica, including the reports of the Irish Manuscripts Commission*
Archiv. Hib.	*Archivium Hibernicum; or Irish historical records*
Bks survey & dist., Wexford	*Books of survey and distribution: being abstracts of various surveys and instruments of title,* Public Record Office, Dublin.
Bodl.	Bodleian Library, Oxford
Cal. Carew MSS	*Calendar of Carew manuscripts preserved in the archiepiscopal library at Lambeth, 1515-74* (etc.) 6 vols (London, 1867-73)
Cal. doc. Ire.,	*Calendar of documents relating to Ireland,* ed. H. S. Sweetman and G. F. Handcock 5 vols (London, 1875-86)
Cal. justic. rolls Ire.,	*Calendar of the justiciar rolls of Ireland,* ed. James Mills et al 3 vols (Dublin 1905-)
Cal. pat. rolls Ire., Hen. VIII - Eliz.	*Calendar of patent and close rolls of chancery in Ireland, Henry VIII to 18th Elizabeth,* ed. James Morrin (Dublin, 1861)
Cal. pat. rolls Ire., Jas 1	*Irish patent rolls of James 1: facsimile of the Irish record commissioners' calendar prepared prior to 1830, with foreword by M. C. Griffith (Dublin, 1966)*
Cal. patent and close rolls	*Rotulorum patentium et clausorum cancellariae Hiberniae calendarium,* ed. Edward Tresham (Irish Record Commission, 1828)

Cal. S.P. Ire., 1509-73 [etc.]	*Calendar of the state papers relating to Ireland, 1509-1573* [etc.] (24 vols, London, 1860-1911)
Cantwell, *memorials*	B. Cantwell, *Memorials of the dead: gravestone inscriptions of county Wexford*, 6 vols (Greystones, 1982-87)
Census Ire., 1659	*A census of Ireland circa 1659, with supplementary material from the poll money ordinances (1660-61)*, ed. Séamus Pender (I.M.C., Dublin, 1939)
Civil Survey	*The Civil Survey, A.D. 1654-56*, ed. R. C. Simington, 10 vols (Dublin, 1931-61)
Cloney, *Narrative*	Thomas Cloney, *A narrative of narrative of those transactions in the county of Wexford in which the author was engaged* ... (Dublin, 1832)
Collect. Hib.	*Collectanea Hibernica: sources for Irish history* (Dublin, 1958-)
Comment, Rinucc.	Richard O'Ferrall and Robert O'Connell, *Commentarius Rinuccinianus, de sedis apostolicae legatione ad foederatos Hiberniae catholicos per annos 1645-9*, ed. Rev Stanislaus Kavanagh (I.M.C., 6 vols, Dublin, 1932–49)
Commons Jn. Ire.	*Journals of the house of Commons of the kingdom of Ireland ... 1613-1791*, 28 vols (Dublin, 1753-91); reprinted and continued, 1613-1800, 19 vols (Dublin, 1796-1800)
Cork Hist. Soc. Jn.	*Journal of the Cork Historical and Archaeological Society*
Curtis, *Ire.*	Edmund Curtis, *History of Ireland* (London, 1936; 6th ed. 1950; subsequent reprints)
D.D.A.	Dublin Diocesan Archives
E.H.R.	*English Historical Review* (London, 1886-)
Extents Ir. mon. possessions	*Extents of Irish monastic possessions, 1540-1541, from manuscripts in the Public Record Office, London*, ed. Newport B. White (Dublin, 1943)
Father Luke Wadding	*Father Luke Wadding: commemorative volume*, ed. Franciscan Fathers, Dún Mhuire, Killiney (Dublin, 1957)
Fiants Ire., Hen, VIII	'Calendar to fiants of the reign of Henry VIII ...' [etc.] in *P.R.I. rep. D.K. 7-22* (Dublin, 1875-90)
F.L.J.	*Finn's Leinster Journal*
Flood, *Ferns*	W.H. Grattan Flood, *History of the diocese of Ferns* (Waterford, 1916)
Hay, *History*	E. Hay, *History of the insurrection in the county of Wexford in the year of 1798* (Dublin, 1801)
H.C.	House of Commons
H.M.C. Rep. I (etc.)	*Historical Manuscripts Commission, first (etc.) report* (London, 1870-)
Hore	P. H. Hore, *History of the town and county of Wexford*, (6 vols, London, 1900-11)
Hore, *MSS*	P.H. Hore, *manuscripts*, St. Peter's College, Wexford.
Hughes, *Patentee Officers*	J. L. Hughes, *Patentee Officers in Ireland* (Dublin, 1960)
I.E.R.	*Irish Ecclesiastical Record*
I.F.C.	Irish Folklore Commission, University College Dublin.
I.H.S.	*Irish Historical Studies*
Ir. Ancestor	*Irish Ancestor*
Ir. Econ. Soc. Hist. Jn.	*Journal of the Irish Economic and Social History Society*

Ir. Geneal.	*The Irish Genealogist*
Ir. Geog.	*Irish Geography*
Ir. Sword	*Irish Sword: the journal of the Military History Society of Ireland* (Dublin, [1949]-)
Ir. Theol. Quart.	*The Irish Theological Quarterly*
Jeffreys, *Castles*	W. Jeffreys, *Castles of county Wexford* (Wexford, 1979)
Jn. Ecc. Hist.	*Journal of Eccesiastical History*
Lecky, *Ire.*	W. E. H. Lecky, *History of Ireland in the eighteenth century*, 5 vols (London, 1903)
Lismore papers	*Lismore papers, by Richard Boyle, earl of Cork* [1566-1643], ed. A. B. Grosart (10 vols, London, 1886-8)
Lodge, *Peerage*	M. Archdall (ed.), *J. Lodge: Peerage of Ireland* (Dublin, 1789)
Lords' jn. Ire.	*Journal of the house of lords (of Ireland), 1634-1800*, 8 vols (Dublin, 1779-1800)
Lynch, *De praesulibus Hib.*	John Lynch, *De praesulibus Hiberniae potissimis catholicae religionis in Hibernia, serendae, propagandae, et conservandae authoribus*, ed. J. F. O'Doherty (I.M.C., 2 vols, Dublin, 1944)
N.L.I.	National Library of Ireland
N.M.I.	National Museum of Ireland
N. Munster Antiq. Jn.	*North Munster Antiquarian Journal*
Ormond deeds,	*Calendar of Ormond Deeds, 1172-1350 (etc.),* ed. Edmund Curtis, 6 vols (Dublin 1932-43)
Ormonde MSS	*Calendar of the manuscripts of the marquess of Ormonde, preserved at Kilkenny Castle* (H.M.C., 11 vols, London. 1895-1920: vol. i, H.M.C. rep. 14, app. vii (1895, vol. ii (1899), index to vols, i and ii (1900, new series, vols i-viii (1901-20)
Orpen, *Normans*	G. H. Orpen, *Ireland under the Normans, 1169-1333*, 4 vols (Oxford, 1911-20))
O.S.	*Ordnance Survey of Ireland*
Past	*The Past: the organ of the Ui Ceinnsealaigh Historical Society* (Wexford, 1920-)
P.R.I. rep. D.K. (etc.)	*First (etc.) report of the deputy keeper of the public records in Ireland* (Dublin, 1869-)
Proc. Belfast, Nat. Hist. and Phil. soc.	*Proceedings of the Belfast Natural History and Philosophical Society*
R.D.	Registry of Deeds, Dublin
R.I.A. Proc.	*Proceedings of the Royal Irish Academy*
R.S.A.I. Jn.	*Journal of the Royal Society of Antiquaries of Ireland*
Reg. St. John Baptist, Dublin	*Register of St John Baptist, Dublin,* ed. E. St J. Brooks (Dublin, 1936)
Reg. St. Thomas Dublin	*Register of the Abbey of St Thomas the Martyr, Dublin* ed. J. T. Gilbert (London, 1889)
Shapland Carew Papers	A. K. Longfield (ed), *The Shapland Carew Papers* (Dublin, 1946)
Studia Hib.	*Studia Hibernica*
Studies	*Studies: an Irish quarterly review*
T.C.D.	Library of Trinity College, Dublin
Wex. Hist. Soc. Jn.	*Journal of the Wexford Historical Society*

For Anne

List of Figures

We are grateful to Matthew Stout, Billy Colfer, Patricia Fagan, Catríona O'Sullivan, Vincent Butler, Ed Buckmaster, Conchubhair O'Fearghail, Paddy Doyle and Jack Burtchaell for their assistance and advice.

List of Plates

We are grateful to The Office of Public Works, Tomás Hayes, Bernard Browne, Fr T. C. Butler, the National Library of Ireland, Pádraig Ó Snodaigh, Catríona O Sullivan, Pat O'Connor, Jimmy MacDonald, John T. Browne, and the Kilkenny Archaeological Society for their assistance in assembling these photographs.

Editors and Contributors

Geraldine Stout,
   Co-Director, National Sites and Monuments Record

Séamus de Vál,
   Parish Priest, Oulart, county Wexford

Billy Colfer,
   Teacher, Wexford Town

Richard Roche,
   Journalist, Scar, county Wexford

Henry Goff,
   Teacher, Enniscorthy, county Wexford

Nicholas Furlong,
   Journalist, Drinagh, county Wexford

Rolf Loeber and Magda Stouthamer-Loeber,
   Pittsburgh

Daniel Gahan,
   Assistant Professor, Department of History,
   University of Evansville, Indiana

Patrick J. Corish,
   Professor of History, St. Patrick's College, Maynooth

Louis Cullen,
   Professor of Modern Irish History, Trinity College

Kevin Whelan,
   Assistant Keeper, National Library of Ireland

Sean Cloney,
   Dungulph Castle, Fethard-on-Sea, county Wexford

Bernard Browne,
Millquarter, Old Ross

T. Jones Hughes,
Professor of Geography, University College Dublin

John Mannion,
Associate Professor, Department of Geography, Memorial University, Newfoundland

Bruce Elliott,
Department of Geography, Queens University, Ontario

John Andrews,
Associate Professor of Geography, Trinity College, Dublin

John de Courcy Ireland,
Director, National Maritime Museum, Dún Laoghaire

William Nolan,
Lecturer in Geography, Carysfort College, Dublin.

1 *Geraldine Stout*

Wexford in Prehistory
5000 B.C. to 300 A.D.

In reconstructing a picture of prehistoric life in this region, we must look to the landscape of the south-east and the debris of human activity which litters its surface. The survival of diagnostic artifacts and monuments to the present day has been affected by many factors such as the nature of former and current farming practices in the region, the degree of superstition attached to a site and the presence of active field collectors and museums within the community. Impressive structures such as the megalithic tombs have dominated the landscape for thousands of years and focussed our attention on the burial customs of a Stone Age community. Similarly, a wide range of weapons and tools dating from the Bronze Age have found their way into private and museum collections. Thus, we are better equipped to discuss the technological developments of that period in Wexford. The physical record is illuminating, despite an inherent imbalance and with it we can visualise the type of environment which appealed to prehistoric man in Wexford and determine to a certain degree his sense of territory or place. It also illustrates a growing awareness by settlers in the south-east of their position in relation to Britain and Continental Europe in this period and the strengthening of communications with these areas, which was facilitated by its maritime location.

Wexford is a maritime county situated on the extreme south-east of Ireland bounded to the south by the Atlantic Ocean with St. George's Channel and the Irish Sea to the east. In broad terms its terrain can be divided into three main physiographic regions; an upland zone in the north and north-west comprising part of the Leinster Mountain range; an intermediate zone which is characterised by gently undulating topography in central Wexford, and thirdly, the lowlands which run in a band along the east coast south of Gorey and incorporate the south-east and southern portions of the county (fig. 1.1)[1]. This lowland belt lies below the 120 m contour and is interrupted only by the mountain of Forth, south-west of Wexford town. A fault-line of volcanic rocks runs on a north-east, south-west axis through the centre of the county

1

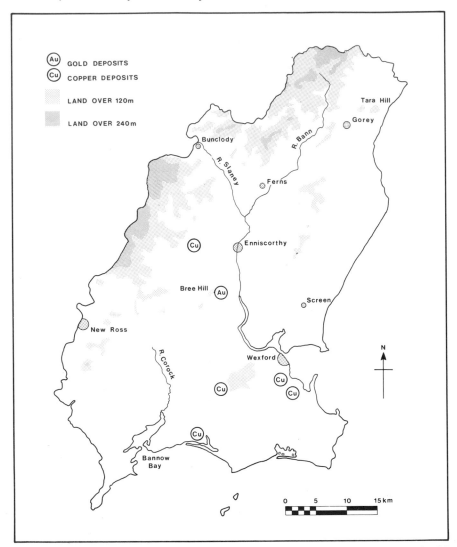

Fig. 1.1: Topographical map of county Wexford showing sources of copper and gold (after Jackson, 1978)

and forms a marked physical feature in the landscape. Wexford is primarily drained by the river Slaney and its tributaries, while the south-western region is drained southwards by the rivers Barrow and Nore. In the main, the soils of the county have developed in glacial material deposited during successive glaciations in the Pleistocene epoch. Generally, these are fertile soils with a wide use range particularly in the extreme west and north-western regions of the county. There are problems with drainage and fertility in the eastern portion of the county including, for example, the heavier, water retentive soils in the north-east, while the Screen area is overlain by morainic sands of low fertility. Included in the mineral wealth of the county is alluvial gold at Bree and low outcrops of copper mineralisation in the south-east.[2]

Mesolithic Wexford

Preliminary evidence indicates that the first Wexford people arrived in the area sometime between c. 5000 b.c. and c. 3000 b.c. A number of diagnostic stone implements have been found in Camolin townland, south of Gorey, and along the eastern coast line between Kilmichael point and Carnsore.[3] These are heavy blades of flint and stone struck from large cores fashioned in a manner similar to implements which were abundant on Mesolithic sites in Larne, county Antrim and termed *Larnian*.[4] The proximity of these find scatters to riverside and shoreline locations hints at the exploitation of numerous resources from a variety of habitats. Fish constituted a significant part of the Mesolithic diet and the rivers in the south-east would have provided ample stock throughout the year.[5] Indeed, a number of Wexford's rivers are associated with runs of spring and summer salmon.[6]

The presence of middens containing an abundance of shell material are a feature of Mesolithic coastal activity. While in Wexford none can be dated with certainty to this period, the midden at Clare Island (pl. i) in Bannow Bay could still prove to be prehistoric in date. The impressive nature of the site and the wealth of animal bone, human skulls and oysters exposed in it's open section was noted as early as 1842.[7] There is also a noticeable absence of pottery and metal from the site.[8] The bone material has been examined by Boxwell, a local doctor and he believed it contained the remains of deer, cattle and pig.[9] This occurrence of cattle bones in the material suggests a post-Mesolithic date for the site, as cattle are known to have been introduced at a later date by Neolithic settlers. There are also indications that some of these mounds have actually accumulated in historic times. This appears to be the case at the Hook peninsula where a group of bone and ivory objects dating from the medieval to the post medieval period may be associated with kitchen middens.[10]

Plate i: The Kitchen midden at Clare Island in Bannow Bay

Despite the absence of diagnostic Mesolithic tools and habitation sites in most of Wexford, it is still possible that Mesolithic activity was more extensive than currently assumed. The lack of systematic field collection and the problems posed by the changes in sea levels in post-glacial times have hindered the study of the period in this part of the country. Because of isostatic uplift in the north-east of Ireland, stable seabed levels meant that this region could be intensively settled. In contrast, the south of Ireland tilted down along a Dublin-Galway axis as the glaciers retreated at the end of the last Ice Age.[11] However, the changes in sea-level in the south may not be as great as previously believed. Woodman has located settlement evidence in Munster especially the area north of the Blackwater, county Cork and in Ballyferriter, county Kerry, which he has dated to c. 4000 b.c.[12]. Here the absence of flint does not appear to have presented a problem to these Mesolithic communities. Excavations at Ballyferriter have produced tools made from a series of locally available volcanic ash and rhyoliths. Based on this Munster experience, field research focussed on the junction of ecological zones could provide evidence for early settlement. It is also possible that early occupation took place on the lowland plain which is now inundated by the sea. An examination of the contouring in the Irish Sea basin suggests that around 7000 b.c. a considerable area of the existing sea floor would have been exposed.[13]

Neolithic Wexford

It is difficult to gauge in detail the process of land clearance (landnam) associated with the development of an economy based on agriculture and its resultant growth in population. Palaeobotanists have identified this landnam phenonemon in the pollen record as indicated by the early appearance of vegetation such as grasses, chickweed, nettle and cereal. Culleton has recently noted the discovery of a landnam record in a peat section on the north side of Forth mountain, which was taking place sometime after c. 4000 b.c.[14] Another significant indication of the intensity of land clearance and early agricultural practice is the occurrence of polished stone axeheads in the county. The production of stone axeheads spanned a period from c. 6500 b.c. to 1500 b.c. in Ireland, so an individual implement cannot be dated more specifically than this unless found in a dateable context. Most are chance finds and conditions suitable for their discovery depend on the intensity of such activities as ploughing, gravel extraction and construction. A recent excavation at McMurroughs Castle, Wexford, exposed a habitation site comprising a pit and hearth, which produced a number of flints and a ground stone axehead.[15] An estimated seventeen stone axeheads and four adzeheads have been recorded for Wexford, a relatively small number when compared with county Meath (142) and county Louth (29).[16] On the basis of surface identification, they appear to have been manufactured from igneous material which is available in the immediate environment of the find spot. They vary greatly in shape and show definite signs of wear (pl. ii). Within this collection, there are a number of potential items of trade or exchange reflecting to a degree the contact

Plate ii: Stone axeheads found at Enniscorthy (A), Mylerspark (B) and Forth Mountain (C)

between Neolithic communities within Ireland. The stone axehead from Garrycullane is a possible porcellanite axehead.[17] This type of stone is very suitable for the manufacture of axeheads and is found in only two places in Ireland, Tievbulliagh on the Antrim coast and Brockley on Rathlin Island. Outside the main concentration of these axeheads in the north-east of Ireland, there is a scattering along the eastern seaboard.[18] The find at Garrycullane would extend that distribution further south-east. There is evidence for very intensive trafficking of these Tievbulliagh axeheads to Scotland and remote parts of England as early as the third millenium B.C. and into the Early Bronze Age.[19] An adze and adzehead of greenstone discovered in a rabbit-burrow at Doonooney has been compared with implements from the Neolithic in Denmark.[20] However it may be more appropriate to look closer to home for parallels, in the light of a more systematic and comprehensive approach being taken of late to the study of stone-axeheads in Ireland.[21]

Included in the Neolithic assemblage of tools are flint implements. A small number of worked flints have been recorded for Cahore, Glascarrig and the Great Saltee Island. Recently, a flint arrowhead was discovered with hazelnut shells and a stone object in Gibberpatrick.[22] Included in the list of recorded flint artifacts are two javelinheads found at Mooresfield townland and Glascarrig.[23] A combination of fine flaking and polishing was used to produce these throwing weapons. An indication of the great value placed on these weapons is demonstrated by their intentional inclusion as grave goods in Neolithic tombs. The main concentration of javelinheads has been discovered in the north-east of Ireland where flint supplies were available, although a number have been discovered in county Wicklow, including one discovered below the cairn of the passage tomb at Baltinglass.[24] The high quality flint necessary to produce such an implement is not readily available in the south-east, so these javelinheads may have been brought in or produced locally with flint transported to the area.

The distribution of the flint and stone artifacts are concentrated around the Slaney estuary (fig. 1.2) and thin out into the uplands. This pattern is further substantiated by the presence of the portal tombs at Newbawn and Bally-brittas, west of the estuary.[25] These simplified tomb types are based on a tripod design with tall portals and lower backstone supporting a massive capstone (pl. iii). The practice of burial in a portal tomb developed within earlier Neolithic communities who are believed to have come from western France in the middle of the fourth millenium b.c. colonising especially north of the

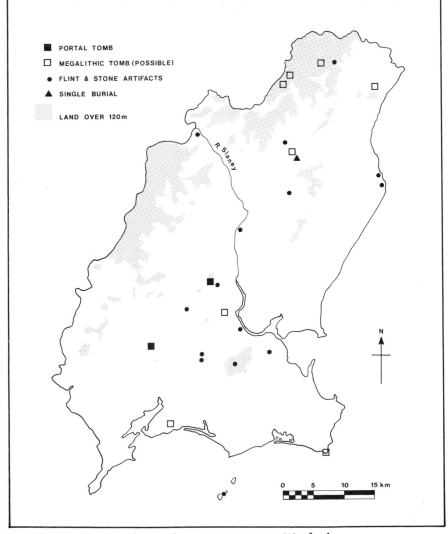

Fig. 1.2: Distribution of Neolithic activity in county Wexford

central plain with extensions as far inland as Tipperary and extending into south-west Scotland and the Isle of Man. These earlier settlers built court-tombs for their dead which comprised a ceremonial court with a passage to this which led into a burial chamber. The development of the portal tomb was accompanied by a further movement of population into east Leinster and settlement along the river valleys. Close connections between both types of tomb builders is exhibited in their pottery, weapons and tools which included leaf end lozenge-shaped arrowheads, javelinheads and hollow-scrapers.[26] The portal tombs at Newbawn and Ballybrittas on the slopes of Bree hill are sited on rolling pastureland along the valleys of the Slaney and a tributary of the Corock and follow the location pattern observed for these tombs generally in the south-east of Ireland and extending across the Irish Sea to Wales and Cornwall.[27]

There is a certain disparity in time between the earliest known *landnam* record at Forth mountain of c. 4000 b.c. and the chronology of the tombs generally recognised in Wexford. There is some evidence to suggest that settlement of tomb builders was more extensive than that represented by the two

Plate iii: The portal tomb at Ballybrittas, on the slopes of Bree Hill

portal tombs previously mentioned. Place-name evidence which may refer to the previous existence of other megalithic tombs in the region includes; the 'Giants Bed' at Ballymore townland; 'Giant's Grave' at Annagh Long and the term 'Druids Altar' which is used with reference to a now destroyed site at Cullenstown near Bannow Bay (appendix 1). This association of megalithic tombs with 'giants' is a popular occurrence. Indeed as early as 1764, it was believed that in the tomb of St Vogues, Carnsore, 'is buried the giant Philim Na thahana ... his grave is still to be seen there, it measures 23 feet in length'.[28] On the ordnance survey six inch for the county, a total of nine potential megalithic tombs have been marked using titles which include 'Cromlech' or 'Dolmen'. Four of these occur on the uplands of north Wexford, namely Baltyfarrell, Aughnamullen, Kilcavan Lower and Ballymore. The site at Barmoney is located west of the Slaney river valley, while St Vogues occurs along the southern coast (fig. 1.2). Cairns such as those at Tara hill and Craan on the summit of Mt Leinster may also enclose megalithic structures.

There is also evidence that in the Neolithic this part of the eastern seaboard was settled by communities practicing a simpler single burial tradition. This custom displays features which are both uniform and exotic in grave goods and ritual, as demonstrated by the excavation at Norrismount.[29] Located on a ridge south of the river Bann, the site comprised a carefully constructed stone box or cist set on a north-east/south-west axis and carefully placed in a round mound. The cist contained the inhumed and partially disarticulated remains of a man in his twenties. Near his head and at his feet were remains of a necked vessel which was decorated with a channel design. This type of pot was also included in six other examples of single burial and has been discovered in court tombs, portal tombs and habitation sites.[30] Kinahan mentions a cist at Cummer containing an urn with a lipped feature which had been opened c. 1877 which is believed to be another example of this single burial tradition.[31] The construction and morphological features of the burial at Norrismount have been compared closely with a recently excavated funerary site at Ashley Park, county Tipperary, which has been dated to the end of the third millenium b.c.[32]

Early Bronze Age Wexford

The introduction of metallurgy into the east of Ireland is attributed to Beaker communities so called after the shape of pot used for domestic purposes and also to accompany their burials. Beaker folk are associated with the establishment of an early dominance in copper and gold working in continental Europe around 2000 B.C. Their appearance in north Britain from continental Europe probably influenced the later adoption of a single burial rite and use of Food Vessel pottery by communities both sides of the Irish Sea. The earliest occurrence of their gold ornaments in Ireland seems to correspond with the beginning of copper and bronze working. Three gold discs of Beaker origin have been discovered in county Wexford, only one example from Kilmuckridge being provenanced. Although these are chance finds, evidence outside this region indicates that these discs probably accompanied individuals to their graves[33] (pl. iv). They are made from fine sheet gold which has been decorated with linear and geometric motifs. Their preference for fine sheet gold work may have stemmed from the properties of gold itself which enabled it to be worked without the necessity of casting. The wheel and cross motif on the Wexford examples compares very well with examples from central Europe

Plate iv: Early Bronze Age gold discs found in county Wexford

where it appears on pin heads. The disc can be seen as a development of the pin head and was permanently attached to a garment using the central pair of perforations. There is evidence for stitching on the circumference of the Kilmuckridge disc.[34] Decoration was applied using a round-pointed wooden stylus which produced a false relief. The borders of the unprovenanced Wexford examples have been elaborated with a ring of dentition and dots have been added to the cross. There is some controversy regarding the source of the ore used in the manufacture of these items but Jackson suggests that this could well have been mined from alluvial sources in Wicklow and Wexford or from a number of shallow surface mines which he has identified in this region.[35]

The type of metal artifacts associated with the Early Bronze Age is limited. Included in the general assemblage are halberds, metal awls, daggers and gold ornaments. However the most commonly produced items were the copper and bronze axeheads. This comes as no surprise in the light of the Neolithic evidence, where one of the most popular artifacts was the stone axehead. Ireland became one of the leading producers of the metal axehead during this period. The production levels observed compare more than favourably with areas such as Iberia and Austria.[36] The present number of axes known in Ireland exceeds 1,017.[37] Many of the types discovered in Wexford are similar in style to axeheads produced in central Europe and north Britain (Appendix II). An examination of these implements demonstrates a development in the method of casting and the desire to produce a more precise, secure and sometimes decorated piece. A hoard of three flat, thin-butted axeheads was discovered on marl under twelve inches of blown sand at Cahore Point (fig. 1.3B).[38] These were probably cast in a stone mould and hammered up on removal to produce a sharp, wide cutting edge. The flanges were also hammered up on the sides to produce a more resistant implement. Because the wedge action of the blade would have tended to split the handle, a stop ridge was later included in the design. This stage in the development is visible on two unprovenanced examples from county Wexford.[39] One of these axeheads is

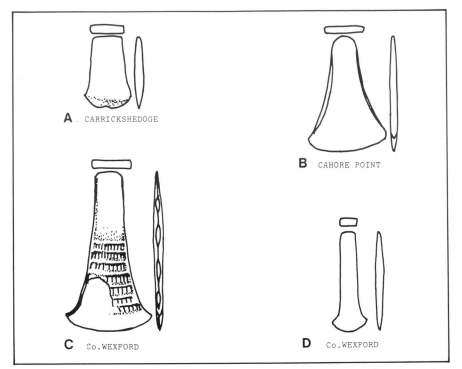

A. CARRICKSHEDOGE

B CAHORE POINT

C Co.WEXFORD

D Co.WEXFORD

Fig. 1.3: **Schematic representation of axehead development in Early Bronze Age Wexford**

decorated on both sides.[40] The ornamentation comprises a series of horizontal ridges which are evenly spaced; the shallow zones between them carry short vertical strokes. The blade had become more curved with short side flanges (fig. 1.3C). A further development involved the side flanges being cast in a clay mould. The axeheads had become reduced in size with a straightening of the sides and an almost semi-circular cutting edge such as the unprovenanced example from Wexford[41] (fig. 1.3D).

An early indication of the organisation of metalworking and the dissemination of its products was highlighted by the discovery of a founder's hoard in a cave in Nash at Carrickshedoge in 1926 (pl. v). This hoard contained three flat copper axes, an ingot and copper cakes, demonstrating a direct link between the smelting process and the final product.[42] As these early hoards rarely exceeded six objects, representing what one man could carry on his back, one could conclude that the first metal workers in Wexford were journeymen.[43] The axes at Nash were a mixture of thin and thick butted examples and were probably cast in a stone mould with a cover. Once cast, the article would have been removed for hammering and smoothing. Many of these early axeheads have side flanges which have been hammered up before clay moulds were introduced and the flanges cast (fig. 1.3A). The ingot in this hoard is probably an unhammered piece which would have been too small to have been dressed for completion. As a final product, it would have been used as a weapon or implement and probably hafted with a wooden shaft. The type of axehead represented in this hoard has been compared with similar axeheads from the south of England which were associated with tanged daggers and used c. 1750 b.c.[44]

In excess of thirty-seven cists or stone boxes have been discovered in county Wexford. These are the most common mode of burial in Early Bronze Age Ireland (appendix III). In 1970, Waddell recorded 637 examples of these burial sites which could be dated to this period.[45] Their general distribution shows a bias towards the eastern half of the country with a notable concentration in the south-east to be seen in Carlow, Kilkenny, Wexford, east Wicklow and south Dublin where they occur on sand and gravel soils. Cist burials are generally chance finds retrieved during land reclamation projects, quarrying or construction works rather than as a result of systematic research. The manner in which they have been discovered in the past has not been conducive to systematic recording, which would allow detailed analysis of the ritual and context of the find. Almost fifty percent of the Wexford sites which appear in the literary record are described as *Kistvaen* with or without urns and no detail of the burial record is included. The most common type of cist in Wexford is the short rectangular cist, a feature of eight sites i.e. Annaghmore

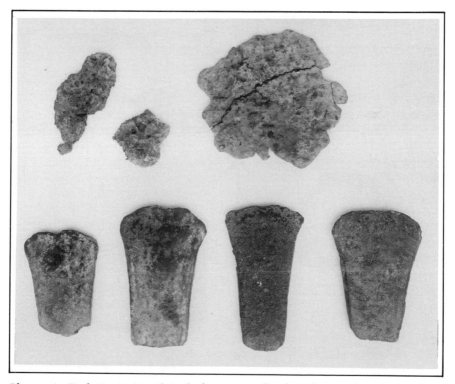

Plate v: An Early Bronze Age hoard of copper axeheads and ingots found at a cave in Carrickshedoge, Nash in 1926

(2), Courtown, Bolinready, Scarawalsh, Oldcourt, Eardownes Great and Ballyduff.[46] Their rectangular plan is sufficiently large to enclose the remains of a skeleton usually in a crouched position. The structure itself can vary in length from 50 cms to 80 cms by 40 cms to 60 cms with a tendency to be orientated east-west, although there are exceptions as at, for example, the cists at Eardownes Great and Ballyduff which were orientated north-east/south-west and north/south respectively. The site at Annaghmore demonstrates their general method of construction (fig. 1.4:1). Four stones were placed on their sides in a pit and roofed with a single capstone. Local shale was generally the stone used. At Bolinready, the side stones were further supported by packing stones (fig. 1.4:2). A number of smaller capstones were used to roof this structure. In some cases dry walling is partly used to build up the sides of the cist, as at Ballyduff and Scarawalsh (fig. 1.4:3). The cist at Ballyduff was floored with slabs (fig. 1.4:3).

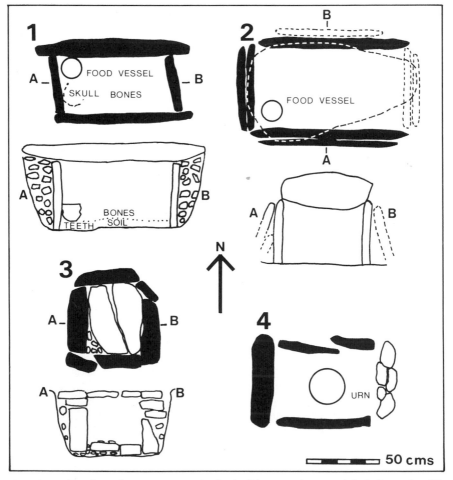

Fig. 1.4: Cist burials in county Wexford: (1) Annaghmore, (2) Bolinready, (3) Ballyduff, (4) Scarawalsh.

The lack of detailed recording makes it very difficult to discuss in any great detail the ritual and grave goods associated with these burials. From the literature we know that a total of thirty cists did contain pottery vessels. The occurrence of an 'urn' is listed in twenty-three examples but the type remains unidentified. In at least thirteen cases, a Food Vessel is included in the grave find (pl. vi). Bowl Food Vessels appear to be as frequent as the Vase form. Both appear to be represented at Knockaskeagh.[47] There were two Food Vessels at

Plate vi: One of two Food Vessels found in cists under a mound in the townland of Ballykale

Kilmuckridge.[48] Cinerary urns which are distinguished from Food Vessels by their larger size are usually found inverted over cremated remains in a pit; however at Oldcourt, Misterin and Scarawalsh, they were found in cists. An enlarged Food Vessel Urn was found in a short cist at Oldcourt and in a cist at Misterin.[49] The cemetery at Scarawalsh contained the only confirmed occurrence of an Encrusted Urn in a cist.[50] There are three recorded occurences of Pygmy Cups with these cist burials.[51] It is also possible that two of these pots were contained in urns with cremated remains at the cemetery in Loggan Upper.[52] Although Pygmy Cups are generally believed to be a miniature accompanying vessel, a pair of these pots at Misterin contained the cremated remains within the cist. The only occurrence of a non-pottery find was a faience bead found with a Vase Food Vessel in the Ballyduff cist.

Where there is evidence for a burial, cremation is twice as frequent as inhumation. Although it is generally believed that we are dealing with a single burial tradition, there are two incidences of multiple burial, at Annaghmore and Ballyduff. At Annaghmore, a child was the first to be buried being later disturbed by the burial of an adult. Also at Ballyduff the traces of the funeral pyre and the cremated remains of two young adults were enclosed within the cist with the Vase Food Vessel set into the south-west corner. This layer produced the faience bead. Where single inhumations have been discovered, they are usually crouched with the Food Vessel at their head, e.g. Annaghmore.

The burials in four cases formed a cemetery. This can be flat and unmarked or in the form of a cemetery mound, which incorporates the cist burials within an earthwork. These cemeteries can contain both cremations and inhumations. The cemetery of Scarawalsh was unique in a number of ways, including the fact that it contained cremations only.[53] At Cummer, there were three cists in a row, all containing urns and Pygmy Cups.[54] The mound at Loggan Upper was a focus for successive burial over a long period of time. It cannot be determined whether or not the actual mound incorporated burials but Westropp noted the occurrence of three urns enclosed in cists near the south-east section of the rampart; about 274 m to the west there was a group of cists near a hollow with human bones and,not far away, were two more urns with ashes and smaller vessels inside.[55] Killincooly More exhibits the same features indicating a similar continuity of place. These sites continued to be a focus for burial despite the various changes in burial ritual. This would imply relatively continuous settlement in the immediate environs. What is difficult to determine is the extent to which we are witnessing a stable population group which is open to ideological changes or the intermittent movement of communities with different traditions into these regions.

The cist burials are mainly concentrated above the 200 foot (61 m) contour in north Wexford with the main distribution centred on the Annagh Hills (fig. 1.5). A second concentration runs in a band on a north-east/south-west axis through the centre of Wexford which corresponds dramatically with a fault line of volcanic rocks. The vast majority of metal artifacts have been discovered along this corridor. This would strengthen the view that we are dealing with a settlement pattern focused in this area in the Bronze Age. The distribution thins out south of New Ross with outliers at Eardownes Great and Shelmalier Commons. There are clusters around Adamstown and Kilmuckridge. The general sparsity of sites on the sands and gravels of the Screen area is exceptional for this monument type. This could be due to the poor state of preservation resulting from intensive tillage. These sands are also much less fertile than the sands and gravels of the central plain.[56]

Amongst the many unidentified 'urns' recorded in the county, eleven Cinerary Urns have been discovered associated with cremation in a pit (appendix III). They were designed to contain the burial remains rather than merely to accompany them.[57] The Collared Urn type was associated with three pit burials in a flat cemetery at Scarawalsh.[58] It was also found in an isolated pit burial at Newtown.[59] The decoration on these pots is confined to the collar. An Encrusted Urn from Ramsfort Park and one from the cemetery at Scarawalsh are distinguished by their plastic form of decoration which is applied in strips and blobs, using a limited range of motifs. Overall decoration is the norm.[60] The urn at Ramsfort Park has a distinct neck emphasised by the use of cordoned decoration.[61] This necked form is peculiar to Enlarged Food Vessel Urns from Ballyvelig and Ballygillistown.[62] In form and decoration, they are related to the Food Vessel Vase tradition particularly in the use of incised decoration although they are usually twice the size of the vases. Only one example of a Cordoned Urn is represented in the record and this was discovered at Ballintubrid, inverted over cremated remains that were accom-

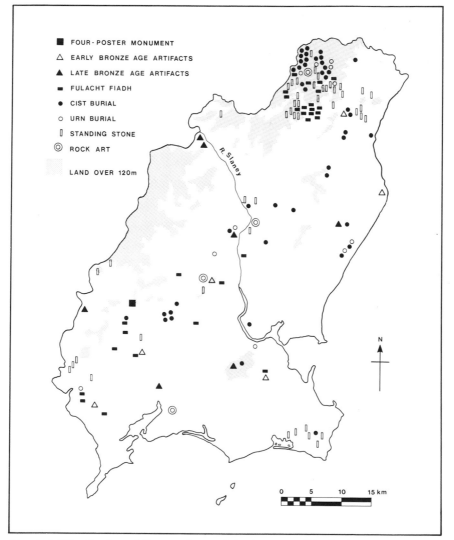

FOUR-POSTER MONUMENT

EARLY BRONZE AGE ARTIFACTS

LATE BRONZE AGE ARTIFACTS

FULACHT FIADH

CIST BURIAL

URN BURIAL

STANDING STONE

ROCK ART

LAND OVER 120m

R. Slaney

N

0   5   10   15 km

Fig. 1.5: Distribution of Bronze Age activity in county Wexford

panied by a battle-axe and a flint chip, (pl. vii). A characteristic feature of this vessel type is applied cordons; in this case, two cordons encircled the upper part of the vessel.

The only pottery association with these urn burials is a Food Vessel Vase associated with the Encrusted Urn at Scarawalsh. The lack of dateable materials makes it difficult to determine the date at which the urn tradition was established and the relative chronology of the various pottery types. A degree of overlap and continuity is indicated by the appearance of the Food Vessel Vase and Encrusted Urn together in a pit at Scarawalsh and the occurrence of urns in cists. Several comments have been made on the similarity in decoration and form of the Encrusted Urn, Enlarged Food Vessel and Food Vase tradition.[63] The distribution of the urn burial is concentrated in much the same area as the cist burial with a tendency to move into the lowlands and south-west Wexford indicating a continuity of settlement (fig. 1.5) There does appear to be a chronological overlap between the various urn types, and the occurrence of both the Collared and Encrusted Urns at Scarawalsh suggested to the excavator internments over only one or two generations., The only non-pottery association which could be used for dating is the battleaxe at Ballin-tubrid. The association of this type of battleaxe with razors indicates a strong tradition in the later part of the Early Bronze Age.[64] It is probable, therefore, in Wexford that the Cordoned Urn is the latest development in the sequence of urn burials.

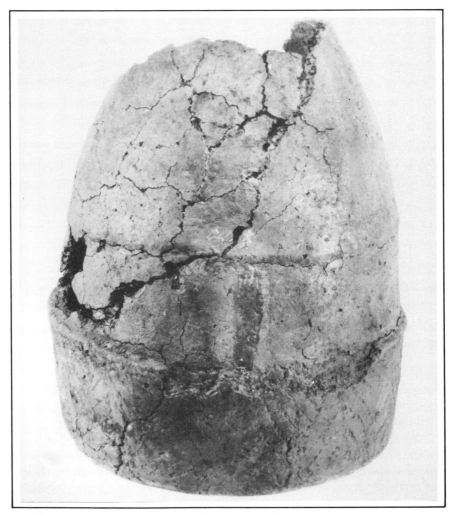

Plate vii: A Cordoned Urn found inverted over cremated remains, a battle axe and flint chip

The standing stone is one of the simplest forms of field monument in the landscape and the most difficult to date. Excavation may be the only potentially profitable method of discovering their date. We know that some of these stones marked burials. In Loggan Lower, a pillarstone marked a cinerary burial of Bronze Age date and was later associated with an inauguration site.[65] At Ballyleigh, the standing stone within the centre of a stone built enclosure of a probable Iron Age date is also associated with burial.[66] A total of four stones in the county have inscriptions in Ogham and three others are carved with rock art: thus standing stones in the county can span in date from the Early Bronze Age to the Early Christian period. However, a constituent part of the megalithic tradition and the desire to build monuments to the dead continued into the Early Bronze Age and is represented in the archaeological record by standing stones which can be grouped or isolated.

In county Wexford, there are at least 47 uncarved standing stones, (fig. 1.5, Appendix IV). These can be divided into three main groups based on their geographical location. There is a large group on the uplands to the north of Wexford, which occur north of Gorey town extending west of Tara Hill to the Craanford area. These are sited on freely drained shale derived drift. The stones around Tara Hill are located on the Macamores, a badly drained soil formed from drift of the Irish Sea. A second group is located south of Waterford harbour on the east bank of the river Barrow and centred on Whitechurch. Just north of this group is Slievecoilta Hill where an early Bronze age halberd was discovered in 1833.[67] Within the Whitechurch group are four standing stones and a stone row.[68] These again are located on the shale derived drift. A fourth stone has recently been added to the stone row as a result of land clearance, which had comprised three standing stones, graded in height.[69] The third group is a tightly knit cluster of sites in the south-east of Wexford situated to the east and west of Lady's Island lake. There are six standing stones in all, three of which are differentiated on the six inch O.S. sheet by the term *Gallan* at Knockhowlin, Bawnoge and Ballyboher (pl. viii). A photographic record of four of these stones taken in 1917 is particularly important as the stones at Knockhowlin and Clougheast cannot now be located.[70] A brief inspection of the extant stones indicates a variance in height from 1.50 metres to 2.10 metres and a tendency for the longest axis of the stones to align north-east/south-west. This is a characteristic of the standing stones in the stone-circle complex in Cork and Kerry and is repeated in a variety of megalithic structures.[71]

Within the county there are three standing stones and one recumbent stone which display rock art, generally ascribed to the Early Bronze Age.[72] These decorated stones are at Connagh Hill near the village of Cummer in north Wexford; Solsborough on the east bank of the river Slaney just north of Enniscorthy; Ballybrennan adjoining the castle there, and finally the Longstone at Balloughton situated to the east of Bannow Bay (pl. ix).[73] A variety of stone was used such as hornblende, schist and granite. The stones can also vary in height from four feet (1.2 metres) to nine feet (3.4 metres). Cupmarks on the stones usually comprise small detached cups without circles tending to be

Plate viii: A standing stone at Ballyboher

two inches (5 cm) in diameter and predominantly located on the south face as at Balloughton and Ballybrennan. These cups can occur singly or in groups as is the case at Solsborough and are associated with long shallow furrows at Balloughton and Ballybrennan. The motifs are usually pocked. In Wicklow and Wexford, with a few exceptions, there appears to be a more limited version of

Plate ix: A standing stone decorated with rock art at Balloughton

the art which elsewhere can include cup and circle patterns and concentric circles with radial and rectilinear lines. Because of the similarity of this art with that of the rock art in Galicia, north-west Spain, contacts with Ireland and Spain in the Early Bronze Age have been suggested.[74] However this art form is represented on megalithic monuments in the north of England and Scotland, which is a more likely source of influence.

Standing stones are also present in groups forming circles or rectangular settings called four-poster monuments. A possible stone circle exists at Carrickbyrne.[75] Here eight stones including one possible recumbent stone form an oval which defines a slightly raised interior measuring 6.1 metres by 4.9 metres. A number of the stones do not appear to be free-standing. At

Clonhasten, two miles north-east of Enniscorthy, the ordnance survey sheet shows six stone circles within an oak wood on the steeply sloping west bank of the river Slaney.[76] These appear on close examination to be a series of terraced platforms defined by a single course of stone embedded in a low embankment. They vary in size and ground plan from 6.90 m x 5.20 m to 7.50 m x 6 m, and are probably the remains of habitation sites of uncertain date. There is a single pillarstone associated with this complex. At Robinstown Great, 9 km. north-east of New Ross on a hill above the river Barrow, a quadrangular setting of four standing stones accompanies an outlying monolith which stands 4.15 m to the south-west (pl. x). This is one of only five four-poster monuments known in Ireland. The other four are in Cork and Kerry.[77] The Robinstown Great design is based on two opposed pairs of stones set with their long axis in line and orientated in a north-east/south-west direction. The presence of an outlying monolith is an unique feature of the Irish sites. This type of megalithic structure occurs more frequently in Scotland and the north of England, where twenty-three certain and thirteen possible examples have been mapped. A number of these sites display rock art and four of the five excavated produced evidence for burials in pits or cists which contained Urn Burials and Beaker pottery. The occurrence of rock art on these monuments and its association with cist burials demonstrates the close link between the various elements of the Food Vessel tradition.

Plate x: A four-poster monument at Robinstown Great

A method of outdoor cooking developed in the Early Bronze Age was prac-tised into the medieval period. The term *Fulacht Fian* or *Fulacht Fiadh* has been used to describe these ancient cooking places. This descriptive term is based on reference to this structure in early Irish literature.[78] The main feature of a *Fulacht Fian* in the field is a horseshoe shaped mound which is composed largely of burnt and shattered stone. Within the concave section of the mound, a stone or wooden trough and occasionally a hearth was accommodated (fig. 1.6). These sites are invariably sited in a wet, marshy area near a ready supply of

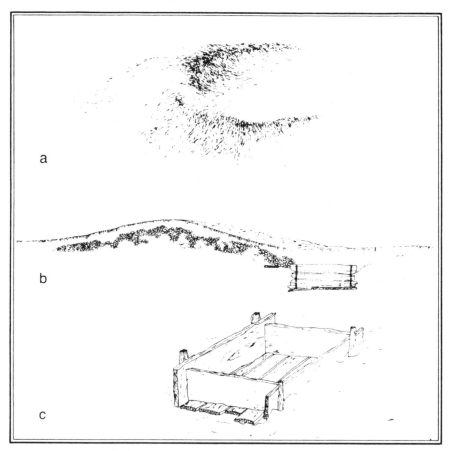

Fig. 1.6: Diagram of a fulacht fiadh, (a) crescent shaped mound, (b) section through wooden trough and mound, (c) view of trough

water such as a spring well, stream or river. The method of cooking involved the heating of stones in a fire in the immediate vicinity which were then deposited in the trough. Once the water reached the desired temperature, the wrapped meat was then placed in the trough. The heated stones were then taken out of the trough and dumped to form the bank which is visible today. Excavation of these sites is often disappointing from the point of view of finds; however, paleobotanical evidence and C14 dating indicates use between the Middle and Late Bronze Age.[79]

In Wexford, there are thirty-six known sites of *fulacht fian* (fig. 1.5, appendix V). They form three main groups i.e. north west of Gorey, centred on Hollyfort, south-east of Enniscorthy and just south of New Ross. These sites are in areas which have produced evidence of settlement in the Bronze Age in the form of artifacts and monuments. At least twenty of the sites mentioned were discovered by Fr Joseph Ranson while assisting the Ordnance Survey with a revision of their maps between 1939 and 1940.[80] Fieldwork undertaken by a teacher's group in south Wexford produced fifteen sites including a cluster of eight sites in Battlestown.[81] The main features of the *Fulachta Fian* in Wexford which Ranson observed were their kidney-shaped ground plan; their location in wet springy terrain in both low and high altitudes and the lack of a local tradition associated with them. These are the main characteristics of *Fulacht Fian* found in other parts of the country as well. The average width of 25 feet (7.49 m) which he quoted is slightly smaller than the nine metres average in Cork.[82] The grouping of *Fulacht Fian* is also a recurrent characteristic of the monument type. Without excavation, we cannot determine whether we are dealing with a number of sites in use at the same time or successive use of one particular place which was desirable for the location of cooking places.

Late Bronze Age Wexford

Hoards were a feature of the Early Bronze Age but they were being deposited in greater numbers and contained a larger array of items in the final stages of the Bronze Age.[83] Palaeobotanical evidence exists for a deterioration in the climate in the later half of the second millenium B.C. and this may have caused a general panic and fear of future calamity.[84] A degree of political unrest is suggested by the occurence of weapons such as spearheads and swords, which now enter the archaeological record. One spearhead dating from this period was discovered near Bunclody[85] and another late Bronze Age sword was found at New Ross (which was altered and used in the rebellion of 1798).[86] Hilltop areas were being settled at this time, for example, Rathgall, county Wicklow.[87] The general absence of evidence for burials from this period suggests that the deposition of these hoards could represent votive deposits associated with a burial ritual.[88] The items included are usually personal in nature. Whatever the varied reason for their deposition, these hoards testify to a period of intensive technological advance with increased exploitation of natural resources. The metal industry was based largely on foreign prototypes from the Baltic region, eastern Europe and Britain.[89] Yet, Irish smiths of this period became important exporters to Britain of such personal ornaments as dress fasteners and pennanular bracelets similar to those discovered in the bed of a stream at New Ross in the last century.[90]

There is a greater variety of material represented in the four Late Bronze Age hoards known from Wexford (Ballyvadden, Enniscorthy, Forth Commons and New Ross) than in those of earlier date (appendix V; fig. 1.5).[91] Their contents can be divided into three main categories; tools, weapons and ornaments. The hoard discovered at Ballyvadden in 1849 contained both tools and ornaments (pl. xi). This hoard is unique in that it is the only Late Bronze Age hoard (out of 130 examples) which was deposited in a pottery container, a feature of hoards on the continent at this time.[92] Amongst the contents were two socketed axeheads, a socketed gouge, socketed knife and a variety of bronze rings. The tools represented are probably those of a carpenter or craftsman working in timber. Socketed axeheads of the bag-shaped variety were the most common

Plate xi: The Ballyvadden hoard of Late Bronze Age date

type of axeheads and are similar in style to those produced in north Germany in the Late Bronze Age.[93] Socketed axeheads have also been discovered as chance finds in Enniscorthy.[94] Another example is provenanced to the county only.[95] The socketed gouge and knife are new types, the former with an origin in eastern Europe.[96] A socketed gouge has also been found at Clonmines.[97] The knife is two-edged with a straight profile from the blade to the socket and is a type developed in western Europe.[98] The purpose of the plain rings in the hoard is uncertain. They are too small to be bracelets and may have been used in horse trappings.[99] A collection of craftsman's tools was also represented in the hoard found in the cleft of rock in a quarry at Forth Mountain in 1906.[100] This hoard contained eight to ten objects when it was discovered, including 'an axe, a gouge and a celt'. Unfortunately, the contents of the hoard were dispersed and the only item which has survived is a socketed gouge housed in the National Museum.

Towards the end of the second millenium B.C., there was a revival in gold working using bar gold as well as sheet metal, represented by a notable increase in the number of hoards deposited at this time which contained gold ornaments of a personal nature. A similar phenomonen existed in the south of England centred on Somerset and termed the 'ornament horizon'. These personal hoards may represent some religious significance associated with the cult of the dead. They also demonstrate the ingenuity of the metalworker during this period and the range of insular developments in techniques and types. Amongst their many achievements is the gold bar torc, a neck ornament dating from the twelfth to the tenth century b.c. and inspired by a prototype in the west Baltic area.[101] There are thirty of these torcs known in Ireland with a distribution concentrated in the south of Leinster, possibly due to the presence of gold in the Wicklow Mountains.[102] A number of these torcs occur in southern Britain and France where they were probably exported by Irish smiths.[103] A hoard found in the vicinity of Enniscorthy contained an assemblage of gold ornaments.[104] Here a gold bar torc was associated with a gold pennanular neck ring which was similar in style to plain bronze rings occurring in the 'ornament horizon' in southern Britain. The gold bar torc was manufactured from an ingot hammered into a rod of square section and of sufficient length to encircle a neck. The terminals taper inwards and were curved back on the ring to form a simple locking device. This bar was sometimes twisted as seen in the example from Tubberduff near Gorey, where a right handed clockwise twist was employed by the smith (pl. xii).[105] This technique was adopted c. 1200 B.C. and is evident on bronze neck rings which originated in the west Baltic area and on ear-rings from the east Mediterranean.[106]

Amongst the more impressive of a wide range of ornaments being manu-

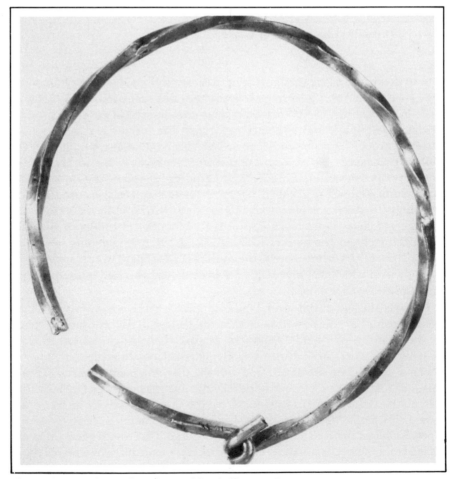

Plate xii: A gold torc found at Tubberduff, near Gorey

factured and worn were gold discs, four of which were discovered by a peasant near Enniscorthy in the Autumn of 1795.[107] The four discs were exactly alike. Unfortunately they were sold to Gurley, an Enniscorthy silversmith who melted two of the discs down and the remaining pair were sent to the Earl of Charlemont, for auction. When compared with the Kilmuckridge and county Wexford discs, they vary greatly both in ornamentation and construction.[108] The style of metalwork is one that was current in Late Bronze Age Europe and was practiced in Ireland particularly in north Munster to produce such objects as gorgets and gold vessels.[109] Eogan believes that the type itself probably developed from Danish or north German prototypes but appeared in Ireland not earlier than the eight century b.c., which is later than the rest of Europe, including Denmark.[110] The discs are composed of three elements, a face plate and a back plate, both held together by a binding along the edge, all made of sheet gold. Ornamentation on the face plate comprises a boss surrounded by multiple circles which is repeated within bands over the whole surface. The back plate is decorated with a network of kite shapes. *Repousse* or relief hammering from the reverse side of the metal is the main technique used to produce this decoration, although a number of the motifs may have been beaten from behind with a die stamp.[111] Over forty of these discs are known from the continent with a distribution that stretches from Hungary to southern Scandinavia. There is only one other definite Irish example from a bog at Lattoon, county Cavan.[112] This distribution underlines the extent of communications within Europe at this time and the general adoption of particular styles.

The achievements of working with gold are manifested in the collection of ornaments discovered in the bed of a stream near New Ross in 1895, which comprised a gold fibula or dress fastener and four pennanular bracelets (pl. xiii).[113] The largest fibula was probably used to fasten a cloak by using loops or double button holes and was made up of five separate parts including the solid bow which was made from a single bar of gold, hammered up from a single ingot and then bent to a bow shape. The cups for the end would have been 'sweated', a procedure which involved surface melting under extreme temperature until the surfaces became molten and could be easily fused. Then the extreme edge of the cup was left thickened and a flat circular band of gold was literally bent around it or riveted on. These cups were internally decorated with a cross-hatched design using a hammer or chisel which produced slight bulges to the exterior. Two of the pennanular bracelets in the hoard had a solid bow but the cups were left thick and then hammered out thin to a bell shape. The edges were then decorated with a series of concentric grooves. As the remaining pair had hollow bows, they were probably produced from a piece of gold plate which had been hammered out and worked around a piece of wood in the shape of a bow. The wood was then burnt out and the two edges of the bow joined by the 'sweating' process.[114] A prototype for the gold fibula in this collection probably came from the west Baltic region but the bracelets are an insular development.[115] The distribution of dress fasteners and their pennanular bracelets provides significant evidence for a trade route from

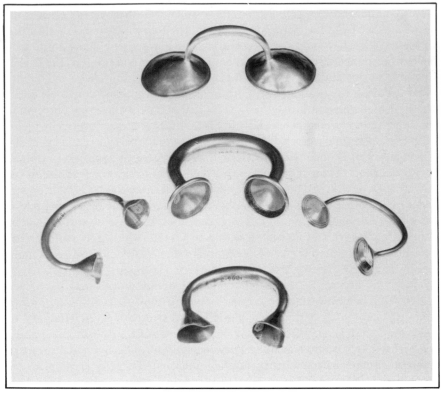

Plate xiii: A hoard of gold objects found near New Ross in 1895

Ireland to north Wales across the Pennines and south to Anglia, possibly extending across the North Sea to lower Saxony in the Late Bronze Age.[116]

Iron Age Wexford

The use of iron became widespread in Central Europe during the latter half of the eighth century b.c. and it is influences from this area that were responsible for the spread of iron-working to western and northern Europe.[117] Small groups of objects associated with the initial stage in the development of iron working have been discovered on settlement sites such as a crannóg at Rathinaun in county Sligo and at two stone ringforts at Aughinish Island, county Limerick.[118] However, it is not until c. 300 b.c. that influences from this area are manifest in the record with the appearance of La Téne or Celtic inspired material. Raftery points to a total absence of La Téne in the southern half of Ireland and concludes that forces other than La Téne must be sought to explain the onset of an Iron Age economy in the south.[119] The evidence for Iron Age activity in Wexford is still somewhat inadequate. What follows, therefore, is a general outline of the possible evidence for settlement, defensive sites and burial customs together with the artifactual evidence for stone sculpture and personal ornamentation (fig. 1.7).

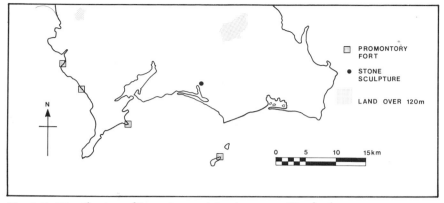

Fig. 1.7: Distribution of Iron Age activity in county Wexford

Outside Wexford, excavations have provided some evidence for settlement in crannógs and ringforts in the Late Bronze Age/Early Iron Age, although the main period of use of both is in the Early Christian Period. There are at least six hundred ringforts in the county but because of the lack of excavation none of these can be ascribed to the Iron Age. Reference has been made in the literature to a crannóg at Clonsillagh near Ballynastragh Demesne and in the northern portion of Wexford estuary an artificial causeway connected Begerin to the other islands.[120] A single piece canoe associated with shoreline settlement was discovered off Cahore Point.[121] Large hilltop enclosures such as that at Ballyleigh may also prove to be Iron age in date.[122] Aerial coverage for the county has produced evidence for large multivallate and single banked enclosures particularly on hillslopes and low lying parts of southern Wexford at Knockanduff and Ballare.[123] Excavation of these sites could throw light on the question of settlement in this period.

The construction of earthen defences cutting off the neck of a promontory or suitable cliff headland is generally believed to date to the Iron Age. Four of these promontory forts have been identified along the south-west coast of Wexford at Nook and Duncannon on the Waterford estuary; at Baginbun in Ramstown and on a site at the north-east end of the Great Saltee Island.[124] In all cases, the sea cliff would have formed natural defences on at least two sides of the site. Because the headland at Duncannon has been garrisoned and built on right up to recent times, there are no traces extant of the early fortifications associated with Dún Conain (the fort of Conan). It is recorded in the *Dinnsenchus* that Fionn MacCumhaill had a residence on Nook and that Conan's fort was 'somewhere near the head of the hill'. Further north of Duncannon is the fortified promontory at Nook. Here the defences comprise an impressive outer fosse and inner bank which runs in a bold curve across the saddle of the ridge. The site is defended by cliffs to the north-west and by a steep grassy slope to the east with uninterrupted views onto the mainland. Its bank is constructed of earth and stone and is 6.5 m wide on average rising to a height of 4 m. In the western section, the fosse was rock cut and is more impressive than in the east where it has silted up and been built on. The fosse is 5 m deep on average and 4.4 m wide. Along its eastern shoreline is a creek which would have provided a water and food supply as well as a place to anchor boats.

The headland at Baginbun (pl. xiv) is surrounded by the cliffs rising abruptly from the sea. The main headland was entrenched by the Normans but the eastern peninsula was fortified in earlier times. An outer embankment was constructed across the promontory and runs along the edge of the cliff which has been undercut by the sea reducing the neck to a width of c. 36 metres. Running across this narrow neck and contiguous to the outer embankment is an internal fosse and bank c. 40 metres long. At the north-east end of the Great Saltee Island, a single earthen bank cuts off the neck of a partially eroded headland. The area enclosed is relatively small compared to the sites at Baginbun and Nook but it is very difficult to estimate the extent of erosion which has taken place here.

Plate xiv: The promontory fort at Baginbun, of probable Iron Age date

Our knowledge of Iron Age burial customs is very much in its infancy. Raftery has summarised the information to date which he divided into two broad categories, native and intrusive; the latter comprises mainly inhumations of Roman or Romano-British origin.[125] There are no known 'intrusive' burials from the county, but there are possible examples of the 'native' type. The ring barrow at Loftus Hall on Hook Head could date from this period.[126] However, there is a general problem with the dating of ring barrows due to their similarity in form throughout the Bronze and Iron Ages. Potential ring barrows have been identified on vertical aerial photographs in the townland of Coolpeach (OS 42) and Ballydaniel (OS 11).[127] There are a number of artificial mounds in the county which have received attention in the literature that could be interpreted as burial mounds.[128] It is almost impossible to date these from a field inspection. Both the earthwork at Kilgorman, southeast of the graveyard north of Tara Hill and the mound at Ardamine churchyard in Middletown townland are thought to be sepulchral mounds. One could speculate that the mound at Loggan Lower itself was funerary in nature and an Iron Age date is suggested by its association with the inauguration of the Uí Ceinnsealaigh.[129]

The cult of the head is a Celtic phenomenon and the representation of the head is found right across Celtic Europe. In Ireland the evidence for this practice is preserved in a series of stone heads, a sword hilt, a horsebit and a wooden carving which can be dated to this period.[130] The stone heads can be dated on art-historical grounds to the Iron Age, using comparative material from Britain and central Europe, particularly the Rhineland. There is a notable concentration of these heads in the north of the country where six of the seven identified groups are located.[131] However, the group of heads from the Piltown area in county Kilkenny share certain similarities with a pair of possible Iron Age heads recently discovered in south Wexford (pl. xv).[132]

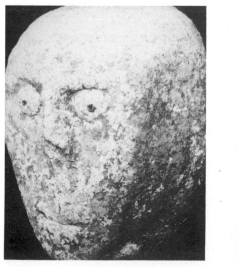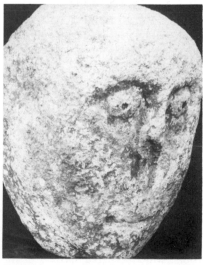

Plate xv: Two possible Iron Age heads from Gibberwell, Duncormick

These two heads stood on tapering stone plinths in a farmyard at Gibberwell near Duncormick. They are slightly larger than life size and it has been suggested that they represent a male and a female. Their main features are a rounded head with a flat face, slit mouth, wedge shaped nose and pointed oval eyes with minimal brows. One of the heads has a 'whistle hole' or perforation at the side of the mouth which is one of the diagnostic features of these Celtic heads. The similarity in style of the heads indicates their probable contemporaneity. Glass has been placed in the eyes and there were also traces of paint. This has caused a certain amount of reservation regarding their early dating: it is quite possible that the heads were interfered with in more recent times.

The artifactual evidence for this period of Wexford's past remains to be discovered. There are two pins from the county in the National Museum collection which are of probable Iron Age date.[133] These provide information on personal ornamentation at the time and their existence indicates contact between Britain and Ireland sometime before the end of the prehistoric period. An ibex-headed and omega type pin are represented. They are both types of ring-headed pin which may have developed in Britain from continental prototypes such as the swan's neck pin.[134] An ibex-headed pin dated to between 400 B.C. and 1000 A.D. similar to our example was discovered in a sandhill site at Dunfanaghy in county Donegal.[135]

Conclusions

The discovery of flint tools of Larnian type along the east and south coast of Wexford indicates that the region was first settled sometime between c. 5000 B.C. and c.3000 B.C. These settlements were in a prime position to exploit the food resources of shoreline and riverside; their impact on the deciduous forests of the interior was marginal. Intensive field-work, particularly focused on the river estuaries along the coast, could change our picture of this period appreciably, unless the effects of coastal erosion have already destroyed a great deal of the evidence.

Palaeobotanical research undertaken in the area of Forth Mountain recorded large scale land clearance and tillage as early as c.4000 B.C. No doubt there was a period of transition when hunting/fishing and agriculture were being practised simultaneously. The presence of cattle bones in the midden at Clare Island in Bannow Bay suggests a mixed economy along the coast. Settlement during the Neolithic appears to have been largely focused around the Slaney estuary, a pattern substantiated by the occurrence of stone axeheads and flints in the area and the position of the impressive portal tombs at Ballybrittas and Newbawn (fig. 1.8). There is some evidence to indicate that the uplands of Wexford had also been settled by this time. Forests were cleared using locally produced stone axeheads. Some of these may have been hafted adzewise to be used for breaking up the ground. A limited assemblage of flint tools, which assisted settlers in their daily activities, have been recovered. A wider range of Neolithic implements has been recorded outside the county

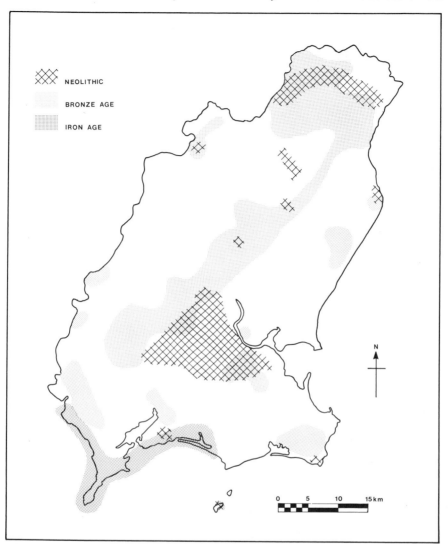

Fig. 1.8: Settlement patterns in prehistoric Wexford

implying either impoverished settlement or incomplete evidence. The only excavated habitation site from this period, at McMurroughs Castle, demonstrates the fragile nature of this evidence. It is difficult to determine the immediate origin of these communities as a similar culture was being practiced across the Irish Sea in Wales and Cornwall but their location along the estuary suggests seaborne contacts. This network of communications among Neolithic communities is further highlighted by the occurrence of possible imported items in the area, such as the porcellanite axehead from Garrycullane and the javelinheads from the county which may have come from north-east Ireland through Wicklow into Wexford. The practice of burial in large stone tombs became less frequent in the later phase of the Neolithic with the adoption of a Single Burial Tradition. There is some evidence to suggest that this ideological and social change was influenced by forces outside the country affecting, in particular, communities in the south-east. In Norrismount the burial of a young man in a single cist accompanied by a finely decorated vessel is representative of this new burial tradition.

The introduction of metallurgy and the adoption of single burial in a cist is attributed in large part to influences from Beaker communities in North Britain. Results from the Norrismount site indicate that a trend towards single burial had already begun in this region during the later part of the Neolithic. An element of continuity is further highlighted by the erection of stone monuments to the dead which extended into the Bronze Age period and was manifested in the form of grouped or isolated stones which are thought to have defined ceremonial areas. In the initial stages of the Bronze Age, contact between Wexford and North Britain may have been largely based on trade possibly in gold ornaments made from fine sheet metalwork. The industry was probably loosely organised, incorporating a number of journeymen smiths. Contacts strengthened during the period and this is illustrated in the gradual development of types and techniques of implements within the county which were being influenced by trends in North Britain and Central Europe. The personalised nature of the objects in the later Bronze Age, such as the gold torcs from Gorey and Enniscorthy, underlines the growing wealth of the population and the establishment of accomplished schools of metalwork in the south-east, exporting their products to south Britain and France. The industry became more centralised and a degree of specialisation emerged with tools for specific purposes being represented in the record. Gold working was still a prominent industry undergoing further developments in the use of bar gold and influenced greatly in style by insular developments in North Munster.

A crouched inhumation or cremation accompanied by a food vessel in a single stone box or cist was the most common mode of burial in north and central Wexford in the Early Bronze Age. With the exception of the faience bead in the burial at Bolinready, grave goods were not included. Generally these cists occur as isolated burials but occasionally they are present within a cemetery which was unmarked or within a cemetery mound. In a number of cases, the cremated remains were contained in a large inverted cinerary urn within the cist. However, this is a later development associated with a decline in popularity of cists and the adoption of burial in an urn, probably influenced from North Britain. Excavations at Scarawalsh indicate a chronological overlap between the use of the various types of urns such as the Encrusted and Collared. The Cordoned Urn at Ballintubrid, with its battleaxe, may represent the latest development of the urn tradition in Wexford. There are no burials dating to the Late Bronze Age identified in the county. Evidence from the excavations at Rathgall in county Wicklow indicates that cremation remained prevalent and that remains were placed in a pit with or without a pottery container.

Taking an overall view of the distribution of Bronze Age activity in the county (fig. 1.8), two distinct regions emerge one north of Gorey and centred on the Annagh hills and a second which occurs in a band running on a north-east/south-west axis through the centre of Wexford corresponding dramatically with a prominent fault-line of drift covered volcanic rocks. Except for possibly the northern uplands and localised areas such as Bree hill and Forth Mountain, there is little overlap with the regions settled by Neolithic communities. The upland bias within this distribution could indicate that its limits have been largely determined by the pattern of survival within the county. However, within the two regions observed, there is a significant correspondence between the artifact and monument evidence; thus we can conclude that they represent areas of intensive Bronze Age settlement. An interesting pattern emerges in the north of the county where the cooking sites cluster on the lower slopes of the hills, whilst the cist burials are on the higher ground. The as yet to be discovered habitation sites associated with this intensive activity could well be located in the intermediate area. Future field-work and excavation should be focused in this region. Such an extensive presence was probably attracted to the mineral resources of south Wicklow. The centralised nature of the metal industry in the Late Bronze Age must have given rise to large population centres. It is possible that the hut sites on a hill overlooking the Slaney at Clonhasten could be the type of settlement evidence for which we should be looking.

The industrial facet of the record, so apparent in the Late Bronze Age, does not exist for the Iron Age in Wexford. Our knowledge of the period is largely dependent on a small number of defensive sites along the south-east coast, potential burial sites and some questionable evidence for stone sculpture and two unprovenanced pins. Some of the ringforts of the county may also have their origin in the Iron Age. Despite the inadequate nature of the evidence, there appears to be an apparent shift to the lowlands in the south of the county (fig. 1.8). In this part of Wexford, a number of large single and multivallate enclosures have been identified which may throw light on the settlement picture at this time, other than the thin evidence gleaned from our knowledge of the defensive sites. The omega- and ibex-headed pins discovered in the county indicate that the contacts with the opposite side of the Irish Sea, so apparent in the earlier phase of Wexford's prehistory, seem to have been maintained up to the end of the prehistoric period.

Appendix I: Megalithic Tombs in County Wexford

S.M.R.	OS Sheet	Townland	Site	Reference
2:28	2	Annagh Long	Megalithic tomb (possible)	Kinahan (1883), p. 154
6:3	6	Aughnamaulmeen	Megalithic tomb (possible) 'Dolmen'	O.S. 6 inch, 1939-40
31:10	31	Ballybrittas	Portal tomb 'Cromlech'	O.S. 6 inch, 1925 Powell (1941), pp. 14, 22; Borlase (1897), 11, pp. 16-17
16:13	16	Ballymore	Megalithic tomb (possible) 'Giant's Bed'	O.S. 6 inch, 1924.
6:2	6	Baltyfarrell	Megalithic tomb (possible) 'Dolmen'	O.S. 6 inch, 1939-40
31:39	31	Barmoney	Megalithic tomb (possible) 'Dolmen'	Powell (1941), p. 22.
31:39	31	Barmoney	'Dolmen'	Powell (1941), p. 22.
46:49	46	Cullenstown	Megalithic tomb (possible)	Butler (1986) , p. 8.
7:9	7	Kilcavan Lower	Megalithic tomb (possible) 'Dolmen'	O.S. 6 inch, 1940
35:52	35	Newbawn	Portal tomb 'Dolmen'	Flood (1912), pp. 13-17; Ó Nualláin (1983), p. 103.
53:37	53	St. Vogues	Megalithic tomb (possible) 'Dolmen (site of)	Borlase (1897), II, p. 417 Lynch et al. (1976), pp. 57-60

Appendix II: Bronze Age Artifacts from County Wexford

OS Sheet	Townland	Find(s)	Reference
21	Ballyvadden near Kilmuckridge	Late Bronze Age hoard Looped socketed axehead (2)	Armstrong (1849), pp. 369-70 Wilde (1857), p. 158 Eogan (1983), pp. 170-1
		Socketed gouge Socketed knife Ring (3) Metal objects (2) Pottery vessel	
25/31	Bree	Early Bronze Age bronze axehead	Culleton (1984), p. 18.
7	Near Bunclody	Socketed bronze spearhead	N.M.I. 1943:55; Culleton (1984), p. 21
17/22	Cahore	Early Bronze Age bronze axeheads (2)	Harbison (1980), p. 1.
40/45	Clonmines	Late Bronze Age socketed gouge	N.M.I. 1968:259; Lucas (1971), p. 219
20	Enniscorthy	Socketed axehead	Ffrench (1891), p. 486
20	Enniscorthy	Bar torc Pennanular neck ring	Eogan (1983), pp. 45-6; Armstrong (1933), pp. 61, 79, 87; Eogan (1967), pp. 139-40
20	Enniscorthy	Late Bronze Age hoard	Eogan (1983), pp. 171-2; Culleton (1984), pp. 24-5
42	Forth Commons	Late Bronze Age hoard including bronze socketed gouge	N.M.I. 1929:3? Eogan (1983), pp. 172-3; Culleton (1984), p. 19
3/6/19	Hollyfort	Spearhead/Ferrules	Ó Broin (1925), pp. 113-4
42	Johnstown	Bronze flat axehead Bronze socketed axehead	N.M.I. 1959:67; Culleton (1984), p. 18
22	Kilmuckridge	Gold disc	Herity and Eogan (1977), p. 112
35	Nash	Early Bronze Age copper axeheads Copper cakes	Bremer (1956), pp. 88-91; Harbison (1980).
29	New Ross	Leaf-shaped spearhead	Eogan (1965), p. 161; Culleton (1984), p. 21
29	New Ross	Gold fibula/dress fastener and four pennanular bracelets	Frazer and Johnson (1923), pp. 776-83; Culleton (1984), pp. 25-6
9	Newtown Barry St. Mary's	Socketed bronze axehead	N.M.I. 1939:48
39/44	Rosetown	Flat bronze axehead	N.M.I. 1938:141;
7	Tubberduff near Gorey	Middle Bronze Age gold torc	Esmonde (1925), pp. 68-70; Culleton (1984), p. 23
?	Wexford	Flat bronze axehead decorated w/slight flanges	N.M.I. 1959:62
?	Wexford	Bronze axehead	N.M.I. 1969:292; Lucas (1977), p. 209.
?	Wexford	Scoketed bronze axeheads (2)	N.M.I. 1959:128-129.
?	Wexford	Socketed bronze axehead	N.M.I. 1959:126
—	Wexford	Gold sundiscs (2)	Ryan (1980), pp. 6-11; Harbison (1977).

Appendix III: Bronze Age Burials in County Wexford

S.M.R.	OS Sheet	Townland	Site	Reference
2:29	2	Annagh Middle	'Kistvaen' with urn	Kinahan (1883), p. 154; Waddell (1970), p. 136; Culleton (1984), p. 55.
2:25	2	Annagh More	Short cist	Hartnett and Prendergast (1953), pp. 46-9; Waddell (1970), p. 136
2:25	2	Annagh More	Short cist	Hartnett and Prendergast (1953), pp. 47-8; Waddell (1979), p. 136
28:6	28	Ballintubrid	Urn burial	Ryan (1975), pp. 132-45; Kavanagh (1986), p. 377; Culleton (1984), pp. 18, 37, 48
16:16	16	Ballyduff	Short cist	Hartnett and Prendergast (1953), pp. 49-57; Waddell (1970), p. 136
25:13	25	Ballygillistown	Pit burial	N.M.I. 1984 1A/84/84.
12:13 12:14	12	Ballykale	'Kistvaens' (2)	Kinahan (1883), p. 159; O'Broin (1925), p. 144; Waddell (1970), p. 136
2:58	2	Ballynabarney	'Kistvaen' with urn	Kinahan (1883), p. 154
2:57	2	Ballynabarney	'Urn' (burial?)	ibid, p. 154
21:33	21	Ballyorley Upper	Cinerary burials	Harte (1925), pp. 95-6
2:33	2	Ballyrory	'Kistvaen'	Kinahan (1883), p. 154; Culleton (1984), p. 55
2:34	2	Ballythomas	Cist	Kinahan (1883), p. 154; Waddell (1970), p. 136
39:41	39	Ballyvelig	Cist	O.P.W.
39:42	39	Ballyvelig	Urn burial	Ó Riordáin (1936), pp. 186-7
39:43	39	Ballyvelig	Urn burial	
42:7	42	Bargy Commons	Urn burial	Ffrench (1898), p. 70; *Past* (1925), pp. 107-14; O.S. Letters, 11, p. 76
2:36	2	Barnadown	'Kistvaen'	Kinahan (1883), p. 154
2:37	2	Barracurragh	Urn burial	Idem
37:78	37	Bolabaun	Cist burials	N.M.I. Record 1, A89/52; Waddell (1970), p. 136
16:10	16	Bolinready	Short cist	Prendergast (1968), pp. 161-2; Lucas (1968), p. 121; Waddell (1970), p. 136
2:38	2	Clonroe Upper	'Kistvaens'	Kinahan (1883), p. 154; Waddell (1970), p. 136
12:15	12	Courtown	Short cist	R.S.A.I. Jn. (1862-3), pp. 144-5; Waddell (1970), p. 136
2:42	2	Cummer	'Kistvaens' with urns (3)	Kinahan (1883), p. 154; Kavanagh (1977), p. 89; Waddell (1970), p. 136.
2:43	2	Cummer	'Kistvaen'	Kinahan (1883), p. 154
2:49	2	Cummerduff/ Loggan Upper	Urn burial	ibid, p. 156
32:27	32	Deeps	Cist burial(s) Urns(s)	Hartnett and Prendergast (1953, p. 57; Waddell (1970), p. 137
48:110	48	Eardownes Great	Short cist	N.M.I. Record, 1961
20:30	20	Enniscorthy	Cist burial	N.M.I. 1975:264-265
6:75	6/7	Near Gorey	Food vessel (Burial?)	N.M.I. 1909:32

OS S.M.R.	Sheet	Townland	Site	Reference
28:4	28	Killincooly More	Flat Cemetery (including short cists)	Esmonde (1902), pp. 68-70 O'Broin (1925), pp. 107-14; Ó Riordáin (1936), p. 188; Waddell (1970), p. 137
34:67	34	Killowen	Urn burials (2)	Kavanagh (1973), p. 567
22:28	22	Kilmuckridge	Cist burial	*R.S.A.I. Jn.* (1887), p. 348; Kavanagh (1977), pp. 89-90; Waddell (1970), p. 137
20:48	20	Kilpierce	Cist?	*N.M.I.* 1A/74/54
20:6	20	Knocknaskeagh	Polygonal cist	Raftery (1968), p. 51; *N.M.I.* 1967:112-114
2:4	2	Loggan Lower	Cemetery	Westropp (1904), p. 321; Orpen (1907), p. 136; Ibid (1911), pp. 270-1; Waddell (1970); p. 137
30:68	30	Misterin	Polygonal cist	Ffrench (1889), pp19-20; Kavanagh (1977), pp. 89-90; Waddell (1970), p. 137
30:66	30	Misterin	Cist burial (2)	Ffrench (1889), p. 20
30:69	30	Misterin	Cist/Pit burial	*N.M.I.* 1931:289
2:54	2	Near Monaseed	'Kistvaen'	Kinahan (1883), p. 159
52:28	52	Mountpill, Tilladavin	Cist burials	*N.M.I.* 1A/57/57.
3:37	3	Mullaun	'Kistvaen'	Idem. Waddell (1970), p. 137
37:29	37	Newtown	Pit burial	*N.M.I.* 1984:112.
30:70	32	Oldcourt	Short cist	Waddell (1970), p. 137
2:60	2	Pallis	Urns (2)	Kinahan (1883), p. 152
6:65/ 7:41	6/7	Ballyowen or Ramsfort Park	'Urn' (burial?)	P.S.A.S. (1876-8), pp. 61-2
20:1	20	Scarawalsh	Flat cemetry	Rynne (1966), pp. 39-46; Kavanagh (1973), p. 567
37:81	37	Tikillin	Food vessel	*N.M.I.* photographic index

Appendix IV: Early Bronze Age Monuments in County Wexford

S.M.R.	OS Sheet	Townland	Site	Reference
6:14	6	Annagh Middle	Standing stone	O.S. 6 inch 1939-40
7:25	7	Ballinacarrig	Standing stone	Ibid.
7:27	7	Ballinacarrig	Standing stone	Ibid.
7:28	7	Ballincarrig	Standing stone	Ibid.
7:29	7	Ballinacarrig	Standing stone	Ibid.
6:20		Ballintlea	Standing Stone	Ibid.
6:21		Ballintlea	Standing Stone	Ibid.
6:49	6	Ballingarry Lower	Standing stone	Ibid.
46:14	46	Balloughton	Standing stone Rock Art 'Gallán'	Kinahan (1883), pp. 39-40 Butler (1986), p. 239
47:56	47	Ballyboher	'Gallán'	Fitzhenry (1913), p. 27
31:42	32	Ballybrennan	Standing stone Rock Art	Kinahan (1883), pp. 40-1
23:2	23	Ballyleigh	Standing stone within enclosure	MacAlister (1937), p. 311
6:8	6	Baltyfarrell	Standing stone	O.S. 6 inch, 1939-40
47:40	47	Banoge	'Gallán'	O.S. 6 inch, 1940
6:23	6	Barnland	Standing stone	O.S. 6 inch, 1939-40
6:10	6	Bolany	Standing stone	Ibid.
6:11	6	Bolany	Standing stone	Ibid.
6:12	6	Bolany	Standing stone	Ibid.
6:17	6	Bolany	Standing stone	Ibid.
6:50	6	Brideswell Big	Standing stone	Ibid.
6:1	6	Buckstown	Standing stone	Ibid.
6:37	6	Clonamona Upper	Standing stones (2)	Ibid.
20:23	20	Clonhasten	Standing stone	Ibid.
53:76	53	Clough East	Standing stone	Fitzhenry (1917), p. 31
2:41	2	Connagh Hill	Recumbent stone	Kinahan (1883), pp. 157-9
6:22	6	Coolintaggart Hill	Standing stone	O.S. 6 inch, 1939-40
4:9	4	Coolmela or Prospect	Standing stones (2)	I.T.A. survey
23:1	23	Curraun	Standing stones (2)	O.S. 6 inch, 1924
6:4	6	Deerpark	Standing stone	O.S. 6 inch, 1939-40
20:50	20/26	Drumgold	Standing stone	I.T.A. Survey
53:19	53	Eardownes Great	Standing stone	Fitzhenry (1917), pp. 25-33
7:11	7	Kilcavan Upper	Standing stone	O.S. 6 inch, 1939-40
20:2	20	Killabeg	Standing stone	Ibid.
39:25	39	Killesk	Standing stone	O.S. 6 inch, 1940
6:33	6	Kilmichael Hill	Standing stone	Ibid.
47:64	47	Knockhowlin	'Gallán'	Ibid.
53:50	53	Loginsherd	Standing stone	Fitzhenry (1917, p. 31
2:4	2	Loggan Lower	Standing stone	Orpen (1907), p. 136.
6:54	6	Monbay Lower	Standing Stone	6 inch O.S. 1939-40
39:1	39	Poulmaloe	Standing stone	O.S. 6 inch, 1940
39:2	39	Poulmaloe	Standing stone	Ibid.
35:25	30	Raheevarren	Standing stone	O.S. 6 inch, 1922
30:35	30	Robinstown Great	Four Poster monument	Flood (1912), pp. 13-17; Ó Nualláin (1984), p. 71
6:51	6	Shrule	Standing stone	O.S. 6 inch 1939-40
20:13	20	Solsborough	Standing stone	I.T.A. survey
7:2	7	Tinnock Lower	Standing stone	O.S. 6 inch, 1940
39:4	39	Whitechurch	Standing stone	Ibid.
39:5	39	Whitechurch	Stone row	Ibid.

Appendix V: Cooking Places or Fulachta Fiadha in County Wexford

S.M.R.	OS Sheet	Townland	Reference
3A:2	3	Askinch Upper	O.S. 6 inch, 1940
5:11	5	Ballyellis/Craanford Area (3)	N.M.I. topographical files
25:19	25	Ballymackesy	Ibid.
35:58	35	Ballynabola	Ibid.
35:59	35	Ballynabola	Ibid.
39:22	39	Ballynamona	O.S. 6 inch, 1940
39:38	39	Ballyvelig	Ibid.
44:21	44/45	Battlestown (8)	N.M.I. topographical files
6:13	6	Bolany	O.S. 6 inch, 1939-40
6:16	6	Bolany	Ibid.
26:21	26	Brownswood	Ranson (1945), pp. 53-5
6:46	6	Craan Upper	O.S. 6 inch, 1939-40
2:39	6	Cummer	Kinahan (1883), pp. 155-6
6:24	6	Drummond	O.S. 6 inch, 1939-40
6:25	6	Drummond	Ibid.
27:53	27	Garrymore	N.M.I. topographical files
39:39	39	Grange	O.S. 6 inch, 1940
42:75	42	Haystown	Culleton (1984), p. 48
42:76	42	Johnstown	Idem
6:32	6	Kilmichael Hill	O.S. 6 inch, 1939-40
6:74	6	Knockbrandon	Ranson (1945), pp. 53-5
6.19	6	Laraheen Hill	O.S. 6 inch, 1939-40
31:12	31	Mackmine	Ibid.
6:52	6	Shrule	Ibid.
34:68	34	Tellarought (2)	N.M.I. topographical file
6:9	6	Tombay	O.S. 6 inch, 1939-40

Acknowledgements

This article is partly based on information collected by the Sites and Monuments Record (S.M.R.) Office and I would like to thank the Commissioners of Public Works for permission to use the S.M.R. database. I am also grateful to Michael Ryan and the staff of the National Museum of Ireland for providing information from their museum register. Figures 1, 2, 5, 7 and 8 were produced by Matthew Stout, figures 3 and 4 were produced by Katherine Daly and figure 6 was produced by Padraic Coffey and reprinted from *Irish Field Monuments* by Conleth Manning, by kind permission of the Commissioners of Public Works. I would like to thank the N.M.I., Thomas Hayes, Bernard Browne and Cambridge University for the photographs used in this article. The text was prepared by Patricia Dunford and Catherine Bannville and I am grateful for their assistance. I am indebted to Gabriel Cooney for a number of helpful suggestions.

Logainmneacha Chontae Loch Garman

An Contae

Cé go bhfuil córas na gcontaetha domhain-bhunaithe i gcúrsaí riaracháin agus
i gcúrsaí spóirt na tíre le fada anois, is córas é nach bhfuil bunús ar bith aige i
seanchas ná i seanstair na hÉireann. Córas atá ann a bhunaigh na Sasanaigh
agus iad beag beann ar na ranna tíre a bhí ann leis na cianta. Is mar seo a
chuireann Tóibín síos ar an scéal: 'Is é an dlí iasachta a chuir gach contae díobh
ar bun, d'fhonn lagú ar an eagras dúchais againn. Agus ba é nós oibre na nGall
san aidhm sin acu ná baile mór mar Phort Láirge nó Gaillimh nó Ros Comáin
nó Dún na nGall a thógaint agus limistéir mór tíre a tháthú leis agus *county* a
thabhairt air.'[1] Is treise fós an chaint a dhéanann Mac Néill: 'Níl údarás ar bith
ón stairsheanchas ná ón mbéaloideas leis na *counties* seo. Níl d'údarás leo ach
cumhacht an tSirriaim ghallda agus an Chrochadóra mar is dá ngnó sin a
ceapadh iad.'[2]

An limistéar tíre a dtugtar Contae Loch Garman anois air, is dúiche ann féin
é, an fharraige ar an taobh thoir agus ar an taobh ó dheas de, agus é deighilte
amach ón gcuid eile d'Éirinn ag na sléibhte agus ag na haibhneacha. Is sa
dúiche seo a bhí cónaí ar an dream ar a dtugtaí Uí Cinsealaigh, an mhuintir a
ainmníodh as a sinsear, Eanna Cinsealach, a mhair sa cheathrú céad, agus le
himeacht aimsire tugadh an t-ainm ar an dúiche a bhí faoina smacht. An t-am
ba mhó a réimeas, ba ionann Uí Cinsealaigh agus Contae Loch Garman an lae
inniú mar aon le cuid de Chontae Cheatharlach agus de Chontae Chill
Mhantáin. Ó am go chéile dhéantaí crapadh ar a gcríocha.

Sa bhliain 598 bhunaigh Maodhóg a mhainistir i bhFearna. Ní dócha go
raibh smacht easpaig aige ar an dúiche ar fad riamh, ach nuair a leagadh amach
teorainneacha na ndeoisí ag Seanad Ráth Bhreasail i dtús an dara céad déag is
mar seo a cuireadh síos ar theorainneacha Fhearna: 'Ó Bheigéirinn go
Míleadhach laistiar den Bhearbha; agus ó Shliabh Uidhe Laighean ó dheas go
dtí an mhuir.'[3]

Lasmuigh d'ainmneacha na n-aibhneacha agus na sléibhte, is iad ainmneacha na ndeoisí agus na bparóistí agus na láithreán eaglasta na logainmneacha is seanda dá bhfuil againn. Bunaíodh na deoisí ar chríocha ársa nó ar ríochtaí beaga, agus i gcás Fhearna níor mhiste a rá gur an Uí Cinsealaigh a bunaíodh í.

Bhí Contae Loch Garman ar na contaetha ba thúisce dár cuireadh ar bun i gCúige Laighean. Tharla sé seo roimh dheireadh an tríú céad déag agus glacadh le hainm an bhaile mhóir ag Inbhear Sláine mar ainm air, an baile ar thug na Gaeil Loch Garman air agus ar thug na Gaill Weysford nó Wexford air.⁴ In *Annála Loch Cé* agus in *Annála Ríochta Éireann* faighimid 'Contae Locha Garman', ach baineann na Ceithre Máistrí feidhm as ainm eile freisin .i. 'An Chontae Riabhach'.⁵ Úsáideann an Céitinneach 'Loch Garman' don chontae agus don deoise chomh maith — 'Fearna nó Loch Garman'.⁶

Na Barúntachtaí

Mar atá sé faoi láthair tá an contae roinnte ina bharúntachtaí. Dála an fhocail 'contae', is téarma é 'barúntach' a d'fheascair as teacht na Normanach. Deich gcinn a áirítear sa chontae ach, ó cheart, níl ann ach ocht gcinn mar tá péire díobh roinnte ina dhá gcuid. Seandúichí Gaelacha is ea cúig cinn díobh, ach déantúis nua an chuid eile agus iad déanta suas as seanchríocha dúchasacha. I gcáipéisí stáit an tséú céad déag agus an tseachtú céad déag is minic a luaitear fearainn agus dúichí a thugann le fios go raibh ainmneacha seachas ainmneacha oifigiúla na mbarúntachtaí nua á n-úsáid ag na Gaeil. I rollaí Paitinne Shéamais I agus i gcáipéisí nach iad déantar tagairt dá leithéidí seo: Kinshelagh's country, Murroes country, McDamore's country, McVadocke's country, Bracknagh territory, Clonehenrick territory, territory of Kilhobbocks, Kilcheele, Kilcooleneline, Farenhamon territory, Farren O Neale. Is as na críocha seo a rinneadh barúntachtaí Ghuaire agus Scairbh Bhailis. Na dúichí dúchais ar barúntachtaí anois iad, is as treibheanna a d'áitrigh iontu fadó a ainmníodh iad.

Fotharta: Eochaidh Fionn Fuath Airt dearbháir Choinn Chéadchathaigh, do réir na seanghinealach, sinsear an phobail ar a dugtaí Fotharta. Ruaig Art ardrí a nia féin as an Mí é agus chuir sé faoi i Laighin. Bhain a shliocht críocha fairsinge amach dóibh féin agus maireann a n-ainm i ndá bharúntacht, ceann acu i gContae Cheatharlach lastuaidh de Bhun Clóidí agus an ceann eile i ndeisceart Chontae Loch Garman. Fotharta Fea a thugtaí ar na críocha thuaidh — Fotharta Uí Nualláin níos déanaí — agus Fotharta an Chairn ar an dúiche ó dheas.⁷

Uí Bhairrche: De réir an tseanchais, ba é Dáire Barrach, Dara mac Chathaoir Mhóir, sinsear an tsleachta seo. Sa dara céad d'fhág a athair le huacht é a bheith ina cheann ar shluaite Ghaileoin. Tá ainm na treibhe ar Shliabh Mairge, barúntacht i ndeisceart Laoise gar do bhaile mór Cheatharlach. D'áitigh cuid acu ar chósta theas Chontae Loch Garman agus thug a n-ainm don bharúntacht ansin.

Beanntraí: Idir an Bhearbha agus an tSláine atá Beanntraí suite. De réir chosúlachta, is mar a chéile an Beanntraí seo againne agus an dream a thug a n-ainm don tríocha céad i nDeasmumhain. Déantar tagairt don dúiche i ndán Uí Uidhrin:

> Ó Bhearbha go Sláine soir,
> cuid críche Cloinne Coisgroigh,
> slógh Beanntroighe na cciabh coam,
> an fhian sheabhcoidhe shúlmhall.[8]

Sna Stát-Pháipéir is minic a luaitear Fásach Bheanntraí, m.sh., the fassaghe of Bentry 1515.[9]

Síol Maoluír: I gcóras an lae inniu tá Síol Maoluír roinnte ina dhá chuid — Síol Maoluír Thiar ar an gcuid siar ón tSláine agus Síol Maoluír Thoir ar an gcuid idir an tSláine agus an fharraige. Fearann na gCinéal nó Críoch na gCinéal a thugtaí ar an gcuid thoir. Is mar seo a labhraíonn Ó hUidhrin air:

> Críoch na Ceinél, caomh an fonn,
> a bhfearonn na bhfód subhdhonn,
> cuan as gartghloine fó ghréin,
> Ó hArtghoile as dual di-séin.[10]

Síol Brain: sin é ainm na barúntachta atá suite sa chúinne thiar theas den chontae. Luann Ó Donnabháin dán Uí Uidhrin ag tagairt don ainm seo[11] — 'Síol mBrain', ach in eagrán Carney 'Síol mBriain' atá ann:

> Ardaicme uasal oile
> Síol mBriain, drong na Dubhthoire.[12]

Dealraíonn sé gur don Dufair a thagraíonn an leathrann seo, dúiche atá suite i mbarúntachtaí Bheanntraí agus Scairbh Bhailis, agus mar sin ní le Shíol Brain a bhaineann an tagairt. Ba léir d'Ó Donnabháin an deacracht agus cheap sé go mb'fhéidir gur áit eile i Síol Brain an Dubhthoir a bhí i gceist.

An Bealach Caoin: Ainmníodh an bharúntacht seo as an sráidbhaile atá suite i lár an limistéir agus ar a dtugtar An Bealach ('The Ballagh') go hiondúil. Tá an bharúntacht roinnte ina dhá cuid — Bealach Caoin Theas agus Bealach Caoin Thuaidh. Is ionann an dá chuid le chéile agus an dá dhúiche Ghaelacha ar a dtugtar sna cáipéisí Gallda 'The Murroes' nó 'Murrowes' agus 'mcDamore's country'.

Fearann Uí Mhurchú is ciall leis an gcéad ainm díobh sin. Uí Fheilme Theas seanainm an dúiche. Mac le hEanna Cinsealach ab ea an Feilimidh as ar ainmníodh an treibh. Bhí dhá chuid sa treibh sin — Uí Feilme (Feilmeadha) Thuaidh i gCeatharlach agus Uí Feilme Theas sa dúiche atá faoi chaibidil againn anseo. Nuair a tháinig córas na sloinnte isteach ghlac príomhchlann an treibhe seo theas an sloinne Ó Murchú (Murchadha) chucu féin agus Fearann nó Críocha Uí Mhurchú a tugadh ar an dúiche. Cuid d'Uí Cinsealaigh ab ea Uí Fheilme.[13]

Críocha Mhac Dháith Mhóir is brí le 'McDamore's country'. Deir Ó Donnabháin gur de shliocht Mhurchaidh na nGael, deartháir Dhiarmada na nGall, Mac Dháith Mhóir.[14] Baintear feidhm as an ainm 'Macamores' coitianta i gcónaí. Mar sin, is ionann Críocha Uí Mhurchú mar aon le Críocha Mhac Dháith Mhóir agus barúntacht Bhealach Caoin idir theas agus thuaidh le chéile.

Guaire: 'Kinshelagh's country' a thugtaí ar thuaisceart bharúntacht Ghuaire — fuílleach na gcríoch fairsing úd Uí Cinsealaigh. Laisteas de sin bhí an 'Bracknagh territory' nó 'the landes of Broyckenagh'.[15] Cheap an Donnabhánach gur talamh bhreac is ciall leis an bhfocal Breacarnach;[16] d'fhéadfaí gur Brocanach atá ann .i. áit a mbíonn na broic flúirseach. Bhí ceantar eile i bhfíordheisceart Ghuaire, dar liom, ar a dtugtaí Coill Hobac, 'territory of Kilhobbocks'.

Scairbh Bhailis: Tá cuid mhaith seandúichí sa bharúntacht seo a ainmníodh as an áit i bparóiste Bhaile Uí Chearnaigh a bhfuil áth éadomhain sa tSláine. An chuid sin den bharúntacht idir teorainn bharúntacht Ghuaire agus an tSláine 'Clonehenrick territory' nó 'Territory of Clonhanrike' a thugtaí air, agus maireann an t-ainm fós in ainm an bhaile fhearainn Clonhenret — Cluain Hanraic — láimh le Cam Eolaing.[17]

Lastuaidh de sin bhí Fearann Ámainn. I litir ón Rí go Chichester sa bhliain 1608 luaitear 'lands of Cloghamon alias Farrinhamon'. Normanach ab ea Hamond le Gras a thug a ainm don cheantar seo agus tá Cloch Ámainn mar ainm ar an sráidbhaile atá suite ar bhruach na Sláine agus i bparóiste Chill Rois. Limistéar tíre ab ea Fearann Ámainn a shín leis an gceantar leathan coillteach, a dtugtaí an Dufair air, idir an abhainn agus na Staighrí Dubha. Sa tríú céad déag faighimid leaganacha mar 'Duffarth' agus 'Dunferch',[18] 'Le Duffer' atá le fáil i státpháipéir lár an tseú céad déag.[19] Tosaíodh ar choillte fairsinge an cheantair seo a leagan sa bhliain 1611 agus i gceann daichead bliain bhí an chuid ba mhó díobh ar lár. Níl fágtha anois díobh ach forais Choill Eachroma i bparóiste Mhóin Airt.[20]

I dtuaisceart na barúntachta tá Fearann Uí Néill suite, dúiche a bhfuil an chuid is mó di i gContae Cheatharlach. Déantar tagairt freisin do cheantar ar a dtugtaí 'Kilcheele' — Coill Chaol (?) — lastuaidh de Chluain Hanraic.

Cuid de na fearainn sin atá luaite — Cluain Hanraic, Coill Chaol, Coill Hobac san áireamh, b'fhéidir, caithfidh gur chuid iad den limistéar ar a dtugtaí 'McVadocke's country' nó 'McDavock's territory'. De shliocht Mhurchaidh na nGael an Mac Uadóg a thug a ainm don limistéar sin, dála Mhac Dháith Mhóir.[21]

Ní miste dúiche eile a lua anseo a ndéantar tagairt di i gcáipéisí eaglasta .i. Uí Dheagha, ceantar i dtuaisceart bharúntacht Ghuaire, a luaitear i *Félire Oengusso*: 'Cell moshílóic i n-Uib Degad i n-Uib Cendselaig.' Ní raibh gaol fola ag Uí Deagha le hUí Cinsealaigh, ach bhí duine de shliocht Ua gCinsealaigh ina thaoiseach ar Uí Deagha san ochtú céad. Maraíodh Dondgal i gcath Ghabhráin sa bhliain 761 agus cuireann an *Leabhar Laighneach* síos mar seo air: 'Dondgal a quo Cellach Bairne .i. taisech Hua nDega' — Dondgal ónar shíolraigh Ceallach .i. taoiseach Ua nDeagha.[22]

Paróistí

Is ar aonaid bheaga riaracháin atá na seanpharóistí bunaithe. Ní miste an téarma 'paróiste' a mhíniú i dtosach báire. Ar an gcéad dul síos, tá na paróistí a cuireadh ar bun sna meánaoiseanna agus ar ranna riaracháin nó 'paróistí sibhialta' anois iad. Ansin, tá na paróistí eaglasta mar atá faoi láthair agus go hiondúil is cnuasach 'seanpharóistí' iad seo. Ní bhaineann siad sin le hábhar na haiste seo.

Is dócha gurb ionann an seanpharóiste, ó thaobh fairsinge de, agus an t-aonad riaracháin ba lú a bhí ann leis na cianta — an baile biataigh.[23] I dtús ré na Críostaíochta ba é a bhí sa pharóiste an limistéar a bhí faoi cheannas aba na mainistreach áitiúla. Ní foláir nó leagadh amach na paróistí tar éis do sheanad Ráth Bhreasail ceist na ndeoisí a shocrú agus, i gcoitinne, is mar a chéile na paróistí san dóú céad déag agus paróistí sibhialta an lae inniu.

I gContae Loch Garman tá 152 paróiste sibhialta; dhá cheann déag díobh atá suite ar theorainn idir barúntachtaí; tá siad roinnte, is é sin go bhfuil cuid acu i mbarúntacht amháin agus cuid eile i mbarúntacht taobh léi.

Tosaíonn beagnach leathchéad d'ainmneacha na bparóistí leis an bhfocal cill. Sa chuid is mó díobh seo is ainm duine a leanann an focal, naomh nó sagart a bhunaigh a chill san áit nó naomh dar tíolacadh an chill, cuirtear i gcás Cill Bhríde, Cill Chaomháin, Cill Chormaic, Cill Chuáin, Cill Gharbháin, Cill Ghormáin, Cill Mocheallóg, Cill Phádraig, agus cuid mhaith eile nach eol dúinn mórán faoin naomh a luaitear. Uaireanta is cur síos ar shuíomh na cille a bhíonn san ainm, m.sh., Cill Easca (b. Síol Brain); Cill Laig (= Loig) in Uí Bhairrche; Cill Uisce (b. Bealach Caoin Theas). Chomh maith le hainmneacha na bparóistí, tá roinnt mhaith áiteanna a bhfuil an focal cill ina n-ainmneacha nach paróistí iad.

Níl ach dornán beag paróistí a bhfuil an focal teampall ina chuid den ainm: Teampall Lúgadáin i mBeanntraí, Teampall Sheanáin i mbaile mór Inis Córthaidh, Teampeall Scuaibe i mBeanntraí, teampall Seanbhoth i Scairbh Bhailis.[24]

An focal Béarla 'Saint' is tús le hainmneacha fiche is a trí de pharóistí agus tá naoi gcinn díobh seo laistigh de Bhuirg Loch Garman. Ainmneacha a cuireadh ar na paróistí tar éis teacht do na Normanaigh cuid acu, ar nós St Margaret's, St Nicholas', St John's, St James', St Peter's, &rl., ach aistriú ar ainmneacha Gaelacha cuid eile acu. 'St Doologue's' a thugtar ar pharóiste i mbuirg Loch Garman. Sa *Leabhar Laighneach* a fhaightear an tagairt is luaithe don naomh agus don áit: Ellóc, agus Cell Moellóc.[25] Sna cáipéisí Gallda is iomaí leagan truaillithe den ainm a fhaighimid: 'Church of St. Alloch' c1172;[26] 'St. Tullog's 1542;[27] 'St. Tullok's' 1597;[28] 'St. Ulock' 1704;[29] 'parish of St. Iologe' 1737.[30] Cill M'Eallóg, mar sin, seanainm an pharóiste.

Sampla eile d'aistriú ón nGaeilge atá san ainm 'St Mullin's' i mBeanntraí. Tigh Moling a thugadh Gaeilgeoirí i gcónaí air. Is do mhainistir a thagraíonn an focal tigh nó teach, agus tá sé le fáil in ainm dhá pharóiste eile — Teach Munna a bhunaigh Munna nó Fiontán (+ 634), agus Teach Moshagra nó Moshagard.

I gcás cuid de na paróistí eile, baintear feidhm as ainm an bhaile fhearainn nó na háite a bhfuil nó a mbíodh an séipéal mar ainm paróiste, ach go minic cuimhnítear ar an naomhphatrún in ainm reilige nó in ainm tobair bheannaithe sa bharóiste, cuirim i gcás Cill Dhiarmada, baile fearainn i bparóiste Chill Chaomháin, barúntacht Ghuaire; Cill Deoráin, reilig i bparóiste Chill Anna; Tobar Mochua Luachra i bparóiste Mhaolanaigh, Bealach Caoin Theas.

Bailte Fearainn

Tá 2,386 bhaile fearainn i gContae Loch Garman, ach san áireamh sin tá cuid mhaith nach bhfuil iontu ach cuid nó codanna den bhaile fearainn céanna; mar shampla, Baile an Mhóta Beag, agus Baile an Mhóta Mór, i bparóiste Ballyhuskard; Crory Lower, Crory Middle agus Crory Upper i bparóiste Ard Chrómáin (Artramon); agus i bparóiste Kilnehue tá Annagh Central, Annaghgap, Annagh Hill, Annagh Long, Annagh Lower, Annagh Middle, Annagh More, Annagh Upper! Chomh maith lena leithéidí sin, tá cuid maith bailte fearainn ar fud an chontae a bhfuil an t-ainm céanna orthu: Baile Beag atá ar sé cinn agus tá dhá bhaile is fiche ann a dtugtar Newtown orthu.

Is Gaeilge atá i dtrí cheathrú, beagnach, d'ainmneacha na mbailte fearainn; Béarla nó meascán den Ghaeilge agus den Bhéarla atá san fhuílleach, agus, b'fhéidir, corrshampla d'fhocail Lochlannaise nó de theanga ársa eile.

Ainmneacha Béarla

I mbarúntacht Fhotharta tá a lán bailte fearainn a ainmníodh as an méid acraí talún a bhí iontu i dtosach báire: Threeacres, Five-acre, Sixacre, Nineacres, Tenacre, Elevenacre, Twelveacre, Nineteenacres, Twentyacres, Fortyacres. Sa bharúntacht chéanna tá roinnt mhaith bailte beaga fearainn a bhfuil sloinne agus -town d'iarmhír leis mar ainm orthu, dála Allenstown, Bricketstown, Busherstown, Ecclestown, Gaynestown, Harristown, Leachestown, Latimerstown, Pembrokestown, Rostonstown, Shawstown, agus mar sin de. Faightear a leithéidí eile ar fud an chontae, agus i measc na n-ainmneacha eile Béarla tá cinn mar seo: Brickpark, Brookfield, Castletown(trí cinn díobh), Cherryorchard, Broomhill. Tá naoi gcinn de bhailte fearainn sa chontae ar a dtugtar Churchtown, trí cinn déag ar a dtugtar Grange, agus ceithre cinn déag a bhfuil Glebe mar ainm orthu. Ba leis an Eaglais an Ghléib agus de ghnáth fiche acra talún a bhí inti. Nuair a bhí tailte á mbronnadh ar dhaoine áirithe sa seachtú céad déag coinníodh an scór sin acraí i seilbh na hEaglaise, cuirtear i gcás, '20a. In Edermyne, next the church, assigned for the glebe thereof' agus '20a. In Bollymore and Ballylamin, next to the church of Skrine for the glebe thereof'.[31]

Cuid de na hainmneacha Béarla, is ainmneacha nua iad a chealaigh seanainmneacha Gaeilge na mbailte fearainn. I paróiste Dhomhnach Mór tá baile fearainn ar a dtugtar Cookstown. An Chúlóg Bhuí a thugtaí air seo agus ba le Sir Walsingham Cooke, Bart., é sa bhliain 1640 (CS)*. I bparóiste Cluana, tá baile ar a dtugtaí Ráithín. Ba leis an gCoirnéal Solomon Richards as Devonshire é agus baisteadh Solsborough air,[32] an t-ainm atá air sa lá atá inniu ann, cé go dtugtaí Ráithín fós air i lár an chéid seo caite.[33] Ainm den saghas

---

*CS = Civil Survey, Wexford.

céanna is ea Borrmount: Eidir-Mhaighin beag a ainm seo gur bronnadh ar Christian Borr é, eachtránaí de chuid Chromail. Agus i bparóiste Chluain Mhór, tógadh caisleán sa cheathrú céad déag san áit ar a dtugtaí Cloch na gCaorach. Atógadh é sa bhliain 1599 agus beagnach céad bliain ina dhiaidh sin dhíol an Captaen Robert Thornhill é le William Alcock a thóg teach mór ar an láthair agus a bhaist Wilton ar an áit.

Tá bailte eile ann a ainmníodh as a n-úinéirí nua agus nach fios dúinn anois a n-ainmneacha bunaidh. Idir Inis Córthaidh agus Bun Clóidí tá Cloch Bheámainn: Cloghveomon 1630,[34] Castle Bemond 1654 (CS), Castlebeaumont 1655 (DS),* Castle Beaumont 1657,[35] Cloughbeman 1714,[36] Clobemon 1807[37]. Is léir, mar sin, gur caisleán is brí le cloch anseo, agus gur le duine darb ainm Beaumont é. Sa bhliain 1395 bhronn an rí, Risteard II, lear mór talún i dtuaisceart an chontae ar Sir John de Beaumont. Is dócha gur leis seo an caisleán as ar ainmníodh an baile fearainn.[38]

I bparóiste Cinn Eich (Tintern) tá Tullerstown: Tolouyston, Tollowyston 1307,[39] Tullowstown 1654 (CS), Tullaghstown 1655 (CS). Ba le John de Tullos (Toulouse) é sa bhliain 1247.[40]

Tá Galgystown i bparóiste Rinn Duáin: Galyestowne 1630,[41] Galgeestowns 1654 (CS), Galstowne 1655 (DS) ach sa tríú céad déag Ballically a bhí air agus ba le John Galgefel é; i 1307 Ballygally an leagan den ainm a bhí in úsáid agus John Galgel ainm an úinéara.[42]

Aistriúcháin

Aistriúcháin ón nGaeilge atá i gcuid de na hainmneacha Béarla, m. sh., Jamestown (p. Eidir-Mhaighin): Ballyshemus 1618;[43] Ballihemus 1654 (CS) .i. Baile Shéamais. Mar a chéile Johnstown (p. Má Dhá Chonn): Ballisoan 1655 (DS), Ballysean c1660 (BSD) .i. Baile Sheoin; Kellystown (p. Adamstown): Ballikelly, Ballykelly 1654 (CS) .i. Baile Uí Cheallaigh. Tá Kellystown eile i bparóiste Ráth Easpaig: Bally-Cally, Ballikelly 1655 (DS). Tugtar Milltown ar Bhaile an Mhuilinn (p. Chill Bhríde): Ballemullen 1630,[44] Ballinmulline, Balinmulline 1654 (CS), Ballimullin 1657.[45] I gcás Dún an Óir (p. Seanros), tá Goldentown mar mhalairt ar Dunanore de réir na Suirbhéireachta Ordanáis.

Ní cruinn i gcónaí an t-aistriú, áfach, mar is léir ón ainm Hook Head. Faoin gceathrú céad déag dhéantaí tagairt do 'Le Hoke',[46] agus bhaintí feidhm go coitianta as 'The Hoke' sa séú céad déag.[47] San am céanna déantar tagairt do 'vicarage of Saint Dowan of Hooks'. Ach i bhfad roimhe sin, i lár an tríú céad déag, Rendevan agus a leithéidí a thugtaí ar an áit.[48] Ryndowane leagan eile ó aimsir Eoin rí.[49] Tá fuascailt na faidhbe le fáil i Féilire Dhún na nGall mar a luaitear an naomh Duán i Rinn Duáin. Naomh de chuid an tséú céad ab ea Duán (Dubhán) a gcomórtaí lá a fhéile ar 11 Feabhra. Dar ndóigh, tá focal duán ann a chiallaíonn gléas marfa éisc .i. 'hook', agus mar sin cuireadh Hook Head mar aistriú ar Rinn Duáin.

Meascán den Ghaeilge agus den Bhéarla a fhaightear in ainmneacha áirithe. Truailliú áiféiseach é Castleworkhouse (p. Cinn Eich). Ní hé teach na mbocht is brí leis an gcuid deiridh de ach an t-ainm Murchadh: Castlemorrougho

---

*DS = Down Survey, Wexford.

1626,[50] Castlemorroghoe 1633[51] .i. Caisleán Mhurchadha. Tá sampla eile den truailliú céanna le feiceáil san ainm Morriscastle (p. Chill Mhucraise): Castle Morcho 1654 (CS), Murro Castle 1659.[52]

Tá scór ainmneacha ann a bhfuil an focal castle ina dtús agus go minic is ainm duine a ghabhann leis. I bparóiste Chill Mucraise tá Castle Annesley. Sa bhliain 1611 deonaíodh réimse talún sa cheantar seo do Sir Francis Annesley, ridire, agus cead aonach a thionól ag 'Ballycaslane'.[53] B'fhéidir gurb ionann an Baile Caisleáin nó Baile an Chaisleáin agus Castle Annesley an lae inniu. Tá Castletown i bparóiste Chill Ghormáin a dtugtaí Baile an Chaisleáin air tráth: Ballycaslane 1618, 1638 (LRR),* Castletown 1654 (CS). Láimh le sráidbhaile na hAbhann Duibhe (Blackwater) tá Castle Talbot: Baile na Móna ainm an bhaile fearainn seo nuair a deonaíodh tailte do Francis Talbot i 1611.[54] I bparóiste St Mary's, Beanntraí, tá Castlemoyle .i. Caisleán Maol, caisleán a bhí gan táibhle, b'fhéidir, nó gan a bheith críochnaithe.

Seanfhocal Béarla ar 'mór' is ea' much' agus tá sé le fáil i ndornán ainmneacha i bhFotharta agus in Uí Bhairrche. Tá péire acu i bparóiste Chill Fhinneog (Killinick): Muchknock .i. Cnoc Mór; agus Muchrath .i. Ráth Mhór. Béarla glan is ea Muchtown i bparóiste Chill Chuáin (Uí Bhairrche), agus cheapfaí gur mar a chéile an t-ainm Muchwood (p. Ard Camrois) ach níl ann ach aistriú ar Choill Mhór: Muchwood 1611;[55] Killmore 1654 (CS), Keilemore c1660 (BSD), Keilmore alias Muchwood 1684.[56]

Baile/Buaile

Maidir leis na míreanna éagsúla a bhfaightear in ainmneacha na mbailte fearainn, ní haon ionadh é gurb é an focal baile an mhír thosaigh is coitianta go mór fada. Is iad na hainmneacha-baile na cinn is flúirsí i ngach páirt d'Éirinn, agus tá beagnach cúig chéad díobh i gcontae Loch Garman. Is é ba bhrí leis an bhfocal i dtosach báire áitreabh, nó láthair tí, nó ionad cónaithe, agus ní go ceann scathaimh a tosaíodh ar fheidhm a bhaint as an téarma le réimse theoranta talún a chur in iúl. Dá bhrí sin, is minic ainm duine ag gabháil leis: Baile Dháith, Baile Dháith Mhóir, Baile Mháirtín, Baile Mhic Sheoinín, Baile Ghearóid, Baile Mhuircheartaigh Léith, Baile Sheáin, Baile Uí Thomaltaigh.[57]

Uaireanta is aidiacht a théann leis an bhfocal baile: Baile Beag — sé cinn díobh; Baile Dubh — naoi gcinn; Baile Breac: Baile Fada, Baile Rua, Baile Uachtarach.

Cur síos ar shuíomh an bhaile a bhíonn ann uaireanta eile: Baile na Bearna — ceithre cinn; Baile an Bhóthair, Baile an Bhealaigh, Baile an Tobair, Baile na Claise. Cur síos de shaghas eile atá ina leithéidí seo: Baile na Caoithe, Baile na gCloch, Baile na nDriseog, Baile na mBriogadán, agus Baile na mBodach!

Uaireanta is deacair, ó na leaganacha truaillithe Gallda, idirdhealú a dhéanamh idir baile and buaile. Tá an dá fhocal in éineacht san ainm Baile na Buaile.[58] Ciallaíonn buaile áit bhlite bó nó páircín féaraigh, agus tá an focal le fáil i dtríocha ainm, m.sh., Buaile Bhán, Buaile Bheag, Buaile Bhuí, Buaile Chruinn, Buaile Dhorcha, Buaile Mhór.[59]

An áit a dtugtar Ballyphilip anois air, is Buaile Philib a bhíodh air uaireanta,

---

*L.R.R. = Lodge, records of the Rolls.

agus Baile mhic Dhonnchaidh Riabhaigh freisin. Ballymacdonnoghreogh 1629,[60] Ballydonnoghreogh 1638 (L.R.R.), Ballydonoghreagh alias Ballyphilip 1685,[61] Bouly-Philip 1753,[62] Ballyphilip 1783, Bolaphilip 1787, Bollyphilip, Ballyphilip 1838.

Tá Buaile an Easpaig i bparóiste Fhearna; agus cé nach baile fearainn é ní miste an áit cháiliúil úd, Buaile Mhaodhóg, a lua. Bíonn cruthanna éagsúla ar an bhfocal buaile sna leaganacha Gallda: bola, boly, boley, boola, booley, bol-. I bhfuaimniú cuid de na hainmneacha-buaile le tamaillín anuas tá athrú ag teacht, m.sh., Bolaboy (Boolabwee), Ballyboy; Boolynavoughran — Ballynavocran.

Cill/Coill

Más deacair idirdhealú idir baile agus buaile, is deacra fós uaireanta breith a thabhairt idir cill agus coill má bhítear ag braith ar na foirmeacha 'béarla', mar seasann Kil-, Kill- don dá fhocal. Má luaitear ainm naoimh leis an réimír is féidir a thuiscint gur cill is brí leis an logainm. Mar a gcéanna, má bhíonn reilig nó fothrach cille san áit. Mar atá luaite cheana, tá beagnach leathchéid ainm paróiste sa chontae a thosaíonn le cill. Chomh maith leo sin, tá trí scór bailte fearainn ann a thosaíonn leis an bhfocal céanna mar aon le dornán logainmneacha eile, seanreiligí agus a leithéid. Astu sin is ainm naoimh a ghabhann le leathchéad díobh.

Tá trí bhaile fearainn ann a bhfuil Cill Bhríde mar ainm orthu, ceann i bparóiste Ballyhuskard, ceann i bparóiste Kiltennell, ceann i bparóiste St James and Dunbrody. (Luadh thuas go bhfuil an t-ainm céanna ar dhá pharóiste.) I measc na naomh eile a chomórtar tá siad seo:-

Beagnait: Cill Bheagnatan, Kilbegnet, p. Chill Ghormáin, Guaire;

Cairbre: Cill Chairbre, Kilcarbery, p. Chluain Mhór, Bealach C., Thuaidh;

Caomhán: Cill Chaomháin, Kilcavan, p. Chill Chaomháin, Uí Bhairrche; agus ceann eile, p. Chill Chaomháin, Guaire;

Cormac: Cill Chormaic, Kilcormick, p. Chill Chormaic, Bealach Caoin Thuaidh;

Cuán: Cill Chuáin, Kilcowan lower agus upper, p. Chill Chuáin, Uí Bhairrche; agus Kilcowanmore, paróiste i mBeanntraí;

Diarmaid: Cill Dhiarmada, Kildermot, p. Chill Chaomháin, Guaire;[63]

Garbhán: Cill Gharbháin, Kilgarvan, p. Chill Gharbháin, Síol Maoluír Thiar;

Gormán: Cill Ghormáin, Kilgorman, paróiste i nGuaire: 'Cill Gormáin in airthur Laighan' — *Féilire Uí Ghormáin* c1630;

Mochua: Cill Mochua, Kilmacoe, p. St Margaret's, Síolmaoluír Thoir;

Pádraig: Cill Phádraig, p. Chill na Manach, Bealach Caoin Thuaidh; agus ceann eile, p. Chill Ghormáin, Guaire; agus paróiste i Síol Maoluír Thoir.

Cé gur soiléir na hainmneacha sna samplaí seo, ní furasta a rá cén naomh atá i gceist i ngach cás toisc an t-ainm céanna a bheith ar níos mó ná duine amháin; cuirtear i gcás Carbhán — bhí triúr den ainm sin ann; bhí ceathrar Cuán ann, agus níos mó na Beagnait amháin ann.

Tá idir pharóiste agus bhaile fearainn i mBealach Caoin Theas ar a dtugtar

Kilmallock; Killmalloke 1547,[64] Killmologe 1654 (CS), Killmollock 1597,[65] Kilmalocker 1659,[66] Killmclogue 1655.[67] Ní raibh an Donnabhánach róchinnte faoin ainm agus tugann sé malairt ainmneacha: Cill Mocheallóg, nó Cill Mo- Shíológ nó Mothíológ.[68] Ach tugann sé na leaganacha céanna agus é ag trácht ar pharóiste Kilmakilloge i mbarúntacht Ghuaire. De réir *Féilire Dhún na nGall*, is ar 13 Iúil a chomórtaí féile Mothiollocc. 'Cell moshílóic in Uibh Ceinnselaigh' atá i *Féilire Uí Ghormáin*, á lua ag Ó hÓgáin; agus tugann *Félire Oengusso* 'Cell moshílóic i n-Uib Degad i n-uib Cendselaig'. Sna cáipéisí Gallda tá na leaganacha seo: Killmakellock 1612,[69] 'church of Kilkelocks' 1654 (CS), 'ye Streame of Killmakelloge' 1654 (CS), Killmackilogue, Kilmclogue, Kilmaclogue 1655 (DS), agus sa naoú déag faighimid Kilmichaelogue. Is dóigh liom gur as sin a tháinig gur 'St Michael's' a thugtar ar pharóiste Ghuaire anois. Luaitear Killmackeloge mar bhaile fearainn i 1633 (LRR) agus is i gCluain Aitinn uachtarach atá fothrach an tseanteampaill. An amhlaidh gur mar a chéile Cluain Aitinn agus Cill Mocheallóg?

Kiltennel an t-ainm atá ar pharóiste agus ar bhaile fearainn i mBeallach Caoin Thuaidh. Sincheal an naomh a raibh baint aige leis an gcill seo, de réir Uí Dhonnabháin — Cill tSinchill. Is sa pharóiste sin atá Cuan Bhaile na Cúirte agus tá tagairt ó 1542 a thugann Baile na Cúirte mar mhalairt ainm do Chill tSinchill: Kyltelyn, otherwise Balnecourt.[70]

Ós ag caint ar naoimh ataimíd, ní miste tagairt a dhéanamh do Templescoby, paróiste agus baile fearainn i mBeanntraí. I lár an chéid seo caite bhaintí feidhm as an leagan Templescobin,[71] agus tá Scobin le fáil sa bhliain 1615. De ghnáth, áfach, ní bhíonn an -n ag a dheireadh. I 1655, (DS) ba chuid de pharóiste Ross-Droite (Ros Droichid) an baile fearainn Templescobie: Templescoby c1660 (BSD), Templeskoby 1659,[72] Templescobye 1629.[73] Déantar soiléiriú ar bhrí an ainm sna leaganacha Laidíne: 'Sacro-Bosco called Tamplescobe 1588; 'church or chapel of Sacrobosco, commonly called Templescobe' 1594;[74] Chapel or Rectory de Sacro Bosco called Templescnobie alias Templescobe' 1619. Mar sin, is é is brí leis an ainm Teampall na Scuaibe Naofa .i. na Coille Beannaithe. An ó aimsir na págántachta a tháinig 'beann-aitheacht' na coille úd? Leaganacha an naoú céad déag a chríochnaíonn le -n, b'fhéidir gur 'scuaibín' (nó scuab íon?) is bun leo. Sa naoú céad déag, ceapadh gur ainm naoimh a bhí i 'Sacro Bosco' agus in 1818 baisteadh 'Church of St Busk' ar theampall de chuid Eaglais na hÉireann a tógadh sa pharóiste timpeall dhá bhliain déag roimhe sin. Níor rófhada go bhfuarthas an botún amach agus díbríodh Busk as féilire na naomh.[75]

Cé nach mbaineann sé go díreach le hábhar, is fiú trácht ar logainm eile anseo — Ballygalvert i bparóiste Chluain Liath (Clonleigh), Beantraí. Ar an gcéad radharc cheapfaí gur sloinne atá sa dara cuid de agus gur Baile Ghailbheirt nó Baile Gailbeir, mar a cheap Ó Donnabháin, atá ann.[76] I dtosach an naoú céad déag faighimid Ballygalworth agus Ballygalwart,[77] ach ní haon chúnamh iad sin. Réitíonn cáipéisí an seachtú céad deág an cheist, áfach: 'Priestowns alias Ballygallsagard 1623,[78] Ballygallsugard 1659[79] .i. Gall-shagart. Cérbh iad na Gall-shagairt seo? Ceaptar gurbh iad manaigh Ghlascarraig iad, sagairt ón mBreatain ar leo an baile fearainn seo.[80]

Coill

Tá timpeall tríocha baile fearainn sa chontae a dtosaíonn a n-ainmneacha leis an bhfocal coill. Ainm crainn a théann leis an bhfocal i gcuid acu: Coill Chuilinn (Kilcullen), p. Theampall Seanbhoth; b'fhéidir gur don áit seo atá an tagairt ón mbliain 1606: 'Killchollinge in the Dufferie'.[81] Tá Coill an Iúir (Killanure) i bparóiste St Mary's, Bun Clóidí, agus Coill Doire (Kilderry) i bparóiste Chill Chaomháin, Uí Bhairrche. I gCillín Cúile (Killincooly), tá Coill na Smután (Kilnasmuttaun); caithfidh gur leagadh cuid mhór de chrainn na coille seo agus gur fágadh na smutáin.

Leanann ainm duine an focal coill uaireanta: Coill Ghiobúin (Kilgibbon), p. Chluain Mhór, cé go b'fhéidir gur Coill Ghobáin atá san ainm mar Killgobbane atá ar léarscáil an *Down Survey*, agus tá 'Kilgibbin alias Kilgobbin' againn ó 1684. Tá Coill Phiarais i bparóiste Theampall Sheanáin, agus Coill Mhac Dhiarmada Rua i St Mary's, Bun Clóidí, Keilmacdermottroe 1654 (CS). Ní luaitear a ainm ach cuimhnítear ar cheird an úinéara san ainm Coill a' Ghabhann (Killagowan), p. Mhaolanaigh.

Coill-ainmneacha eile: Coill Liath (Killeagh) (?), p. Bhaile Bhaldúin, Coill an Iarainn (Killinierin), p. Chill Chaomháin, áit a bhfuil tobar roide, b'fhéidir; Coill Eachroma, fuílleach choillte na Dufaire ar limistéar ann féin é sa séú céad déag.

Tá an t-ainm Baile na Coille ar roinnt bailte fearainn: Ballinakill, p. Arda Meighin, agus ceann eile p. Bhaile Uí Chonbhaigh, Ballynakill, p. Chill Bhríde, agus ceann eile p. Mhóin Airt.

Kyle atá ar roinnt bailte eile: Tá Kyle agus Kyle Little i bparóiste Mhaolanaigh; tá Kyle Lower, Kyle Middle agus Kyle Upper; Coill Mhac Thomáis Rua ainm iomlán an bhaile seo mar is léir ó na foirmeacha seo: Kilmc Thomsrowe, Kilmcthomas rowe 1552,[82] Killmacthomas roe 1610,[83] Keile McThomas Roe c1660 (BSD), Kilmacthomas alias Old Keile.[84]

Móin

Tá breis is dhá scór bailte fearainn a bhfuil Mon- ina dtosach. Móin is ciall leis seo i gcás a leath nó níos mó, ach is léir gur muine an bhrí atá le cuid eile acu ón mBéarlú atá déanta orthu: .i. Money-; tá cúpla sampla eile agus is dócha gur mong an focal atá ann. Ní éasca idirdhealú eatarthu.

Cé go bhfuil leaganacha scríofa ón naoú céad déag a bhfuil 'Money-' ina dtús, is 'ó' atá san ainm Monagear .i. Móin na gCaor, p. Chluana, Scairbh Bhailis,[85] Móin na Gréine, Monagreany Lower agus Upper, p. Mhuine Moling, Guaire: bhí an dá bhaile ann sa seachtú céad déag ach gur Móin na Gréine, mór, agus Móin na Gréine, beag, a thugtaí orthu faoi seach;[86] Móin na Saighead (Monaseed), p. Kilnàhue, Guaire: 'grunda sagittarium' a thug Ó Donnabháin mar aistriú Laidine ar an ainm.[87] An amhlaidh gur fágadh a lán saighead ar an móin tar éis catha fadó, nó, an ndéantaí saigheada as slata na háite?

Rinneadh tagairt do Bhaile na mBodach cheana: tá Móin an Bhodaigh (Monavoddagh) i mBaile na Sláine; i bparóiste Chill Chormaic, tá Monawilling Lower agus Upper: 'Monavullen' an litriú agus an fhoghraíocht áitiúil, Móin an Mhuilinn is bunús leis Monvolling. Monavollim 1654 (CS), Monevooling,

Monnevouling 1655 (DS), samplaí d'fhoirmeacha an seachtú déag. I bparóiste Ballyhuskard, tá Móin Dónaill: Mondonyll 1625,[88] Monnedonnell 1630,[89] Mondonill 1654 (CS), Mondonnell 1655 (DS), Mondaniel. Faoi láthair tugtar 'Mount Daniel' air ar mhaithe le galántacht! Tá bailte fearainn eile ar fud an chontae a thosaíonn leis an bhfocal Mount:- Mountalexander, p. Chill tSinchill, Monyalexander, Mone Alexandr 1654 (CS), Mounthoward, p. Mhuine Molling. Insíonn Sleator (1806) dúinn gur le 'a late bishop of Waterford' an áit agus gur uaidh sin a ainmníodh an baile. De réir dhealraimh, Cúl na Mactíre nó Cluain na Mactíre a bhíodh ar an áit roimh theacht don easpag.

'Munfin' a thugtar de ghnáth ar an dá bhaile fearainn i bparóiste Bhaile Uí Chearnaigh, — 'Mountfin Lower or Ballinturner' agus Mountfin Upper. Monfine alias Monin 1622 (LRR), 'Monfin in the Diffrye' 1631 (LRR), Mongaupum 1634,[90] Monfine 1654 (CS), Monphine, Monfine 1655 (DS), Mountsfin, Mountphin, Moumphin 1699,[91] Mount fin 1714,[92] Munfin 1806, Mt. Fin 1807.[93] Bunús an ainm? Móin Fhionn nó Móin Fhinn nó Moing Fhionn?

In aice le Ros Mhic Thriúin tá Mountgarrett, p. St Mary's, Beanntraí: Móta Ghairead a thugtaí air seo: Mota-Gairead 1599 (A.F.M. — (Ticcearna Mhóta gaireatt (A.F.M.), Montgaret, Montegarett 1549,[94] Mountgarrett 1639, Mongarret 1714.[95] Ba le Richard, Lord Mountgarrett, an áit i 1640 (CS).

Muine

'Money' an gnáth-Bhéarlú ar an bhfocal muine atá le fáil i mbreis is dosaen logainmneacha. Money, p. Carnew, 'Moneyaleboy or Money' 1604,[96] Muney, Moneslaboye 1654 (CS). Muine Sléibhe Buí an t-ainm, mar sin. I Maolanach, tá Moneyboe ach 'Mine vó' nó 'Míne bó' a deirtear muintir na báilte go minic .i. Muine Bhó nó Muine na Bó: Monaboch 1618 (LRR), Muingeneboe 1654 (CS), Monabo 1811, Moneybo, Monyboo 1817.

Moneycross Lower agus Upper, Liskinfere, an dá chuid de Mhuine na Croise: Muynnecraoissee 1618,[97] Munignecroishie, Monecroisse 1630,[98] Muynenecross 1637 (LRR). I bparóiste Theampall Lúgadáin, tá Moneynamough: Monenemoke 1549,[99] Munnenymoagh 1611, Monimogh, Moninimogh 1654 (CS), Moinino c1655 (DS), Monnio c1660 (B.S.D.), Monymough alias Monimoe 1666, Moneymough, Monamough, Monymough 1817, Monanomough 1844[100]. Muine na mBoth is ciall leis an ainm, de réir chosúlachta.

Lios/Ráth/Ráithín/Dún/Caiseal

Tá lios-ainmneacha an-ghann i gCúige Laighean cé go bhfuil siad flúirseach sa tuaisceart. I dtosach báire thugtaí an t-ainm ráth ar áit chonaithe rí nó taoisigh, agus lios a thugtaí ar láithreacha cónaithe na ngnáthdhaoine. Ní heol dom ach aon lios-ainm amháin i gco. Loch Garman .i. Liskinfere, paróiste i mbarúntacht Ghuaire. Lios Cinn Féir an leagan a thugtar in *Eosaí an Phoist;* Cloch Lios Cinn atá in *Ainmneacha Gaeilge na mBailte Poist;* Leskin 1247, Liskene 1425,[101] Leskyn 1552,[102] Leskin 1615,[103] rector' de Leskine 1630,[104] Leskin 1654 (CS), Liskin c1660 (BSD), Liskinfere Church 1811, Liskenfere

1840. Tá baile fearainm agus sráidbhaile sa pharóiste ar a dtugtar 'Clough' .i. Cloch, agus i rith an seachtú agus an octú céad déag thugtaí na leaganacha seo ar an mbaile: Cloghlesken 1604, Clogheleskine 1615 (L.R.R.), Cloghleskin, Cloghelesker 1630,[105] Cloghneskeen 1714,[106] Cloghineskeen 1798, Clough 1807.[107]

I bhFiodh Ard, Síol Brain, tá baile fearainn ann agus Ralph an litríú na Suirbhéireachta Ordanáis ar a ainm. Is é an litriú céanna atá ar léarscáil Gill 1811, ach Rath leagan an seachtú céad déag. Is léir, mar sin, gur ráth an focal atá i gceist. Tá baile fearainn eile i bp. Dhún Chormaic, Uí Bhairrche agus Rath leagan Suirbhéireachta sa chás sin. Tá an focal sin ráth ina chuid de go leor bailte fearainn sa chontae.

Uaireanta leanann ainm duine an focal ráth:- Rathfylane, p. Ros Droichid, Rathfoylean 1745, Rathfoyleam, Rathfoylane 1811, Rathfoylame, Rathfilane, Rathfiland 1826, Rathfinane 1831, Rathfileme, 1834.[108] Tá cuma air gur Ráth Fhaoláin atá ann, ach más ceart na foirmeacha -sam, -eme, b'fhéidir gur Ráth Fheidhlim ba chóir a rá. Tá Ráth Ghearóid (Rathgarogue) i bp. Bhaile Eathain (Ballyanne). B'fhéidir gur le Lonán éigin Rathlannan, Cill Damháin, Fotharta; agus gur le Colm an áit a dtugtar Ratholm, p. Bhaile Bhraonáin. Ní róchinnte a bhí an Donnabhánach faoin gceann deireanach seo: 'First part is from Rath ... but latter ... very uncertain. Cf Rath-Cholaim'.[109] Bhí sé níos dearfa faoi Rathmacknee, paróiste agus dhá bhaile fearainn (Great agus Little) i bhFotharta: Rath Mhic Naoi a deir sé atá ann; gur do threibh Ua nGarchon an Naoi seo agus tagraíonn sé do Ráth Naoi i gCill Mhantáin.

Ba le 'Páidín Buí' an ráth a thugann an t-ainm do bhaile fearainn i dTeampall Lúdagáin, Rathpadenboy 1611 (L.R.R.), Rathpandenboy, Rapadenboy, Rathpendenboy 1654 (CS), Rapadinboy 1659, Raghfadan 1811 agus Rathphaudin. I gCill Naonúir, Guaire, tá Ráth Phiarais (Rathpierce Lower agus Upper, agus Rathpierce Hill); agus tá Ráth Rónáin i bparóiste Mhaol Raincín in Uí Bhairrche.

Deir Ó hÓgáin gurb ionann Rathaspeck, paróiste agus baile fearainn i bhFotharta, agus Ráth na nEaspag a luaitear sna Féilirí Ghaelacha:- Feabhra 16: Aed Glas, epscop Ratha na nEpscop;[110] Aongas espoc ó Ráith na nespoc; Oengas espoc Ratha na nEspoc.[111]

Sna ráth-ainmneacha seo a leanas faightear ainm crainn:- Ráth an Iúir, (Rathnure), p. Ros Droichid agus (R. Upper agus Lower) p. Chill Anna, Rathkyle, p. Chill Gharbháin, — Ráth Choill, más ceart don Donnabhánach, agus Rath Saileach (Rathsillagh) sa pharóiste céanna. I gcás Rathumney, p. Abhainn Dubh, tugann Ó Donnabháin malairt ainmneacha — Rath Omna, Ráth Tumna. Féach na leaganacha eile: Rathubenai 1194, Rathyniny 1604,[112] Rathtumney 1619,[113] Rathymnoy, Rathymney 1625,[114] Rathumny 1654 (CS), Rathtimney 1811, Rathumney 1825, Rathemney 1827.[115] Freagraíonn na foirmeacha -ymney, -imney d'foghraíocht áitiúil an lae inniu. Is sa bhaile fearainn seo atá an sráidbhaile ar a dtugtar Gusserane anois: Raheenaguerane 1838, Rathnacusheran 1841. In ainmleabhair Uí Dhonnabháin tá 'Rathnacusherán, Ráth na g-cosarán', agus b'ionann, dar leis, cosarán agus cosán. Is é is dóichí gur caisearbhán atá i gceist.

Ráth-ainmneacha eile is ea iad seo:- Ráth Dhubh, p. Chill Anna, Ráth Dhearg (Rathyark), p. Mhaol Raincín, Ráth Mhór, p. Oileán Mhuire agus féach go bhfuil Muchrath agus an bhrí chéanna leis sa bharúntacht chéanna i bp. Chill Fhinneog (Killinick). I bhfotharta freisin tá Ráth an Éadain (Rathnedan), p. Bhaile Mór; agus tá Ráth na gCaorach i bparóiste Abhainn Dubh, Síol Brain.

Is flúirsí i Loch Garman na logainmneacha Ráithín ná na ráth-ainmneacha, agus a ndála siúd luaitear ainm duine leo uaireanta: tá ceithre cinn i bparóiste an Bhádhúin Nua i mBeanntraí:- Raheenvarren .i. Ráithín Varain (Warren) is dócha; ansin tá trí cinn láimh le chéile — Raheenaheenedy: Rahinehinedeghe 1637 (L.R.R.), Rahinnikinidie 1654 (CS), Rahinhinnedy c1660 (BSD), Raheenakennedy 1828 .i. Ráithín an Chinnéidigh; 'Raheenarostia or Rochestown': Rahinrochestir 1625[116] .i. Ráithín an Róistigh; agus idir an dá cheann sin tá Raheenaclonagh: Rahincloney 1619,[117] Rahinclough, Rahineclonigh, Rahinnyglonigh 1654 (CS), Rathineclogh 1655 (DS), Rahineclough c1660 (BSD), Rahinclony 1659;[118] Rahinecloanagh alias Rahinaclogh alias Rahinduffe 1684;[119] Rahinclonagh 1787, Raheenaclonagh 1827.[120] Is dealraitheach gur Ráithín an Chluanaigh nó Ráithín na gCluanach — Ó Cluanaigh atá san ainm seo.

I mBealach Caoin Thuaidh tá deich gcinn de ráithin-ainmneacha. I bparóiste Chill Éanach tá trí cinn díobh in éineacht le chéile — Raheen Beg, Raheen More, Raheenpark: 'the Rahines' a thugtar orthu 1618 (LRR), Rahin, The Three Rahins 1654 (CS), The 3 Rahins c1660 (BSD). Más dóibh an tagairt, is inspéisí seo ón mbliain 1612: 'the Rahins, vis., Rahinmorecahire, Rahinmore farginanim and Rahinmoredonell, with their hamlet called Ballinole';[121] agus an ceann seo: 'Rahincahir, Rahyn-Fargananym, Rahinedonell' 1618.[122] Mar sin, Ráthín mór Chathaoir, Ráithín mór Fhear-gan-ainm, Ráithín mór Dhónaill ainmneacha na mbailte; cé nach féidir a bheith cinnte anois cé leis gach baile díobh faoi seach, agus ní fios dom cá raibh Ballinole (Baile an Úill?). Sa pharóiste céanna tá Ráithín Mór eile (Raheen Moor). I Muine Moling tá Ráithín Dearg; i gCill Chormaic tá Ráithín Dubh; Ráithín Loiscthe (Raheenlusk) i nDomhnach Mór; Ráithín na Sceiche, Iochtarach agus Uachtarach, i gCill na Manach. Tá dhá Ráithín Dubh eile ann, i p. Adamstown, agus p. Horetown. I bhFearna tá Ráithín na Gaoithe (Raheennagee), agus tá Raíthín na Uamhan (?) (Raheennahoon) i gCill Chuáin Mór.

Tá trí bhaile fearainn sa chontae a bhfuil Hollyfort orthu, ach aistriú ón nGaeilge is ea an t-ainm i bpéire acu ach go háirithe. I bparóiste Monart atá ceann acu: Rahin Cullen, Rahincullen 1654 (CS), Rathen Cullen, Rathincullen 1655 (DS). Agus deir Ó Donnabháin 'olim Raheencullen but now Holly Fort'.[123] Tá, nó bhíodh, ráth chearnógach i lár an bhaile seo. Ráithín Cuilinn, mar sin, an t-ainm.

Tá an dara Hollyfort i bp. Kilnahue agus más é an baile a ndéantar tagairt dó, Raheencullen a bhí air seo freisin san octú céad déag. An tríú Hollyfort, is i bp. Chill Ghormáin atá sé, ach níl de thagairtí agam dó ach Hollyforth 1830, agus Hollyfort 1831.

I gCill Uisce, tá Tigh an Ráithín: Tenrahin 1618 (LRR), Tanrahin, Tinrahin

1654(CS), Tighinragin 1655 (DS léarscáil), Tighin Raghin c1660 (BSD), Teighuraghan 1669, Tinraheen 1811, Tinnaraheen 1844. Tá Tinnarath — Tigh na Ráithe, i bp. Inse, Guaire.

Níl ach leathdhosaen ainmneacha i Loch Garman a thosaíonn leis an bhfocal dún. Tá Dún an Óir luaite againn cheana i bp. Seanros, agus tá baile agus an t-ainm céanna air i bp. Chluain Mhór, Beanntraí: Downemore 1618,[124] Downenore 1637 (L.R.R.). I Síol Brain tá fothrach na mainistreach cáiliúla Dún Bróithe atá suite i Meirsín, p. St James and Dunbrody, ach tá baile fearainn eile a bhfuil an t-ainm céanna sa pharóiste. Is sa pharóiste céanna arís atá Duncannon: Dunmechanan 1175, Duncanan 1301, Downecannan 1542; Duncannon, Dun-Cannon 1654, Dún Comáin, Dún Cannann.[125] Cheaptaí ó na leaganacha is seanda gur Dún Mhic Canann a bhíodh san ainm. In Uí Bhairrche tá paróiste agus baile fearainn ar a dtugtar Dún Chormaic: Duncomak, Duncomok 1247, Douncormok 1324,[126] Duncormock 1654 (CS), agus tá Dún Droma (Dundrum) i gCill Mhucraise.

Go bhfios dom, níl ach sampla amháin den fhocal caiseal i logainmneacha an chontae .i. i bp. St Mary's, Bun Clóidí, atá an baile fearainn suite: Cashellmore 1685,[127] Cashel anois.

Teach

'Mainistir' a chuirtear in iúl leis an bhfocal teach i gcásanna áirithe. Tá na paróistí Teach Munna agus Teach Moshagra luaite thuas, ach tá suas le tríocha logainm eile sa chontae a bhfuil an focal teach nó tigh ina chuid díobh agus an gnáthchiall leis.

Tigh 'n Chnoic atá ar cheithre bhaile fearainn:- Tiknock, p. Chill Chormaic, Tanknuicke, Tankunick 1654 (CS), Tankennicke c1660 (B.S.D.), Tankennick 1669. Ó na leaganacha sin cheapfaí gur Teach an Chnoic an seanfhoirm. Tinnick, p. Bhaile Bhaldúin, Tanknuck (p. Mylenagh), Tankunck, Tanhnuck 1654 (CS), Tankennicke 1655 (DS). Tinnock, p. Chill Easca (Killesk), Tynknocke 1611,[128] Tinnock, Tincnocke 1625;[129] Tinkniche, Tinknick 1654 (CS). Tinnock Lower agus Upper; p. Chill Chaomháin, Guaire: Tehinknoick 1611,[130] Tineknucker, Tinckknucke 1654 (CS), Tanckennick 1655 (DS), Tinnock 1728.[131]

Tigh 'n Chorraigh atá ar cheithre bhaile: Tincurra, Teach Munna, Tincurragh i gCill Chaomháin agus ceann eile taobh leis i gCill Ghormáin, Guaire; Tincurry, Baile Uí Chearnaigh.

Tá Tigh 'n Chuain (Tincone) i bp. Ard Chaomháin ar bhruach Inbhear Sláine agus tá Tincoon in Eidir Mhaighin; sa chás seo tugann Joyce 'cor san abhainn' mar mhíniú ar cuan.[132] Tigh-ainmneacha eile: Tigh na Bearna (Tinnaberna), Cillín Cúile, Tigh na Carraige (Tinnacarrick), Abhainn Dubh, Tigh na Coille (Tinnakilla), Killurin, Tigh na Srúille (Tinnashrule), Fearna, Tigh na hEasca (Tinnahask), Baile na Sláine, Tigh na Sionnach (Tinnashinnagh), Cill Moshíológ, Tigh 'n tSeiscinn (Tinteskin), Cillín Cúile.

Tobar

Tugann spá a ainm do Thobar an Iarainn (Toberanierin Lower agus Upper), Lios Cinn Féir, Guaire. Fuaim -ng a bhíonn ag deireadh an ainm i gcaint na ndaoine agus tá sé sinn ar aon dul le samplaí ó thús an naoú céad déag; 'Tobbernearing, i.e., the Iron Well' 1806;[133] Tuberneering 1811.[134]

I mB.C. Theas tá Tobar Beag roinnte idir p. Chaisleán Eilis agus p. Chill Uisce. Tá Tobar Dubh i gCill Chaomháin, Guaire, agus Tobar Geal i gCill Chormaic, Guaire: Tobergeall 1654 (CS), Tubbergale 1655 (DS), ach féach an truailliú atá déanta ar an ainm de dheasca dhoiléire scríbhneoireachta sa B.S.D.: Tubbergate, Jobbergate!

Tá Toberona i dTeampall Scuaibe, Beanntraí, agus cheap Ó Donnabháin gur Tobar Eoin a bhí ann; 'Toberone' an 'received name' a tugadh dó.[135] I Maolanach, tá Toberlomina: Tobberlumenagh, Tobberlymenagh, Tobberlumaneh 1618, (L.R.R.) Toberlomny, Toberlony 1654 (CS), Tubberlomney 1655 (DS), Tubberlumney 1826, Tuberlimina 1831.[136] Is é seo Tobar Luimnigh .i. tobar san áit lom sceirdiúil. Ba é lárionad Fhearann Uí Mhurchú é. Más fíor don Donnabhánach, bhí an bhéim chainte ar an tríú siolla i lár an chéid seo caite — Tubberlomina, ach is ar an -in-a chuirtear béim inniu.

Cúl/Cúil

Tá beagnach ceithre scór bailte fearainn sa chontae a thosaíonn le Cool- agus ní furasta a dhéanamh amach an do cúl nó do cúil a sheasann sé. Is cúl atá i gceist sna hainmneacha seo a leanas, dar liom: Coolaknick agus Coolaknickbeg, p. Eidir Mhaighin .i. Cúl a' Chnoic; Coolgarrow, p. Theampall Sheanáin: Coolgarragh 1811, Coolgarriff 1835 .i. Cúl Garbh; tá Cúl Garbh eile i bp. St Mary's, Bun Clóidí, agus Cúl Aitinn chomh maith.

Tá Cúl Broc i gCill Chaomháin, Uí Bhairrche; Cúl Poc i bhFearna; Cúl na Con i gCill Eignigh, Cúl an bhFiach (Coolnaveagh) i gCill Moshíológ; tá sé seo taobh leis an gcarraig ar a dtugtar Carraig an Ghéich (Carriganeagh); Cúl Coll. (Collcull Big, Collcull (Meyler's) agus Coolcull (Shea's)) i dTeach Munna. Tá sé cinn de bhailte a bhfuil Cúl Rua orthu: i gCillín Cúile, i Séipéal, agus i bhFearna; i gCinn Eich (Tintern), agus péire, Cul Rua mór agus Cúl Rua beag, i gCill Ghormáin. In Inse, tá Cúl Buí: Coolboy 1654 (CS), Coolbuoy 1838 agus tá Coolbawn Demesne i dTeampall Lúdagáin.

I bhFearna tá Coolbaun, ach is dócha gur Cúil Bhán an ceart sa chás seo: Culevan, Culvane 1654 (CS). Cúil Íseal ainm baile in Uí Bhairrche, p. Bannow: Coulussyl 1325, Cowlischill 1415, Coylehissell 1568, Coolehishell 1639 (LRR), Coolishill, Colhishill 1654 (CS). Agus tá Coolishal Lower agus Upper i bp. Kilnahue. Cúil Íseal Beag and Cúil Íseal Mór a thugtaí orthu seo — Cowle-Ishelbegg, Cowle-Ishelmore 1618 (L.R.R.), Cowle-Ishellbeg agus Cowle-Ishellmore, Coole-Ishellbeg agus Coole-Ishellmore 1630.(L.R.R.).

Míníonn Joyce[137] an focal cluas: 'a lateral semidetached portion of land, or a long stripe', agus tá sampla de le fáil san ainm Coolnagloose .i. Cúil na gCluas, p. Chill Chaomháin.

Tá Coolstore i bp. Fhearna. Cheap an Donnabhánach gur tuar a bhí sa siolla deiridh de seo .i. páirc a spréití líneadach amach lena ghealachan faoin ngrian — Cúil a' Tuair, agus tá dealramh na fírinne ar an míniú sin as cuid de na seanfhoirmeacha: Cowletoyre, Coolstoyre 1630,[138] Culetoyre, Culletoyre 1654 (CS), Coultoyre, Coultoyle 1655 (DS). Ach tá malairt leagain le fáil —

Cooltogher 1698 — a thugann le fios gur tóchar atá i gceist .i. Cúil a' Tóchair, agus tá tacaíocht ar fáil dó seo ó thagairt níos déanaí fós: 'the Causeway of Coolatore' 1843.

Tá Cúil Seiscinn i bp. Bannow, uí Bhairrche; agus i bp. Kilmannon, tá Coolsallagh: d'fhéadfaí Cúl Salach a thabhairt air seo ach is dócha gur fearr an leagan atá ag Ó Donnabháin — Cúil Saileach.

Cnoc

Tá ceithre scór, ar a laghad, de bhailte fearainn ina bhfuil an focal cnoc, gan trácht ar chnoic ná ar áiteanna eile nach bailte fearainn iad. Dath an chnoic is bun leis an ainm uaireanta agus Cnoc Dubh an t-ainm is fluirsí den saghas seo — sé cinn díobh: trí cinn díobh i S.M. Thoir — p. Ard Cromáin, p. Bhaile na Sláiní, p. Chluain Mhór; dhá cheann i Sc.Bh. — p. Cluana, agus p. Theampall Seanboth; aon cheann amháin i gCill Moshíológ, Guaire.

Tá Cnoc Bán i gCaisleán Eilis, agus ceann eile in Inse, Cnoc Bua in Arda Maighin, agus an dara ceann i Sean-Ros, Cnoc Breac i bp. Kilmannon agus ceann eile i bp. Kilnahue, agus Cnoc Riabhach (Knockreagh) i mBaile Uí Chearnaigh.

Faighimid an t-ainm Cnoc (Knock) i Ráth Easpaig, agus iolra Béarla i gcás Knocks, p. Theach Moshagra. Tá Cúl a' Chnoic (Coolaknick) agus Cúl a' Chnoic beag in Eidir-Mhaighin: Cooleknocke, Coolknockmore, Little-Cooleknock 1618,[139] Coulcunckmore, Coulcuniskmore, Coolknockmore, Coolcunckbeg, Coulcounckbeg 1654 (CS).

Níor mhiste Baile 'Cnoic (Ballyknock), p. Bhaile Mhiota, a chur i gcomparáid le dhá ainm eile: Knockstown, p. Chill Eignigh agus Knocktown, p. Dhún Chormaic. I gcás Knockstown, Baile an Chnoic a cheap an Donnabhánach a bhí ann: Crokston, Cnockston, Cnokston 1654 (CS), Knockstowne c1660 (B.S.D.), Knockstown 1741,[140] Knoxtown c1811.[141] Arbh fhéidir gurb é an leagan deiridh seo atá ceart agus gur sloinne Knox atá ann? An Knocktown i nDún Chormaic, Knocktown(e) an litriú sna tagairtí ach in aon cheann amháin mar a bhfaightear 'Knocktown otherwise Ballyknock' 1741. Is dócha, mar sin, gur Baile 'Chnoic an t-ainm seo.

I Ros Droichid, tá Cnoc Mór, agus ceann eile in Ard Choilm. Agus féach an meascán teangacha atá i Muchknock i gCill Fhinneog.

Is inspéise an t-ainm Cnoc Sceiche Moling (Knockskemolin), p. Chill na Manach. Easpag ar dheoise Fhearna ab ea Moling a d'éag 697. Is dó a thagraítear in ainm an pharóiste Tigh Moling (St Mullin's) agus in ainm an pharóiste Muine Moling láimh le Cill na Manach. Tá baile fearainn eile ar a dtugtar Muine Moling i bparóiste Theampall Lúdagáin. Ní fios dom an fáth a luaitear sceach le Moling, ach tugtar faoi deara ainm an bhaile fearainn Sceach Moling (Scaughmolin), p. Ráth Easpaig.

Go minic faightear ainm planda nó crainn leis an bhfocal cnoc-Knockadilly, p. Chillín Cúile, Knocknadilline 1618 (L.R.R.), Knockedille 1630;[142] Knockadillin 1632,[143] Knockdullin 1654 (CS), — Cnoc na Duille, nó Cnoc an Duillín, b'fhéidir; Cnoc an Iúir, p. Chill Rois agus Knocknalour sa pharóiste céanna: Knockeneloure, Cnockneloure 1654 (CS), Knocknelory 1657;[144]

Knocknelery, Knockdery 1655 (DS), Knocketory 1655 (DS léarscáil): Cnoc na Lobhar brí amháin a d'fhéadfadh a bheith leis an ainm seo; Cnoc na Lobhar nó Cnoc na Leabhar atá ag Ó Donnabháin, ach an saghas crainn atá i gceist: labhras? Cnoc na Saileog (Knocknasilloge), p. Bhaile Bhaldúin, Cnoc na Sceach, p. Chill Chormaic.

Knockaree, p. Chill Rois: tugann Ó Donnabháin malairt ainm air — Knockaree alias Kingsland', agus, mar sin, tugann sé Cnoc a' Rí mar Ghaeilge air. Seanscoil Náisiúnta a bhíodh i gCloch Ámainn sa pharóiste sin, 'Kingsland National School' a bhíodh greanta ar leac an bhalla. An amhlaidh gur bhréag-aistriú é sin agus gur Cnoc a' Fhraoigh ba chóir a bheith ann?

Tá Cnoc a' Mhóta (Knockavota) i gCill Chaomháin agus i bparóiste Charn a' Bhua (Carnew) tá Knocknamota. Tugann Ó Donnabháin Cnoc na Móta ach deir 'no moat here'.

Knocknoran, p. Chill Mhór: Cnoc an Óráin; Knockatober, p. Chill Anna: Cnoc a' Tobair. Taobh le Cnoc a' Tobair tá baile fearainn ar a dtugtar Springmount agus deir Ó Donnabháin faoi nach bhfuil ann ach 'translation of Cnoc a' Tobair'.

Garraí

Tá timpeall tríocha áit sa chontae a thosaíonn leis an bhfocal Garraí agus ainm duine ag gabháil leis an gcuid is mó díobh: Garrycleary, p. Chill Phádraig, Garraí Uí Chléirigh (?); 'Garraidh an Chléirigh' atá ag Ó Donnabháin; Garrygibbon, p. Ard Choilm, Garraí Ghiobúin; Garryhasten, p. Mhá Dhá Chonn: Garihastine, Garrihasten 1654 (CS), 'Garraidh-Hasting' a cheap Ó Donnabháin, agus is dócha gur sloinne dá shórt atá ann — Hastion nó Hestion, b'fhéidir. I gcáipéisí an tseachtú céad déag luaitear baile fearainn eile in éineacht leis seo: Garrihasten & Loggensea 1655 (DS), Log-Inche 1618 (L.R.R.), Loginche 1637 (L.R.R.), Loggins 1643;[145] Logency, Logencye 1654 (CS), Loggonsea 1655 (DS léarscáil); Loggensea c1660 (B.S.D.), Loginch 1699;[146] Loginch 1890.[147] Séard a deir Ó Donnabháin 'Loggage Foord — "Luggage Ford is English",' agus 'Luggage Bridge' atá ar na léarscáil ach freag-raíonn na tagartí thuas 1699 agus 1890 d'fhuaimniú áitiúil an lae inniu, agus dealraíonn sé gur Log Inse is bunús leis an ainm. Sampla é seo de bhaile fearainn a slogadh isteach i mbaile eile. Tá na céadta eile bailte fearainn a ndéantar tagairt dóibh sna Stáit-Pháipéir &rl nach bhfuil tásc orthu inniu ach go maireann ainmneacha cuid acu in ainm páirce nó a leithéid.

I bp. Chill Uisce, tá Garraí àn tSionóidigh (Garryntinodagh): Garrytinod 1618,[148] Garrintinnodee 1630,[149] Garrytinogue 1826, Garrantinode 1838.

Ainmneacha baiste a ghabhann le Garraí- uaireanta: Garraí Dhónaill (Garrydaniel), p. Mhuine Moling, Garrydonnell, Garredonnell 1630,[150] Garrydaniel 1654 (CS), Garrydonneall 1655 (DS). Garraí Risteáird (Garryrichard), p. Chluain Chaoin, Garraí Liam (Garrywilliam), p. Chill Phádraig, Garrylyme, Garrilenie (leg. -leme) 1578 (L.R.R.), Garrileyme 1610,[151] Garrywilliam 1654 (CS), Garry William c1660 (B.S.D.).

Tá a leithéidí seo do gharraí-ainmneacha ann freisin: Garraí Dubh, p. Chill Chormaic, agus p. Abhainn Dubh; Garraí Maol, p. Ballyhuskard, (Garrymile),

agus Garrymoyle, p. Bhaile Bhaldúin, Garraí Mór, p. Chaisleán Eilis, Garraí
Nua, p. Arda Maighin, Newgardine alias Garrinowe 1611,[152] Garrinowe
1618.[153] Garraí 'n Uisce agus Garraí 'n Uisce Beag, p. Chaisleán Eilis; agus
Garraí ' Uisce (Garrynisk) eile, p. Eidir-Mhaighin.

Cluain

Tá cúig cinn is daichead de bhailte fearainn a bhfuil an focal cluain ina chuid
dá n-ainmneacha faoi na foirmeacha clon-, clone-, cloon-. Paróiste agus baile
fearainn is ea Clone i Scairbh Bhailis, mar a bhfuil fothrach suaithinseach
teampaill a bhaineann leis an dara céad déag. Tá trí bhaile i bparóiste Chill
Ghormáin: Clones Lower, Clones Middle and Clones Upper: iolra Béarla atá
anseo, agus seo tagairt ón seachtú céad déag. 'Clones alias Cloones near the
Gorman Water' 1622 (L.R.R.). I Muine Moling tá Clone East and Clone West'
les Clones 1630;[154] Cloun Morchoe, Clounemorchoe, Cloune O Morchoe
1654 (CS), Clonmorrogh Ballagh 1655 (DS léarscáil). Dhealródh sé ó na
samplaí deireanacha seo gur Cluain Uí Mhurchú, nó Cluain Mhurchaidh
Bhallaigh a bhí san ainm; ach tá foirmeacha eile nach furasta a mhíniú:
Cloovarballaghlagg 1655 (DS); Clooverballaghlagh 1655 (DS léarscáil): Is
dócha gur mí-scríobh é -oove do -oon; ach an é an focal lag atá sa deireadh? Sa
bhliain 1641 ba le 'Owen Morchoe' Raheendarrige (Ráithín Dearg) in aice le
Cluain. Tá Cluain eile i bp. Mhá Chluas: Cloune 1655 (DS), Clone 1655 (DS
léarscáil), Clounne c1660 (B.S.D.).

Cluain Dáith: (Clondaw) p. Chill Chormaic, Clonda 1618 (L.R.R.),
Cloundae, Clonedae 1655 (DS), Cluain Haistín (Clonhasten), p. Theampall
Sheanáin: Clonhastin, Clonhasten 1620 (L.R.R.), Clonshastine 1637 (L.R.R.):
Cluain Siúrdáin (Clonjordan), p. Theampall Seanbhoth: Clongurdan,
Clonegurda 1605;[155] Clonecordane 1625;[156] Clon-jordan alias Jordanstowne
1634;[157] Clonjordaine, Clone Jordaine 1654 (CS). Clunin a' Róistigh
(Clonroche) a thugtar ar bhaile fearainn agus sráidbhaile, p. Shéipéal; Clone
Roche 1589,[158] Cloneroshtie 1606,[159] Clonrock, Clonroch, 1654 (CS). Tá
Clonyburn i bp. St Mary's, Bun Clóidí: is dealraitheach ó chuid de na sean-
fhoirmeacha gur le Ó Briain an baile seo agus ní le Ó Broin; agus gur Cluain Uí
Bhriain an t-ainm; Clonyvryn 1621 (L.R.R.); Clonebryen, Clonebryn 1634;[160]
Clone Ibrine 1654 (CS), Clonybren 1655 (DS), Clonybreene 1655 (DS
léarscáil).

Cluain Aitinn (Clonatin Lower agus Upper), p. Chill Moshíológ
Clonattinbeg, Clonattinmore 1612;[161] Cluain Raithní (Cloneranny), p. Chill
Chormáin: Clonanerany 1627;[162] Cluain Saileach (Clonsilla East and West),
p. Chill Chaomháin: Clonsillagh; 1612;[163] Clonsilla 1634 Clonsilla 1634
(L.R.R.), Clownesillagh 1637 (L.R.R.), Clonsillagh 1654 (CS).

Clonmore is ainm do pharóiste agus do bhaile fearainn i mBeanntraí: de réir
Onomasticon Hibernicum, is é seo 'Cluain mór Dicholla Gairbh' arbh é
Maodhóg a phátrún; 'Cluain mór Maodóg' atá ag Ó Donnabháin. Tá bailte a
bhfuil an t-ainm céanna orthu i Lios Cinn Féir, i dTuaim, agus Clonmore
Lower agus Upper i bparóiste Ballyhuskard, B.C. Theas: Clonmore 1654 (CS),
Clonemore, Cloonemoore 1655 (DS) — Cluain Mhór.

Cluain-ainmneacha eile: Cluain Rua (Clonroe Lower agus Upper), p. Chill Naonúir; Cluain Liath (Clonleigh), paróiste agus baile fearainn; Cluain Searrach, p. Dhún Bróith, Cluain na Síóg (Clonnasheeoge), p. Kilmallock.

Goirtín
Tá dosaen bailte ina bhfuil an focal goirtín ina n-ainmneacha:- Gorteen, p. Chill Rois; Gorteen, p. Theampall Seanbhoth: Gurtenphillippe 1605;[164] Gurtin-Philip 1605;[165] Gurtine, Gurttine 1654 (CS), Gurteene alias Gurteenephillip 1686:[166] Goirtín Philib. Láimh leis seo tá Buaile Philib: b'fhéidir gur leis an bPilib céanna an dá bhaile.

Gorteen Lower agus Upper, p. Inse; Gorteens, p. Fhiodh Ard; Gortins, p. Dhún Chormaic; Gortine Great agus Little, p. Chill Meannáin (Kilmannon): Great Gurthens, Little Gurthens 1654 (CS), Great Gurchins, Little Gurchins 1655 (DS léarscáil).

Goirtín Cruinn (Gorteencrin), p. Chill Scóráin; Gurtynchrine, Gurtynechrine 1655 (DS), Gurchingcring 1655 (DS léarscáil). I gCill Damháin, Fotharta, tá Gorteenminogue Lower agus Upper: Gurthemeknock 1654 (CS), Gurthine Minoge, Gurteen Minoge 1655 (DS) Gurthin Minock 1655 (DS léarscáil) Garchinminoge alias Gurtinmonoge 1709;[167] Gurteenaminogue 1811, Gurtaminogue 1826, Gurtumanogue 1833. Cheap an Donnabhánach gur Goirtín na Muineog .i. na dtor, ba chiall leis an ainm.

Mullán
Tá deich mbaile fearainn a thosaíonn le Mullan-, Mullaun-, Mullin. Seasann siad seo don fhocal maolán, nó don fhocal mullán, nó don fhocal muileann. Ciallaíonn maolán maolchnoc nó cnocán cruinn; de ghnáth is ionann maolán agus mullán, ach de réir an Donnabhánaigh, is é an chiall atá le mullán i Loch Garman 'páirc ghlas'. Agus é ag trácht ar an ainm Mullaun i bparóiste Eidir Mhaighin deir sé: 'Mullán, a green field. . . . This is the local meaning.' Agus tá nóta den saghas céanna aige faoin ainm Mullaunfin, p. Kilnahue: 'Mullán Fionn, fair green field; Mullan ought to mean a hill but its local meaning here is green field'.

I bparóiste Chill Naonúir tá Mullaun eile: Mullanegroagh 1618 (LRR), Mollanegroach, Molanegroagh 1654 (CS), Mullinegrogh, Mullegrogh 1655 (DS), Mulane, Mulanegrath 1780.[168] Dhealródh sé gur Mullán na gCruach is brí leis. Tá Mullán na Sméar i bp. St Mary's, Bun Clóidí: Mollanesmere 1621 (LRR), Mullawnasmere 1838, Mullaunnasmear: Mullán Riabhach (Mullaunreagh), p. Mhuine Moling: Molanreagh 1654 (CS), Mullenreagh 1655 (DS), Mullawnree 1841 agus an nóta seo arís ag Ó Donnabháin: 'Mullán riach; mullán = lea field in this part of Leinster'.

Maolán na nGabhar an fhoirm oifigiúil Ghaeilge atá ar 'Mullinagore or Oylegate', ach is é Mullán na nGabhar an leagan a thugann Ó Donnabháin: Mullanegore 1654 (CS), Mullongore 1655 (DS), Mullinagore 1811, Mullinagowr or Oil-gate 1840.[169] Tá Mullán an nGabhar eile, Mullanagower, i bparóiste Ard Chaomháin: Mulannengoure 1654 (CS), Mullenagore 1829, Mullawnagower 1833, Mullawnagour 1838.

Tom/Tuaim

Tá na focail tom agus tuaim le fáil i mbreis is dhá scór ainmneacha agus ní héasca idirdhealú eatarthu. Tuaim (Toome) an t-ainm atá ar pharóiste a bhfuil cuid de i mbarúntach Ghuaire agus an chuid eile i Scairbh Bhailis. Baile fearainn is ea Tuaim (Toom), p. Chluana (Clone), Tomnemctire 1618 (L.R.R.), Tomnemaghtiry 1654 (CS), Toomnemaghtery 1655 (DS), Toommactery 1657,[170] Tomemcterny 1671 (L.R.R.) .i. Tuaim na Mactíre. Luaitear mactíre i mbaile eile — Glentire, p. Chill Uisce; mheas an Donnabhánach gur Gleann Tíre ba bhrí leis ach léiríonn na seanfhoirmeacha an bhrí cheart: .i. Cluain na Mactíre: Clynamicktiry, Clinemucktyry 1654 (CS), Clonmctyre c1672 (L.R.R.).

Tuaim-ainmneacha eile:- Tuaim a' Chorraigh (Tomacurry), p. Mhóin Airt: Tomcorry 1633[171], Toomecory c1660 (B.S.D.), Tomcurry 1686,[172] Tomacurra 1811, Tomahurra 1888. An leagan deiridh seo, is mar sin a fhuaimnítear an t-ainm inniú. Tuaim na nÚll (Tomanoole), p. Mhóin Airt: Tomnanoll alias Tonmenowle 1622 (L.R.R.), Tomnenoule 1629,[173] Tomnenole 1654 (CS), Toomnenole 1655 (DS). Tuaim Fearna (Tomfarney), p. Shéipéil: Tomfarney Lower agus Upper .i. p. Chill Chuáin Mór[174]. Tuaim na gCipín (Tomakippeen), p. Mhóin Airt: Tomnagippine 1654 (CS), Toomnegyppen, Toomnegippen 1655 (DS).

Tuaim a' Duille, is cosúil, is brí le Tomadilly, p. Mhóin Airt, cé gur Tuaim na Daoile is intuigthe as na leaganacha seo: Tomanedilly 1621 (L.R.R.), Tonmedille 1629: (L.R.R.), Tomnedillye 1654 (C.S.), Toomenedilly 1655 (DS learscáil). p. Theampall Sheanáin. Tomnafunshoge .i. Tuaim nó Tom na bhFuinseog (Fuinseoige?): Tomnefunshok 1608,[175] Tomnefoinshoke, Tomnewynshoke 1610,[176] Tomnefinsoige, Tomnefonsoge, Tomnefunshoge 1654 (CS), Tomnefoisoge c1660 (B.S.D.), Toomefanshog 1657,[177] Tomnafinchogue 1826. Ní miste Finshoge, p. Shean-Ros, a lua anseo: Funchoky 1283,[178] Finsoke 1654 (CS), Funshoge, p. Chillín Cúile: Ballefunshoge alias Motenefunshoge 1632,[179] Ffunshoge 1654 (CS), Funshoge, ffunshoge 1655 (DS), Winchoge 1659,[180] Fenshoge 1730, Whinchoge 1800, Finshogue 1828. Baile na bhFuinseog nó na Fuinnseoige, nó Móta na bhFuinseog an t-ainm, de réir chosúlachta.

Ní féidir bheith cinnte de nach tuaim ba chóir a bheith in áit tom i gcuid díobh seo: Tom a' Ghadaí (Tomagaddy agus Tomgaddy little), p. Mhuine Moling; Tom a' Tí (Tomatee), p. Theampall Seanbhoth; Tom Coill (Tom Coyle), p. Chill Naonúir; Tom Coill eile, p. Lios Cinn Féir; Tom Dubh (Tomduff), p. St John's; Tom Dubh eile, p. Chill Éanach: Tomeduff 1612,[181] Tomeduffe alias Parsonston 1618,[182] Tomduffe 1654 (CS).

Tá ceithre bhaile fearainn a bhfuil Tomgarrow orthu .i. Tom Garbh nó Tuaim Gharbh:- (i) p. Chillín Cúile: Tomgarrowe 1654 (CS), (ii) p. Chill na Manach; (iii) p. Adamstown: Tomgarraffe 1629;[183] Tomgarriffe 1639 (L.R.R.), Tomgarrow 1654 (CS), (iv) p. Bhaile Uí Chearnaigh: Tomgarrow 1622 (L.R.R.), Toomegarrow 1655 (DS léarscáil) Toomgarrow 1655 (DS). Agus cuirtear leo sin Tomgar, p. Bhaile Uí Chonbhaigh: Tomgarrow 1618 (L.R.R.), Tomegarrowe, Tomegarrowmore 1630,[184] Tomgarrowes, Tomgarough 1654

(C.S.) Tomgarrowmore alias Tomgarrow 1666, Tomgarra 1811.[185]

I bp. Chill Chormaic tá Tom na Buaile (Tomnaboly Lower agus Upper). I gCluain, tá Tom Salach (Tomsallagh), i gCill tSinchill tá Tom Saileach (Tomsilla) Tomsillagh 1618 (L.R.R.).

Carrán

I logainmneacha Loch Garman ciallaíonn an focal carrán talamh a mbíonn carraigeacha le feiceáil tríthi. Deir Ó Donnabháin: 'Carrán is used to denote land shewing rocks on the surface';[186] agus, 'carrán, rocky land'.[187] Tá beagnach scór logainmneacha a bhfuil an focal le fáil iontu: m.sh., Craan, p. Chill na Manach: Curranmore 1618,[188] Carranmore 1654 (CS) .i. Carrán Mór; Craan, p. Chill Phíopa; Craan, p. Fhearna: Carran, Carrane 1654 (CS) Craan, p. St Mary's, Bun Clóidí: Carankillenure 1654 (CS), Carran 1655 (DS): Craane, p. Chluain Mhór; Craan Lower agus Upper, agus Craanhill, p. Kilnahue; Crane, p. Chluana, Scairbh Bhaillis.

Tá cúpla áit ar a dtugtar Carrán Rua: Carranroe, p. Mhóin Airt; agus Craanroe, p. Eidir-Mhaighin. I bp. Ard Choilm tá Carrán a' Tóchair (Craanatore) Carrantoghchar 1654 (CS), Corrantogher c1660 (B.S.D.). I bp. Bhaile Uí Chonbhaigh tá Carrán a' Chreabhair (Cranacrower): Corrancrory, Curranecrawre, Currancrowre 1630, (L.R.R.), Corancoer 1654 (CS), Carrancroer, Carrancroher 1655 (DS). Carrán Dónaill (Crandonnell), p. Chill Bhríde na Glinne (Kilbride-Glynn): Korandonyll 1552,[189] Currendunell in paroch' de Kilbride 1629,[190] Crandonell 1654 (CS) agus tá an t-ainm céanna le fáil faoin Crandaniel: p. Dhomhnach Mór; agus Crandaniel Great agus Little, p. Chill Treiscne. An baile ar a dtugtar Currawn, p. Thigh Moling: two Carranrowes, Corranroes 1654 (CS).

Easca/Corrach/Eanach

Tá an focal easca le fáil i seacht n-ainm déag, m.sh., Aska Beg agus Aska More, p. Charn an Bhua; Easca Chaol (Askakeel), p. Kilnahue; Easca Saileach (Askasilla), p. Chaisleán Eilis: Askisillagh 1654 (CS), Easca 'n Bhiolair (Askinvillar Lower agus Upper), p. Chill Anna; Easc Fhuinsean (Askunshin), p. Mhóin Airt: Askevishin 1605,[191] Askinfinsene, Askinfinsen 1654 (CS), Asquintian, Asquinsion 1828. Is dealraitheach gurb ionann an t-ainm seo agus Askinch Lower agus Upper, p. Inse, Guaire: Askfunsin 1654 (CS), Askefimsin c1660 (B.S.D.)

I bp. Dhomhnach Mór tá Askingarran Lower agus Upper: Easca an Gharráin, ('quagmire of the copse or shrubbery'), a cheap Ó Donnabháin ba bhrí leis an ainm: Askenegarran 1618 (L.R.R.), Askengarren 1654 (CS), Askengarran 1655 (DS). Ach luaitear Askegarranbane 'in Murrowes' 1637 agus más don bhaile céanna a thagraítear dealraíonn sé gur Easca 'n Garrán Bán is bun leis. Tá Easca na mBó (Askinamoe) i bp. Fhearna.

Focal eile a bhaineann le nádúr na talún is ea corrach: Curragh agus Curraghwood, p. Chill Chaomháin, Corragh, p. Mhá Dhá Chonn: Correcontenemuck 1638 (L.R.R.), Curragh-coolnamuck 1657,[192] a léiríonn gur Corrach Chúl na Muc is bun leis an ainm. Corrach Dubh a thugtar ar cheithre bhaile: Curraduff, p. Theampall Seanbhoth: Curraghduffe, Curragduffe 1654 (CS), Curraduff, p. Chill Rois, ach gur cheap Ó Donnabháin gur Coradh Dubh ba chiall leis: Curraduffe 1618 (L.R.R.), Curraghduffe, Curaghdufe 1654 (CS). Garriduffe 1655 (DS); Corra dubh, black weir — not Curragh' Curraghdduff, p. Mhuine Moling: 'Curraduff or the two Corroduffs' 1618;[193] Curraghduffe 1654 (CS), Curraghduff, p. Bhaile Bhreasail, Síol Brain: 'Currach dubh, black moor'.

Corrach na Buaile (Curraghnabola), p. Chill Chuáin Mór; 'a moore called Corraghinbolie' 1654 (CS), Corrach Mór (Curraghmore), p. Ráth Rua agus p. Chinn Eich; Corrach Leathan (Curralane agus Curralane Oldtown), p. Chill Rois: Curraghlaghane, Curraghlahine 1654 (CS), Carolahine 1655 (DS), Carolaheene 1655 (DS léarscáil) nó an sloinne atá sa chuid deiridh den ainm seo?

Tá cnuasach bailte fearainn i bparóiste Kilnahue, ocht gcinn ar fad, a dtugtar Eanach orthu agus cáilíocht áirithe á n-idirdhealú: fada, mór, íochtarach, uachtarach, láir, meánach. Déantar tagairt do cheann acu, Eanach Mhór, i *Féilire Dhún na nGall;* ag trácht don údar ar Chaoimhín naofa deir sé: 'Atá a bhetha i nGaoidhelg ag Domhnall Carrach mac Ferghail mac Eochadha isin Eanaigh mhor i gCinnsileach.' (Tugtar faoi deara gur focal baininscneach eanach anseo. Mar sin, is dócha gur Buaile na hEanaí is brí le Bolinahaney, p. Chill Rois.) Níl ach dhá Eanach eile ar bailte fearainn iad .i. Annagh, p. Mhuine Moling; Annaghfin, p. Ballyhuskard; agus tá Annagh Cross ar Oifig Phoist, p. Inse, Guaire: Crois an Eanaigh atá in *Ainmneacha Gaeilge na mBailte Poist.*

Áth

'Augh-' is minice a fhaightear in áth-ainmneacha na mbailte fearainn agus áiteanna eile a bhfuil droichid anois, ach tá roinnt bheag ainmneacha ina seasann A- don fhocal: Acloman, p. Tellarought; Athlomman 1307,[194] Aclamane, Aclamaine, Aclaman 1654 (CS), Acclammon 1709:[195] Áth Cholmáin (Clomáin) ba bhun leis, dar leis an Donnabhánach; Assagart, p. Chill Gharbháin; Athsaggard 1654 (CS), Augsagord 1737, Áth Sagairt; Assaly Great agus Little, p. Chill Fhinneog, Foth.: Asali, Asaly 1605,[196] Athsaly, Athsally 1626 ':[197] Áth Sáile a bhrí.

Puiteach nó lathach is ciall leis an bhfocal slaba, agus de réir chosúlachta is leagan de sin atá san ainm Aughathlappe, p. Mhóin Airt: Áth a' tSlapa; 'ford of Aughaclappa', 'the gullet of Aughnaclapa' 1827,[198] Cuireadh clár, ní foláir, mar dhroichead thar an áth ag Áth Cláir: Archlar 1247,[199] Aughclare, Aclare 1654 (CS), Aclare 1659,[200] 'The ford of Aclare 1826.[201] I bp. Theampall Sheanáin tá Aughnagalley: 'the ford of Aghnegally' 1618 (L.R.R.), Aghnegally, Aghnaegally 1654 (CS). Tá an nóta seo ag Ó Donnabháin: 'Áth na gealaighe, ford of the white bellied eel (?) — some think it means "ford of the moon,"[202] Áth na Gealaí, mar sin, cibé ciall atá le gealach anseo.

Carraig

'Carrick' agus, níos minice, 'Carrig' an crot a bhíonn ar an bhfocal carraig atá le fáil in ainmneacha naoi mbaile déag, in ainmneacha cnoc. Ainm paróiste is ea Carrick ar an taobh thiar den Sláine i Síol Maoluír Thiar. Ar an taobh eile den abhainn, i Síol Maoluír Thoir, tá baile fearainn ar a dtugtar Ferrycarrig: 'the passage of ferry over the River of Carge alias Carrick.' Ba chuid den bhaile seo Baile Mhic Seoinín (Ballymacshonean): Ballimackshennan and Carrigferry c1660 (B.S.D.). Is don cheantar seo a thagraíonn an Céitinneach: 'Uime sin do thionóil Mac Murchadha an sluagh soin ré dul d'argain Átha Cliath, is do fhágaibh Roibeard Mac Stiabhna ag tógbháil chaisléin san ionadh darab ainm an Charraig anois .i. dhá mhíle ó Loch Garman amach'.[203]

I mBeanntraí tá carraig a thugann a ainm do bhaile fearainn, Carraig Uí Bhroin (Carrickbyrne): Karebren 1247, Carrykobren 1324, Carrykbryn 1425,[204] Carrigburne, Carrige Birne 1654 (CS), Carrick Byrne Rock 1807.[205] Tugann Brooks tagairt ón mbliain 1234 do 'chapel and house of "Hoel of Karrothobren".' Is ionann Hoel agus an sloinne Howell agus faightear sa cheantar céanna é san ainm Courthoyle New agus Old'[206] Courthoile 1620;[207] Court hill 1654 (CS), Courtell c1660 (B.S.D.), Courtaile 1704,[208] Courtail 1826.[209] Na tagairtí deireanacha seo, léiríonn siad foghraíocht áitiúil an lae inniu. Tá leagan Gaeilge le fáil sa *Leabhar Branach* — Cúirt Óil, ach is dócha gur fearr Cúirt Haol anois, nó Cúirt Héil.

Carraig-ainmneacha eile: Carraig Bheag (Carrigbeg), p. Kilnahue; ceann eile p. Ros Mionóg (Rossminoge); Carraigín, p. Chill Chormaic; Carraigín, sráid i mbaile mór Loch Garman; Baile na Carraige, p. Chill tSinchill (Ballinacarrig); p. Chill Phádraig, (Ballynacarrig); agus p. Bhaile na Sláine (Ballynacarrig).

Tá carraig i gCill Moshiolág a n-ainmnítear baile fearaínn aisti .i. Carriganeagh. Deir Ó Donnabháin, agus eolas a fuair sé ó 'Mr. Butler' á lua aige: 'Carriganeagh or Raven's Rock', mar sin, Carraig an Fhéich an t-ainm.[210] Ní baile fearainn ach cnoc suntasach é Carraig Rua, p. Chill Bhríde.

Leacain

Taobh cnoic is brí le leacain, focal a fhaightear i ndornán logainmneacha sa chontae: Lackan, p. Chill Moshíológ; Lacken, p. Chill Mocheallóg; Lacken, p. Shean-Ros; Lacken, p. Dhún Chormaic. Luaitear an baile i Sean-Ros sa *Leabhar Branach* mar a dtugtar Leacán air. Leacain Darach (Lackendarragh), p. Chill Rois; Glas-leacain (Glaslacken), p. St Mary's, Bun Clóidí.

Maolruain naofa

Tá an paróiste ar a dtugtar Scrín (Skreen) ina luí, cuid de i mBealach Caoin Theas agus an chuid eile de i Síol Maoluír thoir: Scryne 1541,[211] The Skryne 1597,[212] Scrine 1610,[213] Knockneskriny 1638 (L.R.R.), Knockneskrine, Skryne 1639 (L.R.R.), Knockneskrine 1654 (CS). Deir Ranson go dtugtaí Scrín Mhaolruain ar an eaglais anseo.[214] Bhain Maolruain le Tamhlacht in aice le Baile Átha Cliath; d'éag sé sa bhliain 792, agus de réir dhealraimh, choinnítí taise dá chuid i scrín san áit seo. Sa pharóiste tá baile fearainn ar a dtugtar Baile na Lice (Ballynaleck) agus sna seanleaganacha déantar tagairt do Mhaolruain: Leachmulrowne 1578 (L.R.R.), Leachmulrone 1597,[215] Ballinelecky alias Leckmulroane, Ballinlecky alias Leckmulroane 1625,[216] Ballyleckie 1654 (CS), Ballynalick 1830,[217] Ballinaleck 1831.[218] Baile na Lice nó Leac Mhaolruain ainm na háite, mar sin, agus de réir thraidisiún an cheantair cuireadh an leac isteach i ndroichead Bhaile na Lice agus is uirthi a dhearbhaíodh daoine a neamhchiontacht faoi mhionn.[219] In aice an droichid tá Tobar Mhaolruain, agus go dtí le déanaí choinnítí dealbh adhmaid ón gceathrú céad déag den naomh i dtaisce sa cheantar. Goideadh an dealbh sa bhliain 1985 agus ní fios cá bhfuil sí.

Cé go bhfuil roinnt fhánach aistí foilsithe in irisí agus i nuachtáin faoi logainmneacha Loch Garman, níl staidéar dearfach nó saothar cuimsítheach ar an ábhar i gcló fós. Níl san aiste seo ach mar a bheadh sracfhéachaint ghinearálta ar chuid d'ainmneacha na mbailte fearainn sa chontae agus níl trácht ar bith déanta ar an iliomad ainmneacha eile atá ann — fo-ranna na mbailte fearainn, aibhneacha, toibreacha, srutháin, agus flúirse mionghnéithe talún, mar atá cnoic, carraigeacha, coillte, páirceanna, agus na cuaisíní agus cladaigh agus tránna feadh an chósta. Tá iarsmaí d'ainmneacha bailte fearainn nach ann dóibh a thuilleadh le fáil in ainmneacha páirceanna fós, agus tá obair phráinneach le déanamh mura bhfuil siad le himeacht as cuimhne. Níl iarracht tugtha san aiste seo ach oiread ar aois na logainmneacha a scrúdú, ach ní féidir a shéanadh go bhfuil an-chuid d'oidhreacht Ghaelach Loch Garman faoi cheilt sna háitainmneacha.

3 *Billy Colfer*

Anglo-Norman Settlement in County Wexford

The political and military events relating to the arrival and subsequent progress of the Anglo-Normans in Ireland have been extensively researched. Landing initially in 1169 as mercenaries in the service of Dermot Mac Murrough, deposed king of Leinster, by the end of the twelfth century the Anglo-Normans had succeeded in occupying most of the country.[1] The advent of the Anglo-Normans was to prove a watershed in the history of Ireland as the society which they introduced differed culturally, politically and ideologically from the native Gaelic one. The resultant culture clash was inevitable as the conquest of Ireland was never fully completed, allowing friction to continue between the two societies for several centuries.

Following military conquest the occupation of the land was carried out in accordance with the customs of Norman feudalism.[2] The initial step was the granting of land to tenants-in-chief, holding directly of the king by knights' service, and this was followed by a process of sub-infeudation by which the land was distributed to sub-tenants.[3] The manors thus created and the villages which developed on them were populated by settlers attracted from England and Wales. As an added inducement to settlers, the Anglo-Normans established many chartered boroughs as centres of trade and commerce.

This article examines the elements and structure of the feudal society which was established in county Wexford by the Anglo-Normans and identifies features of that society which survive in the modern landscape.

Subinfeudation

After the capture of Wexford in 1169, Dermot McMurrough assigned the town with all its lands to Robert FitzStephen and Maurice FitzGerald and to Hervey de Montmorency he granted the two cantreds on the sea between the cities of Wexford and Waterford.[4] The grant to de Montmorency, identified as the baronies of Bargy and Shelburne,[5] was later confirmed by Strongbow at the time of the sub-infeudation of Leinster.[6] However the grant to FitzStephen and FitzGerald was rescinded by Henry II when he was in Ireland in 1171[7] and the town of Wexford with its lands, corresponding to the present barony of Forth, was restored to Strongbow in 1173[8] and became one of his most important manors in south Leinster.[9] When distributing land through the process of sub-infeudation the Anglo-Normans frequently made use of existing territorial units such as the *baile* and *tuath*.[10] Clearly, this happened in county Wexford as many of the districts granted to Strongbow's knights, such as Offelimy, Fernegenal and Ui Mealla, were based on pre-Norman territorial units. These secondary grants were often equivalent to the cantred, a district which frequently corresponded to the medieval deanery.[11] When the rural deaneries of county Wexford are examined[12] it is clear that, in some instances, they bore a direct relationship to the land divisions established by the Anglo-Normans. This was particularly evident in the south of the county where the three deaneries of Shelburne, Bargy and Forth, were all based on early land grants. The deanery of Shelburne consisted of the seignorial manor of Ross to which was added the manor of the Island after Hervey de Montmorency's death in 1205 (fig 3.1).[13]

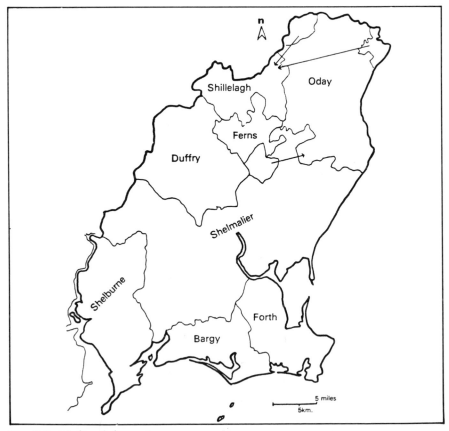

Fig. 3.1: Medieval deaneries

The remainder of Hervey's lands constituted the deanery of Bargy, and the town of Wexford, the present barony of Forth and the manor of Carrick together made up the deanery of Forth. The deanery of Oday in the north of the county was based on the Prendergast fief of Ui Mealla and Kynaloh with the addition of the manor of Glascarrig. Finally the deanery of Duffry between the Slaney and the Blackstairs represented the Prendergast holding of the same name. The large straggling deanery of Shelmaliere, extending right across the centre of the county, occupied an area that would have been frontier or no-mans-land during the period from 1300 to 1600 following the thirteenth century Irish revival. In Bargy alone were deanery and barony boundaries coincident. There is evidence in Tipperary to show that by the end of the sixteenth century the cantreds had been replaced by the modern baronies and it would appear that this also happened in county Wexford as the barony boundaries frequently bisect earlier land holdings and ecclesiastical units.[14]

The sub-infeudation of Leinster by Strongbow has been worked out in some detail and, although there is not sufficient information to determine the exact extents of the principal manors which were established in county Wexford, it is possible to arrive at a reasonably accurate estimate of their areas and locations (fig. 3.2).[15] At least part of the sub-infeudation process had been completed before 1173 as Strongbow's son-in-law, Robert de Quency, who received a grant of the Duffry, was killed in that year.[16] However, it is quite possible that some of the sub-infeudation of Wexford was implemented by Strongbow's successor, William Marshal the elder. Brooks has demonstrated that most, if not all, of the district represented by the modern county was distributed during the sub-infeudation process by either Strongbow or Marshall.[17] This makes it difficult to understand the implications of Strongbow's grant of 'the kingdom of Ui Cennselaig'[18] to Murtough, son of Dermot McMurrough, unless, in fact, some parts of north Wexford and Carlow were left in the hands of the Irish.

There appears to have been nine principal initial grants within the bounds of the modern county. Hervey de Montmorency received Shelburne and Bargy; FitzStephen and FitzGerald held Forth for a short time; Maurice de Prendergast received the largest fief in the county, holding Fernegenal and Ui Mealla by ten knights' fees. On the east coast Gilbert de Boisrohard was granted Offelimy and Raymond le Gros received the manor of Glascarrig. Robert de Quency was granted the Duffry, and the Denne family received the barony of Kayer on the west bank of the Slaney. The manor of Rosegarland, situated between the Owenduff and Corrach rivers, was granted to the de London family and Maghairnidhe, later Adamstown, was granted to the de Heddons.

There was considerable fluctuation during the early years of settlement. As previously mentioned, FitzStephen and FitzGerald lost the town of Wexford with its land in Forth. These then reverted to Strongbow, Lord of Leinster, and were subsequently held as a seignorial manor. A similar fate befell the lands of Hervey de Montmorency in Shelburne and Bargy. After his death without heir in 1205 his lands reverted to William Marshal who, by his marriage to

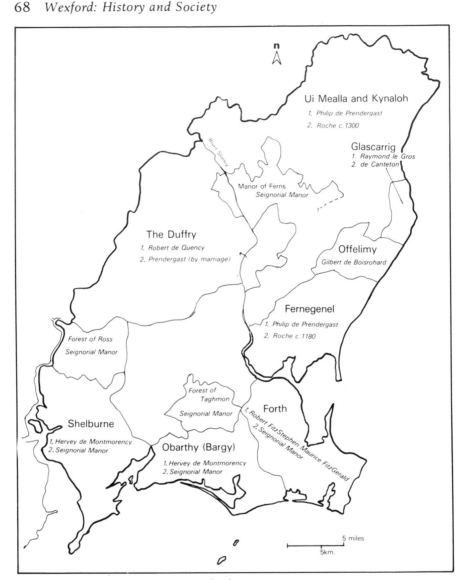

Fig. 3.2: Initial grants, county Wexford

Strongbow's daughter Isabella, succeeded him as Lord of Leinster.[19] As Strongbow retained the forests of Ross and Taghmon as seignorial manors, much of county Wexford was held directly by the lords of Leinster.[20] The manor of Ferns, in the north of the county, containing 160 carucates (c. 48,000 statute acres), appears to have been the largest and most valuable of the seignorial manors in the county.[21] In 1246 the manor of Ferns was worth £81. 15. 0. as compared to £68. 19. 11. for the manor of Rosslare[22] (which was equivalent to the barony of Forth minus the burgage lands of Wexford town.)

Maurice de Prendergast received the largest grant in the county consisting of five knights' fees in Fernegenal and five in a district referred to as

Ayrmellach or Ui Mealla in the north of the county. However. both of these passed to the Roches; Fernegenel about 1185[23] and Ui Mealla towards the end of the thirteenth century.[24] On the other hand the Duffry, which had been granted to Robert de Quency for the service of five knights, passed by marriage to the Prendergasts about 1190.[25] Glascarrig on the east coast which was initially held by Raymond le Gros was apparently passed on to one of his de Canteton nephews.[26] Ballymagir and Adamstown was another important fee which changed hands. The first grantee was Sir Alexander de Heddon but it passed to the Devereuxes by marriage about the middle of the thirteenth century.[27]

Following the division of conquered lands into major fiefs and demesne manors, the organisation of these large units into individual manors was then undertaken. This had to be carefully considered because, once a lord had allocated the various sub-manors within his fief, they became established by hereditary right and custom which was irreversible.[28] The most important of these sub-manors were held as knights' fees by tenants who performed military service in return for their land. The amount of land allocated as a knight's fee varied, sometimes being smaller in peaceful districts. A tenant could hold land worth several knights' fees or alternatively it might be worth only a fraction of a fee. The amount of military service expected per fee was limited by custom to forty days in the year. In Ireland, however, military service was usually on the basis of scutage (the payment of money in lieu of services) and was customarily fixed at forty shillings per knights' fee.[29] These military tenants formed a permanent garrison within the manor as the obligations attached to military service were passed from father to son.[30] Another group of free tenants held their land in perpetuity, not by military service, but by payment of money rent, fixed for ever by their first charter.[31] The kind of settlement planned by the Anglo-Normans required fairly intensive colonisation and this necessitated the enticement of a large number of settlers from England and Wales to inhabit and cultivate the manors. The difficulty of this task is demonstrated by the case of Brother Alan (of Buildwas Abbey) who came to inspect the lands of Dunbrody. He was forced to live in the direst of dire straits in a hollow tree; he reported that the place was a wilderness, the land was worthless, and the natives were ferocious.[32] Not surprisingly the monks of Buildwas decided not to come.

The male members of the Marshal family all died without heir and the Lordship of Leinster was divided among his five daughters in 1247.[33] The Lordship of Wexford, which then became a Palatinate, was allocated to Joan and passed by marriage to William de Valence, Earl of Pembroke. The cantred of Shelburne, which consisted of the manors of Ross and the Island, with county Carlow, constituted the share of Maud, daughter of William Marshal, and passed by marriage to the Bigods, Earls of Norfolk. The first definite information available on the sub-infeudation of county Wexford is contained in two feodaries drawn up in 1247 showing the knights' fees held under Joan and Maud Marshal and their Valence and Bigod descendants.[34] Brooks uses these feodaries and later extents of 1307, 1324 and c. 1425 to identify the holders and locations of knights' fees in county Wexford (appendix 1).[35] A total of sixty-one land grants are identified, ranging in value from one-twentieth of a fee to nine fees, with an overall value of forty-five and seven-twentieth fees. There were twenty-three Bigod land grants not all of which were in the cantred of Shelburne, with a total value of thirteen and a quarter fees. The thirty-eight Valence grants amounted in total to thirty-two and one-tenth fees. As the Valences held Wexford by twenty-two and one-fifth fees[36] this gave them a surplus profit of nine and nine-tenth fees.

Of the sixty-one fees in county Wexford, the locations of forty-eight can be identified with some certainty; five are doubtful and eight are unknown. Brooks does not include an estimate of the extent of each fee and this will be undertaken here. In attempting to map the land held by knights' service, the information contained in the extents will be utilised. The importance of seventeenth century surveys and the boundaries of civil parishes in relation to medieval settlement will also be considered and a review of these is therefore necessary.

Two assumptions can be made: (1) the land-holding pattern at the end of the thirteenth and beginning of the fourteenth centuries reflected the grants made during the sub-infeudation process and (2) in areas of military and political stability, the Anglo-Norman pattern of settlement survived until the middle of the seventeenth century.[37] Therefore an analysis of the information contained in the mid-seventeenth century Civil Survey, when taken in conjunction with earlier material, provides a more complete basis for the study of the Anglo-Norman settlement pattern than could be obtained from a study of thirteenth or fourteenth century material alone.[38] Although reservations have been expressed about the value of the Civil Survey when used in this way, there is significant correlation between the information from earlier sources and that of the Civil Survey particularly as regards the location and extent of settlement in south county Wexford.[39] Consequently the Civil Survey has been used in the preparation of figs 3.3/3.4 on the assumption that it substantially reflects the settlement pattern originally established by the Anglo-Normans in the twelfth and thirteenth centuries. The correlation of manor and parish has been amply demonstrated.[40] It has also been observed that areas of small parishes generally correspond closely to areas of intensive Anglo-Norman settlement.[41] The accompanying map of the civil parishes is based on the first edition Ordnance Survey (1840) of county Wexford with some variations based on the Civil Survey, where earlier ecclesiastical units are shown (fig 3.3).

Place-names found in manorial extents can often be identified with modern townlands whose origins probably belong to the pre-Norman period.[42] These townlands were mapped by the Ordnance Survey in the 1830s and a comparison of boundaries shows them to substantially correspond with the land divisions listed in the Civil Survey. As it seems probable that at least some of these boundaries were used in the sub-infeudation process, the modern townland pattern has been used as the basis for the accompanying map.

The map (fig. 3.4) of the sub-infeudation pattern is of necessity incomplete as the locations of eight fees have not been identified. These are possibly

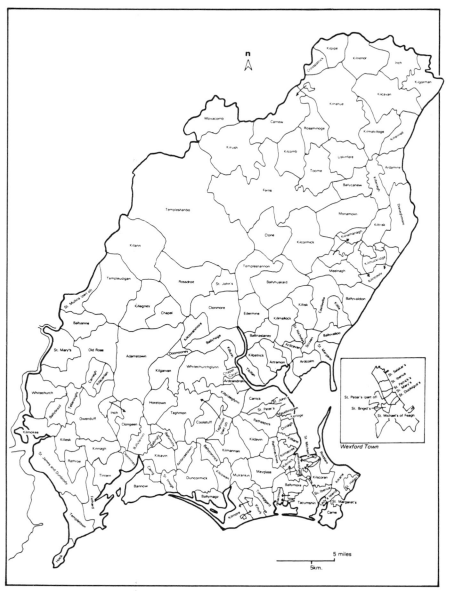

Fig. 3.3: Medieval parishes, county Wexford

represented by some of the blank areas on the map, although some of these must have been occupied by the other categories of manorial tenants.[43] It is not possible to be definite about the extent of a number of the grants, especially the larger manors in the northern half of the county which were sub-divided into a number of parishes. In the closely settled south of the county, the situation was different as in most cases the manor and parish were one and the same. However it is possible to arrive at an estimate of the extent of some of the larger grants. For example, it is known that the manor of Glascarrig consisted of 27 carucates.[44] The carucate is generally thought to have contained about 120 medieval acres of arable land, although an indefinite amount of waste or uncultivated land could also be included. The medieval acre is believed to have been equivalent to about two and a half statute acres.[45] On this basis, the manor of Glascarrig, held as one knight's fee, can be shown to be coincident with the parish of Donaghmore. The adjacent manor of Offelimy

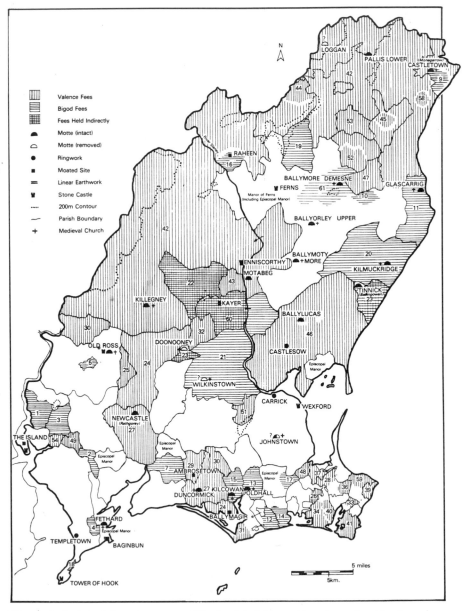

Fig. 3.4: Knights' fees in county Wexford, with associated earthworks (numbers refer to appendix 1)

(Kilmuckridge) was held by two knights' fees and it seems a reasonable assumption that it would be approximately twice the area of Glascarrig. In fact when the area of the adjoining parishes of Meelnagh, Kilnamanagh, Killincooly and Kilmuckridge is calculated it is almost exactly twice the size of Donaghmore. As the fragmented nature of these small parishes suggests an area of close settlement, it seems reasonable to suggest that they represent the two fees of Offelimy. Using a similar method, it is possible to estimate the extent of grants which were not represented by a single parish.

The well-established connection between manor and medieval parish was a feature of Anglo-Norman settlement in county Wexford. Of the sixty-one recorded knights' fees, twenty-nine formed the basis for a medieval parish. In nineteen instances (thirteen in the southern half of the county) manor and parish appear to have been coincident. There would appear to have been two fees in each of the parishes of Tacumshin, Kilscoran and Adamstown. The patchwork of small parishes, therefore, in the southern baronies and halfway up along the east coast reflects dense settlement and small manors. On the other hand the much larger parishes in the northern and north-western part of the county reflect the extensive grants made there which were never densely settled and were overrun by the Irish in the early fourteenth century. The larger grants, Feregenal and The Duffry, were sub-divided into a number of parishes, indicating that these grants were sub-let to other tenants. In a number of instances, for example at Ballyvaldon and Doonooney (no. 23) and Rossdroit (no. 22), military tenants had military tenants of their own.

The size of the knight's fee varied considerably. In county Dublin the service of one knight was worth about 10 carucates (c. 3,000 st. acres).[46] The purpose of military tenure was the creation of a garrison and, as might be expected, the size of a fee depended to some extent on whether the district in which it was situated was at peace or under threat from the Irish. In county Meath, for example, the size of the knight's fee varied from 20 carucates in peaceful areas to 30 carucates in the marches.[47] By comparing a number of grants in county Wexford, it is apparent that the same principle was applied here also. Kilcowan (c. 7 carucates), Mulrankin (c. 8 carucates), Kilcavan (c. 11 carucates) and Ambrosetown (c. 8 carucates) were all held by the service of one knight in the south of the county. Rossdroit (c. 28 carucates) and Glascarrig (c. 27 carucates) were held as one knight's fee in the northern, more vulnerable part of the county. This indicates that the extent of the knight's fee in the frontier zone of county Wexford was up to four times the size of the fee in the land of peace.

In a number of instances the land granted as a knight's fee was held in two separate lots. The most interesting were the fees of Ballyanne (no. 30), Adamstown (no. 24) and Rosegarland (no. 27), all of which had detached manors in what is now the barony of Bargy. As Bargy reverted to William Marshal in 1205 following the death of Hervey de Montmorency this suggests that the holders of these fees had received initial grants in the late twelfth century but were given additional land in Bargy subsequent to 1205. The manor of Duncormick, which went with Rosegarland, subsequently passed the Meylers.[48]

The bishop was one of the principal landowners, occupying six manors principally in the south of the county, at Fethard, Kinnagh, Ballingly, Mayglass, Pollregan and at Ferns itself.[49] He also held extensive lands in other districts, possibly occupied by lay tenants. Following a dispute about various lands in 1226 between John de St John, first Anglo-Norman bishop of Ferns, and Philip de Prendergast, the bishop was granted estates in different parts of the county. These included lands at Templeshanbo, Killegney, Clone and Crosspatrick, as well as in other unidentified areas. In return, the bishop renounced all claim to the manor which he had held on the east bank of the river at Enniscorthy.[50] It is not known when the see lands of the diocese were organised into manors. There are indications that this happened, during the first generation of the settlement, as for example in Tipperary.[51] John de St John became the first Anglo-Norman bishop of Ferns in 1223 and by 1226 there are references to his manors of Templeshanbo and Ferns receiving grants of weekly markets.[52] It is possible that he may have introduced the manorial system to the episcopal lands. The income from these manors, including the boroughs of Fethard, Mayglass and Ferns, amounted to £104 a year in 1282 and would have placed the bishop among the important landholders of the county.[53]

The importance of the seventeenth century Civil Survey in relation to medieval settlement is well established. The manorial system of land tenure led to great continuity of occupation by the same families in districts which were politically and militarily secure. The validity of using the Civil Survey in this way is amply proven in the case of county Wexford as it records that, in the mid-seventeenth century, nineteen parishes were held by proprietors with the same family name as in the mid-thirteenth century and in three other instances some land in the parish continued to be held by descendants of the original grantees. For example, Ballyconnick (no. 30) was held by the Bushers in 1247 and 1640; Kilcowan (no. 15) was held by the Keatings on both dates; Ballybrennan by the Sinnotts and St Helens by the Codds. All of the twenty-two parishes in which there was continuity of tenure were situated in the southern part of the county. It seems clear, then, that the nature and variety of Anglo-Norman settlement in county Wexford was reflected in the pattern of medieval parishes which subsequently developed.

Defensive Earthworks

The first step in the organisation of a fief was the establishment of a principal or *caput* manor and the construction of a defensive strong point. These fortifications usually took the form of a motte castle, but in some cases other types of defences were used as the lord of every manor would not have had the resources necessary to construct a motte castle.[54] Mottes were flat topped earthen mounds usually constructed in a strategic location; sometimes an existing natural feature or an older earthwork might be adapted to avoid the necessity of having to build the entire mound. The mounds were normally surrounded by a fosse, usually with an outer enclosing bank. A timber tower, surrounded by a wooden palisade, was erected on the summit of the mound. In some cases mottes had attached enclosures known as baileys, again usually protected by a fosse and palisade. Mottes varied considerably in size depending on the importance of the builder and the size of the land grant on which they were constructed. In his study of the mottes of the Norman liberty of Meath, Graham has shown that the distribution of mottes bore a direct relationship to the pattern of land grants.[55] Most of the larger mottes with baileys attached were associated with large seignorial manors and principal land grants while minor mottes were usually associated with individual manors. In his study of Ulster mottes, McNeill observed, on the other hand, that baileys were infrequent, except in frontier locations.[56]

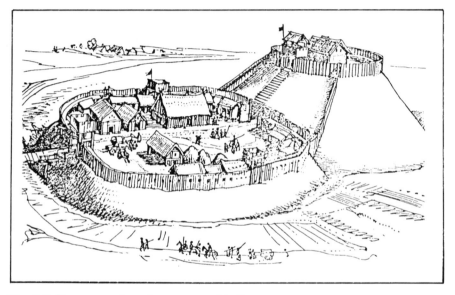

Fig. 3.5: Reconstruction of a motte and bailey

In a provisional list published by Glasscock fifteen mottes are identified in county Wexford.[57] As a result of recent field-work it is now possible to add a further five sites to that list, namely, Ballymore Demesne, Castletown, Duncormick, Kilmuckridge, Old Hall with two possible additional sites at Loggan and Wilkinstown. Two sites at Killincooley and Knockavota, formerly listed as mottes, have proven upon investigation to be other types of earthworks. The motte at Castletown is named from the 1840 O.S. map (Wexford sheet 3) as, due to a change in townland boundary, it is now in the townland of Monagarrow Upper (O.S. 1924). Without archaeological excavation it is not possible to be certain that all of these are actually mottes but in most cases this is indicated by their location within the settlement pattern. This brings to twenty the number of mottes listed in county Wexford and it seems probable that this number would be increased by more intensive fieldwork at a local level. The motte at Newcastle is the only one identified in the county with a surviving bailey. It is accepted that many of the Anglo-Norman mottes were based on existing earthworks, either burial mounds or ring-forts,[58] and it would seem that the bailey at Newcastle may have been based on a ring-fort. The fact that the site was known as Rathgorey would also suggest this. Loggan in the north of the county was described as having a bailey similar to Newcastle[59] and Westropp also described it as having an oval bailey to the south.[60] If the mound at Loggan is a genuine motte it may have been based on an existing burial mound as a number of urns were found nearby in cist burials. However Orpen considered that it was not a motte and so its classification must remain doubtful.[61] (Due to removal for sand, this site has now been almost totally destroyed).

When the mottes are related to Anglo-Norman land grants, their place within the manorial structure becomes clearer (fig. 3.4). The motte at Old Ross is the only one associated with a seignorial *caput* but it must be remembered that there were early thirteenth century stone castles at Wexford, Carrick, Ferns, the Island, Old Ross and Kayer. It is not possible to define the exact extent of the seignorial manor of Ferns but it seems likely that the mottes at Ballymoty More and Ballyorley Upper were connected with it. Ballymore was also probably part of the manor of Ferns and the rectangular motte there must represent the *caput* of the half fee recorded at Ballyregan, (which is the next townland to Ballymore) in 1298. The Prendergasts may have had a motte castle at Enniscorthy, the *caput* of the Duffry, before they built a stone castle there, perhaps in the 1220s. Two other mottes can also be attributed to the Prendergasts; the well preserved Killegney motte which was included in the Prendergast fief[63] and the motte at Motabeg, perhaps the finest in the county, perfectly positioned, with Enniscorthy castle, to control the river Slaney. The three mottes in the north of the county, Castletown, Pallis and Loggan must have related to the other Prendergast fee of Ui Mealla, Castletown motte seems to have been situated on the small fee of Lisbegge (no. 9). Although this was a small fee, the holder, Roger de Hyda, was an important man with lands in other parts of the country also and could possibly have afforded to construct a motte castle.[64]

All of the other major mottes in the county can be related to particular fees. Glascarrig motte can be attributed to either Raymond le Gros or his de Canteton nephews; the motte at Kilmuckridge was located on de Boisrahard's fief and Newcastle motte was on the de London manor of Rosegarland. The de London fief was divided in two, with fees at Rosgarland and Duncormick and significantly there are mottes at both places. Similarly a branch of the Roches held a split half fee at Ballyvaldon and Doonooney, and again there is a motte on each portion. There is no evidence to show that there was a principal motte on the manor of Kayer but it may have been replaced by the thirteenth century stone castle which was built there.[65] There was probably a minor motte at Wilkinstown in the south of the manor where a flat-tapped mound existed until about 1980, in a field known as the moat field, beside the medieval parish church of Whitechurch. No principal motte has so far been identified on the important Roche fee of Fernegenal held by the service of five knights. The motte at Ballylucas was probably in this fief, but, in its present state, would seem to be too small to have been the *caput* of such a large fief. However, in England and Wales the Anglo-Normans used another type of defensive earthwork as an alternative to the better known motte and bailey. These earthworks, known as ringworks, or ringwork castles, were sometimes built so that they were defended on one or more sides by natural obstacles, such as cliffs or steep slopes and only embanked on the exposed faces.[66] The first fortress built by the Anglo-Normans in Ireland was of this type. Built at Carrick, near Wexford, Giraldus described it as a castle built on a steep crag and said that the place, naturally well protected, was improved by artificial means, namely 'a flimsy wall of branches and sods'.[67] These words were identical to the ones used by Giraldus to describe the fortifications constructed by Raymond.le Gros at Baginbun.[68] Recent archaeological excavations at Carrick have shown that the fortress was of the ringwork castle type.[69] The site has yielded thirteenth century pottery, coins and a battle-axe.[70]

At Castlesow, which was in the Roche fee of Fernegenal, there is a good example of a site which would fit into the ringwork castle category. Situated on a high bluff in a loop of the river Sow, the site is protected on three sides by the steep slope. The top, which is about 20m. in diameter is protected by a bank and internal fosse and there is another bank and fosse near the bottom of the slope. In the absence of a major motte it seems possible that the site at Castlesow represents the *caput* of the Roche manor of Fernegenal. There is a double loop on the river at Castlesow and there is another defensive earthwork in the other loop on the opposite side of the river.[71] The Roches sub-infeudated the Sinnotts with part of their lands about 1240[72] with the river Sow dividing the two portions and this could possibly be the reason for the two defensive earthworks in such close proximity. In a study of medieval settlement in the south-west of the county a number of ringwork castle sites were tentatively identified.[73] The most important one was at Templetown on the Knights Templars' manor at Kilcloggan, with others at Boley, Rathnageeragh and Finshoge.

There are two earthworks of another type in the county which are also believed to date to the early stages of Anglo-Norman sub-infeudation.[74] These are the big square forts, each about two acres in extent, of Great Island and Ballymagir. Hervey de Montmorency set up his caput on Great Island, which was known as Hervey's Island for centuries, and it is probable that the moated and ramparted site which existed on the island represented his stronghold. Much of the site has been levelled with only the outer banks surviving as field boundaries. The site at Ballymagir is situated on the de Heddon-Devereux fief and may represent the original manor house. The site, with internal banks 6m. thick and 5m. above the moat, is still occupied by a farm house which incorporates a small stone castle.

The remaining mottes identified in the county can all be identified with smaller land holdings. The mottes at Kilcowan and Oldhall were on the well known half fees of Kilcowan and Mulrankin, held by the Keatings and

Brownes. The classification of the small motte at Fethard would be doubtful but for the fact that it is associated with the medieval church and later tower house. It probably can be attributed to a branch of the Suttons of Ballykeeroge. Only half of the mound, identified by Glasscock as a motte, remains at Johnstown. The rest was removed to make way for the road. The fact that this site is again associated with the medieval church of Rathaspick and a later tower house at Johnstown, now part of the modern Johnstown Castle, would perhaps suggest that it was a motte. The Esmondes are thought to have been established at Johnstown from the earliest days of Anglo-Norman activity in Ireland and this motte may well represent their original stronghold.

It is evident then that the distribution of assumed mottes in the county relates closely to the sub-infeudation process implemented by the Anglo-Normans. Although the whole county seem to have been sub-infeudated originally there is a surprising absence of identified mottes in the whole north-west of the county in what was the manor of Duffry. This area was densely wooded and was perhaps never settled but left to the MacMurroughs. It is noteworthy that of the twenty mottes recorded fifteen have associated church sites. This may indicate that the churches owed their origins to the patronage of the lord of the manor and these motte-church sites must have played an important part in the development of the parochial system in the late twelfth and early fourteenth centuries.

In his study of the mottes of Meath, Graham[75] has shown that mottes were built to form a defensive screen or barrier along the border of the settlement. Similarly in county Wexford the majority of the mottes were apparently constructed in two continuous lines running from south-west to north-east across the county (fig 3.4). They were located across the area which would have been frontier land between the well colonised south,of the county and the thinly settled northern part. This would seem to suggest that the construction and location of motte castles was carried out according to a co-ordinated plan by Anglo-Norman settlers to defend and protect their newly conquered lands.

Moated Sites

Although Orpen referred in passing to rectangular sites surrounded by ditches and ramparts,[76] these earthworks were largely ignored until Glasscock's survey, based on first edition ordnance survey maps, showed moated sites to be concentrated in the south-east, with a distribution which suggested an Anglo-Norman origin.[77] More recently, in 1977, the study of moated sites as a settlement form has been much advanced by Barry's work in the south-eastern counties of Tipperary, Kilkenny, Carlow and Wexford.[78] His extensive fieldwork and research led to the conclusion that moated sites probably functioned as the defended farmsteads of the Anglo-Norman colonists who settled in Ireland in the thirteenth and early fourteenth centuries.[79].

A moated site is defined as an enclosure surrounded by a rectangular or sub-rectangular ditch, usually filled with water. The central platform may or may not be raised above the level of the surrounding land. In the south-east Barry found that the sites vary considerably in area and width of moat but 76% of sites have areas of between 500 and 2,500 square metres with moat widths of between 2 and 7 metres.[80] Since 1977 the results of a number of field surveys and excavations have tended to reinforce the conclusions reached by Barry.[81] The excavations, especially at Rigsdale in county Cork have produced evidence of occupation commencing in the last quarter of the thirteenth century and ending in the first half of the fourteenth century. Empey considers that moated sites were not built as a result of early grants but were the work of a later generation from c. 1225 to 1325. He points out, for instance, that parish churches were associated with early grants and that in no case is a moated site associated with a parish church.[82] However it will be noted later that this was not always the case in county Wexford.

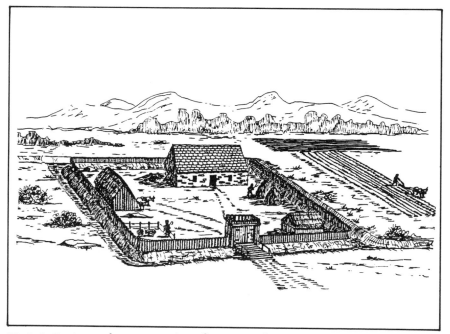

Fig 3.6: Conjectural reconstruction of a rectangular earthwork (by B. Colfer)

There is some evidence to suggest that this secondary phase of land clearance and colonisation may have started in Wexford in 1235. The charter of deforestation issued by Richard Marshal between the years of 1231-4 permitted his free tenants to 'clear, enclose and cultivate' their lands which were within 'the metes and bounds of the forests of Ross and Taghmon'.[83] The placenames mentioned in this charter have been used by Orpen and Brooks to estimate the extent of the areas referred to in the charter and the suggested locations of these districts are indicated on fig 3.7.[84] This distribution map of moated sites is based on the 118 sites listed by Barry in county Wexford.[85]

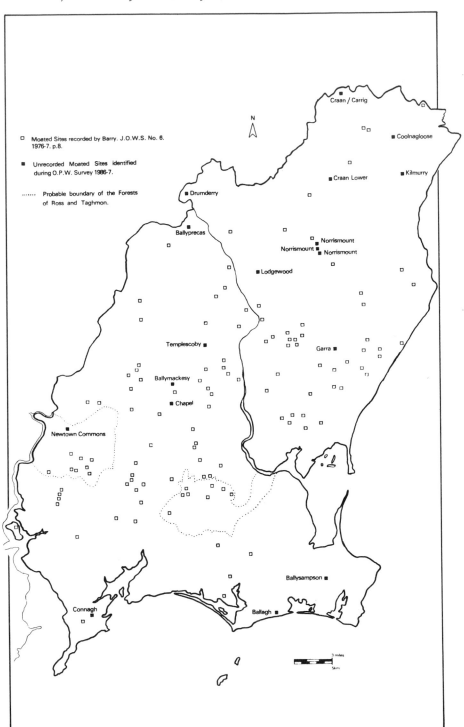

Fig 3.7: Moated sites in county Wexford

Another eighteen sites have recently been tentatively identified during the course of a paper survey carried out for the Office of Public Works by a team led by Geraldine Stout. This survey was based, for the most part, on aerial photographs and maps. While these sites have yet to be verified in the field, the distribution of the additional sites is primarily in the north of the county and this would indicate that settlement was heavier here than previously believed.[86] Clearly there was a concentration of moated sites in the districts described in the deforestation charter, probably constructed during the clearing and settling of these lands subsequent to 1235. The distribution of the sites in the county as a whole follows a very definite pattern. The majority are concentrated in a broad band running from south-west to north-east across the county following, in general, the line of the principal mottes. They were scarcer in the north and west of the county, on the large fiefs of Ui Mealla and Duffry, and almost completely absent in the south.

On the basis of this distribution, and taking other factors into consideration, it would appear that the wave of secondary settlement was confined for the most part to the centre of the county. The manors mostly involved would have been the forests of Ross and Taghmon; the manor of Kayer; the northern part of Fernegenal; the manor of Kilmuckridge and possibly the southern part of the seignorial manor of Ferns. The relative scarcity of moated sites to the north and west would suggest that these areas were never densely settled making it easy for the Irish to recover them in the fourteenth century. The almost total absence of moated sites in the three southern baronies would seem to be due to other reasons. It will be shown later that most of the land of Shelburne was held by the church, principally the Cistercians, on whose lands a manorial system did not operate. Only four moated sites are recorded in the baronies of Forth and Bargy and it seems likely that because the south of the county was densely settled from the very first that there was no need for secondary colonisation and so few moated sites were constructed. Three of the sites in Bargy, namely Ballyconnick, Kilcowan and Ballymagir were on knights' fees and belonged to the initial phase of settlement. The mottes at Pallis, Killegney, Newcastle, Kilcowan, (townland of Hooks), and Wilkinstown may have been abandoned in favour of adjacent moated sites. There are medieval parish church sites at Killegney, Kilcowan and Wilkinstown which would also suggest early settlement.

Nucleated Settlement

MANORIAL VILLAGES
As the Anglo-Norman colony developed in Ireland, a considerable number of English and Welsh settlers became established on the newly conquered lands in the south and east. Manorial villages appear to have been the most common rural settlement form and have been defined as a settlement without borough status but always containing a church and generally, but not necessarily, a castle and mill.[87] In his study of Meath, Graham shows that these villages were

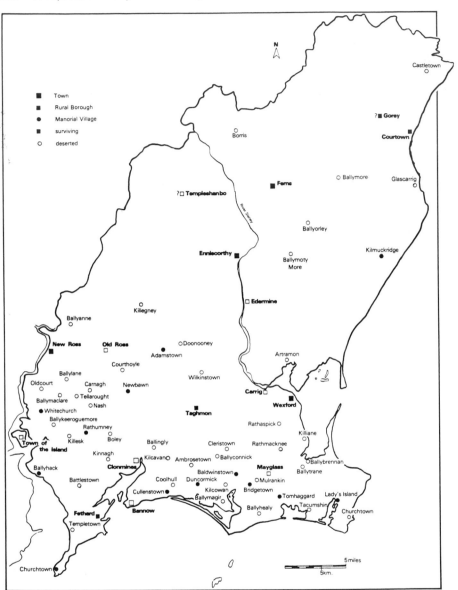

Fig. 3.8: Nucleated settlements: towns, boroughs and manorial villages

nucleated and agricultural in function. Glasscock has focused attention on similar village sites in Tipperary and Kilkenny.[88]

An examination of the Ordnance Survey sheets for county Wexford has produced fifty-four village sites based on church and castle and in many cases a mill also. Some of the castles took the form of a motte, such as at Doonooney and Killegney, but most were tower houses, the majority of which were built in the fifteenth and sixteenth centuries. The distribution map presented here (fig. 3.8) is based on positive church and castle sites which can also be placed in a manorial context by documentary reference. There were many other church sites in the county which are not included here as it is not possible to place them in a manorial context without more intensive study at a local level. It is probable also that many of these churches were of pre-Norman origin and never formed part of a nucleated settlement.

Of the fifty-four villages which have been tentatively identified thirteen survive as settlements in the modern landscape. A number of others, such as Nash and Tacumshin, survive as groups of houses at crossroads. In a study of medieval Shelburne aerial photography has revealed traces of earthworks and old field systems at some deserted village sites[89] and it seems likely that there would be similar remains at other deserted sites throughout the county. The concentration of manorial village sites is very obviously in the south of the county with only isolated examples elsewhere. Of the thirteen which survive as settlements six (Lady's Island, Tomhaggard, Bridgetown, Baldwinstown, Duncormick and Cullenstown) are located in the baronies of Forth and Bargy, indicating stable and continuous settlement. This concentration of manorial villages in the south of the county, in an area where there were almost no moated sites, suggests that manorial villages flourished in this area of early intensive colonisation, where the land-holding pattern remained unchanged in many instances down to the seventeenth century.

RURAL BOROUGHS AND TOWNS

During the twelfth and thirteenth centuries there was an enormous expansion in town foundation all over Europe. Some of the Anglo-Norman adventurers who came to Ireland were involved in this movement or at least aware of it. William Marshal, for instance, was Lord of Leinster for thirty years between 1189 and 1219, but he was also involved in developing his extensive estates in England and France. This concept of town foundation and colonisation was brought to Ireland by the Anglo-Normans and they were responsible for most of the towns and boroughs which were established throughout much of Ireland in the twelfth and thirteenth centuries. The Anglo-Norman barons needed settlers for their newly acquired lands in Ireland and they offered burgess status to attract traders and artisans. Foundation charters to towns granted plots of land to burgesses, within the borough, on which a house could be built and sometimes an outside acreage also. Other privileges included freedom of movement, the right of trial before equals, freedom from certain taxes and the right to self-administration. The privileges conferred by a foundation charter were usually referred to as the laws òf Breteuil, a code of liberties based on the charter of a town of that name in France. In return for these privileges the town founder received revenue in the form of burgess rent, market tolls and court fines and the town became a market-place for the produce of his manors. The number of towns and boroughs that were established in Ireland between 1169 and 1300 seems to indicate that the offer of burgess tenure succeeded in attracting a very large number of urban colonists into Ireland during that period.[90]

Before the arrival of the Anglo-Normans in Ireland the five port towns of

Dublin, Wexford, Waterford, Cork and Limerick had been established by Norse settlers. The importance of these towns is evident from the fact that three of them, Wexford, Waterford and Dublin, were taken over by the end of 1170 and were apparently the first places in Ireland to be given borough status. The inhabitants of Wexford, for example, are referred to as burgesses as early as 1172.[91]

The problems involved in defining a town have been discussed by Graham and Bradley.[92] Graham maintains that settlements upon which borough status was conferred by charter should be classified as towns whereas Bradley points out that only a settlement with certain urban characteristics should be described as a true town.[93] Many manorial villages were granted charters which gave them the elements of a town constitution, although they were never any more than villages in morphology or function. Glasscock described these settlements as rural boroughs, in order to differentiate between them and the chartered boroughs which had true urban characteristics.[94]

A total of fourteen boroughs have been identified in county Wexford (appendix 2). There is also a suggestion that there was a town at Gorey in 1296.[95] In 1223 the bishop of Ferns was granted a weekly market at his manor of Templeshanbo.[96] This is an indication that it may have possessed borough status.[97] It is clear that the system of land grants implemented by the Anglo-Normans had a fundamental influence on the location of settlements which were granted borough status. Most of the settlements which attained importance were associated with primary land grants.[98] Because of a greater choice in selecting an advantageous site, these boroughs had a better chance of long term survival compared to boroughs established on secondary grants where the choice of site would have been more restricted.

In county Wexford there were six boroughs situated on seignorial manors; Old Ross and New Ross on the manor of Ross; Wexford, Carrig and Taghmon on the manor of Wexford and Ferns on the manor of Ferns. Six boroughs were established on major land grants; the town of the Island, Clonmines and Bannow on Hervey de Montmorency's fief; Enniscorthy as the *caput* of the Duffry; Edermine in the Barony of Kayer; Courtown and possible Gorey on the Prendergast fief of Ui Mealla. The boroughs of Fethard, Mayglass and Templeshanbo were situated on episcopal manors and were presumably founded by the bishop himself as it is known that bishops established boroughs elsewhere in Ireland. By the fifteenth century it was necessary to obtain permission from the crown to create a borough but earlier not only the great lords such as the Marshals but also their sub-tenants could create boroughs freely.[99] It can reasonably be assumed that the boroughs on seignorial manors were established by Strongbow or, as in the case of New Ross, by his successor William Marshal. The boroughs on the other manors must have been founded by the various grantees. Hervey de Montmorency's fief escheated to William Marshal in 1205 and although it would appear that the town of the Island and perhaps Bannow were founded by Hervey there is some reason to believe that the town of Clonmines may have been established by Marshal himself.[100]

In Meath Graham has shown that a high proportion of boroughs were established on pre-Norman monastic sites.[101] This association applied in county Wexford also where four of the boroughs, Ferns, Taghmon, the town of the Island and New Ross were established on or near the sites of early Christian foundations. The importance of routeways in selecting sites for boroughs has been commented on and was obviously of importance in county Wexford also.[102] Six of the boroughs were on navigable rivers: New Ross and the town of the Island on the Barrow and Wexford, Carrig, Edermine and Enniscorthy on the Slaney. Four boroughs, Courtown, Bannow, Clonmines and Fethard were on the coast, with direct access by sea to the ports of England and Wales. When Marshal built his bridge at New Ross it also became the lowest bridging point on the river on the main land route between Wexford and Waterford.

New Ross is a good example of a new town established as an economic venture by William Marshal. He obviously realised that the land-locked site of Old Ross had been unwisely chosen and one of his priorities was to establish a port on the river Barrow.[103] The exact date of its foundation is not known but it must have been early in the thirteenth century. Marshal first visited his Irish possessions in 1200 and in his charter to Tintern Abbey in c. 1207 he granted 'one burgage of Ross, on the south side of the bridge' to the Cistercians.[104] New Ross, situated on the tideway of the river Barrow about 34 km. from the open sea, had access to an extensive hinterland along the rivers Barrow and Nore. Marshal's determination to make a success of his new town was epitomised by the construction of a high circular tower at the extremity of the Hook peninsula to act as a light-tower and landmark.[105] His determination was rewarded as by the end of the thirteenth century New Ross was one of the foremost ports in the whole country.[106]

However all of the other speculative boroughs in county Wexford did not enjoy the same success as New Ross. A number would appear to have never been more than 'rural-boroughs' with no locational or economic advantages such as New Ross enjoyed. These included Old Ross, Edermine, Mayglass, Courtown, Gorey, Templeshanbo and possibly Taghmon. The survival of Gorey and Courtown as substantial settlements in the modern landscape owes more to the seventeenth and eighteenth centuries, rather than Anglo-Norman activity. Bradley has pointed out that on a national level only one quarter of all boroughs established by the Anglo-Normans developed as true towns and this was also the case in county Wexford.[107] Of the sixteen probable boroughs, including the doubtful Gorey and Templeshanbo, only four, Wexford, New Ross, Enniscorthy and to a lesser extent Gorey, remain as towns. Fethard, Taghmon, Ferns and Courtown survive as large villages, giving a total survival rate of fifty per cent. A breakdown of the settlements shows that there was a sixty-six per cent survival rate on seignorial manors; forty-three per cent on principal manors and thirty-three per cent on episcopal manors, indicating that the boroughs founded on the more important manors had a greater chance of long term success.

Boroughs failed for a number of reasons, most of which seem to have been economic. The concentration on the development of New Ross would seem to have been a decisive factor in the failure of other towns in the west and south of the county. Old Ross would have been expected to fail as it was in effect abandoned, although it did survive for a time as the *caput* of the manor. The growth of New Ross would seem to have led to the failure of the town of the Island and possibly Bannow and Clonmines as well, although the last two were also hampered by silting in Bannow Bay. The ruins of the abandoned town of Clonmines, where there are extensive remains of medieval features, have been described as the most impressive in the country.[108] Of the boroughs established on the Slaney, Wexford survived as the administrative capital of the county although, as a port, it was never as successful as New Ross. The fact that it was already a thriving town when occupied and fortified by the Anglo-Normans was obviously a major factor in its long-term survival. Wexford's pre-Norman origins are emphasised by the fact that there were five parishes inside the walls of the medieval town, whereas most true Anglo-Norman towns, such as New Ross, were based on a single parish. At Wexford also remains of burgage strips survive outside the walls of the town, not inside as in other Anglo-Norman foundations. The town of Enniscorthy owed its success to a strategic location at the head of the tideway on the river Slaney and also to its early stone castle. Similarly at Ferns, precariously situated in the north of the county, the castle, which represented a major commitment to the location, ensured its continuity as a settlement.

Monastic Grants

The structure and organisation of the church in pre-Norman Ireland differed greatly from the accepted continental pattern. The great Celtic monasteries, under the influence of the Norse raids, had, in many cases, fallen into the hands of lay dynasties or erenachs and this was accompanied by a growing secularisation. By the end of the eleventh century, Ireland was feeling the influence of a continental reform movement and early in the twelfth century several synods, notably Cashel in 1101 and Rathbresail in 1111, began the task of reforming the Irish church and of setting up a diocesan structure based on the European model. The introduction of the continental orders, such as the Cistercians and the Canons Regular of St Augustine, transformed monastic organisation in Ireland and they soon took the place of the old Celtic foundations.[109] In 1158 Dermot MacMurrough founded an abbey at Ferns for the Canons Regular of St Augustine.[110] Although fifteen Cistercian abbeys were established in Ireland before the arrival of the Anglo-Normans none of these were located in county Wexford.[111]

The Anglo-Normans established nine new Cistercian houses in Ireland and two of these, Dunbrody Abbey and Tintern Abbey, were located in the barony of Shelburne.[112] It would seem that Hervey de Montmorency decided to grant land for the foundation of a Cistercian monastery at Dunbrody at an early date after the arrival of the Anglo-Normans in Ireland. Strongbow's charter confirming Hervey's grant to the monks of Buildwas in Shropshire was witnessed by his son-in-law Robert de Quency among others. As de Quency was killed in 1173, Hervey's original charter must have been before that date, perhaps 1172, although there are other difficulties about the dating of the charter.[113] Following an unfavourable report by Brother Alan who was sent over to report on the site[114] the abbot of Buildwas decided not to accept Hervey's grant and offered it instead to St Mary's Cistercian Abbey in Dublin. This proposal was accepted by St Mary's and in 1182 an agreement was made between the two abbeys which gave St Mary's complete jurisdiction over Dunbrody. Monks from St Mary's began work on the abbey in the same year but it was not until 1201 that the monastery was consecrated by Herlewyn, Bishop of Leighlin, a nephew of the founder. Hervey ended his days as a monk in the abbey and after his death in 1205 a monument was erected to his memory near the high altar.[115]

It would seem that Tintern Abbey, the other Cistercian foundation in county Wexford, was established as the result of an incident which occurred on the occasion of William Marshal's first visit to his estates in Ireland in the year 1200, which is the year given in the Irish annals for the foundation of the monastery.[116] While crossing to Ireland Marshal's ship was in danger of foundering and he vowed that, if spared, he would establish a monastery wherever his ship would reach safe harbour. The ship evidently reached shelter at Bannow Bay because it was there, at the head of a small inlet, that he established the monastery, colonising it with monks from Tintern in Wales and naming it Tintern Minor or *Tintern de Voto*. King John's confirmation of a will of William Marshal granting 39 carucates for the foundation of Tintern was made in the year 1200.[117] However, Marshal's charter to the abbey can be dated 1207-13 from the names of the witnesses.[118] The land which Marshal granted to the Cistercians at Tintern was actually part of Hervey de Montmorency's fief but, as mentioned previously, it probably escheated to Marshal after Hervey's death without issue in 1205. This may explain the fact that although Marshal's will giving land to the Cistercians was made in 1200, his actual charter was not given until after Hervey's death.

The foundation charters to Dunbrody and Tintern give much valuable information which can be used to estimate the extents of the original grants. Of the twenty placenames mentioned in the Dunbrody charter, twelve can be identified with townlands in the modern landscape.[119] Nine placenames are mentioned in the charter to Tintern and three of these can be identified with modern placenames.[120] When these placenames are used in conjunction with the possessions of the abbeys at the dissolution in 1539 an accurate estimate of the extent of the lands of the monasteries can be ascertained (fig 3.9).[121] Before his death Hervey de Montmorency had granted some of his lands in Bargy to Christ Church, Canterbury and in 1245 the prior of Canterbury granted these lands to Tintern in return for an initial payment of 625 marks and an annual rent of 10 marks. At the dissolution Tintern still held lands in Bargy and these are also shown on fig. 3.9.

The great military orders of the Knights Templars and the Knights Hospitallers, both of which had been established in the Holy Land early in the

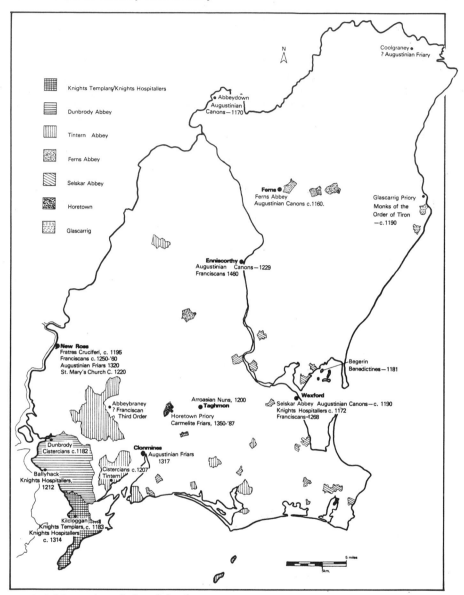

Fig 3.9: Monastic and church lands

twelfth century, were introduced into county Wexford in the early days of the Anglo-Norman occupation.[122] The Templars were first introduced into Ireland by Henry II who had vowed to provide for the support of two hundred Templars as part of his reparation for the murder of Thomas à Becket. Henry's charter, dated 1172,[123] granted to the Templars 'the church of St Aloch near Wexford with the land belonging thereto'[124] apparently referring to the manor of Kilcloggan which was the site of an early Christian monastery founded by Aloch.[125] In subsequent charters of confirmation the words 'near Wexford' were omitted. It is not known when the Templars occupied their lands at Kilcloggan but it was probably before the end of the twelfth century, establishing their headquarters at Templetown which obviously bears their name, as two other areas associated with Templar foundations, Temple House in county Sligo and Templetown in county Louth, were similarly named.[126]

The Knights Hospitallers were also established in county Wexford, at Ballyhack on Waterford Harbour by 1212, and in Wexford town about 1172, perhaps by Strongbow himself.[127] The extent of their preceptory at Ballyhack is not known but after the suppression of the Templars in 1307 the manor of Kilcloggan was granted to the Hospitallers and the two preceptories were merged later in the century. There are no early records available of the size of the manor at Kilcloggan but this can be ascertained by using the extent which was made in 1540 at the time of dissolution.[128] This shows that the manor corresponded to the combined civil parishes of Templetown and Hook (fig. 3.9).

Apart from the great monastic orders about fourteen other religious houses were founded in county Wexford, mostly in the towns. These are shown on the accompanying map with the lands which they held in 1540. The distribution map shows that monastic land was concentrated in the southwest of the county, in the barony of Shelburne. The unusual proximity of the two Cistercian foundations would appear to have been due to the fact that Hervey's land returned to William Marshal allowing him to make a second grant to the Cistercians adjacent to the first one. Significantly, however, a narrow band of lay grants created a 'corridor' between the two communities perhaps for the purpose of preventing friction between them. After the Cistercians and Templars, Selskar Abbey was the next largest landholder with scattered estates in Forth and Shelmaliere. It must be stressed, however, that the lands shown here are those held by the smaller foundations in the sixteenth century and would not necessarily reflect the land holding pattern of earlier centuries.

The Tower Houses

The colonisation and settlement of county Wexford seems to have progressed in relatively peaceful circumstances for most of the thirteenth century. The greatest unrest was apparently caused by a dispute between two Anglo-Norman lords, de Burgo and Fitzgerald, which resulted in the walling of New Ross in 1265.[129] The stable conditions were possibly due in part to the blood relationship which existed between the MacMurroughs and the Marshals and even after the partition of Leinster a new relationship was established between the MacMurroughs and the Bigod lords of Carlow and Shelburne.[130] In 1279 the MacMurroughs were actually in receipt of a fee from the Earl of Norfolk.[131] In 1281 members of the MacMurrough clan visited Roger Bigod in England and were described as his kinsmen.[132] However the MacMurroughs were in rebellion in county Wicklow and after Murchertach MacMurrough, self-styled King of Leinster, and his brother Art were murdered at Arklow in 1282[133] this rebellion seems to have spread to north county Wexford which was recorded

Fig 3.10: The tower house of Rathmacknee

as 'lost and devasted' in 1296.[134] There is evidence also from 1298 to show that the Anglo-Norman colony was coming under increased pressure as in that year waste lands in the county included eighteen and a half carucates in the manor of Ferns; forty-nine and a half burgages in the town of Ferns; one hundred and twenty-eight and a half burgages in Wexford town and twenty three carucates in the manor of Rosslare.[135]

With the death of Roger Bigod in 1306 the lordship of Carlow, with the manors of Ross and the Island, was taken into the King's hands,[136] making it easier for the MacMurroughs to assert themselves and reclaim their lost leadership. From that time on much of county Wexford came under increasing pressure from the resurgent Irish. In the early part of the fourteenth century many of the fiefs recorded by Brooks in the north of the county were described as 'in decay', showing that they had been overrun and abandoned.[137] The plight of the colonists was rendered even more precarious by the events connected with the Bruce campaign of 1315-18 and the great plague known as the Black Death which swept through the country in the late 1340s.[138] During the second half of the fourteenth century the country was in an almost continuous state of war with the Anglo-Norman settlers of county Wexford under constant threat from the MacMurroughs and their allies, the O'Tooles, O'Byrnes and O'Nolans. The campaign of Richard II at the end of the century failed to solve the problem and after his departure the strife continued as before. The MacMurroughs controlled north Wexford and for much of the fifteenth century they actually occupied the great castle of Ferns.[139]

Considering the need for protection it is surprising that few defensive structures were apparently built during most of the fourteenth century. From about the middle of the fifteenth century, however, there was a great building revival which continued for about the next 150 years and it was to this period that the majority of the fortified residences known as tower houses belong.[140] Yet it has recently been shown that some of them may have been built as early as the fourteenth century.[141] The origin of this phase of tower house building in Ireland can probably be attributed to the £10 subsidy which was granted in 1429 to anyone who would build a fortified castle or tower within the Pale.[142] This policy was extended to county Wexford in 1441, when an Act of Parliament was passed for 'building towers upon the waters or river of Taghmon in the county of Wexford'.[143] The 'waters' referred to were the river Corrock, also called the Scar, which flows into Bannow Bay and a small river, or pill, which flows into the Slaney at Polehore (fig 3.11). It was also ordered that these rivers should be dammed so that by deepening the water a greater obstruction would be created. A further order was issued in 1453 that 'none shall break the fortifications of Taghmon in County Wexford nor shall make no ways on the same water from the wood of Bannow to the pill adjoining the river Slaney'. It would seem then that these rivers were considered an important barrier against the Irish and as many as fourteen tower houses were built along them to protect this line of defence (fig. 3.11).

The distribution map of tower houses which is presented here is based on available documentary and cartographic evidence, most of which has been collated in Jeffrey's manuscript.[144] However there are some omissions in this and some seventeenth century plantation castles, which do not belong to the period being dealt with here, are included. These are discussed by Loeber elsewhere in this publication. While comprehensive, this map can not be definitive as there are some problematical sites which require further study at a local level. There is evidence to show that about 170 tower houses existed at one time in the county. About sixty-five of these survive, in various stages of preservation. The vast majority were situated in the south of the county, especially in the baronies of Forth and Bargy, described in 1598 as 'the most civil part, contained within a river called the Pill, where the ancientest gentlemen descended on the first conquerors, do inhabit'.[145]

If, as it is believed, most of these tower houses were built from about 1440 onwards their distribution must reflect the extent of the Anglo-Norman colony as it was at that time. Of the 170 recorded tower houses eighty-six or approximately 50% were located within the pill of Taghmon. Of the sixty-five which survive however, forty or 61% are situated in the same area. This higher survival rate may indicate greater stability and continuity. This continuity is also seen in the many places where the tower house forms part of the modern farmyard complex and indeed in several instances, such as Dungulph, Clonmines and Ballymagir, modified tower houses are still occupied.

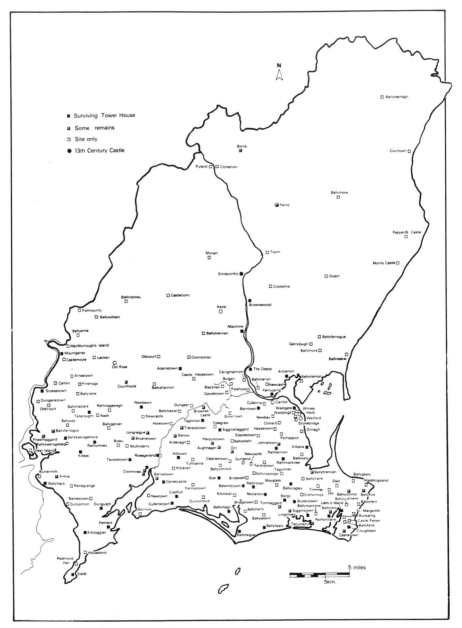

Fig 3.11: Tower houses

Conclusion

Despite the scarcity and uneven quality of available evidence, it appears that all of county Wexford was sub-infeudated in the early stages of Anglo-Norman activity in Ireland. It is obvious that the society which they introduced was of a complex nature with a wide diversity of settlement features. The various elements which are usually associated with Anglo-Norman settlement, including abbeys, military orders, knights' fees, free tenants, demesne manors, boroughs and manorial villages were all to be found in medieval Wexford.

The early motte castles indicate that initially the Anglo-Normans intended to occupy and settle all of the county. This may have been motivated by the fact that much of the best land in the county is in the northern part; the seignorial manor of Ferns, for example, was situated on the Clonroche soil series, one of the most productive and easily tilled.[146] Although the building of a major stone castle at Ferns, early in the thirteenth century, implied a strong commitment to settlement in the north of the county, there was a marked contrast between the subsequent highly successful settlement of the south of the county and the practically total failure of settlement in the north. In fact the progress of the Anglo-Norman colony in county Wexford would seem to have reflected the progress in the country as a whole where expansion continued until about 1300 only to shrink to the area around Dublin, known as the Pale, in the fifteenth and sixteenth centuries. Similarly in county Wexford, settlement in the north came under continuous pressure from the late thirteenth century onwards and by the fifteenth and sixteenth centuries the Anglo-Norman colony was, for the most part, confined to Forth and Bargy within the 'Pill of Taghmon', which could be described as the Pale of county Wexford.

There were apparently a number of reasons why settlement developed in this way. Location and topography were important factors and also the kinship which existed between the MacMurroughs, Marshals and Bigods during the thirteenth century.

The south of the county was flatter and possibly easier to settle, with harbours providing a relatively easy sea crossing to England and Wales. This would have been an important consideration not only in attracting colonists but also in giving them ready access to help and support if required. The north of the county on the other hand was wooded and hilly, although not much of the land was over 200 metres high which is generally accepted as the upper limit of Anglo-Norman settlement.[147] However it was much more open to attack from the Irish and there was no ready access to England by sea. This may have been the reason for the foundation of a borough at Courtown although as a port it would seem to have had only limited suitability. The desirability of the south from a settlement point of view is reflected in the fact that the size of knight's fees in the north was approximately four times those in the south, presumably as an incentive to colonists to take land in the north of the county and by so doing to form an effective garrison.

However this policy does not seem to have been successful and the distribution of moated sites indicates that from about 1250 onwards most of the settlement expansion took place across the centre of the county. By the end of the thirteenth century the county would seem to have been divided into three regions; settlement in the north had been largely abandoned; a frontier zone extended across the centre of the county and the south was securely and densely settled. During the following century it would appear that much of this frontier area was also abandoned and settlement was concentrated in the south of the county.

This is shown in the high number of manorial villages in the south, many of which survive as communities in the modern landscape. Perhaps most dramatically it is shown by the distribution of tower houses and the defence line of the symbolic pill of Taghmon. These tall towers which survive, especially in Forth and Bargy, are a direct reminder of the settlers of Anglo-Norman stock who lived here under constant threat of attack for several centuries. These are not the only reminders. All of the towns, with the possible exception of Wexford, and the larger villages can be attributed directly to the Anglo-Normans and, perhaps most significantly of all, the names of those early settlers still live on, not only in the names of the places where they lived but also in the family names of their numerous descendants.

APPENDIX I: KNIGHTS' FEES
BIGOD FEES

Name of Fee	Parish	Value	Feeholder 1.1247 2.1307	Earthwork	Civil Survey, 1654
1. Slievecoiltia	Whitechurch	½	Keating		The four townlands of Dunganstown, Ballykelly, Whitechurch and Polemaloe held by the Keatings.
2. Tullerstown	Kinnagh (part of)	¼	1. Tullos 2. Keating	moated site	
3. Ballybrazil	Ballybrazil	½	1. Russell 2. Sutton		Four townlands, Ballysop, Ballybrazil, Aclare, Ballykeerogemore held by the Suttons.
4. Chonnach	? Fethard (part of)	¼	1. Maunsel 2. Furlong	moated site	
5. Ballydermot	Old Ross (part of)	¼	le Lu (Lounde)		
6. Ballyinchy	?	¼	Belet		
7. Kilcavan	Kilcavan	1	1. Henry son of Philip 2. John son of Henry		All of the parish, except 3 townlands, held by the FitzHenrys
8. Ballicoan	?	1/10	de Camera		
9. Lisbegge	Kilgorman	1/10	1. de Hida 2. Wythe	Castletown motte	
10. Kilcorkey	Monamolin (part of)	1/5	Bloet		
11. Glascarrig	Donaghmore	1	de Canteton	Glascarrig motte	

Name of Fee	Parish	Value	Feeholder 1. 1247 2. 1307	Earthwork	Civil Survey, 1654
12. Ballyhealy	Kilturk	½	Cheevers		Six townlands in Kilturk held by the Cheevers family
13. Mulrankin	Mulrankin	½	Browne	Oldhall motte	The parish of Mulrankin except the townland of Bridewell, held by the Brownes
14. Tilladavin	Tomhaggard	½	1. le Chanu (Hore) 2. le Rede		
15. Kilcowan	Kilcowan	½	Keating	motte moated site	All of the parish, except for the townlands, of Brownstown and Yoletown held by the Keatings.
16. Ballyrankin	? Kilrush	¼	le Waleis	?Raheen moated site	
17. Ballytally	? Mayglass	½	le Petit		
18. Ballycally ? Galgystown	Hook	¹⁄₁₀	Galgel		
19. Kilcony	?Kilcomb	½	1. de Kernet 2. Levet		
20. Kilmuckridge and Offelimy	Kilmuckridge Kilincooly Kilhamanagh Meelnagh	2	de Borrard	Kilmuckridge motte	
21. Kayer	Clonmore Ballyhoge, Killurin, Whitechurchglynn, Ardcandrisk, Kilbrideglynn, Doonooney	3	de Denne		

22. Rossdroit	Rossdroit	1	de Denne (Held of the Roches of Duffry)		
23. Baldwinstown (? Ballyvaldon) and Ballygormot (? Doonooney)	Ballyvaldon Doonooney	½	Roche	Ballingowan (Tinnick) motte Doonooney motte	
VALENCE FEES					
24. Adamstown and Ballymagir	Adamstown Ballymagir	2	1. de Heddon 2. Devereux	? Scullaboge moated site	Most of the parish of Adamstown and all of Ballymagir held by the Devereuxes.
25. Carrickbyrne	Adamstown (part of)	½	Howell		
26. Ballyregan	Ballymore (part of)	¼	Kernet		
27. Rosegarland and Duncormick	Ballylannan and Clongeen Duncormick	3	de London	Newcastle motte Duncormick motte	
28. Ballygarvey and Trimmer Ballycarran	Kilscoran (part of) ? Ballybrennan	½	de Owemell		
29. Ambrosetown	Ambrosetown	1	Ambrois		
30. Ballyanne and Ballyconnick	Ballyanne Ballyconnick	1	Busher	moated site	Parish of Ballyconnick held by the Bushers
31. Ballyteige	Kilmore	½	Whitty		The townlands of Ballyteige, Crossfarnogue, Neamstown and Newtown in the parish of Kilmore held by the Whittys.
32. Kilcowanmore	Kilcowanmore	½	Keating		The townland of Ballybrittas in Kilcowanmore held by the Keatings

Name of Fee	Parish	Value	Feeholder 1.1247 2.1307	Earthwork	Civil Survey, 1654
33. Ballyfistlane ?Ballycushlane	Lady's Island	¼	1. Purcell 2. Maunsel		
34. Ballymacane	Tacumshin (part of)	½	1. de Akevill 2. Stafford		
35. Ballirodain	?	¼	1. Pincerna 2. de Botiller		
36. Ballyell	Kilscoran (part of)	¼	1. Not 2. Codd		Townland of Codsballyell held by Nich Codd
37. Ballybrennan	Ballybrennan	¼	Sinnott		Parish of Ballybrennan held by the Sinnotts
38. Killagh	?	¼	Stafford		
39. Ballywitch	St. Helens	¼	Codd		Parish of St Helens held by the Codds
40. Ballytory	Tacumshin (part of)	¼	French		Townland of Ballytory and Beting held by the Frenches
41. Carn	Carne	½	Codd		The townlands of Ballyfray, Clougheast, Crossland, Loghinsheare, Churchtown, in the parish of Carne, held by the Codds
42. Ui Mealla and the Duffrey	A number of parishes	9	de Prendergast Ui Mella passed to the Roches c. 1300	Pallis motte Motabeg motte/ Killegney motte	
43. Ballichery	? St. John's	½	de Prendergast		
44. Machrem	? Carnew	¼	de Samford		

45. Gorey	Kilmakilloge	⅛	1. Raymond son of Walter 2. de Neville		Kilpatrick and Tikellen parishes held by the Roches
46. Fernegenal	A number of parishes	5	Granted to de Prendergast but passed to the Roches about 1180. Sinnotts acquired part of it c.1240	Ballylucas motte; ? Castlesow ringwork	
47. Ballycanew	Ballycanew	¼	de Neville		
48. Ballydusker	Killinick	¼	1. de Norath 2. Sinnott		Townlands of Ballydusker and Ballyraine held by the Sinnotts
49. Killesk	Killesk	¼	1. de Ponte Chardun 2. FitzGerald		Townlands of Killesk, Knockagh and Drilstown held by the Barrons (FitzGerald)
50. Rathdouan	?	⅛	de Inttebergh		
51. Balyen ? Ballyhine	Kilbrideglynn	½	1. le Lu 2. Hay		Townland of Davidstown held by the Hay family
52. Liskinfere	Liskinfere	¼	Avenell		
53. Ballicarnall	Kilnahue	½	de Valle		
54. Ballykeerogebeg	Kilmokea (part of)	¼	1. de lá Bell 2. FitzHenry		Ballykeerogebeg held by Mailer FitzHarris
55. Moyamy	?	¼	de Canteton		
56. Ballyforken	?	1/20	Slymack		
57. Monyharly	?	¼	de Herdescot		
58. Torkill (Tarahill)	Kilcavan	1/20	de Katenore		
59. Kilrane	Kilrane	¼	1425 Keating		
60. Mackmine	Clonmore	1	FitzHenry		
61. Ballyregan	Kilbride	½	?	Ballymore Demense motte	

C.I.P.M., III p.222

APPENDIX II: BOROUGHS IN COUNTY WEXFORD

	Name	Reference	Source
1.	Bannow	1283 'burgesses of Bannow'. 1323-4', rent of burgages £8.0s.10d.'	MacNiocaill, *Buirgéisí*, i., p.300. Hore, iv, p.454
2.	Carrick	1307. 'rents of burgages at Carrick 111s 9d.'	Hore, V, p.102
3.	Clonmines	1248: 'assizes and pleas in the ville of Clonmines, 1276, 'the ville of Clonmines has a liberty by grant of William Marshal.' 1306: 'burgesses of the ville of Clonmines.'	Cal. doc. Ire., .i., no.2983 Cal. doc. Ire., II, no.1330. Cal. doc. Ire., V, no.538
4.	Courtown	1280: 'burgage rent of Curtun'.	Cal. doc. Ire., II, no. 1801
5.	Edermine	1324: 'burgesses of Edirdrym (Edermine).	Brooks, *Knights' Fees*, p.45
6.	Enniscorthy	no reference to charter burgesses etc. 1226: 'town of Enniscorthy.' Urban features: early stone castle; religious houses; market place. weekly market.	Hore, vi, pp342-50.
7.	Ferns	1298: '49½ burgages in Ferns.' 1282: 'rent of burgages at Ferns £2.0.0.'	P.R.I. rep. D.K., xxvi, no.26 Hore, vi, p.190
8.	Fethard	c.1200: 'town of Fethard.' 1282: 'rent of burgages at Fethard £6.0.0.'	Hore, iv, p.312 Hore, vi, p.189
9.	? Gorey	1296: 'from the community of the town of Gorey 13s.'	Hore, vi, p.609
10.	Town of the Island	1282: '110s4d. rent of the burgesses of the Island.' 1306: 'burgesses of the town of the Island hold 3 carucates in their burgages.'	Hore, iii, p.207. Cal. justic rolls Ire., ii, p.349
11.	Mayglass	1282: 'rents of burgages at Mayglass 10s.9½d.'	Hore, vi, p.190
12.	New Ross	charter c.1283-6.	MacNiocaill *Buirgéisí*, i, p.300

	Name	Reference	Source
13.	Old Ross	1281: 'The burgh of Old Ross', burgesses of Old Ross.'	Hore, i, p.12-14
		1306: 'burgage land at Old Ross	Cal. justic rolls Ire., p.349
14.	Taghmon	1305: 'burgesses of Taghmon held 5 carucates.' 'profits and perquisites of the Hundred £8.3s.7d.'	Hore, vi, p.418
15.	Wexford	1172: 'burgesses of Wexford.'	Cal. doc. Ire., i, no.39
		1246: 'burgh of Wexford' 1298: '128½ burgages waste in Wexford town.'	Hore, *Wexford*, v, p. 38 P.R.I. rep. D.K. xxvi, no.26.
16.	? Templeshanbo (Senebald)	1226: Grant of weekly market.	Hore, vi, p.342

Forth and Bargy – a place apart

The baronies of Forth and Bargy are situated in the extreme south-eastern part of the county.[1] The region is isolated because of its semi-peninsular position and its clearly defined natural boundaries — the sea on its eastern and southern shores, the mountain of Forth to the north and the Pill (or Corock river) which flows into Bannow Bay on its western frontier. This physical isolation is further intensified by the hostile nature of its coastline. Where it is not bounded by dangerous islets and rocks, treacherous sand-bars and shoals, it is beset by racing tidal currents and unpredictable winds.[2] There are few safe landing-places; even today its small man-made ports of Kilmore Quay, Carne and St Helen's are regularly subject to the wilder excesses of wind and wave. The region's two bigger ports at Wexford and Rosslare lie on the more protected east coast. This is, then, an inhospitable region, bleak and exposed to the prevailing winds from the south-west. Its largely featureless plain is mantled with thin boulder clays, gravels and sands deposited in the second last glaciation. Most of Bargy has stony loams that are moderately well to imperfectly drained, while Forth has well-drained or moderately well-drained loams with pockets of heavy marine clay and some areas of drained sands. Generally the two baronies derive their reputation and high standards of production from careful husbandry over many generations rather than from the intrinsic richness of their soil.[3]

There are today few trees. Indeed there is little evidence of even ancient afforestation and the likelihood is that the region originally had more scrub and furze than trees. The Civil Survey of 1654-56 showed that of 18,249 acres belonging to so-called 'Irish papists' surveyed in Bargy only 67 acres were 'wood'. There is a passing reference to the scarcity of trees in Forth in the anonymous 'Description of the Barony of Forth', written about 1680, referring to the use of furze for roofing houses 'better timber being there deficient'. Small wonder, then, that the area attracted few permanent settlers in prehistoric times. There is little evidence of habitation in the neolithic era as compared with other parts of county Wexford: a dolmen formerly at Carnsore and the remains of a portal tomb on the Great Saltee Island are the only tangible traces of neolithic man in the region. Then, in a later period, there was added to its natural disadvantages the stigma of being an idolatrous waste-land, shunned and feared even by the Celts who settled in other parts of Ireland. This stigma spread from the Druid-infested *Hieron Akron* (or Sacred Promontory) of Ptolemy's map, now Carnsore, to embrace the whole of the Fotharta (Forth) area, a region of supposed idol-worship, pagan practices and human sacrifice.[4] For all its inherent drawbacks and its bad reputation, the region became the cherished home of Celt, Norse, Norman and English, engendering in each successive wave of colonists a fierce loyalty. It was fought over, bartered, planted, plundered; yet it has exerted a strange influence on all who settled within its boundaries.

The two baronies cover an area of 50 square miles, containing 78,850 statute acres. The terrain is generally level, falling gently southwards from the flank of the low mountain of Forth (200 m.) to the coast. It is a largely feature-less, unspectacular landscape, whose inhabitants have tended to invest its few landmarks, such as Forth Mountain, the Saltees, the Rock of Scar and the Hill of Carrig, with undue magnitude and importance. Its shallow valleys run southwards also, carrying small rivers to the sea — the Corock to Bannow Bay, the Duncormick and Bridgetown rivers to the Little Sea, formerly Ballyteigue Lough.[5] The topographical features (the Irish Sea, St George's Channel, Forth Mountain and the Corock river) which isolate the two baronies mirror internally, on a smaller scale, the physical barriers which cut Wexford off from the rest of the country. These natural boundaries have made the south-eastern corner of Wexford into a distinctive physical entity, adding to its isolation and enabling successive waves of settlers to establish self-contained communities there. The *tuatha* of Fotharta and Uí Bairche were early territorial expressions of this distinctiveness. Fotharta derived its name from a people called the Fotharta who were descended from Eochaidh Fionn Fuathart, a brother of the celebrated Conn of the Hundred Battles, a king who lived in the second century A.D.[6] Bargy commemorates the Uí Bairche, a family which apparently lived in this area. The two modern baronies preserve the boundaries of these two ancient *tuatha*, an indication of the precision of their natural frontiers and also of the exclusiveness of the entire area. Though the barony as such is an obsolete division abolished in 1898, the distinctive personality of the two baronies is reflected in the unusual degree to which the term 'Forth and Bargy' has survived in modern spoken usage and consciousness.

Early Settlement

Evidence of the existence of Mesolithic (7,000-4,000 B.C.) inhabitants in south Wexford is scant but pieces of worked flint flakes (Larnian flints) have been found at Carnsore, tentatively dated to the period between 5,000 and 3,000 B.C.[7] These earliest peoples were semi-nomadic hunters, gatherers and fishers, supplementing their meat and fish diet with nuts and wild fruit. Some of these early nomads left traces of their stay in the form of a kitchen-midden on Clare Island in Bannow Bay, which contained quantities of animal bones and oyster shells.[8] The first farmers moved into Ireland about 2,500 B.C., clearing forests for crops and grazing. They have left scant evidence of their existence apart from their stone edifices, ranging from court cairns to portal dolmens and passage graves. South Wexford, however, is poor in such remains. The 1840 Ordnance Survey map shows a dolmen at Carnsore but this has since vanished, though its capstone remains among the boulders of the beach and there are remnants of a possible small dolmen on the Great Saltee.[9] A number of standing stones survive, for example those at Cotts (near Broadway), at Slad and at Balloughton. These date from the Early Bronze Age (2,000-1,200 B.C.) and may have been boundary markers or burial monuments.[10] Early man has left few other traces in Fotharta and Uí Bairche. Even bronze tools and arms are extremely rare: two axeheads were found at Johnstown, a palstave (type of axe) was found on Forth Mountain and socketed gouges were discovered at Clonmines.

New migrants came with the advent of the Iron Age (about 300 B.C.). These were the Celts, reputedly tall, fair-haired Goidelic (Gaelic)-speaking people who hailed from central Europe, bringing new technology, new art forms and a new language. It is related that some of those Celts landed in south-east Wexford, perhaps through what is now the estuary of the Slaney.[11] They must have penetrated into Fotharta, for very soon the region around Carnsore became notorious for its druidic rites and idol-worship. Its notoriety spread, probably through Phoenician sailors, as far as Alexandria in Egypt where in the second century A.D. the Greek cartographer Ptolemy marked on his map of Ireland the *Hieron Akron* of Carnsore.[12] Ogham stones were another form of monolith dating from pre-Christian times. Examples have been found on the Great Saltee Island, at Bannow and at Cotts (Broadway).[13] Some of these stones had inscriptions representing a family name and descent from some pagan god; early Christian missionaries often erased the pagan god's name, as happened with the stone found at Bannow, in order to banish his worship.

Christianity

This part of Wexford was probably Christianised before the arrival of St Patrick. Welsh missionaries were apparently working here before 432 and have left names and relics in The Hook, where Brecaun founded a tiny monastery, and at Begerin in Wexford harbour, where Ibar founded a church. The advent of Christianity to south Wexford in the fifth century heralded a decline in druidism but the early Church included in its observances and rubrics a recognition of the old pagan sites. Thus, wells associated with druidic rites became holy wells dedicated to Christian saints;[14] crude churches were built on or near ancient raths or dúns, as at Mayglass, Tomhaggard and Carnsore and the great stone structures marking pagan burial sites were often christianised by the incision of crosses or other Christian symbols on them. It is likely that the capstone of the Carnsore dolmen was so marked with the

T-cross which is still visible on its underside. It is called St Vauk's Stone after the saint who founded the small monastery at Carnsore in the seventh century, and who built a tiny church on the site of what may have been a pagan burial.[15] With the spread of Christianity came monasticism and the founding of small communities of hermits and monks in isolated places. There is some evidence of such monastic settlements in Fotharta and Uí Bairche at Lady's Island, at Carnsore, on the Great Saltee and at Cullenstown.[16]

The Norse

In the last years of the eighth century, marauding Norse began to appear off the coast. In the ninth century, they plundered Begerin in Wexford harbour where St Ibar had his church; they burned Taghmon, a famed monastic centre founded by St Fintan. They may well have landed and later settled at other points on the south Wexford coast for they have left Norse names on land-marks from Bannow Bay to the Slaney estuary — Selskar (Seal's Rock) in Bannow Bay, the Saltees. (Salt Islands), Scar (Rock in Bargy and estuary at Bannow), Mablehaven (The Little Sea), Tuskar, Carnsore and Wexford (Weissfiord), the harbour of the mudflats.

As their raiding parties eventually settled, the Norse probably controlled the entire southern part of the county embracing Fotharta and Uí Bairche, pene-trating inland to Scar, where the rocky outcrop known today as the Rock of Scar would have provided them with a vantage point unsurpassed in the area. Their strong settlements at Waterford and Wexford would have dominated the southern coast; they had a base, too, in Bannow Bay where they mined lead and silver at Barrystown. However, it was in Fotharta that their sway extended most and lasted longest. Here, in what eventually became known as the cantred of the Ostmen, they had their farms, supplying the trading port of Norse Wexford, and here they remained, another stranger people, until the twelfth century.[17] So, to the Celtic blood of the tribes already settled in Fotharta and Uí Bairche was now added a new strain. Out of this exotic racial cocktail came families with names such as Ó Lorcain (Larkin), Uí Beaccan (Boggan), Ó Dubhthuigin (Duggan and Doogan), Uí Bairche itself (Barrigry) and the ubiquitous Dubhghaill (Doyle), all names which are still found in the region. These families remained in isolated independence in south Wexford, owing allegiance sporadically to the rulers of Uí Cheinnsealaigh, though these seldom had any effective authority in south Wexford.[18]

The almost unchallenged presence of these Norsemen in Fotharta for about 300 years can surely be taken as another indication of the area's exclusivity. Had Fotharta been of any value to the kings of Uí Cheinnsealaigh, they would certainly have banished the Norsemen in the early stages of their settlement. Yet it seems the Mac Murchadh allowed the foreigners of Fotharta and Uí Bairche to stay, a concession they regretted in the early years of the eleventh century when the Norse-Irish under Ó Lorcain burst out of Fotharta and Uí Bairche and assumed command of the entire kingdom of Uí Ceinnsealaigh. It was not until Dermot MacMurrough appeared on the scene that the Norse-

Irish were driven back into their enclave, there to remain, again in isolation, until the Norman incursion in 1169. In addition to the placenames and family names which they bequeathed to the area, the Norse also left another persistent legacy — the great seafaring tradition of south Wexford that finds expression in a thriving fishing industry in Kilmore Quay, Carne, Rosslare and Wexford itself and also in the many generations of sailors who have found livelihoods and fame in the navies of numerous nations.

The Normans

The history of Fotharta and Uí Bairche was to change irrevocably after the Norman landings at Bannow Bay in May, 1169. Uí Bairche was to see the first skirmish after the landing when local forces, probably Norse-Irish, unsuccessfully challenged the foreigners at the ford of Duncormick.[19] The newcomers marched across Uí Bairche and Fotharta to take the Norse port of Wexford and consolidate a bridgehead for further incursions. Maurice FitzGerald landed at Wexford with 140 men later in 1169.[20]

With the subjugation of south Wexford, the colonisation of Fotharta and Uí Bairche began. While recruiting the Cambro-Normans in Wales, Dermot MacMurrough had promised grants of lands to their leaders. Maurice FitzGerald and his half-brother Robert FitzStephen were promised in fee the town of Wexford and the two adjoining cantreds.[21]FitzStephen did get Wexford but the other two cantreds 'that lie betwixt the towns of Wexford and Waterford, along by the sea', i.e. Uí Bairche and Shelburne, were given to Strongbow's uncle, Hervey de Monte Marisco, who had been sent over to Ireland to watch his nephew's interests.[22] When Hervey became a monk at the Abbey of the Holy Trinity in Canterbury in 1179, he bestowed all his lands in south Wexford to the Abbey. These were later transferred to the Abbey at Tintern. The Norse in Fotharta were taken under special protection as 'the King's Ostmen'. The first area granted by Dermot to the Cambro-Normans was Fotharta and Uí Bairche. Dermot was 'king of the foreigners' (Norse) by virtue of his natural son Donal's victory over them in 1161 and he had exercised a right not only to rule them but also to grant their lands. Thus Uí Bairche was given to Hervey and this grant may well have represented Dermot's revenge on the Larkins and also a measure of the expendable, unattractive nature of the area itself. There are extant several references that make it plain that the Cambro-Normans themselves were not greatly impressed by the lands in Fotharta and Uí Bairche which they had been granted. The new colonists were to turn this previously underutilised area into a productive, self-sufficient enclave which won the commendations of many commentators and cemented the distinctiveness of the two baronies. With Strongbow's appointment in 1173 as King Henry's Viceroy in Ireland, the enfeoffment of lands already conquered and occupied by the Cambro-Normans gathered momentum. The old Ostman territory in Fotharta, stretching south from Wexford town to Rosslare, was enfeoffed to knights and planted with commoners. Hervey de Monte Marisco was confirmed in his grant of Uí Bairche and a similar plantation took place there. Thus, to the Norse-Irish elements in the baronies, there was now added a further racial mix of Welsh, Flemish and English, with Norman barons planted in the manors and villages. In the process of colonisation the new settlers assimilated much of the local organisation and land-divisions of the indigenous inhabitants. It was Norman practice when colonising a territory to allow the indigenous working peasantry to remain and to mobilise them into the new manorial system as hewers of wood and drawers of water. Despite the view of Orpen that the original Norse-Irish were driven from south Wexford by the colonists, it is likely that most of the local population remained in the area.[23] This may be deduced from the survival of Norse-Irish family names in Forth and Bargy; it may also be deduced from the local nomenclature, which retains Gaelic names for parishes, townlands, fields and topographical features. Of the 40 ancient parishes in Forth and Bargy, 36 retain Irish names. In Bargy, nearly 49 per cent and in Forth, nearly 40 per cent of all townlands still carry Irish names.[24]

Land division proper in Forth and Bargy began with the setting-up of the manorial estates. The sub-infeudation of the two baronies was very intensive: the many sub-tenants were drawn initially from the ranks of both the Cambro-Normans and their Welsh and Flemish mercenaries and subsequently from English migrants. The Norman manors, expecially in south Wexford, were not vast demesnes and probably did not exceed 600 or 700 acres at most.[25] This was unusually diminutive. The very high incidence of Norman, Welsh, Flemish and English surnames (then and now) is proof of the intensive colonisation and sub-infeudation of these baronies from the highest level of lords, barons and knights down to the humble level of artisan, labourer and betagh.

Detailed evidence of the manner in which the occupied territories were parcelled out in knights' fees is available in late medieval inquisitions. The documents derive from the circumstances of the partition of Leinster in 1247 among the daughters of William Marshall, Earl of Pembroke, whose sons had all successively died without issue.[26]

The feodaries contain the names of the military tenants and here we find the same names which survived in a proprietorial classification in the Civil Survey returns 400 years later, names (in the case of Forth and Bargy) such as Keating, Stafford, Synnott, Codd, Prendergast, Neville, Devereux, le Poer (Power), Lambert, Hay, Wadding, Roche (de Rupe), Whitty, Rochford, Barry and others. Indeed the most remarkable feature of the continuum in Forth and Bargy was this survival of the old gentry, the Catholic land-owners whose ancestors had been the original Cambro-Norman colonisers of the twelfth century.

A comparison of these lists of old proprietors with the names of dispossessed land-owners of 1664, following the Cromwellian confiscation and settlement, shows the same family names surviving in the same areas; Stafford in Ballymacane, Devereux in Ballymagir, Codd in Clougheast, Whitty in Ballyteigue, Keating in Kilcowan, Synnott in Ballybrennan, Hay in Tacumshane, Lambert in Ballyhire and so on.[27]

Many commentators have noted this continuity of land tenure: as early as 1680, one of them observes:

> 'The ancient Gentry and Inhabitants of that Barony deryve their originall Extraction lineally from England, theyre predecessors haveing beene officers in the Army under the conduct of Fitz-Stephens, who first invaded Ireland. Suddenlie after the conquest thereof, distinct allotments of land according to theyre respective qualityes and merits were assigned to them, which untill the Cromwellian usurpacion and Government, they did, during the 500 years, almost compleat, without any diminution or addition, peacablie and contentedlie possess; never attained nor convicted of any crime meriting forfeiture ... '[28]

This 1680 writer further noted that these families could not be forced or induced to quit or alienate their possessions and took care always to confer their estates on their male progeny or next male heir. He also pointed out how they had expanded into the territory north of Wexford harbour and pushed up towards Enniscorthy.

Consolidation of the colony

The consolidation of the south Wexford bridge-head and the expansion of the Norman colony in Leinster in the twelfth and thirteenth centuries afforded the settlers in Forth and Bargy a long period of comparative peace and stability. After the turbulence of the initial attacks and counter-attacks, we find only occasional references to unsettled conditions in the region. The local chieftains, Ó Lorcain and Ó Dubhthuigin, are found fighting on Strongbow's side in 1175[29] and there is a reference to the 'fierceness of the barbarous people living in the neighbourhood' in a report on the site of Dunbrody in nearby Shelburne made in 1182.[30] Apparently the settlers were not being allowed to take unhindered possession. In this period of consolidation the colony in Forth and Bargy began to take shape. The first step in the occupation of the area had been the construction of central motte-and-bailey strong-points. Such mottes and baileys stood, for example, at Duncormick, Kilcowan and Wexford itself.

It was not until they had consolidated their military occupation and acquired greater security that the Cambro-Normans in south Wexford began to build their stone castles. The first of these were erected in the thirteenth century and from then until the sixteenth century most of Wexford's 365 stone castles were built.[31] A comparatively greater number than in any other part of Wexford were built in Forth and Bargy and their gaunt grey ruins still shadow many farmyards, overlooking the more modern dwelling-places of the descendants of the men who first built these grim strongholds.[32]

Contemporaneously with the building of their first stone castles, the colonists also erected churches and abbeys. The first Norman churches were usually small, attached to the manors; their ruins can be seen in many places in Forth and Bargy. Of abbeys, the two baronies saw none, apart from the reconstructed Selskar in Wexford town which housed Augustinians.[33] The granting of tithes to religious orders went hand in hand with the secular organisation of the manors and, with the building of manorial chapels, parishes began to take shape. Very often these corresponded with the holdings of tenants and took their names from the original tenancy-holders. Ambrosetown (Bargy), for example, got its name from the Ameroys family.

Besides the large number of tower-houses in Forth and Bargy, the two baronies also had many chapels. To the scattered crude churches of the native clergy and hermits, the Cambro-Normans added chapels in almost every manorial division, sometimes building on old holy sites, as at Mayglass, Tomhaggard, Tagoat, Churchtown and Lady's Island. Many of these were dedicated to saints venerated especially by the colonists, superceding the Celtic saints after whom the sites were originally named. Thus Tomhaggard was dedicated to Anne and James whereas it had originally been dedicated to St Mosacer who died about 650; Tacumshane was rededicated to St Catherine replacing St Fintan, the old Irish patron of the place.

Raids on colony

Although there appears to have been no concerted war-effort by the Irish against the Forth and Bargy colony in the thirteenth century, the settlers had to maintain a strong guard at all times. There was always the threat of attack — postponed temporarily through the payment of the so-called *Black Rent* to the MacMurrough Kavanaghs. So we find Adam de Rufe, in June 1305, telling the Court of Pleas that, when the Liberty of Wexford was in the King's hands, he took £20 of the money of Joan de Valence and spent it on guards to protect Wexford 'from the malice of the Irish of the mountains of Leinster'.[34] It was Joan's brother Aymer who had completed the walling of Wexford town towards the end of the thirteenth century. The colony's relatively peaceful period was soon to end. The Irish revival of the fourteenth century brought war to the heart of the region. In 1331, the Irish of Leinster, led by Donal MacMurrough Kavanagh, recently elected king of the province, 'assembled themselves and went to the county of Wexford and destroyed all that country to Corcornan. Richard FitzHenry, and other Englishmen subjects, met them and killed 400 of them, and many of them fleeing home to their country were drowned in the river called Slane'. FitzHenry was enfeoffed of Kilcavan (Bargy) at the time. Five years later, the Irish had their revenge on the colonists and on the FitzHenrys in particular. In 1336, a battle took place in which the colonists were defeated with the loss of their leader, Sir Mathew FitzHenry, Baron of Kilcavan, and 200 of his men.[35] This encounter marked the beginning of the attacks and encroachments which continued for nearly 300 years, until the Pale of Wexford consisted of little more than Forth and Bargy.

The harassment of the colonists in Wexford by the Kavanaghs had gone on since the late fourteenth century. Initially Dermot Mac Art Kavanagh, who destroyed and burnt Carlow in 1377 set out 'to extend the territory, and dominion of his ancient race, by recovering for them the greater part of the county of Carlow and three parts of the county of Wexford'.[36] The fourth part of the county of Wexford, obviously Forth and Bargy, remained unrecovered. The colonists could maintain contact with Dublin only by hazardous and roundabout ways through hostile country and the main channels of communication were by sea to the capital and England. The fifteenth century proved to be calamitous for the people of Forth and Bargy. Art MacMurrough, taking advantage of the absence of many colonists on feudal service in England, launched a new campaign against the south Wexford colony in 1406 and two years later broke through the outer defences and attacked Forth and Bargy. The *Book of Howth* records that MacMurrough 'burned and destroyed a great part [of Forth and Bargy] and stayed for the night at Ballitege, and on the morrow before his departure would have forced Ballitege'.[37] MacMurrough apparently was unable to take the castle at Ballyteigue at that time but undoubtedly wreaked havoc throughout the remainder of the baronies.

The government in Dublin immediately took steps to protect its English colony in south Wexford by extending Aymer de Valence's defensive works to include the baronies of Forth and Bargy. In 1408 John Neville of Rosegarland was appointed bailiff of the waters between Ross and Wexford; these included the strategic pill flowing from near Taghmon into Bannow Bay, and also the pill of Polehore flowing north into the Slaney. It was not until 1441 that the government set about seriously fortifying this vital six-mile river line. In 1452 it was enacted that towers be built on the river of Bannow at Scar, Barrystown, Rosegarland, Slevoy, Horetown, Harperstown, Taghmon, Sigginshaggard, Traceystown, Moulmontrey and Brownscastle. So the gap southwards from Taghmon was effectively closed to raiders and when Parliament in 1453 further enacted that 'none shall break the fortifications or strengthenings of Tamon in the county of Wexford, nor shall make no ways on the said water from the woods of Bannow to the pill adjoining to the river Slaney', the seal was set on the total isolation of Forth and Bargy for centuries to come. The records of the remainder of the fifteenth and all of the sixteenth centuries reveal a continuation of the war by the Irish on the Wexford colonists, and retaliatory raids by the colonists against the Irish. At the opening of the sixteenth century, the Wexford Pale consisted of little more than the baronies of Forth and Bargy. The revolt of the Leinster Geraldines had serious repercussions in Bargy. The Presentments of the Juries which reported to the Commission sent down from Dublin in 1537 reveal Bargy in a turbulent state, with massive attacks by Geraldine forces on Ballymagir, Mulrankin and Bannow. The attack on Ballymagir, seat of Sir Nicholas Devereux, leading knight of the Wexford Pale, took place on August 3, 1534 and involved 1,000 men under Caher Mor M'Piers (Birmingham), Gerald Boy Prendergast, The MacMurrough and Edmund Duff, chief of the Clan Ceinnsealaigh. They burned Ballymagir, killed and wounded several people and took spoil valued at £800.

The raids on Mulrankin were carried out by the Butlers in 1534 and 1535 and the town of Bannow was raided by Butler gallowglasses and kerne on their way back from Mulrankin in 1535. As late as the year 1600, Sir George Carew was informing the Privy Council that the rebels in Leinster 'have been making havoc of the good subjects, as lately in the English baronies of Wexford', and later in the same year Donal Spáinneach and Feagh Mac Hugh's sons were reported to be rooting out all who refused their subjugation, especially in the county of Wexford ... 'the most ancient English county in Ireland'.[38] In the meantime, other events had overtaken the colonists in Ireland. Henry VIII had broken with Rome and his new religious policy and initiation of a fresh effort at conquering Ireland had some unusual results. The fact that both the 'Irish enemies' and the 'English rebels' in Ireland professed the Catholic faith gave them a common cause. Thus, when Elizabeth I sought to impose Protestantism generally, she was resisted forcefully and the old religion soon became a unifying influence leading to a common resistance to English rule. It would seem that, once again, Forth and Bargy were the exceptions to this general rule. The dissolution of the monasteries did not impinge on them to any great extent since there were no great monasteries in the region. English law continued to prevail in the baronies and the Irish continued to look upon the colony as English. Thus, in Elizabeth's reign, the MacMurrough Kavanaghs, this time led by Brian McCahir Kavanagh, once again swept down on the Wexford Pale (1572). Robert Browne of Mulrankin was killed in a raid. When the Wexford colonists mobilised to resist Brian McCahir, they were defeated in a battle near Dunbrody.

Despite the continued raids and attacks on the enclave, the south Wexford colonists maintained their English Pale. Life in the baronies of Forth and Bargy at the time must have been difficult. Houses and crops were burned by the Irish in their assaults, prisoners and hostages were taken, cattle and horses were driven off. Only the doggedness of the colonists and their fierce determination to hold on to their castles and lands saw them through. Even the Reformation failed to shake the foundations of the colony, although a member of one of its great land-owning families, Alexander Devereux of Ballymagir, the last Catholic Abbot of Dunbrody, was consecrated Protestant Bishop of Ferns in 1539. Church properties in the two baronies which had been confiscated were leased back to local land-owners who largely remained true to the old faith.

The years between the Irish victory at the battle of the Yellow Ford (1598) and the summer of 1600, when Mountjoy over-ran the territory of the MacMurrough Kavanaghs, saw the Wexford Pale at the mercy of the Irish. It was at this difficult time that great numbers of the colonists went back to Pembroke. Nobody there could understand their English, so fossillised had it become.

When the Earl of Essex, Sir Robert Devereux, was returning from the ill-fated Munster expedition, with an army 'weary, sick and incredibly diminished in numbers', he decided to visit his kinsman, Sir James Devereux, at Ballymagir. He crossed from Passage to Ballyhack, sent the main body of his depleted army to Enniscorthy and he himself marched with his bodyguard via Tintern, Duncormick and Killag to Ballymagir. His Englishmen were safe in Bargy. There is a tradition that Sir James had to sell three townlands to pay for the three-day victualling of the troops and the great hall which he built for the occasion still stands, roofless, at Ballymagir.

The last big attack on south Wexford occurred in April, 1600, when a large force of Irish under Dónal Spáinneach, Feagh MacHugh's son, Edmond McBrian Kavanagh, Thomas Roche and the Butlers of Mountgarrett, raided Bargy, burning Taghmon and everything in their path to Bannow. Even though this was the last large-scale attack on the colony, the inhabitants continued to be harassed until the final defeat of the Irish at Kinsale.

The changed conditions in Ireland under the first two Stuarts tended to diminish the isolated character of the Wexford Pale. While its inhabitants were still loyal to the English crown and entirely English in sympathies, they had a strong bond in their common religion which tied them to their Gaelic neighbours. The 'old English', whether of the Great Pale or the Wexford Pale, paid the same penalties for conscience's sake. Their religion nominally barred them from holding government office, from the protection of the law, from university degrees, from keeping a school and imposed on them the obligation of paying a recusancy fine. Sir John Davies, Attorney-General of Ireland, reported in 1616 that 'though the county of Wexford, being ancient and inhabited by people of English race, have our laws and government so long amongst them, that our business there was usual, according to the manner of assizes in England'.[39] Yet the Wexford jury had to be threatened before they could be induced to return a verdict against recusants, so strong was the bond of religion and so loyal to each other were the Wexfordians.

Loyalty to the old religion was accompanied by a marked tolerance towards followers of the Protestant faith. A report on the Barony of Forth, written about 1680, remarks on the 'neighbourlie human good offices being betwixt them [Protestant ministers] and the native inhabitants; discrepancy in principles of faith or points of religious worship no way exciting discord, animosity, aversion or opprobrious contumelie in word or act, one or the other'. This was taken as proof of 'an evident demonstration of the innate pro-penscion of the inhabitants to humanity and affection of tranquillity'.[40] South-east Wexford, comprising the baronies of Forth and Bargy, was left relatively untouched by the confiscations of the early seventeenth century. The 'old English' of the two baronies were retained in their ancestral holdings by James I, unlike the Gaelic small-holders in north Wexford who suffered grievously and to all intents and purposes disappeared after the subsequent Cromwellian confiscation.[41]

Dissolution of the colony

The Great Rebellion of 1641, however, brought war once more to south Wexford. The town of Wexford was a major seaport for the Confederates. The 'old English' and the Irish joined in defence of their common religion. Every family in Forth and Bargy was represented on the Confederate side and later paid the penalty through confiscation and transplantation. The Confederacy failed. Cromwell, the victor in England, arrived in Ireland in 1649. He entered county Wexford on 29 September, accepted the surrender of Enniscorthy castle and took Wexford by storm on 11 October. There followed the massacre of citizens in the Bull Ring, the plunder of churches, mansions and castles, the destruction of statues and tombstones throughout south Wexford. Detachments of Cromwellian troops were stationed in Wexford, and later in Drinagh, Killinick, Taghmon and Kilcavan. Fr Nicholas Meyler of Tomhaggard was murdered while celebrating midnight Mass at Christmas in 1653 in a 'knock' of furze at Linziestown. The castles of the colonists, which had held out against so many onslaughts by the Irish, were reduced to ruins. In the subsequent Cromwellian plantation, practically every land-owner in Wexford lost his estate — 621 in all. In the Barony of Forth, where there had been 125 Catholic land-owners, nearly all the 'old English' were banished and their lands confiscated. In the restoration and Declaration of 1660, only a few got their holdings back. These included Col William Browne of Mulrankin. As Browne's descendant, the historian Kathleen Browne, records, 'some of the descendants of the old proprietors settled down in succeeding years as tenants under the new Cromwellian owners, others became mixed-up with the peasantry, others went to foreign lands. All the smaller gentry, owners of from 200 to 500 acres, vanished'.[42] Paradoxically the later Cromwellian plantations ensured that Wexford, and especially Forth and Bargy, would become a region of moderately-sized estates with many resident landlords, leading to rural stability and prosperity.[43]

The names of these Cromwellian planters included Grogan, Harvey, Boxwell, Nunn, Edwardes, Richards, Palliser, Stannard, Jacob, Barrington, Waddy, Lett, Hatton, Hughes, Hobbs, Ram, Walker, Jones, Wilson, Le Hunte, Cliffe, Boyce, Swan, Tench, King, Jeffares and Sheppard. Grogan, Harvey, Boxwell and Lett were names later associated with the insurrection of 1798; their liberal and humanitarian attitudes were unusual among the Puritan landlords who were given the estates of the old Catholic gentry. Whatever else might have been said about the new colonists, their blunt honesty, industry and progressive farming ideas soon won them a grudging acceptance. Yet the old families survived, if not as owners of estates, then more likely as tenants and even as labourers of the newly-planted Cromwellian landlords. 'None of the Cominalty or plebian natives of that Barony [Forth] was transplanted or banished . . . only such as were signally known and accused to have persevered in their loyalty in bearing arms for his Majesty of England. . . . Some gentry of that barony preferred exile before transplantation into Connaught . . .'[44] So by living as labourers or small-holding tenants, the remnants of the old aristocracy held on in their ancestral neighbourhoods and by their perseverance and industry built up their farms and fortunes again over the years.

It is from the period 1649 to 1653 that one can date the dissolution of the 'English Pale' of Forth and Bargy as an exclusive cultural entity. What the Irish had failed to do over 500 years, Cromwell, the English republican, achieved in less than five. His so-called Settlement smashed the hegemony of the old Anglo-Norman land-owning families, introduced religious strife into an area which had been monolithically Christian for 1,000 years and posed a threat to the unique culture of the Forth and Bargy region. The badge of that culture was the strange dialect spoken by the inhabitants of the two baronies, a dialect that evolved with the isolation of the area. The first mention of it is found in Stanyhurst's *Description of Ireland* (1577) when he wrote: 'They have so acquainted themselves with the Irish as that they have made a minglemangle or gallimafrie of both languages and commonlie the inhabitants of the meaner sort speak neither good English nor good Irish'.[45] As Stanyhurst himself probably had little, if any, Irish, it is doubtful if he knew the content of Irish in the dialect. In fact, it is small enough. Sir Henry Wallop, writing in 1581, was probably nearer the truth when he wrote that the people of Forth and Bargy 'generally speak ould English'.[46]

A tenable explanation is that the dialect branched off from the main-stream of English speech at the time of Chaucer, who was actually writing when the construction of the Taghmon Line was isolating the two baronies completely. It has since been proposed that the dialect is a form of conservative English which by the reign of Elizabeth I differed widely from the English spoken at the court.[47] There are elements of Norman French and Flemish in the dialect, reflecting the presence of those nationalities among the early colonists and from the sixteenth century, when the English language was on the decline in Ireland generally, Irish began to influence the dialect also.[48]

We are not so much concerned here with the essence of the dialect as with its symbolism as the vernacular of an isolated colony and as the badge of a unique and distinctive culture that survived precariously almost down to our own day. The old dialect (called Yola) helped to preserve traditions, customs, a way of life for many centuries and to make Forth and Bargy a truly alien enclave in Ireland. The stay-at-home disposition of the people of the region and the fact that they rarely married outside their own districts helped to preserve the dialect. Thus the introduction of new colonists with a new form of English by Cromwellian planters caused the first cracks in the cultural mould. The dispersal of the old gentry was another; as a cultural elite they carried away with them much of the powerful tradition of the two baronies which was never replaced. Yet the dialect survived the Cromwellian transfusion and was spoken widely in the baronies until well into the eighteenth century. It continued to be spoken in Forth until at least 1850; there are still many words and phrases of the dialect in common use in the two baronies today, for example, 'chi' (a small quantity), 'to kurk' (to sit on the hams), 'to taape' (to tilt), 'a scolyoon' (an apron).

The decline of Yola was inevitable. In the seventeenth century, the medieval way of life was passing everywhere. The new Grand Jury roads were opening up even such isolated areas as Forth and Bargy.[49] Wexford itself was declared an open town in 1759 and its gates dismantled. The people of Forth and Bargy began to feel the winds of change whipping around their snug houses. As the isolation of their region relaxed, the use of the dialect waned. Yet the area still clung to many of its archaic customs and traditions and continued to pride itself on other attributes consolidated by time and usage — the industry and sobriety of its inhabitants, the good husbandry of its farmers, the neatness of its homes, the general appearance of progress, prosperity and rural stability. Numerous observers have commented on these attributes. 'The Barony of

Forth, on all emergencies of public concern in the said county, precedeth and hath pre-eminence', said the anonymous commentator of 1680.[50] Arthur Young, in 1776 and 1779, saw many comparisons between the baronies of Forth and Bargy and England, especially in their orderliness and way of life. The young Chevalier de la Tocnaye, touring Ireland a few years before the 1798 Insurrection, noted: 'The inhabitants of the barony of Forth...have never mixed with the Irish and still speak a singular language which is more akin to Flemish than the modern English. They are like the Flemish also in manner and marry among themselves. Their houses are cleaner and more comfortable than those of the other inhabitants and they are also so much more clean in person that they appear quite as a different race...'[51]

A correspondent of *The Irish Farmers' Journal* in 1814 wrote: 'The inhabitants of these baronies are enabled by the industrious and skilful management of their farms, to avail themselves of the comforts and decencies of life, in a degree seldom to be remarked in any country, among the lower orders. Their habitations...are neat, cleanly and commodious....A regular system of interior cleanliness and comfort is observed....In each house is a manufactory of almost every article necessary for home consumption, even to the making of their sacks and ropes....'[52]

Amyas Griffith, who visited the two baronies in 1764, was another who was impressed by the industry and appearance of the inhabitants:

'The plebian sort live better than the generality of any of their kind I fancy in the Kingdom ... they dwell with those who will reward their labours and use them as fellow creatures. These poorer sort of people have all snug commodious cabbins, with good doors, but no locks; you may travel all over this barony [Forth] and not see one, either on door, chest or cupboard. They ... depend on the honour and honesty of each other and scorn to surmise or suspect that their neighbours would be guilty of such unmanly and ungenerous actions as to steal. ... They are the most indefatigable and hardest working people you have ever heard of; they commonly rise at 4 in the morning, and pursue their labours until 12, they then eat a hearty meal and go to sleep till 2'

(This south Wexford custom of mid-day rest, called 'enteet' or 'taking a sahsty', persisted well into the twentieth century). Griffith continues:

'They commonly dispose of their offspring very young, the men marry at 18 or 20, to girls of 14, 16, etc'. He says that the practice of co-habitation for a month before marriage was common in the baronies and mentions some unusual wedding customs which in any other community would be regarded as licentious.[53]

Further eulogies of Wexford, and Forth and Bargy specifically, came from Mr and Mrs S. C. Hall, writing in 1842. They referred to

'the skilfully farmed fields, the comfortable cottages, the barns attached to every farmyard, the well-trimmed hedgerows, the neat gardens stocked with other vegetables than potatoes, and the acre of beans — the peasantry are better fed than we have seen them in any other part of Ireland, and have an air of sturdy independence. ... They are a proud

Plate xvi: Harristown house, Ballymitty, home of the Ennis family. It was built c.1735. It later became the home of the Meyler family

Plate xvii: the Etchingham family home at Bearlough, Rosslare, c.1930

people — proud of their ancient names, and their advanced civilisation'.[54]

The Penal Laws were applied as harshly to Forth and Bargy as elsewhere in Ireland but because of the unusual relationship between Protestant landlord and Catholic tenant in south Wexford the rigours of the laws appear to have been tempered considerably. Thus we find Luke Wadding with sufficient Protestant friends, both lay and clerical, in 1678 to guarantee his acquittal at his Wexford trial; a Quaker landlord, Jacob Poole, providing a site for a Catholic chapel in Kilmachree in 1796; liberal Protestant landlords like the Harveys of Bargy Castle and the Grogans of Johnstown Castle permitting Catholic chapels on their estates. This was the period when the old Catholic families of Forth and Bargy gave many of their younger sons and daughters to religion, being able to afford to educate them abroad, as they recovered politically and economically after the Cromwellian confiscations.

The baronies remained largely undisturbed during the insurrection of 1798. Several reasons have been adduced for this, apart from the vaunted peace-loving attributes of the inhabitants. Though the region had some influential leaders of the United Irishmen (Cornelius Grogan, Bagenal Harvey and John Colclough), the organisation itself was skeletal in the baronies. There was not the same religious antagonism between Protestant and Catholic as was prevalent in north Wexford and remarkably good relations existed between landlord and tenant, with several of the liberally-minded Protestant gentry openly espousing the nationalist cause. These were looked upon as leaders and their tenants turned out in force for the battles of Ross and Horetown, while the folk at home provided camps, hospitals and provisions for the fighting-men. Only two chapels in the area were burned, both by the retreating Wexford garrison on its way to Duncannon. After the rising, Forth and Bargy soon returned to its normal peaceful ways.

Similarly, during the famine years in the mid-nineteenth century, Forth and Bargy apparently saw little distress. Though the potato crop failed, as elsewhere in Ireland, the people of the two baronies were not totally dependent on it for sustenance. The area was one of the great grain-growing regions of the country, with massive exports of barley and oats, while meat, beans, turnips and other root crops were plentiful. Forth and Bargy, probably because of the rich supply of food available there, was one of the few areas in the entire country whose population increased in the decade between 1841 and 1851. That decade saw the population of the baronies increase from 37,756 to 38,036. Kathleen Browne gives a vivid picture of the baronies at this time. 'The people lived in comparative comfort, especially in the Baronies of Forth and Bargy. ... There were few shops, and almost every article of household requirement was made at home, soap, candles, starch, ink, etc. Flax was grown, even on farms of five acres, and went through the whole process of manufacture on the spot, though the linen was sometimes sent to a central bleach-green. There were weavers in every parish and the wool for thread, blankets and the strong warm frieze worn by men was all prepared at home. A black sheep was kept in every flock, as the natural black wool never became 'rusty'. Peasant women wore a strong serviceable linen called 'lincey', and a mixture of linen and wool called 'lincey-wolsey'. There was no enamelled and very little tinware and coopers had a busy time making churns, 'keelers' and firkins for the dairy. The women took much pride in keeping them as white as constant handscrubbing with freestone or fine gravel could make them, while the hoops shone like silver. Cheese was made in large quantities. The farm kitchen, with its snow-white dresser, pewter plates and dishes, brass candle-sticks,and wooden trenchers and noggins, was a delight to all beholders. Out-doors there was a similar exhibition of thrift, order and comfort. The love of flowers seems, in particular, characteristic of South Wexford'.[55]

Ms Browne also refers to the busy windmills whirling their sails. There were many windmills in the baronies (one of the reasons why the region was called 'Little Flanders'). As there were few strong rivers in the region, watermills were scarce.[56] The flat, unsheltered landscape and fairly constant winds, however, together with the Flemish traditions in the area, provided the right conditions for wind-mills.[57] In the 1850s, according to Richard Griffith, Forth and Bargy had 24 windmills, more than any other similar area in Ireland. As recently as 1903, ten of these windmills were still operating, when only three were operating in the rest of the country.

Apart from providing corn for their own use and as animal feed-stuffs the farmers of Forth and Bargy became major producers of grain for the distilleries of Dublin and the markets of Britain. From this alone came much of the prosperity that marked the area so distinctively.

There were several social characteristics that distinguished the baronies too, apart from their industriousness, neatness and order. One was the remarkable recovery of the old Catholic landowning families in the nineteenth century, not only to the complete ownership of their ancestral lands but also their accession to positions of power and influence in the church, politics and nationalist organisations. Their recovery began with the introduction of the Poor Law system in 1838 and the decline of the powers of the Grand Jury after the Famine. From then on, tenant-farmers, shopkeepers and publicans, who tended to be drawn from the ranks of the Catholics, for the first time got their hands on the reins of elective power. As early as 1861, the representatives of the tenant-farmers on Wexford District Poor Law Union Board of Guardians, men such as James Browne, Thomas Murphy and John Walshe, were acting as chairmen of the Board, admittedly in the absence of the landlord chairman. By 1886, Wexford Union Board of Guardians had three tenant-farmers as chair-man, vice-chairman and deputy vice-chairman. This was the period of Land League and National League activities and the names of the old Catholic families of Forth and Bargy crop up with increasing regularity as members of League branches, Boards of Guardians and as M.P.s — John Barry and Peter ffrench (M.P.s), Edmund Hore, William Pettit, Michael Sinnott, John Culleton, Michael Browne, James Devereux, Arthur Keating, Mathew Parle, William Stafford, John Codd, Andrew Cullen, Walter Harpur, Patrick Lambert, Nicholas Roche and Gregory Rossiter (Guardians). In April, 1887, another sort of milestone was passed. Nicholas O'Hanlon Walshe, a member

Plate xviii: the Windmill at Tacumshin c.1952

of the evicted family of Knocktartan and himself a convict, was elected as a rate-collector by Wexford Board of Guardians, much to the dismay of many of the Protestant landlord ex-officio members, two of whom left the meeting in disgust when Nicholas was called in after being elected. In the same year, a Catholic, Dr J. R. Cardiff, was elected coroner for south Wexford, 'the first time', as he himself pointed out, 'that the appointment was in the hands of a nationalist'.[58] In the new County Council elections of April 1899, an 'entirely nationalist council' was returned in county Wexford.[59] Again the old Catholic family names predominate: in the South Wexford divisions James E. Meyler (for Bannow), Edmund Hore (Rosslare), Michael Browne (Bridgetown) and John J. Roche (Taghmon) were elected. By September, 1908, 'over three-quarters of the county of Wexford had been sold under the Land Purchase Acts' (back to the tenant-occupiers, that is) and it was expected that the remainder would be sold before long.[60] By 1909 only isolated groups of evicted tenants, such as those of the Boxwell estate in Duncormick, had not been reinstated. The wheel had turned full circle.

A second remarkable characteristic of Forth and Bargy has been the phenomenal contribution in personnel to the Catholic Church made by the leading 'old Catholic' families of the area. The number of priests, nuns and brothers coming from these families over centuries must surely be unequalled in any other similar region in Ireland. The reasons for this unique contribution have been adduced as including staunch loyalty to the Church over many centuries, the tradition of service in the cause of the Catholic faith, the comparative wealth of the 'comfortable' farmers and business people of Forth and Bargy which enabled them to educate their sons and daughters at home and abroad for the Church, and the example of neighbouring families. This provision of recruits to the Church continues down to this day.

Other marks of the old Forth and Bargy colony and way of life that survive to the present are the relics of the Yola dialect in everyday speech, the unusual customs such as mumming, the singing of old Christmas carols, the placing of funeral crosses at wayside holy sites and the survival of many of the neat thatched houses so often mentioned by commentators in the past.

What were the chief reasons, then for Forth and Bargy's differentiation and exclusivity? We have seen that its geographical isolation tended to develop exclusivity among the region's inhabitants, from the early Celts, through the Norse, to the Normans. The alien (as opposed to indigenous) character of the culture imposed by the Normans on the area and stoutly defended by them concomitantly with their defence of their lands set them apart as well. That culture included not only a different language and social mores but also a new legal system and new land laws. They introduced innovative farming methods and stamped their distinctive traits of industry, thrift, stolidness and sobriety indelibly on the face of the region. Forth and Bargy became synonymous with progressive farming, neat, comfortable homesteads, a hard-working, tolerant, undemonstrative people, but also doggedness, inter-marriage, clannishness and strong local loyalties.

By far the most remarkable feature of the continuum in Forth and Bargy was the survival, over an unusually long period and through various vicissitudes, of the old Catholic elite and land-owning gentry whose twelfth century ancestors had been the original Cambro-Norman founders of this unique colony. There were many factors involved in this survival — the isolation of the Forth and Bargy region; its natural boundaries to which were added the defences of the colonists; its proximity to Wales and England, sources of physical and moral sustenance in times of need. Over and above these considerations, however, stand out the personal attributes of the colonists themselves — their courage and tenacity, their stubborn loyalty to the land of their adoption in south Wexford. While English law prevailed there, they felt secure in their tenancies, so they defended English law with all their might. First and foremost, their fight was always for the lands they had been granted and held in the face of numerous difficulties.

Their long struggle for survival brought out many fine qualities among them — bravery, determination, stubborness, pride. Despite the passage of centuries, these qualities can still be found among the people of Forth and

Bargy. Time has brought many changes and the baronies are no longer the isolated enclave they once were. Physical and cultural frontiers have diminished with the advent of the railway, the motor-car, radio, television. Yet even the casual visitor to this corner of Ireland will come away with the strong impression that here, indeed, is a place apart, inhabited by a people apart.

5 *Henry Goff*

English conquest of an Irish barony. The changing patterns of land ownership in the barony of Scarawalsh 1540-1640

During the century between 1540 and 1640, the first tentative steps were taken by the English crown to settle the land question in Ireland, a problem that was to continue to dominate Irish politics for almost four centuries. The attempts at land settlement were part of a political and social revolution that saw the entire country reduced to English authority between 1534 and 1691. These first attempts at land settlement in early modern Ireland comprised the 'surrender and regrant' policy of Henry VIII and Elizabeth as well as the Tudor and Stuart plantations. They were followed in the second half of the seventeenth century by the Cromwellian, Restoration and Williamite land settlements. Before 1641, the confiscation was aimed primarily against the Irish but after that date, all catholic proprietors, comprising mainly Irish and Old English, found their lands subject to forfeiture, unless they could prove 'constant good affection' to the English parliament.

There have been few, if any, in depth examinations of the dissolution of the great Anglo-Irish lordships and the replacement of the Irish system of land ownership by the English system. This paper examines how the Tudor and Stuart policies of land settlement took effect in a specifically Irish region — the barony of Scarawalsh in north Wexford. It charts the coming of the New English, the decline of the MacMurrough Kavanaghs (the great Gaelic lords in the area) and the emergence of the new towns, Enniscorthy and Gorey.

The conquest of Scarawalsh: a pattern established, 1540-1610

This study is concerned with the changing patterns of land ownership in Scarawalsh between 1540 and 1640. The barony of Scarawalsh, approximately fifteen miles from north to south and fifteen miles from east to west, is situated in north-west county Wexford and bounded by county Wicklow on the north, by county Carlow on the west, by the barony of Bantry on the south and by the baronies of Gorey and Ballaghkeen on the east.[1] In all, the region covers an area of 106,659 statute acres.[2] The River Slaney, entering the barony at Bunclody in the northern end flows through its centre towards Enniscorthy and divides it in two, with the eastern portion being slightly larger than the western. Up to the seventeenth century, the area now represented by county Wexford was divided into two distinct parts — Forth, Bargy, Shelbourne, Shelmalier and Bantry 'commonly called the English baronies' and the remainder of the county 'commonly called the Irish countries'.[3] The failure of the Irish during the nine years war and the ensuing efforts to extend the area of English administration resulted in another attempt to shire the northern part of the county. It was set down by inquisition on 18 January 1606 that 'the territories commonly called the Irish countries, shall be divided into three several baronies to be named and distinguished as follows viz. the barony of Ballaghkeen, the barony of Scarawalsh and the barony of Gorey'.[4]

The barony of Scarawalsh comprised the following territories: 'the Duffry, the lordship of Enniscorthy, Farrenvarse, Farrenhamon, Farenoneile, Fasaghslewboy, Clunhanricke, the lordship of Ferns, Kylcolnelyen, Kilhobucke and the bishop's lands both sides of the Bann'.[5] That the writ of the crown did not extend to Wicklow and north Wexford even in 1606, when the inquisition was taken, is clearly evident in the failure of the jury to set down with any accuracy the sizes of the territories that were included in the new barony.[6]

Since this study is concerned with the changing patterns of ownership in the barony of Scarawalsh in the century between 1540 and 1640, the first require-ment is to establish who actually owned and occupied the land in 1540. By 1540, most of county Wexford (including the liberty of Wexford, which was confiscated from the earl of Shrewsbury in 1536) had by various means become vested in the crown.[7] Under the acts of absentees of 1380 and 1536 title to lands of the absentee overlords (earl of Shrewsbury, duke of Norfolk and Lord Berkeley), was resumed by the crown and all those areas in the county which had passed out of royal control were surrendered in 1395 when Art MacMurrough Kavanagh formally submitted to Richard II. An alternative crown title to most of the area was established by the attainders of Francis Viscount Lovel and Thomas, earl of Kildare and the subsequent confiscation of their property.[8] The dissolution of the religious houses in January 1541 further increased the king's possessions in the area.[9]

From 1540 on the crown granted various estates in county Wexford to numerous individuals. The lands of the dissolved religious houses, the manors of the royal castles and lands confiscated on account of the attainder of the owners were more readily available for distribution and constituted the largest portion of the grants in the years immediately following 1540. The crown's claim to the remainder lay dormant until the first decade of the seventeenth century.[10]

In 1540 there were three religious houses in the barony of Scarawalsh — the Franciscan friary in Enniscorthy and the Augustinian abbeys at Ferns and Downe.[11] There were also three crown manors in the barony at the time located at Enniscorthy, Ferns and Clohamon.[12] Although nominally in the legal possession of the absentee overlords, the northern portion of county Wexford

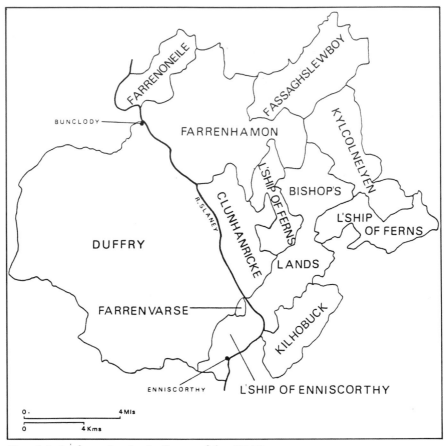

Fig.: 5.1: Irish territories in Scarawalsh c.1540

including the barony of Scarawalsh, along with most of Carlow and south Wicklow was controlled and occupied by the MacMurrough Kavanaghs, titular kings of Leinster, who administered Gaelic laws and customs in the area. Fig. 5.2 shows the distribution and location of the crown possessions in 1540. The attempts of the legal owners to gain possession and the resistance of the occupants, mainly Kavanaghs, were the dominant features in the struggle for the control of Scarawalsh from 1540 to the end of the century.

The Kavanaghs before 1540 were in an extremely strong position controlling a large area of 'low Leinster', comprising most of county Carlow and the northern two-thirds of county Wexford. Among the factors which contributed to making the Kavanaghs the pre-eminent Irish family in the area were the historical importance of the MacMurroughs, nominal kings of Leinster, the size of the various septs, the extent of their lands, and the nature of the terrain which was easily defended. Their alliances with the Fitzgeralds was also an important factor with Garret Óg helping Cahir MacInnycross become MacMurrough in 1531 despite the opposition of Dowling Kavanagh, who was supported by Skeffington, the lord deputy.

In a direct attempt to curb the power of the Kavanaghs, Sir Richard Butler was appointed constable of Ferns castle in 1538 in place of Cahir MacInnycross. The removal of the Irish Kavanagh and his replacement by the Anglo-Irish Butler was a significant step in the introduction of English rule and in the corresponding decline in the power of the Kavanaghs. Thereafter no Irishman was appointed to the important position of constable of the strategic Ferns castle. In fact Butler himself was the last Anglo-Irishman to hold the position as after him the constableship was always granted to a New English soldier, in keeping with crown policy.

The arrival of St Leger in Ireland as lord deputy had significant consequences for crown policy and in particular for Irish landowners. There was an immediate and perceptible change in the policy of the crown towards the Irish lordships. General reform of the Irishry was still the intention but St Leger aided by Thomas Cussack proposed that this be done by conciliation. Cahir MacArt offered to administer English law and customs in his area and further proposed that the northern portion of the then unshired county Wexford 'be made a county by the name of Ferns' with himself as sheriff. Not

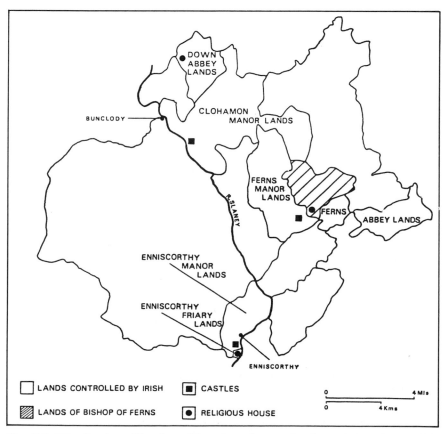

Fig. 5.2: Distribution of lands and location of crown lands c.1540 in Scarawalsh barony

surprisingly, this latter offer was not accepted but St Leger, who was anxious to assimilate the Irish lordships to the polity of the crown, accepted Cahir's submission and summoned him to the parliament. A period of two and a half years elapsed before the Kavanagh preliminary surrender and regrant submission was formally signed in September 1543.[13] This was probably due to the dispute over who should succeed Cahir MacInnycross as MacMurrough.

The formal agreement was signed at New Ross on 3 September 1543 between 'the principal men of the nation of the Kavanaghs'[14] and the representatives of the crown omitted two important clauses that were a standard feature of most other preliminary surrender and regrant submissions.[15] The Kavanagh agreement did not repudiate papal jurisdiction and it contained no provision for any representative of the Kavanaghs to attend parliament. Under the terms of the 1543 agreement, the Kavanaghs recognised the right of the crown to the castles and manor of Ferns, Enniscorthy, Clohamon and Clonmullen. In return, it was agreed that the 'Kavanaghs shall make a new partition and division of all their lands'.[16] They also agreed to cultivate their lands in the English fashion, to banish their 'idlemen' and not to demand coyne and livery.

This agreement marked the formal conclusion of the first stage in the three stage process that came to be known as 'surrender and regrant'. The next stage of the actual process of surrender and regrant required a further indenture and in the case of the Kavanaghs, this indenture had not been signed when England's foreign wars resulted in the suspension of the surrender and regrant policy at the end of 1543. The 1543 agreement stabilised the relationship between the crown and the Kavanaghs but it did not resolve the dispute about succession to the chieftaincy of the sept. Gerald macCahir of Garryhill continued to press his claim and on the death of Cahir MacInnycross, the MacMurrough, in 1545, Cahir MacArt had to engage in pitched battle against his kinsman Gerald before he was acknowledged as leader of the Kavanaghs.[17]

When St Leger was sent back briefly in 1550 to replace Bellingham , who had been appointed to the former's position in 1548, he tried to revive his conciliatory initiative. In the case of the Kavanaghs, this entailed negotiations leading to the second stage of the surrender and regrant process and attempting to resolve the question of the chieftaincy succession. As a result of St Leger's efforts, Cahir MacArt publicly renounced the title of MacMurrough in Dublin in 1550 and in return was created Baron of Ballyanne for life in 1554 and leader of his sept; Maurice Kavanagh was created *tánist* and baron of Coolnaleen.[18] Such was the desire of the crown to settle the question of succession and proceed with the surrender and regrant of Kavanagh lands that the crown actually recognised the position of *tánist* and included it in the formal patent. When Cahir died the following year, Maurice succeeded to the chieftaincy of the clan and Cahir's son Dermot received a patent appointing him *tánist*.[19]

This attempt to impose primogeniture on the succession to the chieftaincy failed as the office reverted to the Garryhill sept in the person of Moriertagh Óg in 1580. However, the attempt begun by St Leger to anglicise this branch of the family succeeded to the extent that the principle of primogeniture operated with regard to the succession of land in Cahir MacArt's immediate family. Despite the fact that the final stage of the surrender and regrant process was not implemented until 1571,[20] the lands of St Mullins descended first in 1555 to Cahir's oldest son Brian (d.1572), to Brian's oldest son Morgan (d.1626) and to Morgan's oldest son Brian (d.1662).[21] In the area of social reform, the policy introduced by St Leger also met with some success in that Brian (d.1572) sent his two sons and two daughters to school in England.[22]

By the end of St Leger's final period as lord deputy in 1556, little further progress had been made in the attempt to bring the Kavanagh lordship under the English sphere of influence. The policy of persuasion and education advocated by St Leger was replaced by attempts during the deputyships of Bellingham, Crofts, Radcliffe and Sussex to cow the Irish lords by force; given the size of the army, the lack of finance and the indecisiveness of the queen; this policy of coercion had little hope of succeeding. When the policy of conciliation towards the Irish lords was abandoned, it became necessary to secure the defence of the Pale and it was this consideration which dominated the policies of Bellingham and his successors. They felt that English interests in Ireland could best be promoted by enlarging the Pale and providing for its defense by garrisons on the Calais model.

This idea had first been introduced in 1538, but was developed further under Bellingham and his successors. North Wexford and Wicklow were divided into three administrative zones and English captains supported by soldiers were appointed as seneschals to rule each area with Sir Jacques Wingfield taking charge of the area inhabited by the O'Byrnes and O'Tooles and Captain Nicholas Heron, based at Leighlin Castle, being appointed seneschal of the Kavanaghs.[23] The seneschals were expected to finance themselves by collecting rents and dues that had formerly been collected by the Gaelic chieftains of their areas but crown lands in the vicinity of the garrisons were also granted to them. These grants served the dual purpose of augmenting the seneschals' income and encouraging them to extend the jurisdiction of the crown.

Heron's attempts to administer English law in the area occupied by the Kavanaghs met with a fair degree of success. Lord Lieutenant Sussex wrote in 1562 that 'the Kavanaghs be brought to such obedience as they live at the commandment of Captain Heron and under obedience of the laws'.[24] In his role as lessee of crown lands, Heron also made a significant contribution to extending English jurisdiction in Ireland. He was the first person to make a determined attempt to occupy crown lands leased to him in the Gaelic area of north Wexford. He received a grant of the manor of Ferns in 1558 and this was followed by a grant of the abbey of Ferns in 1561. To these were added Enniscorthy friary and manor in 1555 and 1556.[25] From the time that he received the first lease, Heron set about taking actual possession and, despite opposition from the Kavanaghs, met with a good deal of success. The effectiveness of his seneschalship and the manner in which he took possession of the crown lands was recognised by the new lord deputy Sidney who arrived in

Ireland in October 1565, when Heron, alone of all the old seneschals, was confirmed in office.

The arrival of Sidney marked a turning point in the conquest of Ireland. The policies of Sidney's predecessors were based on the need to defend the Pale. Sidney on the other hand arrived in October 1565 with a clearly outlined programme for the conquest of Ireland and a commitment from Elizabeth and the English privy council to provide him with sufficient finance and soldiers to implement the scheme.[26] In dealing with the Gaelic lordships, Sidney continued the system of seneschals but he redefined their role. The first seneschals had been appointed with the main objectives of keeping order and securing the Pale against attack. Under a directive from the new lord deputy, the seneschals were now given the additional duty of leading the Irish to an acceptance of the common law, culminating eventually in the shiring of the regions.[27] All of the old seneschals, with the exception of the successful Nicholas Heron, were replaced by Sidney's appointees and new sherriffs were also appointed to counties Wexford, Carlow, Kilkenny, Queen's Co. and King's Co. in 1566. Later that year, Sidney accompanied the judges on their circuit through Leinster. The work of the seneschals proved effective. Quarterly sessions were introduced and the jurisdiction of the crown was gradually extended to include low Leinster.

Nicholas Heron's role in this regard was particularly important as were the activities of his successor, Thomas Masterson, who was appointed constable of Ferns castle early in 1569.[28] Masterson had arrived in Ireland five years previously in 1564 and was appointed sherriff of Kilkenny in 1568.[29] He was a native of Wichmalbank in Cheshire and a descendant of Robert Masterson, whose landholdings there dated back to the time of Edward I.[30] His father, also called Thomas, married Margery, daughter and co-heir of Roger Mainwaring, escheator of Cheshire. Thomas (junior), the second oldest son in the family of six sons and four daughters, was, like many other second sons, obliged to choose a military career and seek his fortune overseas.

Having been appointed constable of Ferns castle, Masterson also purchased Heron's interest in the abbey lands of Ferns in March 1569.[31] He continued to pursue Heron's aggressive policy against the Kavanaghs and took possession of the abbey lands, despite opposition from the Kavanaghs. The Kavanaghs greatly resented the intrusion of English soldiers into lands previously occupied by themselves and also objected to attempts to bring them under English jurisdiction. They needed little encouragement then to join the Butlers in rebellion in 1569. Sidney wrote in December of that year 'the Kavanaghs [who] for the most part first rose by provocation of the Butlers, have ever since remained in actual rebellion'.[32] The promptings of the Butlers may have been the deciding factor in causing the Kavanaghs to rebel in 1569, but the ill-feeling caused by the activities of Heron and Masterson was also an important factor.

In June 1570 two of the lesser Irish septs under Kavanagh control, the MacDavymores and the MacVaddocks of north and east Wexford, agreed to surrender their lands and receive them back by letters patent.[33] In March of the following year, Sidney concluded a similar agreement with Brian MacCahir Kavanagh 'chief of his name and sept called *Sliocht Diarmuid Lamhdhearg*' on behalf of Brian and all the other gentlemen and freeholders of that sept.

Thus the third and final stage of the surrender and regrant process for the Kavanaghs, begun by St Leger in 1543 and continued by him during a subsequent lord deputyship in 1550, was finally completed by Sidney in 1571 for some branches of the family. The final result was very different to that envisaged by St Leger in that patents were granted to a much larger number of minor landowners in 1571, with a view to undermining the power of the leaders of the sept. The patents ensured however that the lands now held by a title, valid in English law, remained in the possession of the Kavanaghs right up to the end of the century and in some cases up to 1640.

As a result of their involvement in the rebellion of 1569, the Butlers lost possession of their huge estates in the baronies of Scarawalsh, Bantry and Shelmalier. The loss was only temporary as they recovered most of their former possessions through their kinsman, the earl of Ormonde. Ormonde regained the lands of St Johns and Kilcarbry near Enniscorthy but, instead of returning them to the Butlers, he conveyed them to Nicholas White.[34] White's grandson sold his interest in the lands to Daniel Mullineux of Newlands in county Dublin in 1599. The latter was very active in granting mortgages to Irish landowners in the area during the early years of the seventeenth century.[35] The remainder of the Butler lands in county Wexford descended to Edward Butler. He settled in the area just south of the border between Bantry and Scarawalsh where he created the manor of Kayer. He succeeded also in increasing the extent of the Butler holdings by granting mortgages to the Irish landowners in the Duffry and foreclosing when they were unable to redeem the mortgages.[36]

During the 1570s, most of the Kavanaghs were securely in possession of their own lands, now held by patent from the crown. The extent of the lands allocated to the Kavanaghs in 1570 was considerably smaller than that claimed and occupied by them for centuries and this was a source of friction between the Irish and the new patentees who were attempting to gain possession of what was assigned to them by royal patent. The Kavanaghs also seemed to be still in occupation of most of the Butler and Sinnott lands in Wexford.

By the year 1572, the year after the signing of the surrender and regrant agreement with the Kavanaghs, the crown properties in Scarawalsh were in the hands of two men, both resident in county Wexford. Richard Sinnott, residing at Ballybrennan, held leases on Enniscorthy friary and manor lands, the lands of Clohamon and Downe and the lands of Donal O Morrow. Thomas Masterson, residing in Ferns, held the leases on Ferns manor and abbey lands. Both men were also patentee officers of the crown. Sinnott was vice-seneschal of Wexford and Masterson was constable of Ferns castle and seneschal of county Wexford. The families of both men were also related by marriage in that Richard Sinnott's son, Walter, was married to Thomas Masterson's daughter, Mary.[37] Between 1572 and 1580, both men consolidated their positions and title. Masterson received new patents confirming him as seneschal of county Wexford and the liberties of Wexford and as constable of Fern's castle.[38] His hold on the Fern's abbey lands was secure and although he did not succeed in obtaining a lease in his own name to Fern's manor lands, he did obtain a new extended lease from Edmund D'Arcy.[39] Sinnott was confirmed as vice-seneschal and in 1575 received new twenty one year leases to Enniscorthy manor and friary lands, the lands of Donal O'Morrow and the lands of Clohamon and Downe.[40]

The Kavanaghs and their followers bitterly resented the intrusion of Masterson and Sinnott into lands which the Irish regarded as theirs by inheritance. Led by Brian MacCahir and Dónal Spáinneach (so called because he had gone to Spain with Stukely), they offered armed resistance to the new 'legal' owners of the land and much of the area was laid waste. The property of Masterson was a prime target and during the summer of 1579 the abbey and castle of Ferns and the manor of Clohamon were burned.[41] In March 1581 Henry Wallop, vice-treasurer of Ireland, wrote 'the county of Wexford, and divers parts adjoining, is far out of order (with) the Kavanagh in rebellion in great numbers.[42] With the rebellion in Munster collapsing as Desmond's allies and followers deserted him, lord deputy Grey turned his attention towards Leinster and led 400 footmen and 100 horsemen into the county in June 1581 in an attempt to put an end to Dónal Spáinneach Kavanagh's resistance.

Because of Grey's success and the continuing campaign of Masterson and Sinnott, the Kavanaghs were forced out of eastern Scarawalsh. They crossed the Slaney and took refuge in the dense woods of the Duffry in western Scarawalsh. In a final attempt to crush the Kavanaghs' resistance, Masterson, accompanied by Sir William Russell of Arklow, entered the Duffry in the summer of 1582 and met 'a whole troop of the Kavanaghs to the number of 100 swords, whom they charging did break and cut in pieces'.[43] This incident resulted in the submission of the remaining Kavanaghs and effectively ended their resistance. Pardons were issued to Dónal Spáinneach, the other leading Kavanaghs and their supporters, notably the O'Briens of the Duffry in May 1582.[44] In July of the following year Brian MacBrian Kavanagh and his followers were pardoned in consideration of their good service in apprehending Walter Eustace, brother of James, late viscount Baltinglass. This marked the end of the Kavanagh rebellion. From then until the outbreak of hostilities at the beginning of the nine years war in 1596, the area was relatively peaceful, with only occasional forays being made against the new landowners.

In Wexford the defeat of the Kavanaghs was not marked by the wholesale forfeiture of their lands. Those who submitted were pardoned and allowed retain possession of their estates. Although there were no wholesale confiscations of land from the Irish in Wexford, the rebellion of 1579-83 did have important implications for the English landowners in the area. Both Sinnott and Masterson were well rewarded for their activities on behalf of the crown during the rebellion. Sinnott received the manor of Rosegarland in 1582 and he also received a new forty year lease of Enniscorthy manor and friary lands and the lands of Dónal O'Morrow 'in consideration of his having received no benefit from the premises during the late wars from the adjoining rebels'.[45] Masterson was equally well rewarded. In December 1581 he received the lands of Clohamon and Downe, surrendered by Sinnott, and two years later, in November 1583, he received a new sixty year lease to these areas to run from the expiry of the 1581 lease.[46] He also received new patents to the manor and abbey of Ferns 'in consideration of his service and to encourage his sons to continue in their father's steps'.[47]

In addition to the threat from the Kavanaghs, Masterson was also at logger-heads with Thomas Colclough, the other most prominent representative of the New English in county Wexford. Colclough was a native of Bluerton and Woolstanton in Staffordshire and had first arrived in Ireland in 1542.[48] In May 1557, he had purchased the lease of Tintern Abbey and in August 1576 the queen had granted the lands to Colclough in fee.[49] Despite numerous attempts, Colclough had not succeeded in obtaining a crown office and was particularly envious of Masterson who had obtained a number of crown offices in Wexford, despite arriving in the county much later than Colclough. It may have been the difficulties involved in trying to defend his six different holdings that forced Masterson to reconsider his position and decide to concentrate his energies on defending the four holdings based in his own name — Ferns manor and abbey lands and the lands of Clohamon and Downe. Masterson yielded up his interest, as assignee of Richard Sinnott, in Enniscorthy manor and friary lands to Henry Wallop at Easter 1586.[50]

Wallop was born about 1540.[51] He was the oldest son and heir of Sir Oliver Wallop of Farleigh-Wallop in the county of Southampton and nephew and heir of Sir John Wallop, governor of Calais. Elected M.P. for Southampton, he served on a number of committees in parliament and in July 1579 was appointed vice-treasurer to the earl of Ormond in Ireland. Wallop's interest in Wexford dated back to the summer of 1581 when he had been a member of Grey's expedition against the Kavanaghs. The aspect of the area that had most attracted his attention was 'the quantity and goodness of the woods which are marvellous great'.[52]

Wallop was only too well aware of the commercial possibilities of exploiting the huge oak forests of the Slaney valley. He was also deeply interested in plantation as a means of proceeding with the conquest of Ireland.[53] After a good deal of preliminary investigation, Wallop decided to invest his money in a small plantation in the Enniscorthy area. He commenced purchasing lands from the Irish. This is quite clear from a letter he wrote to Walsingham in January 1586 when he referred to 'the woods ... but none of his majesty's neither belonging to the house of Enniscorthy or otherwise but appertaining all to freeholders of the Irishry, at whose hands, I have and am to buy them'.[54] Shortly afterwards, at Easter 1586, Wallop purchased Sinnott's interests in the manor and friary lands of Enniscorthy.[55] In addition to lands acquired from the Irish and from Sinnott, he also obtained an extensive tract of ground amounting to 1,500 acres on a ninety nine year lease from Hugh Allen, bishop of Ferns.[56] These areas belonged to the established church, but, like all the other lands of the established church in the diocese, they were let at low rents on very long leases.[57] The bishop's lands acquired by Wallop directly adjoined his Enniscorthy properties and stretched from the River Slaney right up along the Bann river to Ferns.[58]

In the matter of land acquisition, Wallop did not confine his attention to the barony of Scarawalsh. He also obtained leases to the abbey lands of Selskar in Wexford town, Adare in county Limerick and Athlone. Enniscorthy was however his main investment. These grants were enrolled in Chancery on 4 November of the same year. Permission was obtained on 1 February 1597 to alienate Adare abbey to Sir Thomas Norris, while Wallop retained possession of Enniscorthy.[59] This grant to Wallop was the basis of his possession of Enniscorthy, a possession that was to remain relatively intact through the four main upheavals in ownership in county Wexford during the seventeenth century and has persisted right down to the present day in the form of ground rents payable to Wallop's heirs by the occupants.[60] Wallop did not personally supervise any of his properties in Ireland. He returned to England in April 1589 and did not come back to Ireland until July 1595. During his six year absence, he did not resign his position as vice-treasurer but continued to administer it by deputy. Henry Wallop died on 14 April 1599 and his oldest son, also called Henry (1568-1642), succeeded to the Enniscorthy property.[61] This second Henry had acted as his father's deputy in Dublin while Oliver, second son of Henry (senior), looked after Wallop's properties in Wexford, but he was killed in a skirmish with the Kavanaghs in May 1598. From the time that the 1579 rebellion was finally put down in 1583 both Wallop and Masterson enjoyed relatively peaceful occupation. This peace, with only occasional exceptions, continued for a period of about ten years up to the outbreak of the nine years war.

The lord deputyships of Perrot and Fitzwilliam saw an emphasis on 'amiable persuasions' rather than military conquest. This manifested itself as the 'composition of Connacht' and in the so-called 'native plantation' in the McMahon and McKenna country of Monaghan. In Wexford, those members of the Kavanaghs who had not been included in earlier surrender and regrant arrangements benefitted when the process was revived by Elizabeth. Two of these were Dermot MacMaurice Kavanagh and Cryon Kavanagh who occupied lands in the Clonhenret/Camolin/Raheen area, along the eastern border of Scarawalsh as well as lands in Ballyduffbeg, Ballyduff and Tullabeg just over the border in the adjoining barony of Gorey.[62] By a commission issued in November 1591 to Thomas Masterson, the seneschal and several assistants, the lands were surrendered the following month and were regranted to Dermot and Cryon Kavanagh by patent from the queen in April 1592.[63]

Under the terms of the patents of surrender and regrant to the Kavanaghs, the rights of the minor landowners were safeguarded. The commission authorising the surrenders contained clear instructions that the lands of Dermot MacMaurice and those of 'his freeholders' were to be differentiated. He was then to receive a patent to his lands 'with provision that he confirm the freeholders in their rights'.[64] How this was to be achieved was made clear in the patent granting legal title to Dermot. The lands of the minor landholder Cryon

Kavanagh were conveyed to Dermot with the following instruction 'the last four (townlands) had belonged to Cryon Kavanagh MacDonnell of Rahincormackmore, county Wexford and are to be reconveyed to him by Dermot'.[65] This safeguarding of the rights of the minor landowners was an important feature of the surrender and regrant process under Elizabeth and is in stark contrast to the treatment meted out to the Irish under the Stuarts.

As we have seen above, the longer established English landowners in the barony also fared well under Elizabeth. Both the Sinnotts and the Butlers retained possession of most of their lands under Tudor rule in Ireland. One of the main factors that contributed to the prominence of the various members of the Sinnott family in the political life of the county and their success in retaining possession of their estates was undoubtedly the legal expertise of some of the family members.[66] The two families above, the Sinnotts and the Butlers, were part of a leading landed and social elite in county Wexford during the second half of the sixteenth century. This elite also included the leading merchant families in Wexford as well as the new English landowners and the more important Irish landowners. Intermarriage between small groups of families was widespread. There were close marital ties between the Butlers, Devereuxs and Kavanaghs.[67] The new English Masterson family of Ferns had marriage ties with both the Sinnotts and the Butlers but, significantly, not with the Kavanaghs. Thomas Masterson's daughter married Walter Sinnott of Ballybrennan who was killed in 1580 and his son Richard married as his second wife Joan, daughter of Richard, third Viscount Mountgarret. When Richard died in 1627, he left four daughters as co-heiresses who were married to Edward Butler of the manor of Kayer, Walter Sinnott of Rosegarland, Nicholas Devereux of Ballymagir and Robert Shee of Upper Court in county Kilkenny.

Among the first to take up arms in Scarawalsh at the beginning of the nine years war in 1596 was Dónal Spáinneach. A contemporary account states 'Dónal Spáinneach and his kinsmen who also pretended to be much at the devotion of Sir Henry Wallop ... took up arms against the queen and challenged the house of Enniscorthy possessed and sumptuously built by Sir Henry Wallop'.[68] It was further reported that 'Hovenden, an Englishman, but a papistical traitor took Dónal's son and carried him to the earl of Tyrone, with the consent of his father, as a pledge of his fidelity to the earl'.[69] Kavanagh's reason for supporting O'Neill was made quite clear. Kavanagh still looked on the lands of Enniscorthy as belonging to himself and his followers and he looked on Wallop as an intruder.[70] The Kavanaghs and O'Byrnes joined in a formal agreement in August 1596 in preparation for the forthcoming war. The O'Tooles, Owen O'More and some members of the Butler Family in county Wexford were also parties to this agreement.[71] The initial efforts of the Irish and those Anglo-Irish who supported the rebellion were not too successful. The capture and execution of Feagh MacHugh O'Byrne in May 1597 was a serious setback but the rebels in the south-east recovered from his loss and scored a notable victory over the crown forces.[72] This confrontation took place just outside Enniscorthy on 19 May 1598 when Wallop, Masterson and Colclough joined forces, amounting to about 400 soldiers and were opposed by Dónal Spáinneach Kavanagh, Owen O'More and Walter Reagh Fitzgerald, a member of the Kildare family that had lost most of its lands earlier in the century. The new English forces were heavily defeated and 'there was slain of the queen's soldiers 309 persons and the rest put to flight'.[73] Among those slain was Oliver Wallop, second son of Sir Henry, and Leonard Colclough, brother of Sir Thomas Colclough. Richard Masterson, the seneschal, had a narrow escape when his horse was killed. About eight of the rebels were killed, including Brian Reagh Fitzgerald, who died shortly afterwards from wounds received in the battle. Wallop and Masterson, who between them occupied about one eighth of the barony of Scarawalsh, were forced to retire from their lands and were effectively confined to their castles at Enniscorthy and Ferns.

Even after the signing of the Treaty of Mellifont, Wallop and Masterson found it difficult to regain possession of their estates because of the guerilla warfare. Edmund MacBrian O'Byrne, one of the Wicklow O'Byrnes, and James Butler, a party to the agreement in 1596, along with about 100 followers engaged in guerilla warfare against Masterson for some years in the north of the county and Dónal Spáinneach pursued a similar course against Wallop in the Enniscorthy area. Sir John Davys wrote to Cecil in 1604 'many Robin Hoods yet live in the woods. Dónal Spáinneach and his followers have lately committed a murder . . . and yet this man has been pardoned twice in twelve months and now he sues for a further pardon'.[74] However the superior military forces and organisation of Masterson and Wallop prevailed and within a couple of years they had regained effective control. After the debacle at Kinsale the rebellion collapsed and O'Neill submitted at Mellifont in March 1603. The wholesale confiscation hoped for by English officials and adventurers did not take place. However, contrary to the position that obtained in the remainder of Ireland, a number of the minor landowners in Wexford were attainted and their lands were confiscated.[75] Most of these minor landowners were located in the specifically Irish area of the Duffry in western Scarawalsh, an area that had been particularly troublesome during the war and this may have accounted for the forfeiture of lands in the area. Most of the holdings were quite small ranging in size from four to thirty five acres but a couple of holdings extending to about 300 acres were also confiscated.[76] The lands were all held from the crown, with the title going back to the surrender and regrant process of the sixteenth century.[77]

Lands confiscated from the Irish because of complicity in the rebellion were granted to patentee officers of the crown. Most of the Duffry area was granted to George Carew, vice-chamberlain of the king, in April 1604 and he sold them to Sir Thomas Colclough of Tintern.[78] The remainder of the Duffry region was allocated to Sir Henry Brounker, president of Munster, in 1605 but he sold his interest in the lands back to the occupants, who were mainly O'Briens and they were still in possession in 1640.[79] A similar course of action was pursued by Sir James Hamilton, later appointed a commissioner in the court of wards, when he received a patent for the lands of Maurice Kavanagh of Coolnaleen, (parish of Kilcomb). He also sold his interest in the estate back to Kavanagh, the occupant, who was still in possession in 1640.[80] Brounker and Hamilton were also involved in a much more insidious threat to the titles of the Irish land-owners, when individuals of an unscrupulous nature were encouraged by the crown to seek out ancient title to lands. This device had been used by Peter Carew in 1568 but it was used with increasing frequency during the later Elizabethan and early Stuart period. In 1605, the estates of George Talbot, earl of Waterford and Salop, situated in north east Scarawalsh and occupied by Dowling MacBrien Kavanagh, were declared forfeit to the crown under the statute of absentees. The area was granted to Sir Henry Brounker, who sold them to Dowling MacBrien Kavanagh in whose possession they remained until they were again claimed by the crown and included in the north Wexford plantation.[81] Similarly the estates of the duke of Norfolk and Lord Berkeley were also forfeited to the crown under the statute of absentees. A good deal of Scarawalsh was included in this forfeiture, including the area occupied by Dónal Spáinneach and the manor of Ferns leased by Richard Masterson.[82]

Dónal Spáinneach's properties were granted to Sir James Hamilton. He immediately sold the lands back to Kavanagh, who eventually succeeded in obtaining legal title to the property in 1621.[83] Richard Masterson however did not receive the expected patent to the manor of Ferns. Instead the castle and lands were granted to Lord Audley, who used his position as councillor of state to acquire the patent.[84] Masterson protested but James ordered that the patent be confirmed to Audley to hold until the lease expired and that a fresh patent be issued to Masterson.[85] Following this direction from the king, Masterson received in June 1609 a grant of all the areas occupied by him, with the exception of those passed to Audley, 'to hold for ever as of the castle of Wexford in common socage'.[86] Included in Masterson's grant were estates previously occupied by Dónal Spáinneach, who disputed the former's title to the property.

The dispute was settled in Masterson's favour in the court of chancery in the easter term of 1610. While the crown's title to the area granted to Masterson was being researched, it was discovered that the crown had a legal title to practically all of Wexford between the River Slaney and the sea. It was this discovery which provided the legal basis for the plantation of north Wexford. Before examining the implications of the plantation for the landholders of north Wexford, ownership and occupation in the area and in the barony of Scarawalsh in particular needs to be assessed. Fig. 5.3 sets out the distribution of lands in Scarawalsh about 1600 and also shows the holdings of the two major landholders, Masterson and Wallop, in the area at the time.

In 1540, Scarawalsh, in the legal possession of the crown, was occupied entirely by the Irish, mainly MacMurrough Kavanaghs. By the end of the century, the situation had changed considerably. The position of the Irish landholders was seriously eroded and in the period under review, they lost possession of approximately 40 per cent of their land in the barony. At the turn of the century, the Irish occupied only about 60 per cent of the area of the barony and only a small portion of this, approximately a quarter, was held by a

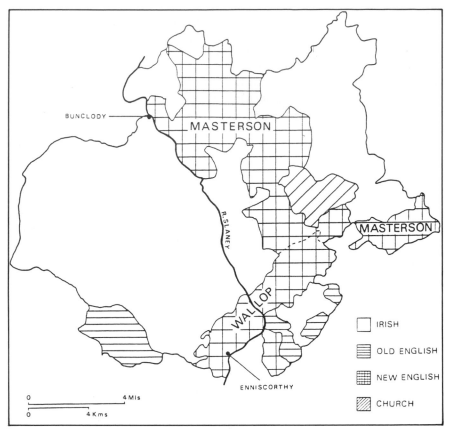

Fig. 5.3: Distribution of lands of Wallop and Masterson c. 1600 in Scarawalsh barony

title good in English law. The main beneficiaries during that period were the New English, in the persons of Henry Wallop and Thomas Masterson. Between them, they owned and occupied about 35 per cent of the barony in 1600. The main basis for their holdings were crown manors and confiscated friary lands but Wallop in particular had augmented his holding by purchase from the Irish and also by the acquisition of church property. The remaining 5 per cent of the barony in 1600 was in the hands of the Old English, mainly Butlers and Sinnots. The bulk of their estates was acquired by mortgage foreclosure from the Irish, but all their lands were held by title good in English law. The erosion of the Irish landholdings in north Wexford and the success of the New English and to a lesser degree, the Old English in property acquisition was hastened considerably by events during the first two decades of the seventeenth century.

Scarawalsh and the plantation of north Wexford, 1610-18

The crown had, during Elizabeth's reign and during the early years of the reign of James, encouraged New English to establish crown title to estates possessed

by the Irish and longer established English proprietors. The people who discovered crown title to such areas were well rewarded, usually by being granted
leases of the 'discovered' lands at very attractive terms. A new impetus was
given to the discovery of titles when the courts ruled that land acquired by
tanistry (1606) and gavelkind (1608) was not held by a title valid in English
law. In 1609, Samuel Mullineux of Newlands in county Dublin took
possession of Tomgarrow, Mountfin, Tomanoole, Ballywilliamroe and
Ballinakill, all in the barony of Scarawalsh 'under pretext of a supposed title'
from the O'Briens of the Duffry.[87]

There was quite clearly some kind of an understanding between Chichester
and Masterson leading up to the plantation. Masterson was granted a new
lease of all his lands 'to hold for ever, as of the castle of Wexford, in common
socage' by patent dated 7 June 1609.[88] He acquired his title to these areas
under the commission of surrender and sale of lands on defective titles. A
number of Irish and Old English proprietors including Art Mac Dermot
Kavanagh, William Browne of Mulrankin, and Patrick Peppard also surrendered their lands but in their case regrants were suspended and their properties were not restored[89]

Masterson, like Mullineux in the Duffry, started to take possession of lands
in the Clohamon area which had been included in his new patent.[90] Members of
the Kavanagh family, the long time occupants of the area, disputed the right of
Masterson to take control of what they considered to be Kavanagh lands. The
dispute was settled in the court of chancery in the Easter term of 1610, when
the court ruled in favour of Masterson on the grounds that the crown was the
rightful owner of the region and was fully entitled to make a grant to
Masterson.

The crown advanced two separate claims to the lands of north Wexford. The
first claim to the area dated back to the fourteenth century when Art
MacMurrough Kavanagh and his allies had on 7 January 1395 submitted to
Richard II and signed a covenant in which they agreed to relinquish to the king
all their estates in Leinster.[91] The crown's title to the area as outlined above is
genuine to the extent that the facts receited are beyond dispute, The question
does arise — how could MacMurrough and his allies surrender lands that they
only held in trust during their leadership, which in the Irish system of
ownership were not theirs to surrender?

Lest any deficiency should be detected in the first title, the crown also
advanced a second claim to the lands under the act of resumption passed by
Poyning's parliament of 1494-5.[92] It was under the authority of this act that
the area was confiscated.[93] Once it became clear to James that a valid title for
the crown had been established, he authorised Chichester to implement a
scheme of plantation. Thus in June 1611, a writ of resumption was issued
from the court of chancery to the sheriff of Wexford directing him to seize for
the king's use all the lands 'from the river of Slaney (South) to the Blackwater
of Arklow (North) and from the sea (East) to the bounds of Carlow and Kildare
(West)'.[94] The next step in the legal process of confiscation was to empanel a
local jury in county Wexford to find the title for the crown.

At first the local jury brought in a verdict of *ignoramus* on 4 December 1611.[95] Five recalcitrant jurors were censured. 'Walter Bryan, Edmond Sinnott, Edmond Codd, James Butler and Thomas Codd (were) condemned to pay fines of £ 30 English apiece and to be imprisoned during pleasure'.[96] A new jury was assembled consisting of the eleven who had found for the king and these were joined by Sir Thomas Colclough, a member of the commission, and John Murphy, who was appointed as an undertaker in the ensueing plantation. Not surprisingly, this new jury found that the king's title to the lands was valid.[97]

The story of the plantation of north Wexford is extremely complicated and difficult to unravel because no less than four different schemes were drawn up and partially implemented between 1612 and 1618.[98] The fourth and final scheme of plantation was drawn up by the English privy council following receipt of recommendations from St John but it was not actually implemented until the spring of 1618.[99] Based on the grants in the patent rolls, the total amount of land in north Wexford confiscated and granted to undertakers servitors and existing occupants was 84,900 acres.[100] Eighteen undertakers, all New English and mainly patentee officers of the crown, received 28,000 with estates ranging in size from 1,000 to 3,800 acres. Patents amounting to 3,100 acres were issued to seven servitors. These were all New English, with one exception, and patents ranged from 300 to 800 acres.[101] The remaining 53,800 acres were granted to the existing landowners in the area. The ten with the largest land holdings received new patents and had their holdings raised to the status of manors. The new patents were issued to three Old English for 6,100 acres, three New English for 12,800 acres and to the four most prominent Kavanaghs, for 6,900 acres.

The re-organisation of land ownership in the planted area was completed by granting patents to selected persons from among those Irish and Old English owners who had occupied over 100 acres before the plantation. Those who had occupied less than 100 acres were dispossessed but were given the option of staying on as tenants of the new patentees. Altogether, patents were granted to approximately 120 Irish landowners for 23,000 acres, while about twelve Old English, mainly Sinnotts, received patents amounting to 5,000 acres.[102] Under the fourth and final scheme of plantation, the land of north Wexford was allocated thus:

New English	43,100 acres	50%
Old English	11,100 acres	14%
Irish	30,700 acres	36%
Total	84,900 acres	100%

By March 1618 most of the patentees had taken possession of their estates and Sir Henry Dowcra, vice-treasurer, was writing that the plantation at Wexford 'was now thought fully accomplished'.[103] While those who had received patents may have been satisfied, the occupants who had been dispossessed because they were regarded as unsuitable or had not sufficient land to be made freeholders were far from happy. Petitions were addressed to James, a deputation led by Patrick Doran went to London and almost 200 of the natives went to Dublin to protest.[104] Some of the objections took on a more violent nature when the protestors vented their anger on the property of the new undertakers. The lord deputy reported to the English privy council in 1619 that 'idle people and wood kern ... infested ... the woods of low Leinster, near the plantation of Wexford' and 'some desperate rogues inhabit the fast places of the counties of Wexford, Wicklow and Carlow and have lately made an attempt upon a house in Enniscorthy'.[105] The intimidation of the undertakers and their tenants was widespread as the protestors attempted to undermine the plantation. St John and the Irish privy council reported to the English privy council in 1620 that

Maurice MacEdward Kavanagh, a bastard of that ever rebellious race of the Kavanaghs, with a crew of wicked rogues gathered out of the bordering parts, entered into the plantation, surprised Sir James Carroll and Mr Marwood's houses, murdered their servants, burned their towns, and committed many outrages in these parts, in all likelihood upon a conspiracy among themselves to disturb the settlement of those countries.[106]

A number of the protestors were committed to prison while the more vocal among them were deported to Virginia, possibly as indentured servants.[107] These severe actions had the desired results in that they removed the most troublesome of the agitators and while protests continued sporadically for some years they were badly co-ordinated and ineffective. The new patentees remained in control.

The security of the plantation was improved by the erection of a corporate town in the planted area: Enniscorthy, at the southern end of the planted area was granted a charter in 1613[108] and expanded quickly to become the major centre of commerce for the newly planted area. In January 1618, St John proposed that a new town be built on the escheated lands in order to improve the defence of the undertakers.[109] Similar provision had been made in Ulster for the erection of corporate towns on escheated lands. Accordingly, a charter was granted for the town of Newborough on 10 October 1619 but the town was more commonly referred to as Gorey, taking the name from the townland and barony in which it was located.[110] Sir Lawrence Esmonde was appointed the first sovereign and practically all the burgesses were undertakers who had received land in the plantation.

The north Wexford plantation was one of a series authorised by James after the apparent success of the larger scale Ulster plantation in 1609. These smaller confiscations were all directed at the distinctively Irish areas of Wexford, Leitrim, Longford, Westmeath, King's County and Queen's County. The importance of the Wexford experiment lies in the fact that it was the first of these smaller plantations. The method by which the crown acquired title and the scheme as it finally evolved in Wexford were used in all subsequent Stuart policy The north Wexford plantation was the first to be based on the resurrection of ancient crown title. It demonstrated that the ancient surrender of land by Irish chieftains was regarded by the crown as legally binding and also that the acts of resumption passed by various Irish parliaments constituted adequate legal title to Irish lands. As a direct result of the plantation in north Wexford, there was a dramatic change in the structure, nature and character of land ownership in the planted area of two and a half baronies. The native Irish share of the area dropped from 75 per cent to 36 per cent, the Old English increased their share marginally from 11 per cent to 14 per cent and the New English boosted their share from 14 per cent to 50 per cent of the total.

While the transfer in ownership was the dominant feature, the change in its nature was no less dramatic. The number of people who actually owned lands decreased drastically and the ownership of the land became concentrated in fewer hands. Although there was a dramatic change in ownership, there was little change in occupancy. The native Irish who lived and worked on the land continued in that capacity.

The change in the character of ownership was also quite significant. The New English who owned half the area were few in number, controlled very large holdings and were in the main absentee landlords interested in a quick return on their investments. The position of the Old English owners was practically unchanged, with the owners obtaining new title to most of their estates. The Irish landowners, however, suffered severely as a result of the plantation. Although still retaining 36 per cent of the barony, the Irish were much reduced in number with only about 124 of them receiving patents.

Scarawalsh after the Plantation, 1620-40

The plantation of north Wexford, once the final allocation of the area had been accomplished, was in many respects a disappointment to those who had initiated the scheme. Ownership of a significant portion of the planted area had been transferred out of the hands of the long established native Irish owners and into the hands of the New English proprietors, but not in the manner envisaged by James and his advisers. Less than one half of the original 24 New English undertakers and servitors had taken possession of their estates and of these only a few complied with the conditions of plantation in respect of buildings and tenants.[111] The remaining undertakers or servitors never made any serious attempt to occupy their lands but sold their interests, usually to one of the adjoining New English proprietors who remained.[112] In many cases the lands were let to the natives who were discontented because they had no security of title and in general the Kavanaghs in Wexford remained 'a hardy and unquiet people'.[113]

In this way, between 1620 and 1640, the eleven New English proprietors who retained possession substantially increased the size of their holdings and established themselves as the dominant landowners in north Wexford. Of these eleven New English patentees in the planted area in 1640, five of them owned lands in the barony of Scarawalsh. Three of them, Francis Annesley, Sir Richard Wingfield and Nicholas Loftus received land in county Wexford for the first time under the scheme of plantation, while the remaining two,

Richard Masterson and Henry Wallop, held land in Wexford before 1610 but had also received grants of land confiscated from the Irish at the time of the plantation.

The most successful of the new undertakers was Francis Annesley.[114] By 1620, he had the biggest holding of all the New English in the barony with 6,444 acres in Ballaghkeen, 1,324 acres in Gorey and 2,530 acres in Scarawalsh, giving him a total of 10,308 (C.S.) acres of profitable land.[115] The second of the new undertakers who retained possession of his estate in Scarawalsh was Sir Richard Wingfield.[116] In February 1618 a patent was issued to Wingfield for 1,700 acres in the territory of Kilcheele, the premises being created the manor of Wingfield.[117] Wingfield consolidated his hold on his estates and like Annesley increased his holding until by 1640 his heirs owned 2,350 acres in Gorey and 400 acres in Scarawalsh.[118].

Of all the seven servitors appointed in 1618, only three were in possession of lands in north Wexford in 1640. One of these was Nicholas Loftus with a much reduced acreage, another was the native Irish Henry Murphy with the same acreage that was granted to his father in 1618, while the third patentee, William Plunkett, was the only servitor to actually increase his holdings between 1618 and 1640. From his initial grant of 400 acres, Plunkett, probably from his departing neighbours, increased his holding to 3,600 acres.[119] A clear indication of how he acquired some, at least, of the land is given in the *Civil Survey* which refers to him holding a further 400 acres which were mortgaged by Thomas Masterson.[120]

In general, those undertakers and servitors who remained consolidated their positions at the expense of the Irish and Old English and also of those New English who sold out. All three groups of landowners lived in somewhat uneasy harmony and the situation with regard to landownership was in a constant state of flux as the three groups and various individuals within each group sought to consolidate their positions. In addition to the suspicion and distrust which existed between them, all the landowners, irrespective of grouping, had to cope with the changing economic circumstances. Of the three groups, the New English, with their political influence and financial expertise, were by far the best equipped to cope with the changing situation. Between 1620 and 1640 they continued to consolidate their position as the most powerful and extensive landowners in Scarawalsh and such was their success in coping with the changing economic and political circumstances that they were in an even stronger position in 1640 than they had been twenty years previously.

We have already examined the progress of the new undertakers and servitors above. We turn our attention now to the New English, who were established in the barony before the plantation, to examine in greater detail how they fared under the plantation scheme and how they coped with the changing political and economic situation between 1620 and 1640. The most successful of these was Richard Masterson of Ferns. Masterson was one of Chichester's and St John's principal assistants in the preparation and implementation of the north Wexford plantation and he was well rewarded for his co-operation. In all, he received patents for 12,340 acres in four manors.[121] Masterson did not retain possession of all four manors, Ferns, Clohamon, Cloghlesking and Ballychargene.[122] He himself occupied Ferns manor but he sold the manor of Clohamon, which also included the abbey lands of Downe, to George Calvert, first lord of Baltimore, and settled most of the remainder on various members of the Masterson family.

Henry Wallop was not included in the original list of patentees for the plantation in north Wexford but when the number of patentees was increased under the final scheme of plantation he received, on 12 December 1618, almost 800 acres of the confiscated area immediately adjoining his own estates to the east and south of Enniscorthy.[123] Wallop had a marked impact on the life of Enniscorthy town and the surrounding district. In all he brought between thirty and forty English families to Enniscorthy and most remained settled there until forced to move by the war in 1641.[124] Despite his protestations that he was intent on civilising the natives, Wallop's motives for the plantation in Enniscorthy were clearly economic. His main aim was to exploit the vast oak forest of the Slaney valley.

Because he resided in England, Wallop administered his Irish estates through an agent. Roger Mainwaring of Nantwich in Cheshire was appointed constable of Enniscorthy Castle and steward of Wallop's property in Enniscorthy in 1612 and held this position until his death in 1637. Wallop himself died in 1642 and was succeeded by his only son Robert (1601-67), who also succeeded to his father's Enniscorthy properties, which at that time included 3,690 acres in Scarawalsh and 1,492 acres in the town and liberties of Enniscorthy.[125]

The third New English landowner who was established in Scarawalsh before the plantation was Sir Thomas Colclough of Tintern. All of Colclough's lands at that time were situated in western Scarawalsh, an area that was not affected by the plantation. Colclough was not resident in the barony at the time, being based at Tintern, but there was a great deal of acrimony between Colclough and Masterson, who had replaced him as constable of Ferns Castle. Wallop wrote about the 'dissention between Mr Masterson, seneschal there and Mr Colclough, an English man, the best of that country'.[126] Given the prominent part played by Masterson in the allocation of the lands under the scheme of plantation, it is hardly surprising that Colclough was not a beneficiary. He concentrated his energies instead on acquiring lands directly by purchase from the Irish, which he did with considerable success.

The Scarawalsh lands were conveyed to Dudley Colclough in 1628 when he was fifteen years of age. Dudley went to live in Monart which was situated on his lands in the Duffry area of Scarawalsh and married firstly Katherine, daughter of Patrick Esmonde of the house of Johnstown in north Wexford and secondly Mary, daughter of Sir Patrick Barnewall of Brickstown. Because of his marriage to Katherine, one of the three co-heirs of Patrick Esmonde, Colclough acquired further lands in northern Scarawalsh including the townlands of Ballyshonock, Ballynastragh and Garryhasten in the parish of Moyacomb.[127] Dudley Colclough inherited substantial properties from his father in 1624. He astutely added to these properties by purchase and mortgage foreclosure from the Irish and increased it further by marriage alliances until in 1640 he possessed the biggest landholding in the barony, with 11,885 acres to his credit.[128]

The relative peace of the early seventeenth century following the disturbances and wars of the sixteenth century helped to create a favourable climate for economic development. However, the Irish money system was in a state of chaos and it was difficult to develop the economy because of the conflict of interest between Ireland and England in many aspects of trade. Many landowners found themselves in severe financial difficulties.

The Irish were the landowners most at risk between 1600 and 1640. Official crown policy aimed at a huge reduction in their numbers. That a large number of Irish landowners lost possession of their estates is beyond doubt. The decline in their numbers can be calculated with a fair degree of accuracy for the area encompassed in this study. At the time of the plantation, approximately 124 Irish received patents to lands in the two baronies of Gorey and Ballaghkeen and the half barony of Scarawalsh. By 1640 the number of Irish people owning land was only one third of what it had been a mere twenty years earlier. Much of this land was sold or mortgaged to the New English. In the western portion of the barony of Scarawalsh, Henry Wallop and Thomas Colclough bought up quite an amount of Irish land. Colclough, in particular, acquired a great deal of land from the Irish and from a grant of 1,000 acres received from the crown in 1604, he built up his holding mainly by purchase but also by mortgage foreclosure, until in 1640 his son owned 11,885 acres in the barony of Scarawalsh.[129] The evidence is that a very large number of Irish landowners lost possession of their estates by mortgage foreclosure.[130]

Who acquired the land from the Irish? Most of the commercial transactions in the barony of Scarawalsh involving purchase from the Irish or the granting of mortgages to them were carried on by four people, Thomas Colclough, Samuel Mullineux of Newlands, county Dublin,[131] William Turner 'an apothecary in Dublin'[132] and Edmund Hire, a merchant from Wexford.[133] Between 1620 and 1640, the amount of land owned by the Irish was gradually being reduced. By 1640, the actual share occupied by the Irish declined from the 36 per cent of 1620 to approximately 27 per cent in 1640. At the same time there was a substantial decline in the number of landowners as the smaller and weaker men were forced out. The available lands became concentrated in the hands of a lesser number of owners. In 1608, it was recorded that there were twenty five principal Irish landowners in Scarawalsh, as well as a number of lesser landowners. By 1640, there were only seventeen Irish landowners altogether in Scarawalsh.[134]

The Irish were not the only landowners who found themselves unable to cope with the changing economic conditions. Many of the Old English landowners also experienced difficulties and were obliged by economic circumstances to take out mortgages on their properties. Among these were many of the leading Old English families in county Wexford during the early seventeenth century. However, there appears to have been one very important difference between the Irish and Old English mortgagors. Where the Irish mortgaged their lands to merchants and speculators from the towns, the Old English in county Wexford who required mortgages obtained them from other Old English families in county Wexford and in almost all cases redeemed the mortgages and retained possession of their lands. Walter Sinnott, the chief Old English beneficiary under the north Wexford scheme of plantation, fared very badly between 1620 and 1640 and in fact lost possession of the entire 3,900 acres granted to him in 1618. The loss of Sinnott's lands can be attributed primarily, if not solely, to his fondness for drink and even now, three and a half centuries later, it is obvious that he was a chronic alcoholic. He travelled 'from place to place up and down the country drinking wherever he went and spending all he could get'.[135] In 1618 under the scheme of plantation, the Old English had received patents to approximately 14 per cent of the lands of the planted area. By 1640, because of inability to cope with the political and economic pressures, the size of the Old English holding in the area had been reduced until it accounted for only about 6 per cent of the total area. In Scarawalsh, the biggest holdings belonged to Edmond Butler of the manor of Kayer in the barony of Bantry. An inquisition taken in 1617 showed 'the town and lands of Glanderick, Monglass, Kiltrea, half of Caim, and the woods of Aughrim are in the possession of Edward Butler and his heirs'. In 1640, Butler was still in possession of most of these lands extending in all to 1,470 acres but part of them had been lost to Dudley Colclough.[136] The next largest Old English holdings were those of Edward and David Sinnott who occupied 1,710 acres, which showed a big reduction from the 9,000 acres granted mainly to the Sinnotts in 1618.[137] In terms of loss of prestige and power, the Old English suffered more than the Irish between 1620 and 1640.

While the weaker and occasionally the larger landowners were losing possession, a number of the Irish were succeeding in the battle to survive. By far the most important of these were the more able members of the once omnipotent Kavanagh family. Of these Dónal Spáinneach was the most influential and in 1621 he received a patent granting him full title to most of his lands in Wexford and Carlow by free and common socage. The premises were created the manor of Clonmullen with 500 acres in demesne.[138] Most of these lands were situated in the Duffry area of Scarawalsh. Also included in the patent were grants to a number of lesser Kavanaghs, mainly members of the O'Murrow sept. The patent also confirmed their lands in Coolnaleen, Tullabeg and Ballymunny to a member of the O'Doran family, hereditary poets to the Kavanaghs, to hold in free and common socage. This development was rather surprising as the bards at that time usually got short shrift in the distribution of land. Four other members of the Kavanagh family surmounted the obstacles posed by the changing economic and political situation and were still in occupation of their estates in 1640. These were Brian Kavanagh with 1,800 acres, Morish Kavanagh with 890 acres, Derby Kavanagh with 550 acres and Daniel Kavanagh with 230 acres.[139] After the Kavanaghs, the second largest Irish landowners in the barony of Scarawalsh were the O'Briens. The O'Briens were more numerous than the Kavanaghs and the Down Survey lists seven O'Briens as owning 7,021 acres.[140]

Among the more important landowners recorded in the Civil and Down Surveys is Lord Baltimore (George Calvert) but, despite the large acreage credited to him in 1641, his connection with north Wexford was slight. The significance of his arrival in Wexford lies in the fact that it was due to his religious beliefs. Excluded from the English privy council because he refused to take the oath of supremacy, Baltimore settled briefly in Wexford prior to establishing a colony in America. Calvert purchased the manor lands of Clohamon and Abbey of Downe lands from Richard Masterson for a sum of £1,600.[141] Nominally, the manor lands of Clohamon and the Abbey lands of Downe contained 2,000 acres but correlation with the ordnance survey shows it to contain almost 7,000 statute acres.[142] George Calvert was succeeded by his son Cecil who became the second Lord Baltimore and took possession of his father's lands. Cecil is listed as the owner of Clohamon and Downe in both the Civil and Down Surveys and appears in both as a protestant. Calvert appears to have leased the land back to the Mastersons as Oliver Masterson was in possession of Clohamon in 1641 and Edward Masterson occupied Ballycarney.

In order to conclude the survey of ownership in the barony of Scarawalsh in 1640, it is necessary to refer briefly to the holdings of the established church. During the second half of the sixteenth century, the value of the see had decreased greatly. Most of the lands were passed away in fee at very low rents until in 1615 the Regal Visitation found that the value of the see had been reduced from £400-£500 per annum to £66.6.8.[143] Among those who obtained church lands at very low rent for long leases was Henry Wallop. Despite strong opposition from successive bishops Wallop and his heirs managed to hold on to the lands of the bishop of Ferns. In August 1634, just three months before he died, Bishop Ram addressed a petition to the lord deputy and council in which he stated that his two bishoprics of Ferns and Leighlin yielded less rent than the amount at which their first fruits were taxed. He asked that the people who received these grants from his predecessors be summoned by writ to Dublin and forced to bring their deeds with them. In particular, Henry Wallop (d.1642) was accused by the bishop of holding sixteen ploughlands in the neighbourhood of Enniscorthy, at the minimal rent of £4 a year.[144] While the parties were ordered to appear in Dublin Castle on 8 August, Wallop appears to have retained possession of the lands as they were still in his possession in 1640. The church lands in 1640 in the immediate vicinity of Ferns comprised approximately 2,000 acres in Lower Ferns, Kilboro, Kilthomas and Bolinaspick.[145]

Having discussed the general patterns that emerged in landownership in Scarawalsh between 1540 and 1640 and having examined the roles played by various individuals in the formation of these patterns, it is necessary to outline briefly the overall situation with regard to landownership *c.* 1640. This is a relatively easy undertaking, given the scope and nature of the surviving sources. Figures quoted below are based on the *Down Survey* for catholics and

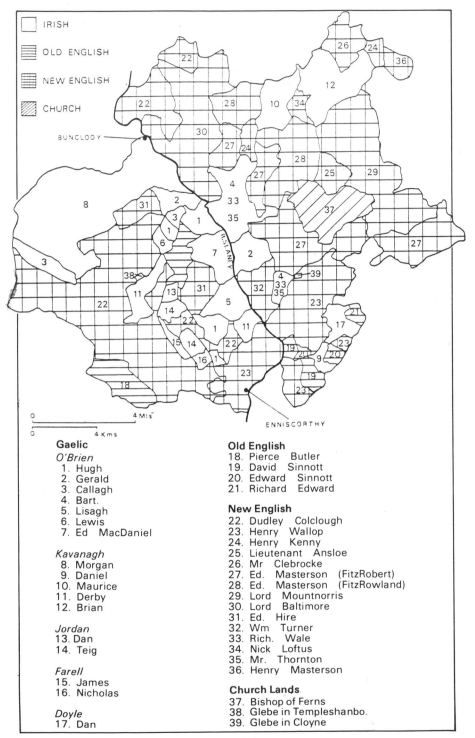

Gaelic

O'Brien
1. Hugh
2. Gerald
3. Callagh
4. Bart.
5. Lisagh
6. Lewis
7. Ed MacDaniel

Kavanagh
8. Morgan
9. Daniel
10. Maurice
11. Derby
12. Brian

Jordan
13. Dan
14. Teig

Farell
15. James
16. Nicholas

Doyle
17. Dan

Old English
18. Pierce Butler
19. David Sinnott
20. Edward Sinnott
21. Richard Edward

New English
22. Dudley Colclough
23. Henry Wallop
24. Henry Kenny
25. Lieutenant Ansloe
26. Mr Clebrocke
27. Ed. Masterson (FitzRobert)
28. Ed. Masterson (FitzRowland)
29. Lord Mountnorris
30. Lord Baltimore
31. Ed. Hire
32. Wm Turner
33. Rich. Wale
34. Nick Loftus
35. Mr. Thornton
36. Henry Masterson

Church Lands
37. Bishop of Ferns
38. Glebe in Templeshanbo.
39. Glebe in Cloyne

Fig. 5.4: Individual proprietors in Scarawalsh c.1640

on the *Civil Survey* for protestants, but the *Civil Survey* has helped in some cases to determine individual catholic owners.[146] In some instances, the Irish system of partible inheritance survived and a number of owners are given as holding land collectively. Based on the sources quoted above, the lands of Scarawalsh were occupied in 1640 as follows:[147]

Table 1

		Name	Acreage
Irish	7	O'Briens	7,021
	4	Kavanaghs	6,997
	3	Jordans	511
	2	Farrells	160
	1	Doyle	602
	17		15,291
Old English	2	Sinnotts	1,710
	1	Butler	1,470
	1	Edward	126
	4		3,306
New English		Dudley Colclough	11,885[148]
		Ed. Masterson (Fitzrobert)	5,099
		Ed. Masterson (Fitzrowland)	3,444
		Ed. Hire	1,014[149]
		Wm. Turner	800
		Henry Wallop	5,082
		Lord Mountnorris	2,530
		Lord Baltimore	2,000
		Brian Kavanagh	1,900
		Henry Kenny	1,660
		Mr Clebrocke	800[150]
		Mr Thornton	666
		Richard Wale	667
		Lieut. Ansloe	500
		Ed. Wingfield	400
		Henry Masterson	120
		Nicholas Loftus	100
	17		38,567
Church lands		Bishop of Ferns	1,900
		Glebe in Templeshanbo	24
		Glebe in Cloyne	22
			1,946

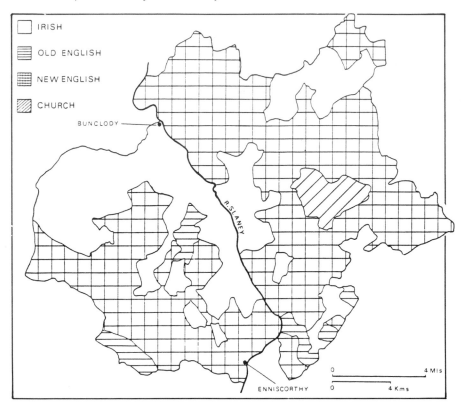

IRISH

OLD ENGLISH

NEW ENGLISH

CHURCH

BUNCLODY

R. SLANEY

ENNISCORTHY

4 Mls

4 Kms

Fig. 5.5: Distribution of lands by ethnic group in Scarawalsh, c.1640

Distribution of land of Scarawalsh *c.* 1640

Irish	17	15,291	25.9%
Old English	4	3,306	5.6%
New English	17	38,567	65.2%
Church		1,946	3.3%
Total	38	59,110	100%

The extent to which the old order of landownership had changed in the century between 1540 and 1640 was quite remarkable. The long established Irish and Old English owners who between them held all the lands of Scarawalsh in 1540, owned only one third of the area between them in 1640. In the intervening one hundred years, the New English had succeeded, by various means, in acquiring two thirds of the entire lands of Scarawalsh. With the passing of the old order, much of the old way of life disappeared and the Irish literature of the age resonates with bardic indignation for the destruction of the society that sustained them.

There was a dramatic change too in the number of landowners. Hundreds of minor Irish landowners lost possession of their lands by sale or forfeiture, particularly during the first two decades of the seventeenth century. By 1640, there were only thirty eight landowners altogether in Scarawalsh, the largest barony in Wexford, comprising almost one fifth of the total lands in the county. Only seventeen of these landowners (less than half the total) were Irish. Those Irish landowners who survived did so by adapting to the new economic situation and in particular by acquiring a title good in English law.

6 *Nicholas Furlong*

Life in Wexford port 1600-1800

'King of loughs in this lough of the south,
Loch Garman of the famous poets,
Wide and winding haven of the ships,
Gathering place of the buoyant boats'.[1]

Wexford port had significance and a brazen personality out of all proportion to its physical size imposed on it from the earliest times. Wexford's geographical situation rendered it the capital and port of a small but vibrant province. County Wexford was isolated from the rest of Leinster and Ireland before the arrival of the great mould breaker, the railway. There were only three comfortable land exits and entries, through mountain terrain, the Scullogue Gap, the Slaney valley at Bunclody and the Arklow Gap. Sea travel up to the time of the railways was easier, cheaper, economically rewarding and practised as a fine art by thousands of sailing families, inheriting centuries of tradition on river, harbour, coast and ocean. Moreover, Wexford soils grew malting barley, an export crop which for quality and profit to grower and processor was without equal in Europe. Wexford was the nearest safe harbour in Ireland to England, Wales and mainland Europe, for vessels of medium bulk. It was these factors which put a specific imprint on Wexford and at the same time bestowed a cosmopolitan outlook upon its men, women and children. Unlike inland communities, they were accustomed daily to sailors, foreign vessels, passengers, cargoes, the gossip and lore of cities and civilisations from Pembroke, Bristol, Rotterdam, Dunkirk, Bordeaux, Cadiz and points west across the Mediterranean as far as Constantinople and up through the Black Sea to Galatz on the Danube. The names of streets, squares and sights in those foreign ports were household words in the Faythe. It is not coincidence that the south part of the Bullring under the old Tholsel where the fish stalls were congregated was known down to recent times as *'The Piazz'* (pronounced 'Pee-Adz')

150

That culture then bestowed a cosmopolitan outlook on Wexford's natives, an understanding and an appreciation of cultures across the seas brought close to them by constant contact. The atmosphere of Wexford from 1600 to 1800 would be recognisable to today's old salts. There were taverns and merchant houses, shops, fights, murderous skippers and 'hard chaws' and, in a maritime economy, sailors' wives on the look-out for the house money. There were the drinking bouts and rows between deep water and shallow water sailors; there was rivalry between the sailors' enclaves around the Faythe and Maudlintown and the land employed families of the John Street area. These divisions lasted to our own time when an invisible but powerful boundary in Rowe Street divided south from north, Volunteer from Harrier, Gaelic quarter from Viking sector. There was another common denominator. The overwhelming bulk of the population refused to conform to Protestantism and remained loyal to the old religion. This factor, along with the international political significance that that choice signalled to London, added a major dimension to the character of the town.

The reign of Elizabeth consolidated English settlement in Ireland, along with a vigorous persecution of those actively professing the Roman Catholic faith. Of its nature as a much used port, Wexford became embroiled to the hilt in the Counter-Reformation. The priests of the Counter-Reformation made their earliest appearances in places like Wexford, for the first contacts of Ireland with the religious renewal in Catholic Europe must have arisen to a great extent from chance business and social relationships. In Wexford, whose people had the sea in their blood, the foreigner was no stranger to the quays. Once the movement had begun, it grew like a snowball. A family sent a boy abroad; some years later the young man came back as a priest but a different type of priest.[2] The Elizabethan executions in Wexford made Catholicism and treason synonymous. Matthew Lambert was executed for hiding in his mill two priests and Viscount Baltinglass (who had openly declared for the old religion). Sailors including Robert Meyler, Patrick Kavanagh and Edward Cheevers were executed for carrying priests to the continent as was Patrick Hay, merchant. Two Wexford students, Peter Meyler from Spain and Christopher Roche from Louvain, captured on the way home, refused to take the Oath of Supremacy; Meyler was executed in Galway, Roche died in London after torture.

At the start of the new century, King James VI of Scotland succeeded to Elizabeth's throne as James I of England. Both his father and mother were Catholics and James was baptised and confirmed a Catholic. The immediate reaction in Wexford was to restore to the old religion the churches administered by the Established Church.

On the accession of King James I, the citizenry thought it appropriate that any taint of irregularity should be exorcised from their temples and so a Jesuit priest, Fr Coppinger, was appointed to the town. The Church of St Patrick was also retained by the Catholics for some years. It was made clear that the Government would not tolerate this. To general astonishment, the pressure under James was more sustained and pernicious than under Elizabeth; James' persecution also intended to cripple professing Catholics in their property. The political content of the repression can be accepted easily. At the turn of the century, and for long after, the principal continental enemy of England was Catholic Spain. There had been underground contacts and active exchanges between Spain and Wexford port. '... at Wexford one Father Archer and divers other Jesuites and Seminaries are lately landed [out of Spain] who are commonly the forerunners to such attempts [to aid the Spanish] *by preparing the peoples minds fitt to receave them, as these will soone be most apt in regard they are farr gone in popery and superstition, and most devilishly bent to doe mischief.*[3]

Despite the political turmoil and religious strife, Wexford contrived its survival commercially, politically and ecclesiastically by the facility of running, or appearing to run, with the hare while still hunting with the hounds. On 25 April 1603, the Lord Deputy Mountjoy acquainted Cecil that 'Wexford in Leinster has with some insolence set up the public exercise of the Mass' and that he has written 'commanding them on their allegiance to desist'. The Lord Deputy writes to him again on the 26th, so important did he consider this matter of the public performance of the Mass and encloses a copy of a letter received from the Sovereign of the town of Wexford. According to Fynes Moryson, the Lord Deputy wrote on 26 April, 1603, to the Sovereign of Wexford, that 'whereas they excused their erecting of popish rites by the report they heard of his Majesty's being a Roman Catholic, he could not but marvel at their simplicity, to be seduced by lying Priests to such an opinion, since it was apparent to the world H.M. professed the true religion of the Gospel, and ever with careful sincerity maintained it in his Kingdom of Scotland, charging him and those of Wexford upon their allegiance, to desist from the disordered course they had taken in celebrating publicly the idolatrous Mass; lest he, at his coming up into those parts should have cause severely to punish their contempt shewn to his Majesty, and the laws of his kingdom'. This admonition produced the following letter from Francis Bryan, sovereign of Wexford, on 23 April, 1603.

Supposes, that he [the Lord Deputy] has been informed by the Lord Bishop of this Diocese that he [the Mayor], with the Masters and Commons of this town, entered into all the Churches of this town, especially into St Marys, taking thither armed men, dispossessing the Ministers, not naming the Bishop but an ordinary man, and having Mass said in the Churches openly; 'whereupon your Lordship and others of H.M.'s Privy Council directed warrant and commandment to me for redress of the premises. For answer whereof it may please your Lordship to be advertised that long before the decease of our late Sovereign Queen Elizabeth, and since, Mass was daily and openly said in certain houses, whereunto all the Inhabitants of this town (very few excepted) did resort; which of long time, as also the priests themselves and the places of their abode, have been well known to the Lord Bishop of this Diocese, who never accused any Priest dwelling here of any traitorous crime, of which I never knew any of them guilty. And after the joyful proclamation that was made here of the most mighty and undoubted

King James, that now is, whose Majesty, by common judgement of all here (few excepted) is thought to be Catholic, and by reason of the great multitude of people which resorted into these houses wherein formerly Mass was said, and had not sufficient room, We [the Mayor and Commons] without armour, or any opprobrious words used towards the said Lord Bishop, or any others, entered with a Priest unto the Churches, and in one Church named St Patricks, which was ruinous, (the rest continuing as before), Mass is said, which the People think will be graciously accepted of his most Royal Majesty, and will in no way be hurtful to His Highness or to the State or good government of this his Realme, without either meddling with tithes or any livings of the Church by any Catholic priest, or other man whatsoever.

Assures his Lordship of the most firm obedience and loyalty of this poor Corporation to H.M. and hopes for his lordship's favourable construction of the premises and gracious dealing towards this poor Corporation'.[4]

A dilemma of the first years of the century received exceptional notoriety with the return and subsequent missionary work of a young Wexford towns-man. His name was William Furlong. Furlong's wealthy parents, Patrick Furlong and Margaret Stafford, had conformed to the Church by state established. William was sent to Oxford University, where he studied law and subsequently converted to Catholicism. William Furlong then left for Spain where he entered the Cistercians. He came back to the port of Wexford in 1609, where he worked feverishly. Despite restrictions, the numbers of Wexford people he persuaded to return to the old religion were notable and it included his father and mother. There was no resisting the gentle and per-sisting reformer. At the time of his death, he was venerated in Wexford town as a saint; his burial place in St Patrick's churchyard became a place of pilgri-mage. All these issues excited fireside, forge, dockside and tavern debates over the first half of the seventeenth century amongst a Wexford populace that for its day was exceptionally well informed on European affairs. The question remains of the early sixteen hundreds; who then if not the locals frequented the Established church services? The conclusion is inescapable that it was natives and Government officials of the English nation. Be that as it may, there were other matters to claim public attention. King James bestowed a royal charter outlining many rights and privileges on Wexford town in 1609. In 1612, the port's great comfort, herrings, were so abundant off the coast of Wexford and the fishery so profitable that many boats were attracted from Devonshire and Cornwall.[5]

The busy marine scene attracted the usual predatory attention of pirates, especially in the first two decades of the seventeenth century. The nonchalant acceptance of piracy is little remembered because it was clandestine as was much of Wexford's political manoeuvres at the same time. In 1613, the King and Council wrote to the Deputy Chichester complaining of continual appli-cations by merchant strangers for restitution of their property taken by pirates. Occasionally, pirated goods were redirected with the connivance of the port's authorities, which provoked considerable hostile publicity.[6] Other sensations smote the body politic at the same time.

Richard Wadding was elected Member of Parliament for the town of Wexford but was not returned. Described as 'a known, malicious papist', he was also deprived of the mayoralty of Wexford for refusing to take the Oath of Supremacy. A member of the delegation from Irish Catholics to King James, he was flung into jail with his colleagues by that monarch after the delegation made its plea. Like many other of the Wexford town merchants, he belonged to a long established landed family of Norman origin in south Wexford, the Waddings of Ballycogley.[7]

Public amusement was given a fillip in 1621 when a charter of freedom was conferred upon the guild of butchers. Itemising self protection, market rights and a closed shop clause, the mayor and corporation received in return a privilege: 'Ane wee the foresaid John Busher etc. Bouchers, for our selves and our successors for ever covenath, condicioneth and agreeth and by theis presents undertaketh that two tymes ever yeare they will upon their owne costes and chardgs have a bull bayting at the Common Playne of Wexford yerly for ever, viz., at Bartlemas Day and Hallantyde, [i.e. August 24th and November 21st] and the hids of them to bee given unto the Maior for the tyme being for ever as aforesaid'.[8] Thus, the bloody spectator sport of bull baiting, imported from Spain, was introduced to the Wexford crowds and the arena where it took place was given the name which is almost part of the life blood of Wexford natives, the Bull Ring. A specially selected bull was firmly tied by the neck or head to a stake or large boulder in the Bull Ring and every savage, hunting, ratting or worrying dog available was let loose on the beast until, after several hours, it was harrassed and worried to death. The practice, it was believed, rendered the flesh more tender. This spectacle was carried out for almost 170 years.

In the ecclesiastical culture of inner Wexford, there was another constant throughout the ages and that was the presence of one of the most powerful spiritual influences in Christendom, the mendicant Friars Minor of St Francis. Of unambiguous Counter-Reformation ambience, they had comprehensive contacts and were well informed at the highest level in the Papal and Catholic courts of Europe. There is no doubt whatever that those contacts were known in London and to English officialdom in Wexford. The personnel of the friary were all Wexford natives and, as the names suggest, of the county's important 'old foreigner' families. There was a further intimate connection at the highest possible level in the order to mainland Europe through Fr Luke Wadding, OFM, historian, theologian, confidante of King Philip III of Spain. Here was a man who declined the red hat, arguing that he could serve his country more effectively in a position less prominent than that of cardinal; a man who received votes in the conclaves to elect a Pope in 1644-5, a man of scholarship and international diplomatic finesse, founder of St Isidores Irish college in Rome and official representative of the Irish Roman Catholic hierarchy in the Roman curia. Wadding was a kinsman of the Rossiters of Rathmacknee castle outside Wexford town.[9] The Wexford Franciscans and their charitable ministrations were regarded with affection by the people. Yet, the friars were eyed by the authorities with unambiguous hostility and, justifiable suspicion. Fr Richard Sinnott was elected guardian for two separate periods prior to 1642. Sinnott was a friend and fellow student in Portugal of Fr Luke Wadding. He had been a professor of theology in Kilkenny (1620-4) a senior definitor of the Irish province (1624) and was guardian of St Isidores in Rome (1633-4). In 1642, he was sent to Enniscorthy to re-establish the community there and repair the church. The quality of the personnel in Wexford friary (which is testimony both to the importance of Wexford town itself and to the friary's remarkable but unobtrusive European and Roman contacts) is further emphasised by the appointment in 1648 of Fr Paul Sinnott as guardian of Wexford friary at the time of the Confederation of Kilkenny. Sinnott had been in the papal diplomatic service and was Pope Urban VIII's special legate to the Ottoman Turks. Wexford, the port of the Confederation, was given that calibre of churchman. From 1634 to 1649, a Franciscan, Peter Stafford, was parish priest of Wexford as well. There were twelve friars of outstanding experience and academic merit in the community in 1649. Documents discovered in Wexford friary in March, 1983, bear further testimony to the firmest possible links between the Franciscans and the Spanish throne between 1608 and 1671.[10]

The Franciscans were enabled in 1622 to rebuild, occupy and minister from their church outside the Keyser Gate, a fact attributable not just to a relaxation in the penal laws but to the cunning legal subterfuges of the Wexford merchant family of Turner. After the Dissolution, the Franciscan property came into the hands of Paul Turner. Turner allowed the friars back in the reign of the Catholic Queen Mary (1553). Elizabeth I dashed their hopes (1558) but by 1562 Turner was in control of the property again. 'By a clever legal device, however, the friars allowed all their property to be vested in the hands of Paul's son, Nicholas'. He in fact acted then as syndic (lay agent or manager of the property) for the friars. In turn, Nicholas's son, Edward, succeeded his father as nominal tenant. Technically, the Turners were the tenants of the property, but the friars continued their fifth century of service to Wexford town, albeit from outside the walls. This was an amicable Wexford solution to a Wexford problem.[11]

An urgent letter from the Lord Deputy Falkland on 23 June, 1626, recorded the assembly of a Spanish expeditionary force, an assembly known to Patrick Turner, mayor of Wexford.[12] It can be seen with hindsight that Wexford was well situated to live dangerously. One experience must have impressed itself on thousands of Wexford's sea faring men — the public celebration of Catholic church rituals and norms in every port from the Spanish Netherlands to Cadiz when contrasted with the penalised observances in their home port. The women of the Faythe, Selskar, The Piazz, Paul Quay, the Stone Bridge or the Bullring were hardly likely to conceal that contrast under their oxters.

A flavour of the social life in Wexford town in 1635 is conveyed by William Brereton's report on his entertainments by the mayor, Mark Cheevers. Cheevers was eminent in public life and held lands at Growtown, Taghmon. He was Chief Justice of Leinster in 1643, president of the Wexford council of Confederate Catholics in 1642 and was married to Joan Itchingham who is thus presented by Brereton:

'... the Mayor, a well bred gentleman, an Inns of Court man, who is counsellor, a gentleman that hath an estate in the country and was Knight of this Shire for last Parliament invited me to dinner as also to supper with the judges. He is an Irishman, and his wife Irish in a strange habit, a threadbare short coat with sleeves, made like my green coat of stuff, reaching to her middle. She knew not how to carve, look, entertain or demean herself. Here was a kind of beer (which I durst not taste) called charter beer, mighty thick, muddy stuff; the meat nothing cooked or ordered'.[13]

Wexford's self esteem was further emphasised in the appointment of Catholic bishops of remarkable stature. Until 1626, the diocese was ruled by Daniel O'Druhan, a skilled counter-Reformation priest, a graduate of Salamanca in Spain. His successor was a Ross man, John Roche. He was a graduate and later Rector of Douai. Of his own volition, he chose to return to Wexford rather than become the first Irish Cardinal, which was a distinct possibility. He signed his letters 'J. R. Turner', the initials signifying himself while the use of the Turner surname indicates that the mercantile family were sheltering him, as they had sheltered the Franciscans.[14] The Turners were symptomatic of a growing clutch of wealthy, well-connected Catholic merchants in the town. He was succeeded by Nicholas French, parish priest of Wexford, a native of Ballytory castle whose mother was Catherine Rossiter of Rathmacknee castle, one of the great powerhouses of seventeenth century Wexford Catholic culture. He was consecrated in the middle year of the Great Rebellion, November 1645.[15]

The Great Rebellion

'*God bless the King of Spain,*
For but for him we should all be slain'
(A Great Rebellion song popular in Wexford Town.)[16]

The Great Rebellion in Wexford port with its destruction after eight years of free rein is the stuff of Wagnerian drama, almost to the sordid end. The rebellion gave Wexford's vast majority a taste of freedom to which they were not accustomed for well over a century. It lasted but eight years and culminated in annihilation. The Great Rebellion began effectively on 3 October 1641 with a 'monster' meeting at Ferrycarrig hill of the principal gentry and burgesses to consider the state of affairs, the stagnation of trade and the distress and poverty so prevalent in the whole county.[17]

The rebellion achieved form and effect just before Christmas 1641. Wexford port was declared in rebellion on 21 December and out of its own resources mustered 800 men in arms with Colonel Nicholas Stafford of Ballymacane being Governor. The town's determination can be estimated against the 1,500 men mustered for the rest of the county at the same time.

Apart from the Spanish-English antagonism festering for over half a century and the Counter-Reformation missionary zeal in Wexford, there was a further economic depression in a town so dependent on the harvest of the sea. The succulent Wexford herrings had forsaken the coast and instead of the customary full and plenty 'the town was much impoverished and decayed. Their quays go to ruin and are in no good repair; there belonged sometimes unto every great merchants house seated on the shore either a quay or a part interest in a quay or a private way to the quay. Their haven was then furnished with 5,000 sail of ships and small vessels for fishing and is now naked'.[18] The fuel for rebellion was plentiful and everywhere. At the outset, it is doubtful if ever a revolt was so universally supported in county Wexford or Ireland. The supreme council of the Confederate Catholics, as the broad union of Irish racial groups, factions, political and regional groups was called, was seated at Kilkenny. Wexford became the major port of that Confederation, the port through which gold, arms, provisions and armour passed from mainland Europe. In the early days of 1642, a frigate laden with ammunition arrived in Wexford from Dunkirk sent by Owen Roe O'Neill, the great Ulster chief of men.

Let us now look at the streets of Wexford to measure its effect on a citizenry who could now do as they wished, free of colonial administration and threat. That there was shrill triumphalism, celebration, revenge, cruelty and a thorough overthrow of the previous English administration, religious and civil, cannot be denied. Parades, cheers, songs and throngs exhausted themselves, while the women of Wexford had an insatiable appetite for jeering abuse which helped settle old scores with those they had been compelled to acknowledge as their betters, reluctantly. The following depositions give a view of events seen from the English aspect.[19] 'In the early summer of this year, the rebels made a declaration in the town that they would not suffer English man, woman or child, beast or dog of English breed, or anything that was English to remain alive, and before the faces of several Protestants burned all the Bibles they could meet with, saying (in disgrace and contempt of religion) "What will you do now, your bibles are burnt?" and all the women were most mischievous, violent, and cruel in expressing all hatred and practising all cruelties, as robbing and stripping naked men and women of the distressed English, and the very children of the Irish were as forward to their power as the men and women were'. Another (F.2 11, 43) adds 'The Irish women of the rebells doe deport and demean themselves more wickedly and violently farr than the male rebels in theire actions and the young impes that can but throw a stone are forward to act and express their malicious and rebellious affections'. William Whalley. (F.2, 11, 48). 'About this time the colours of the King of Spain were hung out of the windows of the town, carried up and down the streets and into the Market Stalls [Corn Market] with a piper playing before them, the common people shouting 'God bless the King of Spain, For but for him we would all be slain', and finally placed upon the Castle.' Several prizes were brought into harbour — Captain Doran being the chief Naval Officer — and it was seriously proposed to send out the English Protestants in two boats and sink them in the sea. It was at this time too that the head of Captain Ashton, killed at the attack on Redmond's Hall, 20 July, was brought to Wexford and after being kicked up and down the streets was hung upon the wall.

Catholic church rubrics were restored with great fuss and pomp but those restorations paled when compared with the exuberant entry into Wexford of the representative of the Pope, Cardinal Rinuccini. He entered the town of Wexford on the evening of Holy Saturday 1642, receiving a tumultuous welcome. Cannons saluted from the walls and from ships in the harbour. Bands played, military guards of honour were drawn up. The corporation of Wexford formally received him. Citizens blazed away with firearms into the sky in salute. A solemn liturgical reception was held in the church dedicated to St Peter, Prince of the Apostles. (St Peter's Square today.) Next day, Easter Sunday, Cardinal Rinuccini himself sang the Easter Mass in Wexford. He remained in the town until the following Wednesday but it is also recorded that he spent some time in Rathmacknee castle with the powerfully connected Rossitters.[20]

We must withdraw from the well recorded daily account of the logistics, maneouvres, naval, military, ecclesiastical and political, of war in Wexford, 1642-9. It is an inviting task for another arena. The early triumphs of the Confederation turned to disaster. The mix of old Irish, old foreigner, royalist and nationalist, did not gell sufficiently to maintain and win a national revolt, despite the overseas effort. Ultimately, Ireland and Wexford collapsed before Cromwell's single minded fanaticism. Wexford's collapse is surprising, for its defenders were well equipped to give a good account of themselves. 'Surely never since the time a shout brought down the walls of Jericho was any town so well provided and so defensible surrendered so easily'.[21] Following the surrender of Wexford castle, (outside the walls then, as its modern successor, the military barracks, is now) the taking of Wexford by storm, street by street, square by square, church by church, was an effusion of havoc. The red maw of war opened and consumed the armed and unarmed alike, men, women and children. Of the 2,000 dead enumerated by the Cromwellians, many were drowned in the panic to get anyway across to Ferrybank. The Franciscan friars were savaged in church and street. There is no doubt that even modest intelligence would have marked them out to Cromwell or any ambitious London administrator as dangerous enemies of England's interests and England's religion. Wexford, having entered the lists so unambiguously and finally taken in siege, could hardly expect anything less than slaughter from troops who were zealots for England's security and fundamental reformed religion.[22] Cromwell reported of the capture of Wexford, 'It hath pleased God to give into our hands this other mercy. For which, as for all, we pray God may have all the glory. Indeed your instruments are poor and weak, and can do nothing but through believing — and that is the gift of God also'.[23] There are several Cromwellian and Wexford estimates of the casualties, all of them guesses.[24]

With the conquest of Cromwell, a deep gash was cut across the abnormal, for open triumph and self government were not the norm. They were abnormal in Wexford. The Wexford that had developed to 1649 in good times and bad, in government, society, religion and commerce, was uprooted, violated, outraged, banished. Comparisons of similar cultural and martial shocks are not easy to come by in history but Wexford's ravishing in 1649 was in microcosm the sack of Byzantium by the Moslems or in more proximate comparison the sack of Norse Waterford by the Norman mercenaries under Strongbow. In Wexford 'a great spoyle and havock was made of many rich commodities, so that now we are inforced to seek further for a Winter retirement, and want that refreshment which else the place might have afforded in the declining of the year'.[25]

A regime of ruthless dispossession and virulent apartheid was introduced by the victors who determined that at long last a 'Solution' was to be carried through. A sample of the new laws for the remaining inhabitants of Wexford town shows the spirit of a regime that was never, ever forgotten or forgiven.[26]

To ye 1st. That no Irish Papist be permitted to live in the Town of Wexford after ye 1st of May next, but such as shall have particular orders to to do from ye General and Commissioners of ye Com. Wealth, or some [one] authorised by them to give Lycenses in that behalfe.

To ye 2nd, 3rd, 4th, 5th, and 6th Proposals. The said Colonel Sadlier and ye Commissioners of Revenue at Wexford, Lieut.-Col. Overstreet, Lieut.-Col. Puckle, Captain Dancer, Captain Tomlins, Mr Withers, Mr Cleburne, and Mr Dobson, or any 5 or more of them, are forthwith to consider how many Sea-men, Boatmen, fishermen, Packers, Gillers, Coopers, Masons, Carpenters, and Labourers of ye Irish Nation there bee in Wexford, Rosse, and other Port townes within ye said Precinct, and to certify ye same to ye said Comrs of ye Com. Wealth, with their names, the number of their families, and how many of each they judge absolutely necessary to bee continued in ye said Town after ye 1st May next, with their Reasons why they judge them so necessary.

To ye 7th. The Irish women, though Papists, ought to continue with their husbands who are English and Protestants in the English Quarters, but that neither they nor their husbands are to bee permitted to live in any Garrison.

To ye 8th. There will bee a Declaration or Generall Instructions or Rules suddenly published and sent into ye severall Precincts touching such Irish who are become Protestants, and resort to hear the Word preacht, to which such Irish of ye Town of Wexford, Rosse, and other Port Townes are referred.

To ye 9th and last. That noe Lycenses bee given to any, either English or Irish, for ye selling of Strong Drink to bee consumed within dores. And that all Lycenses granted contrary to ye late Declarations published in that behalfe bee forthwith revoked. And ye Justices of the Peace within ye said Precinct are to see the same observed accordingly.

Dublin, 13 March, 1653[-4].   Signed by FLEETWOOD, CORBET, AND JONES.

The 'great looting' and robberies began to consolidate in 1650. Any farmer or property owner bearing the designation 'Irish Papist' was dispossessed, transported to Connaught or the Barbados, their soils and hearths bestowed on the Cromwellian soldiery in lieu of wages. Soon the names in Wexford town bore a most unfamiliar ring. Christian Borr became Mayor; Lt Col. Throgmorton, Commander of Wexford Garrison; William Cleburne, Collector of Customs; Sadleir, Sherriff of Wexford, Withers, Quartermaster to the Garrison; Hussey, Kett, Cook, Bodle, Wakefield, Rich, Camby, Andrewes, Stodder, Tomlins, Overstreet, Dowse; names as odd as the Normans and Flemish four and a half centuries previously, with the exception that the Cromwellians were enemies, invaders, looters, while the Normans and Flemish had been hired mercenaries.

Since the furtive do not record their steps we have no way of knowing when exactly Wexford's basic population seeped back into town and county. It is nevertheless clear that the call of Carrigeen, St John's Gate, Cornmarket, Faythe, Boker, Bull Ring and Selskar was as potent then as it is even yet to the exile. As well, workers, tradesmen, hod carriers and sailors were needed. Bit by bit, they returned, aided no doubt by a growing, locally wise *mafia*. Some came, as did a great many land owners, to accept the role of tenants in their own houses and properties. It was not easy. The Cromwellian council at Dublin ordered in February 1656, seven years after the taking of Wexford, that all 'Irish Papists' were to be removed from sea port towns and not to be allowed to inhabit within two miles.[27] The English inhabitants of Wexford apply at the same time to the Commissioners for an enlargement in the leases of their houses.[28] Ten years after Cromwell, his government had four men of Wexford vintage in the town gaol for not transplanting — Devereux, Barron, Murphy and Doyle.[29] The friars were never overlooked. At Easter in 1654, four friars had the misfortune to be captured and identified. All four were taken and hanged in the neighbourhood of the friary chapel.[30]

With the restoration of the Monarchy and the return to London of Charles the Second, we find again entries in records of recognisable old Wexford names. In the roll of attorneys admitted to practice in Wexford precinct, there is listed Walter Walshe, Nicholas Meyler, Maurice Prendergast and William Keating. This achievement at so important a level suggests at least the settled return to home by the less eminent. If they hoped for a return of their property and homes, they were grievously mistaken. Wexford's wits were taxed to maximum fluidity in the several decades following Cromwell. A Wexford wag, Brendan Hearne, was wont to exclaim in times of calamity that 'God never shut one door but that he shut six or seven more to keep it company'. That was never so true as in the case of Wexford port where to one torment several others were added from unexpected and bizarre origins.

The Roman Catholic bishop of Ferns, Nicholas French, was compelled to take flight. He died as assistant bishop of Ghent after twenty-six years of bitter exile. The sturdy house he built in Peter Street in the 1640s still survives, one of the few buildings to have remained in its original form since that violent chapter. His successor was Luke Wadding, of New Ross, (not to be confused with the eminent Rome based Franciscan of the same name, but a kinsman nonetheless). The mother of Bishop French, and the mother of Bishop Wadding were *both* Rossitters of Rathmacknee castle. In 1683, the year of his consecration, Bishop Wadding wrote that there were but twenty one secular priests in the diocese, and but forty Catholics in Wexford town. This presumably means that forty attended Mass in the thatched chapel he built in High Street. He had first declined consecration, writing, 'I am little inclined to it because of the present state of our people, because of the extreme poverty of everyone here, the uncertainty of the times and a hundred other reasons'. A state of misery prevailed. The state of misery bore down heavily on the families of the 'old foreigners', the *Sean Gall*, who had been powers in the land and who bore their contempt for the Cromwellian confiscators down to this very day. I have heard contempt cascade from the lips of Brownes, Roches, Prendergasts, Furlongs, Sinnotts, Codds, Devereuxes, Esmondes, Waddings, Staffords, Lamberts, Rossitters and many others expelled from lands held for over 450 years. Their contempt was lubricated by the snobbery that nobler blood flowed through the veins of the expelled than through the Cromwellians' who were aristocrats 'neither by blood, station, birthright or breeding'.[31]

Solomon Richards wrote in 1682 of Wexford:

'It was in good order and very populous since the last Rebellion, but much depopulated in its taking by Oliver Cromwell. Since that time brought by the English into a flourishing condition, but now about two thirds of it lyes in ruins through the decay of the herring fishing. The greatest number of the inhabitants are Irish but the magistracy are all English or Protestants'.[32]

Into this culture providence tossed a few more phials of violently interacting chemicals. With the connivance of two powerful families, the Plunkets and Colcloughs,[33] the Franciscans succeeded in occupying their old premises and rebuilding their chapel on the ruins of the old, giving us basically the friary church we still retain. This manoeuvre was facilitated by the fact that the friary was outside the walls of the corporate town. This new symbol was accompanied by another. Charles the Second died in 1685 and was succeeded by James II, an avowed Roman Catholic. He devised and bestowed a special charter of rights on Wexford in 1687 and in the same year thoroughly frightened the ascendancy by appointing a Roman Catholic, Richard Talbot, Earl of Tyrconnell, Lord Lieutenant of Ireland.[34] In 1688, revolution erupted in England against James and it succeeded. In Ireland, his battle was continued against the usurper, William, and the Boyne became immortal. In rapid succession, Wexford port was held and lost for James II. William of Orange 'sent 1,000 horse and dragoons to secure the maritime town of that name and head of the shire'. His troops found Wexford abandoned with a good store of provisions and ammunition left behind. So another era of popular confusion was ushered in to accompany political persecution and the impression of even more bitter penal laws against the unreliables. Now, instead of one clearly recognisable king, there were two kings, bringing barely tolerable consequences on an already overburdened population. William and his Queen Mary were *de facto* rulers, and Protestant; James II was Roman Catholic and believed by many the true and anointed monarch. The Roman Catholic church and major European powers recognised James and so Catholics adhering to that position invited (and received) political and religious persecution.[35]

Wexford faced into the new century with a new penal code imposed, although there were few enough of old Wexford stock in residence. Recent research suggests that the population of the port in 1700 was c.1,000.[36]

The first forty years of the eighteenth century are almost mirror images of the first forty years of the seventeenth in Wexford port. The persecutions indicated on the statute books to be against Catholicism were winked at, for the Establishment would have been aghast at a mass conversion of Catholics.

This factor enabled the Wexfordman and woman of 1700 to connive at survival. To an extent there was mutual connivance. Priests and bishops slid in disguise through the port, to and from the seminaries of mainland Europe. They had to be very careful and Wexford sailors even more careful about their passengers. Two friars were betrayed in 1702. One was transported after eight years of gaol to the American plantations, the other vanished without trace. The successor of Luke Wadding in 1691 was yet another kinsman from the remarkable family of Rathmacknee castle, Michael Rossitter, dean of Ferns. His appointment was the first to signal a new lurking peril. He was nominated by the exiled Stuart monarch, James II, ratified by the Holy See and consecrated. He escaped expulsion by registering himself as parish priest of Rathmacknee and was cared for in seclusion amongst his surviving friends in his old home environs.[37] In 1704, he was one of only three Catholic bishops in the whole of Ireland.[38]

As recently as 1722, three friars were identified when they came ashore on Wexford's quays and were promptly exiled. Nevertheless an extraordinary degree of normality in parish life was maintained. Sunday masses, sermons, the teaching of cathechism to children were regulated for in the diocesan statutes of 1722. There were thirty five holy days in the year, the only holidays the people had. Most priests had no house of their own, lodging instead with wealthy parishioners.[39]

The rival Stuart line continued in exile in Rome. Bishop Rossitter's successor in 1709 added fuel to hostility in his appointment. John Verdon, vicar-general of the Archdiocese of Armagh was nominated bishop of Ferns by the 'old pretender', James III, in Rome. The Established church bishops were appointed by the *de facto* monarch in London, the head on earth of the Church of England, Protestant and reformed. Verdon ruled the diocese from Wexford town in an age of constant mortal and physical peril for just twenty years. The friars, numbered about four, carried on their service in Wexford at the worst of times. The guardian who officiated from 1714 to 1719 had actually been for five years a member of the usurped royal court, chaplain to the Stuart king James II in whose presence he had frequently preached. A prudent strategy evolved. The friars could no longer quest openly from door to door for fear of discovery so they used the old practice of questing at parish masses, 'questing at the altar' as it was called. They provided sermons on such occasions at least six times a year and were awaited with excitement in rural parishes where such occasions provided much colour and high drama. People from country parishes where the friars visited and quested still come to the friary in Wexford to make their Easter duty, but they have most likely forgotten the reason why.

Throughout the period, the tension between the London bulwarks of the Williamite succession and the supporters of the Stuart succession reached at times a tempo of terror. The supporters of James III in Wexford and Ireland were the more feared, for they had been conditioned for revolt, any day, any time. Any person with an objecting mien was labelled 'Jacobite' by the Establishment powers firmly entrenched in Wexford.

This factor was so real, of such daily importance in the port of Wexford that the marvel is that it was forgotten. The king in exile in Rome, James III, kept the realm and territories of England in a state of paranoid suspense for an incredible sixty years. He launched three civil wars in England with the unambiguous aim of restoring the House of Stuart. The situation was of active significance in Wexford port particularly until 1786, in other words almost a complete century. The town remained a rigidly controlled Williamite town. Nonetheless the seat of Catholic government was there, however silent. That cannot be without significance. The port still meant contact with the great Catholic powers and colleges. In this climate of delicacy the new bishop was nominated by James III, in 1728, after the death of John Verdon, a choice ratified by the Holy See. He was a Franciscan of the highest calibre and experience, Ambrose O'Callaghan, who had formerly been guardian of St Isidore's College in Rome. Bishop O'Callaghan escaped molestation and in 1737 built a dwellinghouse for himself in the garden of the friary at a cost of £85.00.[40] Internal Catholic church dissent only surfaced with the death of Bishop O'Callaghan in 1744. The Franciscans ably proposed another Franciscan James Nugent, for the See of Ferns to James III in Rome. The secular parish clergy postulated Nicholas Sweetman for bishop. Despite the Franciscan lobby in Rome against him, Nicholas Sweetman was nominated for the diocese of Ferns by James III, ratified and consecrated.[41] He never forgot the vigorous Franciscan opposition to his candidature. A Newbawn man, a graduate of the college of St Iago in Salamanca, Spain, he returned to enter with vigour the home mission, as a fearless outspoken man.[42] He lodged in Back Street, Wexford, over the shop owned by John Murphy, close to the lodgings of his own two Wexford town curates. It was not long until he turned on the Franciscans, demanding his right of residence in the bishop's house built in the friary garden by his predecessor. The Franciscan superior, Fr Walter Paye, replied firmly: 'The house is the property of the Franciscans'.[43] The bitter dispute between Sweetman and the friars simmered for twenty years.[44] One can but speculate on the reactions of clergy, secular and regular, or for that matter the whole citizenry to the dispute.

The 1750 Wexford town gives the imagination less work to do. One can touch the squares, the streets, the buildings, the graveyards, the churches in use. To our oldest citizens who remembered the Tholsel and the first years of this century, the comparison was indeed far easier as many of the first photographs demonstrate[45]: the same unpaved streets, the cobbled shores, the Cornmarket and Back Street as the shopping centre. Church services in the friary could almost be used as a time table for today. There were six Masses on Sundays and Holy days. The church was well equipped in furniture and vestments. On Sunday evenings, there were sung Vespers and every night there were evening prayers. The full ceremonies of Holy Week and Eastertide were carried out to the full, much as they were until the post-Vatican 2 changes in rubrics. The devotion known as the 'Stations of the Cross' were introduced in 1746, a striking innovation. The old Mass house in Mary's Lane was still used as a place of devotion throughout the century. It still survives, along with its distinctive atmosphere.[46]

Entertainment in Wexford prospered with the foundation of the Bethesda Theatre in Corn Market (the premises occupied by Mr Patrick Kelly) in the 1730s. The sharp critical faculties and sophistication of Wexford's audiences were honed when Dublin bound actors and actresses from London performed there before opening in the capital. That unbending critical appraisal has greeted all stage works down to this decade.

The Riots, 1757

The temper of Wexford's men and women could only absorb so much and the Government gave the generality of the work force and merchants little room for permanent tranquility. The general anger in the countryside about farm rents, evictions, penal restrictions and the legacies of confiscation had to overlap onto the market places and wharves of Wexford, expecially since the export of farm produce to Dublin and overseas was so predominant. Yet it is a matter of surprise that the reasons for the ferocious riots in Wexford town in early 1757 were terror of famine and rising prices of all foodstuffs. The riots took place to prevent the export of grain and food because of that terror. Wexford port was ravaged by a chaos not experienced since Cromwell's infestation over a century before. There was no police force, no troops in the barracks and the nearest troop of dragoons was at Ross.

It was with the greatest of difficulty that an alarming situation of civil warfare was calmed. Some idea of the duration of the riots can be gleaned from letters to Dublin on 12 Feb. 1757, following the furious crowds stripping ships of their sails, bursting open granaries and even houses.[47]

Dear Sir,

The mobs of this town have committed such outrages that there's no knowing where it will end. We have all thought proper to send a memorial to the Government and hope you'll be so good as to deliver it and get us a command of soldiers if possible and some orders to the Mayor in regard to them.

James Tottenham, Esq.

Examination of John Royse, Hearth Money Collector of Wexford Sworn and saith that about Monday or Tuesday last, he the Examinant, being on his collection in the town and suburbs of Wexford was insulted by a mob of people of a considerable number and threatened to have his legges cut off, if he attempted taking a Distress from one of them that headed them who was armed with a Curriers knife or piece of a Scythe and this Examinant is therefore afraid to proceed on his duty in collecting His Majesty's Revenue of hearth money in the said town and suburbs.

Signed John Royse

Js. Tottenham, Mayor

An agreement brought about between the merchants, corn dealers and shipping interests restored Wexford's people to a measure of docility or at worst latent hostility.

"Every person who has exported any corn since Jan 25, 1757, or shall export any to Michaelmas next, shall deliver up into a proper storehouse one barrell out of every score so exported at the following prices:

For every barrell of barley 8 shillings
For every barrell of barley, oats 6s. Beans or Peas 10s, Rye 15s.

Which shall be delivered out to the poor only in small quantities at the aforesaid prices by a proper person etc., etc. And we further agree that none of us will presume to ship off any kind of meal, potatoes, wheat or eggs or fowl on any pretence whatever'.[48]

The list of twenty five signatories includes only eight of Cromwellian flavour — Joseph Attwood, Thomas Frankland, Samuel Batt, Richard Bennet, Bostock Jacob, William Scofield, John Emerson and George Hobbs. The other seventeen were predominantly Anglo-Norman origin (John Bryan, Lawrence Sinnott, Nicholas Heron, Patrick Scallan, Luke Corish, Thomas Sinnott, Thomas Codd, John Codd, Joseph Barry, James Heron, Richard Codd, David Lacey) with only a few (John MacCarthy, Pat Carty, Matthew Hughes) of possible Gaelic origin. This breakdown gives us a good indication of the overwhelming continuity in mercantile life in Wexford of the old Norman-descent families, even in the late eighteenth century.

In 1764, an intimate glimpse of the streets of Wexford was afforded by Amyas Griffith who sent a chatty piece to the *Dublin Magazine*.[49] Griffith imparts vital information especially in the elusive area of population which can be guessed at from house numbers. Allowing an average of 5 per house, the indications are of a significant increase in population and that, one would assume, is of the older established town families.

'It [Wexford town] before Cromwell's time was well enclosed, part of the walls are yet standing, with four gates, one at each quarter of the town. The Main Street from the West-gate to the Barrack-gate is about three-quarters of a mile in length. Outside of the West-gate is a fine Spa, reckoned by skilful physicians an infallible cure for many disorders,   *   *   *   among others the scurvy, gout, and decay. It creates an appetite and certainly dispels melancholy, &c. Beyond the South [or Barrack] gate stands the barrack, a large, low building forming a little square. I have heard it can contain 4 Companies completely. From this barrack runs a very broad street upwards of a mile in length named the Fierth, commonly styled Faith. The cabbins which compose this suburb or outlet are very snug and commodious, and the dwellers are a set of the most industrious people on the earth. Their employments are mostly weaving nets or spinning hemp.

'To return to the town. In the midst or heart of the Main Street is the bull-ring, where the Court-house, with an excellent clock, &c., stands.   *   *   *   About 50 yards from the Court-house, southwards, is the new Church, which, (when finished) in miniature will come nigh in beautiful structure, workmanship, materials, &c., to any in Dublin. Between the Church and Barracks, a little above the Jews [*sic*] Bridge, lies the gaol, it is but ordinary, yet built exceeding strong, with a court-yard, &c. In John-street, north-west of the town, is the Chapel; it is one of the prettiest I have ever seen, with a friary, garden, &c., belonging to it. The Chapel yard is esteemed the best walk about the town. We have a prodigious number of other streets, lanes, and quays, as the Flesh Market, Corn Market, Back Street, Shambles, Keizars lane, Ferry-boat quay, Medow's quay, Bennett's quay, the Common quay, Gibson's lane, the Custom house quay, which is the chief or principal of all the other quays, half of which I have not mentioned. The Custom-house quay is small, but vastly pretty, with seats all round, a good warm watch-house, and an excellent Custom-house, with convenient stores, &c.

'I procured the number of houses in the town and suburbs from a Collector of the Hearth money who told me there were exactly to a house, 1300, and in the confines of the walls 650 good slated houses.

'For ale and oysters Wexford is noted as having the best on earth. The chief exports are Corn, which annually exceeds upwards of 2,000,000 barrels [*sic*], herrings, beer, beef, hides, tallow, butter, &c., and they trade to all parts of the globe, but in particular to Liverpool, Barbadoes, Dublin, Norway, and Bordeaux'.

In another part he says the Wexford imports are brandy, rums, sugars, wines, dyestuffs, porter, fruit of all foreign kinds, salt, timber and hops. He concludes these remarkable notes by stating that:— 'Wexford is as celebrated for its fine women as for its beer and oysters'.

The so called 'Protestant Ascendancy' claimed the eighteenth century in Wexford town and county government as well as in comprehensive influence. In the latter half of the eighteenth century however, another strand is discerned in the fabric of the old port town. People of recent English origin, inhabitants of Wexford, members of the 'establishment', are none the less found to establish roots of enduring affinity in Wexford town. In short they have been captivated by what passes as the Wexford charm or atmosphere, its marriage to the sea, its beautiful hinterland. By no means were they birds of passage who having fulfilled a colonial or ecclesiastical posting left at their convenience. The outstanding contributions to Wexford for generations are exemplified in names which come easily to the tongue, like Elgee, Hadden, Hughes. It is difficult to state with any degree of certainty when these roots found agreeable nourishment but one is tempted to attach significance to the erection in 1760 of a brilliant successor to many previous churches on the site of the earliest Christian oratory of St Ibar or Iberius. This, the parish church of the Anglican communion, has been described as a Georgian gem. Churches outside the main stream also dropped anchor in the eighteenth century. The Presbyterians assembled on the site of their present church in Anne Street in1681 and a congregation has gathered there ever since. The first Methodist church was erected in the eighteenth century in Allen Street below St Patrick's Square. The direct ancestor of the distinguished Wexford historian, George Hadden, who arrived at that time, was one of the lay preachers of the Methodist founder, John Wesley.

Bishop Sweetman had built a sturdy house and apartments for himself in High Street just on the fringe of St Patrick's Square. Here, he carried on his diocesan government with tight efficiency and firmness. In High Street, behind closed doors, he ordained his priests for what was called the home mission. After ordination, they took ship from Wexford port to France or Spain to continue their studies in philosophy and theology.[50] Sweetman lived vigorously beyond the normal span of years, a mighty presence in Wexford town and throughout his life an unrepentant Stuart supporter. Towards the end of his days, the sting began to go out of the penal laws as far as observance and practise was concerned. He appointed a nephew as coadjutor bishop and a grand-nephew as a parish priest of Wexford and treasurer of the diocese. Sweetman was in his forty second active year as bishop of Ferns and in the ninety first year of his life when he died peacefully in his High Street home. One of the biggest and longest funerals ever held in Wexford town, escorted him to the family resting place in Clongeen. His successor, James Caulfield, coadjutor and parish priest of Ross, was of a different mould. He accepted the London status quo and was an out-spoken, singleminded loyalist even when that meant insult and commercial injury to his flock.

Most of the accrueing national bitterness was given the euphemism 'agrarian', and if the people of Wexford in their busy followings of sea-faring, river boating, fishing and merchandising, appreciated little of the bestialities, the humilitations imposed on their rural fellow countrymen, they had not long to wait until the common cause was forced upon their attention.

Wexford's citizens had since 1769 been in receipt of that wonder of communication, the newspaper. In addition to news brought home by ship and digested according to whim, there were now propagators of news, local and international, rival newspapers and rival views. The *Wexford Journal* was first in the field. Printed and published in the fashionable sector of the town at 96 North Main Street (the premises' Queen Anne style windows are still a feature) it later became the *Wexford Independent*. A whole new dimension was added to light the imagination and complement rumour from overseas.

Items of gossip and port news dominated the local news.[51]

WEXFORD, October 1784.
Yesterday evening, Admiral Sir Hugh Pallifer, bart, and the lady of Captain Walters, arrived in this town from London.

The prisoners confined for debt in the Marshalsea of Wexford, gratefully acknowledge to have received, by the hands of the Rev Mr Elgee, the sum of twelve shillings, a donation from the gentlemen of the jury held at the Tholsel on the 25th instant.
Monday last, a woman in the Faith was lately delivered of three girls, which make up five children of whom she was delivered within eleven months — the mother and the children are in good health.

Birth. At Harperstown, the lady of James Boyde, of Rosslare, Esq. of a son and heir.

Married. Yesterday, Mr James Jeffares, of Rathronan, in this county, to the agreeable Miss Goodison, of Garryduff, with a fortune of £1,000.

The news of arrivals in Wexford port gave details of the ship, the port she had left, the owner and the cargo:—[52]

Arrived:-
Polly of Wexford, from Milford, Fortune, coals. Lively of and from Newport, Griffey, ballast. Molly, of and from Cardigan, Lewis, culm. John of Wexford, from Whitehaven, Rack, coals. William and Margaret of Wexford, from Dublin, Leary, ballast.

Sailed:-
Catherine of Arklow, Doyle, ballast. Adventure of Wexford for Dublin, Hays, corn. Catherine of Wexford. Sally of Wexford for Dublin, Scallan, corn. Robert of and for Irvine, Ross, ballast. Phoenix of and for Carmarthen, Roberts, ballast.

The publisher of the *Wexford Chronicle*, Thomas Millet Vize, knew what the people wanted, especially when it related to a world port frequented by Wexford sailors on the Black Sea grain run.

Wexford toward the last quarter of the eighteenth century had become a fashionable town with all modern conveniences and ease of transport. It became a place where the town houses of the landlord classes packed a few of the town's most important streets, Georges Street, Selskar Street, and Main Street. The Winter season became a riot of social occasions, balls, private parties, musical evenings. The Colcloughs of Tintern Abbey surpassed their peers. The upper storey of their Georges Street town house was turned into a small theatre where visiting players entertained their friends. Harveys, Hughes, Letts, Esmondes, Derinzys, Nunns, the Marquis of Ely, Tottenhams, Boltons, Rowes, Kyans, Herròns are but a few names from the catalogue of bigger landowners who 'spent the season in the town'. They spent most of their incomes in Wexford where the participants in the serving and catering areas prospered.[53]

Three years after the death of Nicholas Sweetman in 1786, an event took place which changed the world. In 1789, the untamed teemed out of their lairs in Paris and hurled the established norms of civilisation and order into desolation. Fear, never ending fear, lodged in the hearts of the London establishment. Though firmly in control in Ireland and certainly Wexford, there was none the less the prospect of a repetition of Paris by a population which outnumbered them by ten to one. Liberal members of the Protestant establishment drew different conclusions. If the news came back to Wexford by ship and news sheet, eye witness accounts also came back to one of Wexford's most highly regarded Protestant landlord families, Caesar Colclough of Tintern Abbey and Georges Street. Colclough later went to France bursting with admiration for the revolt. He joined the Revolution's foreign supporters, but his every footstep was monitored by English intelligence.[54] The Roman Catholic church was thoroughly assaulted in the French Revolution so it needs no explanation to defend the horror loudly propagated by James Caulfield all over Wexford and his strategically placed diocese. The world had indeed changed on the streets of Paris.

In the 1770s Wexford port and county generally were enjoying commercial prosperity. The old spirit and heart had revived everywhere, (even though former masters like the Roches of Garrylough were but tenant farmers to a Cromwellian, Le Hunte, whose inherited confiscations did not prevent him being nominated one of Irelands 'landed gentry'.) The high quality malting barley which was grown with facility supplied no less than 242 small malt houses throughout Wexford.[55] These malt houses were able to maintain up to 100 vessels shipping malt from Wexford port to Dublin distilleries, and that is apart from the mainland Europe grain trade. At the beginning of the decade, a tranquility seemed to settle. The horror of revolt along with a ripple from the streets of Paris was also sampled on the streets of Wexford in 1793.[56] Like most ghastly martial struts, it could have been avoided. Sixteen men were arrested, drinking in a tavern, two of whom had arms. The two with arms were sent to Wexford gaol to stand trial, the remainder were released. Rural Wexford was outraged and a huge assembly of protestors marched on Wexford town to release the two men. Fifty soldiers of the 56th Regiment under the command of a veteran of the Spanish Wars, Major Charles Vallottin, marched out to meet the riotous assembly. The two groups met at the northern end of John Street. Vallottin went forward to parley and a young man, John Moore, the apparent leader of the crowd, came forward. He bore a scythe across his shoulder. They had just exchanged a few words when Vallottin caught sight of a red coat officer apparently in the crowd's hands. He instantly plunged his sword into Moore. Moore managed to sweep his scythe into Vallottin. Both man collapsed and the military commenced firing. In the pandemonium, a great many lives were lost. A Wexford Militia officer, Captain James Boyd, returning with his men from patrol, lay in ambush for the fleeing hundreds at Bettyville where he had no difficulty inflicting heavy casualties. Eleven lay dead in John Street. The remaining dead were exposed until identified; amongst them were four Protestant freeholders. Eight men were found hiding in a hayloft at John Street; one died from his wounds, two became informers, five were put on trial. The five were hanged on Wexford's execution theatre, the Windmill Hill. The bloody episode was known by the old people in Wexford of the last century as the 'First Rebellion'.[57] No one in Wexford had ever witnessed violence remotely of its kind. The shock which resulted from the sight of many people, some of them friends and acquaintances, shot dead, hanged, wounded in homely environs was severe but the shock which compounded the heinousness was the alacrity with which the military opened fire and the alacrity with which Captain Boyd and the Wexford Militia ambushed the crowds running for their lives. Wexford town and Wexford county were never the same again. In 1793, the private manufacture of pikes began. They were made quietly, in great numbers and hidden away. The feeling gained currency that there would be need of them. The pike became a guarantor of some security.

Not a few writers have noted that in the various stupefactions of the eighteenth century, the 'lower orders' approached ecstasies when confronted by the rare or even not so rare. A coloured man, for example, was a matter of wonder, a story teller, a questing friar, a pattern, a strange foreign ship, a fox hunt, even, it was said, a rising pheasant, called a halt to work. It is therefore true to say that were it not for the outbreak of frightful and total war in Wexford streets at the beginning and end of the 1790s, the erection of Wexford bridge, the first Wexford bridge, would have easily overshadowed all other events. In concept, design, preparation and anticipation, this overwhelmed all peace-time sensations by leagues. The millenia old ferry and ferry rights on the site of the new bridge had to be debated at length and proper compensation made. The monied classes had to be stimulated to support a private enterprise which planned toll gates at either side for income. What was then a mighty expanse of river was boldly tackled by the talented American designer Lemuel Cox. When it opened in 1795, it created excitement and traditions which lasted to its demise. It was Wexford's grand parade where boys and girls walked across and along, again and again, dressed in their best. Young, old, rich, poor used this beautiful promenade and Cox saw to it that they had facilities for entertainment as well. Militia bands played on the new bridge regularly, one of which was of a detachment still notorious in the folk memory of Wexford, the North Cork Militia.

The total warfare and war conditions, the planning, the government, reprisals, capture and recapture, executions, braveries, atrocities, revenges, nobilities and heartbreaks of Wexford town during the long hot summer of 1798 provide too great a canvas to adequately colour on these pages.[58] The ideals of the French Revolution and the United Irishmen were fermenting in so respectable a street as Georges Street for years before the outbreak. The names of the inhabitants, the visitors, the owners of town houses is like a catalogue of the hanged; Keugh, Harvey, Colclough, John and Henry Shears, Grogan. Whatever Wexford knew of the United Irish plans and membership, the upper echelon of which in Wexford town and area was mostly of the Protestant and landlord class, the quayside wharves and taverns could not possibly be un-aware of the mighty armada being assempled by Napoleon from Dunkirk and Dieppe to Le Havre. What may not have been known was that their own proxi-mate coastline was one objective for an April, 1798 landing. The bishop of Ferns James Caulfield was, to judge from his every utterance, very well aware of the course of events at home and overseas. In November 1797, a letter from him was read at all the Masses in the friary outlining with chilling, prophetic accuracy what would happen if the disaffected did not hand up weapons or renounce and abjure with sincere contrition any and all unlawful oaths of combining or conspiring with United Irishmen 'which are only bonds of iniquity'.

Whatever about pure patriotism, love of freedom and equality, idealism or simple revenge, there was one other gross stimulus to despair and revolution visited upon Wexford town that year. In 1796, the price of barley to farmers was twenty six shillings per barrel. In 1797, that market and stability was slashed to nine shillings a barrel, indeed even less. The Colcloughs of Tintern, influential landlord family though they were, could only procure 5/- per barrel.[59] Labourers of all trades and none became unemployed. Worse was to ravage the port of Wexford. In 1797, in addition to a further increase of duty and an increase on malt and malt house licences, the Government decided to end the carriage bounties on grain shipped to Dublin. The shipping of Wexford malt alone had earned annually around one sixth of all the Dublin carriage bounties on grain and flour. The loss could not be made good from new export bounties, for malt was not exported. The last goad to revolt for a more prosperous segment of Wexford society arrived. A new act outlined the regulation of licensed maltings. The legislators insisted that the quality of malt delivered to Dublin brewers would thereby be improved. The effect of the bill was catastrophic in Wexford. Half the 242 maltings in the county closed as they were judged too small to license. Apart from the malsters, millers and ship owners, the suffering was extended to labourers who lived by malting, sailing on sea or river, farm work or work based on farm produce. The United Irishmen exploited the catastrophe to the full. 'Incendaries were sent down from Dublin to fan the disaffection. A visible change took place in the temper and manner of the lower classes', noted Rev Thomas Handcock in Enniscorthy. 'There were surly expressions. Men stayed later than formerly in public houses. There were threats, whispers, and hints when the lower classes were drunk or angry of revenge upon enemies'.[60] It is no mystery that amongst the names of executive rebels in 1798 there are to be found so many malsters and millers; nor so vindictive a killer of loyalists on Wexford bridge as the sea captain and innkeeper, Thomas Dixon, with his wife Moll.[61]

The spectre of punishment made its appearance to the people of Wexford town on 26 April, 1798. It was the North Cork Militia under the command of the Earl of Kingsborough. They arrived with much pomp as they marched through the streets to Wexford barracks. They were accompanied by their women and children. The officers were Orangemen and there were Orangemen in the ranks as well as a number of Irish speaking Catholics. Their entry into Wexford created a more than usual stir, for they openly displayed Orange devices and emblems, Orange medals and Orange ribbons on their uniforms. Based in Wexford barracks they went into action countywide without delay. One of their sergeants, Thomas Honam, invented and widely used the torture known as the pitchcap.

The rebellion in Wexford county exploded unexpectedly in an unexpected place under an unexpected leader. The revolt started with a skirmish at the Harrow, grew rapidly, rolled over county Wexford, moblike at first. The successful leader was an obscure country curate, Fr John Murphy of Boolavogue.[62] The town of Wexford saw its garrison and Yeoman Cavalry unit cross Wexford Bridge on Whit Sunday morning to disperse and punish that threatening mob of malefactors assembled on Oulart Hill. That night an officer and two or three soldiers, the only survivors, staggered back across Wexford bridge to tell of defeat and slaughter. On 31 May, that army of revolutionaries was before the gates of Wexford, having swept through the county, from Camolin south, capturing Enniscorthy as well. The same night, they were in occupation and the people of Wexford, whether in fear or in favour, gave the rebels the welcome, the feastings, the hero's greetings not experienced there for over 150 years. The United Irish Directory in Wexford had another ingredient to contend with for better or worse: a priest in revolt with them who had preached and worked against revolt. Be that as it may, in a few more days, the south-east corner of Ireland from Wicklow town to the Hook was cleared totally of Government troops. The way was open for an unhindered French landing.

Wexford town has not produced a minstrel to sing of her own part in that insurrection against terrible odds and very little has been heard of two separate Wexford town units who fought throughout the rebellion. The Wexford seamen's 'Faythe Corps' and the 'John St Corps' fought under Fr John Murphy, Edward Roche and Miles Byrne in the ill-fated thrust to Dublin, and the long last stand in Laois, Carlow and Kilkenny.

By summer's end, the hurricane of 1798 had blown itself out. Wexford county was in ashes, Wexford town numb with shock, continuing reprisals and transportations. Revenge for atrocities, church burnings, killings, perjuries, courtmartials, terminated the eighteenth century. Wexford's people on street square, church and chapel, had now seen in their own intimate streets the red maw of war and hate, the utmost in brutality, the burning of rebel-filled hospitals, the doing to death of hundreds, the guilty and innocent, on street corner and Wexford bridge, the Government of revolt with flag flying, the subjugation of the county by twenty thousand troops under six army generals and a ruthless commander, General Lake. To that may be added the dispatch of Wexford's national and intellectual leadership. After 1798, the Act of Union of 1800 seemed scarcely to be of cosmic importance to Wexford.

It is easy today to contemplate recovery in retrospect but the generation which had fought and lived through 1798 became silent. It took two generations, together with no small measure of prudence and pride, to rejoice. Indeed so great was the danger of reprisal and damage to life, business and prospects for those who survived that for almost forty years the old policy of running with hare and hound obtained. 'The horrible blank in the folk memory',[63] is one of the impenetrable mists which swathes the last years of the eighteenth century in Wexford.

There is no source material for the flavour or the personality of a town. I have relied on much minutiae which on inspection becomes not minutiae at all but the heart of European history. How our predecessors reacted to the culture imposed on them by geography and history is a fascinating story. They walked the same streets that we walk, watched the sun dance to morning over Curracloe and Rosslare, looked at the very same hills of Screen, the harbour waters, the Slaney valley and the distant blue of the Blackstairs. They spoke with that phonetic phenomenon, the real Wexford accent, developed over the centuries from an admixture of Gaelic, Norse, Norman, Flemish, Welsh and English tongues. They had the fears, pleasures, ambitions, nobility, loyalty and degradation that is the lot of all human life. If that is borne in mind, it may well be possible to glean from these glimpses a fellowship with the people who left us such a complex inheritance. Thereby, it will be possible to recognise an atmosphere, a personality and a spirit that is no stranger to ourselves today.

7 Rolf Loeber and Magda Stouthamer-Loeber

The lost architecture of the Wexford Plantation

The Wexford Plantation was a success, although severely disrupted by the rebellion in 1641. Even after the Cromwellian confiscation, it left a permanent impression on the ownership of land in north Wexford. This paper examines the lost architecture of the Wexford Plantation, an undertaking made possible largely because of the discovery of a contemporary survey of the plantation castles in that county. This document, together with other sources, allows us to gain a glimpse of the colonial society then being intruded into the area. We will first sketch the background of the Wexford Plantation, provide descriptions of the planters' buildings, and consider these buildings against the backdrop of the existing architecture of the native inhabitants.

The Wexford Plantation was the first colonial settlement undertaken by the Dublin government after the massive introduction of British settlers into Ulster at the beginning of the century. While its history has been elusive, an examination of available records provides ample evidence for its infamous reputation, acquired because of the government scheming that led to confiscation of large tracts of land belonging to families of old Gaelic and Anglo-Norman stock. This was followed by protracted conflict between dispossessed individuals and the government in Dublin, a conflict which eventually reached the Privy Council in England. The confiscation of land, in the words of its main proponent, the Lord Deputy Chichester, was 'to raise thereby a more civil plantation and more firm to the State than hitherto hath bin ... (because) the meer Irish ... (are) meer Intruders into the Kings Right and Possessions. ...' Lands were to be appropriated from the local inhabitants although some of them were descended from the Anglo-Norman invaders; others, particularly the Kavanaghs, though not of Anglo-Norman descent, had welcomed the initial Anglo-Norman conquest in the twelfth century. In fact, the Anglo-Norman conquest never fully penetrated the far northern part of the county. Despite the protests of native landowners, James I insisted that they be replaced by 'some more civill and better inhabitants ...', and that buildings and fortifications be made 'for the security of the country ... (for which he was willing to give away) our owne lande as were in the plantation of Ulster'.[1] The weak grounds on which the government had made its case was a title dating back to the time of Richard II, which had subsequently come to the crown but had escaped notice for about 200 years. Although the commission sent over to enquire into the proceedings of the plantation produced a second and more accurate survey, which led to a slight reduction in the size of lands lost by the original owners, the effect remained ultimately the same. English grantees obtained large tracts, ranging from 1,000 to 3,000 acres of fertile land. The confiscation took place totally in north Wexford. (fig 7.1), encompassing the baronies of Gorey, Ballaghkeen North and South, and the eastern portion of the barony of Scarawalsh, (stretching from the river Arklow in the north, along the coast, cutting across the land westward, omitting the barony of Shelmaliere East, over to the river Slaney on the south and to Enniscorthy and the border with county Carlow on the west). The territories reserved for the plantation were identified by the names of the Gaelic septs living there, i.e., the Kinshelaghs, MacMurrough Kavanaghs, and O'Morchoe.

The Wexford Plantation territory consisted of the surviving Gaelic area in county Wexford; the rest of the county had been solidly planted by Old English families to the virtual exclusion of Gaelic landowners.

The motivation for the Wexford plantation in the early seventeenth century can be traced to changing conditions in the preceding century. As early as 1534, Sir Patrick Finglas had called for the suppression of monasteries on the lands of the McMurroughs and for the settlement of 'lords and gents out of England'. In 1562, the Lord Deputy Sussex expressed his confidence in the amenability of the Kavanaghs to English law; they answered summons of all the Dublin Courts, served on juries, and were constables of the royal castles at Ferns, Clohamon, and Ballyloughan (the latter in county Carlow). In the mid-sixteenth century, the Lord Deputy Sir James Crofte had given orders 'for inhabiting the lands of O'Morrowes country' but neither of these initiatives led to a settlement of planters. North Wexford had few monasteries, aside from those at Enniscorthy, Downe, and Ferns. Confiscation of these properties did not take place until the second half of the sixteenth century and only in the case of the Franciscan Friary of Enniscorthy did a substantial plantation take place. It was begun about 1586 under the leadership of Sir Henry Wallop, who for self-defense had ordnance mounted on his residence. He promoted also the building of a fort at St Mullins in south Carlow in 1581 in order to strengthen his plantation and protect access to the town of New Ross along the river Barrow. Its remains consist of a regular pentagonal fort with five bastions on top of the hill. As far as is known, the rest of the region was not much affected by new settlers during most of the sixteenth century.[3]

The government's next manoeuvre was to shire north county Wexford in 1606. Within four years a fort was built as a garrison for troops five miles northeast of Gorey, called Fort Chichester after the Lord Deputy (now named Fortchester). Its first constable was Capt Denis Dale (also known by a Gaelic version of his name, Donagh O'Daly), who had built the fort at his own

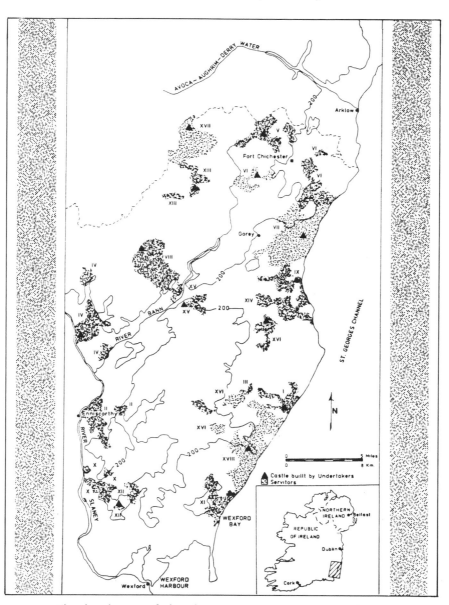

Fig. 7.1: The distribution of the plantation sites in county Wexford. Legend of probable site and name of the grantee (also called undertaker) in parenthesis: **I**: Castle Annesley (Francis Annesley); **II**: Drumgold (Francis Blundell); **III**: *Location unclear (Conway Brady);* **IV**: Ballycarney (Sir James Carroll); **V**: Newtown (Walsingham Cooke); **VI**: Limerick (Sir Lawrence Esmond); **VII**: Prospect (Sir Edward Fisher); **VIII**: Monasootagh (Thomas Hibbotts); **IX**: Middleton (Sir Roger Jones); **X**: Edermine (Nicholas Kenny); **XI** Ballynaclash (John Langhorne); **XII**: Rahale (Sir Adam Loftus); **XIII**: Monaseed (William Marwood); **XIV**: Tomduff (William Parsons); **XV**: Milshoge, Norris Mount, or Medhophall (Henry Piers/Edmund Medhop); **XVI**: Ballyvoodock also called Sampton (George Trevelyan/Sir Arthur Chichester); **XVII**: Ballynabarney (Sir Richard Wingfield)

TABLE 1: THE SETTLERS AND THEIR PLANATIONS IN COUNTY WEXFORD

Settler	Position	Date of first grant***	Date of regrant	Number of acres	Name of the manor	Location	Location on Fig. 7.1	Alienated to, or descended to (date)
(Sir) Francis Annesley (later Baron Mountnorris) (d. 1660)	Clerk of the Pells of the Exchequer	1612†	1618	1,000	Annesley (later Camolin)	Castle Annesley	I	—
(Sir) Francis Blundell (d. 1625)	Surveyor-General of the Exchequer	1613	1620	1,000 (1,500) (1621)	Blundelston	Drumgold	II	Sir Henry Wallop (1630)
Conway Brady	Queen's footman and Irishman	1618		600	?	?	III	
Sir James Carroll (d. 1639)	Remembrancer of the Exchequer	1612	1618	1,000	Slane-Carroll	Ballycarney	IV	— Thorentone, Richard Wale, & Bartholomew Breine (1640)
Sir Richard Cooke (d. 1616) later his son Walsingham Cooke	Secretary of State & Chancellor of Exchequer and commissioner of Wexford plantation	1612†	1618	1,500	Cookestown	Newtown	V	Sir George Sexton and Mathew Ford (1624)
Sir Lawrence Esmond (later Baron of Limerick) (d. 1648)	servitor and native commissioner of Wexford plantation	1612	1618	1,500 (2,000) (1621)	Esmond	Limerick	VI	
Sir Edward Fisher	servitor & commissioner of Wexford plantation	1612	1618	1,500 (2,000) (1621)	Chichester (1612) Fisherstown (1618)	Prospect	VII	Edward Chichester (1641)
(Sir) Thomas Hibbotts	Chancellor of the Exchequer	1613	1619	1,000	Hibbotts (1613) Monasootagh (1619)	Monasootagh	VIII	Sir Francis Annesley (1641)

Name	Role	Date	Date	Acreage	Settlement	Proportion	No.	Subsequent holder
Sir Roger Jones (later Viscount Ranelagh) (d. 1644)	relative of Sir Arthur Chichester	1612	1618	1,000	Jonestown	Middleton	IX	Lord Esmond, then Piers Synnott (1636)
Nicholas Kenny	Escheator of Leinster and commissioner of Wexford plantation	1622	1622	500	Edermine	Edermine	X	Henry Kenny (1622)
John Langhorne	son-in-law of Sir Arthur Chichester	1613		1,000	Langhorne	Ballynaclash	XI	Sir Adam Loftus (1620), then to George Cheevers
Sir Adam Loftus	Privy Councillor	1613	1619	1,000	Rahaile	Rahale	XII	Richard Stafford (1621)
William Marwood	Deputy Remembrancer of the Exchequer	1613	1618	1,000	Castle Marwood	Monaseed	XIII	Henry Masterson (1641)
(Sir) William Parsons	Surveyor-General & commissioner of Wexford plantation	1612	1618	1,000 (1,500) (1621)	Coolag (1612) Parsonstown (1618)	Tomduff	XIV	Sir Walsingham Cooke (1641)
Henry Pierse (d. ca. 1622)	Secretary to Sir Arthur Chichester	1613	1620	1,000	Piersetown-Ewinch (1613) Medopall (1620)	Medhophall	XV	regranted to Edmund Medhop, who died in 1620; subsequently probably conveyed to Sir Francis Annesley
Capt. George Trevelyan (d. 1620)	Servitor and nephew of Sir Arthur Chichester and commissioner Wexford plantation servitor							
& Capt. Faithful Fortescue (for Sir Arthur Chichester, d. 1625)	Lord Deputy	1613	1618	2,000 (3,000 + 1,000)** (1621)	Sampton	Ballyvoodock	XVI	Sir Francis Annesley (1621)
Sir Richard Wingfield (later Viscount Powerscourt)	Marshall of the army and commissioner of Wexford plantation	1613	1618	1,000	Cromwell (1613) Wingfield (1618)	Ballynabarney	XVII	

†Letters patent not enrolled (Anal. Hib. xxxi (1984). pp. 96-7).
**In 1621 the 3,000 acre Sampton estate is mentioned as belonging to Sir Arthur Chichester, while Capt Trevelyan held another 1,000 acres.

expense. It probably was situated on a woodland pass, although this is no longer ascertainable, and was intended to protect the county against raids from the Kavanaghs. Access to north Wexford from the Pale was through this pass as the main Dublin road ran south along the narrow Wicklow coastal lowland.[4]

The government sponsored Wexford Plantation really got under way only after 1610. The history of this settlement has remained elusive for several reasons. Early estate accounts for the individual plantations have not apparently survived. Even more disappointingly, the structures that the grantees were obliged to build under plantation conditions no longer stand out in the landscape.

Development of a locational policy The Wexford Plantation was comparable to that of Ulster in the sense that there were relatively few existing castles which could be confiscated and reused; hence, the need to select strategic sites for new castles invulnerable to attack by the displaced and disgruntled natives. In 1611 an unknown official, possibly the Lord Deputy Chichester, recommended that the Gaels be transplanted from the inland borders of their territories to the region near the sea to facilitate the building of castles for British settlers in the border territory, thereby providing a buffer zone between the Irish in county Carlow and the Irish in county Wexford.

Simultaneously, the Surveyor-General Sir William Parsons stressed the need for the British to settle on the coast of county Wexford because, except for here, the coast from the 'Glinns' in Ulster to Waterford had been planted with Englishmen. Ultimately, the plantation commissioners in Wexford agreed to both options, that is, to locating British settlers near the sea and servitors (as army officers were called) in the higher ground towards the Wicklow and Carlow borders. Chichester travelled through the area to identify all the places fit for the servitors to build.[5] The debate over the siting of castles was revived in 1616 when, after repeated protests from the native inhabitants, a redivision of the plantation lands was undertaken. The Lord Deputy Chichester desired that the Irish, together with some English planters, would be situated on the lowlands, while servitors would have

'those seats and chief places of habitation upon the mountains and fastnesses, in which castles or houses of strength, framed and composed of lime and stone, are to be built by them for the better securing of those territories to the King, and suppressing the licentious liberty of the neighbours'.[6]

This plan was adopted; ultimately, seventeen grantees (then called 'undertakers') instead of the proposed twenty five received lands, mostly 1,000 or 1,500 acre tracts (table 1), mainly in the low lying areas (fig. 7.1). The castles of one group of settlers encircled the new plantation of Gorey within a radius of three to eight miles. Two servitors were placed along the coast, and another two occupied places in the higher areas towards Carlow and Wicklow. Another group of planters occupied virtually all the coastal lands.[7] This carving out of planter estates caused a great dislocation of the native inhabitants, many of whom were forced to move from their former homes.

The grantees The new grantees of the plantation lands in Wexford were an odd assortment of individuals. On the one hand there were several veteran servitors, some of whom had served on the continent, such as the Lord Deputy Chichester, Sir Richard Wingfield, and Sir Lawrence Esmond. Esmond and Edward Fisher later served as constables of strongholds in Leinster. Esmond was the only grantee who already had been a resident in south county Wexford; his adoption of the protestant faith undoubtedly removed a major obstruction to his qualifying as a settler. Moreover, of all plantation commissioners, he was the most familiar with the local situation in north Wexford. A contemporary writer characterised him as 'an expert, prudent, and resolute Commander, of a sedate and composed spirit ... of sanguin Complexion, of an indifferent tall stature, compact, solid, corpulent body with robustious Limms ...'.[8]

Among the people who benefitted from the Wexford Plantation were four relatives of Chichester: his son-in-law Langhorn, Sir Roger Jones, William Parsons, and Capt George Trevelyan. Chichester was probably responsible for selecting the commissioners who supervised the initial stages of the Wexford Plantation and, not surprisingly, all of them received tract of lands as a reward for their labours (Parsons, Cooke, Wingfield, Trevelyan, Fisher, Esmond (see table 1). Conway Brady, an Irishman by birth, became a grantee because of his direct connection with the court in England.[9]

Chichester played a major role in organising and developing the plantation, and then became the largest recipient of plantation land under the cover of at least two relatives, Capt George Trevelyan and Capt Faithful Fortescue. Chichester had previously sold his own land in Devon, and at the age of thirty six had arrived in Ireland for the second time with nothing beyond his pay and his expenses as a soldier to support him. At the end of his life, he was the owner of over 100,000 acres in Ireland. His considerable ability as a governor was wedded to a cunning and a willingness to deceive which enabled him to amass a vast estate in Ulster, centred around Belfast Castle, Carrickfergus, and the Inishowen peninsula. It is probably not coincidental that three other of his associates received plantation estates, first in the barony of Dungannon in county Tyrone, and later in Wexford.[10]

Many of the other planters in Wexford either had received or shortly were to receive additional land grants in other parts of the country. For example, Thomas Hibbotts acquired part of Con O'Neill's estate in county Down. The nucleus of Sir Richard Wingfield's estate was closer at Powerscourt in county Wicklow. In contrast, Francis Blundell was soon to purchase plantation lands in Leitrim and Offaly; later he became an investor in the West India and the Africa Companies.[11]

Wexford is unique among plantations of the period in that it did not lead to a single new grantee coming over from Britain; rather, many of the bene-ficiaries were Dublin officials, particularly members of the Court of Exchequer (see table 1). These included the Chancellor Cooke, and his successor, Hibbotts; the Remembrancer, Carroll, and his deputy, Marwood; the Clerk of the Pells, Annesley; and finally its Surveyor-General Blundell.

This is especially ironic in view of the fact that the persistent protests of the former owners were brought before this court rather than to one of the other courts in Dublin. At the Exchequer, the native inhabitants must have witnessed a great perversion of justice considering that so many of the court officials stood to gain directly from the confiscations. Predictably, the native inhabitants did not receive redress for their complaints.

A singular figure in this court was Sir James Carroll, an Irishman, whose father had settled in Dublin. Sir James undoubtedly was a Protestant, whose frequent mention in contemporary documents evokes the image of an entrepreneurship more typical of the New English. His name often appears in records of land grants in many parts of Ireland; he also displayed an interest in civic affairs such as the erection of a work-house in Dublin and keeping that city's streets free from beggars. He was elected mayor of Dublin four times, and can be credited with quelling a disturbance associated with the 1622 election and with preventing the return of Roman-Catholics. In the same year he also issued a proclamation to enforce the laws against Jesuits and other seminary priests. He became insolvent in 1620, just at the time that he was supposed to build in county Wexford; years later it was said that he was almost 'sunk' by the expense of building his residence there (see Ballycarney). His life was plagued by impending crises, such as large debts for his estate in Armagh leased from Trinity College, from whom he also had leased 6,000 acres in Donegal, but he was forced to sell his lease in 1618. These personal financial problems appear to have dogged him despite the fact that he was deputy Treasurer-at-War under the very capable Sir Thomas Ridgeway. After his re-election as Mayor in 1925, the Lord Deputy temporarily forbade him to execute the position because of the many judgements and outlawries against him. Carroll ended his mayoral career when he was forced to resign in 1634 after being fined by the Star Chamber for committing extortions. His wife, who died eight years earlier, was described by James Ware as an 'infamous strumpet'.[12]

Another official from the Court of Exchequer whose name will recur repeatedly in the following pages is Francis Annesley, later Baron Mountnorris. He was a peculiar man, who had gained much power in Dublin, and had skilfully used his influence to amass a large estate in the Ulster plantation, as well as holdings elsewhere in Ireland. Very little is known about how he financed these acquisitions. One thing is clear, though; he surpassed all Wexford planters in carving out a large personal territory by acquiring four plantation estates in county Wexford which in 1641 amounted to over 11,000 profitable acres, not to mention the unprofitable land. Unlike Sir James Carroll, his fortune did not wane until the rebellion, when he and his son claimed the loss of £4,000 in yearly income and £10,000 in personal estate.[13]

The fact that many of the grantees were based either in Dublin or its neighbourhood and were owners of several other plantation estates scattered across a number of counties must have weakened the Wexford Plantation from the beginning. Few of the grantees could be expected to become resident planters and devote the necessary energy to improving their newly acquired lands. On the other hand, the Wexford Plantation did serve to cement human ties, such as intermarriage between those families who settled permanently on their estates as in the case of Fisher on the one hand and Cooke and Marwood on the other. Other less formal but nevertheless important ties must have been responsible for the fact that four of the Wexford planters — Esmond, Parsons, Jones, and Loftus — later were granted tracts of lands in the Ranelagh Plantation in county Wicklow, immediately north of county Wexford.[14]

Plantation conditions Settlers in Wexford were not bound by the many plantation conditions imposed by the government on the Ulster planters. Grantees with 1,000-1,500 acres of land were to build a defensible castle or house of 24 by 24-30 feet at the minimum, with a height of 24 feet, exclusive of the roof and battlements. Those with 500 acres were to build a defensible house without specified dimensions. As to building materials, stone or brick was prescribed, but no mention was made of the building of a bawn or court as in Ulster. All grantees were allowed four years to comply with the plantation conditions and were not required to personally reside on the property. Another condition was that they would not sell the property to 'any mere Irish being not of English blood or surname'.[15] Interestingly, this did not exclude the old Anglo-Norman families, who had suffered under the plantation. Unlike the planters in Ulster and Munster, the grantees in Wexford apparently were not obliged to settle British tenants on the lands, or to keep them armed for the defense of the plantation.

Grantees' buildings Progress with the plantation was slow which is not surprising given the opposition from the local population. Only two of the grantees (Sir Lawrence Esmond (see Limerick) and Sir Edward Fisher (see Prospect)) who received lands in the first series of letters patent in 1612-3 (see table 1) had fulfilled their conditions four years later. Esmond and Fisher had been responsible for the initial survey of the area in 1611.

The opportunity for building was limited in the interim as a result of the protracted conflict over the division of the county. This delay led to a second and final series of letters patent most of which were issued in 1618. The following years were punctuated by occasional attacks by the natives on the settlements, culminating in 1620 in the burning of houses and cabins, and the killing of inhabitants at the plantation of Drumgold (q.v.) and Ballycarney (q.v.), the estates of Sir Francis Blundell and Sir James Carroll, respectively.[16] A survey undertaken by Sir Thomas Rotheram in 1621 indicates that the majority of plantation castles were constructed in the years from 1618 onwards. An almost contemporaneous report on all Irish plantations was prepared by one of the grantees, Sir Francis Blundell, Clerk of the Commissioners for Defective Titles. He was satisfied that the planters, considering the danger of the work, had looked 'more upon their owne service then anie present profit ...' by building 'faire and strong castles, houses, and bawnes upon their proportions and thereby made that part of the country strong and defensible against an Irish enemie'.[17]

According to Rotheram's report thirteen of these seventeen grantees had built or were in the process of building in 1621, which was close to the deadline stipulated in the second series of letters patent. Thus, by all appearances, the Wexford Plantation had a high compliance rate in terms of the buildings completed on time. However, it became largely an absentee landlord settlement. The only individuals mentioned in 1622 as sometimes resident were Sir Francis Annesley (see Milshoge) and William Marwood (see Monaseed). Four years later, the then Lord Deputy Falkland complained that only two of the grantees permanently lived on the land (perhaps the same ones as in 1622) and that many had sold their properties. He observed that their houses were small but was more concerned that the owners had let their lands 'in a manner altogether to the Natives, who have assurance of their possessions and are much discontented . . . If better order be not taken for settling that plantacon it may prove not only unprofitable but perilous'. In contrast, the settler, Sir Francis Annesley, wrote that 'for soe much circuit of ground . . . there are not so many good buildings in any [plantation] Territory in Ireland' as in Wexford.[18]

The plans of the plantation buildings in Wexford resembled those in Ulster. The usual lay-out showed a main house with one or two flankers adjoining a walled court or bawn, about 12 to 13 feet high, which was reinforced by one or two flankers (see fig. 7.6). Some of the castles consisted of two main buildings as at Monasootagh and Limerick. The largest residences were at Monaseed, Tomduff, and Limerick. These structures can be contrasted with five small castles, each 40 by 24 foot (see Ballyvoodock, Ballynabarney, Castle Annesley, Middleton, and Rahale, and fig. 7.2 for a typical example).[19] Prospect, Monaseed, and Limerick had large walled gardens and orchards adjoining. Although it is likely that the castles were preceded by temporary buildings which were used until the final residences were finished, these were not mentioned in the 1621 survey.

Only rarely has the name of a craftsman who helped to erect one of the plantation castles come down to us. One such instance concerns a Dublin bricklayer, Peter Harrison (see Killybegs in the appendix). At three other sites, Middleton, Tomduff, and Prospect, the plantation buildings were of brick but otherwise stone and lime were the most common building materials (i.e., the local small shaly stone that required much lime). The Civil Survey of 1654 mentioned few stone houses other than the plantation castles. These were probably occupied by leaseholders and are mentioned at the Monasootagh and Prospect estates. It seems likely that other tenant buildings were made of timber or sods, straw, and wattle; however, these were not listed in contemporary surveys.

No architects' names have been connected with any of the known plantation buildings. However, documents make it clear that as early as 1609, the Clerk of the Royal Works in Ireland, Samuel Molyneux, regularly lived on his property at Mountfin and surrounding lands opposite Ballycarney within easy reach of plantation patrons. He was a colleague of one of the planters, Sir Francis Annesley, who held the post of Clerk of the Works but Annesley himself is not known as an architect.[20]

It is quite possible that Samuel Molyneux was responsible for the building of the pleasant residence at Mountfin (fig. 7.1) which unfortunately was pulled down circa 1970 (pl. xix). It showed a degree of sophistication that was rarely found in Irish architecture of the sixteenth century. A main square block had four tower projections. Symmetrically placed chimney stacks adjoined the towers and obstructed their defensive capacity. The house had regularly spaced windows and one classical moulded string course that broke the monotony of the wall surfaces. When the photograph was taken, the walls must already have seriously bulged, considering the wall ankers in the right hand tower, connected to the other frontal tower by three steel cables, running in front of the house. Because of its non-defensive design, the house probably originally stood in a walled enclosure.[21]

Plate xix: Mountfin, on the river Slaney, just outside of the plantation area

Towns The Wexford Plantation, like other plantations in this period, was to have a plantation town. Directions to that effect were given by King James I in 1618, who specified that it be surrounded 'with a good and sufficient wall . . .', to be built within seven years, at the expense of the settlers and the native inhabitants. This town, initially called Newborough, became the town of Gorey. It was incorporated in 1619 by royal charter, issued to several protestants, including grantees such as Sir Edward Fisher, Sir Adam Loftus, and Edmund Medhop. According to the poll tax account of 1659, 15 adult Englishmen and 74 Irishmen were living there. Apparently its defenses were not very strong, for it was taken at the time of the rebellion. According to a deposition, its 'houses are burnt and fallen downe. . . .' The Down Survey map shows a fort and town walls, which in all likelihood were made not of stone but of sods.[22]

In addition, plantation villages sprang up at Limerick, Monaseed, and Tomduff, but have been long since swept away. Virtually nothing is known about the appearance of these villages or their occupants, trades, and wealth. Probably the largest was Tomduff, where 200 families had settled before 1641. Some of the planters built churches such as the one at Tomduff, or the chapel at Limerick. A government account states that the planters had attracted many English people and families from the Pale to work as tenants on the plantation estates. Judging again from the poll tax account of 1659, the Wexford Plantation must have led to a reasonably high immigration rate (given the low rate of population change from 1641-59), because concentrations of Englishmen could then be found all along the coast and inland towards county Carlow. Examples of settlers were a clothier at Prospect and a carpenter at Camolin, who both claimed losses as a result of the 1641 rebellion. It is significant that the proportion of English in the unplanted area south of the Wexford Plantation remained much lower. One of the grantees obtained a license to build tanneries on his estate at Drumgold. Otherwise, with the exception of some timber industry on a few estates, the main source of income must have been the cultivation of wheat, barley, and oats, and to a lesser extent from pasture. The government tried to influence the type of agriculture pursued in the plantation by specifying that settlers and native inhabitants set aside one in each hundred acres for the cultivation of hemp and flax; it is unclear whether or not this was an economic success.[23]

Buildings of the native inhabitants The emergence of plantation castles should be seen against the backdrop of the then existing architecture in the area. Contemporary descriptions, even by government officials organising the plantation, have rarely revealed the appearance of older buildings in north county Wexford (see below). More is known about the architecture of the south of the county. In the sixteenth century, a transition took place from tower houses with adjoining hall to an elongated rectangular plan, usually with one corner tower (as at Slade, Fethard, Dungulph, Coolhull, and Bargy). These residences often had many other defensive features, including battlements, a bartizan, and sometimes a stone vault (little is known about their bawns or courts) and are therefore called 'hall type fortified houses'. They all are located on the south coast of the county; there is no evidence that this architectural innovation penetrated north county Wexford.[24]

The latter area had been relatively inaccessible for many centuries because of the woods in the Leinster Mountain range on its western and northern flanks. In the sixteenth century, the two principal Norman castles, Enniscorthy and Ferns, had come into the hands of Sir Henry Wallop and Sir Richard Masterson respectively and continued to be lived in. In addition, towns and manors, dating back from around 1300, could be found at Gorey, Courtown, Glascarrig, Edermine, Ferns, and Enniscorthy. Their thin spread over the northern area clearly suggests that the Anglo-Norman infiltration had not been strong. This conclusion is also supported by the scarcity of surviving tomb sculpture dating from the Norman settlement.[25] Only the sites at Gorey and Courtown (see Prospect) became plantation centres in the early seventeenth century.

The principal Gaelic inhabitants of the area were the Kavanaghs in the north and east, the Vadick and Wafer families in the north, the O'Morchoes mostly in the west, and the O'Breine's and Kenshalaghs in the east. The dominant sept was the Kavanaghs. Domhnaill Spáinneach, the last member to assume the ancient title King of Leinster lost land with the establishment of the Wexford Plantation, like most of his compeers. Interspersed with the Gaelic Irish were Old English families such as the Synnotts, the Peppards, the Esmonds, and others. According to a contemporary document, these Old English had only recently moved into the area and had 'not long since obtained part of those lands from the Irish'.[26]

A few stone castles mentioned in the Civil Survey of 1654 were situated in the southern part of the plantation area, especially in the corridor along the river Slaney, with a virtual absence of castles in the north. Documents show that by 1654, with only one exception, the Gaelic Irish no longer owned castles but lived instead in stone houses which presumably had few defensive characteristics. Others must have lived in timber or wattle and clay structures but these were not listed in documents of the time. The virtual absence of castles with Gaelic Irish ownership was a result of the government policy which left the few remaining castles in the hands of the Old English, particularly members of the Synnott family. They and others may have continued using the sod moats or enclosures dating from medieval times, as the plantation papers mention native inhabitants living at a number of such sites. Their castles were very similar to the one lived in by Sir Morgan Kavanagh, at Clonmullen (county Carlow) just outside the plantation area. It probably was a conventional keep, described in 1635 as 'an old, high, narrow and inconvenient building; the stairs leading up into the dining-room and chambers being narrow and steep, like a steeple stair ...'[27]

Little is known about new buildings erected by the Gaelic Irish or the Old English. One early seventeenth century house, Huntington Castle, built by a member of the Old English Esmond family, still stands at Clonegal in county Carlow, again just outside of the plantation area (pl. xx). It consists of a three storey tower (discounting the many later additions), on a rectangular plan, with a staircase in the half-round projection at the rear. This building has many affinities with plantation architecture elsewhere in Ireland.

The scarcity of medieval tower houses in the plantation area itself suggests that timber dwellings remained common here which is not surprising considering that woodland covered its borders with Carlow and Wicklow, and also mantled its central area in the Screen Hills; other woods occupied the shores of the river Slaney.[28] An example of a timber residence, probably at Tincurry on the east bank of the river Slaney, was described in 1635 by a travelling Englishman as 'as handsome an Irish hall ... as I ever saw in this

Plate xx: Huntington Castle (county Carlow) on the perimeter of the plantation area

kingdome, and if Sir James Carroll will part with his house [i.e., the closeby Ballycarney] it stands most conveniently to be occupied herewith.... This were a brave seat for a younger brother ...' It was then in the hands of Derby Cavanagh, a member of one of the principal branches of the Kavanaghs.[29]

According to an initial plantation plan, the native inhabitants were also obliged to build a stone house or tower for those with 1,000 or 500 acres, respectively, while those with 120 acres were to construct an enclosure with a strong ditch planted with quicksetts. Whereas stone or brick was specified for the grantees and servitors, natives were allowed to use stone or earth. These initial building conditions were later abandoned, however, probably out of fear that the natives would build defensible residences. Instead, a clause was inserted in the letters patent to native inhabitants prohibiting them conveying their lands to other Irishmen not of English blood or name for a longer period than three lives or 40 years. Contemporary sources repeatedly indicate that the plantation caused a large displacement of native families. Sheriffs and soldiers are known to have broken open the doors of houses belonging to those who refused to budge in order to forcibly eject these Irishmen, their wives and children. Subsequently, some were even transported to Virginia. Not surprisingly, one correspondent commented in 1630 that Chichester's plantation in the country of O'Morchoe 'has extirpated the Irish almost quite'.[30]

The plantation area was reasonably peaceful in the 1620s and 30s up until 1641, judging from the account of Lord Anglesey, the son of Sir Francis Annesley, who had been resident at Camolin (see Milshoge) before the rebellion. He wrote that, 'there never was more unity, friendship and good agreement, amongst all sort and degrees (of Roman Catholics and Protestants) ... I remember very well the summer before the rebellion, the titular Bishop of Ferns coming on his visitation in the county of Wexford, where I then dwelt. At the request of the Popish priest, I lent most of my silver plate to entertain the said Bishop with, and had it honestly restored'.[31]

The peace was shattered in 1641. The rebellion that had started in the plantations in Monaghan very swiftly spread to Wexford. Within a month the Lord Justices in Dublin reported to England that the rebels in Wexford had taken the castle of Limerick and Fort Chichester, considered 'places of good strength and importance', while 'all the cattle and houses of the English with all their substance are come into the hands of the rebels ...' Fort Chichester had already passed into private hands in 1618 and thus lost much of its function. It probably was neither strong nor well-maintained when it was taken by the rebels in 1641. Settler residences suffered badly as a result of the rebellion and its aftermath: by 1654, at least eight out of the original thirteen known principal residences had been ruined or were in decay.[32]

In the wake of the Cromwellian conquest that followed the rebellion, more confiscations of native properties took place. Among the many plantation estates that initially had changed hands, five estates had come into the possession of Roman Catholics before the rebellion.[33] These estates were reconfiscated, thus repeating the cycle of plantations. In the following centuries, change and decay affected the Wexford Plantation castles to such an extent that in most instances their location and appearance was forgotten.

The following pages contain a listing of the grantees' castles including their plans which are based on the descriptions in Rotheram's survey, other records, and our 1977 and 1986 field notes of the sites. Although Rotheram's survey gives the dimensions of the structures, the plans presented here are primarily conjectural and will need to be validated by archaeological methods. The listing in the text of government initiated plantation castles is complemented by an appendix containing descriptions of buildings held by other settlers in north county Wexford.

Grantees' Buildings

BALLYCARNEY (Ordnance Survey 1/2 inch, Sheet 19, 97.48), on the river Slaney, about five miles north of Enniscorthy. This estate was granted in 1612 to Sir James Carroll, Mayor of Dublin, and regranted to him in 1618. It is very likely that he occupied the lands as early as 1617, when the former Irish owner, Dowling McBryan Cavanagh, complained about Carroll's taking possession. The plantation was attacked by another Kavanagh in 1620, when houses on the estate were burnt, and servants were murdered. Apparently, Carroll had not yet started building the main residence, which was listed as being under construction when the 1621 survey was taken. At that time, the foundation was laid for a bawn of 74 foot square. When Sir William Brereton visited the area in 1635, he found Sir James Carroll's 'new and stately house, which hath almost sunk him by the charge of building the same'. It is likely that this 'great English' house was burnt by the Irish during the rebellion, but that the nearby village was largely preserved. The poll tax account of 1659 lists 39 Irishmen and 4 Englishmen in 1659. The Civil Survey records in Ballycarney 'A large stone house, two mills & two wears upon the river Slane(y)'. A drawing made in 1840 (pl. xxi) shows two towers, one broad-based and three storeys high judging from its three string courses. It had small windows (larger windows were probably inserted at a later date), was capped by battlements and had an external chimney stack, all typical of early seventeenth century plantation architecture. The tower was more slender than the contemporary Huntington Castle at Clonegal (pl. xx), dating from 1625, and probably was no more than additional living quarters which complemented the main house that has long since vanished. A second tower probably complemented the other towers as flankers to the former court, which according to tradition had two other towers opposite them. There are no surviving fragments of this four-towered court and its main residence above the ground.[34]

Plate xxi: Drawing of Ballycarney in 1840

BALLYNABARNEY (8.70), 8 miles nnw of Gorey, close to Wingfield House. This property was granted in 1613 to Sir Richard Wingfield as the manor of Cromwell but was renamed the manor of Wingfield in a regrant five years later. The 1621 survey describes the building on this estate as similar to that at

Sampton (see Ballyvoodock, fig. 7.2). It apparently survived the rebellion because the Civil Survey of 1654 shows it as an intact manor house at Ballynabarney, together with a ruined castle, close to the present Wingfield House. A visit to the latter site in 1977 revealed no traces of these buildings.[35]

BALLYNACLASH (14.32), on the coast, 7 miles sse of Oulart. The land of Ballynaclash and adjoining property had been granted to John Langhorne or Langherne, a son-in-law of the Lord Deputy Chichester, in 1613 and again five years later. Within the next two years the estate had been sold to another planter, Sir Adam Loftus (see Rahale), from whom it passed to George Cheevers, a Catholic, sometime before the rebellion. The 1621 survey indicates that a castle had been built, similar to Sampton Castle (see Ballyvoodock, fig. 7.2). Ballynaclash castle was mentioned shortly after the rebellion as a 'small plantation house' of two-and-a-half storeys, lived in by George Cheevers, who disagreed with others that it was fit to serve as a garrison. According to the present owner of the property, there were formerly remains of a ten-foot high tower in the garden near where there is a slope in the land. The remains of that tower and of the older house on the site, close to the present house, have been demolished.[36]

BALLYVOODOCK (14.36), close to the coast, 4 miles se of Oulart. The estate was granted as the manor of Sampton to Capt George Trevelyan in 1613, for his services as commissioner for the plantation. In fact, Trevelyan, the nephew of Lord Deputy Chichester, received the lands as a concealed grant to the Lord Deputy, who wrote that he had passed the lands to Sir George 'to secure myself', because of the 'great sums of money laid out by me ...' for the Wexford plantation. At the same time, the transfer to Trevelyan was intended as a dowry for Trevelyan's wife, which, as it happened, was not superfluous as Trevelyan died in 1620. Annesley had received letters patent for the estate in the preceding year. Its precise ownership is unclear from the documents, however, for in 1621 Chichester valued the estate as 'a hundred pounds upon the rack ...' (i.e. at a rack rent), while Annesley the lessee, thought that it could be purchased for £1,000 to £1,100. It is not known who was responsible for building the rather small castle which consisted of a two-and-a-half storey house with a small court (fig. 7.2). The evidence from the Civil Survey indicates that Sampton Castle was ruined in 1654. It was located at Ballyvoodock, which had been the choice of a grant for a market in 1618. There is no trace of the castle other than a slight mound and a field called the 'castle field' near Ballyvoodock House.[37]

CAMOLIN See Milshoge

CASTLE ANNESLEY (19.41), on the coast, 6 miles east of Oulart. The area around Castle Annesley, probably including Castle Murrough (also called Morriscastle), was granted in 1618 to Sir Francis Annesley as the manor of Annesley. In all likelihood, Castle Annesley formed the centre of the estate.

The 1621 survey mentions a small castle built by Sir Francis, similar to that at Sampton (see Ballyvoodock, fig. 7.2). However, the Civil Survey of 1654 does not show a stone building on the Castle Annesley site. Remains on the site consist of a small, round, two storey high tower with five pistol loops. Judging from the fragments of wall attached to the tower, it was not a corner tower, but abutted to a straight wall, possibly from the back of a house.[38]

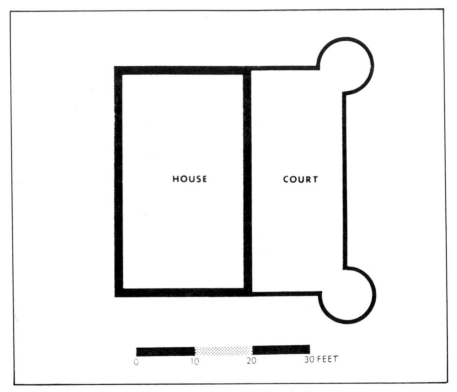

HOUSE

COURT

0   10   20   30 FEET

Fig. 7.2: Conjectural plan of the castle at Ballyvoodock

CASTLE MARWOOD See Monaseed

CASTLE MURROUGH See Castle Annesley

DRUMGOLD (98.39), about one mile east of Enniscorthy. This estate was granted to Sir Francis Blundell in 1613 and again in 1620. By the latter grant he was obliged to build a castle and a bawn within two years. He also obtained the rights for the fishing of salmon in the river Slaney, the customs for timber brought over the river or land and a license to build tanneries. The 1621 survey mentions the estate but does not show that anything had been built there. However, a plantation apparently existed, since there is a record of one of Blundell's tenants threatening in 1620 to burn the plantation houses there.

Blundell sold the property before 1630 to Sir Henry Wallop, the owner of the large estate at Enniscorthy. As the Civil Survey does not mention a stone building on the site, it is unlikely that the plantation conditions for building were adhered to here. Neither the Down Survey nor the six-inch Ordnance Survey showed a building on this site.[39]

FISHERSTOWN See Prospect

JONESTOWN See Middleton

LIMERICK (15.66), 4 miles north of Gorey. The estate of Lemanagh and surrounding lands were granted in 1612 and again in 1618 to Sir Lawrence Esmond. Its Irish name was subsequently anglicised to Limerick. Esmond was one of the few among the first series of settlers to adhere to the plantation conditions as was noted in a government document of 1617, at which time he probably already had built at this site. The 1621 survey (fig. 7.3) shows a residence that undoubtedly was the largest among the known plantation castles of the area. Two houses, each of two-and-a-half storeys, stood back-to-back. Each faced a court with flankers on the corners and there was a gate house at the smallest court. Little is known of the social life at Limerick Castle other than a late seventeenth century account that Lord Esmond maintained 'always a numerous Retinue of well accomplished young gentlemen, well accoutred and compleatlie armed with excellent serviceable horses ...' The Lord Deputy Strafford stayed at the castle in 1637.

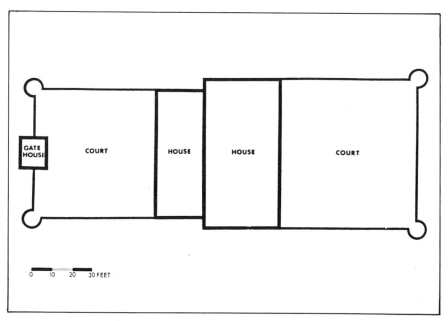

Fig. 7.3: Conjectural plan of the castle at Limerick

Remains on the site consist of one round flanker with pistol loops; the flanker was 20 feet in height in 1840, but is only about six feet high now. The site of the main house may coincide with the present farm buildings. Another ruined castle was mentioned in 1659 at Ballynestragh, the site of the now ruined country seat of the Esmonds that succeeded Limerick Castle. A third, surviving Esmond castle still stands at Clonegal called Huntington Castle (see pl. xx), and is said to have been built in 1625 by Sir Thomas Esmond, a son of Sir Lawrence. A fourth castle was built or rebuilt by the latter at Ballytramon, on Wexford harbour, after its acquisition in 1625.

To return to Limerick Castle, it is clear from Sir Lawrence's letters that he often resided there. At the rebellion of 1641, it was defended by '140 able men well armed', and must have survived intact. Only at the siege of the castle in 1649, four years after Lord Esmond's death, was it burned, allegedly by its defender, Sir Thomas Esmond. An account of that time described the building as a 'very stately and defensible House . . .'' The *Civil Survey* of 1654 mentions a ruined manor house and a castle, probably the one at Ballynestragh. Subsequently, the lands were confiscated and passed into the hands of an absentee landlord, the Duke of Albemarle. A survey made in 1669 survives among his estate papers and gives the following description: 'The manor house was a large Stone Building, situated on the southside of A large Hill, but in the time of Rebellion was all Burnt to ye Ground only ye Wales, some say by S(i)r Thomas Esmon(d)e order. To it Joynes A large Garden & orchard, & severall verie large vines Against ye House wale. And from it Eastward is A long stragling Irish Towne. At ye East end A Chapple. And about ye Middle of it A Reasonable good slate House in w(hi)ch Mr Daulton lives, though badly in repayre & all ye rest to ruine. . . .' According to a late seventeenth century document, Lord Esmond was buried at the chapel at Limerick in 'a sumptuous tomb'. The adjoining town, according to the poll tax account of 1659, must have been one of the largest ones in the area with its 11 Englishmen and 55 Irishmen. At the Restoration, the property passed to the Duke of Albemarle, an absentee landlord. However, eventually the lands were returned to the Esmonds.[40]

MEDOPALL See Milshoge

MILSHOGE (7.52), one mile south of Camolin. The 1621 survey indicates that the property was originally granted to Henry Piers, secretary to the Lord Deputy Chichester but a comparison of the lands in Piers' letters patent of 1613 do not agree with the townland names in this area. Piers sold his property to Edmund Medhop or Medhope, Clerk of the Pleas of the Exchequer, Chirographer of the Common Pleas, and Clerk of the House of Commons in 1615. The latter obtained a grant of lands in 1621, which were to be created the manor of Medhopall (sic). The grant stipulated that he was required to build a house and bawn within three years. Medhop married a sister of Sir Francis Annesley but died soon after receiving the lands. His widow resided at another plantation property in Ely O'Carroll (county Offaly) which had also been granted to Edmund Medhop. After Medhop's death, the Wexford lands passed to Sir Francis Annesley. The 1621 survey noted that nothing had been built on the land, but about 30 years later, according to the *Civil Survey*, there was a castle at 'Melsoigne', which refers to the townland of Milshoge. The actual site, however, could have been at the adjoining townland of Norris Mount (named after Annesley's baronial title of Mountnorris). The six-inch Ordnance Survey of 1841 shows a square structure on the site, with four projections at two corners, possibly flankers for defense, adjoining a large formal garden. This house was pulled down 20 years ago.

To complicate matters even further, a townland called Medophall Demesne (sic) is located on the opposite site of Norris Mount, name after the second grantee. Although it is not clear when a residence was built here, it certainly was occupied in 1672 by a Lady Rotheram. The 1841 Ordnance Survey map shows a rectangular house with two ranges of outbuildings, which must refer to the georgian residence which no longer exists on the site. However, the Ordnance Survey also shows a square garden, laid out in a formal seventeenth century fashion.

Nearby Camolin (formerly called Knockangarrow, see under Monasootagh) became the centre of the Annesley estate. Only the stable block now survives on the latter site, which probably was contemporaneous with the brick house which dates from the late seventeenth or early eighteenth century and stood here until about thirty years ago. According to the *Civil Survey* of 1654, Lord Mountnorris owned over 11,000 acres in the baronies of Scarawalsh, Gorey, and Ballaghkeen. He had acquired this large estate primarily through purchases of other plantation lands.[41]

MIDDLETON (20.55), one mile south of Courtown. This property was granted to Sir Roger Jones in 1618, although Sir Roger had been nominated as grantee as early as 1612. The 1621 survey noted a bawn of 40 feet square, defended by two flankers, and within the bawn a brick house of two-and-a-half storeys, measuring 24 by 30 feet. The castle was therefore very similar but slightly smaller than the ones at Ballyvoodock, Ballynabarney, and Rahale. The property was acquired by Lord Esmond (see Limerick) prior to 1633 at which time he sold it to Piers Synnott. The *Civil Survey* of 1654 notes a 'stone house decayed' on Piers property and refers to it as Coranvready, possibly the Irish townland name prior to the introduction of the name Middleton. The poll tax account of 1659 shows 7 English and 27 Irish living there, an adequate number to suggest a small village. Inspection of the site in 1986 showed no clear remains, although the present Middleton House, dating from the nineteenth century, may incorporate some aspects of the older house.[42]

MONASEED also called CASTLE MARWOOD (8.65), 5 miles nw of Gorey. This estate was granted in 1613 and again in 1618 to William Marwood, and he was given the license for a market in 1615. The 1621 survey records a large structure, consisting of a two-and-a-half storey house adjoining a bawn with gate house (see fig 7.4). There was also a walled orchard of 268 by 161 foot. In

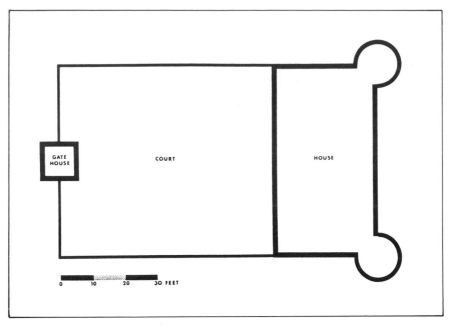

GATE
HOUSE

COURT

HOUSE

0   10   20   30 FEET

Fig. 7.4: Conjectural plan of the castle at Monaseed

the preceding year, the Kavanaghs surprised 'Mr Marwood's houses', probably adjoining this castle, and burnt the town. The property was sold to Henry Masterson, who styled himself as of Monaseed in his testimony of losses resulting from the rebellion, which he estimated at £3,000. He related that he had been forcibly expelled from his dwelling house, lands, and farms, losing an income of £390 per year. The *Civil Survey* of 1654 indicates that the castle was ruined; at this time, the building and a mill were still in the hands of Henry Masterson. As only four Irishmen lived at Monaseed, according to the poll tax account for 1659, the village must already have decayed by that time. Our survey in 1977 did not locate any traces above the ground in the townland called Monaseed Demesne.[43]

MONASOOTAGH (5.57), about 3-1/2 miles nne of Ferns. This estate was granted in 1613 and regranted in 1619 to Thomas Hibbotts, successor to Sir Richard Cooke, Chancellor of the Exchequer. By 1621 Hibbotts had built a house of two-and-a-half storeys, adjoining a tower and bawn, with another house on its other side for offices (see fig. 7.5). According to the *Civil Survey* of 1654 it had passed to Lord Mountnorris by 1640, at which time it contained a castle at Monasootagh, a church, and a small stone house at Cnocangarrow (Knockangarrow). The later location was later named Camolin (see Milshoge) and was a former residence of one of the main branches of the Kavanaghs. There are no traces of the castle at Monasootagh, which must have stood close to the present hamlet of the same name.[44]

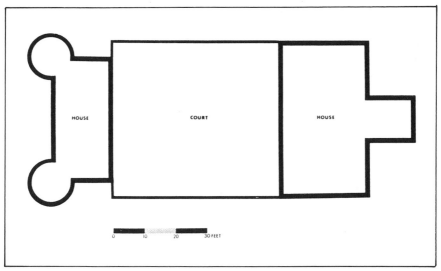

Fig. 7.5: Conjectural plan of the castle at Monasootagh

NEWTOWN (18.71), 7 miles north of Gorey, adjoining the Wicklow border. This estate was granted in 1612 to Sir Richard Cooke, Chancellor of the Exchequer, but the letters patent do not appear to have been enrolled. Six years later, Sir Richard having died in the interim, the estate was granted to his son Walsingham Cooke as the manor of Cookestown. The 1621 survey indicates that a stone castle probably stood on this site with a flanker in the rear housing the staircase (see fig. 7.6). The building was then unfinished. The property was sold to Sir George Sexton and Mathew Ford in 1624. The location of the castle is apparent from the *Civil Survey* of 1654, which mentions Ford being in

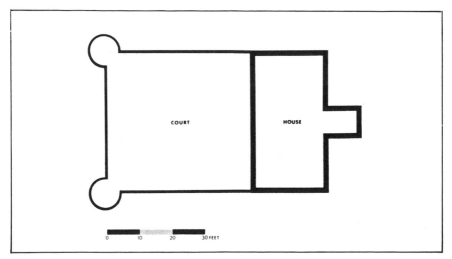

Fig. 7.6: Conjectural plan of the castle probably at Newtown

possession of a ruined castle, two mills, and a manor house, probably intact, at 'Ballynowe', which was later anglicised as Newtown. About five years later, only two Englishmen are mentioned in the poll-tax account of this site; another nine are listed on other lands of this estate. This plantation should not be confused with Walshingham Cooke's estate at Tomduff, which he had taken over from another grantee, William Parsons, thereby exchanging the upland property for more fertile coastal lowlands near the south. A visit to the site in 1986 did not reveal any evidence above the ground of a former castle.[45]

NORRIS MOUNT See Milshoge

PROSPECT (20.60), also called Fisherstown, 3 miles north of Courtown, almost on the coast. This estate was first granted to Sir Edward Fisher in 1612 as the manor of Chichester and regranted six years later as the manor of Fisherstown. He was one of the few initial grantees who fulfilled the plantation conditions by 1617. The castle mentioned in 1621 as 'verie fayre' was made of brick (see fig. 7.7). Even the flankers to the house contained good lodgings. There was a garden nearby, enclosed by a wall measuring 110 by 72 foot. The area was rocked by an earthquake in 1624. Because of Fisher's 'extraordinary plantation' here, he was (unsuccessfully) nominated as a Privy Councillor. Sir Edward also built a residence close to Dublin in Phoenix Park.

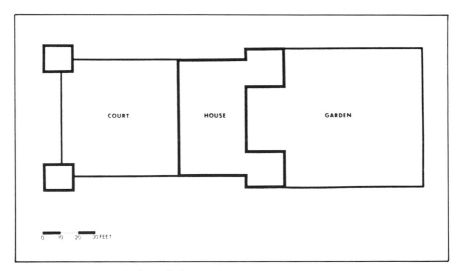

Fig. 7.7: Conjectural plan of the castle at Prospect

It later became a vice-regal lodge; this site is now occupied by the Magazine Fort. In 1654 the manor house at Prospect was 'decayed', at which time it was in the hands of Edward Chichester, to whom it had passed by marriage (it probably is shown as a tower-like feature on the Down Survey). In addition, there were the following structures: a decayed stone house at Ballymoney; a stone house, apparently in repair on the lands of Kilbride and Courtown; and a mill in repair elsewhere. It is likely that the latter farm was leased to John Cooke, who in 1642 reported his losses resulting from the rebellion. These included such unusual possessions (for a tenant) as his 'divers books and pictures found in his Studie', which caused the rebels to see him as 'a dampened puritan unworthy of anything to live. . . .' In 1659, the population on the Prospect estate consisted of 18 Englishmen and 44 Irishmen, mostly centred at Kilbride, adjoining the former site of Courtown House. The estate passed in 1711 from John Chichester to James Stopford, the father of the first Earl of Courtown.[46]

RAHALE (2.31), 6 miles sse of Enniscorthy. A castle, similar to Ballyvoodock (q.v., see fig. 7.2), was built here by the grantee Sir Adam Loftus, whose residence in Dublin was at Rathfarnham Castle. After receiving a grant of the lands in 1619, he soon afterwards conveyed them to Richard Stafford, probably of Old English stock. The castle on the site is noted in the 1621 survey and had a moat around it with a drawbridge fed by the river Sow. It stood close to a ford across that river and may have had a small village nearby, since the poll tax account of 1659 mentioned 32 Irish living there in the absence of any Englishmen. The adjoining townlands, Mill Lands and Bleachlands, refer to the economic activities of the villagers. The 1654 *Civil Survey* lists a ruined stone house at the site, which in 1640 was in the hands of James Stafford, an 'Irish Papist'. The property passed in 1668 to Sir Hans Hamilton. According to Jeffrey, the site of the castle was on the Maher farm, at the castle field, where there was a mound of 120 feet square, surrounded by a deep and wide ditch. Local tradition dates the demolition of the castle to 100 years ago. In 1986 we were unable, even with local help, to locate the site. However, Barry in his list of moated sites mentions a raised platform of 1.2 metres with a 5.50 metre wide wet moat in the townland of Mill Lands, which must be the Rahale site.[47]

SAMPTON CASTLE See Ballyvoodock

TOMDUFF (16.50), also called Parsonstown, 5 miles sw of Courtown. This estate originally had been granted to the Surveyor-General, Sir William Parsons, first in 1612 under the name of the manor of Coolag and later in 1618 as the manor of Parsonstown. The 1621 survey mentions that Parsons built, probably at this site, a 'fayre castle or house', 28 foot high (fig. 7.8), with asymmetrical flankers and a bawn. It is not clear whether Thomas Ricroft, a freemason, who farmed Ballywalter on the Tomduff estate at least as late as 1641, was involved in building the castle. The estate was subsequently leased or conveyed to Sir Walsingham Cooke, another settler (see Newtown), whose daughter had married the son of Sir William Parsons. Cooke resided here on the eve of the Rebellion of 1641 when he completed a burial vault for his wife and grandchild. After the rebellion, he claimed to have expended £2,000 on building, enclosing lands, erecting a new church and chancel, and constructing dwellings for more than 200 families that had settled there. In terms of

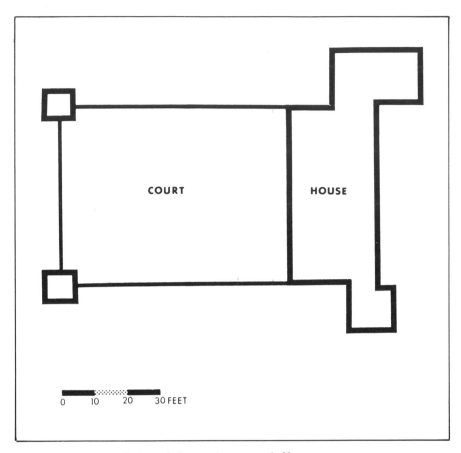

Fig. 7.8: Conjectural plan of the castle at Tomduff

personal household goods, he claimed that he lost £2,000. He buried his wife in a vault at the site made in 1641, probably in the overgrown graveyard close to the present ruins. The ruined manor house and a mill were listed in the *Civil Survey* of 1654. An Arthur Parsons is mentioned as being of Newenham (also called Tomduff) in 1678-80, while a probable descendant, William Parsons of Tomduff, died in 1705. Buildings still standing on the site in 1977 consisted of brick structures now used as barns which are difficult to date. Their location was quite strategic; they are situated on high ground, sloping steeply toward the Owenavorragh river, where there presumably was a ford or even a bridge. A nearby townland is called the Brick Park, suggesting the presence of a brick industry here. The six-inch Ordnance Survey map of 1841 shows various buildings, but none that resembles fig. 7.8 in plan. The plantation village here is no longer in evidence. The lands eventually descended to the Earl of Courtown.[48]

WINGFIELD CASTLE See Ballynabarney

Appendix 1

OTHER PLANTATION SITES

CASTLE ELLIS (9.37), 8 miles ssw of Enniscorthy. The lands had been granted in 1618 to an Irishman Henry O'Murrogho. However, by 1641, they were in the hands of William Sacheverell who claimed considerable losses due to the rebellion. It is not clear whether the castle on the site was renovated or replaced by another building. There are no remains.[49]

KILLYBEGS (20.67), immediately west of Inch in the north-eastern part of the area. This site probably was not part of the government sponsored plantation, but was mortgaged by its Irish owner William Doyle of Fortchester (Fort Chichester) to the merchant Thomas Wakefield, Mayor of Dublin, and one Plunkett. In a deposition after the rebellion, the former mentioned that he had spent £200 in building there. It probably was a brick house, as a Dublin bricklayer, Peter Harrison, was employed on the site by Wakefield.[50]

RAMSFORT (15.62), one mile north of Gorey. Thomas Ram, the protestant Bishop of Ferns and Leighlin moved his see from Ferns to the new plantation town of Gorey in 1620, where he completed the bishop's palace in 1630. An inscribed stone from this building had the following verse inscribed on it:

> This house Ram built for his
> succeeding brothers:
> Thus sheep bear wool, not for
> themselves, but others.

Ram died in Dublin in 1634 but his body was carried to Gorey, where it was buried in a chapel built by him. The palace, including the bishop's library, was burnt by the rebels in 1641, when the town was sacked. His son Abel Ram built a house close to the town called Ramsfort which was also burnt around this time. The *Civil Survey* mentions the site as 'a ffort in repaire & a decayed Mill', which may indicate that its residence, as the name suggests, was situated in a fortified enclosure. It probably stood on the site of the present country house, built in 1751.[51]

CLOHAMON (93.55), on the river Slaney, 9 miles nnw of Enniscorthy. This manor dates from medieval times. In the sixteenth century, the lands were granted to an Englishman, Thomas Masterson, from whom it passed to his son Sir Richard Masterson, seneschal of the county, who did not restore the building since its partial burning in 1597. The last patent to Masterson in 1610 mentions the structures at the site as 'a bawne, an old tower near the river Slane(y), and another tower near the Manor gate ...' Masterson was considered a 'native' rather than a potential settler for the Wexford Plantation. Although he was nominated to build three castles, there is no evidence that he ever did so. Instead, he sold the property shortly before 1625, for £1,600 to Sir George Calvert, Lord Baltimore. This English peer had been principal secretary to James I but after his resignation had given up the protestant faith to become a Catholic. The intolerance for Catholics in England drove him to Ireland, which had become the home of other Catholic exiles. He had received a grant of plantation land in Longford in 1621, which he gave up in preference to the Clohamon estate in county Wexford. He must have known the area well since he had been one of the commissioners sent from England in 1613 to report on the progress of the Wexford plantation. In Calvert's case, it meant a major move, since he had recently completed the building of a charming and unique country house, Kiplin Hall, in Yorkshire. His colonial interests spanned two continents. He had been granted a vast tract in the Avalon peninsula in Newfoundland in 1622, where he founded a settlement and he eventually became the only Roman Catholic to be granted, by the English king, a fiefdom on the American continent in the form of the province of Maryland.

Before striking out across the Atlantic ocean, Calvert, with his family and retinue, moved to Masterson's manor house at Ferns where he stayed during the rebuilding of Clohamon during the fall of 1625. A year later, he occupied the new buildings. The only known description of Clohamon dates from 1635 and is from the traveller, Sir William Brereton, who characterised it as 'a brave house, but of no great strength, nor built castle-wise'. This tantalising, brief description evokes a question as to whether or not the building was in any way similar to Calvert's Kiplin Hall. The latter was unique, even in England, with its rigorous symmetry from all four sides. Even though its architect is unknown, Calvert may have received inspiration from his architecturally minded friend, Sir Henry Wotton, or from Palladio's *Quattro Libri* (1570), or Serlio's *Book VII* (1618). Calvert's own apparent sophistication in building was evident at Clohamon but this awaits archaeological confirmation. The town and its adjoining village appears to have survived the initial stages of the rebellion in 1641 but the town and perhaps the house were pillaged by the English army early in 1643. An account of this time mentions the village of Balleparke (Ballinapark, close to Bunclody), part of the Clohamon estate, 'which had been an English plantation, but now full of Rebells (although there were) 'some distressed English which escaped from the Irish and came to the armie'. Clohamon itself, though, was the true centre of the Calvert estate, judging from the fact that at the end of the 1650s the town was among the largest in north Wexford with its 14 Englishmen and 80 Irishmen. However, by that time Calvert was dead and his son a permanent resident in Maryland. The manor house, which was in decay in 1650, was a ruin in the eighteenth century and is now gone.[52]

Acknowledgements

The authors are grateful to Mr and Mrs S. Johnston and Kevin Whelan for their advice and for showing us several sites. R.J. Hunter kindly provided a transcript of Rotheram's survey, and gave inspiration in several ways to write this chapter. The map was drawn by Mary Guercio, while the plans were prepared by Will Mayer. The authors are greatly indebted to Celia Eatman and S. Johnston for their thoughtful comments on an earlier draft.

8 *Daniel Gahan*

The Estate System of County Wexford, 1641-1876

During the period 1641-1878, landed properties in county Wexford became progressively smaller and more fragmented; the confiscations of the Cromwellian. period may have initiated this process but it developed a momentum of its own over the ensueing two centuries. In addition, the ethno-religious composition of the landed class of the county also changed so that, while the New English protestant element held a monoply of landownership at the end of the seventeenth century, the Old English and Gaelic catholic element had gained a major foothold among the landowning class by 1876. Combined with these changes, however, are two important elements of continuity in the agrarian history of the county. First, even as late as the mid-nineteenth century, there was still a noticeable contrast between Wexford's southeastern baronies and the rest of the county in terms of estate size; smaller estates in the south reflected the legacy of the manorial system which had been established on the basis of small properties. Second, the catholic landowners who entered the county' landed classes between 1782 and 1876 joined its lower levels only. The result was that by 1876 there were two estate systems in Wexford, one based on relatively large properties, with long-established protestant ownership, the other based on small estates, many of whose owners were catholic and new to the proprietorial classes. These combinations of change and continuity demonstrate the complexity of Wexford's agrarian history and indicate that, by and large, the Wexford pattern of proprietorial change is broadly similar to that of other counties which bestrode the old Gaelic/Norman frontier.[1]

The influence of the past on the land system of Wexford in the seventeenth century is evident from an examination of the geography of the two basic territorial sub-divisions in the county, the civil parish and the townland. The areas of these sub-divisions reveal a pronounced difference between the southern and northern areas of the county (fig. 8.1). The boundaries of the civil parishes of Ireland are generally believed to reflect the outlines of proprietorial

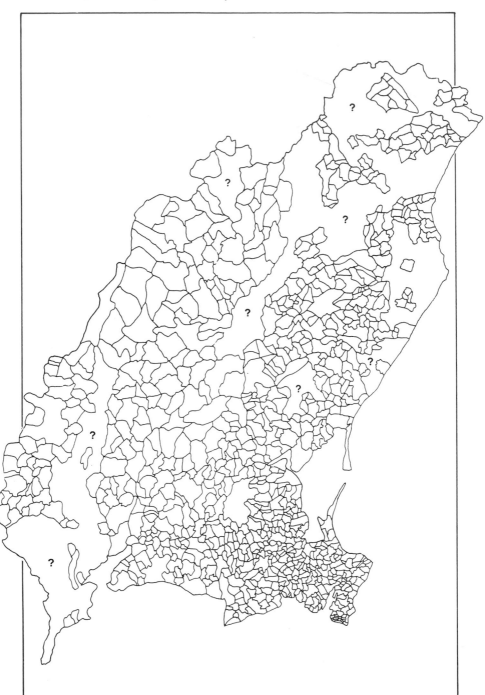

Fig. 8.1: The townland structure in Wexford in the mid-seventeenth century (based on the Civil Survey)

divisions at the time they were drawn up in the late Middle Ages.[2]

In county Wexford there is a significant difference in parish size and degree of fragmentation between the southeastern baronies of Bargy, Forth, Shelmalier and South Ballaghkeen, where parishes were quite small, and the north-western baronies of Bantry, Scarawalsh and Gorey where they were much larger. This pattern suggests that the manors established by Norman settlers in Bargy and Forth may have been much smaller than properties in the Gaelic north and west of the county.[3]

The network of Wexford townlands also reveals the influence of the past. Fig. 8.1, which is based on Johnston's superimposition of the Down Survey on mid nineteenth century Ordnance Survey maps, demonstrates the contrast between the southeast and northwest of the county in terms of average townland size.[4] Thus, while townlands were extremely small in Bargy and Forth and also quite small in most of the barony of Shelmalier (East and West) and in much of Ballaghkeen (North and South), townlands in the northern and western baronies of the county were much larger and were especially large in Scarawalsh and Bantry.[5] While townlands of one hundred acres or less were very common in southeastern parts of the county, townlands of up to five hundred acres or more were the norm in the north and west. These two distributions demonstrate the importance of the northwest/southeast contrast in the county. However, while the variation in the size of parishes is explicable by the presence of the manorial system in the southeast and its absence in the northwest, the difference in townland size begs another explanation.[6]

The small townlands demarcated by Petty in Bargy and Forth may have been fully enclosed, compact farms by the seventeenth century. The far more extensive townlands in north Wexford suggest that land here was farmed on some type of 'pre-enclosure' basis. We know too little about the socio-economic history of Gaelic north Wexford before the seventeenth century to tell whether a rundale-based or an extensive pastoral agriculture was locally predominant;[7] indeed, it is possible that the land system simultaneously contained elements of rundale tillage and extensive pastoralism.[8]

The geography of the estate system of the county prior to the Cromwellian confiscation suggests that this difference between the north and south of the county was replicated at the proprietorial level also (fig. 8.2). This map provides a reasonably accurate picture of the pattern of landownership in the county in 1641. A striking regional contrast exists between the Norman baronies of Bargy, Forth, Shelmalier, and South Ballaghkeen, where estates were very small, and the Gaelic baronies of Gorey, Scarawalsh, Bantry and North Ballaghkeen, where estates were unusually large.[10] Indeed, many of the estates in the southeastern baronies were almost small enough to be run as yeoman farms, being no more than one to two hundred acres in extent, while the extensive properties in the north of the county often exceeded several thousand acres.[11] Moreover, these rather large properties of one thousand acres and more tended to be very compact. The resulting geographical pattern of landownership is simple and would lead one to conclude that many of these estates were large enough to function as well-integrated socio-economic

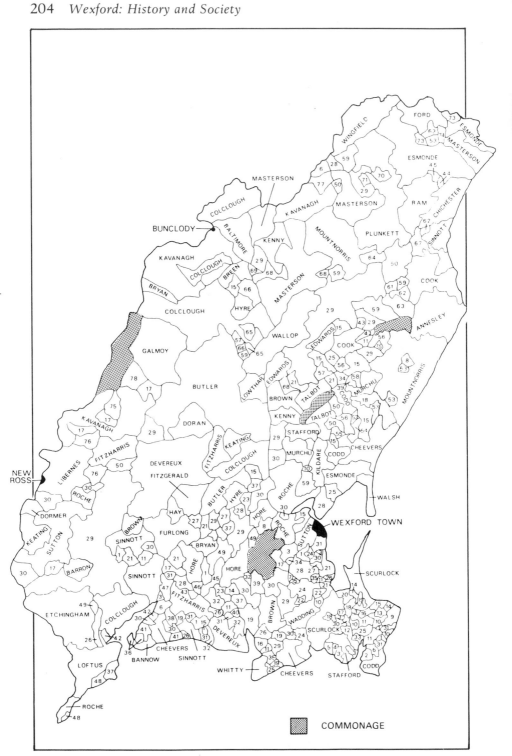

Fig. 8.2: Landownership in Wexford c.1640 (based on the Civil Survey)

Numbers refer to fig 8.2

1 CODD	40 PATRICK
2 MELLARD	41 CULLEN
3 HAY	42 DUFFE
4 JERVIS	43 GILES
5 SIGGINS	44 STRONG
6 BARRY	45 LOFTUS
7 DAKE	46 CANNING
8 FURLONG	47 CHURCH
9 LAMBERT	48 LEWIS
10 STAFFORD	49 SUTTON
11 BROWN	50 MOUNTNORRIS
12 FRENCH	51 SMITH
13 DORMER	52 FITZHENRY
14 BUSHER	53 MURCHU
15 SINNOTT	54 FAGAN
16 FITZNICHOLS	55 EUSTACE
17 FITZHARRIS	56 KENNY
18 TALBOT	57 CONNOR
19 KEATING	58 SATCHELL
20 WALSH	59 MASTERSON
21 ROCHE	60 WALLOP
22 ROCHFORD	61 MURTHA
23 RUSSELL	62 KINSELLA
24 ROSSITTER	63 KAVANAGH
25 TURNER	64 FARRELL
26 WHITTY	65 O'BRIEN
27 WADDING	66 McDANIEL
28 ESMONDE	67 REDMOND
29 UNKNOWN	68 BREEN
30 DEVEREUX	69 WALL
31 CHEEVERS	70 RAM
32 MEYLER	71 WADDOCK
33 SCURLOCK	72 WAFER
34 DORAN	73 DOYLE
35 NICKSON	74 PLUNKETT
36 COLCLOUGH	75 GRIFFIN
37 HORE	76 MOUNTGARRETT
38 BISHOP	77 SLEABROOK
39 PRENDERGAST	78 McENROND

units.[12] If this is true, and if one may assume that the cash nexus was not very common in this society by 1641, then the relationship between many of the owners of these large properties and their general populations may have closely resembled that of a Latin American lord with his subject peasantry.[13] This view of the estate in the north of the county as 'neo-manorial' is crucial to the discussion which follows, particularly since, as in the Latin American example, the lords of such properties would have been, in most cases, aliens in the sight of the general rural population.[14]

Fig. 8.2 also reveals that there was a pronounced geographical dimension to what might be termed the 'ethno-religious' pattern of landownership at that date. While the landed class of Wexford tended to be dominated by families of Norman or so-called Old English origin in 1641, a number of New English landowners were already present, concentrated in the northern half of the county. Bearing in mind the importance of the Stuart plantations and other early modern assaults on the Gaelic landed elite in Wexford, this pattern is hardly surprising. Thus, those areas of the county which had already been confiscated in the second decade of the seventeenth century were now in the hands of New English protestants and were declared unforfeited; these areas are left blank in fig. 8.2. Unforfeited areas were located mainly in the northern baronies although there were a few such tracts in Shelburne in the southwest. Most but not all of the confiscated areas of the county were in the hands of the families with Old English surnames, many of whom still held land inside the former Norman colony. The Esmonds of Gorey barony are a good example of a southern Old English family which expanded its holdings at the expense of defeated Gaelic families following the Nine Year's War. The largest estates in the county were those of the Annesley/Mountnorrises in the baronies of Gorey and North Ballaghkeen and the Wallop estate around Enniscorthy (both New English), and the very large property of Pierce Butler, a landowner with Norman forebears in Bantry.[15] Moreover, in the southern part of the county Old English family names also dominated the landed elite — Scurlock, Cheevers, Butler, Esmonde, Stafford, Wadding and Devereux were especially prominent.[16] The Old English element was at the height of its economic and political power in county Wexford just prior to the Cromwellian period, having wrested much of the northern lands from their age-old Gaelic rivals in the first decades of the century and having maintained their position in the south. On the other hand, the presence of so many New English names among the landed elite of the north is indicative of the very different experiences of the two halves of the county since the beginning of the Tudor conquest.

Fig. 8.3 details the location of estates in 1660/1703; it is a composite map drawn from the data in the Books of Survey and Distribution and incorporates official changes in landownership made between 1660 and 1703. This map does not take into account transfers of land sold privately and consequently should not be accepted as a perfectly accurate picture of Wexford's estate system in the latter year. The confiscations produced an estate system which was based on significantly smaller and more fragmented properties. Small units were more common in northern parts of the county in the late seventeenth century than had been the case in 1641, even though 'northern' estates were still on average larger than 'southern' estates'. This pattern is illustrated in statistical terms in table 1 which summarises the size distribution of the properties of the county after the confiscations. Half of the land surveyed was owned by individuals with estates of 3,000 acres or more, and landlords of this size accounted for eight percent of the landed class.[17] Twenty-two percent of landowners had estates of 100 acres or less, estates small enough to be worked directly by their owners. However, over half the landowners of the county, or 51 percent, owned properties of 100 to 1,000 acres in extent and 19 per cent owned properties of 1,000 to 3,000 acres. These figures suggest that land-ownership was fairly widely distributed in 1660/1703 and that the typical estate was in the range of 500 to 1,200 acres, with larger properties being the exception rather than the rule.[18] By the early eighteenth century, many of the larger estates had become fragmented. This feature of the estate system has an important bearing on the general evolution of landownership over the ensueing century and a half. Very few large estates in the study area consisted of a single contiguous tract; this was particularly true of large estates owned by aris-tocrats such as the Earl of Anglesey. Fragmentation was evident on smaller estates, although to a lesser degree. Such fragmentation and the prevalence of very small estates in Bargy and Forth may have inhibited the emergence of a neo-manorial pattern of social and economic relationships which developed in other colonial societies. Indeed, the small average estate size in county Wexford, if compared with the extensive properties of Eastern and Central Europe at this time, would suggest that most members of the Wexford class were far less powerful and less wealthy than their counterparts in many other pre-modern societies.[19]

Table 1

Size Distribution of Estates in County Wexford, 1660/1703

Acres (Plan)	Number of Estates	% of Estates	Number of Acres	% of Land Surveyed
0-99	52	22%	2,236	1%
100-299	48	20%	8,812	4%
300-999	73	31%	42,213	17%
1,000-2,999	46	19%	73,720	29%
3,000 plus	19	8%	119,997	49%
Totals	238	100%	246,978	100%

Source: Books of Survey and Distribution (County Wexford).

The significance of the municipalities as a landowning group declined markedly between 1641 and the end of the confiscations. In 1641 there were large tracts of municipal land in the vicinity of several towns and these tracts were quite extensive in some cases, particularly that of New Ross. In 1660/1703, however, the various municipalities owned a mere 2,000 acres or

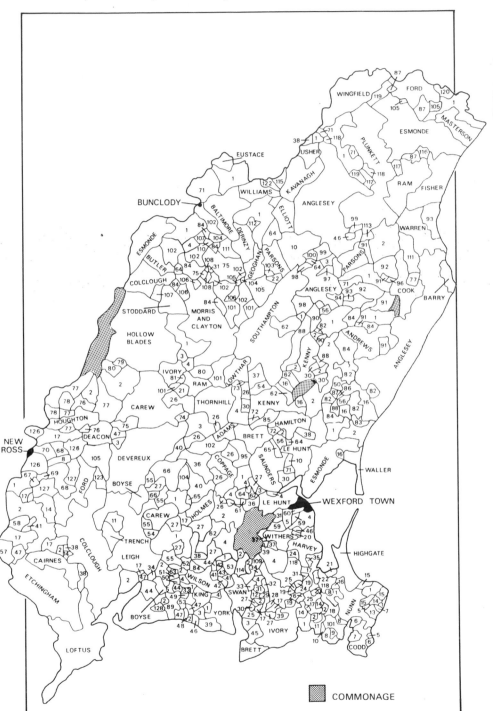

Fig. 8.3: Landownership in Wexford c.1703 (based on the Book of Survey and Distribution)

Numbers refer to fig 8.3

1 UNKNOWN	44 DUKE OF YORK	85 WILLIAMS
2 ANGLESEY	45 BARKER	86 STAFFORD
3 DILLON	46 WALSH	87 THORNHILL
4 BORR	47 LEIGH	88 REDMOND
5 CODD	48 COX	89 HASSELS
6 WADDY	49 JACKSON	90 EDWARDS
7 NUNN	50 THOMPSON	91 WARREN
8 NEALE	51 LORD	92 MASTERSON
9 JONES	KINGSTON	93 FOUNTAIN
10 CHURCH	52 GROWER	94 DORAN
11 OLIVER	53 JENKINS	95 DEVEREUX
12 HART	54 RIDGES	96 KAVANAGH
13 DEAN	55 SCOTT	97 CRADDOCK
14 HOLMES	56 RAM	98 COURTHROP
15 EDWARDS	57 ORMONDE	99 MOUNTNORRIS
16 TALBOT	58 GIFFORD	100 GIBSON
17 IVORY	59 HUDSON	101 BARRINGTON
18 JACOBS	60 HARVEY	102 COLCLOUGH
19 OUSLEY	61 EVANS	103 CORBETT
20 MILLER	62 RICHARDS	104 WAKENHAM
21 WILLIS	63 DREW	105 PLUNKETT
22 WHITE	64 WHEELER	106 CAREY
23 QUIN	65 HOLMES	107 COTTERELL
24 KNOX	66 GATRIX	108 MORRIS
25 ROWE	67 SHEPPARD	109 BISHOP
26 COLLINS	68 ROSS	110 WATKINS
27 HORE	CORPORATION	111 PARSONS
28 ANSLOE	69 DRAKE	112 CARROLL
29 CLIFF	7. WINKWORTH	113 MASTERSON
30 BRETT	71 ESMONDE	114 RADFORD
31 ELLIOTT	72 LE HUNTE	115 BLACKWELL
32 RUSSELL	73 SHEEN	116 HOLLOW BLADES
33 BEASLEY	74 DEACON	117 SANDES
34 SMITH	75 BUTLER	118 ALBEMARLE
35 HARVEY	76 WARREN	119 WINGFIELD
36 THICKNESS	77 KAVANAGH	120 MULES
37 BROWN	78 HAWKINS	121 ANDREWES
38 LOFTUS	79 MEADOWS	122 UNDERWOOD
39 DEVEREUX	80 BARRINGTON	123 GRIFFIN
40 STANNARD	81 HARTING	124 CAIRNS
41 BISHOP	82 LONG	125 CORBETT
42 CHANDLER	83 MURPHY	126 MOUNTGARRETT
43 FOSSY	84 KENNY	127 CROONHORE

one percent of land surveyed and this represented a mere remnant of their former possessions. Since most of the former Liberties were transferred to the new Cromwellian landed classes, the shrinkage of such municipal holdings marks an important stage in the integration of the county into the larger English colonial system. Such a transfer is indicative of the more powerful positions which local landowners had now acquired vis-à-vis the townsmen who had been relatively independent since the twelfth century.

The confiscations of the late seventeenth century also had a great impact on the ethno-religious composition of the Wexford landowning class. Table 2 presents a statistical summary of the distribution of landownership by ethnic group in 1660/1703. For the purposes of constructing this table, landowners have been divided into three groups based on their surnames, i.e. New English, Old English and Gaelic Irish; while this is hardly a totally reliable method, it is sufficient to illustrate the general impact of the confiscations.[20] As the table shows, 176 of the 234 landowners listed for the county in 1703 were of New English protestant background. These 176 landowners represented 64 percent of the landed class and held 88,871 acres or 76 percent of the land surveyed. In contrast, landowners with Old English surnames accounted for only 16 percent of the landed class and held 17 percent of the land surveyed, while landowners with Gaelic surnames accounted for a mere ten percent of the proprietorial class and held only eight percent of the land surveyed. Surnames do not always indicate religious affiliation but it would seem that, as a result of the Cromwellian/Williamite confiscations, landlords of New English protestant background came to completely dominate the county at the expense of the Old English element.

Table 2

The Ethno-Religious Pattern of Landownership in County Wexford, 1703

Ethnicity	Number of Landlords	% of Landlords	Number of Acres Held	% of Land Held
New English	76	74%	188,871	76%
Old English	38	16%	41,646	17%
Gaelic	24	10%	16,593	8%

Source: Books of Survey and Distribution, County Wexford.

Ironically, the Cromwellian conquest and confiscation of Wexford may have lessened the chances of rural Irish society becoming totally dominated by aristocratic landowners in modern centuries. As the county entered the eighteenth century, individuals with aristocratic titles were a relatively unimportant element of the landed class. Table 3, which illustrates this point, shows that only four percent of the proprietors in 1703 had aristocratic titles and held 15 percent of the surveyed land. Landowners who had been knighted or who bore military titles were also relatively unimportant. Untitled landowners, on the other hand, made up 87 percent of the landlords listed in the Books of Survey and Distribution and held 71 per cent of the land surveyed. This situation contrasts markedly with many continental societies where land-ownership was almost the exclusive preserve of the aristocracy.[21]

Table 3

Titles of Landowners in County Wexford, circa 1703

Titles	None	Aristocrat	Knight/Mil.
No. Landlords	207	9	21
% Landlords	89%	4%	9%
Acres Held	174,440	37,460	35,210
% Acres Held	71%	15%	14%

Source: Books of Survey and Distribution, County Wexford.

In spite of these sweeping changes, there was some degree of continuity in the geography of the Wexford estate system during the seventeenth century. There remained a pronounced regional pattern to the distribution of large and small estates in the county similar to the pattern of 1641 (fig. 8.3). For example, there was still a noticeable difference in the size of estates in northern and western as opposed to southeastern baronies just as there had been in 1641, in spite of the fragmentation caused by the confiscations. This point is clearly illustrated in table 4, which summarises the statistical differences in estate sizes among the baronies in 1660/1703. The largest estates were to be found in Shelburne, Bantry and Gorey, with average sizes of 1,099, 1,033 and 992 acres respectively; estates in Bargy and Forth, on the other hand, averaged a mere 394 and 271 acres respectively. Moreover, many of the properties in Bargy and Forth were owned by individuals whose names did not recur in any other part of the county and who, therefore, probably constituted a local resident gentry, of very modest means.[22]

Table 4

Average Estate Size in County Wexford by Barony, circa 1703

Baronies	Average Estate	Baronies	Average Estate
Shelburne	1,099 acres	Scarawalsh	880 acres
Bantry	1,033 acres	Shelmalier	770 acres
Gorey	992 acres	Bargy	394 acres
Ballaghkeen	883 acres	Forth	271 acres

Source: Books of Survey and Distribution, County Wexford.

It is important, before leaving this discussion of the structure of the estate system of county Wexford in 1660/1703, to examine the position of the most important families in the power elite of the county, in terms of the location and extent of their landed property. Such an examination is essential partly because it will give a better sense of the composition of the power elite, and also provide a backdrop for a similar discussion of the personnel of that elite a century and a half later. For the purposes of this discussion the county has been divided into three large sections; the northern or 'panhandle' area, the central area, and the south.

The northern 'panhandle' of the county, composed of the barony of Gorey and the northern portion of North Ballaghkeen, was dominated in 1703 by several large estates, the most prominent of which were the large tracts owned by the Annesley family or the Earls of Anglesey. By 1703 the Angleseys owned a total of some twenty four thousand acres in county Wexford. The largest of the Anglesey tracts was located in the parishes of Ferns and Kilcomb, with a second large holding running along the county's east coast from the parish of Donoughmore to Ballyvalloo. The Angleseys also owned several other more compact properties in Ferns and Ballycanew parishes and numerous smaller tracts scattered throughout the southern half of the county.[23] The property of the Esmondes, another large landowning family, included extensive lands in the north, centred mostly on the manor of Limerick in the parish of Kilcavan, just north of Gorey; they also owned smaller tracts of land on the western border of the county, around Clonegal and in the southeastern corner of East Shelmalier, within the confines of the old Norman colony. Both the Annesleys and the Esmondes remained prominent figures in the social and political life of the county well into the nineteenth century but their landed property had diminished to insignificance by the time of the Great Famine.[24] The Ram family, in possession of a modest estate around Gorey in 1660/1703, incorporated the property of Sir Walter Plunkett, an absentee, early in the eighteenth century and remained a very prominent landed family in the barony of Gorey into the nineteenth century. Another important family in this northern panhandle, the Mastersons, once a powerful Old English family with a large estate in Ferns, were confined to a modest estate near Castletown and another small property around Monaseed in 1660/1703.[25] They too would gradually fade from the ranks of the propertied classes over the course of the eighteenth century. Other estates in this area were those owned by the Fishers, who were in possession of the parish of Ardamine, formerly the Chichester estate and later to evolve into the core of the large and scattered Courtown estate; and that of the Wingfields, later to become the Viscounts of Powers-court, which corresponded to Wingfield Manor in the hilly northwest corner of Gorey barony.

The central portion of the county, the baronies of Scarawalsh and the southern portion part of Ballaghkeen, was dominated by more modest landowners than the northern panhandle. However, there were three exceptionally large properties here; the estates of Morris and Clayton in Scarawalsh, parish of Monart; the Earl of Southampton's estate, an absentee property around the town of Enniscorthy and corresponding to the parishes of Templeshannon, St Mary's, St Johns and Clone; and the long strip of Anglesey territory running down the central portion of the east coast. The Earls of Southampton, like the Earls of Anglesey, were absentees and the lands around Enniscorthy would remain in the hands of English absentee aristocrats through the nineteenth century. The remainder of the baronies of Scarawalsh and Ballaghkeen were dominated by medium-sized estates. As the data in the Books of Survey and Distribution indicate, some of these properties were outlying portions of the estates of large landlords whose main holdings were in the northern panhandle, but many of them belonged to individuals without title whose names do not recur elsewhere in the county and who, presumably, were mostly resident landlords of fairly modest means.

In the southern portion of the county, large estates were to be found in a broad corridor of territory in the southwest, including much of the baronies of Bantry and Shelburne; the parishes around the town of New Ross were an exception to this generalisation since they had numerous small properties, many of them quite fragmented. The large estates in this area included that of the Hollow Sword Blades Company of London, which would sell off its holdings very early in the new century; the estates of the Carews of Castleboro, encompassing a very large tract around the present village of Clonroche in the parishes of Killegney and Chappel; the Devereux lands, which consisted of a large, compact estate that corresponded to the parish of Adamstown;[26] the Leigh estate, centred on Rosegarland and including the parishes of Clonleigh and Ballylannon; the Colclough estate, corresponding to the former Cistercian lands of Tintern; and the Etchingham and Loftus estates, which occupied the peninsula of Shelburne barony in the extreme southwest corner of the county. The four resident families in this group, the Carews, Devereuxs, Leighs and Colcloughs, undoubtedly formed an important coterie of large landed proprietors in this section of the county and their properties were all located in what had been the frontier zone of the old Norman colony. The close correspondence of the boundaries of these estates to those of the civil parishes suggests that they were built on the basic outlines of much earlier property units such as the monastic lands which once dominated this barony.[27]

In areas where small estates were the norm, it is more difficult to determine which families were locally dominant. The economic base of many of the landowners in such areas could not have supported a very lavish lifestyle. There were a few moderately large estates in the southeast which should be mentioned. For example, the Saunders estate in East Shelmalier and the Le Hunte estate adjacent to it were quite large compared to most properties in the immediate area. Similarly, amidst many small properties in Bargy and Forth were a few moderately large estates such as those of the Highgate, Borr, Nunn and Ivory families. Although none of these properties were very extensive, the position of their proprietors in the social and political life of the locality was probably quite important during much of the eighteenth century.

By 1703, therefore, the county's landed elite was clearly a varied group presiding over a rather complex estate system. Properties were relatively small compared with those found in some pre-modern societies, and far too small or fragmented in most cases to allow for the development of any real neo-manorial features. The landed elite itself was almost exclusively New English Protestant in origin and was predominantly of 'commoner' background. This elite, which consisted of close to three hundred families, was made up of a handful of large absentee proprietors, e.g. the Anglesey, Wingfield, Plunkett, Southampton, Etchingham and Loftus families; a small number of large resident landowners, e.g. the Esmonde, Devereux, Colclough and Leigh families; and a very large number of moderate to small landowners, some of whom may have been absentees, but the vast majority of whom were probably resident.[28] While this landed elite was only in place for a generation or two at most by 1660/1703, it is clear that the general geographical outlines of the estate system of the pre-Cromwellian era had been maintained by them in spite of an overall tendency toward fragmentation. Thus, the contrast between the north and west and the south and east of the county was maintained.

How then did the general geographical features of this estate system and the composition of its landed elite change over the course of the ensueing century and a half? From the evidence of Griffith's valuation, the process of fragmentation continued during the eighteenth and early nineteenth centuries; by 1850 the average estate was even smaller than had been the case in 1660/1703. Concomitantly, by 1850 many of the landed families who had been prominent in the area in 1660/1703 had disappeared and some of their former properties had been dismembered. In spite of these important developments, however, there was also a strong degree of continuity.

For example, while the composition of the landed classes changed in terms of personnel, it did not change in terms of its dominant ethnic group; the landlord of New English descent was still the main figure in the area's power elite. Furthermore, the northwestern/southeastern dichotomy in estate size was still visible, albeit less so than in 1660/1703.

The principal source for this section of the discussion is the data of the Primary Valuation of Tenements, an extremely reliable land survey which has been used to reconstruct a map of all the estates of the county in 1850. Names of immediate lessors have been superimposed onto a townland map of county Wexford (fig. 8.4). It should be noted here that the location of properties within individual townlands as indicated on this map is only an approximation, in those cases where townlands were divided among several lessors; however the impression of the general location and extent of estates in 1850 which this map provides is reasonably accurate and will serve as a useful illustration for our discussion.[29]

Fig. 8.4 clearly illustrates the extent to which the estate system of county Wexford had become more fragmented by 1850 compared with 1660/1703. There were far more properties in the county in 1850 and the average estate size was about half what it had been in the early 1700s.[30] This fragmentation may have been partially the result of sales of parcels of large estates which took place over a long period of time. Such sales were probably made at the transition from one generation of landowners to another since the practice of entail would have artificially constrained the land market of the county. It is also possible that many of the smaller landlords on the 1850 map had emerged

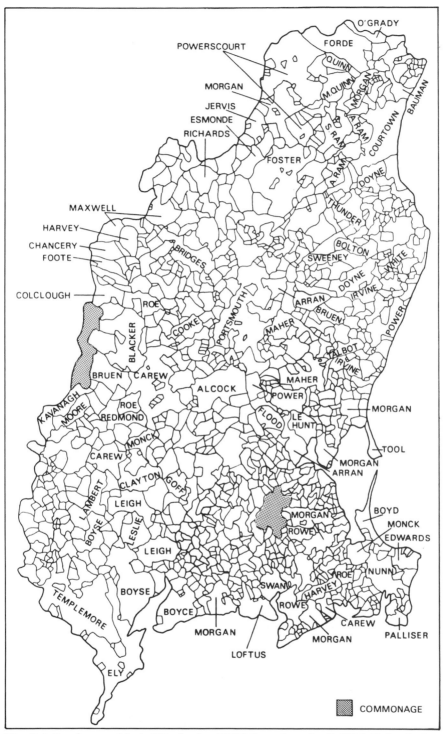

Fig. 8.4: Landownership in Wexford, c.1850 (based on the Griffith Valuation)

from the ranks of the larger tenantry in the countryside or better-off merchants in nearby towns. These individuals may have bought land directly or may have acquired an interest in the land through mortgages. There is also the possibility that some of the small estates delineated in the 1850 map were surviving middleman holdings. A middleman tenancy could have remained autonomous as late as the 1850s or beyond, if it were based on a lease of lives renewable forever, which practically gave ownership rights to the tenant; the land would probably have been bought and sold as if held under outright ownership.[31] In this sense, therefore, it is justifiable to consider such properties to be estates in their own right.

In spite of the changes outlined above, certain general features of the Wexford estate system were not completely altered between 1660/1703 and 1850. Thus, the smallest estates by far were still to be found in the southeast corner of the county and estates elsewhere, particularly in the north and west, were much larger by comparison. In more specific terms, many estates in the southeast consisted of only a few hundred statute acres, while estates in the north and west frequently exceeded a thousand statute acres.[32] Alongside this continued divergence between the southeast and the rest of the county in terms of estate size, it is also significant that the areas of greatest fragmentation in the north and west of the county were precisely those areas which had been most heavily fragmented at the close of the seventeenth century i.e. the southern part of the barony of Ballaghkeen, the area of Shelburne and Bantry baronies around New Ross and the barony of Scarawalsh. Elsewhere in the county, particularly in most of the northern panhandle, in the area around Enniscorthy and in most of Bantry and Shelburne, estates were still quite large. In all areas, landowners with New English surnames continued to predominate.

A closer look at the various regions examined for the 1660/1703 map reveals the local importance of continuity and change. The estate system of the northern panhandle of the county changed very little in its general outlines between 1660/1703 and 1850. Thus, the Powerscourt estate in the northwest corner of this area, formerly known as the Manor of Wingfield, was still intact within largely unchanged boundaries. In this northern panhandle were also the Forde, Quinn, Ram, Morgan, and Courtown estates. The Forde property was owned by the Fordes of county Down, an absentee family; the other four owners of these large estates were residents of Wexford. The Ram and Quinn properties were rather compact but the Courtown estate had outliers in several places across the northern half of Wexford, many of them in areas formerly belonging to the Earls of Anglesey. The Morgan estate of Gorey barony was the property of Hamilton Knox Grogan Morgan, the scion of the Grogans of Johnstown. This family's property was extensive and widely scattered in tracts of moderate size throughout the county, but especially in the southeastern and northern baronies.

The most conspicuous change in the estate system of the northern panhandle was the virtual disappearance of the once extensive Esmonde estate. At one time occupying the entire parish of Kilcavan, this estate had shrunk to a remnant around the manor of Limerick, to be largely replaced by the Quinn estate and several smaller properties nearby. Overall, therefore, the northern panhandle of the county, which had been dominated by large estates in the late seventeenth century, continued to feature large properties in the mid-nineteenth century even though many of the landed families who had owned property there in 1660/1703 had been wholly or partly replaced by 1850.[33]

The central portion of the county, like the northern panhandle, was also characterised by continuity and change in the evolution of the outlines of the estate system. Only one of the four large properties present in this area in 1660/1703 was still largely intact in 1850. This property, the manor of Enniscorthy, remained in the hands of English absentee aristocrats, the Earls of Southampton in the late seventeenth century and the Earls of Portsmouth in 1850; apart from a few erosions on its southern edge, the boundaries of this estate were almost completely unchanged since 1660/1703. The land belonging to Morris and Clayton in Monart parish in 1660/1703 had been replaced by numerous small properties by 1850. A similar development had occurred in the case of the Anglesey estate, which had run along the east coast of the county from Donoughmore to Ballyvaloo; this property had been replaced by several estates of moderate size, i.e. the Guinness White, Power and Irvine properties, along with some other smaller estates.[34] Apart from these changes, however, the general pattern of the estate system in central Wexford was maintained between 1660/1703 and 1850.

In the southwest of the county, in the baronies of Bantry and Shelburne, several of the landowning families which had been established before 1700 were still present in 1850. The Carew and Leigh estates remained intact, as did the Etchingham and Loftus properties, now the Templemore and Ely estates; their owners had risen into the ranks of the titled nobility in the interim. The Colclough family, on the other hand, had almost disappeared from the ranks of Wexford's landed class, although branches of the family still held a few small scattered properties elsewhere in the county, expecially in the barony of Scarawalsh. Three new large landowners had joined the elite of this area by 1850: Blacker in the parish of Killann, Alcock south of Enniscorthy, and Boyse in place of the Colcloughs in Shelburne.

Between 1660/1703 and 1850, properties in Bargy and Forth became smaller and more fragmented as well. There is little indication, however, that there was any major change in the overall structure of landownership. Thus, there continued to be a handful of modest estates interspersed among the many tiny properties of the area. Most of the larger estates had changed hands; however, it appears that the social and political position of their owners probably did not alter appreciably over the century and a half. In all, two of the larger estates in this area were still intact by 1850, the Nunn estate in the extreme south of Forth and the Boyse estate in the southwest corner of Bargy. The Highgate estate and the Esmonde property in Shelmalier had both changed hands, the former acquired by the Boyds and the latter broken into several smaller units, two of which were owned by Hamilton Knox Grogan

Morgan. Additionally, the various Borr estates had passed into the hands of several smaller landlords.

The evidence outlined above suggests that between 1660/1703 and 1850, the estate system of Wexford was characterised by profound change combined with some notable continuity. There was apparently a gradual replacement of many older landed families by newcomers; estates became on average much smaller and more fragmented; the difference in estate size between the southeastern baronies and the rest of the county lessened. However, the ethnic composition of the landed elite did not change appreciably in spite of the fact that land purchase was open to catholics from 1782; as the surnames mentioned above indicate, landlords were still overwhelmingly of New English protestant descent and few of them held aristocratic titles.

The contrasting behaviour of larger and smaller estates is further highlighted by an examination of the distribution of landownership in Wexford at the end of the third quarter of the nineteenth century. The 'Return of Landowners in Ireland, 1876' allows us to observe the culmination of the process of fragmentation described above, and demonstrates that by 1876 the county had, to all intents and purposes, developed two distinctive estate systems: one a system of relatively large properties, characterised by considerable stability, the other a system of small properties, characterised by extreme fluidity.

For the purposes of this section of the discussion, the data from the 1876 return have been analysed to determine the size distribution of estates and the ethno-religious composition of the landed population at that time. A summary of this analysis is presented in table 5.[35]

Table 5

(a) Size Distribution of Estates in County Wexford, 1876

Acres	1-99	100-299	300-999	1,000-2,999	3,000-9,999	10,000-15,000
No.	656	197	199	93	27	5
%	55.7	16.8	16.9	7.9	2.3	0.4

(b) Proportion of 'Non-English' Surnames in Each Estate-Size Category, 1876

Acres	1-99	100-299	300-999	1,000-2,999	3,000-9,999	10,000-15,000
Totals	655	197	188	93	27	5
Non.Eng.	505	39	12	12	4	0
%	77.1	19.8	19.6	12.9	14.8	0

Source: Return of Landowners in Ireland, 1876 (County Wexford).

The statistics presented in table 5 lead to several conclusions concerning the nature of Wexford's estate system just prior to its final downfall. First, extremely small estates were very numerous in the county by 1876, reflecting the fragmentation which had taken place by the mid-nineteenth century and further disintegration of properties between 1850 and 1876. In all, 656 properties, or 55.7 percent of the total in 1876, were less than 100 acres in extent. Properties of 300 acres or less numbered 863 or 72.3 percent of estates in the county. However, there were still 331 properties of one thousand acres or more and five of these contained between ten and fifteen thousand acres, suggesting considerable resilience on the part of the large estate despite the increasingly widespread distribution of landownership which these figures indicate.

Second, unlike 1850, individuals with catholic surnames had become very numerous among the landowning population by 1876. However, the catholic landlords were confined almost exclusively to the ranks of the smaller land-owners. Thus, 77 percent of landowners with less than one hundred acres had 'Non-English' surnames and therefore were probably catholics, while only about twenty percent of those owning estates in the 100-1,000 acres range had such surnames. Landlords with Non-English surnames were practically absent from the larger ranges.

These patterns suggest that any erosion of the protestant grip on land-ownership which was taking place after 1850 was occurring, not in the larger estate categories but in the smaller. Many of the tiny catholic-owned properties which show up in the 1876 returns may represent parcels of land sold in hard times by protestant landowners to larger catholic tenants or to catholic townsmen. These small estates represent the filtering of large numbers of catholics into the landed classes but this influx was largely limited to openings in the lower ranks of Wexford landed society. Therefore, while the Wexford estate showed signs of fraying around the edges by 1876, in terri-torial terms at least, it had declined relatively slowly at the centre. One might argue with equal justification that by 1876 there really were two estate systems in the county: one a protestant-owned system which was character-ised by large properties of one thousand acres or more, the other a pre-dominantly catholic-owned system, characterised by smaller units, most of which did not exceed three hundred acres and many of which were actually less than one hundred acres in extent. Most of the protestant estates were probably *rentier* properties while many catholic estates were small enough to be worked on a direct commercial basis.[36]

In addition to these differences between smaller and larger properties, it is also significant that the rate at which land was changing hands between 1850 and 1876 in the smaller estate categories was far greater than the corre-sponding rates of turnover in the larger categories. Table 6 has been con-structed using data from Griffith's valuation, along with data from the 1876 return. The 1876 return has been searched for names surviving from the Griffith list in 1850. This analysis has been conducted for the baronies of Gorey, Scarawalsh, North Ballaghkeen, South Ballaghkeen and the northern half of Bantry. The technique will not produce an absolutely accurate measure of the survival rate of landlords but it is sufficient to provide a tentative picture of what happened in the four decades following the Great Famine.[37] Thus, as table 6 shows, there was a strong direct relationship between estate size in 1850 and the chances of a particular family maintaining possession of its land between that date and 1876. At least two thirds of families holding more than a thousand acres in 'North' Wexford in 1850 still held land in 1876, while barely more than a quarter of those holding estates of less than three hundred acres seem to have survived this period. These statistics suggest that the catholic estate system was not only newer and based on smaller properties than was the protestant system, but also that this catholic system was characterised by an unusually high rate of turnover in landowners. In a certain sense, the catholic system seems to have all the hallmarks associated with capitalist commercial agriculture in that it was part of an extremely fluid land market in which only a minority of individuals seemed to survive for more than a generation, even though many of these small estates may have been operated as *rentier* properties.

Table 6

Size Distribution of Estates Belonging to Families Retaining Landed Property in 'North' Wexford, 1850-1876

Acres	1850 Totals	No. of Survivors	% Surviving
1-99	292	77	26.4
100-299	128	61	27.7
300-1,000	113	66	58.4
1,000-2,999	53	42	79.2
3,000-10,000	12	8	66.6
10,000-15,000	3	2	66.6

Sources: Griffith's Valuation; Return of Landowners in Ireland, 1876.

In conclusion, then, it is clear that the pattern of landownership in Wexford did undergo significant change from the mid-seventeenth to the mid-nineteenth century. Such a transformation is hardly surprising considering that the process of commercialisation was taking place over these centuries. Estates became smaller and the internal functioning of such properties changed in response to this reduced size. Additionally, a large number of the landed population of the county was catholic by 1876. As a counterpoise to these developments, however, one must also note that the vast majority of medium to larger estates were still in the hands of protestant landowners at this date, some of them descendants of landowners who had been established in the county for generations. Moreover, the contrast between the southeastern part of the county and the northwestern sections in terms of average estate size was still apparent in the nineteenth century; in the old Norman colony landed estates were still far smaller than in the old Gaelic areas.

The juxtaposition of old and new is the most important feature of Wexford and its estate system in the centuries discussed above. This duality is arguably characteristic of all land systems; however, the colonial nature of Ireland's system makes such a duality doubly important. In this situation the contrast between old and new, continuity and change, is all the sharper since the old is personified by an entrenched protestant colonial landed elite and the new by a rising catholic element which represents a slowly emerging but powerful challenge to that entrenched class. While it is difficult in the absence of other studies to determine if the process of gradual estate fragmentation character-istic of Wexford occurred elsewhere, one may surmise, considering the patterns which the county obviously shares with other areas of the southeast of Ireland, that this was at least a regional pattern. Thus, while the preser-vation of some distinction, in terms of estate size, between the southeastern and northwestern baronies of Wexford over a period of almost seven centuries is in itself remarkable, equally important is the fact that, although excluded from the landed elite for almost two centuries, the catholic population had numerous representatives in that class by 1876. If many of these landowners were working their property directly, then the overthrow of the landlord system in the late nineteenth and early twentieth centuries involved the mere culmination of a complex socio-economic process which had been taking place since at least 1782, and possibly as early as 1641. In essence, one could argue that the seventeenth century confiscations, by fragmenting the estates of Wexford to the extent that they did, made further fragmentation as a result of economic forces likely and laid the basis for the gradual erosion of vulnerable parts of the estate system over the century and a half following their completion.

Acknowledgements

I am grateful to Theodore Wilson and the Hall Centre for Humanities, University of Kansas, for pro-viding the resources which made my work on the article possible. I would like to thank Vincent Butler for his painstaking work on the maps.

Two Centuries of Catholicism in County Wexford

There was a time when history books began by saying who the king was: now they are more likely to begin with an account of how people lived. Something similar has happened to religious history: it is less about bishops and clergy and more about the experiences of people. This has not made its writing any easier, partly because so much of the surviving source-material comes from bishops and clergy, but partly too because it may develop into a kind of 'social study' in which the religious experience is in some danger of being ignored. 'Religion' for the historian is very much a blanket-word that can range from mystical experiences to fairly crude forms of social control. The historian will probably feel safest at the social control end but he cannot afford to stray too far from the centre of where religion and society intersect, which in all Christian traditions is called 'the church'.

Some time in the 1570s it was becoming clear, in county Wexford as in other parts of the dominions of Queen Elizabeth I, that a choice might have to be made between two churches, between being what was to be called a Catholic and what was to be called a Protestant. In Wexford as in Ireland generally the great majority took the Catholic option despite the fact that it posed severe political problems. In consequence, the Catholic reform movement consolidated at the Council of Trent had to establish itself in Ireland in quite unique circumstances, a combination of political loyalty and religious disloyalty that slowed down the reform, by comparison with a countryside like northern Italy, to take an example from the opposite pole. It has even been argued that in some respects the reforms begun at Trent were not really established in Ireland until late in the nineteenth century. This would suggest a study terminating with the episcopate of Thomas Furlong (1857-1875). By then the Catholic church in Wexford had certainly taken on the stamp it was to retain until less than a generation ago — still Tridentine at the core, but Tridentine as modified particularly by the Catholic Enlightenment and by Ultramontanism. Three centuries of Wexford Catholicism would need a book

222

to handle properly — the recent excellent study of nineteenth-century Wexford town ends in 1858, with Thomas Furlong just becoming bishop, and runs to fifty pages.[1] What I propose here is something more modest — a survey that ends with the death of Bishop Nicholas Sweetman in 1786. It might well be argued, for reasons I trust will appear in the following pages, that even by this date Catholicism in county Wexford had reached a degree of approximation to the Tridentine pattern that was not attained in some other places until the best part of a century later.

By the 1570s, then, it was gradually becoming clear in Ireland that the religious situation posed itself as a choice and probably as a conflict. The Council of Trent had closed in 1563, having drawn up the master-plan for the pastoral revitalisation of the Catholic Church. The Elizabethan religious settlement had already lasted for more than a decade, and the papal excommunication of the queen in 1570 was a declaration of war in the name of Catholic Europe. Particularly as the might of Spain began to be drawn into the conflict, England saw itself as a threatened outpost of Protestantism, a 'beleaguered isle'.

Yet at the time of the papal excommunication a contemporary might well have judged that county Wexford, and indeed Ireland as a whole, would go the way of the church now by law established. The county fell into two sharply contrasting parts. In the north, the various Kavanagh clans were slowly being drawn into obedience to the crown. There was no question of the loyalty of the 'English' south with its landed gentry and two sizeable towns, Wexford and New Ross. Its people had for long years been fending off the Kavanaghs from their own resources and any help in this was welcome. The two mid-century bishops, Alexander Devereux (1539-66) and his nephew John Devereux (1566-78), were of the great gentry family of Ballymagir. Neither was likely to put his bishopric at risk for reasons of conscience, but on the other hand neither was likely to lead a religious revival.

However, traditional religious ways were deeply rooted, even if they were not well prepared to face the debates generated by the Reformation. A late-seventeenth century observer recalled the eighteen churches, the thirty-three chapels and the many wayside crosses in the barony of Forth that survived until the 1650s. At the same time the Catholic bishop, Luke Wadding, listed among his possessions 'two old script carol books', surely an indication that the still surviving Kilmore carols have a pre-Reformation origin. Another observer, Solomon Richards, Cromwellian officer turned landlord, was describing its great pilgrimage centre, Our Lady's Island, one of the immemorial holy places indulgenced by Pope Paul V at the beginning of the seventeenth century.[2] Historians are beginning to emphasise the complexity of the cultural challenges posed by the sixteenth century, and how much compulsion and instruction, 'sword' and 'word' was needed even in England to secure acceptance of the Reformation.[3] Irish historians are considering how limited was the power of 'sword' and 'word' at the disposal of the government in Ireland.[4]

Something of a crisis came to 'English' Ireland with the religiously-motivated revolt of James Eustace, Viscount Baltinglass, in 1580. Wexford became a focus in the suppression of the revolt, mainly because Baltinglass's close companion was a county Wexford Jesuit, Robert Rochford, and their unsuccessful attempt to escape through the port of Wexford brought a number of local people into peril (already in 1577 a spy's report from St Malo had named two Wexford merchants, Jasper Codd and Richard Sinnott, as assisting James Fitzmaurice in the invasion plans he was plotting on the continent).[5] When the lord deputy arrived in the town to execute justice in June 1581, quite a number of people were in gaol. The chief among them was Sir Nicholas Devereux of Ballymagir, though one may doubt if his offences were primarily religious. The lord deputy described them only as 'matter worthy death', proved, he alleged, by Devereux's own confession. The jury acquitted him: one did not lightly find against so powerful a magnate, whose family would still be there when the lord deputy was gone.[6] The necessary victims were found among poor men, Matthew Lambert, a baker who had given shelter to Baltinglass and Robert Rochford, and a group of five sailors who had unsuccessfully tried to get them passage abroad. The names of three of the sailors are known — Robert Meyler, Edward Cheevers and Patrick Kavanagh. They publicly proclaimed their loyalty to the Catholic faith; when pressed on how he reconciled this with his admitted loyalty to the queen, Matthew Lambert simply replied that he was an unlettered man quite unable to deal with such questions. All were hanged, drawn and quartered.

That same year two other men from Wexford were imprisoned and died of hardship. Patrick Hay, a merchant and shipowner, had been imprisoned for quite some time, charged with sheltering priests and bishops and conveying them abroad. So had Richard French, a priest, accused of exercising the Catholic ministry. In 1588 Peter Meyler, a student from Wexford, who had fled to Spain, was captured in Galway on his journey home, and was hanged, drawn and quartered when he refused the oath of supremacy. In 1590 Christopher Roche, another Wexford student who had gone to Louvain, was captured in Bristol, again on his journey home. He too refused the oath of supremacy and died in prison in London.

The details of all these except Christopher Roche were recorded before his own death in 1599 by another Wexford Jesuit.[7] He signs his name in Latin 'Joannes Holingus', which may be safely translated as 'John Howlin'. He was careful to weigh his evidence and his vivid account of Matthew Lambert and his sailor-companions must surely derive from an eye-witness, who quite possibly was Howlin himself. 'Jesuits and seminary priests' were seen by the government as the great enemies of its religious policy. John Howlin and Robert Rochford were both born in Wexford in the early 1540s. Rochford became a Jesuit in Rome in 1564. He returned to Ireland about 1576 and, as already noted, became the close companion of Baltinglass. He escaped with him to Spain in November 1581. In 1588 he sailed with the Armada, and was among the many who did not return. Howlin became a Jesuit at a mature age, in 1583, again in Rome. He spent his last years in Lisbon, where he died in 1599. He was the effective founder of the Irish college there.[8]

The Catholic Reformation relied on the revitalisation of established religious orders as well as the institution of new ones, spearheaded by the Jesuits. In pre-reformation Ireland the orders of friars, who by then had almost all adopted the observant reform, had a good reputation. There had been six friaries in county Wexford before the Reformation, Franciscans in Wexford, New Ross and Enniscorthy, Augustinians in New Ross and Clonmines, and Carmelites at Horetown. All six had been dissolved in the reign of Henry VIII, but in Ireland generally the friars continued their ministry, though details are hard to come by. The Franciscans were particularly prominent as opponents of the new religious settlement. The Catholic diocesan clergy in the reign of Elizabeth are even more a *gens lucifuga*. With them, stiffening was provided by the 'seminary priest'. At the centre of Trent's plans for reform had been the good bishop, overseeing the work of good priests. Good priests were to be provided by a new institution to train them, the seminary. By about 1580 the 'seminary priests' were beginning to have some impact on Ireland. Trained in mind and morals as priests had not been trained before, they were able to instruct people and stiffen the older clergy who wished to resist the changes — it is very unlikely that Richard French, who died in prison in 1581, had had a seminary training. By the end of the reign of Elizabeth there were enough Catholic priests to provide a service of discreetly-celebrated Masses, and the great majority of people went to Mass, not to the service in the queen's Prayer Book. At least so Francis Bryan, the mayor of Wexford, claimed when he wrote to the lord deputy on 23 April 1603, justifying the Catholics for having had Mass said in one of the churches in the town when news arrived that Elizabeth had died. Nearly everybody went to Mass anyway, he said, and now that the queen was dead they felt it made sense to have Mass in the churches.[9]

By now it had become increasingly clear that the bulk of the people of Wexford, like those of Ireland as a whole, had taken a decision without parallel in Europe: they had opted for a religion which was not that of their civil ruler, even when, as was certainly true of English Wexford, they wished to give that ruler full allegiance in civil matters. This position was not easily accommodated in the political thought of the early seventeenth century. It caused many problems and in the end brought disaster.

That the decision had been taken is clear from the reports of the Church of Ireland bishop, Thomas Ram (1605-34).[10] He was able to man his parishes, but he had only about six 'preaching ministers', all of them 'New English', that is, either born in England or of families who had come to Ireland since the reformation. The rest, of Old English or Old Irish stock, could be licensed only as 'reading ministers', that is, to read prepared sermons. Their religious outlook must have been uncertain, sometimes, it might be suspected, even to themselves. They were certainly not able to stand up to the Catholic ministry, an increasing number of whom had a seminary training. By now the Irish had their own seminaries in continental Europe, the first of them at Salamanca in 1592. Of the hundred students who entered Salamanca between 1592 and 1617 ten were from Wexford. The information they gave when admitted discloses a network of Catholic schoolmasters in Wexford and New Ross — in all, thirteen are named.[11] In 1612 Ram listed the Catholic priests with what already appears as a certain helplessness.[12] Among the laity, he said, the propertied classes were lost to recusancy, though, he claimed, 'the poorer sort' would go to church except that they feared their recusant masters would dismiss them. It is quite likely that he was told this, but it is at least fairly likely that it was not the full truth. As far as the propertied classes were concerned, the issues were finally clarified in the parliament which met in 1613. Its principal purpose was to introduce stiffer laws against recusancy, and the government used very questionable methods to secure a majority. This led to a protest to the King by the Catholic members, and in the end no new anti-Catholic laws were passed. All six of the Wexford members (James Furlong and Thomas Wadding representing the county, John Turner and Robert Talbot representing Wexford town, and James Fitzharris and Matthew Shea representing New Ross) supported the Catholic petition.

It was just about this time that a Furlong from Wexford was making a name for himself as a miracle-worker. He was a Cistercian, Father Candidus, born William Furlong in 1576. His parents, Patrick Furlong and Catherine Stafford, were at least going with the tide in religious matters, for they sent him to Oxford, but like some other Oxford scholars he went to Catholic Europe and became a Cistercian in Spain. He returned to Wexford in 1609, and soon had a reputation for power and holiness that brought many to the Catholic Church, including his own father. He died in 1616, and was buried in St Patrick's churchyard.[13]

In November 1607 the pope appointed Daniel O'Druhan vicar apostolic of the diocese of Ferns.[14] This policy, of putting a priest not in bishop's orders in charge of a diocese in difficult circumstances such as existed in Ireland, had been begun by Pope Clement VIII (1592-1605). Daniel O'Druhan first appears in history in 1583 as an Irish priest seeking financial support from the university of Salamanca. He got enough to allow him to pursue his studies there, and, finally, in 1591, money to take him home to Ireland.[15] Particularly after his appointment as vicar apostolic he had to move cautiously, at times using the alias 'James Walsh', for to Ram and others, either as Daniel O'Druhan or as 'James Walsh', he was the 'reputed bishop of Ferns' or at least 'the elect of Ferns'.[16] They knew he was in charge. Just four references to his activities as vicar apostolic have survived, three of them in Franciscan sources.[17] On 19 November 1626 Thomas Fleming, the Franciscan archbishop of Dublin, wrote to the cardinal secretary of state saying he had died two months before.[18]

By the time Daniel O'Druhan died the diocese of Ferns had a bishop, though Archbishop Fleming did not know this. His name was John Roche, and he was an outstanding example of the new generation of clergy of the Catholic Reformation.[19] His father was a lawyer in New Ross, and both he and his wife Joan were active recusants. John Roche went to Douai in the Spanish Netherlands to study for the priesthood (a struggling Irish college had been in existence there since 1594). In 1606, a few years after his ordination, he was put in charge of the college. The next year, 1607, he entered the service of Guido

Bentivoglio, the papal internuncio at Brussels, and became his trusted adviser particularly in the affairs of Great Britain and Ireland. He followed this gifted papal diplomat to Paris in 1616 and to Rome when he became a cardinal in 1621. In 1622 the Irish bishops nominated Roche their agent in Rome. Here too he and Luke Wadding the Franciscan succeeded in establishing an Irish seminary.[20]

He had been nominated bishop of Ferns on 29 April 1624, but his con-secration did not take place until 25 April 1627. The reason for the delay was that he was a serious candidate in the contentious nomination to Armagh, vacant since Archbishop Peter Lombard died in Rome on 5 September 1625. In the event, the Armagh nomination went elsewhere. Roche was consecrated bishop of Ferns, and left immediately to return to Ireland. On his way he went to Douai and Paris, to bring himself up to date on Irish problems in these centres. In Paris he had to wait to cross to England until the end of the war with France, which had broken out at the beginning of 1627. When it ended in April 1629 he immediately crossed to London, where he had discussions with the English Catholics and also at the court of King Charles I. By the end of July he had arrived in Dublin.

It was only natural that he should take a leading part in the general reorganisation of the Catholic church in Ireland. Here we are concerned only with his work in the diocese of Ferns, where, however, all the Irish problems presented themselves in microcosm. His own people, the Old English, were still wealthy, merchants in the towns and landowners in the countryside. Now as a body firmly committed to the Catholic church, their central problem remained that of combining civil obedience with religious disobedience. It was getting harder, and the next few decades were to show that it was impossible. While the church had a large measure of practical toleration it functioned altogether illegally, and priests and especially bishops had to move cautiously. The bishop lived in Wexford town. He frequently used the alias 'J.R. Turner', which indicates that he lodged with the Turner family, passing, no doubt, as a relative returned from abroad. The Turners were wealthy merchants and their story is itself a microcosm of the Old English community. In the early days of the Reformation they had had no scruples in grabbing their share of monastic spoils, but now they were committed Catholics. John Turner, mayor of Wexford in 1609, had been among the active recusants in the 1613 parliament. His son Patrick repeated these roles, mayor in 1626, M.P. in 1634. A brother, Thomas Turner, was a Catholic priest of the diocese of Ferns.

Another problem facing the Old English community was that of defining what they had in common with the Old Irish because both were now Catholic. The Old Irish had been conquered in a war that had been savagely waged and had already lost much of their wealth as a result of plantation. The Old Irish of Wexford had suffered severely in the plantation of 1618. About 150 local occupiers received grants, most of them Old Irish. Some of these accepted the established church. Some Old English recusants also got grants, and, to complicate matters further, a few of the New English planters were themselves recusants. The plantation also introduced a Protestant tenantry, a minority, but in some places a substantial minority, second only to that in the planted Ulster counties. Bishop Roche knew no Irish, and while he did visit the area in person he relied heavily on Daniel O'Breen, a priest known as 'Donal Spáinneach' because he had studied in Spain.[21] He was to minister in Wexford until he was put to death on 14 April 1655.

The Council of Trent had laid heavy obligations on the diocesan bishop. All pastoral care was to emanate from him. This pastoral care was to be exercised primarily through the parish priest in his parish, and even the religious orders came under the bishop's authority when they ministered to the people. It was not easy to build a Tridentine parish system in Ireland, but priests were appointed to localities as opportunity offered and the fact that Irish Catholicism for the future was not to be as centred in the parish church as Trent had envisaged left it with a certain 'domestic' character that was to prove a strength.

The regular clergy too posed problems for a bishop in the Irish situation. The Franciscans in particular had been in the front line of opposition to the Reformation when there were not many others there. All the religious orders had grown used to an independent mission, backed by faculties direct from Rome. Two friars had been proposed for the bishopric of Ferns in the 1620s — Walter Cheevers, a Franciscan, and John Murphy, a Dominican. The Franciscans had houses in New Ross and Wexford, and a few Jesuits were working in New Ross. There were also two Cistercians, and these posed involved problems even more intractable than those of the friars. Yet John Roche managed to live in peace, even with the Cistercians. When he died a Cistercian epitaph saluted him as 'outstanding for his learning and his courtesy'.

The preaching of the Catholic Reformation in some ways challenged the old religious observances, with their customary incrustations of pre-Christian inheritances that were sometimes hard to reconcile with any kind of Christianity. To begin with, it insisted on religious instruction. Here the Jesuit and the Calvinist may have had more in common than would have occurred to them. For the Catholic, this religious instruction was to be the basis for regular sacramental practice, and the sacraments were to be seen as occasions of personal regeneration, not, as they had at least to some extent appeared in the past, occasions for the strengthening of the kin-group.

In 1635 John Roche reported on his stewardship to the Roman authorities. As might be expected from one who had spent his formative years in Catholic Europe, there is a certain note of disappointment running through it. Yet while he may have felt his success limited, a report a few years later by the Church of Ireland Bishop Andrews made it clear that few in county Wexford would be Protestant.[22] Bishop Roche may have felt it might take some time to make them Tridentine Catholics, but he had thirty good diocesan priests and good relations with the friars. As was only to be expected, the new preaching of these priests was most effective with the better-off, especially in the towns. The old ways were harder to change as one moved out the country and down the social ladder.

He died in Kilkenny on 9 April 1636 while on a visit to Bishop Rothe of

Ossory. Death seems to have come suddenly. He was buried in Kilkenny, probably with the Rothe family in St Mary's, but no stone or inscription marks his grave. With him the final step had been taken to change the Catholic structures in county Wexford from a loosely-organised mission into a diocesan church.

On 23 October 1641 the dispossessed Catholics of Ulster rose in arms. With some hesitations the Old English Catholics made common cause with them, and soon most of Ireland was controlled by a Catholic government sitting in Kilkenny. The Irish Confederate Catholics insisted they were loyal to King Charles I, but had been forced to take action in defence of their threatened liberties. At this same time groups in England and Scotland were taking rather similar actions. In all three countries it was to lead to a decade of war.

The Irish Catholic alliance was uneasy because the Old Irish and the Old English wanted different things. The Old Irish wanted a restoration of the lands they had lost in the plantations, and this disposed them to press for a full restoration of the Catholic religion. The Old English, on the other hand, were inclined to settle for a confirmation of the toleration they had enjoyed up to this in practice but not in law, all the more so as they were anxious not to jeopardise the considerable wealth they still possessed by any imputation of rebellion. Yet the town merchants, who had been in many ways the leaders of the Catholic Reformation, were more willing than the landed gentry to press for a full restoration of Catholicism.

The Confederate Catholics controlled all of county Wexford and Wexford town became a kind of naval headquarters for them. The churches were taken over and Catholic rites restored. The highlight of the decade was the visit by the papal nuncio, Archbishop Rinuccini, at Easter 1647. By this time the diocese once again had a bishop. He was Nicholas French, of gentry stock from the barony of Forth. His father was John French of Ballytory and his mother Christina Rossiter of Rathmacknee. He had entered the Irish college in Louvain on 13 December 1627.[23] He was then twenty-four years of age, and already, it would appear, ordained. On completion of his studies he returned to Wexford. He was consecrated bishop of Ferns on 23 November 1645.

Rinuccini wrote an account of his visit in his diary. Though this has been lost, a contemporary writer has preserved its substance.[24] On Tuesday of Holy Week, 13 April, he left Kilkenny for New Ross, where he celebrated the liturgy of Holy Thursday and Good Friday. He was in Enniscorthy for Holy Saturday, and that afternoon he sailed down the Slaney to Wexford. A flotilla of boats set out to meet him, and his welcome in the town was tumultuous. Cannon thundered from the walls and from ships in the harbour; bands played and a military guard of honour was drawn up as he was officially received by the corporation. The liturgical reception took place in St Peter's church, and the next day he sang the Mass of Easter. He remained until Wednesday, a little overwhelmed by the warmth of his welcome, which he described as the greatest manifestation of loyalty to the Holy See he had received in Ireland.

The religious commitment was beyond question, but the political problems remained, and in the end they split the Confederate Catholics. Rinuccini sailed from Ireland on 23 February 1649 leaving half of them excommunicated, and when Oliver Cromwell landed at Ringsend on 15 August he found the divided country an easy prey.

His troops stormed into Wexford on 11 October. That day is for ever imprinted in blood and fire in the town's history.[25] When he appeared outside the walls negotiations began. Within the town counsels were divided. It could be defended successfully only by admitting a garrison from the forces who had opposed Rinuccini, and at least some of the townsmen were unwilling to do this. They asked for the continuation of Catholic worship, leave for the garrison to withdraw, and full legal protection for the lives and property of the inhabitants. Predictably, Cromwell refused, but he did offer quarter to the garrison, the private soldiers to go free, but the officers to yield themselves prisoners. He would also undertake to protect the town from plunder. While the negotiations were still in progress Captain James Stafford, the commander of the castle at the south end of the town, surrendered it to Cromwell. The indications are that he represented a party, how large it is impossible to say, who would have nothing to do with those who had opposed the nuncio and considered the terms offered by Cromwell not ungenerous. No doubt they also had in mind the slaughter at Drogheda just a month before, when the town had been taken by storm and about 2,600 people slaughtered.

Whatever the motives of Stafford and his party, things went horribly wrong. Control of the castle allowed Cromwell's army to enter the town, where they simply ran amuck, slaughtering indiscriminately. Two thousand people died — the figure comes from several sources, including Cromwell himself — and about three-quarters of them were civilians.[26] Cromwell's account of the slaughter has its reticences, for it had taken place because his army had got out of control while negotiations were still in progress. He speaks of his troops meeting a 'stiff resistance', but in effect contradicts this by admitting that his own losses were 'not twenty'. He also makes it clear that what resistance there was ended in the market place, that is, the Bull Ring, where to this day a plaque recalls the massacre. It has been claimed that the tradition of the massacre in the Bull Ring is not mentioned by any contemporary, and first appeared in print in the Abbé MacGeoghegan's *Histoire d'Irlande* (Paris, 1758-62). However, it is clear that MacGeoghegan's narrative here depends on a book published in London in 1663, *Flagellum, or the Life and Death, Birth and Burial of Oliver Cromwell, the late usurper, by S.T. Gent.* 'S.T. Gent' is James Heath (1629-64), an extreme royalist who had served Charles II in his exile in the 1650s. While he is clearly very biased, he was well placed to gather accounts of Cromwell in Ireland from Irishmen who also served the king in exile. He gives a brief account of the storming of Wexford on pp 86-7, but in a list of *Errata* on the page preceding p. 1 he adds to this account (the fact that the addition to his text is clearly an afterthought need not mean that he had first heard the story after his type had been set, for he did not have a very ordered way of putting things together). This is what he has to say:

Most abominably and barbarously cruel was he in this place, for, near 200 of the better sort and the beautifullest Women of the City, having (upon the Town being entred) fled to the Crosse, and with the Command of their charming eyes, and those melting tears, prevailed upon the Soldiers for quarter, now at his coming thither, and after a laughing jeering enquiry what they did there, and other mocking insultations, were commanded to be knock'd on the head, which those that promised them life nobly refusing, he commanded another Regiment to encompass them, and then most horibly massacred them all.

Heath's account makes Cromwell personally responsible for the massacre, against the wishes of his reluctant soldiers. In fact, it was not Cromwell but his soldiers who got out of control. Yet while it is Heath's venemous bias against Cromwell which leads him to introduce this twist into his story, his whole point would have been lost unless there was a story to twist: and Cromwell's own account, it will be recalled, makes it clear that the killing — or, as he put it, the resistance — did in fact end at the market cross in the Bull Ring.

Seven Franciscans died in their church, where their names are still inscribed: five priests, John Esmond, Peter Stafford, Raymond Stafford, Paul Sinnott and Richard Sinnott, and two lay brothers, Didacus Cheevers and Paul Rochford. The evidence for their killing comes from a first-hand source, Francis Stafford, who had been guardian of the friary for many years.[27] He gives vivid details of their murder and eye-witness accounts of signs and wonders that accompanied their killing and the general massacre. There are in addition some accounts by Bishop Nicholas French.[28] He was not in the town when it was stormed, and so escaped with his life. He repeats the account of a general slaughter, and adds that his own house was sacked, and that here his chaplain, his gardener, and a boy of sixteen died. The buildings of the town also suffered severely. Cromwell lamented that it was now useless as winter quarters for his troops, and in a report to the archbishop of Paris dated 18 November 1651 Bishop French claimed that two months after the sack the surviving Catholics, to the number of 6,000, were ordered out of the town in the winter weather, and that scarcely twenty managed to remain.[29] That many of them fled abroad is clear from the list in the petition made by the former inhabitants on 4 July 1660 after the Restoration.[30]

New Ross surrendered without resistance, and the unexpected defection of much of Munster gave Cromwell the winter quarters he so badly needed. The last resistance petered out early in 1653, and the English commonwealth was free to do what it wished in Ireland.

The commonwealth settlement was concerned with two broad issues, land and religion. All propertied Catholics who had not died or fled abroad were to be transplanted to four counties of Connacht. In a kind of new Pale bounded by the Barrow and the Boyne, the hope was to remove all Catholics. It could not work and it did not work, and by the Restoration in 1660 there was still great confusion.[31] The Irish Catholics lost their property, but by no means all of them went to Connacht. They remained even in the towns, not just the labourers and tradesmen but some of the former merchants. In the countryside, numbers of the former landowners got large farms on advantageous terms from the officers of the Cromwellian army who were the new landlords in Wexford. Mixed with these people going down in the world were people coming up in the world. In this way there emerged the class of 'middlemen' who were to have an important role in the years to come. There was still a Browne at Mulrankin and a Wadding at Ballycogley. The Furlongs of Horetown ended up at Templescoby, and Devereux of Mount Pill at Tom-haggard. This same emergence of middlemen can be seen a century later, when the Shapland Carew family of Castleboro let out their rich lands, now apparently being brought under intensive cultivation for the first time. They let them townland by townland, about half to Protestants and half to Catholics. The religious affiliations can be distinguished with fair certainty. Those who received leases for lives were Protestants, while those who received leases for a maximum of thirty-one years were almost certainly Catholics, who could not receive any longer lease under the provisions of the Penal Code.[32]

It was when summoning New Ross to surrender that Oliver Cromwell had proclaimed 'I meddle not with any man's conscience', but it was a difficult principle to apply in practice in the mid-seventeenth century. 'Popery' could not be tolerated because it was contrary to scripture, as was the 'prelacy' of the established church. The Act of Supremacy was repealed, and people were not compelled to attend services contrary to their conscience, but evidence has survived of prosecutions for contumacious refusal to hear the word of God. Yet the evangelising mission under the commonwealth was very ineffective, and part of the general confusion in which it ended was the unresolved question of the complete lack of legal status of the Irish papists it was now accepted would not become Protestants.

Catholic priests were pursued mercilessly. While the war lasted, numbers of them were killed. At the beginning of 1653 it was decided to expel all priests by extending to Ireland the English statute of 1585 which had made a priest guilty of treason by the very fact of his presence in the country, and very many were in fact expelled. Numbers, however, continued to be incarcerated in the 'transit camps' set up on the western islands of Aran and Inishboffin — for example, Francis Stafford, O.F.M., who had escaped the massacre in Wexford, was held in Inishboffin in the late 1650s — and some managed to continue a ministry, so furtively that it has left little documentation. One who continued his ministry was Daniel O'Breen. He had been a senior priest of the diocese under Bishop John Roche in the 1630s, and was now an old man. He was arrested several times, but was released on one pretext or another, until he was at last hanged at Wexford on Easter Saturday, 14 April 1655. With him died another diocesan priest, James Murphy, and Luke Bergin, a Cistercian. They were buried in the grounds of the ruined friary.[33]

In this one decade many of the gains of the mission of Catholic Reformation had been seriously eroded. Yet the Catholic propertied classes who had been a kind of keystone of these gains were still present in some numbers, though they had lost all their property. It was natural that their hopes should be high at the Restoration in 1660, but in fact there was little restoration of Catholic wealth in Wexford. The whole question of the Restoration land settlement is still to be explored in detail, but there is no doubt it will have its surprises. For example, a Robert Leigh appears as a proprietor in Rosegarland, on land which had been forfeited by Marcus Sinnott.[34] Robert Leigh was an Old English Catholic, younger brother of John Leigh, who had forfeited nearly 1,000 acres at Rathbride, county Kildare. Robert had done service for Charles II in his exile, and after 1660 not merely was John restored in Kildare but Robert received lands in Wexford. But in Wexford very few Catholic landowners were restored. The merchants who had hung on in the towns were also greatly impoverished, but they began again to mend their fortunes, just as members of the former landowners began to build a more modest prosperity as middlemen.

The mission of the clergy was reconstructed more slowly, especially because Rome did not nominate bishops in the 1660s. Nicholas French, the bishop of Ferns, had gone to the continent early in 1651 on a rather despairing mission to seek help for the Irish Catholics. He had been so involved in the political events of the 1640s that he had no hope of being allowed to return to Ireland, and he ended his days in Ghent on 23 August 1678. Ten years earlier he had named Luke Wadding as his vicar-general. Wadding had been born in Wexford town about 1628. His father, a younger son of the Wadding family of Ballycogley, had moved into the town to make his living as a merchant. Luke fled from Ireland on 7 October 1651 — he himself gives the date — and studied at Paris, where he was ordained, and taught at Paris in some capacity for a number of years. When he returned to Ireland in 1668 he settled first at New Ross and then moved to Wexford. In 1671 he was appointed coadjutor to the exiled bishop, but deferred his consecration, pleading that he could work more successfully as a priest in such difficult times. It is not known when he was consecrated, but a document of 20 June 1684 refers to him as a bishop. He was fortunate in not having been consecrated bishop when the 'Popish Plot' erupted at the end of 1678, for he could claim in all honesty that he was neither a bishop nor a vicar-general (this office had lapsed with the death of Bishop French the previous August), and he had such good relations with the Protestants in the town that they gladly seized the excuse to acquit him. He fled from Wexford when it fell to the Williamite armies in 1690, but returned after the fall of Limerick in October 1691. He died the following December and was buried in the restored Franciscan friary.[35].

With Luke Wadding it is for the first time possible to study in detail the work of a Catholic bishop in Wexford. Little has survived for John Roche's episcopate, and most of the efforts of Nicholas French went into the political affairs of the Confederate Catholics. The detail for Luke Wadding comes almost altogether from one document, a notebook into which he entered many details of many things, and which has been preserved among the manuscripts of the Irish Franciscans.[36] The first thing that might be noticed is the steadily improving lot of the Catholics of the town, including the bishop himself. In a letter written to Bishop French from New Ross on 1 February 1672 Wadding had described his own extreme poverty and the poverty of the people of the town.[37] Yet his notebook shows a number of Catholics in Wexford in reasonably comfortable circumstances. They included his brother-in-law,

Thomas Dulan, husband of his dead sister, Nell (two brothers, Peter and John, were merchants in Bristol and Drogheda respectively), Edward and Mary Wiseman, who lodged him for ten years, and Anthony Talbot, in whose name the bishop's house was taken when he finally managed to get one of his own in 1684. In March 1685 he was awarded a pension of £150 a year by King James II.

Luke Wadding brought to his ministry a well cultivated mind. His extensive library of about 700 works was well stocked with works of theology and spirituality (the spirituality, it is worth noting, being of the Jesuit or Salesian school, not of the Jansenist). It also contained literary works in English and French, with some indications of a predilection for the English 'Metaphysical' poets, Crashaw in particular. These find some echo in his own little book, *A Small Garland of Pious and Godly Songs*, published at Ghent in 1684, which helped to stabilise the tradition of carol-singing at Christmas (it has already been noted that in his library there were two 'old script carol books' taking this tradition back to before the Reformation).

This then was the man who set out to build up again the Catholic mission in the diocese of Ferns and especially in the town of Wexford. In 1671 he began the Catholic parish registers, continuous since that date, a record of Catholic parish life unique in Ireland. In 1674 he began to build a chapel inside the walls of the town. It took time, but he succeeded in completing it and furnishing it well. I know of no other references to chapels being built in Wexford at the time, but the correspondence of his neighbour Bishop John Brenan of Waterford and Lismore, shows the Catholic chapel or 'Mass-house' now being built if the landlord was willing to give a site, as he usually was.[35] The chapel, as the place of religious instruction and sacramental life, was at the centre of the Tridentine plan for Catholic reform. Instruction and sacramental life were at the centre of what Bishop Wadding tried to do in Wexford. He distributed beads and medals by the gross, some brought from France but others bought locally in Wexford and New Ross, and prayer-books and catechisms by the dozen.

His notebook also provides evidence that despite the calamities of the 1650s Catholics and Protestants were learning to live together in Wexford. A practical compromise had been worked out, whereby the Catholics were allowed to seek the rites of their own church if they — or at least the wealthier of them — first paid fees to the Protestant minister. There are several entries in the notebook about a close personal friend, 'Mrs Shapoland, Ellen Bond', who was a Catholic married to a Protestant. She and the bishop shared tastes in music and gardening, and he was careful to see that she got reading-matter to help her faith. Naturally she had been married by licence from the Protestant bishop, but her marriage is entered in the Catholic register, as are the baptisms of her children. As has been seen already, Bishop Wadding's good relationship with the local Protestants helped to protect him during the 'Popish Plot' of 1678.

There are other documents which throw light on Catholicism in Wexford in the late seventeenth century. Two were prepared in connection with an *English*

Atlas proposed by the publisher Moses Pitt about 1680. The Irish section was never published, but the reports were printed by H.F. Hore in the nineteenth century.[39] One was by Robert Leigh, whom we have met already. Because he was himself a Catholic, he was reticent on the subject of religion, but he does provide information on social history, such as that the principal merchants of New Ross were Catholics, and that the former proprietors in the barony of Forth were now tenants on the lands they had previously owned. This latter statement is confirmed by the author of the second account, Solomon Richards. Richards had been an officer in Cromwell's army, and had been rewarded with lands in Wexford. He is quite interested in what he regards as the superstitions of popery, and he has left us the first detailed description of the pilgrimage of Lady's Island. He notes that 'the chiefest or more meritorious time is between the two Lady Days of August 15 and September 8.' He describes the pilgrims making the circuit of the island, understandably concentrating on what he regarded as the more superstitious aspects, and regrettably making no mention of any details of the prayers or devotions.

The third document, also edited by H.F. Hore, is the most interesting from the religious point of view.[40] It is concerned solely with the barony of Forth. The author's name is not given, but it is clear from the text that he was a native of Forth, a Catholic, and quite probably a priest. The particular attention he pays to the Sinnott family suggests strongly that it was his own. He too refers to the pilgrimage at Lady's Island, but gives no details of the devotions. He lists the churches and chapels reduced to ruin in the 1650s, and mentions the many wayside crosses now defaced and broken. The people, he said, keep patron days very devoutly, by penance and the Eucharist, followed by a feast and entertainment, 'cheerfully, piously and civilly'. They are very 'precise and exact' in keeping the Church's fasts. At wakes and funerals there are no 'rude eiulations or clamours', as in so many other parts of Ireland. They are hard-working and industrious: there is 'hardly any vagrant native beggar'. Even before Cromwell, though there was scarcely a native Protestant, the ministers of the established church lived peaceably among them and received their tithes and offerings.

There was a brief period of euphoria after the accession of a Catholic king, James II, in 1685. In 1687 it was decided to issue new charters to the towns, and Catholics appeared again on the corporations of Wexford and New Ross. There were Catholic mayors, Patrick White in New Ross and Edward Wiseman in Wexford, both closely connected with Bishop Luke Wadding. The bishop, as has been noted, received a royal pension of £150 a year. When James II came to Ireland and called a parliament for May 1689 the towns and the county returned Catholic M.P.s.[41] The euphoria did not last for very long. The country was again conquered, and 'the Protestant interest', severely shaken by the events of the reign of James II, was determined to make its position impregnable. This it did by the legal enactments that have come to be known as the Penal Code. These laws had two principal thrusts — against the possibility of political power and the landed property which was the basis of political power ever again being concentrated in Catholic hands, and against the practice of the Catholic religion. Whatever may have been the original

Plate xxii: Robert Leigh of Rosegarland

intention of the legislators, only the first of these aims was taken seriously for very long. By about 1730 Catholics were free to practise their religion provided they accepted the social and economic consequences, and repeated attempts to induce foreign Protestants to settle in Ireland are a clear indication that the government had accepted that this was the only way to increase Protestant numbers there.

The legislation against the Catholic religion was directed in the first instance against the clergy. The Banishment Act of 1697 ordered all regular clergy, bishops, and all exercising ecclesiastical jurisdiction to leave the kingdom by 1 May 1698. Most of them went. The Registration Act of 1704 ordered all parish priests to register with the clerks of the peace at the next quarter sessions, and to produce two laymen to go surety of £50 each for their good behaviour. These registered priests enjoyed legal toleration in the parishes for which they registered, but as no provision was made for successors it was clearly envisaged that the Catholic priesthood would die out in a generation. The system broke down in 1709, when registered priests were required to take an oath of abjuration of the Stuart cause. Only a handful took it, and the government was left with no control over a church it lacked both the will and the means to suppress.

Some years ago I summarised the history of the Catholics of county Wexford under the Penal Code.[42] Little new source material has been published since, but it might just be noted that the more recent developments in the writing of history would lay more stress on the social and economic background of the Catholics at this period. However, the new approach, as far as Wexford is concerned, is still in the form of questions rather than answers, at least until the end of the eighteenth century. For example, our understanding of things would be greatly deepened if we could put faces on the names of the laymen who went surety for the thirty-four priests who registered in county Wexford in 1704. Those who went surety for a number of priests represent the surviving Catholic landed families, at Rosegarland, for instance, or Mohurry. Elsewhere, there are only tantalising glimpses. For example, there was a Michael Downes who lived at Ballygarvan and registered as parish priest of Dunbrody and Owenduff. His guarantors were Mortogh Bryan and William Sinnott. All three surnames appear in the area as landed proprietors who lost their lands in the 1650s. However most of our information still concerns the clergy. From it we can extract a good idea of what they set out to do and what they considered they had achieved. This, it need scarcely be added, may not represent exactly what was in fact achieved.

The Catholic Reformation had lived through so many upheavals in the seventeenth century that it need come as no surprise that its aims were only imperfectly achieved. A French Huguenot, Baron de Courthiez Rousele, had hard things to say on the superstition and ignorance he found among people in the vicinity of New Ross about 1690.[43] True, he was not an unprejudiced witness, especially as it was a very uncertain time for Protestants, and most especially for Huguenots, but there is evidence from other parts of the country to lend some credence to what he had to say. Yet the thirty-four priests registered for county Wexford in 1704 had for the most part a good preparation for their ministry. Twenty-three are noted as having been ordained abroad, which is proof that they had had a seminary training. Some of the eleven ordained in Ireland may well have gone abroad after ordination for theological studies, though a number of these had been ordained not too long before 1704, and, judging by their family names and places or ordination, were not natives of the diocese. The bishop, Michael Rossiter, remained by registering as parish priest of Killinick. His guarantors, Thomas Sutton and William Wadding, were from Wexford town. Thomas Sutton was also one of the guarantors of David Roche, registered as parish priest of Wexford. Both priests had been close friends of Bishop Luke Wadding. All three, the two priests and Thomas Sutton, appear against the same background of a merchant community surviving through all its misfortunes.

This list of clergy for 1704 is the first of seven for the eighteenth century. The others are dated 1731, 1739, 1744, 1753, 1772, and 1785.[44] Between them they must account for most of the Catholic clergy over the period. The succession of bishops was henceforth unbroken, and the diocesan organisation was consolidated in the long episcopate of Bishop Nicholas Sweetman (1745-86). His family is also a very interesting one, and we are gradually coming to know more about it.[45] Early in his episcopate Pope Benedict XIV had in 1751 thoroughly reorganised the Catholic mission in Ireland and given new stability to the building up of a church on the Tridentine model.

Even before this it is clear that a parish organisation that was to prove permanent was well on the way to being stabilised. A set of diocesan statutes for 1722 has survived in the Franciscan House of Studies at Killiney.[46] A report by Bishop Verdon on the state of the diocese of Ferns in 1715 exists in the archives of Propaganda at Rome, but it has not been published.[47] The 1722 statutes, also drawn up by Bishop Verdon, do provide a very fair idea of the state of the Catholic church. There is a reasonably well-organised parish life, in that the parish priest can reside permanently and provide the services of his ministry. It is not easy to staff the parishes and it appears that some of the priests are not permanently attached to the diocese. Running right through the regulations is the concern to ensure that there is Sunday Mass, at a fixed time and place, that there is decent equipment for Mass, that there is a sermon, and that catechism is taught to the children. There is some problem about Mass-vestments and chalices, in that it appears that in the really bad days, especially after 1709, these had been entrusted to the laity for safe keeping, and that some laity were unwilling to surrender them when better days came, and these better days were at least in sight by 1722. As well as Sundays, there were still twenty-five holydays of obligation during the year. They were the only holidays people had, but it was not always possible to observe them because so many employers were Protestants, and by the end of the century the number had been considerably reduced. The priest, it appears, lodged with the laity, and the indications are that some priests had to move round from house to house like schoolmasters. Friars helped in the parishes, but were not parish priests. The

Plate xxiii: Bishop Nicholas Sweetman

Banishment Act of 1697 was by now completely ineffective — bishops were being appointed in growing numbers, and there were great numbers of friars in the country. It is clear that the bishop was able to go round on visitation fairly regularly.

In 1731 each Protestant bishops was ordered to make a report to the House of Lords on 'the state of popery' in his diocese. Their detailed reports were printed in the *Lords' Journals*, and have been reprinted in *Archivium Hibernicum*. The report on the diocese of Ferns noted thirty-one 'mass-houses', twelve of them described as 'recently built'.[41] In eleven places there is a 'moveable altar in the fields', in other words, a 'Mass-rock'. These Mass-rocks cluster in four areas: one around Templetown and the Hook; the second taking in most of the Barony of Forth and part of Bargy; the third stretching from Enniscorthy to Oulart; and the fourth from Kilrush to Ballycanew. This geographical concentration can only indicate that in these areas the landlord would not allow a Mass-house to be built, for the local fortunes of the Catholic population depended much more on the goodwill of the landlord than on the letter of the law. There were forty-four diocesan priests, 'besides itinerants', friaries in Wexford and New Ross each with four friars, and a lone friar at Clonmines. Fourteen 'popish schoolmasters' were listed.

The long episcopate of Nicholas Sweetman (1745-86) saw the stabilisation of the Catholic mission in the diocese of Ferns. This was the third time a parish organisation had been attempted; the first was at the beginning of the seventeenth century, and the second was after Cromwell. This third attempt, based on the registrations of 1704, was to prove permanent, though when Nicholas Sweetman received his documents of appointment in the crisis year of 1745 he could have had very little assurance that this would be so. These documents would have described him as having been proposed for the see of Ferns by 'James III, king of Great Britain and Ireland'. Another Jacobite invasion was under way, and in 1744 the local authorities had been ordered to list carefully the popish clergy in their localities.[49] In 1751 Bishop Sweetman was denounced to the administration as a Jacobite and was brought to Dublin and put in prison. The person who denounced him was not very credible — a priest named James Doyle, who can fairly confidently be described as the worst troublemaker among the priests of the diocese. The bishop was released after interrogation.[50]

When he came to die in ripe old age in 1786, the dismantling of the Penal Code was well advanced as far as religious practice and even landholding was concerned, but it was already beginning to appear that political rights might be the sticking point. These were the problems of a new age, essentially problems for the next bishop. Despite the fact that the Stuart cause had in effect died with the Old Pretender in 1766, and notwithstanding his release in Dublin in 1751, there can be no doubt that Nicholas Sweetman died as he lived, a Jacobite. In 1774, as part of the first steps towards dismantling the Penal Code, a new oath of allegiance to the Hanoverian kings to be taken by Catholics was drawn up. It was quite acceptable to the Catholic laity, and after some initial hesitation the clergy also accepted it. The first Relief Act in 1778 extended benefits only to Catholics who had taken the oath of 1774. On 3 April 1779 Bishop Sweetman's coadjutor, all the clergy of the diocese and 'a vast number of laity' assembled at Wexford courthouse to take the oath.[51] The old bishop did not take it, nor did he take it to the day of his death.

In many other ways he appears as 'a gentleman of the old school', rigid in the demands that he made on himself and on others. We should be slow to use the word 'Jansenist', for all the indications are that this increasingly imprecise word is not the best one to use to describe the severe and anxious strain that developed among middle-class Irish Catholics in the eighteenth century. In 1756, when Bishop Sweetman decided he could no longer combine his episcopal duties with the parish care of Wexford, he appointed a Jesuit, Edward Devereux Keating, as parish priest; and when the Jesuits were suppressed in the universal church in 1773 he wrote a very angry letter to Archbishop Carpenter of Dublin.[52] The best label to pin on him, if there is any use in such exercises, is 'Catholic Enlightenment' — sober, practical, distrustful of new devotions, especially the more emotional ones, anxious to see that the round of duties perceived as demanded by the church be faithfully discharged.

The mentality appears clearly in the brief memoranda he jotted down before beginning his parish visitation in 1753.[53] He was to enquire into the diligence of his clergy in preaching and teaching, in keeping their chapels in good order, in keeping their registers of baptisms and marriages. He noted 'I am to recommend to them a little decency in their habitation and dress' and 'on the day of visitation I am always to dine at the pastor's own house as frugally as he pleases' (this does not necessarily mean that every priest had a house of his own — most of the priests in what survives of the 1744 listings lived in lodgings — but it does imply that each parish priest could be reasonably expected to entertain the bishop on visitation).

On the whole, the bishop was pleased with what he found: a frequently-recurring phrase is 'all things decent and well'. When there is trouble the comment is pointed. There are priests who do not preach — Pat Walsh, 'negligent in instructing his flock', Thomas Furlong, 'careless in exhorting his flock'; John Fitzhenry of Bannow, 'an honest, indolent man, who neither preaches nor teaches his flock' (a comment that shows Bishop Sweetman at his most incisive, as does what he says of Edmund Murphy — his church was in good order, 'but himself discontented with many of his flock, and they so with him'). Of Brian Murphy of Rathgarogue he noted carefully: 'I was told that the pastor minded dogs and hunting more than his flock, and that he did not give Mass at Rathgarogue on holydays'. Even in 1753 there was the priest who could not stop building, Henry Masterson of Camolin, 'at odds with his flock, through his own fault, as he built or threw down chapels in his district or caused it to be done unaccountably without the Ordinary's [i.e., bishop's] leave; nay applied to Protestants for said purposes, and abused his flock for applying for justice to the Ordinary'.

There is an obvious improvement since 1722 and 1731, in that the parish system has become more stable and is functioning well, but there is still evidence of poverty, some of it slatternly enough — bad chalices, bad altarstones, bad vestments. Sometimes, but not always, the bishop notes if a sermon were preached, and whether it was in English or Irish. A recent study, using later census-material to try to estimate the proportion of Irish speakers in much earlier decades, concludes that Irish was spoken by a significant number of people in only two baronies of county Wexford in the decade 1771-1781 — perhaps 6 per cent of the barony of Bantry and 13 per cent in the barony of Shelburne.[54] These were a kind of overspill from the strongly Irish-speaking areas of Kilkenny to the west of them, but even in Bantry and Shelburne Irish died with the great famine. The question of language has some pastoral significance. Catechesis of an Irish-speaking population was more difficult because catechetical material was scarcer, and, not just in Wexford, the number of priests who could instruct in Irish with ease and fluency was relatively small.

On the whole, then, Bishop Sweetman could be reasonably content with his priests. Naturally, he could have done with more of them. This complaint is to recur through the century, though the 1731 list indicates that already, even if quite illegally, there were assistant priests or 'curates' in some parishes. In 1796 Bishop Caulfield returned 'less than eighty', including regulars and diocesans, for a Catholic population he estimated at about 114,000, that is, one priest for about 1,500 Catholics.[55] In this the diocese of Ferns was better off than most. Reasonably firm statistical information becomes available only in 1834. By then increasing population and increasing poverty had led to a real crisis in some dioceses. Tuam, for example, had one priest for 4,199 people. Ferns was the best in Ireland, but even here the ratio had slipped to one for 1,941.

If the bishop could have done with more priests, he had some he would have been better without. In eighteenth century conditions there were limits on how a Catholic bishop could exercise his authority, but there were times he had to take action. Under interrogation in Dublin in 1751 Bishop Sweetman instanced 'one Hagan who practised physick without a licence'.[56] This man seems otherwise unknown, but the bishop's 1771 diocesan regulations indicate that other priests may have been tempted into the practice of a brand of clerical 'physick', those 'who read exorcisms, or gospels, over the already too ignorant, and by such ecclesiasticks too much deluded people, or act the fairy doctor in other shape . . . Under the foregoing article I comprehend those who bless water to sprinkle sick persons, cattle, fields, with'.[57]

The case that got the bishop into most trouble was the suspension of three priests in 1751 — Nicholas Neville, Nicholas Collier, and James Doyle. Nicholas Neville appears up to this in a very respectable light. The 1744 listing had noted him as 'popish priest of Ferns generally at the house of Patrick Doyle of the same place' (the priest at Ferns in 1731 had been Daniel Doyle). Nicholas Collier had been sailing a little more stormily: the 1731 list had returned him as assistant priest at Kilcommon in the present parish of Annacurra, but in 1744 he was listed as 'a priest without a parish at Anagh with an old woman'.[58] But whatever it was that had lost him his appointment Nicholas Collier was living quietly in comparison with James Doyle. He appears in the 1731 list as the priest in Edermine, apparently curate to the parish priest in Templeshannon, for it was the appointment of Patrick Sinnott to Templeshannon that led to the trouble, culminating in Doyle beating him 'treacherously and enormously' on 3 September 1751. For this he was suspended, and in retaliation he denounced Bishop Sweetman to the government. Twenty years later the bishop was still pursuing what appears to have been the indestructible James Doyle as an 'infamous and incorrigible couple-beggar', that is, a priest who made his living by officiating at clandestine marriages.[59]

There could, then, be problems in disciplining the unruly, but the general picture that emerges from the 1753 visitation indicates that these were an exception. In the diocese of Ferns the majority of the clergy even in the worst times had had a seminary education, and by the second half of the eighteenth century it was the rule. The progress of a young man to the priesthood may be traced in detail in the diary kept by John Kavanagh, now in the possession of the Irish Passionists. Born 'in a pleasant vale named Annagh near the town of Gorey' in 1749, he showed a taste for his books from an early age, and at the age of twenty decided to become a priest. In 1774 he was ordained, and then, as was the custom, went to the Irish college at Nantes for his theological studies. He was one of the many who did not return because they found a congenial post in *ancien régime* France, in his case a chaplaincy in the navy.

To turn from the clergy to the laity is to enter a world of greater uncertainties. It has already been noted that the great confiscations of the seventeenth century did not reduce everyone to a common misery. Still, in the whole of county Wexford the surviving Catholic landed proprietors were a tiny handful. Not all were as fortunate as the Hay family, who had lost their lands in the barony of Forth under Cromwell, but had managed to acquire lands at Ballinkeele between Ballymurn and Glenbrien before the Penal Code forbade the purchase of land by Catholics. At the other end of the scale were former landowners reduced to real misery. In his 1722 statutes, Bishop Verdon speaks of people reduced to such poverty as to be in real need of charity. More important, because more numerous, were the middlemen, of whom as yet we know so little, people like the family of Miles Byrne of Monaseed, with whom past sufferings and lost lands were such a lively memory. A clause in Bishop Sweetman's 1771 diocesan regulations is very revealing. The congregation at Sunday Mass, he declares, is not to be kept waiting 'for any person whatsoever', but, he immediately adds, 'at least, this compliment must not be paid to anyone oftener than three times in the one year'. Wexford may have had no Catholic landowners, but it did have its equivalent of a Catholic gentry. The start of Mass would be delayed — at least three times a year — if Mr Byrne of Monaseed was late.

These diocesan regulations of 1771 are very informative on the Catholic church that was emerging with some confidence from the penal laws.[60] The keeping of feast and fast was obviously a matter of great social as well as religious importance — it gave cohesiveness to the Catholic community if only by marking it off from the Protestant one. The same social role is fulfilled by the spiritual observances at the heart of the Catholic Reformation — instruction in the faith and sacramental practice, centred on the Sunday Mass.[61] A full service of Sunday Mass was provided. There appears to have been no problem about a priest saying two Masses on Sunday if necessary, though elsewhere this was to be a real problem even much later. Instruction was given on Sundays in the form of a sermon, and also by catechesis of the children. In 1796 Bishop Caulfield said that here the priest was assisted by the teachers, by young men preparing for the priesthood, and by the 'recently established' Confraternity of Christian Doctrine. Baptisms and weddings took place in the home, though church registers were kept (or at least the regulations required them to be kept — comparatively few eighteenth century registers have survived). The funeral Mass was also in the home, though Bishop Sweetman's regulations seem to indicate that, unlike some other parts of the country, the priest also attended in the cemetery.

Over much of Ireland the pastoral problem of confession and communion was met by the institution of 'stations of confession', that is, confessions and Mass in designated houses through the parish at Christmas and Easter times. The origins of the practice are obscure, but it can be seen fully established in Munster in the 1780s. It is doubtful if it ever became a feature of Catholic life in county Wexford. It was certainly not there in 1796, for Bishop Caulfield, speaking of the shortage of priests, says that they sometimes have to spend twelve hours or even more *in the confessional*. In his 1771 regulations Bishop Sweetman does speak of 'stations', but, while it is impossible to be completely certain, it does appear that these 'stations' were days of general confession and communion, but in county Wexford even then frequently held in the church and on Sundays. In 1831 the provincial synod of Dublin urged that this be made the universal practice, and in 1850 the synod of Thurles, not completely successfully, made it mandatory in the whole of Ireland. As already noted, Ferns was better supplied with priests than other dioceses, and the indications are that already by the 1770s the parish church provided the sacrament of penance, Mass and communion, and that Christian instruction which the Tridentine Reformation had seen as underlying all Christian life.

Catechesis of children was also provided by the growing number of 'private schools ... under the vigilance and direction of the parish priests' as Bishop Caulfield described them in 1796. There is no direct evidence from the eighteenth century to show how effective this church direction of schools was in county Wexford. The extensive Cashel visitations of the 1750s[62] would suggest something close to a system of parish schools in that diocese, but the vivid descriptions of his many schoolmasters left by John Kavanagh indicates that they were a race of rich idiosyncrasy, living partly on fees but partly by the patronage of the better-off Catholics in town and country, and not as amenable to clerical vigilance as Bishop Caulfield might like to think. The master who brought most misery to Kavanagh's young life would doubtless have considered himself a religious man. 'He was', says Kavanagh, 'a confounded drunkard who was not less ignorant than his predecessor, but far more fierce, wicked and severe. His masterpiece, or what he most professed, was the catechism, and whipping of his pupils, in which he spent the better part of the day, and a sermon each afternoon, which was generally interrupted by the sobs of his whipped pupils'.

So, by the late eighteenth century the structures of the Tridentine Reformation were established in Wexford to an extent that remoter areas did not match for perhaps another century. Direct evidence as to how effectively they were working begins to appear about a generation later, quite early in the nineteenth century, but this indicates that they were working well. Naturally, superstitions lingered, those superstitions which all the sixteenth-century reformers, Catholic and Protestant, had tried to eliminate. A bishop of the Catholic Enlightenment like Nicholas Sweetman would not have liked 'priests that act the fairy doctor', but it was hard to put them out of business. What was most to be regretted was the way the eighteenth century Catholic bishops set themselves against the traditional pilgrimages. The civil law forbade them and the local authorities tried to stop them, because all gatherings of Catholics were regarded as dangerous. In 1777 the sheriff and grand jury of Wexford had ordered all magistrates to be vigilant in suppressing them.[63] Six years earlier, in 1771, Bishop Sweetman had denounced them even more strongly — 'meetings of pretended devotion, or rather of real dissipation and dissoluteness'. He was not altogether wrong, but the question, unanswerable, of course, persists — how much of this degeneration of the traditional pilgrimages had been caused by their neglect by a clergy whose theological training in eighteenth-century seminaries would not have made them very sympathetic to such ancestral practices, even those as hallowed by tradition as Lady's Island?

As already noted, the influence of the Tridentine Reformation was strongest in the towns and among the better-off. We are reasonably well informed on Wexford town, though much still remains to be found out about its people; people like Thomas Sutton, clearly wealthy, for he went surety for several priests in 1704, and held the lease of their chapel and house for the Franciscans — precariously enough, for as a Catholic he could have a lease for only thirty-one years, and in the panic of 1744 there was talk of filing a bill of discovery to get possession of the premises, which, it was felt, would be very suitable for a Charter School.[64] The Franciscan chapel was the only one in Wexford. The chapel built by Bishop Wadding had been damaged when the Williamites took the town, and because it was inside the walls the Catholics were not allowed to repair it. The friars and the parish clergy had to share the Franciscan chapel which was outside the walls. This generated tensions, and the tensions generated correspondence and information.[65]

By about mid-century there were five or six friars in the house, a parish priest with an assistant, and normally a young priest doing a kind of 'internship' before receiving his own appointment. The bishop also lived in the town — indeed Sweetman, consecrated bishop in 1745, retained the parish of Wexford until 1756. With so many clergy to be supported, it is not surprising that one of the disputes concerned the Sunday collections. In the end it was agreed to divide them equally between the friars and the parish clergy. Each friar had his own possessions, even his own money. It was a regulation of the house that each of them should leave his books to the friary in his will, and in this way a rather notable library was begun, though its biggest single benefactor was a diocesan priest, John Wickham, parish priest of Templeshannon, whose 260 volumes came to Wexford friary when he died in 1778.[66]

There were six public Masses on Sundays and three on weekdays. On Sunday afternoons there was the office of vespers, well attended by the laity it would seem, for care was taken to have the vespers of Sunday recited 'as the laity have them in their manuals and are best accustomed to them' (at that time even a relatively minor saint's feast took liturgical precedence over the Sunday office). The chapel was well equipped with plate and vestments — some of what belonged to the friars is noted as having come from the friary which had existed in New Ross, while some of what belonged to the parish clergy way well be the same as things listed by Bishop Luke Wadding about eighty years before. There is Benediction regularly too — the friars would like to have it oftener, but the bishop thinks it is already too often. Neither does he approve of the Stations of the Cross, erected by the friars in 1747. The Catholic Enlightenment was indeed austere in its devotions.

But behind this almost bourgeois normality there was what Edward Hay called quite simply 'my civil degradation as a Catholic'.[67] When Nicholas Sweetman was under questioning in Dublin in 1751 he had to assure his interrogator that he 'never rings a bell but at the altar,' for to summon people to public worship was the prerogative of the established church. He further had to give assurance that it also got its due deference in that Catholics had their banns of marriage published and their marriage fees paid there, even though they continued to be married by their own clergy and have their children baptised by them, and the registers of births and marriages begun by Bishop Luke Wadding were carefully continued. When the Penal Code began to be dismantled the laws against the practice of religion went easily enough, if only because they had long been in practice disregarded. So did the laws against Catholics acquiring land in freehold. The sticking-point came over what Edward Hay called 'civil degradation', in other words, political rights for Catholics. With first the American Revolution and then the French Revolution making this question topical, the better-off Catholics were left with a substantial sense of grievance. The instincts of the older generation, like Edward Hay's father, Harvey, or Bishop Sweetman, or indeed his successor Bishop Caulfield, had been to keep their heads down, but this would not content younger men. When their political grievances fused with the basically economic grievances of the poor the result was the explosion of 1798.

There is a lot we do not know about 1798, but the issues are gradually clarifying. In particular, we are beginning to see why it was such a sectarian outburst on both sides. The Irish Volunteers have on the whole had a good press — the Dungannon declaration, the freedom of the parliament in College Green, among other things. Enniscorthy liked to boast it had the oldest Volunteer corps in the country, founded, curiously enough, in 1766, ten years before the declaration of American independence.[68] What happened was that a militia force formed in Enniscorthy in 1766 turned itself into a Volunteer corps when these began to be formed in 1778 to deal with the problems raised by the withdrawal of the army to fight in America. In 1781 a rumour that the Catholics of the county proposed to raise a Volunteer corps was met with thinly disguised threats, and no Catholic was admitted into any Volunteer corps in Wexford. The new tensions showed county Wexford to be very polarised in religious matters.[69]

The declared purpose of the Enniscorthy militia of 1766 had been 'to rid the county of the houghers or Whiteboys'. They must have appeared to the Catholic poor very much in the role of 'B Specials', armed to defend the Protestant interest. Yet although there was a widespread 'Whiteboy scare' at the time the evidence seems to show that there were few if any Whiteboys in county Wexford. Bishop Sweetman was also very severe in his condemnations of the Whiteboys — his regulations of 1771 speak of 'the accursed Whiteboys' and a pastoral letter read in all churches on 16 July 1775 used similarly strong terms.[70] His successor, Dr Caulfield, was equally condemnatory, urged on by his forceful neighbour John Thomas Troy, the bishop of Ossory. Now there were serious Whiteboy disturbances in the diocese of Ossory, but still very few in county Wexford, and those at the very margins of the county. The first serious disturbances were in 1793, and all accounts agree that they were purely agrarian, this at a time when in the north of the country the organisation of Catholic poor, the Defenders, were quickly absorbing political ideas inspired by the French Revolution. A good deal of social history is still to be unravelled before we can really understand 1798.

10   *L. M. Cullen*

The 1798 rebellion in Wexford: United Irishman organisation, membership, leadership

I

The key question of the extent of organisation among the 1798 rebels in county Wexford remains unresolved; indeed it has been assumed that there is not a problem of organisation for which to account. The almost universal assumption is that there was little organisation. Charles Dickson wrote thirty years ago:

if . . . further proof was required that County Wexford was forced into the war, it would be found in what I believe to be a fact beyond question, namely, that it would be difficult to point to a single entirely willing insurgent in the whole county.[1]

His only exception was for the extreme north of the county, 'the only part of County Wexford where the Society of United Irishmen made much progress before the rising'.[2] While there is evidence in Anthony Perry's confession of attempts at organisation further afield, Dickson drew the conclusion that 'Perry had no high opinion of the state of the organisation elsewhere in the county', and that 'the Society met with no enthusiastic response except perhaps in the north of the county'.[3] His overall conclusion was that

That minority of them who had taken the oath as United Irishmen did so, with those constitutional objects alone in view. There was nothing of the Jacobin about them.[4]

Thomas Pakenham's view is similar. He describes the absence of organisation, confining it to the border with Wicklow and to the middle classes mainly within that fringe.[5] However, though its range is on his account confined, his recognition of organisation within those limits is very positive, and has been strongly criticised by Thomas Powell for whom United Irishman organisation was a very minor factor in the Wexford rising. For him, in his excellent study of the background to the rebellion, there was (even taking Perry's evidence into account) both little organisation and little contact with the Dublin Society.[6]

248

His conclusions were that 'it was primarily a peasant movement' whose 'leadership was fragmented and local', and that 'indications are that the middle-class leaders were drawn into the movement after it had already begun'.[7] Purely economic unrest explains the movement and he even went so far as to assert that 'it seems perverse to attempt to account for the enthusiastic solidarity of the Wexfordmen in rebellion by any other means'.[8]

Thus, while the three main modern historians of the rebellion may disagree in emphasis, the basic conclusion is broadly similar. Moreover, it simply confirmed an already long-standing view of the rebellion. The returns seized in Oliver Bond's house on 12 March contain no reference to United Irishman strength in Wexford, and almost immediately after the rebellion they were highlighted by Wexfordmen anxious to extricate themselves from legal or more general accusation to justify the argument that they had been merely driven into rebellion by their loyalist opponents. Powell makes a point of stressing that there is no mention of Wexford in three separate reports dated 19, 20 and 26 February.[9] On this evidence it would seem probable that 'even if the United Movement was officially organised to some extent in county Wexford, its communications with the provincial and national committees were not very close'.[10] A later seized return of 19 April with no reference to Wexford seems to bear out further the absence of organisation.[11] It is, however, a different return: one of military organisation, not of general political affiliation to the movement as the earlier returns were, and it is so incomplete or inconsistent in some of its internal detail that it is no reliable guide at all to the presence or absence of general military United Irishman organisation within a county. The various returns were published in the report of the secret committee in the autumn of 1798. They were known to government from an earlier date but there is no evidence that they had an influence in accounting for the complacency of government in relation to Wexford. That complacency pre-dated the seizure of the returns and seems to have been due to the scale of the exercise conducted by Lord Mountnorris, unparalleled in other counties, to administer the oath of allegiance in the districts in Wexford where loyalty was most in doubt in late 1797. Complacency in Wexford led to complacency in Dublin; the harassed officials in the Castle were fully occupied by complaints from elsewhere and were relieved by a sudden drying up of the complaints from Wexford which had made their appearance in the previous year. The returns therefore merely reinforced an existing complacency, though when the rebellion finally broke out, Cooke was driven to write the oft-quoted remark that 'Wexford, the peaceable, the cultivated has been and is the formidable spot. You will recollect there were no returns, no delegates from Wexford. How artificial'.[12] Gordon (who was familiar from clerical residence with the Mountnorris and Stopford estates) mentions in passing in a footnote that Mountnorris had prevented extra troops being sent to the county.[13] The evidence suggests that not only did Mountnorris prevail on opinion in Dublin but that his endeavours calmed protestants in Wexford. Mountnorris's role is the single most neglected aspect of Wexford's story on the eve of the rebellion and the most critical factor. He is difficult to judge because little of his correspondence survives and because some subsequent opinion was hostile to him. This was either because he had opposed the spread of the United Irishmen, or because he was regarded as betraying the catholics. Edward Hay himself was in his company on some of his pacifying missions.[14] Mountnorris entertained catholic priests in his own home and also sometimes dined in the home of the catholic parish priest of Camolin, Frank Kavanagh.[15]

Miles Byrne has a few unfavourable remarks on him, and, less defensibly, Edward Hay comments bitterly and more explicitly on him. However, against these hostile references must be counterbalanced reference to his good opinion among contemporary catholics, some favourable comment in later catholic opinion in the Luke Cullen manuscripts and the fact that on that authority Mountnorris was one of those who arranged in the aftermath of the rebellion for Billy Byrne to recruit for the British army.[16] In one fleeting glimpse in the Rebellion papers on 5 September 1798 Mountnorris is seen as acting in support of the release of a rebel.[17] The decisive factor in changing some catholic opinion of him seems to have been the summary court martial and execution of Father John Redmond. Opinion in Wexford was, however, too polarised in the aftermath of the rebellion for unsupported assertions to be accepted too readily. Yet, the traditional hostile view gains some credence by Gordon's acceptance of the report that Mountnorris had actually ordered Father Michael Murphy's head to be cut off after his death.[18] An impressionistic view based on the scanty evidence is that Mountnorris may have been a rather lightweight, shallow man, prone to court popularity. The tone of his letters to subordinates is slightly ingratiating.[19] Yet, he may well emerge finally in a more favourable light than hostile opinion of him suggests and his opposition to over-severe measures prior to the rebellion was certainly in itself wise. Mountnorris's role had a two-fold importance in the immediate background to the rebellion. On the liberal side he was the focal point of the violently contested election of 1797 and his pacifying mission in 1797 and 1798 convinced both Dublin Castle and for a shorter period and less completely Wexford protestants of the good intentions and good order of Wexford catholics. Without Mountnorris, there would have been either no rebellion in Wexford or a very different one.

Given the large number of courts martial and prosecutions of rebels extending over several years after the termination of the rebellion, the practical benefits for those accused and their apologists of playing down the existence of conspiracy in the county were very real. At one level contemporary polemics seemed to throw the responsibility onto the loyalist party by suggesting that their highhanded law-and-order tactics had occasioned the rebellion (Mountnorris by opposing them even before the rebellion had already made this an issue). At another level, they served as a vital defence argument for those accused of involvement. Edward Hay and Thomas Cloney were harassed by accusations which dragged on through 1799; Edward Roche, one of the military leaders, was in prison until his death in 1799. Prosecutions and executions proceeded at least as late as 1801 for lesser fry accused of crimes. In the excitement of the times, even loyal catholics like Philip Hay, Sir Thomas

Plate xxiv: The Earl of Mountnorris

Esmonde and his cousin Laurence Doyle were arrested and charged. Hence the question of organisation was not solely an academic one useful for the polemics which had taken the place of battle from the autumn of 1798, but an argument of real value especially for those who had been implicated but were now desperately struggling either to establish their innocence or secure more favourable treatment. The secret report on its publication in the autumn of 1798 was quickly seized on by Wexford polemicists as one of the weapons in their armoury. Luke Cullen, referring to information gathered in 1825, makes the issue much clearer;

I asked a man named Doyle who had given some details of battles and meetings to Mr Ed Hay why that gentleman said so little in his book about his devoted friend and cousin Mr Fitzgerald. He said that when he spoke of Mr Fitzgerald to him on the above occasion, Mr Hay preserved a silence which I understood afterwards was that he hoped that he would be allowed to return home and was [sic] on that account designed to say as little as possible about him lest it might retard his return.[20]

If the famous returns seized in 1798 in Dublin revealed no United Irishman presence in Wexford, and if the argument developed that there had been little Wexford involvement in treasonable activity, it is hardly surprising that leadership was also played down. Edward Hay in his book made a point of saying that the organisation in Wexford was comparatively smaller than in other counties and dismissed the topic so speedily that it suggests that he would have found further comment on the subject embarrassing.[21] His book contains a single reference to his own brother John Hay and its brevity suggests that there was little scope for defending his innocence. For Hay, such combination as there was among United Irishmen was due exclusively to fear of Orangemen, and these fears were entertained even by people of respectability.[22] As time proceeded assertions of absence of organisation became even more positive. Thomas Cloney writing in 1832 was not only vague on the topic but his views became more explicit as his writing proceeded. At the outset, he described organisation as 'having but partially taken place in the county Wexford'; some 180 pages later he was asserting that 'no organised political confederacy (existed) in that county even to a limited extent'.[23]

The awkward fact that catholics had arms to surrender in quantity on the eve of the rebellion was potentially damaging. Much use had therefore to be made of the argument that terrorised catholics simply procured arms in order to have something to surrender and thereby obtain a protection. Gordon mentions one such episode to illustrate the depth of the terror, not to suggest that it was a frequent occurrence.[24] Hay, using Gordon's instance, suggests that the urge to acquire arms for this reason was widespread.[25] There is a single instance of this sort in the evidence collected by Luke Cullen[26] and again, as in the case of Gordon, no wider deduction about the practice is remotely implied. There is no other evidence whatever for the practice. In fact, it seems an inherently improbable practice and the evidence all seems to stem from Hay's effort to widen the import of what Gordon had reported. Kavanagh's popular history which professedly relied on tradition as well as written sources merely relies on Hay for this issue.[27] However, on this topic as on others, Cloney had no difficulty in making sweeping claims:

Such was the terror which prevailed that numbers who were never United Irishmen went in and assumed the character, procured some kind of weapon, which they never possessed until the day they thought it necessary to produce it, and thus did they furnish the magistracy of the county with lists of both real and feigned United Irishmen.[28]

Flogging and picketting were also seen by Cloney as a factor which recruited people through fear into the United Irishmen.[29] It is hard to understand why the fear of flogging led people to become members of an organisation which did not exist in the county. Given the polemical nature of the contemporary writing on 1798, the sources are shot through with such impasses.

The two main catholic contemporary accounts of the rebellion were written by Hay and Cloney. Thus the potent myth was created that even the possession of arms proved nothing. Gordon, who had unwittingly created its basis says very little about organisation, merely confining himself to a comment that the county was 'very recently and but partially organised.'[30] The reason for the absence of further attention to the issue in Gordon's pages is that his primary concern was with the aftermath of the rebellion, the thorny question of repression or pacification, and exaggerated claims of protestants. It was not his concern to go over ground which protestants were raking up about the extent of conspiracy. His own view is revealed in a throw-away comment in a footnote: 'the people were so determined on insurrection. . . .'[31] Thus Gordon cannot be really relied on, as he often is, to prove the absence of conspiracy. As he lived in the region of the rebellion, was fair-minded, and the admission is not in the interests of his basic task of challenging the extreme loyalist view of a general conspiracy among catholics, it is a small but significant point.

II

If the case is made that there was no organisation or preceding conspiracy, then the responsibility for the rising and for the sectarian animosities must be thrown onto popular feeling, popular organisation and in the last analysis the Defenders. No one adopted this line of argument at the time. The only feature of the period is the loose use of both the terms 'Defenders' and 'United Irishmen' by some contemporaries. Not even Cloney, writing later and quite prepared to take liberties with truth, made this point, though secret agrarian societies were by then abominated by all levels of society. Only later writers have made this argument. Kavanagh did not do so in his popular history though in later editions he printed a communication from a correspondent that in his part of the county (i.e. to the west of the Slaney) the 1798 rebellion was known as the second rebellion and the 1793 unrest as the first rebellion.[32] It has become the basis on which later historians have drawn a distinction, seeking to play down United Irishman organisation and to attribute the sectarian and emotional features of 1798 to popular organisations. The loose use of contemporary language all comes from the protestant side, and historians like Musgrave, anxious to establish the depth of the catholic conspiracy, were eager both to trace the conspiracy back to the Whiteboy rising in the 1760s and to report instances of Defender organisation or activity. None of the contemporary commentators on the catholic side seems to have made the distinction.

The thin evidence accounts for the vagueness and ambivalence of modern assertions. There is no clear statement of the importance of Defender organisation in Dickson's book; yet he later made the assertion in an article that the Defenders were 'especially strong in County Wexford'.[33] In his history he speaks of organisation 'more on the lines of the Defender organisation', 'in the succession of Defenders' and of 'the Defenders in Wexford unlike elsewhere being absorbed into the United Irishmen only to a limited extent'.[34] Importance is attached vaguely to the influence of past Defender activity.[35] Thus the assertion is made frequently by Dickson, but evidence is at no stage adduced which would bear out the importance attached to the issue. Much earlier Lecky had written of Wexford as 'an important centre of defenderism'.[36] He concluded that there was 'little positive political disloyalty ... till shortly before the rebellion of 1798' and more explicitly that 'scarcely any steps had been taken to form United Irishmen in Wexford into regiments'.[37] Powell in a later examination of the evidence pointed out the problems of Defender associations. The 1793 unrest was west of the Slaney whereas the 1798 rebellion had its origins to the east of the river: he concluded that there was no evidence of a Defender movement prior to 1798.[38] Yet even he, disallowing as he does a popular conspiracy, is thrown back onto resting the case on popular disturbances and lower-class movements. He speaks of 'pre-existing societies' and 'the earlier experiences of local combinations' and is forced to the conclusion, even when faced with much use of the term United Irishman, that

it is probable that as in the case of the defenders the term 'United Irishman' was often applied to organisations and activities which might not be strictly entitled to it and so one should not be too quick to accept its use in stated evidence as trustworthy.[39]

We are faced here ultimately with an ambivalent picture; as in the case of Dickson, some of the case rests on dubious arguments. Dickson, for instance, seems to give weight to the Defenders because the middle class were of 'recent origin' and hence would not carry much weight.[40]

Caesar Colclough at Duffry Hall near the border of Wexford and Carlow was the single most regular Wexford correspondent of the Castle. As a barrister and a man whose disposition closely attached him to the liberal political group in Wexford county, he was in a position to accurately observe what was taking place and his outlook was not obscured by the wild fears or prejudices that coloured many of the Castle's regular correspondents. In a letter of 7 April 1798, written while on circuit at the assizes at Clonmel, he contrasted the variety of oaths administered by agrarian rebels in Waterford and the absence of United Irishman support for the defence of the accused with the situation in Wexford and Wicklow:

I think 'tis plain that though great disturbances exist yet the county [Waterford] is not organised as other places are — that is evident from the various and different oaths which have been tendered and from the prisoners being left to defend themselves as they may without any aid from the committee [provincial committee] as is the case in Wicklow and in Wexford.[41]

He noted that the absence of respectable people from the business was reflected in the performance of the petty juries which he saw as 'excellent, keeping a happy medium between the severity of the Wicklow and the laxity of the Wexford ones. . . .' Kemmis, the state solicitor, had an equally bad opinion of the Wexford juries.[42] This evidence, coming from a liberal and an official source suggests that political alienation reached as far as the juries hearing serious charges in the county. Another indication of the political nature of the background is that Luke Cullen dismissed Musgrave's statement of the Defenders having come to Ballymurtagh in 1792 as absurd.[43]

Emphasis on popular movements meant that leadership could be dismissed as a factor in the outbreak. Powell saw the middle classes as being drawn in only after it began.[44] For Dickson the case is even more specific;

It is difficult to determine with certainty whether all these persons were willing or unwilling insurgents. My own opinion is that it is impossible to describe any one of them as a *willing* insurgent, though no doubt when they were finally compelled to take the field there were varying degrees of reluctance.[45]

One of the most oft repeated assertions is that prominent catholics were summoned by the rebels and that they had no alternative to complying. This assertion was made by Hay who included his brother John among those so summoned (it is his only reference to his brother).[46] The reliability of these assertions is not very good. Indeed, elsewhere in his volume Edward Hay alleged that protestants were accusing people whom they had formerly induced to join the United Irishmen, itself a rather damning admission of conspiracy whose significance seems to have escaped Hay.[47] Even in the case of the notorious Thomas Dixon, Hay was anxious to eliminate any suggestion of military rank:

His denomination of captain was owing to his being master of a sloop which traded to and from Wexford.[48]

Gordon on the other hand took pains to describe him as a sea captain who became a United Irishman captain.[49]

The statement that death threats were used by the rebels to acquire their middle-class or landed leaders has often been made. Hay is circumspect on this issue, except in the case of his brother, whom he represents as joining the rebels under the menace of a threat to harm him and his family in his own home. Much later the general assertion is made more baldly by Holt.[50] Here, as in other instances, the argument is pushed to its extreme by Thomas Cloney.

He represented Cornelius Grogan as having acted as a commissary because the alternative was his execution by the rebels and the merchant Patrick Prendergast as assuming civil office because refusal would have meant certain death.[51] He insinuates the same for Keugh and Edward Fitzgerald.[52] Cloney is remarkably vague as to the circumstances in which he was himself summoned. He represented himself as acceding to the wishes of the second of two bands which approached him on 29 May; 'louder and more peremptory in their demands ... I joined the people'.[53] The assertion that rebels had participated under the threat of death was made in the immediate aftermath of the rebellion and some fair-minded protestants and army officers seem to have accepted its *prima facie* validity as a defence. Thomas Cloney, who was well-connected and able to generate a sizeable amount of Protestant support for himself, even obtained a letter from Sir James Foulis who wrote on 1 October 1799 that

he [Cloney] found it prudent to accept of a command among the rebels; indeed according to their maxim a refusal or evasion would have been certain death.[54]

Dickson has mentioned his puzzlement as to statements made in the course of the rebellion by Philip Roche and Esmond Kyan to loyalists that they faced death from the rebels.[55] Were Roche and Kyan thinking forward to a possible line of legal defence? Given the ferocity of loyalists to convict rebels and their patent bias, fair-minded people anxious to halt the vindictive campaign that seemed to make even a second rising possible, were hardly likely to adopt too legalistic an attitude towards arguments which might help to save rebels from an unscrupulous and frenzied campaign, devoid of all wish to find common ground for a peaceful future.

Cloney quite specifically stated that he was not an United Irishman on at least three occasions in his book.[56] Dickson, in regard to Cloney's relationship to Robert Emmet's conspiracy, is obliged to remark that 'with regard to his subsequent movements there and in Dublin he is lacking in candour'.[57] Indeed his disregard for truth comes through at several points through his volume. In 1801, failing to observe the terms of his release, he falsely represented that he was in Wales while he was still in Ireland and his memoirs revealingly show approval of tampering with the date of a letter.[58] The entire book is characterised by a marked inconsistency which makes any general observations by Cloney suspect. He claimed in his defence in 1799 that 'political subjects scarce ever occupied my mind and I was perfectly contented with those laws and that constitution under which I felt myself prosperous and protected'.[59] Yet a different state of mind is revealed elsewhere where he says he would not have been involved 'were it not that I beheld my country in chains and bleeding at every pore under the whip of the executioner and the bayonet of the mercenary'.[60] More startlingly he observed that 'nor could I be brought, though death stared me in the face, to submit to laws of any villain's making'.[61] He believed that 'protection and allegiance are reciprocal obligations ... if one is withdrawn, the other cannot be expected to continue'.[62] As for the claim that he was uninvolved in the public life of the county, he concedes by impli- cation the charge that he had refused to drink the health of George Ogle at a

Plate xxv: Rev James Gordon

Plate xxvi: Edward Roche

Plate xxvii Esmond Kyan

Plate xxviii: John Henry Colclough

public banquet 'some little time previous to the Insurrection', and he also regarded himself as 'very generally known to all classes'.[63] In these circumstances his denial of United Irishman membership can hardly be regarded as compelling. Even less trustworthy is his statement that on his arrival at the Three Rock Mountain from Vinegar Hill on 29 May 'I found all disinclined to assume authority, or avow their rank if they had been invested with any'.[64]

In the case of John Hay, Cloney claims that he was not a member and was ignorant of the conspiracy:

From his long residence abroad and consequent removal from the scene of Irish politics, he was too much a stranger to be involved in the secret confederacies which were organising previous to the crisis of 1798. Accordingly when his neighbours flew to arms, he remained at home ignorant of their preparations and intentions.[65]

It would seem to be on Cloney's authority that Dickson refers to Hay as 'a most unwilling insurgent'.[66] Much could be said on John Hay. Suffice it to mention at this stage, in weighing up Cloney's assertion, that he had been a guest at one of the Wexford political dinners in April 1798 mentioned by Barrington in which other guests included John Sheares.[67] Cloney himself inconsistently makes the significant admission that John Hay 'witnessed the repression of his countrymen with the indignation natural to a generous mind'.[68] Hay had been back in Ireland since 1793 and on at least two occasions Edward Roche, an undoubted United Irishman, acted as witness for him in property transactions.[69]

When Edward Roche had surrendered himself and in August 1798 sought the terms of the amnesty, he represented that he had been going (by implication to Wexford) to find out why Edward Fitzgerald had been put in confinement when he was met a quarter of a mile from Fitzgerald's house by a crowd of several hundred people, unknown to him, some of whom fired a shot at him while one man presented his gun to shoot until stopped. Turning back, he was faced with an even greater crowd of people. According to his statement 'he proceeded where the greater crowd of people were, being fully determined to know the reason, let whatever happen, even at the risque of his life. When he came up to them they asked him would he join them, when he answered knowing it was no use to deny it'.[70] This account is quite interesting. Like Cloney's account it represents a sequence of two crowds, the second larger and allegedly more menacing; as in Cloney's case, the statement avoids the assertion that his life was threatened, while implying it. Other aspects of Roche's statement are interesting. Roche gives the date as 27 May. If this is meant to be the daylight of 27 May, it is quite erroneous, intentionally or unintentionally, as he had already thrown in his lot with the rebels during the night. If, as was the case, he was abroad during the night on business which was not yeomanry business, his real intentions are more open to question and it may have been the intention of the memorial to obscure the fact. The reluctance to admit membership explicitly is quite understandable, especially where, as in Roche's case, he is seeking a favourable decision. Even in the case of individuals like William

Michael Byrne (of Park Hill, Wicklow) who in effect admitted their guilt, a similar claim was made, Byrne claiming that 'of me, it has been said without any positive proof that I was actually one'.[71]

III

All biographical accounts have latched onto these claims which have supported powerfully the argument that there had been no previous organisation or even conspiracy in county Wexford. There is a striking contrast between the literature on Wexford and that on the West and Ulster. The sustained argument that there was no organisation in Wexford contrasts with the specific recognition of deep United Irishman involvement in the north and of significant activity in Mayo. A comparison between Hayes and Dickson is illuminating. While Dickson goes to great lengths to discount United Irishmen involvement in Wexford, Hayes for the west goes to the other extreme, tending if anything to exaggerate the extent of involvement and the degree of enthusiasm of the Mayo rebels.[72] Kavanagh in his history of the rebellion in Wexford made a big issue of non-involvement. He claims that the organisation had made little progress because of the opposition of the priests and the character of the people which was adverse to secret societies.[73] He contrasted the high degree of organisation in Ulster with its absence in Wexford: in the latter place 'there existed no previous organisation'.[74] In Ulster the United Irishmen failed because it was a secret society which lent itself to penetration by government agents. He argued that resistance in Wexford was effective precisely because it did *not* derive from a secret society. Thus the case for a near-spontaneous rebellion grew. Kavanagh is coy about the roles of his own maternal grandfather, John Prendergast, and his paternal grandfather Jeremiah Kavanagh of Ballinamonabeg, who joined the insurgents at Oulart and in whose public house ahead of the battle the county leaders of the United Irishmen had met.[75] In the case of John Prendergast, an admission emerges that United Irishman organisation existed in the area 'but very few joined them'[76] and the subject is disposed of by saying that the old man was 'unwilling to talk of his experiences in the rising'.[77] The problem is to some extent resolved by emphasising the role of clergy as leaders, not indeed as United Irishmen but as individuals who stepped forward to defend the people against oppression and impossible odds. There is the distinctly odd statement by Kavanagh that the catholic priests redeemed themselves by fighting with the people.[78] John Murphy was singled out as 'their wisest and bravest leader . . .'.[79] In this way the concept of the priest leader emerges to a degree which did not exist in contemporary accounts or indeed in later accounts in the first half of the century. In Byrne's account it is clear that the priests involved were only some of a number of leaders and Luke Cullen's informants do not provide any exceptional role for John Murphy. Kavanagh's emphasis on Murphy serves a three-fold purpose. First, it removes the emphasis from the disturbing possibility that there was popular responsibility for the rising. Second, it disposes of the awkward example of Murphy's role by turning him into a man in a heroic mould. Third there may be some element of local patriotism in choosing him as the hero of the county.

Kavanagh used the accounts consistent with his thesis that the rebellion was not an organised affair:. 'The pages of Hay, Gordon, Cloney, Teeling and Plowden have been diligently perused . . .'.[80] The absence of Byrne's memoirs is remarkable. This is no accident. He says that Byrne was too young to be of consequence and claims that his narrative is 'very interesting, but inaccurate in some important statements'.[81] The only substantive acknowledgement of Byrne seems to be an admission that Monaseed, Byrne's birthplace, furnished many brave insurgents.[82] The reason for ignoring Byrne is very clear. His avowal of the existence of the United Irishmen in the county and his acknowledgement of cold-blooded and ruthless acts by the rebels was much too uncomfortable for the thesis maintained by Kavanagh; hence his account was for all practical purposes ignored.

Byrne's book is a very important work. Dickson's conclusion is that it is 'difficult to overestimate the value of his work'.[83] Though slightly partisan in his outlook, Lecky, judicious and cautious in his use of sources, relied extensively on Byrne. In fact on close examination Byrne's work is even more interesting. It is intended as an explicit rebuke of the apologetic tone adopted by catholic commentators on the rebellion and as an effort to assert the political intent that lay behind the rebellion. His widow wrote in 1868 that 'I publish the memoirs he had written in the hope they might be of use to his fellow countrymen, particularly that of the rising generation'.[84] Kavanagh's dismissal of Byrne is inexcusable. While he may have been very young and his military responsibilities junior, he served through the campaign in Wexford, its borders and the midlands and knew the chiefs closely in these campaigns. His own background moreover was remarkable. He had met James Edward Devereux at his own Monaseed home when Devereux was on his way to London as one of the five delegates to carry the Catholic petition to George III; Robert Graham, the Wexford United Irish delegate, was a relation on Byrne's mother's side; Murt Mernagh, a United Irishman captain, was a relation; through a Monaseedman, Ned Fennell, he had met Perry in 1797 and frequently went on errands to his home subsequently; Nicholas Murphy, only a few years older and a United Irishman captain, was one of his closest friends and he met the United Irishman organisers Putnam McCabe and Mathew Doyle at Nicholas Murphy's house.[85] A step-brother in Dublin, Edward Kennedy helped organise the defence of United Irishmen prisoners before the rebellion and was later a state prisoner.[86] No writer was as well-qualified to write about the United Irishman presence in the county; unlike the other writers (including Holt who wrote only after his return) he lived outside Ireland and had no intention to come back. He could accordingly write with none of the prevaricating quality that characterises all the written rebel accounts without exception.

He made a point of defending the 1798 priests: 'how unfeeling and uncharitable and unjust it is of those Roman Catholic historians who have taken upon them to write of the insurrection of Wexford, to condemn, and endeavour to tarnish the reputation of those priests who fought so bravely at the head of the people, in their efforts to expel the common enemy'.[87] He describes Father Murphy as 'a fine specimen of what a people are capable when resolved to be firm',[88] a point which may imply United Irishman sympathies on Murphy's part. As far as the lay leaders are concerned, he was anxious to defend their political purpose. In particular, he criticised de Beaumont's book (a bad book on all accounts) which 'does no justice to the many distinguished Irish protestants who sacrificed themselves and their lives and fortunes in the cause of the independence of their country …a perusal of his work would convey the idea that none but the poorest and most miserable peasantry of Ireland were engaged in the effort to shake off the yoke of England … The facts are different. . . .'[89] Byrne is anxious to assert the significant input of both Protestant and Catholic middle class into the 1798 rebellion.

Byrne had read all the published accounts of the rebellion and its times. Wolfe Tone, Hay, Musgrave, Gordon and McNeven are all mentioned by name. He is critical to the point of contempt of Edward Hay. He casts aspersions on Hay's judgement and elsewhere notes that Hay's 'presence at the Irish camp could have been dispensed with', a comment made in a specific context but which may convey a deeper disdain.[90] Significantly, Cloney's book is not referred to on a single occasion, an omission so extraordinary that it can only have been intentional. Dickson is not correct in saying that Byrne used Cloney's work.[91] Cloney is however referred to more frequently than most and in terms which are extraordinarily favourable (and which imply awareness of the book):

His long imprisonment and suffering are well-known to every true Irish patriot. I feel at a loss for expressions to do justice to the memory of Mr Cloney; I knew him well, and as I shall have to speak of him often before my narrative is finished, I shall endeavour to make amends for any omissions of what could have redounded to his honour.[92]

This paragraph appears to hint at the lack of candour in Cloney's own account and to seek to make clear that he was a committed United Irishman, a point absent from Cloney's own volume. Thus, quite in contrast to the lacklustre and evasive account by Cloney himself of his appearance at the camp on Vinegar Hill, Byrne very deliberately states that 'the brave and dauntless Thomas Cloney of Moneyhore, joined the camp on the 29th May, at the head of a splendid corps of fine determined fellows'.[93] It is on this note that Cloney is introduced in his narrative. Elsewhere he also emphasises Cloney's initiative in sedition. Thus a long account of Cloney's wishing to see Emmet and of his subsequent relations with him flatly contradicts Cloney's version.[94] In relation to Cloney's mission to General Lake, which is presented in Cloney's version as an instance of his co-operative or peaceful attitudes, Byrne tersely comments that 'I am persuaded that the brave Cloney always felt the deepest anguish that he had accepted this fruitless mission'.[95] There is no undue amount of inaccuracy in Byrne's account; given the distance in time from the events and his youth during the events in question it is all the more remarkable. Dickson has pointed to the conflict of fact between William Barker's memorial of 12 November 1798 in which he claimed that he joined the rebels under menace, and Byrne's account purportedly based on contacts with Barker in 1803 in France.[96] The error, while material in itself (Byrne stated that Barker escaped court martial, while he was declared innocent by the court), does not seem central to Byrne's account. Barker indeed seems to fall into the category of those rebels who made use of the intimidation argument to support their protestations of innocence. The case simply establishes that the imperfect machinery of justice worked in favour of rebels as well as against them, due to the presence of fair-minded army officers and local protestants as well as partisan ones.

IV

The Rebellion and State of the Country Papers in Dublin Castle do not throw much light on Wexford on the eve of the rebellion or in the preceding year and accordingly they have been used to support the contention that there was little or no organisation in Wexford on the eve of the rebellion. However, the papers have never been systematically appraised as a documentary source. Either they have been mined for the isolated evidence contained in letters or negative conclusions have been drawn from the fact that evidence fails to surface in them. Their inherent character as an archive has never been appraised. They reflect the role of complex networks of individuals. Letters frequently reveal the character of the individual who wrote them; where much information obtrudes, it reflects ideological or political influences operating on individuals and the dissemination of fears or political propaganda along well-identified lines rather than merely the response of individuals to local events or happenings. Absence of comment does not suggest the absence of events which gave rise to concern; instead, it may reflect local circumstances or even relative immunity to the insidious network of Castle loyalists who were intent on stirring up loyalist panic to engender pressure for sterner law and order methods. In 1796 and 1797 the papers were mainly taken up with northern issues, where the situation was without exaggeration seriously out of hand. Apart from the north midlands, elsewhere the only really widespread reporting was from Cork and Waterford which has extensive troubles, largely United Irishman in Cork, mainly agrarian in Waterford (even Musgrave was later to concede rather unwittingly the economic basis for discontent in this region),[97] In the west some moderate opinion occasionally reported fear of politicisation activated by the migration of catholics from east Ulster: this fear reached as far south as county Clare.[98]

In South Leinster reporting was extensive only from Carlow and Wicklow. In Carlow the troubles as measured by the Rebellion papers date back to August/September 1797, the correspondence becoming more extensive and shrill with time. Moreover, the correspondence reflected not just local fears but the epistolary dimension of the pre-occupations of a handful of magistrates, notably the Rochforts and Robert Cornwall. In June 1798 William Elliott, an undersecretary in the Military Department in the Castle, recollected that the Orange associations had been 'formed and promoted by Colonel Rochfort and some other gentlemen in the counties of Wexford and Carlow'.[99] So notorious was the initiative in Carlow that the founding of a Grand Lodge there had been reported in the Dublin press as early as 13 January 1798.[100] The influence of the Rochforts radiated into the neighbouring counties as well. A meeting of the Queen's county magistrates had been postponed in January for Colonel Rochfort's attendance and there the magistrates (except for Pole) were in favour of proclaiming the county.[101] The Rochforts and Cornwall had links too with the Montgomery and Keating families in Kildare and there too the Order took shape.[102] The Rochforts had close links with Wexford as well. Quite apart from his magistracy, Colonel Rochfort had been a candidate in the bitterly contested Wexford election of 1797. As he drew little support at the polls in an election which saw the two Wexford parties marshall their voters with vigour, he can only have had links with Wexford figures who stood outside the mainstream of its loyalist or liberal politics. The two conflicting Wexford groups had some lines of communication among themselves as witnessed in the electoral negotiations between Cornelius Grogan and Lord Ely, or in loyalist acceptance for a time of the apparent success of the Mountnorris pacification campaign launched in late November 1797. In consequence Colonel Rochfort's Wexford contacts would seem to be with relatively obscure individuals in the west of the county. It is possible too that the small Blacker estate in this region may have proved a point of support for the spread of Rochfort's Orange associations. Captain William Blacker of Armagh had acquired a small Wexford estate by marriage. Though largely absentee from the county, his position as a county grand master for Armagh in April 1798[103] may have had some significance for the early stages in the growth of the Order in Wexford. One of the early lodges in Carlow had as its master Moses De Renzy, a member of a minor landed family based at Clobemon in Wexford.[104] The first lodge within Wexford was headed by Hunter Gowan of Mount Nebo, likewise a minor gentleman outside the county's political networks. Significantly Hunter Gowan seems to have been an active magistrate in January when the general approach in the county was low-key. At the first meeting of the national Grand Orange Lodge in Dublin on 9 April, Robert Rochfort and Hunter Gowan as grand masters for Carlow and Wexford respectively were present.[105] In May, Carlow had no less than ten lodges, Wexford one, and Wicklow three.[106] The initial spread of the Order in south Leinster outside the main gentry network seems to be confirmed in the pattern of its early spread in Wicklow where Benjamin O'Neill Stratford was one of its early adherents and where two of its three Orange lodges were at Carnew and Tinahely.[107] The impetus for its growth seems to have come from gentry — usually minor gentry — within regions where the presence of a prosperous, articulate and(as they saw it) subversive Catholic middle class seemed to threaten the Protestant interest. It spread more slowly in adjacent districts within the same regions. Indeed it may even have been the relative complacency of the main gentry political interest in these regions which triggered off the more combative outlook of lesser fry. The most marked complacency of all was evident in Kilkenny and Kildare, though the situation was deteriorating in both counties. The absence of magistrate reports from Kildare is particularly noteworthy, because it was the county which had made the most progress in popular organisation in Leinster and the situation was far more serious there than elsewhere. Clearly the local gentry were more easy-going, more confident of their abilities to operate within the parameters of existing civil law, and some were implicated in or sympathetic to United Irishmen aims.[108] It is noteworthy that in the disarming of Kildare in April and May more heavy reliance was laid on the army than on local magistrates; in Wicklow too, despite the fact that the county was a staunchly Protestant one in gentry terms as opposed to the crypto-catholic profile of Kildare, reliance on the army even earlier than in Kildare suggests a lack of confidence in the readiness of the main county establishment to push things along at a fast pace.

Expressions of fear and reporting of crime had been marked in the Castle's correspondence from Munster in November. Lord Shannon and Sir Richard Musgrave were prominent, pointing to an establishment framework making the case to the Castle for more active measures. Once the proclamation of west Cork was achieved, Lord Shannon's own views displayed complacency: a marked cycle in some although not all loyalist correspondence betrayed a political motivation aimed at achieving a wider array of legal powers. Alarmist fears surfaced again in February in the aftermath of several murders. Munster fears and Munster predilection for harsh law and order measures drew on a longstanding tradition of its establishment. Colonel St George, a magistrate assassinated on the borders of Cork and Tipperary had previously been representing to the Castle that he would establish order even if he had to burn every house in the district, starting with his own tenants.[109] Expressed in these terms in January, the sanguinary outlook of St George is extraordinary, betraying a high-handed and arrogant frame of mind not evident in gentry circles in most of Ireland. Later when Queen's county was disarmed, the only detachment which showed a wish to destroy the country 'indiscriminately' was one commanded by John Beresford's nephew, Lord Waterford.[110] The purpose of correspondence in March was to represent the situation in the worst possible light with a view to force the Government to take stiffer measures. The letters should not be seen as an objective assessment of the situation and the opposition to Abercromby becomes explicit in Musgrave's case.[111] Two distinct groups were now about to coalesce. The first was the powerful grandee group of Munster closely linked through Lord Shannon and the Beresfords with the Castle and relying more on their political influence there than on any strength on the ground in their own districts. The second was the lesser gentry in and on the fringes of the great heartland of catholic wealth in Leinster which ran from Carlow through Kildare to Meath. Relatively isolated in power from a political establishment and, even when drawing on the support of their own protestant tenantry, surrounded by a predominantly catholic population which was in contrast to Munster both prosperous and politicised, they quickly saw the benefits of the Orange Order as a protection for their interests. The two Rochforts, Robert and John Staunton, becoming members of the first Dublin lodge no. 176 in February 1798[112], are the key figures in the link-up between the two streams. Lodge no. 176, as McClelland has noted, from the time of its founding on 4 June 1797 'rapidly became the lodge which the nobility and gentry joined and it soon began to act as the ruling body'.[113] By April, as fears deepened, the distinction between two streams of gentry thought began to disappear and the stage was set for the sudden spread of the Order beyond its relatively narrow confines at the outset of the month.

The situation revealed or perhaps even concealed by the Castle papers is complex. The relative absence of correspondence from Wexford and Kildare in the winter and spring of 1798 is striking. These two counties, the former with a highly liberal gentry faction as well as a strongly loyalist one, the latter, with a liberal gentry with a tradition of opposition to the establishment, both seem to be silent. In the case of Kildare the silence points to a deep cleavage between the local gentry and the Dublin establishment as the evidence in Kildare of subversion was considerable. In the case of Wexford, which had a strong loyalist faction, the situation is particularly complex. Wexford had been by no means behind other southern counties in evidence of the spread of sedition in 1797. If anything, it was ahead of many counties with a fair number of letters appearing in particular between late April and early June. Moreover, with the exception of one alarmist letter from Stephen Ram on 12 November and two letters from Lord Ely, the bulk of the evidence comes either from political moderates (Caesar Colclough, Lord Mountnorris, Thomas Knox Grogan) or from a loyalist, Reverend Thomas Handcock, quite an exceptional figure who was very much his own man. It is thus much more telling evidence than that from figures in other counties who had every political reason to exaggerate the extent of unrest. Indeed, when we proceed to survey the evidence of action on the ground, it shows that the political moderates supported wholeheartedly all action against sedition which stopped short of the Insurrection Act. July and August 1797 were totally silent in the Castle correspondence from Wexford (this period approximates to the election and its immediate aftermath). The fact that law and order was not an issue suggests that at that stage a divide in the county did not exist on that particular subject. Indeed a very large number of justices of the peace actually petitioned government on 16 October to appoint a special commission to try those already arrested in the county.[114] A split surfaced only in November when the north Wexford justices of the peace on 20 November disagreed on the proclaiming of 16 parishes. At this stage, there is some evidence of greater apprehension. Robert Cornwall had reported in some alarm on the situation in Carlow with Wexford in mind as well; Ram had written on 12 November; Lord Ely forwarded a small file of letters on 6 December.[115] Thus, some slight evidence in the Castle papers and more telling evidence from the magistrates' proceedings in Wexford tells us that a sharp division had emerged in November. The stories filtering out of Munster or the concerns displayed by Carlow magistrates may have influenced events. In one sense, what happened was political beçause Mountnorris, who opposed the proclaiming, was faced with a revolt against him by the loyalist middleman justices of the peace on his own estate; the area proclaimed, though not confined to his estate, was largely centered on it. Some moderate magistrates (notably the Grogans) supported the proclaiming: the political nature of the decision seems to be reflected in the fact that the area embracing the Grogan estates of Monaseed and Castletown was not included in the areas recommended by the magistrates for proclaiming, although both estates were hotbeds of the United Irishman organisation. The Grogans had very nearly given their support to Ely during the 1797 election. This was not an altogether surprising move; quite apart from Cornelius Grogan's political ineptitude, the 'liberal' candidate John Maxwell Barry (given his wildly anti-Catholic record) could not have appealed to the opposition in any county other than a highly politicised one such as Wexford, entranced by Mountnorris's personal influence.

Indeed the fact that a John Maxwell Barry appeared as country grand master of the Orange Order for Cavan in April 1798 suggests how off-putting Mountnorris's stand must have been for radicals, as opposed to the opportunistic political coalition which joined battle with the county's loyalist establishment in the 1797 election.[116] Given hostile comment by Hay and Byrne on Mountnorris, one senses that the Grogans (through the political sentiments of the United Irishman tenants on their north Wexford estates or through the close personal links of Cornelius Grogan with the county's gentry United Irishmen) may have favoured a more radical political stance than that of Mountnorris; they may have disliked Mountnorris's clearcut stance of a conservative but highly politicised pursuit of a middle ground. In other words, the dislike of Mountnorris revealed in the pages of Hay and Byrne may not reflect a response to his stance during the rebellion and his part in the court-martial and execution of Father John Redmond so much as an existing dislike which preceded the rebellion. Irish county politics were complicated, based on quirks of personality and family as well as on real issues.

The magistrates' political decision of 20 November was followed immediately by Mountnorris's campaign to obtain declarations of loyalty from catholics. This campaign began within November itself, in other words before the lord lieutenant had actually given effect by formal proclamation to the magistrates' wishes and before any measures can have been taken under the terms of the Insurrection Act within the county. Mountnorris's campaign was an ambitious one, involving his own appearance and that of some sympathetic gentry at the chapels: there is no parallel in other counties for such an orchestrated series of meetings for the purpose of administering an oath of allegiance or for such an exclusive identification of a single individual with the process. It seems to have impressed many protestants, and as their stand on proclaiming seems to have been dictated less by fear than by immediate political considerations, there were few reasons to prevent them from being convinced of the significance of Mountnorris's apparent success. Thomas Handcock had been seriously concerned by the situation in his district both in

May and in October.[117] However, on 3 December in the wake of Mountnorris's initial success, he actually wrote that

We know of no disposition to turbulence or disloyalty now existing in any part of the said parish. We see the generality of the inhabitants of our parish as quiet and as industriously employed as in the most peaceful times.[118]

Ely wrote to the Castle on 6 December, not so much expressing fear, as relaying other people's correspondence to the authorities.[119] It is outwardly a calm letter and it had no follow up from him. No correspondence from Wexford followed until a letter came from Caesar Colclough on 31 January. Even more remarkably there was a single letter in February and March and that from a non-regular correspondent, Charles Tottenham of Ross.[120] Tottenham in all probability reflected the deteriorating situation on the Carlow border of Wexford; some evidence would suggest that panic there preceded a changed atmosphere in the rest of the county by a significant interval of several weeks. Indeed the epistolary calm of Wexford contrasted with the sombre sentiments of the State solicitor, writing from Wexford, on 28 March after the Assizes.[121]

By this time evidence on the ground of organisation and arming was becoming hard to disregard. Orange sentiments and membership began to spread farther afield in the county in April and the political calm was beginning to break down. Alarmed letters reached the Castle from Clonegal dated 8 and 23 April.[122] Handcock stated that there were scarcely ten Orangemen in Enniscorthy in April, almost all in the North Cork militia.[123] His conceding that there were other Orangemen there is, however, significant, and could give credence to Cloney, who, when referring incidentally to Anthony Rudd, stated that he was considered to have been the first Orangeman in Enniscorthy.[124] In other words, it may be the case that the Order's emergence there roughly coincided with the arrival of the North Cork and had been confused with the regiment's presence because of its high profile Orange sentiments and the lateness of the spread of the order outside the north-west of the county. The fact that the Order was slow in acquiring highly-placed individuals within the county would also make its progress seem obscure. However by 16 May the Rev William Lyster of Wexford is returned as a member of Verner's lodge in Dublin;[125] it is tempting to assume that he is a member of the same family as J. H. Lyster, Lieutenant of 'Ogle's Blues', or yeomanry cavalry. Hunter Gowan, Archibald Jacob, Hawtrey White and James Boyd (who had Armagh associations) were singled out in the famous rebel proclamation of 9 June. While this has been assumed to be because of their excesses in law and order (and the proclamation explicitly states this) it may also have been because of an association with the spread of Orange sentiments or activity. If so, along with the Lysters, these four may have provided the nucleus of a spread of Orange association in the east of the county. The very lateness and rapidity of its spread would help to explain why popular opinion was unaware how far it had actually permeated local protestant society: it would also account for the tendency so evident in east Wexford once the rebellion began to equate all protestants (bar quakers) with Orangemen.

As early as 26 November Colonel Rochfort in neighbouring Carlow had been sceptical of the benefits of administering the oath of allegiance: 'the priests at all their chapels have told their flocks that any oath taken under the influence of fear is not to be kept and that the letter only offers the oath of allegiance, but no surrender of arms'.[126] The first magistrate to come to a similar conclusion in Wexford seems to have been Charles Dawson of Charlesfort near Ferns; another magistrate, Hawtrey White, summoned the priests in his district to his house on 19 May, having, according to Musgrave 'positive information, that some of the farmers who had made such declarations of their innocence, were possessed of considerable quantities of those weapons'.[127] In the interval in April, faced with growing loyalist scepticism and the likely proclaiming of the county, Mountnorris organised another great wave of chapel declarations.[128] This was well-intentioned, but at this stage with mounting evidence of Orange sentiments and of spreading United Irishman organisation, the meetings arguably added to polarisation. The deceptive calm of preceding months, by the very rapidity of its collapse, now added to protestant fears; in turn the incipient adoption of the Orange Order by loyalists undid what good Mountnorris had achieved and sent numbers into the United Irishmen or won them back for the Organisation. Opinion polarised very swiftly, especially north and east of the Slaney, the area most politicised in 1797 in the election and in the law-and-order debate revolving around the proclaiming of 16 parishes in November. It was in these areas that the first active magistrates had appeared; here, too, they were faced with the largest, longest-established and most determined concentration of United Irishmen.

Certainly Handcock had revised his outlook once again ahead of the outbreak of the rebellion, and even Caesar Colclough (who had a concerned though relaxed view of events) had shifted his ground somewhat. On 23 April, while he felt there was no real necessity to proclaim his part of the county, he concluded that 'it may be a wholesome preventative, inconvenient as it may be to me, to absent myself from term'.[129] Colclough proceeded to administer the oath of allegiance. By 8 May the Bishop of Ferns Eusebius Cleaver was seized of the great protestant fear in its most credulous form.[130] The fact that the moderate Caesar Colclough was still the only regular correspondent of the Castle in April and early May shows too that the changed pace of events in Wexford was not in the hands of the grandees who might have succeeded in keeping things in rein, but in the hands of frightened or credulous magistrates on the ground, a prey to the Orange outlook creeping across the county border. These magistrates were in active political conflict with Mountnorris, the man who was not only the county's largest landowner but who was also in acres easily the larger potentate in the area where the rebellion was about to break out. There was no consensus on law and order as there was for instance in county Kilkenny, where the calming presence of Lord Ormonde and a measure of gentry consensus may have been the chief factor in keeping events from getting out of hand. Had the task of law and order not led to a split, enforcement would have been more moderate and restrained; more importantly, the absence of a divide on the issue would have removed from the United Irishmen one of their main propaganda arguments — that law enforcement was patently partisan.

V

There is significant evidence of United Irishman organisation in county Wexford. In sharp contrast to the later evasive tone of contemporary catholics, evidence of organisation abounds once one turns to analyse the sources afresh. Local magistrates were familiar with United Irishman ranks and the significance these held in the organisation or for effective legal proceedings against individuals. Cloney reported that the loyalist magistrate Lyster 'not being certain of the rank I held, but wishing to make sense of it, he began with that of general descending through the intermediate gradations down to that of captain'.[131] Because the concept of rank was well-defined in the county, it was even applied to the priest leaders. Thus, following his sources, Luke Cullen recorded that fathers Michael and John Murphy were variously described as captain or colonel.[132] The most loosely used title is that of general precisely because the rank did not exist within United Irishman structures. It would be possible to argue that ranks were created on the field and, indeed, in the courts martial, evidence exists of a formal ceremony precisely for that purpose.[133] However, while this may have happened, it is clear that ranks were not normally appropriated or employed casually with the exception of general (a need which itself arose because the United Irishman structure had not provided for the designation of effective field commanders). The terms and the distinctions are made far too precisely to have been merely created in the heat of a sudden war or by casual imitation of what existed elsewhere in terms of United Irishman structures. The rank of captain in particular seems to have conveyed quite specific authority.[134] Court martial evidence even refers to a dispute between two rebels as to which was the more senior captain.[135]

If rank refers to previous involvement in United Irishman organisation, it then becomes a vital clue to the extent of United Irishman organisation and it can illuminate conditions in Wexford on the eve of rebellion just as readily as it does in other counties. The list found in Mathew Keugh's house, reported in Musgrave, has never received the degree of analysis it deserves.[136] It contains 17 names. One of these is that of a priest Father Nicholas Stafford of River Chapel. His exact position is not made clear, but his listing in this company must be regarded as compromising to say the least. Esmond Kyan is given the rank of major of brigade: this rank certainly did not exist in the organisation and its significance is not quite clear. There is one lieutenant: this rank did not figure in the formal constitution of the United Irishmen but evidence for it is overwhelming from sources for the Society everywhere and the lieutenant seems to have been a supplementary captain. These issues apart, the list identifies three colonels and 12 captains (including the one lieutenant). The colonels are John (*recté* Anthony) Perry of Inch, Edward Roche of Garrylough, and Edward Fitzgerald of Newpark. Given the fact that Esmond Kyan is distinguished by a grade which is above that of captain, it is possible that he too was a colonel. He is reputed to have been a British artillery officer and one of Luke Cullen's sources cites his United Irishman rank as colonel.[137] Byrne too in observing that Perry and Kyan 'were well known to have merited the rank they obtained in the United Irish system' seems to imply that they had a similar standing.[138] The evidence so far brings out the existence of one colonel in the north of the county at Inch and of two in the Newpark-Garrylough districts, both districts known hotbeds of rebel activity. Under its revised constitution of 27 August 1797, a colonel would imply authority over as many as 1,200 men.[139] If to these three designated colonels, Kyan is added and if Cloney and Kelly are also considered to be colonels, six colonels then stand identified. If so United Irishmen organisation in at least six regiments could have embraced 7,200 men on paper. This would not include a further possible regiment (for the barony of Forth) under Matthew Keugh, and which may not have been fully organised at the outbreak of the rebellion. If we look at the names of the captains in the Matthew Keugh list, we can find support for the existence of the three colonels identified in the list, with a hint of organisation further afield. Regiments could have in theory between four and ten captains, so that six regiments would imply a grand total of between 24 and 60 captains.

Regiment in Inch-Monaseed region (Gorey barony)
Captain Martin Myrna of Limerick
Captain William Carton of Ballyclough
Captain Nicholas Murphy of Monaseed
Captain Patrick Redmond of Coolgreany
Captain Denis Doyle of Gorey
Captain James Doyle of Gorey
Captain Martin Quin of Clough

Original 'Ballaghkeen' regiment
Captain Philip Murphy of Peppard's Castle-gate
Lieutenant John Tissin of Coolatore

Regiment in Castlebridge (East Shelmaliere)
Captain Rossiter of Saunder's court
Captain Nicholas Dixon of Castlebridge

Possible regiment in north-west of county
Captain Edward Synnott of Kilrush

Captain Nicholas Dixon is the brother of the notorious Thomas Dixon who from other sources we can assume to be a United Irishman captain. Nicholas Murphy is the man much mentioned in Miles Byrne's memoirs and said by him to have been 'one of the first to correspond with the county members'.[140] Martin Myrna could conceivably be a misreading of Murt Mernagh, a relation of Byrne's. This list, obviously incomplete, provides a total of 11 captains (including one lieutenant), a number by no means insignificant and certainly disposing of the argument that United Irishman organisation did not exist in the county. The fact that only two captains were named for the region around Castlebridge and none for the district around New Park, both of which were locations of Colonels, of itself suggests an obvious addition to be made of between 6 and 18 captains. In itself the list would not put the county on a par with other counties. As far back as 10 November 1797, and on a day marked by the discouraging circumstances of the county having been proclaimed, no less than twenty-six Wicklow captains came together at a meeting.[141]

While the number of captains underlines the scale of organisation in the Monaseed-Inch district, the presence of two colonels in the Newpark-Garrylough districts highlights the strength of the Society in the region where the rebellion actually broke out on 26 May. The very centre of disloyalty hinged on Le Hunte's yeoman cavalry; Fitzgerald and Roche were respectively lieutenant and sergeant in it. The pattern of clear identifications of individuals for this region and for the extreme north of the county also suggests less intensive organisation in the intervening belt. In support of this, Gordon noted that 'the people in the neighbourhood of Gorey were the last and least violent of all in the county of Wexford in rising against the established authority'.[142] Hay similarly states that the rebellion took place across the middle of the county, unsupported from north and south; he regarded the Gorey District as within this belt asserting that there were more United Irishmen there than in any other part of the county.[143] He also makes it clear that he regards the tumults in Wexford as being occasioned by multitudes from the north,[144] though failing to make it clear that the 'northern' region from which they came was uncomfortably close to the town as Castlebridge. All these considerations give added significance to the comments of the State Solicitor, writing from Wexford town, in March 1798 after the assizes at which the cases of a number of Kilcormick men had been heard: 'though this county appears quiet yet I think it is in a bad state from the great number of those United Irishmen which are in this county and I understand this town is the worst part of the county'.[145]

The fact that the organisation took root in two regions of the county which were widely separate is at first sight puzzling. In fact there were close family ties between north and south which help to account for the pattern. Byrne tells us that the mother of Nicholas Murphy, so active in the early United Irishmen, was 'of the family of Roches and nearly related to General Edward Roche and other families of the town'.[146] He also identifies the house of Mrs Rossiter, a cousin of Nicholas Murphy in Wexford. Edward Roche was married to a sister of Thomas Dixon, brother in turn of Captain Nicholas Dixon and cousin of the priest Thomas Dixon who had been transported.[147] We thus get some insight into a powerful circle. Colonel Anthony Perry was married to one of the Fordes of Ballyfad in the north of the county and even held land from them. The Fordes were a very comfortable catholic family and Perry's family ties through the Fordes with the Hays of Ballinkeele and Fitzgeralds of Newpark would have given him access to those families. The comfortable catholic families seem to be found in two belts, one across the far north of the county and the other in the Castlebridge-Blackwater-Ballinkeele region, with an intervening belt in which the protestant middle interest dominated. The spread of the United Irishmen in Wexford, north and east of the Slaney, seems to have largely followed this distribution of the middle classes, with much support in the north and south and less in the intervening Protestant layer.

Perry's confession was not made public · at the time and hence contemporaries were able to make their assertions in the post-rebellion polemics about the absence of organisation without realising that what they said was in part contradicted by this testimony.[148] His evidence tends to confirm the pattern which has been described though as we shall see its scope raises some problems of its own. Perry took the United Irishman oath in the summer of 1797 in the house of the attorney Mathew Dowling in Dublin. Dowling, who seems to have had Wexford connections in his own right, was also Perry's first cousin.[149] He then attended a meeting at John Forman Kennedy's. On his return, on dates which are not known and over a period which can not be precisely estimated, he attended four successive meetings which are identified in his confession, one in the house of Moses Kehoe at Castletown, one in his own barn, a third at Robert Graham's at Coolgreany and a fourth in the mill of Thomas Howlet at Inch. At this last meeting the parishes of Kilcavan, Kilnahue and Inch seem to have been organised into a baronial committee. Howlet then proceeded to Ballaghkeen and organised a baronial committee there. Robert Graham went twice to see Edward Fitzgerald of Newpark. The reason for these visits to Newpark was that the United Irishmen envisaged the election of county officers and even had the individuals in mind: Bagenal Harvey as treasurer, John Colclough (of Ballyteigue) as secretary and Perry as delegate. They were faced with the problem that, under the constitution, a county committee structure, with representation on the provincial committee, could only exist if at least three baronial committees had been formed. This helps to date the period of activity and confirms that the pace of organisation was quite hectic. The old constitution of 10 May 1796 provided for three baronial committees as a basis of electing a county committee, whereas the new constitution of August 1797 introduced a larger and more ambitious structure which not only increased the number of layers of intervening committees but required four baronial committees as the basis of county organisation.[150] The dilemma about forming a third baronial committee thus antedates the activity to August 1797 unambiguously. It is perhaps easy to postulate that the creation of an Edward Roche regiment did not simply reflect the intensification of membership but was a strategy intended to increase the number of baronial committees in an effort to meet the Society's revised constitutional requirements.

However, Wexford was not represented in the Dublin United Irishmen and this would suggest that other difficulties arose subsequent to August (quite apart from the increase in the required number of baronial committees from three to four) which prevented the county's United Irishmen from perfecting their organisation. This requires some explanation as superficially it would seem not too difficult, if further baronies were reluctant to enlist on a sufficient scale to justify baronial committees, to intensify the organisational structure in the districts where the organisation was already strong. An example would be the south Ballaghkeen/Shelmaliere region, where Fitzgerald's baronial committee seems to have been divided subsequently into two, embracing roughly south Ballaghkeen, and Shelmaliere East respectively.

However, first of all the formal problem must be addressed. The United Irishmen, largely city-based in their national leadership and dominated disproportionately by professional men, especially lawyers, were intensely bureaucratic in approach. Copies of the constitution were circulated to guide the local organisers and these documents quickly came into the hands of the government, so that ironically the authorities had a very good idea of its structures and phraseology, though rather little clear idea outside Ulster of its actual members. As an illustration of bureaucratic procedures, when Reynolds became Treasurer for Kildare, he was told by McCann, Secretary of the provincial committee in Dublin, that 'unless he brought up the returns from the county committee of Kildare he could not be admitted to the provincial'.[151] This was the dilemma that Wexford faced in formal terms. It was not so much that Wexford could not make returns but that these returns had no standing until county organisation existed in accordance with the constitution.

Hence, while contacts undoubtedly existed, Wexford did not feature in the returns. The Dublin-based informer Francis Higgins was able to report 284 United Irishmen in October 1797.[152] Moreover, prominent United Irishmen either visited or were expected in the county. Caesar Colclough warned in June 1797 that Lord Edward Fitzgerald was expected at Castletown.[153] McCabe also visited the county on organising trips and Mathew Doyle of the better-organised county Wicklow was also deputed to aid in this organising effort. According to Byrne,

Mathew Doyle, who resided on the way between Ballyarthur and Arklow [at Pollahoney] was appointed by the provincial chiefs to travel in the adjacent counties, to give instructions to the Societies, and to report on their progress. Putnam McCabe was frequently sent from Dublin on the same mission ...[154]

Byrne has reported meeting both Doyle and McCabe in Nicholas Murphy's house. What was the position of Robert Graham when, according to Byrne, he missed the fatal meeting of 12 March in Oliver Bond's house in the capital when most of the Leinster delegates were arrested? Clearly the position is different from the situation in the preceding summer when Graham was not one of the three county officers who were proposed. It is not clear that he was a fully accredited delegate or, unless the County organisation had been perfected, that he would have been received. The possibility nevertheless exists that four baronial committees had been formed by the Spring of 1798. However, given the speed of organisation in the preceding year between June and August, subsequently progress seems to have been slow and the absence of any Wexford returns in the February lists means that no fully acceptable returns had been drawn up since August. In other words the position is that even if Graham had been bringing full returns it would have been for the first time. The question would therefore still arise as to why it took so long to get properly established returns. The answer to this must lie in Mountnorris's campaign to adminster the oath of allegiance with the help of the priests: the oath very specifically renounced membership of the United Irishman organisation. The oath was administered mainly in the region proclaimed in November 1797 but was also administered in some parishes not proclaimed (e.g. Kilnahue). It is quite likely that this sustained effort, the most remarkable one in Ireland, undermined the thrust of local United Irishman recruitment. The fact that the oath was administered with the support and frequently the presence of a nobleman closely identified with the Catholics made it all the more persuasive. Moreover, while it seems to have convinced Wexford protestants of the loyalty of catholics, it also had the result of deferring resort to more active policing of the region concerned. The relative inactivity of magistrates deprived the United Irishmen of their greatest local propaganda asset. Only in April did the position change and this must have helped recruitment as well as winning back to the fold those United Irishmen who had succumbed to the siren song of Mountnorris and the parish clergy. Byrne makes a point of referring to the efforts of the clergy to contain the advance of the organisation.[155] It is quite likely that these developments had an impact outside the region as well. Though some early manifestations of United organisation appeared on the Carlow border of the barony of Scarawalsh and in the barony of Bantry, the subsequent progress seems to have been decidedly slow.

Perry's account presents its own problems. After all, it has even been used to support the contention that the United Irishmen made little progress in the county. It is puzzling in some respects. Thus, though he was clearly deeply involved in the organisation, the confession gives no information on what happened after the early months. It is possible that Perry concentrated simply on his own district and may have been out of touch with what took place subsequently elsewhere. Yet the abrupt nature of the termination of his testimony is quite curious. Moreover, while the testimony names individuals, it avoids giving military ranks and some prominent United Irishmen in his district such as Nicholas Murphy are not named at all. Only three hypotheses can be advanced in the present state of our knowledge. First, Perry by giving some information was able to ease the pressure to extract more information (apparently under torture) from him. Secondly, the information was sufficient to implicate Harvey, Colclough and Fitzgerald, thus providing the basis for arresting them and this by justifying their arrest satisfied the magistrates. Third, the outbreak of the rebellion, and Perry's own escape, brought to an end an interrogation which had simply proceeded as far as an invaluable deposition and would have been resumed later. This latter possibility seems unlikely, as the magistrates' enclosure suggests they were content with what they had, simply noting that Perry was 'ready to come forward to substantiate the evidence produced by his information'.

VI

We have now got a fairly clear picture of the state of organisation of the county. The north of the county from Monaseed to Inch and Coolgreany is the clearest case, mainly because of Byrne's memoirs whose purpose was to put the record straight. No historian has avoided giving credence to Byrne apart from Kavanagh who simply dismisses the book out of hand for very thin reasons. The list in Mathew Keugh's house and Perry's confession provide good supporting evidence. Second, the United Irishmen were very strong in a region running from Kilcormick to Castlebridge and even Wexford town. Organisation began very early here and significantly it, rather than the extreme north of the county, is more reported on in the letters in the Castle. As early as 23 March 1797 Mountnorris reported on an assembly of 50 men at Blackwater.[156] Moreover, just as the Perry confession suggests that United Irishman cells were already creeping into the county independently of Perry, there is even clearer evidence for the Kilcormick region that the first steps in organisation preceded the more middle-class attempts to politicise the county on United Irishman lines. Handcock's letter of 18 May brings out the nature of the early attempts in Kilcormick: 'the principal distributor of them [seditious letters] there was a Charles Nowlan, nephew and clerk of a Timothy Nowlan, pawnbroker in Greek Street Dublin. He associates while so employed much with a man named M'Guire, a schoolmaster of a neighbouring village but a native of the north of Ireland'.[157] Again, Lord Ely in May had information against a carman operating between Dublin and Wexford.[158] The nature of these early propagandists points to the danger of relating non-middle-class activities to the ranks of agrarian rebels. The sharp definition given to Defenders as an organisation separate and distinct from the United Irishmen is due largely to an implicit and unchallenged assumption limiting radical well-defined aims to the middle classes and relegating all other discontents to an underworld of ill-defined and unrelated discontents. Moreover, the well-defined nature of some of the activity at this stage is witnessed in the fact that these early rebels had made attempts to suborn members of the small detachment of the Clare militia at Enniscorthy. It was this more than anything else which heightened the alarm of Handcock, Ely and the moderate Alcock of Wilton.[159]

The absence of any hint of agrarian discontent and the clear distinction implied by Caesar Colclough, who actually lived in the district where the 1793 unrest had been evident, between oaths in Wexford and the agrarian ones of Waterford makes an appeal to Defender or agrarian rebels most unconvincing. By 30 September an affidavit about United Irishmen at Kilcormick was sworn before Hawtrey White[160] and Handcock in a chatty personal letter to the army officer with whom he had cooperated over the suborning of the soldiers at an earlier date wrote pessimistically in October that

You will find this county very much inclined to turbulence if no worse. United Irishism is spreading over it very rapidly — six of my parishioners were after all my preaching — deposited safely in gaol on Monday — and between you and me I believe there are some hundreds of them, alike deserving of it. They are disciples of Mr Nowlan, encouraged to adopt his principles by the *mild* disposition of government towards him.[161]

Nor was Handcock's assessment merely a loyalist one. Mountnorris's letter of 5 October referred approvingly to the activity of the magistrate concerned,

Hawtrey White, a tenant of his, and commented on the presence of unrest in a wide arc across the north of the county as well.[162] Handcock himself sought a commission of the peace apparently in the aftermath of these developments, and was formally appointed on 9 December. While the outlook of Cleaver, bishop of Ferns, later a very timid loyalist, was complacent on 12 September, Stephen Ram in the nearby town of Gorey displayed real fear by 12 November.[163] Both loyalists moreover were on the fringe of the district of which we are speaking. In that district — Kilcormick and Castlebridge — the atmosphere may be conjured up somewhat in comments recorded by a farmer informant of Cullen's who retrospectively defended the reputation of Edward Turner of Newfort, murdered by the rebels after the rebellion broke out.

Why do you entertain such a bad opinion of him ... Mr Turner met often parties of us coming home in the mornings after boozing all the night, singing party songs and often with green boughs in our hats. He has advised us in the most kindly way and never never injured a man.[164]

The growth of evidence of this sort led magistrates to seek firmer action, either the special commission requested by a meeting on 16 October, or the proclaiming settled on for part of the affected area by a divided meeting of magistrates on 20 November. The active magistrates in these days of October and November were to be found in the regions where the rebels were strongest: Hunter Gowan in the north and Hawtrey White on the most disaffected parts of the Mountnorris estate. Hunter Gowan was emerging as the most active magistrate in the north-west: he seems to display more external influences coming in from Carlow and Wicklow, whereas the other magistrates were locked into an ongoing political tussle. Magistrates like Hawtrey White seem to have operated in harmony with Mountnorris in October; in November, when the question of the Insurrection Act came up, a divide emerged. It was in the north-west of the county that the Orange Order made its first and most prominent appearance in the county, and its spread elsewhere even in the Enniscorthy region must have occurred only in and after April when loyalist fears rekindled. There, in the middle of the county, the distribution of the hardline political sentiment roughly occupied a stretch of land on either side of the Slaney from Enniscorthy south to Wexford town, corresponding to a rough radius centred on the Bellvue residence of George Ogle, leader of the county's hardline party. The party existed too in Wexford town and on the estate of the Boyds near Rosslare. James Boyd, who was mayor of Wexford in 1793[165] when the rebels marched on the town and who might have particular fears, may have been a member of the Boyd family in Wexford who were beneficiaries under the will in 1776 of Richard Jackson,[166] the landlord of Forkhill in county Armagh on whose estate the family of the schoolmaster Barkely was horribly mutilated in 1791. This incident had powerfully impressed loyalists, and was much used in loyalist propaganda throughout the 1790s. If Orange sentiments and organisation suddenly grew in April, then the popular obsession with Orangeism is not a mirage. An obsession with colours as a symbol of party was marked on both sides.[167] The much-quoted episode of the

Dixons seizing the orange-coloured fire screen at Colonel Le Hunte's house at Artramont becomes less irrational in this context and may even have been a cynical attempt to exploit this fear by turning popular rage against Le Hunte, a local enemy of the Dixons. The Quakers have been noted in almost all modern commentaries as having been immune from this popular rage. Most dissenters were regarded as being unassociated with government policy or establishment outlook. Indeed in Waterford a loyalist regarded the Quakers as opposed to the government.[168] Although they may not have been overtly so in the climate of the 1790s, there was little danger even in highly politicised Wexford of anyone confusing anglicans with their emotive and political attachment to the establishment with other protestants.

The north-west of county Wexford, the region in the shadow of the Blackstairs mountains and stretching south to New Ross, presents problems. There is less evidence of organisation there and it does not fit into the picture painted by Perry. Indeed, Perry's account is quite explicit in bringing out its backwardness in organisation. According to him, Howlet and Darcy's mission to the barony of Scarawalsh was a failure. Perry's account refers to the barony of Scarawalsh, in the centre and extreme north-west of the county, not to the barony of Bantry and it should not be accepted too readily or conclusively as a general description of the situation. Indeed, the north-western parts of the county had close family links with the rest of the county. Not only had the Esmondes property at Clonegal, on the Carlow border, but John Esmonde, then living there, was a United Irishman in 1792.[169] Thomas Cloney at Moneyhore in the barony of Bantry was connected by marriage with Thomas Synnott of Kilbride on the other side of the Slaney near to the centre of political radicalism in the county. Perry's description of the Scarawalsh response would have referred to the period of June to August 1797. An account exists (how well founded we do not know) of a futile visit by Perry himself and 'Lord Edward Fitzgerald' (probably Edward Fitzgerald of Newpark) to Myles O'Connor, parish priest of Ballindaggin in the Duffry to establish the United Irishmen.[170] It is clear from the letters of Caesar Colclough, who lived in the north of Bantry district and who was the most regular Wexford correspondent of the Castle, that sedition already existed within the region. Indeed, as early as 29 May 1797, he had information that seditious papers, already circulating in county Carlow and in other parts of Wexford, were to be posted up in sundry parts of his district.[171] Some of his own tenants were observed on a journey to a part of Kildare where 'the people to a man are sworn'.[172] Mogue Kearns, a curate from this region, later involved in the rebellion, had spent some time in Clonard on the borders of Meath and Kildare. More alarmingly still, Colclough was to report 10 days later that

The son of a man of respectability in this neighbourhood had been in Dublin and had been sworn ... he is of the better sort and a well conducted man and one who could have considerable influence ... the young man's name is Kelly and he is nearly related to Mr Ferris the wine merchant'.

As a wine merchant named Ferris is listed in the Dublin directories from 1781, this is a significant relationship between the region and Dublin. There is no reason to think that this Kelly is not 'Kelly the Boy from Killan'. According to Colclough, Kelly had already sworn in a man and he administered the oath of allegiance to Kelly 'much astonished how government should have such good information'.[173] Coinciding roughly with the abortive attempt to harness Scarawalsh, Kelly's experience may explain why progress was slow in this region. Compromised by his action, or adhering to his oath of allegiance, he may not have responded to further overtures. Cloney, a young man from Moneyhore, remarkably similar in age and social position to Kelly, denied receiving overtures and in his memoirs claims that, if he was sitting in the dining room in Rudd's Inn in Enniscorthy at the same time as McCabe the United Irishman organiser, it was by pure coincidence.[174] Cloney's record for truthfulness is too poor for his denial to carry much weight.

A factor which may have hampered recruitment in west Wexford is that the region, unlike Wexford east of the Slaney, had few loyalist magistrates. Its dominant landlord interest was opposed to the county establishment. Maxwell Barry contested the election in 1797 as the Mountnorris candidate and Thomas Cloney and his father at the request of one of their own landlords, Phayre, campaigned for him. Thomas Kavanagh of Borris had land in the region and Caesar Colcough of Duffry Hall was a tolerant man linked by blood to the liberal political interest and having catholic relatives. To the south of the region its two great landowners, Carew and Alcock, were also on the liberal side. There was no law-and-order caucus of landlords in the region, and from what evidence we have of attendance at meetings of magistrates within the county the region was poorly represented. Alcock attended the April 1798 meeting to oppose the proclaiming of his district. In the light of such a landlord interest neither the election nor the law-and-order issue would have polarised the population to the same extent as on the Mountnorris estates. Its politically benign landlords would have carried more weight with Catholics than the landlords or middleman gentry east of the Slaney, many of whom were already vociferous loyalists, even if the success of Mountnorris's campaign had led them finally to stay their hand. Significantly, Cloney himself draws a sharp contrast between the Protestants around his home and those around Enniscorthy where there was 'a knot of the descendants of Cromwellian settlers ... liberality in a Protestant of rank in that quarter was rare'.[175]

The benign political profile of the region may explain why the most persistent evidence of organisation in this region stems from the Wexford hinterland of Clonegal, a strongly loyalist village on the Carlow side of the Wexford-Carlow-Wicklow border. As early as September 1797, information revealed the active swearing in of United Irishmen on the Wexford side of the village.[176] It was in this region too that the most precise reports of activity appeared in March/April 1798 after the comparative silence of preceding months. John De Renzy, a member of a small landed family with landed interests in both counties and postmaster in Clonegal, reported to the politically ardent postmaster general John Lees on 8 April 1798 that at Lacy's, a local distiller, 'there are constantly emissaries from Dublin and at which place the principles of United Irishism have been industriously disseminated by almost frequent visitors from Dublin....'[177] John James, a county Wexford magistrate of very minor social status, reported from Clonegal a fortnight earlier that 'instead of the rebellious being discouraged or decreasing in numbers or enterprise they are daily gaining strength and becoming more daring'.[178] Indeed, it seems likely that, as Protestants revised their views after the complacency of preceding months and as the appearance of Orange sentiments or organisation added to Catholic fears, previous hesitancy like that of those originally approached in Scarawalsh or of Kelly further afield in Bantry dissipated, and the Bantry/Scarawalsh region, hitherto behind eastern Wexford, now began to organise. The loyalist families of Killan and Old Ross had already taken refuge in New Ross before the rebellion broke out.[179] As early as April, James had expressed the fear that 'the few remaining well-affected Protestants will be forced ... into the association of the disaffected'. Elsewhere Protestant families were taken by surprise by the rebellion. Father Philip Roche had been transferred to Bantry in the winter of 1797 as curate to Thomas Rogers, parish priest. Roche lived at Poulpeasty. Another priest, a curate also of Roger's prior to his suspension two years previously, Thomas Clinch, was also involved in the rebellion, as was Mogue Kearns a curate from the Duffry.[180] The fact that three of the priests involved in the rebellion either held or had held office in this region points to a rapid spread of disaffection on the eve of the rebellion. Roche's past association with east Wexford may also explain Father Michael Murphy's move on 26 May to Kilthomas Hill, inexplicable as it would be if he was motivated simply by fear, or ties to his local parishioners at Ballycanew.

Cloney's protestations of his non-involvement at this time are not compelling because of his own untruthfulness. There were also some family ties between the region and the already highly organised district east of the Slaney. Thomas Synnott, a man of about sixty years, and of 'very independent property',[181] husband of Cloney's paternal aunt, was involved in the rebellion and figures in the recollections collected by Luke Cullen. He lived at Kilbride, about four miles east of Enniscorthy and joined the rebels in time for the attack on Enniscorthy. Moreover, Thomas Handcock, a tough but observant loyalist, referred to Cloney as a person 'of whose treason I had proof' and when Cloney demanded an interview with him in Enniscorthy in the days immediately before the outbreak, Handcock took the precaution of not granting it to him in his own house 'but took him to the markethouse, in which was the main guard'.[182] There is a striking difference of emphasis between Handcock's and Cloney's version of their conversation and Handcock seems to have regarded the protestations of Cloney and others of fears of massacre by Orangemen 'as a pretext for arming and rising by the Roman Catholics'. This suggests that he cut a more forceful figure than the fearful one projected in his own account and that he made explicit assertions about the Orange menace, a common attitude among United Irishmen in fact. The pains taken by Byrne to draw a contrast between the manner of Cloney's coming to Vinegar Hill on 29

May as described by Cloney himself and as Byrne saw it are also significant. Moreover Cloney himself refers to Kelly as 'Colonel Kelly'[183] and in the Luke Cullen memoirs, dispassionate in their detail and usually precise in their reference to rank, Cloney is described as a Colonel.[184] Cullen collected little information from west of the Slaney.[185] Cloney himself refers to his volunteering his services at Vinegar Hill to John Kelly of Killan, Robert Carty of Birchgrove, and Michael Furlong of Templescoby (a statement which suggests their common leadership profile as otherwise they should have come under the direction of more notorious rebels) and describes 'the bold peasantry of our respective neighbourhoods ... all brave men of the barony of Bantry'.[186] Byrne shows them as in charge of active units as early as 30 May.[187] The Bantry men are later described as two battalions of 500 men led by 'Colonel Kelly' and by Cloney respectively.[188] The battalions at their largest swelled to 1,500 men. Byrne describes recruits in the early days of the rebellion as 'pouring in particularly from the barony of Bantry and the country leading to Ross'.[189] Combined with the relatively early recrudescence of Protestant fears in this region, the apparently compact organisation of the Bantry men suggests that a degree of military cohesiveness had been attained by the time of the rebellion. Cloney was not press-ganged in a confused fashion into some form of leadership at the camp but seems to have operated at the head of a well-defined group of west-Slaney men. Incidental mention of individuals from his own region scattered across his memoirs also serves to bear this out.

The use of the term colonel is in fact remarkably sparing in all surviving accounts, both published and unpublished. Apart from some casual attribution of the rank in one source (and many years after the rebellion) to clergymen, only seven Wexford figures seem to bear the attribution. We may regard Perry, Fitzgerald and Roche as certain, Kyan as a possible, and Kelly and Cloney as probable late-appointed colonels whose districts were quite well-organised on the eve of the rebellion. In fact, one of these two regiments should include the Edward Synnott of Kilrush (near Clonegal) named in the Keugh list. It is likely that Cloney was the commander of the southernmost regiment embracing Bantry and Kelly of a regiment from the more northern districts of Bantry and the western and northern parts of Scarawalsh. The fact that 1,000 men gathered at Oulart would reflect a high proportion, above half the paper strength, of two United Irish regiments, those of Fitzgerald and Roche. Thomas Synnott's later joining in action would suggest a separate organisation and hence a possible third regiment to the north and east of the Kilcormick-Castlebridge core: Cloney described him as leading 1,000 men at Vinegar Hill on 28 May.[190] As Synnott lived well to the north of the Newpark-Castlebridge region and Esmond Kyan seems to have been similarly located, it is just possible that Kyan was a member of this contingent and even its colonel. Significantly Byrne seems to bracket him with Perry in leadership status, and hence by implication military rank.[191] This regiment would correspond also to the presence at the otherwise isolated location of Coolatore of a captain in the list found in Keugh's house. This is probably the Ballaghkeen baronial committee and regiment described in Anthony's Perry's confession as the second unit formed in the county. Curiously, no leadership figures are clearly described for it in that confession. Kyan and Synnott by social position and prominence seem however its likely leading figures, and, while neither Kyan nor Synnott can be identified in action on 26 May, the districts in which they were located had significant ties with the events and some of the personalities of 26 May. John Murphy was a curate in Kilcormick parish adjoining Oulart; a Synnott, a son of a rich farmer,[192] and hence conceivably a son of Thomas Synnott, was present at the battle of Oulart, and though Morgan Byrne resided at Kilnamanagh, near Oulart, his brother, also an United Irishman, lived close to Enniscorthy. Nicholas Synnott, the parish priest of Oulart, actually resided at Kilbride, a fact which further illustrates the close ties across a very broad district. Baronial committees and regiments do not seem to imply precise geographical boundaries. In particular, the original Ballaghkeen unit, if correctly identified, embraced districts on both sides of the boundary between Ballaghkeen and Gorey baronies, just as Ballaghkeen barony at large was later the base for two separate regiments.

The fact that John Murphy first moved north on 26 May seems to suggest action by a Ballaghkeen unit, just as his movement south in the course of the night bears out the focal importance of Edward Fitzgerald and his regiment centred on New Park. Moreover, John Murphy's prominence on 27 May, which is often exaggerated, can be attributed in part to the fact that the leading lay figures of the regiment, Kyan and Synnott, for whatever reason, did not join in the action on 26 or 27 May. In fact, while Fitzgerald's regiment was the third regiment formed in the county, the spread of the United Irishmen in his district seems to have led to the division of his unit into two regiments in the months preceding the rebellion, one based on Newpark (South Ballaghkeen) under Fitzgerald and the other on Castlebridge with Edward Roche as its colonel. In this way, accepting Perry, Fitzgerald and Roche as certain colonels, Kelly and Cloney as probable colonels, and Kyan as the possible colonel of a known Ballaghkeen unit — the second unit formed in the county but of whose leadership we know little — we arrive at a figure of six regiments. This would, at a book strength of 1,200 men per regiment, indicate a possible paper strength of 7,200 men, scattered across Wexford north and east of the Slaney and west of the Slaney, in the barony of Scarawalsh and some of Bantry. This, though late in the day, compares fairly favourably with what we know of other Leinster counties, although it would fall far short of county Down with at least 23 colonels on the eve of the rebellion. The fact that only three colonels are identified in the Mathew Keugh list would tend to suggest both that the list was a relatively early one and that, Gorey and Ballaghkeen apart, the other regiments were late-formed.

South of Wexford town the United Irish seem to have been slower to form any organisation in depth. They had a base to start with in the membership of Bagenal Harvey of Bargy Castle and John Colclough of Ballyteigue. In this region too there were, apart from Harvey, several other Protestant United Irishmen — John Boxwell of Sarshill, Henry Hughes of Ballytrent, and his brother-in-law Nicholas Grey.[193] Mathew Keugh in Wexford and William

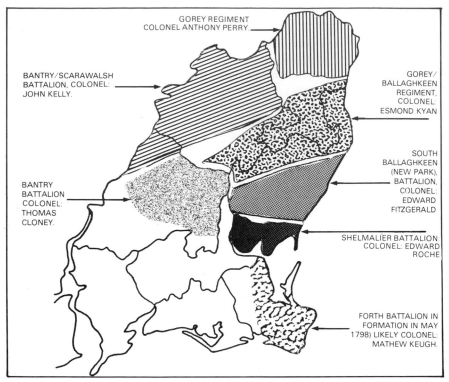

GOREY REGIMENT
COLONEL ANTHONY PERRY

BANTRY/SCARAWALSH
BATTALION, COLONEL:
JOHN KELLY.

GOREY/
BALLAGHKEEN
REGIMENT,
COLONEL:
ESMOND KYAN

SOUTH
BALLAGHKEEN
(NEW PARK),
BATTALION,
COLONEL:
EDWARD
FITZGERALD

BANTRY
BATTALION
COLONEL:
THOMAS
CLONEY.

SHELMALIER BATTALION:
COLONEL: EDWARD
ROCHE

FORTH BATTALION IN
FORMATION IN MAY
1798) LIKELY COLONEL:
MATHEW KEUGH.

Fig. 10.1: United Irishman Organisation, Wexford, 1798. Tentative location of regiments, May 1798

Hatton, a member of the county committee, were other examples of Protestant United Irishmen in, or in the vicinity of, the town. It was the one area of the county where there was a significant Protestant presence in the organisation in 1798. Elsewhere in the county, Perry and Sparks seem to be unique. The Harvey-Grogan political axis accounts for this group and though Cornelius Grogan was not himself a member, his home was one of the focal points of dissidents' meetings. At popular level, the Society made slower progress in Forth but it was in evidence by the end of 1797: one of Lord Ely's informants reported a change in 'the present state of this once peaceable barony', and the receipt of a threatening letter by one of his landlords, Nunn.[194] Harvey himself was administering the oath of allegiance and gathering firearms as late as 26 May and Byrne later rightly made the point that if firearms existed, then the United Irishmen were present. Mathew Keugh was probably the colonel for the district. Certainly, he stated to Elizabeth Richard's mother that 'I am now colonel', when in the course of the rebellion she addressed him as 'captain' in Wexford.[195]   The real strength of the organisation as opposed to its paper strength is hard to make out for any county. It involved the creation of two streams of organisation, military and civil, and oaths were administered to men and officers in addition to the ordinary oath. Those who took the oath did not necessarily take the military oath. On the other hand all those who held military office had to hold civil office as well. United Irish committees did very little work and the posts, military and civil, to some extent simply conferred prestige. Thus, even in county Kildare, one man indicated preparedness to join the United Irishmen provided he could be assured of becoming a colonel.[196] The prospects of any effective organisation were greatly precluded by the democratic but insane position of all committees and offices being subject to election every three months. All contemporary accounts bring this out. The fact that all military offices were represented on the civil command structure meant that it is impossible to maintain seriously, as Dickson did, that individuals were unaware of the military plans of the organisation. This was all the more inevitable because the collection of money and its use and transfer to the central organisation were conducted through the county committees. Thus, while individual United Irishmen may not have been aware of what was involved, no member of the upper baronial or county committees could have been unaware of exactly what was happening. Perry's confession makes it clear for instance, that Ballaghkeen barony was not simply 'organised' (i.e. had a civil committee structure), but 'arm'd' (i.e. had a military organisation under a colonel sitting on an upper baronial civil committee).[197] The context thus also implies comparatively early military organisation i.e. in 1797. Almost all United Irishmen assumed that revolution would be bloodless and the jejune workings of the committees may have helped to reassure some that it was all very harmless. Penetration of the militia would paralyse the forces of authority, it was assumed, and especially if rebellion was linked to French invasion (the moderates attached importance to this) loyalists would readily accept a *fait accompli* because their political leaders, the 'oligarchs' (much abused by the United Irishmen), did not represent the real feelings of the people they professedly represented. Hence, no member of baronial and county committees could really plead ignorance of the Society's military designs, though they may foolishly have been confident of a bloodless revolution. On the other hand the mere fact of being on committees did not *ipso facto* establish that a man held military rank.

The strange workings of the county committee in Kildare, the best-organised Leinster county, led by the intended military leader of the United Irishmen, should disabuse historians of the idea that the organisation's ineffectiveness was simply due to the impact of the arrest of so many of the leaders on 12 March 1798. Any strength the organisation had was on the ground in proportion to local determination rather than to the strange group of vain, ambitious or idealistic people who dominated county and provincial structures. There is no evidence whatever, for instance, that Bagenal Harvey held military rank in the organisation. He was wildly radical in his sentiments as early as 1792 and this combined with his vanity[198] may have been responsible for his becoming commander-in-chief. He is at no stage credited in any surviving account with the rank of colonel. John Colclough also was a United Irishman but, according to Taylor, after he had accompanied Fitzgerald to Enniscorthy, 'retired with the intention of re-entering his prison'.[199] He did not have military rank as far as we can judge and this would help to explain why, though he was on the rebel side, he never appears in a position of military prominence. Indeed, it is highly likely that Edward Hay was a United Irishman in the civilian sense and this accounts further for the coyness of his book. It is interesting to speculate why some catholics of local prominence — and both Colclough and Hay had a very high profile in Wexford life on the eve of 1798 — were assumed into positions of military leadership and others among the rebels were not. It throws doubt on the suggestion that catholics or protestant liberals were press-ganged into military leadership. Individual United Irishmen military officers, especially if politically moderate, may well have had doubts about the advisability of a rising when the occasion presented itself without the presence of the French to which they had attached importance, but whatever their own attitudes the position seems to have been that, when the rebellion broke out, those who held military rank found themselves confronted literally or morally with the situation of having to assume the authority they had held. Compromised practically or morally, they took the field, in some cases no doubt propelled along by subordinates who had a less clear view of what it all implied.

Mathew Keugh, if he was a colonel, would have been the leading United Irishman military officer to the south of the Slaney. Connected by an astute marriage to the Grogans, he moved intimately despite his own modest family background in the gentry radical circle and had been deprived of his commission of the peace in 1792 because of his advanced sentiments. He was, however, heartily disliked by more conservative society and Mrs Brownrigg claimed that 'the gentlemen of the county all disliked or shunned him, and he was ever reckoned a dangerous and disaffected man'.[200] The finding of the list in his house seems to be a compromising factor, especially as it relates essentially to people who held military rank already ahead of the rebellion. Indeed, according to Mrs Brownrigg, 'General Lake was in possession of *letters* that proved he had carried on the plan for *5 years* and had been one of the most active agents in Ireland for the cause'.[201] The fact that, as governor of the town during the rebel occupation of it, he attempted to establish good order was a valid legal defence plea but not in historical terms a particularly good point to establish his position as a totally innocent man caught up against his will in what happened. The whole problem of running a large town during a rebel occupation for three weeks was a daunting task. The rebels seem to have made serious attempts to cope with the police and material demands it entailed, facilitated no doubt by the fact that the military campaigns tended to keep the more committed rebels in the field almost constantly. In some respects, it is the most fascinating single aspect of the rebellion, an achievement whose significance has been underestimated because of loyalist intent after the rebellion to make as much political capital as possible out of the massacres on Wexford bridge on 20 June in the dying hours of the occupation. Indeed it was precisely the throwing back on Wexford of rebel units as they were defeated across the county that made law and order increasingly unmanageable in the final days of the rebellion. The accusation that Bishop Caulfield and other prominent Catholics failed to advert to the fatal events in a compact town loses relevance, given the constant tumult of the final days.

The clergy are the last and most intriguing single category to discuss. As mentioned earlier, the role of the clergy tended to be enhanced in later tellings of events, starting with Kavanagh's account. Even Musgrave, despite seeing the hand of the clergy in everything, in detail gives as much prominence to the lay as to the clerical leaders. In the Cullen memoirs which reflect the perspective of humble participants and in Byrne's account, though individual clergymen are active, their individual role is not particularly prominent. Indeed, putting the detail together it seems clear that the pattern is that the pace was not set by clergymen on the day of the outbreak but that to the extent that they came to the fore, they did so in the subsequent days. Thus, on the first and second day, from Cullen's account, John Murphy's role seems overstated. His prominence seems to grow from the hours before the attack on Enniscorthy and Philip Roche, the other clergyman with the most commanding role in the rebellion, seems to have been in obscurity for the first few days before coming to prominence from 31 May. For all practical purposes, Dickson concedes that Philip Roche, Kearns and Clinch were members of the United Irishmen.[202] He sees the two Father Murphy's as trapped by circumstances. To this list should certainly be added Thomas Dixon of Castlebridge: in Bishop Caulfield's list, in a letter from Bishop Caulfield to Archbishop Troy in September 1798, often ignored or glossed over, Dixon is stated to have been suspended a year previously on suspicion of 'Uniting'.[203] There is no evidence that his suspension was instrumental in his subsequent arrest and prosecution on charges of swearing in United Irishmen. Indeed, it was his own cousin Fr James Dixon of Castlebridge who according to a letter of Caulfield on 6 December 1798 was 'one of the first who complained to me of his cousin-germain on account of his agitations and encouraging the people to unite, and for which I removed and censured him'.[204] Because this cousin, Father James, who was arrested after the rebellion is considered on good authority to have been innocent, the benefit of it seems to have been extended to Thomas Dixon. Father James Dixon himself was brother to Nicholas and Thomas, who were both United Irishmen: Fr Thomas Dixon thus illustrates the depth of United Irish penetration of Castlebridge, and James Dixon was a victim of the post-rebellion loyalist fury, because loyalists had difficulty in seeing how, as in the case of the Esmonde or Hay families, individual members could have different views on the issues of the day.

As for the two Father Murphys, they can not be acquitted as easily as Dickson suggests. Caulfield had described John Murphy as 'giddy'; his advice in the course of 25 and 26 May in the Luke Cullen Mss. seems to be equivocal, Murphy suggesting even on 25 May that people should resist.[205] In particular as his bishop was actually in the area on 26 May exhorting the people to submit, Murphy's actions seem like an act of ecclesiastical as well as civil rebellion. Even Kavanagh, who does not seem to have had access to Cullen's memoirs and hence was probably drawing on independent local traditions brings out the ambivalent quality of Murphy's role in referring to 'the hitherto wavering mind of Fr Murphy'.[26] As for Michael Murphy, he joined the encampment at Kilthomas on the night of 26 May or the following morning.[207] Hay suggests that Michael Murphy first dallied in his district and was swept along with the multitude.[208] This seems at variance with the facts. Kilthomas is 6 miles west of Gorey and was a somewhat odd location for a curate at Ballycanew to resort to. Indeed Kavanagh mentions that Nicholas Murphy was a nephew of Fr Michael[209] and, if so, this may suggest a political motive. Moreover, according to Kavanagh, the mother of John Prendergast, Kavanagh's maternal grandfather who was involved in the rising, and an admitted United Irishman in the region, was a sister of Father Michael Murphy.[210] Thus, he had family ties in two hotbeds of United Irishman activity and for him, like Father John Murphy, an United Irishman tie is not implausible. Indeed, Kavanagh also mentions the recollections of an old lady, a relative of Father Michael, relating that she was present when he entered his brother's house to summon a nephew forth.[211] It is true that both Father Murphys had been active in securing oaths of allegiance from parishioners for Mountnorris but this was in the very altered circumstances of late 1797 or early 1798. The declarations for which Mountnorris secured support in April were very different, amounting to general political statements. As far as both catholics and loyalists were concerned, the situation had totally changed since late 1797 and neither catholics nor protestants can have seen themselves as being inconsistent in assuming very different attitudes and behaviour in April. As for other clergy, Nicholas Stafford's appearance on a list of United Irish leaders found in Mathew Keugh's house is a rather compromising piece of evidence. Three other clergy come up in Caulfield's list (excluding Father John Redmond who must be regarded as innocent), about whom we know little. Caulfield's list makes clear that no less than six of the clergy had been suspended or otherwise warned. A number of the clergy had a drink problem, which in Irish terms is related to a gregarious life and hence were open to the political attitudes that their parishioners were assuming. Even Kavanagh's ancestor, John Prendergast, in Kavanagh's rather coy account, is permitted the significant admission that, apart from priests who opposed the movement, 'others of them, however, had lived abroad, and had seen what liberty was, and loved it, thinking that their fellow-countrymen should enjoy the same rights as people in other countries'.[212]

VII

The situation was now deteriorating in Wexford. Even when things were better, as far back as January, Laurence Doyle of Springhill (a relation of Sir Thomas Esmond's and lieutenant in Grogan Knox's corps) who was loyal, had been proceeded against.[213] By now, loyalists were well and truly of the opinion that the sentiments of loyalty in the final round of declarations had been 'imposed on them by their landlords and admitted by the priests without the knowledge of the people'.[214] Opinion was already inflamed by the recent assizes. In Wexford, the Kilcormick men arrested in September had come before the assizes and were acquitted by the jury.[215] At the Wicklow assizes, just ahead of the Wexford ones, the cases brought against a large number of Wicklow and some Wexford men on the strength of the informer Cooper were thrown out by direction of the judge. Other cases resting on Cooper's information, due to be heard at the Wexford assizes were dismissed by the judge in the light of the collapse of Cooper's testimony in Wicklow.[216] Both sides drew from these events contrary conclusions. Loyalists concluded that the existing law was inadequate; resort would be necessary to the powers of the Insurrection Act and its provisions extended to the whole county. Their opponents made political capital out of the fact that at the assizes charges were thrown out or the accused acquitted. The proclamation of the entire county followed on 27 April, as loyalist fears mounted and Orange sentiments crept in. On the other hand, this provided the propaganda and fear factor which helped United Irishman recruitment and encouraged the rethink that we may perhaps attach to Fathers John and Michael Murphy who in quite good faith had helped to secure the oaths of allegiance of their parishioners in November or January. Opinion was further inflamed by the holding of the quarter-assizes at Wexford on 23 May. At the quarter-assizes, sentences passed by individual magistrates under the Insurrection Act were appealed but confirmed. The cases heard included the appeal of Father Thomas Dixon.[217] In other words, in Wexford as in Wicklow the cases were vigorously contested in the courts.

The magistrates assembled in Wexford on 23 May took advantage of the occasion to pass a resolution directed specifically at the part of the county with which they were familiar. For some time efforts to secure the surrender of arms had been proceeding afresh in the county. The resolution now passed referred to the system 'generally adopted by the inhabitants of the several parishes of this county' and then proceeded to indicate that if the inhabitants of the other parts of the county failed to surrender arms within fourteen days, the magistrates would apply for free quarters.[218] The intent of the resolution is reflected in the location of the centres of magistrate activity over the next few days. The administration of oaths and gathering in of arms began in Oulart immediately. The little village was the nerve centre of the surrounding parishes, which incidentally had few resident gentry or magistrates. It was beside important north-south and east-west roads, and had the only inn — and general shop — in the region offering accommodation to travellers. On the evidence of the Luke Cullen Mss, Oulart was the centre recognised by the Kilcormick men for the surrender of arms. The tension was enormous because the yeoman cavalry were on constant patrol day and night[219] and, as shown in the evidence of Luke Cullen's informants, any assembly of men, even the turf cutting for Father Murphy on 25 May, came under constant surveillance.[220] It is possible that this assembly may have had a less innocent purpose than the appearances. Certainly, given the strong United Irishman presence in the area, surveillance of the activity was not in itself unjustified. The fact that Thomas Donovan who was with Murphy on the turf bank was also with him further north at the Harrow on 26 May when the first resistance took place is not purely incidental, especially as Luke Cullen's informant seems to suggest a similar outlook for both Donovan and Murphy.[221] On 26 May a large number of people had come into Oulart and were addressed by Bishop Caulfield who on his return from Dublin made his first halt there:

He exhorted the people to relinquish their wild notions of insurrection, to live in peace and charity with each other, and threatened the disobedient to the laws with the heaviest of God's chastisements.[222]

Similar activity proceeded elsewhere in the disturbed region. On 25 May, for instance, Edward Hay recalls helping the magistrate Edward Turner to gather in arms at Turner's residence at Newfort and the following day Turner moved on to conduct the same activity from the residence of Edward Fitzgerald at Newpark.[223]

The delicate situation in the region was also now being influenced by news from further afield. United Irishmen, as made clear in Byrne's narrative, in Byrne's region where magistrate action resumed earlier than in Boolavogue, were already for several days in hiding not only for fear of arrest but in expectation of an imminent order to rise. The same expectation must have existed in the Slaney region. Two developments, or rather news of them, now gave events an impetus of their own. First, news of the Carnew and Dunlavin massacres, according to Cullen's information, reached Kilcormick on Saturday morning 26 May. News of the Leinster rising must have reached county Wexford as quickly or even more quickly: indeed, Handcock's account suggests that the news reached his district in county Wexford on 25 May and it was certainly in Wexford town on 26 May.[224] Such news would have altered the situation radically. As long as arms were demanded from rebels in isolation from events elsewhere, it was very difficult not to cooperate: the alternative was their acquisition by the authorities by more brutal methods and further oppression. There is an irony in the fact that, through the slowness of news to spread, rebel leaders like Harvey were party to arms collection, after the expected rebellion had broken out and that Fitzgerald's own residence was a centre of collection at the request of, and in the presence of, the magistrate Turner on Saturday 26 May. If arms were surrendered at Fitzgerald's, they would not necessarily be lost to the rebels. The final irony was Fitzgerald's own arrest at much the same time as a few miles to the north the rebels were marching away from the ambush of Lieutenant Bookey. Such news would have altered the situation radically. If rebellion had actually broken out, then the whole question of surrendering arms had to be seen in a new light and resistance for the first time made sense. This is what seems to have happened in the Oulart area where arms collection had gone on for several days and was planned to take place on 26 May as well at Edward Fitzgerald's house in the very heart of the rebel country. Kilcormick seems to have been the only area where people had held out against the Mountnorris-administered oath because they had regarded it as too strict; they had finally signed only under heavy pressure from Mountnorris.[225] Some did not co-operate in arms collection now and certainly, according to one of Luke Cullen's informants 'there were some choice spirits among us that could not be induced to surrender theirs, even by

those who had the strongest natural claims on them'.[226] Others regretted that
they had surrendered arms the preceding day and it is easy to relate their regret
to the filtering into the district of news of the Leinster rising. In the course of
Saturday, an effort was made to stir up action:

During the day there were some gentlemen going through the people and spoke thus to
them. Well John this is fine weather. Yes sir. Have you all your spring's work done? No
sir. It is a pity to loose this fine day from your work. To another Well Tom you were
always an early man with your work. Yes sir I endeavour to keep up with the season. I
suppose you have all thrashed a long time ago. I have sir. Have you your turf cut and all
your weeding done. Not all sir. Then I wonder at a wise man like you to loose this fine
day. Why sir, these are strange time and very dangerous gentlemen of our enemies are
determined our being here today will not remove the danger. Such were the significant
hints of Mr John Hay and one or two more that were there on that day.[227]

Quite apart from the ceaseless patrolling, violent magistrate acts — some
floggings and house burnings — added to the general tension and the rebellion
broke out in the evening roughly twenty-four hours after news of the Leinster
rising had filtered into the county. The news had given a new urgency to the
acts of both loyalists and United Irishmen and a cycle of events now made a
local rising inevitable. The possibility of a plan for action in concert with
United Irishmen from further afield both to the north and the south cannot be
discounted. In Wexford, on the authority of Elizabeth Richard's diary entry for
26 May, there were reports that the neighbourhood of Gorey and of Oulart was
much disturbed. Handcock, acting on discovery of a design to seize the market
house in Enniscorthy and to carry off all the arms lodged there, had them
destroyed in public view. At about six or seven o'clock, he was shown a letter
written by an officer 'hinting at some expected disturbance'.[228] Was this some
plan for action in the troubled Oulart region where magistrate activity was
now concentrated, where the United Irishmen were numerous, and where
some arms had not been surrendered? John Murphy's force at the Harrow
between 8 and 9 p.m. on Saturday night seems to have been unexpected by
Lieutenant Bookey's patrol which had left Ferns to reconnoitre the troubled
Kilcormick district at the end of a day of rumours. The attack on the patrol
took place at 10 p.m. Kavanagh's history suggests that the Boolavogue men
had been attacked on their way to surrender their arms in Ferns and fighting
their way home were *then* led by Murphy.[229] This is patently false, as arms were
actually being surrendered at Oulart on both 25 and 26 May. Later testimony
from the family of Burrowes, the rector of Kilmuckridge, intimates that they
had been warned in the late evening of a possible attack and had strengthened
their house at Kyle a few hundred yards from Oulart village with the presence
of nine or ten armed men.[230] Rather ironically, this act by a respected and
fearful protestant seemed menacing to locals, given the disarming activity
under foot among catholics, and may have helped to draw attention to the
house. With the patrol defeated, the next step was to add to the stock of arms.
Burrowes' house, strongly fortified, seemed the obvious point to proceed to
and it was now laid under siege and overcome with little delay. It is stated in
contemporary and later accounts that a detachment was sent off after the

Harrow to Camolin to raid Lord Mountnorris's house for arms.[231] It seems unlikely that it happened on the night of 26 into the morning of 27 May, because the loyalists had not vacated Camolin and because, if the arms had been acquired, there was time for the rebels to get the arms to Oulart hill for the battle on the afternoon of 27 May, whereas all accounts make it clear that the rebels were still badly armed on that occasion. As events were extended in these hectic first days over a long time span embracing night hours as well as day, action undertaken on the night of the 27th into the morning of the 28th has been unwittingly brought back to the early hours of the 27th. The number of guns seized at Camolin is said to have been 800 and is the prime reason for the success of the attack on Enniscorthy.

Murphy's assembling of men at the Harrow and at Burrowes' house at Kyle was only one of several assemblies before or after midnight on Saturday 26 May. At about the same time as Murphy opened his action at the Harrow another group, about 30 or 40 strong, assembling at Blackwater, met George Sparks, a protestant gentleman. Apparently they had expected to meet Edward Fitzgerald, and Sparks proposed to send a deputation to Fitzgerald when he failed to turn up.[232] Sparks was almost certainly a United Irishman:

One of those rare individuals of his class, he loved and associated with the people ... possessed of a great deal of action, just what the county Wexfordmen loved, he played ball, leaped etc with the young men, kept a pack of hounds and hunted with them twice a week. In fact he was a kind of idol amongst them and in a country like that exclusively catholic he was looked on as a United Irishman by Hawtrey White, Jacob and Boyd ...[233]

They could see the distant flames of Burrowes' house on fire. It is this observation which makes it possible to time their action as independent and contemporaneous with Murphy's elsewhere. At this stage, Murphy's contingent marched to Castleellis, where they were joined by Sparks' Blackwater contingent and, now swollen to 400 men, they proceeded a mile south to the village of Ballinamonabeg.[234]

Turner had been at Fitzgerald's house up to 10 p.m., and it was only at Ballinamonabeg that the rebels heard that 'in the dead hour of night' Fitzgerald had been arrested. In fact, Ballinamonabeg may have been a pre-arranged meeting point. Taylor, whose account is very accurate and well-informed in a number of respects, also states that the rebels had been ordered to assemble there.[235] Not only did Murphy and Sparks in unison converge on it from nearby Castleellis but Edward Roche and some of his United Irishmen from farther south, not so far involved in the action, now linked up there with the more northern rebels. Edward Roche in his yeomanry regimentals was accompanied by some five or six men from his regiment. In his later plea for clemency, Roche represented that he met up with the rebels when on his way from Turner's company to Wexford to ascertain Fitzgerald's fate. This would date his meeting with the rebels to the early hours of the morning, but the truth of his claim is thrown into doubt by the fact that, from what we know of Turner's movements, he would have been south of Ballinamonabeg if he

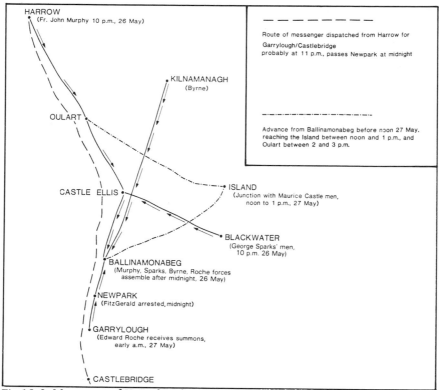

HARROW
(Fr. John Murphy 10 p.m., 26 May)

KILNAMANAGH
(Byrne)

OULART

CASTLE ELLIS

ISLAND
(Junction with Maurice Castle men,
noon to 1 p.m., 27 May)

BLACKWATER
(George Sparks' men,
10 p.m. 26 May)

BALLINAMONABEG
(Murphy, Sparks, Byrne, Roche forces
assemble after midnight, 26 May)

NEWPARK
(FitzGerald arrested, midnight)

GARRYLOUGH
(Edward Roche receives summons,
early a.m., 27 May)

CASTLEBRIDGE

— — — — — — — —
Route of messenger dispatched from Harrow for
Garrylough/Castlebridge
probably at 11 p.m., passes Newpark at midnight

—·—·—·—·—·—·—·—·—·—
Advance from Ballinamonabeg before noon 27 May,
reaching the Island between noon and 1 p.m., and
Oulart between 2 and 3 p.m.

Fig 10.2: **Movement of United Irishmen, before and after midnight, 26 May, 1798**

parted company with Turner, and could have joined the rebels only if he was going, not to Wexford as he implies, but in the opposite direction.

Ballinamonabeg is very close to Fitzgerald's residence, a fact which makes its selection as a rendezvous very plausible, and hints very strongly at the likelihood that Fitzgerald was the expected military leader of the rebels in the region. Moreover, 'the Wexford delegates of the United Irishmen', according to Kavanagh, met in session in the public house of Jeremiah Kavanagh.[236] He was later to accompany the insurgents to Oulart. He had himself an interesting background: he had been to America, and had fought under Washington.[237] He is thus more likely to have been a willing rebel than an involuntary one. During the early morning the rebels were sighted by Hawtrey White and the yeomanry cavalry from Gorey who had been alerted to events: when they arrived, they could distinguish even the leaders of the rebel army at Ballinamonabeg, in two divisions led by Roche and Murphy respectively.[238] Hawtrey White's forces retreated, and at an indeterminate time, probably quite early in the morning, the main body of the rebels moved away to Meelnagh and then the Island, where they were still at 1 o'clock. Their movements were probably first dictated by Hawtrey White's retreat, and later their advance to Oulart hill was prompted by news of the advance of the combined militia/yeomanry force brought to them by the leaders after their hasty departure from Ballinamonabeg.

Reinforcements were now joining the rebels from across a wide district. As well as Roche, Morgan Byrne of Kilnamanagh — on the far side of Oulart — had arrived at Ballinamonabeg.[239] He was nephew to Luke Byrne who was to become prominent in the following days[240] on the rebel side. There were in fact two Byrnes at the battle of Oulart, Morgan and his brother Peter.[241] They must be included among the committed United Irishmen. Luke Byrne is described as sanguinary by Taylor, perhaps inspired by private access to the memorandum written by Handcock which refers to him as 'a most sanguinary ruffian'.[242] Even a rebel account refers to him as a 'voilent (sic) man',[243] and the more public testimony of Hay is to a man 'whose sanguinary disposition I was well aware of'.[244] When they arrived at the Island, the rebel force was joined by recruits from Maurice Castle. A fracas ensued in which two Castleellis men, John and Michael Redmond, were lost to the rebel division almost immediately as a result of one being killed, and the other withdrawing: 'by this wanton murder they lost two young officers as brave, intelligent and as high-souled as any connected with the wide system of United Irishmen'.[245]

Because Turner, the sole magistrate living in the immediate proximity of the preceding hours' events, brought the fateful news to Wexford in the early hours of the morning, the army from Wexford moved north at 11 a.m. to quell the rebels. Later that morning they reached Ballinamonabeg. According to Kavanagh, the United Irishmen leaders, receiving news of the advance of the army barely in time, only escaped by the skin of their teeth.[246] As the burning of Kavanagh's took place around mid-day[247] and the main rebel army only reached Oulart by 2 or 3 p.m., this suggests that the rebel leaders had long remained behind in deliberation. Fitzgerald's arrest, if he was the planned leader, would account for a good deal of confusion and indecision and long-drawn-out deliberation, reflected also in the absence of the emergence of any very clear leader at this stage. In social position, Fitzgerald was easily the highest of those holding the rank of colonel within the county. How effective he was as a man we do not know. Mrs Brownrigg, a hostile witness made more acerbic by captivity in Wexford town, recorded that 'the young man is, as I am told, both weak and stupid'.[248] Byrne, while in no way hostile to Fitzgerald, tends to be critical of him, in contrast to his more favourable views on other leaders of the rebels. He observes that Fitzgerald 'knew nothing of military affairs'[249] and attributes the decision to make a last stand on Vinegar Hill to both Fitzgerald and Roche.[250] Fitzgerald may well be another example of the socially well-placed United Irishman colonels, selected more for their position than for their capacity. Fitzgerald's arrest would help to explain the circumstances in which, over the next few days, non-military figures rose to play military roles, whether clergymen like the two Murphys or Philip Roche, or the civilian figure of Bagenal Harvey. Edward Roche, no more than Murphy, emerges as a dominant figure in the events of 27 May and if one assumes some personal incapacity or failure on Roche's part to assume wider authority on that day, it would underline the scale of the vacuum which Fitzgerald's arrest created, and how a wholly unexpected leadership emerged for the rebellion. Harvey's reluctance to assume the office of commander-in-chief can be explained in part by the fact that he can only have foreseen for himself civil, not military, responsibilities.

The success of gathering the rebel forces together quickly at Ballinamonabeg was due to the early despatch of news from the Harrow. One of Kavanagh's informants described how Jeremiah Donovan (a son of Tom Donovan, and a nephew of Morgan Byrne) disguised as a groom (this probably means yeoman cavalry uniform) with fictitious letters directed to Mountnorris, brought news of the Harrow to Castlebridge.[251] A man residing two miles to the south of Oulart who happened to be living out of doors through fear on these disturbed nights, related to Luke Cullen seeing a horseman proceeding in the Wexford direction shouting: 'get up and fight or you will be burned or butchered in your beds. The country is in a blaze all round you'.[252] Cullen's informant followed him a mile south as far as Fitzgerald's gates where he found the cavalry drawn up. This would obviously have been Boyd's cavalry despatched from Wexford and the messenger was witness to what must have been Fitzgerald's arrest. Perhaps the messenger had even been charged to convey the news of the Harrow to Fitzgerald. The hour would have been around midnight, the time suggested by Edward Hay who was actually in Fitzgerald's house for these events. It would be consistent too with the time necessary to take a message from a short action beginning at the Harrow at 10 p.m. It would also explain why Roche could arrive so promptly at Ballinamonabeg. Indeed, the messenger's function may have been to relay the news successively to both Fitzgerald and Roche. The messenger, probably because he was in yeoman uniform, was, according to Luke Cullen's informant, not impeded by the yeomanry at Fitzgerald's gate. The sequence of events in which the messenger must have sighted the cavalry at Fitzgerald's gates would also explain how Roche would have been made aware so early of Fitzgerald's fate. The fact that the arrest took place at midnight also underlines further the inconsistency of Roche's account, as Hay states that Turner's activity terminated at 10 p.m. and that he later aroused Turner, whereas Roche states in his memorial that he parted from Turner in the knowledge that Fitzgerald had been arrested and then proceeded towards Wexford. The fact that a messenger was despatched south by Murphy to Castlebridge also seems to imply that Murphy can not have been acting except in liaison with the United Irish leadership. The taking of Fitzgerald to Wexford was not the occasion of news of the revolt being conveyed to Wexford. He was removed before the news spread in the region, and the cavalry returned with their prisoner to Wexford unaware of what had happened a few miles to the north and before the movement of men summoned by the messenger would have alerted them to the occurrence of greater events. The news was brought into Wexford by Turner still later in the course of the short night of the 26th into the morning of the 27th. Hay in his account claims that he aroused Turner after Fitzgerald's arrest in order to secure the arms lodged in Fitzgerald's house and which were left there untouched by the cavalry. Hay's account is however very general: clearly he was anxious not to dwell on the circumstances close to the heart of the early action on the night of the outbreak and to put his own presence in the most favourable light. It implies that, at the time that Turner was aroused, Hay was still unaware of what was afoot, as he claims that his arousing Turner saved him from the rebels as the house was shortly afterwards raided by them. Because Turner's news contained details of house burning, his departure from Newfort would seem to have been in the aftermath of the move of both Hawtrey White and the rebel forces to the north, when both sides unleashed an orgy of house burning on the countryside. The rebel messenger's call did refer to the country being ablaze, but at midnight that could only have referred to the district around the Harrow and Kyle. It is clear that Boyd's cavalry returned to Wexford with their prisoner, blissfully ignorant of what was already beginning to unfold a few miles to the north.

The army, summoned from Wexford by Turner, reached Ballinamonabeg around mid-day on the 27th of May. They refreshed themselves in Kavanagh's public house — the drunken drummer features in several accounts — and then burned it down. Kavanagh, the proprietor, had retired with the rebels and fought at Oulart. The fact that his premises were burned down suggests not so much the unrestrained vindictiveness of the troops as an awareness of where the sympathies of the proprietor lay. By 2 or 3 p.m. the rebel army took up its position on the hill of Oulart, chosen no doubt as the highest point in the region; shortly afterwards the Wexford army reached the rebel positions and in the late afternoon the first large-scale action of the rebellion had taken place. Far from Murphy being the obvious leader of events, his role was fairly limited at this stage. The tactics of the rebel army in the early hours of the morning when confronted at Ballinamonabeg with Hawtrey White's forces seem to have been dictated by Sparks.[253] Although one of Cullen's informants described Murphy as 'our principal leader', this phrase may be coloured by hindsight and by the legend that grew up around Murphy. He notes in fact that Roche and 'a few others were engaged in council and preventing disertion' and also that Morgan Byrne by his address and riding through them prevented desertion. Murphy himself at this stage 'was but of little use to us'.[254] About half the rebel forces seem to have deserted or avoided participation in the combat.

The outcome of Oulart provided the catalyst for the wider conflict that now developed. Evidence of well-defined co-ordination responding to what was taking place in Kilcormick rather than to purely local events is to be seen in the events of the thirty-six hours or so from dawn on the morning of the 27th. When Murphy's forces after Oulart raided Camolin Park between the night of the 27th and the morning of the 28th, Paul Murray, standard bearer of the Monaseed United Irishmen, was present and seized the flag of the 1782 Volunteers.[255] In the course of the daylight hours of the 28th as the rebel army moved south, it drew in the units of the United Irishmen from other locations. At Scarawalsh bridge, the Monaseed men, presaged already by the presence of their standard-bearer at Camolin Park, joined the main force. Michael Murphy joined the rebels at Balliorel hill[256] and Thomas Synnott with a further contingent of east-Slaney men made a junction with them. On the 29th, Thomas Cloney and Michael Furlong led a contingent of Bantry men to the victorious rebel camp at Vinegar Hill. The Wexford United Irishmen contingents had now all joined the rebels and the lack of clarity about those United Irishmen under the colonelcy of Mathew Keugh suggests that organisation in the barony of Forth was still far behind that of the other units. While the campaigns moved backwards and forwards across much of the county over the succeeding three weeks, it is noteworthy that no further accretions took place to the rebel leadership. The well-defined pattern in which the units and their leaders emerged within the three days from the late evening of the 26th May gives the lie to the argument that the rebels were mere frightened crowds of peasants and that they had acquired their leaders simply through a process of intimidation of suitable middle-class figures.

11 *Kevin Whelan*

The Role of the Catholic Priest in the 1798 Rebellion in county Wexford

We are still at an early stage in our efforts to understand the 1798 Rebellion in county Wexford, a series of events which seared contemporary consciousnesses and whose afterglow lit the fuse of many explosive myths.[1] In particular, the participation of Catholic clergymen as active rebels nurtured a rich but mainly adventitious growth of folklore: this accretion of later legend reached its apogee in the emotional scenes of the '98 commemorations in 1898, 1938 and 1948, commemorations which in Wexford were orchestrated by Catholic priests, not least Fr Patrick Kavanagh and Canon Pat Murphy (popularly known by the soubriquet ''98'.) On this occasion, for once, the Catholic clergy could be shown to be on the 'right' side in a popular agitation; as their legendary role loomed larger and larger, so actual events were displaced and receded in the popular consciousness. This highly developed mythology has obliterated the actual role of the clergymen involved: Fr John Murphy's 'mighty wave' has swept aside the complex, enigmatic clerical configuration of 1798 in Wexford and only the 'patriot priest' image has withstood the inundation. This paper attempts to remap the clerical topography of '98 before the all-powerful, all-simplifying 'mighty wave' overran it.

A detailed combing of the scattered documentation establishes a figure of 85 priests in county Wexford in 1798 (appendix 1.)[2] Of these, a maximum total of eleven can be regarded as having been actively engaged in rebellion: one of these (John Keane) can be disregarded as mentally unbalanced. This leaves a sizeable minority of ten who can clearly be demonstrated to be rebels. Of equal interest are the seventy four who were either active loyalists or kept a very low profile in the rebellion. Three of them (James Dixon (transported) John Redmond (executed), William Ryan (murdered)) came to grief in the hysterical post-rebellion period — totally innocent victims of a frenzied Protestant backlash. Many more suffered personal intimidation and harassment and also the burning of their chapels. This backlash was unjustified — many of the priests had striven hard to prevent the rebellion, had opposed its spread and worked to

296

soften its acerbities in their local contexts. The accumulation of detailed material from a wide variety of disparate sources supplies a basis for making a general assessment of the role of the Catholic clergy in 1798 in county Wexford.

In the protracted build-up to the rebellion in the turbulent 1790s, two parties had clearly emerged on the Catholic side. On the one hand were those who favoured a conservative low profile image, content to await a continuing thaw in establishment attitudes and hastening the melting process by a conciliatory, deferential stance to local authority figures. The Catholic bishop, James Caulfield, epitomised this group, who tended to be the older, propertied Catholics. On the other hand was a younger, more aggressive Catholic middle class grouping, who pressed strongly for the repeal of the penal laws and agitated for the rapid advancement of Catholics on the legal, social, economic and political fronts. This group was fronted by James Edward Devereux of Carrigmenan and Edward Hay of Ballinkeele and others associated with it were Edward Sweetman (Newbawn), Edward Fitzgerald (Newpark), Edward Sutton (Wexford), Patrick and Mathew Sutton (Enniscorthy) and John Henry Colclough (Ballyteigue) — in other words, the younger, burgeoning Catholic middle class in the county. This group was abrasive, anti-Government, anti-establishment, and secularised: it was also the group from which the later United Irish leadership in the county was to evolve.

In the 1790s, these two groups were in competition for the loyalties of the non-politicised Catholic masses in the county and were less than friendly to each other. Inevitably, this division had repercussions for the clergy of the county. Bishop Caulfield was especially opposed to the hardline Catholic politics promulgated by the younger men, seeing them as direct implants from atheistic French revolutionary principles. He described the leader of the Catholic Committee (James Edward Devereux, recently returned from France) as 'a young hot-headed libertine and more attached to the committee than to any other order now existing. Yet he has acquired an amazing influence on the people by his haranguing and specious promises of total emancipation'.[3] He accused them also of anti-clericalism: 'The spirit of this town [Wexford] is now [1792] violent beyond belief and a general sullenness pervades. It seems to be the plan adopted to give the clergy nothing if they do not come into their measures'.[4] Caulfield may have been correct in suspecting the religious orthodoxy of this group: when examined before the Privy Council in 1798, William Byrne of Park Hill in neighbouring county Wicklow described himself as a 'nominal Catholic' who 'believed every religion equally good'.[5] In this type of climate, one understands why Caulfield felt increasingly out of control prior to the Rebellion: 'You know of old that they [the people of Wexford] would not be managed by me. T'is true the times are changed now [August 1799] nor have they now the leaders who led them astray or set them mad in them times'.[6] In a bitter comment after the execution of John Hay in 1798, he observed 'I hope they [Edward and John Hay, Edward Fitzgerald] will now see the differences between their principles and mine'.[7] On another occasion, he described Edward Hay as a 'dangerous man'.[8]

Caulfield tried hard to impress his conservative line on his clergy and with a great deal of success. In the immediate build up to the events of the summer of 1798, only a tiny handful publicly dissented from Caulfield's cautious line, although some of them must have felt some sympathy for the radicalism of the United Irishmen. Their bishop was suspicious of those who did not whole-heartedly toe the conservative line. Thus, on two separate occasions, he refers to Fr John Murphy as 'giddy' and, in Caulfield's terminology, this meant that Murphy possessed political sentiments which veered to the popular side.[9] As a result, the bishop, to use his own words 'reproved, reprimanded and threatened him'.[10] In cases of obvious infection by the new radicalism, Caulfield moved decisively. Fr Philip Roche had been curate in Gorey. There is a revealing comment from Miles Byrne that Roche 'knew of the many inhuman deeds committed by the Orange Magistracy of that area'; this suggests that Roche had wholeheartedly adopted the local United Irishmen's perspective on the law-and-order issue and that his sympathies were publicly known.[11] In Caulfield's view, he had 'begun to agitate' and had become 'obnoxious'. Accordingly, he was subjected to 'reprimanding, admonishment and in-struction' by his bishop, before being peremptorily despatched to the far end of the diocese to the Cloughbawn/Rathnure area.[12]

However, the vast bulk of the clergy were obviously of the same opinion as their bishop and the senior clergy in particular were impeccably conservative. This shows in a number of ways. Fr John Shallow, in Adamstown parish, vehemently opposed the United Irishmen:

'From the time I supposed the doctrines and tenets of the United Irishmen were disseminating or making strides in my parishes or neighbourhood, I did combat and deprecate them in the best manner I could . . . from my altar as also in private, as analogous to, and flowing from French atheistical revolutionary principles, and derogating from, and repugnant to, the established laws of the land and the law of God. . . . I did also use my influence and utmost endeavours to preserve the people committed to my care, by inculcating obedience to their beloved Sovereign, King George the Third, from the many favours he bestowed on them and the gratitude they in consequence owed him. I did also in the same public manner declare the oaths of the United Irishmen entirely void and null, . . . as sinful and damnable to be taken but still more to be adhered to, from the Roman Catholic Cathechism which I held in my hand and explained from the altar'.[13]

Shallow had invited the local magistrate, John Heatley, to Mass at Newbawn and Adamstown to hear him preach this sermon. Francis Kavanagh, vicar-general of the diocese, stated that, in the year prior to the Rebellion, 'I uniformly reprobated the proceedings of the United Irishmen as tending not only to disunion amongst fellow subjects but to disloyalty and sedition. I always condemned their Oath or test as unnecessary, equivocal and insidious'.[14] John Redmond, curate in Camolin, deliberately turned away United Irishmen on their knees from their Easter duty in the spring prior to the Rebellion.[15] In other cases, the priests co-operated with the local yeomanry and magistracy in attempting to keep their congregations under control. Many of them allowed the magistrates to speak from their altars in a bid to keep their parishes quiescent: others collaborated in the search of arms. Andrew Corish of Kilmore parish was 'to direct the people to keep order in the parish and not to appear in numbers but keep proper hours'.[16] Caulfield had explicitly ordered his priests to follow the magistrate's advice in these matters. The chapels were obvious locations for United Irish recruitment to take place. In an early example in May 1797, a Dublin pawnbroker had been observed distributing propaganda at the chapel gate in Boolevogue.[17]

The opposition to the United Irishmen by the clergy was on a number of levels. Firstly, there was the spiritual argument against their oath bound structure. Frank Kavanagh described their oath of association as 'contrary to the doctrine of the Roman Catholic church, which condemns all association oaths not sanctioned by lawful authority'.[18] Secondly, there was the ideological argument that the United Irishmen were inspired by atheistic principles which were inevitably hostile to established religion in all its manifestations.

'The clergy were not so stupid as not to know that all this was leading to their own degradation, that, although they might be spared for the moment, they would soon be forced to yield to those new masters, as the clergy in France, the only advocates of the poor, had been forced to do.'[19]

Thirdly, there was the political argument that a quiescent low-key approach by Catholics had created a benevolent attitude which was already reflected in the repeal of some of the penal laws: the United Irishmen disrupted this gradual process, destroyed Catholic unity and gave the authorities an opportunity to delay further concessions. For example, on 10 February, 1798, Michael Lacy, parish priest of Kilmuckridge, had published an address in the *Freeman's Journal* on behalf of himself and 500 of his flock. In this, he criticised the United Irishmen's principles as 'tending to sow the seeds of discord between Protestant and Catholic and to revive old prejudices against each other'.[20] Fourthly, there was the social argument that the United Irishmen were divisive and destroyed the natural links between clergy and people and substituted anarchy in place of it.

'The strength of religion being paralysed, the paternal influence of the clergy was destroyed and the curb being thus plucked from the mouth of the multitude, they have become what we have of late seen them, unmanageable by Civil laws and abandoned to their passions and profligacy'.[21]

Michael Lacy also felt it necessary, in the face of this threat, to get his congregation to swear 'to maintain the present arrangement of property'.[22] Finally, there was the conspiracy theory held by the clergy which argued that the United Irishmen were controlled by a narrow, self-serving coterie 'who promoted ebullition in the social mass, in the hope of disengaging their active spirits from the dregs, where nature and fortune placed them, to float like scum on the surface of confusion'.[23]

Bishop Caulfield summarised his opposition in a sweeping denunciation:
'The uniting of Irishmen for the late Rebellion was hatched in the dark, or

was communicated by private whispers; it was recommended by specious promises, impressed by flattering prospects, enforced by threats and menaces, denouncing death and destruction on the persons and properties of those who refused to unite and to cooperate and the union was secured and sanctioned by a solemn oath. The people, in general, more credulous than wise or virtuous swallowed the bait and joined in the diabolical confederacy, adhering to their perjurous oaths more strictly than to their baptismal vows, or the most sacred ties of conscience, religion and the express word of God. All this accumulation of misfortunes was brought on the country by the machinations of crazy, ambitious, revolutionary adventurers, through the credulity of the incautious and ignorant multitude'.

The end product was to create

'an armed and inebriated rabble, screaming for revenge: a rabble which, besides that fury which multitudes cause by reverbations, the envy of former superiority, the hatred stirred up against the name of religion to which that superiority had been exclusively attached, the accumulation of private spite, the pain of late severities experienced and probably of some real injuries, combined with the unabated rage of a newly armed horde of slaves, pushed onwards to a project of which they had no ideas but such as were insolent, violent and cruel'.[24]

A local example clarifies the general role of the senior clergy. On the Wexford-Carlow border at Clonegal, we can trace the activities of a small United Irish cell in the autumn of 1797.[25] This cell was largely composed of craftsmen and labourers (three labourers, two tailors, two slaters, a carpenter, a carman) plus a schoolmaster, a publican and three farmers. The cell had also infiltrated Lacy's distillery in Johnstown and maintained links to Dublin through it.[26] However, this cell was exposed when its recruiting efforts came to grief and the local magistrate, Durden of Huntington Castle, despatched them to Carlow gaol. In the meantime, the local parish priest, James Purcell, was quick to move against them. In a strongly worded address, published in the Dublin and Carlow newspapers, Purcell declared his parishioners 'unalterable attachment to his Sacred Majesty, King George II and that most excellent constitution which his mild and paternal reign has restored to us'. He goes on to

'lament the success of some incendiaries in our parish and we blush at the weakness of many of the lower order of our Communion, who, through ignorance, have been misled by their wicked artifices. We rejoice, however, that the delusion was short lived'.

Purcell proceeds to lash the United Irishmen:

'We are perfectly satisfied that the emissaries of those turbulent factions called United Irishmen, are as much the enemies of Catholicity as they are of our King and Constitution and we solemnly and sincerely pledge ourselves, should persons of such description attempt to disseminate amongst us seditious, levelling or irreligious principles, that we will drag such miscreants to the bar of justice and prosecute them to the utmost rigour of the law'.

There are a number of interesting points in this harangue, signed by 1,561 of

Purcell's parishioners.[27] Firstly, there is the assault on the 'lower classes' as 'ignorant' which masks Purcell's fears of their politicisation and a consequent challenge to their control by their social 'betters' (including the priest) and ultimately a breakdown of the accepted moral economy. Purcell himself lived adjacent to the crossroads nucleation of the Watch House village, a confused jumble of small thatched houses which contained the agricultural labourers, distillery workers, carmen, poachers and blacksmiths who were becoming United Irishmen. This strongly conservative view was that of an old man of 79, trained on the continent and with the lower expectations of a Catholic clergyman whose decisive formation was in the first half of the eighteenth century. Similarly, he follows a strong law-and-order line, hopes for a gradual amelioration in the conditions of Catholics by a piecemeal policy and supports the existing class system by attacking the 'levelling' principles of the United Irishmen. In all these ways, he was merely articulating the mainstream opinion of the Wexford clergy in the period prior to the rebellion.

In the winter of 1797, a portion of north-east Wexford (the Maccamores area) was proclaimed and placed under martial law because it was considered to be in a dangerous state by some of its magistrates.[28] The powerful local political magnate, the Earl of Mountnorris, saw this as unjustified and also as threatening his credibility with the government. In November 1797, he organised an impressive display of conspicuous Catholic loyalty in the area specified, using the Catholic priests and their chapel congregations to forcibly make the point. The congregations and priests affected were those of Ballygarrett (Nicholas Redmond, Nicholas Stafford), Oulart (Nicholas Synnott), Ballyoughter (Frank Kavanagh, John Redmond), Boolevogue (John Murphy), Kilmuckridge (Michael Lacy), Blackwater (David Cullen), Ballycanew (Michael Murphy) and Ferns (Edward Redmond).[29] These parishes formed a homogeneous block in north-east Wexford, effectively covering both the old north Wexford plantation area and also Mountnorris's political heartland. This area was to remain at the hub of the rebellion.

In April 1798, when events had finally begun to outstrip the ability to contain them, Mountnorris organised another series of public displays of Catholic loyalty, to reassert his ability to keep his area quiet.[30] The congregations and priests involved were directly equivalent to those of November, with the addition of Castlebridge (Michael Redmond), Crossabeg (Redmond Roche), Gorey (John Synnott) and Kilrush (Edan Murphy).

This display of public loyalty also included the taking of a loyal oath, containing a specific anti-United Irishman component. An example from Kilrush in the *Freeman's Journal* of 1/3/1798 signed by Rev Edan Murphy and 514 parishioners illustrates the general tone:

'We, the R.C. inhabitants of Kilrush in the County of Wexford this day assembled at the chapel of Kilrush, holding in abhorrence the barbarous outrages lately committed and seditious conspiracies now existing in this Kingdom by traitors and rebels styling themselves United Irishmen, consider it incumbent on us thus to vow and declare our unalterable attachment and loyalty to our beloved sovereign King George III and our determined resolution to support and maintain his rights and our happy Constitution ... and we do pledge ourselves to cooperate with our Protestant brethern of this Kingdom in opposing, to the utmost of our power, any foreign or domestic enemy who may dare to invade his dominion or to disturb the peace and tranquility of this country'.[31]

This spectacular co-operation with the local clergy was sufficient to allow Mountnorris's views to carry the day in Dublin. It may also have successfully stunted the growth of the United Irishmen in the winter of 1797 and the spring of 1798. However, the vigorous public role of the priests on the 'establishment' side may have caused some resentment in their flocks. In May of 1798, Alexander reported from the New Ross area that 'the zeal of the R.C. priests to prevent rebellion began to be talked of in their own community'.[32] Yet, not all the priests who supported Mountnorris's orchestration may have been entirely happy with his political tune. The presence on these lists of priests later to be associated with the rebels (John Murphy, Michael Murphy, Nicholas Stafford) suggests that events deteriorated rapidly in late spring/early summer. It is noteworthy that the Boolevogue parishioners, headed by John Murphy, had been the only ones to complain in April 1798 of the severity of the oath.[33] Clerical dissent had already displayed itself in the known association of two priests with the United Irishmen, an association so prominent that Bishop Caulfield had suspended them from their clerical duties. These men were Thomas Dixon and Edward Synnott.

Dixon was born into a family who occupied an important mercantile position in the corn village of Castlebridge, strategically located in a toll-free position over the water from Wexford town.[34] The family were millers, corn-factors, malsters and brewers; they also owned the most important public house and shop in the village. As such, they had wide reaching economic and social tentacles stretching through the Castlebridge/Screen/Blackwater area, one of the main hotbeds of early United Irish organisation in the county. The family had marriage links with at least two other families prominent in the United Irishmen — the Roches of Garrylough (with whom links stretched back through a couple of generations) and the Furlongs of Templescoby in distant Bantry.[35] Fr Thomas Dixon himself appears to have been a gregarious, convivial individual, who threw himself wholeheartedly into the day-to-day life of his parishioners. However this laid-back style of operation on Lady's Island came to the attention of his bishop, who suspended him in 1794 for 'drinking, dancing and disorderly conduct'.[36] After a chastening interval, he was stationed as curate in Blackwater parish but he became involved with the United Irishmen there in 1796 and 1797 (presumably centred on the activities of George Sparks) as well as maintaining his care-free lifestyle.[37] Curiously, it was another clerical member of the Dixons, James, who reported his cousin's political activities to Bishop Caulfield: James' two brothers, Thomas and Nicholas, were already deeply involved in the United Irishmen. Fr Thomas Dixon was again suspended and, practically similtaneously, he was accused by one of his parishioners of having attempted to recruit him as a United Irishman in a Wexford tavern. He was arrested and convicted of this offence late in 1797. His appeal was heard and lost on 23 May 1798, in the traumatic week prior to the outbreak of rebellion. His sentence of transportation engendered considerable hostility in the local United Irishmen and had an escalatory effect on their combative streak. Elizabeth Richards noted the mood of 'sullen melancholy' in Wexford town as a result of this judgement.[38] Dixon was placed aboard a tender at Duncannon to await transportation, contracted fever and died in the first week of June 1798. His memory lived vividly, not least with his cousin, Thomas Dixon, who orchestrated a flamboyant public execution of Francis Murphy, the man who informed against him.[39] Loyalist Catholics had no time for him: Caulfield described him as a 'notorious agitator' and a contemporary pro-Catholic pamphlet described him as 'a priest some years degraded from his office and excommunicated, the dishonour and scandal of the clergy'.[40]

At the same time, Edward Synnott, curate of Kilrush since 1793, had also become involved in the United Irishmen, at the other extremity of the disturbed area on the Wicklow/Wexford border. His name is found on the list of United Irishmen captains found in Mathew Keugh's house, which appears to date to 1797.[41] His activities were brought to the attention of Caulfield, who suspended him for being yet another 'notorious agitator' who did 'much mischief' by his 'agitations and uniting'. Caulfield also claimed that he was 'prone to excessive use of spirits' and that this hastened his death from pneumonia in the winter of 1797.[42] There is a hint of a possible relationship with the family of the well connected Thomas Synnott of Kilbride (Oulart) whose relatives included the Cloneys of Moneyhore, the Dorans of Oulart and the Roices of Tinnacross — all committed United Irishmen.[43]

Both these priests, then, shared a common background — strong family links with the United Irishmen, a drink problem, a history of confrontation with their ecclesiastical superiors. A third priest was also involved with the United Irishmen well before the Rebellion but he seems to have evaded Caulfield's intelligence network. This priest was Nicholas Stafford, a native of Ballyvoodock (Blackwater), where his family were neighbours and associates of the Murphys of Kilnew, the adjacent townland, where another rebel priest, Michael Murphy, was born.[44] In the seventeenth century, the Staffords were landowners in Ballyvoodock but by the end of the eighteenth century they were merely small farmers.[45] The priest's family is probably descended from the seventeenth century branch. Stafford was curate at Riverchapel in the late 1790s. Like Fr Synnott, his name is listed as a United Irishman captain on the document found in Mathew Keugh's house, believed to date to 1797.[46] Musgrave accuses him of being a 'notorious rebel' and certainly he became a fugitive after the Rebellion and was suspended by Caulfield.[47] He never again ministered openly in the diocese, retiring to his homeplace, where he died of T.B. in 1811. In 1798, he was 45 years old and still only a curate, which suggests that his bishop did not have a high opinion of him.

However, these three priests were in a minority compared with the concerted opposition of the Catholic clergy to the United Irishmen. To counteract their effect, the United Irishmen adopted a number of strategies.

One of these was to circulate rumours that the priests were in the pay of government. This rumour was so prevalent, even after the Rebellion, that Caulfield felt obliged to specifically repudiate it in a pastoral letter. He denied that he was 'fee'd, bribed or pensioned by government and that to a considerable amount: of course, that, as a mercenary, I censure and condemn the measures of United Irishmen and Revolutionists'.[48] A second line of attack was to concede the priest's authority in spiritual matters but to deny it elsewhere. Thus, on one occasion, the Franciscan, Patrick Lambert, was preaching a sermon advocating lenient measures during the occupation of Wexford town when he was peremptorily interrupted: 'Man, go mind your own business in the chapel. We know how to mind ours'.[49] A third strategy was to approach potentially sympathetic clergy with a view to neutralising their opposition. Thus, Anthony Perry and Edward Fitzgerald approached Miles O'Connor, the parish priest in Ballindaggin with a view to allowing a branch of the United Irishmen in the parish.[50] In this case, O'Connor was a distant relative of the Hay family of Ballinkeele and may have been assumed to sympathise with that family's well known political sentiments.[51] Ballindaggin was also the parish where Adam Colclough of Duffry Hall lived, a gentleman believed to be sympathetic to the cause.

The United Irishmen deliberately cultivated clerical contacts. Fr John Murphy, for example, was on visiting terms with both the Hays of Ballinkeele and the Fitzgeralds of Newpark prior to the rebellion. Through kinship links, they would have had a natrual *entrée* to many priests. Edward Roche of Garrylough had a brother, Redmond, parish priest of Crossabeg.[52] Patrick O'Brien, the schoolteacher who was the United Irishman captain in Piercestown parish, was a nephew of John Corrin, parish priest of Wexford town.[53] William Lacy, an active United Irishman in Enniscorthy was brother to Fr Michael Lacy, parish priest of Kilmuckridge. Nicholas Murphy, prominent in the Monaseed United Irishmen, was a nephew of Fr Michael Murphy, who was in turn related to the Roches of Garrylough, the Prendergasts of Knottown and the Whelans of Ballymartin, all families with close United Irish connections.[54] Michael Clinch, the United Irish captain in Kilrush, was brother to Fr Thomas Clinch.[55] Patrick Redmond, captain in Coolgreaney, was a nephew of Edward Redmond, parish priest of Ferns.[56] Thomas Synnott of Kilbride was a brother of Nicholas Synnott, parish priest of Oulart, who lived in the same house as him.[57] We have already commented on the Dixon family. Bernard Downes (parish priest of Tintern) was uncle to Michael Downes, captain in the Adamstown area.[58] Close family ties of this magnitude must have placed great strains on the Catholic clergy.

The United Irishmen may also have made concerted efforts to recruit or appeal to the many priests who were marginalised in the ecclesiastical structure of the time. It is certainly a remarkable fact that no parish priest in the county (with the possible exception of Bryan Murphy) succumbed to their appeal: of the ten who obviously took part on the rebel side in the 1798, only three (John Murphy, Philip Roche and Nicholas Stafford) were officially accredited priests of the mission. Indeed, of these three, Roche had already fallen foul of the bishop while Murphy had been reprimanded by him. Of the other seven, John Byrne was a maverick Carmelite and six (Thomas Clinch, Thomas Dixon, Mogue Kearns, Bryan Murphy, Michael Murphy, Edward Synnott) were suspended or unemployed. This suggests that the clerical appeal of the United Irishmen was to the marginal men, who had already fallen foul of the official church bureaucracy. As the case of Thomas Dixon exemplifies, some of them were 'men of the people', gregarious individuals with a strong social profile. In this respect, it is worth noting that at least seven (Clinch, Dixon, Kearns, Ml. Murphy, Philip Roche, Byrne, Synnott) had a noticeable drink problem. The nature of Irish rural social life made drink an occupational hazard for those who desired to participate fully in the life of the people: weddings, wakes, christenings, funerals, dances, fairs, stations, patterns — all were associated with very heavy drinking. The rebel priests may have been drawn to this open, relaxed lifestyle, reflected in their active participation in field sports. Mogue Kearns was a well known Duffry hurler and weight thrower, John Murphy was an expert handballer, Thomas Dixon was fond of dancing. Kearns and Murphy linked up for grouse-shooting expeditions on the Blackstairs.[59] Such men, deeply immersed in the quotidian stream of community life, may have found it especially difficult to swim against the United Irish current. Their wavering tendencies in the spring of 1798 reflected the conflicting claims on their allegiances.

The unemployed or suspended priests may have been pressurised in a less subtle way. The suspended priest in Irish folk tradition was credited with supernatural potency, expecially as a thaumaturgist, and the 'power' was particularly associated with those who had been silenced for a drink problem. John Keane from Ballymader (Bannow) was obviously accorded this status in his local community,[60] However, such priests were very directly exposed to the good will of their host communities and may have felt the need to swim with the tide. As the Anglican bishop of Killala, Joseph Stock, accurately observed:

> 'The almost total dependence of the Romish clergy of Ireland upon their people for the means of subsistence is the cause why, upon every popular commotion, many priests of that communion have been ... in the ranks of sedition and opposition to established government ... The peasant will love a revolution because he feels the weight of poverty and has not often the sense to perceive that a change of masters may render it heavier. The priest must follow the impulse of the popular wave or be left behind on the beach to perish'.[61]

These pressures were accentuated on the suspended or unemployed priest, of whom six became involved in the rebellion.

According to Veritas, Michael Murphy, who lodged in Ballycanew, had never been called to a curacy on account of 'his incapacity and riotous temper'.[62] Mogue Kearns had been dismissed by Bishop Delaney of Kildare and Leighlin from his job as curate in Clonard on the Meath/Kildare border and had returned to live in Enniscorthy, near his native Kiltealy.[63] Thomas Clinch had been suspended in 1796 for drunkeness by Caulfield and had also moved into

Enniscorthy. Bryan Murphy, the parish priest of Taghmon had apparently been suspended and a curate (Denis Kelly) was sent to perform his duties. John Byrne, the Horetown Carmelite, would have been entirely dependent on 'questing' in the local area. All of these (the two Murphys, Kearns, Clinch, Byrne, Keane) would have felt themselves very much under an economic whip-lash. These men were typical of a section of the eighteenth century Catholic clergy which had emerged under a lax ecclesiastical discipline — badly trained, easy-going, heavily secularised, leading a relaxed, open lifestyle. Bishop Nicholas Sweetman's visitation in 1753 had picked out a number of such priests in the Ferns clergy — Rev Bryan Murphy (Rathgarogue) who 'minded dogs and hunting more than his flock', Rev Michael Kennedy (Kilrush) 'neither very instructive or edifying to his flock', Rev Edmund Dempsey (Oulart) 'not himself very zealous or diligent in his duty', Rev John Fitzhenry (Bannow) 'an honest, indolent man'.[64] Caulfield had a classic example of the genre in his diocese between 1795 and 1798 — a Fr Carton 'who has been in Ferns about three years and has hunted, sported, visited etc. but never said mass or asked leave to say it. He has been idling from one gentleman's place to another in the style of a Buckeen, without observing fast or abstinence etc'.[65] The '98 priests, then, were coming out of a well-established clerical tradition.

We can now pick out some of the central elements in a profile of these priests — men of the people, with a history of conflict with their ecclesiastical superiors, possibly with a drink problem, who had close family links to the United Irishmen. Some of them may also have felt frustrated in their ecclesiastical careers. John Murphy, for example, was aged 45 and was still a country curate: by contrast, John Corrin, grandnephew of the bishop, had been appointed parish priest of Wexford town within a year of his ordination and was obviously on the fast track. Nicholas Stafford, like Murphy aged 45, was a similarly obscure country curate in Riverchapel. Philip Roche had been rusticated to Cloughbawn. So even these three serving on the mission had little stake in their ecclesiastical future. It is also remarkable that of the eleven clergy involved only three were south of a line from Wexford to New Ross, although this area (especially Forth and Bargy) supplied the bulk of the diocesan clergy at the time.[66] The three southern priests were Keane (Ballymader, Bannow) Bryan Murphy (Ballybeg, Taghmon) and John Byrne (probably from the Horetown area). Mogue Kearns was from Kiltealy in the Duffry while the other seven had a strong northern profile. Michael Murphy (Kilnew) and Nicholas Stafford (Ballyvoodock) were from neighbouring townlands in Blackwater parish; Thomas Dixon was from Castlebridge and Thomas Clinch from Oulartwick (Camolin). John Murphy was born at Tincurry (Ballycarney) and Philip Roche at Monasootagh (Boolevogue). Edward Synnott was probably born in the Oulart/Kilrush area. All seven of these had also served in northern parishes — Roche (Gorey), Ml. Murphy (Ballycanew), John Murphy (Boolevogue), Stafford (Riverchapel), Dixon (Blackwater), Synnott (Kilrush), Clinch (Killaveney). It was in these northern parishes that the United Irishmen penetrated soonest and most effectively. It is revealing that the rebel priests came disproportionately from the two areas most heavily infiltrated prior to '98 — the Blackwater/Castlebridge area (Dixon, Ml. Murphy, Stafford) and the Oulart/Boolevogue area (Roche, John Murphy, Clinch, Synnott). There is another minor axis in the Rathnure/Kiltealy area, associated with Kearns and Roche.

Their family background may also have influenced these men to become rebels. Thomas Clinch's grandfather had fought at the Battle of the Boyne before settling at Knockanure (Kilrush), whence the priest's family moved to Oulartwick; his cousins Michael and William Clinch were involved in the United Irishmen in the Kilrush area, with Michael being the local captain.[67] A mentally retarded nephew of Clinch's was murdered by the yeomanry at Scarawalsh in the week before the rebellion — an incident which may have precipitated his involvement.[68] Mogue Kearns' family were small farmers on the upper slopes of the Blackstairs mountains at Kiltealy and his mother was related to the Kellys of Killann, whose son John was a major catalyst in the spread of the United Irishmen in that area.[69] Mogue's two brothers (Martin and Patrick) and his four cousins (Michael, Mogue, Roger and Stephen Kearns of Ballychrystal) were all active rebels. John Murphy's father, Thomas, farmed seventy acres at Tincurry and was also involved in bacon-curing in Enniscorthy.[70] Tincurry townland in 1776 had ten Protestant families (three Pipers, Ellard, Britton, Tatlock, Sparks, Hawkins, Webster, Kinch) and the Murphys were the only substantial Catholic presence.[71] John's brothers (Mogue and Patrick) fought throughout the campaign as did his cousin James Whitty of Tomgarrow.[72]

The family background of Thomas Dixon and Nicholas Stafford has already been commented upon. Michael Murphy came from a centrally placed family in Kilnew (Blackwater) which had many kinship connections in the east of the county. A sister was married to John Prendergast of Knottown, another sister was married to a Whelan of Ballymartin, his nephew, Nicholas Murphy, was a United Irish captain in Monaseed, his mother was related to the Roches of Garrylough. When the rebellion broke out, all these men fought, as well as Michael's two nephews in Ballinoulart (James and John), whom he personally collected on his way to Ballyorrill hill to join in the attack on Enniscorthy.[73] We knew little about the family background of the other priests: it is possible that Philip Roche (born Monasootagh) was related to the Roches of Garrylough, although this is never explicitly mentioned. An additional point must also be made: many of these priests were living close to their family homes, as was generally the case in eighteenth century Wexford. Tincurry was close to Boolevogue (John Murphy), Kilnew to Ballycanew (Ml. Murphy), Kiltealy and Oulartwick to Enniscorthy (Kearns, Clinch). This proximity would have facilitated close relationships with their families and accentuated the pressures on them to pursue the same paths as them. All of this has to be pieced together from evidence that is, at best, fragmentary; yet, this discussion allows us to make a number of generalisations. The rebel priests were drawn from families with close links to the United Irishmen, or who fought when the rebellion commenced (Clinch, the two Murphys, Kearns, Dixon, Synnott). All their families had a background of local prominence or prior status (John

Murphy, Stafford, Clinch) and were predominantly of farming stock with an occasional mercantile involvement (Dixon, John Murphy).

Once the rebellion started, a number of priests came to the fore. Most important of these was Fr John Murphy, who was closely involved in the initial sequence of events in Boolevogue. He was a close friend of Tom Donovan, the most prominent (and well connected) local United Irishman, who seems to have made the running in the early events at the Harrow.[74] Sympathy with his parishioners, family ties, friendship with United Irishmen, opposition to stern law-and-order measures, frustration in his ecclesiastical career — all these factors may have fed into his decision to participate in the Harrow flashpoint and the battle at Oulart Hill. With the leadership structures of the United Irishmen in disarray as a result of the arrests of Harvey, Colclough and Fitzgerald, Murphy found himself thrust into a position of leadership which he may not have wanted. His primary motives seem to have been defensive rather than offensive — thus, his well-known reluctance to fight outside county Wexford. For the crucial attack on Enniscorthy, another clerical leader joined the fray — Michael Murphy. Murphy was an unemployed priest, living in lodgings at Ballycanew, close to his brother's family at Ballinoulart.[75] He was hot-tempered and had a drink problem, for which reasons Caulfield refused to have him on the mission after his return from Bourdeaux. Murphy was publicly known to be involved with the United Irishmen in the spring of 1798 and was forced to go 'on the run' at the start of May, a month prior to the open outbreak of rebellion. As soon as it did, his lodgings in Ballycanew were raided and burned by the Camolin yeomanry and the man with whom he lodged, James Kenny, a tanner, was shot, indicating how well known both Murphy's and Kenny's sympathies were known locally.[76] On hearing of the victory at Oulart, Murphy returned to the Ballycanew area, mobilised the local young men (including his two nephews) and joined forces at Ballyorrill hill with John Murphy, prior to the attack on Enniscorthy.

From west of the Slaney, two more priests joined the rebel forces. Mogue Kearns, fond of both drink and fighting (according to Bishop Caulfield) with known links to the Defenders and a high local profile as a sportsman, was one.[77] He fought vigorously at the Battle of Enniscorthy, armed only with a whip, leading the Duffry men. From further south at Poulpeasty, Philip Roche had also immediately thrown in his lot with the rebels. Roche's probable involvement with the United Irishmen in the Gorey area may not have been severed by his transfer west. Despite his notorious drink problem, this larger than life figure eventually succeeded Bagenal Harvey as leader of the southern army, after the failure to win the Battle of Ross. Thomas Clinch also joined the rebels in Enniscorthy. Being a man of huge stature and flamboyant dress (wearing a crossbelt over his vestments and carrying a scimitar), he was a prominent figure on Vinegar Hill and actively engaged in the fighting.[78]

The other priests associated with the rebels seem to have been more in the nature of 'hangers-on'. John Keane, 'the blessed priest of Bannow' was mentally unhinged and had a serious drink problem.[79] His main contribution to the rebel cause was the liberal dispensing of holy water, scapulars and blessings as he made his way through the rebel camps, mounted on a pony 'led by two men, who cried out, in a loud voice "make way for the blessed priest of Bannow"'. Caulfield described him as an 'idiot' and 'a weak poor fool' and he escaped any repercussions after the rebellion because of his mental disability.[80] John Byrne was a Carmelite at Horetown in a convent which was petering out and he attended the rebel camps in the south of the county. Caulfield described him as 'a drinking, giddy man'.[81] Bryan Murphy, a shadowy figure, had become parish priest of Taghmon in 1789 but was deprived of it three years before the Rebellion by Caulfield, who describes him as a 'reptile'.[82] Little is known of his actual involvement in the events of the rebellion but he was accused by some of having issued the fatal order to burn Scullabogue barn.

The two clerical military leaders — John Murphy and Philip Roche — both displayed many weaknesses as commanders. However, they could command tremendous loyalty from their followers and inspired undisciplined, makeshift soldiers to fight with astonishing bravery and perseverance. Thomas Cloney, who fought alongside them, makes the following observation:

'Not like laymen, it is not only their relatives that avenge injuries inflicted on Catholic clergymen; the whole Catholic community feel insulted by any outrage committed on men who, in the hour of affliction and misery, console and relieve them, not only affording them the comforts of religion but dividing with the poor their scanty means, to assist, either in raising them from the bed of sickness or enabling their poor families to consign them to their tombs, with that decency which the poor Irishman considers one of the First of Duties'.[83]

In part, they drew also on the power vested in the sacerdotal aura: stories soon circulated of the priest's invulnerability to bullets, perhaps helped by the two Fr Murphy's willingness to show spent bullets in their hands to credulous followers.[84] Philip Roche provided written 'gospels' (scapulars containing a protective prayer) to his men as a safeguard against injury.[85] Even in death, the priest's power lived. After Michael Murphy's brutal treatment in Arklow, a rumour soon circulated that the priest's consecrated right hand had refused to burn despite the most intense efforts to get it to do so. The secular United Irish leaders resented the power of the priestleader. Edward Hay commented bitterly that they 'assumed the priestly character *when it suited them*' and acidly comments 'not one of the priests who took up arms . . . escaped a violent and sudden death, clearly indicating a providential fate'.[86] Cloney commented 'I never approved of seeing a clergyman in arms'.[87] Philip Roche's frequent drunkenness was a particular source of concern.

While these few men were definitely on the rebel side, the bulk of the diocesan clergy remained strictly loyalist. For them, it was a trying time. The first priority was to protect their non-Catholic neighbours. One strategy was to take them (or their valuables) into their house. William Synnott, parish priest of Enniscorthy, did this with the aged rector of the town, Rev Joshua Nunn.[88] A second strategy was to baptise Protestants as Catholics, a service which was much in demand and which was performed by many of the priests

— Shallow (Adamstown), Cullen (Duncormick), Downes (Tintern), Doyle (Davidstown), Stafford (Lady's Island), O'Connor (Piercestown). In many cases, the priests were importuned to perform this service and did it under duress. Andrew Corish of Kilmore explained to a would-be Catholic 'Except for protection from the fanaticism of the ignorant multitude, the ceremony [is] useless'.[89] Others pretended they had performed the ceremony, so as to mislead their congregations; Fr Thomas Rogers (Cloughbawn) encouraged the belief in public that the local Protestants had converted and were going to mass, so as to ensure their safety.[90] Few priests had any scruples about issuing certificates stating that 'the bearer has done his duty' to protect Protestants from fanatical rebels. They also accommodated the Protestants at Mass — so much so that the 'grand gallery' in the Franciscan chapel in Wexford was packed with converts for Sunday Mass.[91] On request, priests made specific interventions. John Sutton and Michael Lacy went to Vinegar Hill at the behest of local Protestants to see if they could get members of their families released. John Shallow went to Scullabogue barn at the request of the Lett family on a similar rescue mission. Others, under coercion, went to the rebel camps, for example, James Doyle of Suttons parish.[92] He had received a threatening letter on 14 June from Philip Roche at neighbouring Lacken Hill camp, who promised to ravage Suttons parish if Doyle did not lead the men from that parish to the Lacken camp forthwith. The reluctance of south Wexford to become involved was a major feature of the events of that year: in most respects, the rebellion was a north Wexford phenomenon.[93]

In Wexford town, the Franciscan friars, especially Lambert, Broe and Scallan, were very actively involved in trying to soften the acerbities of the rebel occupation of the town and, in particular, to counsel clemency for the prisoners.[94] Corrin, the parish priest, was very active in this regard — averting a massacre at the gaol, stopping the massacre on Wexford bridge in the dying days of the occupation, signing protections for the many refugees trapped in the town. This policy of protecting and comforting local Protestant families was strongest in south Wexford, where such families were a vulnerable minority. Edward Murphy, parish priest of Bannow, wrote protections which he pinned on the entrance gates of Protestant houses: he also wrote notes in French to at least one local Protestant family telling them 'to fear nothing'.[95]

The priest's response to the rebels was uniformly negative. Some admitted that they had lost their power as a result of their opposition to the rising. Edward Murphy in Bannow wrote during the Rebellion: 'The power is passing from all who do not go entirely with the people: the priest can now lead to evil but hardly to good'.[96] Mrs Brownrigg commented: 'The priests were all benevolence but, alas, they had no power: their influence had long ceased over the minds of the people'.[97] Some were afraid for their own safety. 'The priests of Enniscorthy, taking no part in the rebellion, were afraid to remain in the town'.[98] John Redmond of Camolin, identified as an 'orange priest' because of his public opposition to the rebels, was in constant hiding in Protestant houses during the course of the rebellion.[99] His parish priest, Frank Kavanagh had to flee Gorey for similar reasons.[100] James Doyle, parish priest of Davidstown, expressed his hopes during the rebellion that an army would be sent over from England to defeat the rebels. while admitting 'I have lost my influence with the people'.[101] Their descriptions of the rebels was uniformly hostile: 'a drunken and infuriated rabble (Franciscans in Wexford), 'traitors' (Rev Edan Murphy), 'I never will give one of them the rites of the church' (John Shallow), 'An armed and inebriated rabble', 'a newly-armed horde of slaves', 'insolent, violent and cruel' (Veritas).[102] They were also horrified at the activities of the rebel priests, lacerated in one of their polemical tracts as 'excommunicated priests, drunken and profligate couple-beggars, the very faeces of the church'.[103] The Wexford Franciscans stated 'we hold in abhorrence the conduct of the few misguided clergymen who joined the rebels'.[104] Bishop Caulfield described them as 'renegade, abandoned, reprobate priests who perverted their ministry by joining the Rebellion'.[105]

The rebel's perception of the priests who opposed them was equally bitter. One leader, when handed a protection written by James Doyle and Miles O'Connor, jabbed his sword in it, saying 'why should such fellows as Mr Doyle and Mr O'Connor meddle with the business then going on, as they are known to be averse to it'?[106] John Shallow, after refusing to hear a rebel's confession, was told 'Hell would be his bed, he was worse than any Orangeman and he would pay for it'.[107] Frank Kavanagh considered himself as having been 'publicly and repeatedly threatened by the rebels'.[108] In the aftermath of the rebellion, John Sutton, curate in Enniscorthy, was the sole witness against Patrick Beaghan for the murder of Rev Samuel Heydon.[109] On Sutton's word, Beaghan was convicted and executed. According to family tradition, the public animosity to the family was subsequently so great that no one else of the name Sutton ever again became a priest in county Wexford.[110]

The aftermath of the rebellion saw severe harassment of Catholic clergymen in north Wexford. John Redmond, whose loyalty was impeccable, was summoned by Mountnorris to Gorey, went there unsuspectingly, where immediately 'he was treated as if manifestly guilty before trial, knocked down in the street and rudely dragged by some Yeomen'.[111] After the most perfunctory courtmartial, he was hanged on Gorey Hill on 22 June and Mountnorris himself, according to Miles Byrne, fired a brace of bullets through his dead body.[112] Bishop Caulfield reported that even Mountnorris's own Protestant servant considered him a totally innocent man, whose 'crime' was to be present at Camolin Park in an effort to prevent the rebels looting it.[113] He was a blameless victim of Mountnorris's personal fury at what must have seemed to him a bitter personal betrayal by the Catholics of his area, led by their priests. Similarly, James Dixon fell victim to his family connections when he was arrested at Milford (Wales) where he had gone after the rebellion with the local landlord family, the Le Hunte's of Artramont.[114] At his subsequent courtmartial in Waterford, it was alleged that he was present at various battles in north Wexford, but it is certain that he was confused with his prominent brothers, Nicholas and Thomas. Thomas's notoriety tainted his brother, who was initially sentenced to death, which was then commuted to transportation and he was shipped off to Botany Bay. A number of priests were courtmartialled for their alleged involvement with the rebels. Edward Redmond (P.P. of Ferns) was tried in April, 1799 in Enniscorthy on a charge of having led his parishioners to the Battle of Bunclody but was acquitted.[115] Michael Lacy (P.P. of Kilmuckridge) was arrested by General Needham, courtmartialled at Oulart and acquitted on a charge of having been present at Vinegar Hill, when he proved that he went there only at local Protestant's requests.[116] James Doyle (P.P. of Suttons parish) was acquitted of a courtmartial charge of having been present at the rebel camp on Lacken Hill when he produced the threatening letter sent to him by Philip Roche.[117]

Others were physically harrassed in a protracted campaign of intimidation which lasted until 1801. Their family links to the United Irishmen and the conspicious role of a few priest leaders made them a visible and emotive target for the Protestant backlash. Rev William Ryan, who lived at Cooladangan on the Wexford-Wicklow border, was murdered on the night of 14 December, 1798, supposedly by a contingent of the Castletown Yeomanry.[118] In June 1799, Frank Kavanagh and his curate John Barry were visited by a drunken party of the Gorey Yeomanry. Kavanagh managed to slip out but Barry and his servants were badly beaten and cut with swords.[119] Patrick Cogley (P.P. of Monagear) was accosted while on a sick call in October, 1799 by two local Protestants and struck over the head with a large stone.[120] Also in 1799, Fr Nicholas Redmond (P.P. of Ballygarrett) was visited by the local yeomany: he escaped but his niece and housekeeper were murdered.[121] In the winter of that year, John Corrin had the windows of his house repeatedly smashed in Wexford town.[122] In December 1800, Edward Newport (curate in Castlebridge) was visited by a party of the local yeomanry at his house in Ardcavan and was forced to flee. While sleeping rough in a nearby thicket, he contracted a fatal chill from which he died in February, 1801.[123]

All of this was taking place against a background of protracted chapel burning in north Wexford.[124] Thirty-two of the total of 63 chapels burned in the country as a whole were situated in north Wexford — 50 per cent of the total. The best insight into this troubled and little commented on period after the rebellion is the detailed correspondence of Bishops Caulfield and Troy.[125] Their letters vividly evoke the inflamed sensibilities, bitter animosities, fears and uncertainties of that time. Propertied and influential Catholics kept their heads down, as a welter of accusations reverberated in hard-line Protestant circles. The Catholic clergy were literally in the firing line, with a concerted effort being made to banish them from north Wexford, a campaign which was partially successful for a period. The campaign was conducted by the rank and file yeomanry, especially the poor Protestants, with the connivance (at least) of their leaders and the support of the bigots Ogle, Boyd and Wilson. The voice of liberal Protestantism was muted. As a result, the clergy suffered badly. The devastating impact of the rebellion in the county is seen in the very low figures given for the value of Catholic parishes there in 1800 — an average valuation of only £30.[126] Many priests were simply forced out of their parishes through continued intimidation. These included John Synnott (Gorey), Patrick Cogley (Monagear), Nicholas Synnott (Oulart), Mark Barry (Kilrush),

John Barry (Camolin), Michael Lacy (Kilmuckridge), Frank Kavanagh (Camolin), Patrick Stafford (Kilanerin), John Cooney (Kilmuckridge), Edward Redmond (Ferns), Nicholas Redmond (Donoughmore), and Francis Fitzgerald (Carnew). Bishop Caulfield observes 'I could hardly get a priest to venture to the Mackamores, to the neighbourhood of Gorey or Camolin, so much afraid are they of the yeomanry of them parts'.[127] The pressure was especially fierce on those associated with the rebels. Bryan Murphy in Taghmon suffered a nervous breakdown.[128] Nicholas Stafford was hunted out of Riverchapel and forced to live the rest of his life quietly at home at Ballyvoodock. John Byrne, the Carmelite, suffered an excruciating death when visiting Waddy at Clougheast Castle. Waddy, believing that the priest was about to attack him, lowered the portcullis which fell on the priest, pinning him to the ground, where he was left to die.[129] For one clergyman, the pressure was too extreme. William Synnott of Enniscorthy resigned his parish in the aftermath of the rebellion and retired to Wexford town.[130]

Conditions only gradually stabilised in the north of the county, when local magistrates began to curb the activities of the night raiders and to guarantee the safety of the priests. Patrick Cogley, for example, only returned to Monagear once he had his guns restored to him and had a guarantee of protection.[131] A clampdown on the chapel burning and a more impartial attitude to law enforcement quietened the area and things gradually reverted to normality. Even in the worst times, some Protestants had stood by Catholic priests. Jonas King of Barrystown, the most influential landlord in Bannow parish, exerted himself to extricate the parish priest, Edward Murphy, from various charges levelled against him.[132] The Le Huntes of Artramont interceded on James Dixon's behalf. The local Protestant clergyman, William Sutton, testified that Bernard Downe's behaviour as parish priest of Tintern was 'exemplary, irreproachable and loyal'.[133] John Shallow and John Corrin had no difficulty in getting local Protestants to vouch for their good behaviour and Corrin was held in great affection by Wexford town Protestants for his good offices in the Rebellion.

The complex patterns of response by the Catholic clergy in the rebellion of 1798 in county Wexford were cast in the shadows by the penumbra of the 'patriot-priest' in the nineteenth and early twentieth centuries. This detailed investigation has attempted to place the priests in the context of their times, to make them and their motivations more real and human and to illustrate the multi-layered complexities of Wexford society in the late eighteenth century. It is a fragmentary portrait, cobbled together from the most unpromising of materials — scattered, patchy, enigmatic. It does, however, in conjunction with other pioneering investigations, help to make more understandable this crucial episode in the history of the county.

Acknowledgement

I would like to thank Larry and Molly Mythen, Fr Lory Kehoe, Louis Cullen and Monsignor Patrick Corish for help with this paper.

Appendix I: The Catholic Clergy of County Wexford in 1798

Diocese of Ferns

Enniscorthy	William Synnott, John Sutton
Ballindaggin	Miles O'Connor
Bree	Mark Devereux
Cloughbawn	Thomas Rogers, Philip Roche
Davidstown	James Doyle
Ferns	Edward Redmond, Miles O'Connor
Kilrush	Edan Murphy, Mark Barry
Monagear	Patrick Cogley, John Murphy
Bunclody	Edward Cullen, James Stafford
Oylegate	Francis Lacy
Oulart	Nicholas Synnott
New Ross	William Chapman, Edward O'Flaherty
Adamstown	John Shallow
Cushinstown	Patrick Doyle
Templetown	Robert Barron
Suttons Parish	James Doyle, James Murphy (?)
Tintern	Bernard Downes, Peter Doyle
Wexford	John Corrin, James Roche, Philip Stafford, James Caulfield (Bishop)
Mayglass	Aidan Ennis, Laurence Comerford
Bannow	Edward Murphy
Blackwater	David Cullen, Thomas Dixon
Castlebridge	Michael Redmond, James Dixon, Edward Newport
Crossabeg	Redmond Roche
Glynn	Peter Devereux
Kilmore	Andrew Corish, ? Whitty (?)
Ladys Island	Mun Stafford, Thomas Browne
Piercestown	Roderic O'Connor, Patrick O'Toole
Rathangan	James Cullen (Collins), Patrick Codd (?)
Taghmon	Bryan Murphy (Suspended), Denis Kelly, Denis Ryan
Tagoat	Thomas Carroll, Mark Cooney (?)
Gorey	John Synnott, Patrick Stafford, D. Murphy
Tomacork	Francis Fitzgerald
Annacurra	James Brennan
Ballyoughter	Frank Kavanagh, John Redmond, John Barry
Ballygarrett	Nicholas Redmond, Nicholas Stafford
Kilmuckridge	Michael Lacy, John Cooney

Unemployed or Suspended:
Mogue Kearns, ? Carton, Thomas Clinch, Michael Murphy, John Keane, ? Hendrick.

Augustinians	J. C. Butler, William Doyle, Joseph Rosseter, John Crane.
Franciscans	Patrick Lambert, Thomas Scallan, Patrick Petitt, Mathias Colfer, Richard Synnott, John Broe.
Carmelites	John Byrne, ? Reville

Diocese of Kildare and Leighlin

Clonegal	James Purcell.

Archdiocese of Dublin

Castletown	William Ryan (Curate).

Appendix II

The following letter from Bishop James Caulfield to Archbishop Troy of Dublin (dated 2 September 1798) gives the most detailed listing of the rebel priests of 1798. It was given by Troy to Plowden, who used it in his book. The original does not now appear to be extant.

1. Thomas Dixon of Castle-bridge, had been curate at the Lady's Island for some years; but for drinking, dancing, and disorderly conduct, was suspended about four years ago. After some time of apparent amendment, he was sent to assist Rev. David Cullen of Blackwater, where he relapsed into his former pranks, and was suspected latterly of being active in the accursed business of *uniting,* for which I interdicted and suspended him above twelve months ago. He was afterwards apprehended, tried, and convicted here, and sent on board the tender lying at Duncannon Fort, where he took a fever and died.

2. Rev. Thomas Clinch, native of Camolin, had been appointed curate to Rev. Thomas Rogers in Bantry; but turning out a most beastly drunkard and unfit for duty, was suspended about two years ago, and remained so. He joined the rebels, and was killed in their retreat from Vinegar Hill.

3. Rev. Mogue Kearin or Kearns of the Duffry had been employed by Doctor Delany for some time, but latterly dismissed. He was notorious for drinking and fighting; and joined the rebels, among whom he made a gigantic figure, and was hanged at Edenderry.

4. Rev. John Murphy, curate to Rev. Patt Cogly of Boolyvogue, ever giddy, but not noted for immortality, was the first to commence the rebellion and became a signal general in it. He had been apparently but not really dutiful to his superior. He was whipped, hanged, beheaded, and his body burnt in the county Carlow, at Tullow.

5. Rev. Philip Roche, alias General Roache, had been curate to Rev. John Synnott of Gorey; had been a proper man and would be useful, but indulging in excess of drinking, and beginning to agitate, he became obnixious and was removed. He was afterwards sent curate, after reprehension, admonition, and instruction by his superior, to Rev. Thomas Rogers in Bantry, the other extremity of the diocese, last winter: I heard nothing remarkable of him there, till he joined the rebels and soon became a leader. He was hanged here and his body thrown into the river the 22nd of June.

6. There is another reptile, Rev. Bryan Murphy, who was very active in the rebellion. He had been *deprived* and suspended about three years ago. Nevertheless he had address enough to procure a protection when the rebels were routed, and remains undisturbed.

7. There is a Rev. Mr. Byrne, a Carmelite, at Goff's Bridge, who shewed himself a very zealous, active rebel. He also got a protection. He was a drinking, giddy man. I advised him to quit the diocese and threatened suspension.

8. Rev. John Keane, under censures the greater part of his life for drunkenness and other irregularities. He is a weak poor fool. He has not been questioned, nor is he worth notice.

9. Rev. John Redmond, curate of Rev. Francis Kavanagh, a most regular, attentive, zealous priest, without reproach ever until the accursed rebellion; whether he joined them through terror, as was the case with some, or volunteer'd, I know not. He surprized me more than all the rest. He was hanged near Gorey on the 21st or 22nd of June last.

12 *Sean Cloney*

The Cloney Families of County Wexford

The name Cloney, which has been found to occur with greatest frequency in counties Carlow and Wexford, is assumed to be of Gaelic origin.[1] The oldest recorded Cloney memorial in county Wexford is that to William Cloney in Rossdroit cemetery near Clonroche and is one of at least seven Cloney gravestones in close proximity to each other which indicates a family relationship between those named on them.[2] While some affinities are authenticated on the stones by use of such words as 'his son', 'his sister', 'his wife', in other cases the exact kinship has to be assumed on the evidence of known dates of births, perhaps used in conjunction with the deceased's place of residence. The inclusion of various people on the same memorial generally suggests that those named belonged to the same family.

Family tradition has held that Tominerly (a townland immediately west of Clonroche village) was 'where the Cloneys came from', so William, who was born in 1676, most likely lived there; he died aged 70 in 1746. There is no information as to whom he married but it is reasonable to assume that his marriage took place about 1699, because a son, James, later described as of Tominerly, was born in 1700 and would appear to have been the eldest, since other sons were to leave Tominerly soon after that period, to establish branches of the family in other districts of county Wexford.[3]

A memorial in St Mullins churchyard in county Carlow commemorates not only a Rev Laurence Cloney, P.P. of Graiguenamanagh for 49 years, but his brother, Thomas, of Ballycrogue, county Carlow and also a third brother, Matthew, who died at Harristown; they were aged 96, 99 and 90, respectively; all were born about 1700. Because of their longevity and the recurrence of these christian names among William Cloney's descendants, one is inclined to consider the possibility of a family connection. The further possibility is raised that, with a return to a less tense situation in the country following the Battle of the Boyne and Treaty of Limerick, William Cloney may have, in addition to his holdings in county Carlow, rented land near Clonroche, where he might even have found a wife, in addition to the land.

316

James Cloney of Tominerly married a Catherine Delany and died aged 94, when he was succeeded by his only son, John and two daughters; one, Margaret, married Martin Howlett; the other married a Bolger of Taghmon, whose daughter married a Raynard, also of Taghmon; but his son again, one James Raynard, was rather wayward in the opinion of contemporary Cloneys.[4] In 1780, Tominerly was held from the Carews by Joseph Martin Cullimore, a Quaker middleman, but was leased to James and John Cloney two years later; that family were probably sub-tenants of the Cullimores before then. In 1804, John was tenant of 54 acres 'for 3 lives' and was prosperous enough not to have fallen into arrears with his rent in 1821.[5] John married a Catherine Fizhenry and died in 1844, aged 90, leaving no son, so he was the last of the name in Tominerly. Under the terms of his will he bequeathed 'six great coats, six cloaks and twelve blankets to the most indigent and deserving poor in my neighbourhood'.[6]

His family comprised three daughters; the eldest, Mary, married a man named Rogers and remained in the home until her death in 1865; her sister, Margaret, married a Devereux and the third sister, Johanna, married her cousin, Garrett Cloney, of Old Ross.[7] Like the county Carlow Cloneys already mentioned, both John and his father, James, lived in excess of four score and ten years. Moneyhore, Old Ross, Blackhall and later Ballymoty, Dungulph and Lambstown were residences of the family during the seventeen and eighteen hundreds, with the graveyard at Whitechurch, Glynn, in addition to Rossdroit, becoming a family burial ground. The earliest date on a Cloney memorial in Whitechurch is 1777, erected to the memory of a Cohsty Cloney, née Kavenagh, who died then, aged 75. Her husband, (possibly William) was presumably a son of William Cloney of Tominerly. The original William's youngest son, a Thomas Cloney, together with his wife Anastasia, were the next to be buried in Whitechurch and it may be presumed that they lived at Blackhall (Glynn) where he died in 1794. Their eldest son, Thomas, born in 1752 married a Johanna Roche and definitely resided at Blackhall. The next succeeding generation saw a Laurence, who died in 1893, aged 82, at Blackhall, while his brother Martin, resided in Lambstown until his death in 1878, aged 74. Although Martin married Margaret Walsh, there is evidence that the male members emigrated to the New World; his son John, died in Toronto, Canada in 1923 aged 78 and his brother Thomas and sister Johanna also died in America. Martin's third brother was John, the owner of Blackhall. He died in 1878 aged 80, having earlier married a Mary Sinnott. They had a daughter, Catherine, who died in Ballyhogue and one son also named John, who married a Mary Hanlon. When only 42 years old, he died in 1888 leaving a son, again named John, (he died in 1903 aged 21) as well as three sisters, Catherine, Johanna and Mary. All three sisters married three brothers of the Butler family in the neighbourhood.

Apart from William's, the oldest Cloney tombstone in Rossdroit is that to Garrett (born in 1707) and to his wife Elizabeth.[8] Although the inscription does not give the place of residence, there can be little doubt that it was Moneyhore, where his son, Denis, born in 1738, succeeded him. As Elizabeth was only 18 when that son arrived and as she lived to be 60 years of age, no doubt other children followed but authenticating them is not easy. One girl married a Thomas Sinnott of Kilbride;[9] a boy, Martin, born 1729, married an Eleanor Pierce; another girl, Anne, born in 1737, later became a Mrs Summers.

There are a number of townlands named Kilbride in county Wexford but the evidence in Cloney's *Narrative* points to the one near Ballaghkeen, in Oulart parish, where the Synnotts were an important and long established family. James Synnott held a castle at Oulart in 1607 and the family had a Catholic chapel built there in 1753.[10]Nicholas Synnott was P.P. Oulart and Ballaghkeen (1766-1823) and lived at Kilbride.[11] The *Narrative* refers to this Thomas Synnott, at 60 years of age, leading 1,000 men, under fire, across the Slaney river above Enniscorthy, prior to the insurgent assault on that town.[12] Although playing a prominent part in the rebel victory at Enniscorthy, Thomas Synnott escaped the fate of many who played lesser roles during the rebellion; after the final defeat at Vinegar Hill, he was allowed to resume living at his home in Kilbride, mainly due to the good offices of influential Protestant friends. About a year and a half later, in December 1799, Thomas Cloney, having narrowly escaped transportation to New South Wales, was brought back to Wexford Jail from Geneva Barracks in county Waterford. He immediately sent word to Moneyhore that his sister should come to visit him. He directed her to convey letters to his counsel, Peter Burrowes, and other friends in Dublin and to Thomas Synnott at Kilbride. This indicates the confidence and trust in which he held his uncle by marriage. 'Mr Synnott on hearing her melancholy tale, lost no time in setting out for Dublin and on his way met General Grose who knew him, had his carriage stopped and came and walked some distance with him. ... The General kindly urged him to use all possible expedition in his journey and gave him such other advice as he deemed necessary for his guidance'.[13] Thomas Synnott of Kilbride appears to have been a prominent and respected figure before and after the rebellion, a significant achievement for a Catholic in that troubled period.

Among those elected freemen of Enniscorthy in 1754 were 'Garot (sic), Thomas, Denis, and Mat Cloney' and there is a mention of a William Cloney 'of Curnecody' (Courtnacuddy) in 1775.[14] Those obviously were men of influence to merit mention in the records of Enniscorthy; although some could have a father-son or uncle-nephew relationship, the indications are that Garret, Denis and Martin belonged to Moneyhore and Thomas to Blackhall.

For two centuries after the time of Sir Thomas Colclough (1564-1624), his descendants played a leading role in the affairs of Enniscorthy, as well as in a large area of northwest Wexford, stretching to the Blackstairs mountains. Like their neighbouring landed family in that area, the Carews of Castleboro, the Colcloughs were noted for their liberality and tolerance.[15] It is not surprising, therefore, that a certain concordance of purpose and close friendship developed between them and the Cloneys of Moneyhore, who could be described as middlemen, leasing about 300 acres in four farms from the Phaires.[16] During the 1700s, the Colcloughs owned and controlled the borough of Enniscorthy; Caesar Colclough was portreeve of the town for an unbroken period of 43 years until his death in 1766.[17] By having their friends such as members of the Cloney family elected freemen, the Colcloughs secured a base on which they could rely for support. By giving that support, the Cloneys in turn would have had their own standing in the county considerably enhanced. This strong solidarity between the two families from the barony of Bantry continued well into the nineteenth century. The young men probably shared common aspirations for a new political arrangement in Ireland, un-fettered by the devious machinations of the Dublin Castle establishment. It was in such a political atmosphere that the young Duffry Hall Colcloughs, the scion of the Moneyhore Cloneys and the last of the male Tintern Colcloughs were reared.

Very much smaller than the large mansions and extensive estates of the gentry, the Cloney leasehold in Moneyhore was a good example of a middle-man's situation in the mid-eighteenth century. The homestead comprised a solid, stone built house with slated roof and equally well constructed farm buildings, centrally located relative to the accompanying farm land, some of which would have been sub-let to small holders and cottiers, situated on the fringe of the holding. These people lived in small, mud-walled, thatched cabins, sometimes grouped together to form a type of scattered village, as at the crossroads of the Leap, near Moneyhore. Many of these small holders were accomplished in a wide variety of skills and their products were greatly in demand, not only by their neighbours, but also by the local middleman, who was their immediate landlord. Moneyhore was a centre of considerable importance since a fair was regularly held there on the fair green, which was situated within a quarter mile of the Cloney residence. A village developed in the vicinity of the green and the only public house in the parish was located in Moneyhore for the convenience of fair-goers. The last proprietors of that establishment were Thomas and Honoria Cloney; she was the last licensee and died in 1875.[18] No doubt a family relationship existed between their ancestors and those of Thomas Cloney but documentary evidence of that is not available.

Nearer the fringe of the Cloney property, the trade of blacksmith was carried on at the cross of the Leap for over two centuries by the family of Duggan; the last one of eleven generations, a Michael Duggan, died in September 1981. Cloney states that 'John Doogan, an ingenious smith and a very intelligent man' was a tenant of his father's (Denis Cloney).[19] The use of the words 'ingenious' and 'intelligent' indicate that Cloney held that particular man in high regard and it is significant that the cross and forge at the Leap were frequently referred to in Cloney's courtmartial. Was Duggan's forge a nerve centre of the United Irishmen's organisation? Forges were popular meeting-places and discussion centres up to recent times. Duggan's forge was located on an important cross-roads; it was on the property of a local middle-man, Cloney, who was an United Irishman. On Whit Tuesday, 1798 after the capture of Enniscorthy, the rebels, mostly from the barony of Bantry, assembled outside Duggan's forge on the cross of the Leap, before marching in a body to join their victorious comrades at Vinegar Hill.[20] John Duggan probably supplied weapons to at least some of the party. Earlier a galloping horseman had arrived from Enniscorthy shouting, 'Victory! Victory! Never were tidings more joyfully heard, nor eagerly listened to'.[21] It was the awaited signal to join the revolt. Some days later, on the 5th June in the early morning with the opening of the assault on the town of New Ross, Cloney tells us that two of his fathers tenants, Philip Lacy and John Duggan — 'approached me and put their arms about me with such feeling that they could scarcely speak and after an affectionate embrace they said, "you are now going into battle and we declare if you fall we shall not survive to carry home the sad tidings to your father and sisters". Well did those true-hearted Irishmen redeem their pledge, for they both fell at the Three Bullet Gate, through which we all entered the town'.[22] This passionate, almost feudal allegiance to their local leaders was a feature of the rebel's attitude in 1798. Obviously the 25 years old Thomas Cloney commanded great local prestige and loyalty.

Plate xxix: A typical forge scene at Evoys of Ballyshannon Lane

Denis Cloney at Moneyhore, probably returning to his grandfather's home district where he rented land, chose for wife a Mary Kavanagh, daughter of Felix Kavanagh and Catherine Furlong of Ballybeg, county Carlow. These Kavanaghs apparently were people of some consequence, since they had a strategically located family vault in St Mullins churchyard.[23] According to his son, Denis Cloney 'rented large tracts of land, both in the counties of Wexford and Carlow, a good part of which his father left him in possession of, and the remainder he acquired by industry, and altogether they would, if let, produce him an interest of several hundred pounds a year'.[24] An example of his methods can be cited. In 1791, he and John Hawkins, an Enniscorthy attorney, rented the lands of Mangan in Scarawalsh for £113: they sublet them for £207 to a host of undertenants, leaving a profit rent of £94.[25] Denis and Mary had one son, Thomas, born in 1774, and three daughters, Catherine[26] probably called after her maternal grandmother, then Helen, probably called after her maternal grandaunt, Helen Kavanagh, and a third to whom Cloney refers but is named neither there nor on any known tombstone.[27] Possibly she died soon after the 1798 Rebellion and may have been named Elizabeth, after her paternal grandmother. It appears that their mother, Mary, died aged 30 when Helen was born in 1782 but Denis lived to see his son, Thomas, take a leading part in the Rebellion in county Wexford during the summer of 1798. No doubt the distress and torment of seeing his only son and heir under real threat of execution for his treasonable activities hastened the old man's demise, which occurred in October of the same year.[28]

It is not intended to dwell here at great length on the military engagements in the life of Thomas, later known as 'General' Cloney of Moneyhore, as much information may be obtained from his *Personal Narrative of 1798*, the literary style of which reflects his education in Bristol, England. Socially the Moneyhore Cloneys were well connected and well regarded. Prior to the 1798 rebellion, Carew of Castleboro had assembled a large party of mounted farmers and middlemen, predominantly Catholic, on his spacious lawn, where they practiced drilling, with a view to forming a yeomanry unit. The Cloneys of Moneyhore were amongst them. Carew, because of his liberal leanings and the suspect composition of his corps, was refused permission to form the unit.[29] The Cloneys had also close political ties to the Colcloughs and worked with them on election campaigns. As well, the Cloneys mingled socially and in the hunt with local Protestants and landed families, like the Carews of Castleboro. They even loaned money to their head landlords, the Phaires. Even more so, the Cloneys had close ties to other middleman Catholic families in their area — the Furlongs of Templescoby, the Sweetmans of Newbawn, the Downes's of Adamstown, the Kellys of Killann, the Carthys of Birchgrove and the Devereuxs of the Leap. The leadership of the United Irishmen was drawn from these prominent Catholic families. Tom Cloney used his kinship and social connections to form a chain linking the various United Irish cells together: for example, his uncle by marriage, Tom Synnott of Kilbride was a United Irishman across the Slaney in the Oulart area. Other possible United Irishman relatives were the Cloneys near Glynn and Old Ross, Michael Doyle of Arnestown, Quigley of Donard and Kavanagh of Turra (St Mullins).

Thomas Cloney was well regarded by his Protestant neighbours, expecially the Whitneys, Carews, Letts and Robinsons, all of the Carew estate, but his standing in the eyes of the Kavanaghs of Borris is the most intriguing. Cloney's family held land in county Carlow from these Kavanaghs for many years and he gives the impression of having a strong attachment to the landlords of Borris. It seems quite reasonable to suppose that somewhere in the past there was a close blood relationship, which would also explain why so many of Cloney's friends, but especially his mother's relations, the Kavanaghs, were to be found among Mr Kavanagh's yeomen. 'It gives me no small degree of pain', wrote Cloney, 'to be one of this body which made the attack on the mansion of Mr Kavanagh' in the hope of obtaining badly-needed arms and ammunition after the Battle of Ross.[30] That enterprise ended in failure for the attackers and it is practically certain that, when the rebellion was crushed, Mr Kavanagh would have been given information that the attacking party was led by Cloney. A few years later, on 1 October 1803, Mr Kavanagh 'expressed his great unwillingness' to enforce a Government order which he had received to arrest Cloney and he said that 'if there were any possible means by which it could be avoided, it would give him great pleasure to adopt such'.[31] A year later, Kavanagh used his very considerable influence with Lord Clifden and also with the Government to have Cloney released from prison, where he had been confined under conditions of unnecessary severity. In addition, Kavanagh offered £5,000 bail for the prisoners 'peaceable and good conduct' should he be granted his liberty. Kavanagh of Borris was generous to an extraordinary degree to a rebel who had led an armed assault on his mansion home a few years previously; some definite measure of kinship between them would provide the possible reason for that generosity.

Because of the uncertainties which the future held for him, Tom Cloney denied any involvement with Robert Emmet in hatching conspiratorial plans for another rebellion in the first years of the nineteenth century but the truth, in all probability, was otherwise.[32] There is a marked reticence on the part of Cloney concerning his involvement with the activities of Emmet and his ill fated insurrection of July 1803. He mentions certain comings and goings by Henry Hughes of Ballytrent to the home of a relative, Quigley of Donard, over that particular weekend when the revolt occurred in Dublin. Although Cloney admits to being in Quigley's house with Hughes, the *Narrative* merely states that they were all on 'business'. Myles Byrne states that, after the '98 leaders' return from exile in England, which took place in February 1803, he resided in Dublin and soon afterwards he attended a dinner party in George Nowlan's Hotel in Maynooth given by a Mr Butler of Wexford, at which Cloney was the guest of honour.[33] Before the celebrations ended, a meeting was arranged by Byrne between Cloney and Emmet, which took place at the green at Harold's Cross the following evening. The account described Emmet as 'slight and under the middle size; Cloney almost gigantic, being six feet three or four inches tall and well proportioned'.[34]

The subsequent pattern of events is revealing. Cloney continued to reside in Dublin until he departed for Graiguenamanagh on 21 July 1803; he spent the 22nd in the vicinity of Borris and was at Quigleys of Donard (2 miles east of Ballywilliam) on the 23rd, the day of Emmet's Rising in Dublin. Henry Hughes arrived at Donard on the 24th and a messenger arrived there with the news of the Dublin events on the 25th.[35] Cloney was arrested and brought before the Attorney General about the 1st October following and committed to the tower of Dublin Castle. Then at the end of February 1804 he was transferred to Kilmainham Jail before being released on medical grounds following the intervention of Kavanagh of Borris about the 1st November 1804. One is left to conclude that the Government believed Cloney to be deeply involved in a treasonable conspiracy with Emmet and only failed to prosecute for lack of evidence. Byrne quotes Cloney as saying after his meeting with Emmet, 'I have heard a great deal about that young gentleman's talents, but certainly he far surpasses anything one can imagine'.[36] The agreed plan was that the various counties would rise in revolt when the metropolis, Dublin, was 'in the hands of the people'. It is against this background that the meeting of Hughes, Quigley, Cloney and the messenger from Ross at the house in Donard should be viewed.

During the brief 1798 campaign, Thomas Cloney spent considerable time with his cousin, Martin Cloney, in Old Ross, during the first days of June, before the rebel attack on New Ross, which began on the 5th. The rebel army, after the capture of Wexford town, had reformed into two divisions, one of which moved towards the north of the county, while the other made its camp on one of the county's most distinctive landmarks, the twin-peaked Hill of Carrickbyrne, three miles east of Old Ross. The objective was the capture of New Ross and the opening up of the country across the River Barrow. It was at this stage of the campaign that Cloney is said to have sketched out a plan of attack to take the town, using the kitchen dresser in Old Ross as a writing table.[37]

Before Cloney went into exile on 7 September 1801, he had spent a considerable period in prison, both before and after his courtmartial which began on 5 July 1799. Temporarily liberated to settle his affairs on 12 February 1801, he was beset by many problems regarding leases as well as difficulties in collecting monies due to him. He relinquished his interest in the lands and other property which he and his family had held in Moneyhore from the Phaires. Prior to the '98 rebellion, good relations existed between the two families, well illustrated by the *Narrative* passage: 'My father was always an independent tenant and never refused to contribute to the accommodation of a needy landlord; both his purse and his name were frequently at Col Phaires service', but after the rebel defeat 'all ties of friendship,were now severed by party spirit, all obligations cancelled'.[38] Cloney's last meeting with Col Phaire was a heated one and it was apparent that the former rebel leader was no longer regarded as a suitable tenant of the Moneyhore leasehold, which then passed to the Keatings, a prominent middle-class Catholic family.[39]

The aftermath of the rebellion saw Cloney in some financial difficulties because of his complete inability to vigorously press for the payment of rents due to him, notwithstanding the fact that he was obliged to pay his own head rent to Phaire, who may also have defaulted on his loan repayments to Cloney. During his time in Liverpool where he spent his enforced exile, the rebel leader was permitted substantial freedom. He 'made excursions to some of the manufacturing towns of Lancashire and Chesire and attended some of the Chester meetings, which are generally very grand'.[40] Back home in Wexford, his grandmother and sisters obtained lodgings in the town of New Ross. Property held from Kavanagh of Borris provided his income for the remaining fifty years of his life.

His sisters both died when aged 35, Catherine in 1811 and Helen in 1817.

He states that he was sorely grieved by their deaths, but there is no evidence that he ever contemplated marriage.[41] Thomas Cloney devoted all his adult life to politics, beginning with his early association with the Colcloughs which persisted through the rebellion and its aftermath. Subsequent to his release from prison, he was actively involved with the Carews and the Tintern Colcloughs (John and Caesar) in various elections; he supported the Catholic Board, the new Catholic Association and the agitation for the repeal of the Tithe Laws. He was arrested along with Daniel O'Connell and six others in 1830 for campaigning for the repeal of the Union of Great Britain and Ireland.[42] Cloney was a great admirer and staunch supporter of John Colclough, 'a good private friend'[43] up to the fatal duel in 1807 when the pride of the Tintern branch fell mortally wounded at the hands of his fiancee's brother, William Alcock of Wilton. He was present at all stages of that tragic *affaire d'honneur*, from the incident when the challenge was thrown down to the bloody climax on the field at Ardcandrisk. Colclough's enemies galloped from the field 'with great expedition and unbounded exultation' while 'the remains of the lamented patriot were carried from the field and placed in a chaise [a light horse drawn carriage], seated as if living, with his friends, Mr Henry Colclough and Mr Thomas McCord at either side of the body'. Cloney then relates how he rode with Colclough's friends, some in carriages, others on horseback, towards Wexford and when approaching the town, he went

> 'up to the carriage in which my friend, Mr McCord was seated [he was Colclough's agent]. Not knowing that our departed friend was in the same carriage, I stooped to the window to ask Mr McCord what arrangements he proposed making about the funeral and other questions concerning the burial in Tintern and the giving of the necessary notice to the public of the county, with a view to ensuring a large turnout at the funeral. When Mr Henry Colclough [who was of the Duffry Hall branch and lived at Mount Sion, county Carlow] saw me stooped at the carriage window next which he sat, he conceived that I bowed as if taking leave of my lamented friend and he took the hat off the head of the deceased to return my salute. I cannot describe the sensation I felt at that moment. I could scarcely support myself in the saddle'.[44]

It is safe to assume that he must have been subjected to an agonising period when compiling the manuscript of his narrative, as he was obliged to be extremely cautious in everything he wrote; he was very well aware that he still had formidable enemies who had not forgotten '98. On completion of the manuscript, he was faced with the problem of attracting a sufficient number of subscribers to enable him to have it published. The list of subscribers makes an interesting catalogue of those with a liberal party viewpoint in the region about 1830. Many of those named were Cloney's Whig associates against the Tories in the various elections held in the first decades of the nineteenth century. Surprisingly there is no Colclough on the list; they were dead or scattered. Caesar of Tintern lived mainly in France or England after 1820 but there was a copy of the book in Tintern Abbey in the possession of the late Miss Biddulph Colclough who died in 1983. A limited edition was at last brought out by

James McMullen of Dublin in 1832. It is still regarded as a valuable work of reference for students of those troubled times. His continuing interest in improving the conditions under which so many of his fellow countrymen laboured ensured his active involvement in the politics of the first half of the nineteenth century. It is not surprising, therefore, that he worked actively with the Liberator, Daniel O'Connell, in the struggle for Catholic Emancipation.[45] O'Connell was a very astute politician and commanded support from a wide range of opinion in Ireland. While he championed constitutional means, he also saw merit in the veiled hint of a physical force tradition. The presence of the old '98 leader on a platform with him conveyed that message very clearly.

The death of O'Connell in 1847 and the onset of the Great Famine cast a dark cloud over the country but a fresh idealism fired the Young Irelanders in 1848, when three of the leaders, Thomas Francis Meagher, William Smith O'Brien, and John Blake Dillon visited Cloney at his residence, Whitehall, Graiguenamanagh, county Kilkenny. Meagher stated that they 'were carried by that gallant throng [the people of Graiguenamanagh] to the house of the venerable, dear old man, who still enjoys upon this earth the homage and the title won, in earliest manhood, beneath the insurgent flag of Ireland' and on meeting them, the old 'General' embraced O'Brien 'with all the fondness of a father and affectionately welcomed them all into his house'.[46] No doubt, advice was sought by the youthful party and generously given by the old warrior but the revolt a short time later at Ballingarry, county Tipperary, was a fiasco, with the leaders being afterwards transported or obliged to flee the country. The following year, 1849, Charles Gavan Duffy, having visited the old veteran at Whitehall, remarked that 'his heart was heavy; two failures such as he had shared (with a half a century between them) quenched the light of hope and perhaps life itself, which cannot exist without it'.[47] That light went out for Cloney on 22 February 1850 and he is buried with his mother and members of her family (the Kavanaghs) within the walls of what still remains of a monastic building in St Mullins. 'General' Cloney's remains have an honoured place. Every July on Pattern Sunday, his memory is perpetuated, not only by the people of St Mullins but by many others from much further afield, when an emblematic pike is placed on his grave and that of other '98 men in the cemetery.

The Cloneys of Old Ross

Yet another son of the before-mentioned William Cloney of Tominerly, Sylvester, was born in 1707 and subsequently married a Catherine Cullen. He became tenant of the farm and corn-mill at Millquarter, near Old Ross under a lease granted by 'Andrew Ram of Coolattin in the County of Wexford'.[48] The Cullens may possibly have been former tenants but either way Sylvester was the first Cloney to reside in Old Ross and work the corn-mill which existed there at that time.[49] He died at the age of 87 in 1796. Since the Cloney farm in Old Ross was not a very large holding (about 35 Irish or 60 statute acres) the principal income of the family was derived from the milling enterprise for which two streams were harnessed to provide water-power. For a considerable time during the first half of the nineteenth century, if not during an earlier period as well, the same water also powered a small woollen mill on the Cloney farm.[50] For generations, it was always referred to as the Factory, although it was a rather small building and probably did not employ more than two men in its operation. It could have been described as a carding mill, since the principal operation was the carding or combing of the wool fibres, rendering them suitable for spinning into thread. It is probable that the Cloney factory worked on a commission basis. When the sheep were sheared in summertime, the owner of the wool brought it to be washed, dried and carded, after which it would be brought home for the womenfolk to spin into thread on spinning wheels, which were to be found in many homes in those times.

A distinctive feature of the Old Ross district was its large colony of German Protestants from the Palatinate region, who were settled there by the Ram family, with such names as Hartrick, Hess, Harman, Jekyl, Horneck and Whitney.[51] The writer was often told by his uncle, Dean Thomas Cloney, that it was mainly due to the custom given to the Cloney mills by their predominantly Protestant neighbours in this colony that Sylvester and his descendants were enabled to successfully weather many financial crises and even to accumulate sufficient funds to educate many family members to the priesthood.

Plate xxx: The Old Ross dwelling house and mill

An 1818 lease of the mill farm to Martin Cloney of Millquarter states: 'that part occupied by Martin Cloney is by odds the worst part of that town-land, it being mostly a steep shingly brow [i.e. hillside] encompassed by a swampy bog, with a sandy bottom, such as not to admit of anything like permanent drainage. There is a very good corn mill on these premises with two pairs of stones and a constant supply of water. However, that business lately has been indifferent. The dwelling house is a tolerably good one. This man has drained a little, however, from the nature of the soil it cannot be permanent'.

In 1782, Martin Cloney's lease was for 32 acres, at a yearly rent of £ 30. In 1792, the farm, in consideration of the mill, was valued at the steep price of £ 2 per acre, which reflected the tillage boom of the Napoleonic era.[52] The mill always artificially inflated the rent of the farm.[53]

In spite of imputations that Thomas Cloney was implicated in the burning of Old Ross Church during the '98 Rebellion,[54] the most cordial and warmest relations always existed between the Old Ross Cloneys and the descendants of their Palatine Protestant neighbours.[55] Old Ross is in the R. C. Parish of Cushinstown and the baptismal and marriage records of the parish church there give the names of a number of Cloneys but with little other information as to interfamily relationships or domicile until near the mid-nineteenth century.[56] A study of those records, while not providing absolute proof, never-theless gives a good indication as to which generation the various named people would have belonged. Sylvester's son, Martin, presumably the eldest, was born in 1758 and succeeded to Old Ross on his fathers death in 1796, if not before, while there appears to have been five daughters. Catherine married Thomas Cummins, Johanna married Daniel Murphy, Elizabeth married James Fitzhenry, Mary married John Roche and Anastasia probably remained a spinster. A second son, John, married a Mary Kavanagh; they had, as far as can be deduced, two sons, Patrick, born 1778 and Garrett, born 1776. Nothing further is known about this Patrick; he may have died young, but Garrett had a son, Denis, in Ballymoty (4-5 miles east of Enniscorthy), who having married an Allice (sic) Murphy, died in 1897, apparently without issue. The above mentioned Martin Cloney of Old Ross married Bridget Neville of Ballinaboola in 1785. The Nevilles, who held about 150 acres (much of it part of the Bog of Ballinaboola) were next door neighbours of the Cloneys.[57]

Immediately after the Battle of Ross in 1798, Martin gave shelter and a bed to his cousin Thomas.[58] Martin's situation in the aftermath of that Rebellion must have been rather delicate, since his relationship to and possible sympathy with the rebel leader was well known to his Palatine neighbours. Aggravating the prevailing tensions would have been the knowledge that Old Ross was the only Protestant church burned during that strife-torn period; of even greater moment was the terrible atrocity at nearby Scullabogue Barn, where so many innocent Protestant prisoners were burned to death.[59]

As 'the only propertied Catholic living in the Old Ross area',[60] Martin Cloney must have played a very significant part in the reduction of tension and the re-establishment of trust and good neighbourly relations with the many

Palatine families among whom he lived and whose corn he ground and whose wool he processed, until his death in 1832, aged 74. Bridget, his widow, died in 1839, aged 84, having had a family of five sons and a daughter, Catherine. In 1813, one son Michael, married Mary Phelan; another Matthew, married Maria Browner in 1803.[61] John married Honora Harrington in 1804; she bore him three children, Patrick, Eleanor and Joany but he later married a Bridget Harrington, who bore him two further daughters, Johanna and Anne. Honora and Bridget were probably sisters and all his children were born between 1805 and 1825. This recurrent pattern of marrying sisters implies a closely supervised family marriage strategy.

Thomas, another of Martin's five sons, married Eleanor Devereux of Dungulph Castle in 1817.[62] Two of Eleanor's brothers had taken part in the battle of Ross in 1798 and were obliged to emigrate to America to escape execution or the lesser fate of transportation.[63] The parents, John and Mary, required a son-in-law with experience of the trade to manage their wind and water mills at Dungulph; they may have arranged the match with Martin, the father of Thomas; such arrangements were quite common then and later. John Devereux and Martin Cloney were both millers, would have regarded themselves as middlemen, had a history of family participation in 1798, had similar political inclinations and were probably well known to each other for many years. Devereux of Dungulph, an Irish speaker, was known locally as Seán Rua Devereux (Red John Devereux). In his role as middleman he held the farm of Kinnagh (immediately south of Ballycullane) which had been in the hands of the Devereux family for centuries.[64] He also held the farm of Ballinruane and had succeeded the Lynne family in Dungulph around 1780.[65] Although he was a Catholic he was on the vestry committee of Fethard church in 1792. Bishop Devereux had granted the townland of Battlestown to his relative Stephen Devereux in 1522.[66] Like the Devereuxs of Dungulph, the Battlestown Devereuxs were implicated in 1798.[67] Cloney refers to John Devereux of Sheilbeggan, probably another relative, who was subsequently transported to Botany Bay.[68]

Dungulph Castle and well over 400 acres had been the property of the Whittys of Ballyteigue (near Kilmore) but it was granted to the Loftus family in 1666; it was the residence of Henry Loftus until he moved to Redmond Hall, later known as Loftus Hall, in the later 1670s.[69] There was a church and small graveyard just south of the castle and a little further on towards Poulfur is a disused water-mill, one of two in the townland. The other is quite close to the castle and northwest of it, while at a similar distance northeast of the castle is the site of a windmill. On the 1840 Ordnance Survey map, this last water-mill is referred to as a 'flour mill' so one can assume that it was employed to grind wheat and probably Indian corn (maize) into flour for bread. The windmill would have been used to grind oats, barley and possibly beans into meal for animal feed. Almost certainly one of the mills would also have carried on the process known as 'shelling oats', in other words making oatmeal (for porridge), the production of which only ceased at Dungulph water-mill in the early 1950s. In Seán Rua's time, that mill was a square stone building with

Plate xxxi: Dungulph Castle, c.1840

two lofts and a ground floor, built where the side of the valley sloped steeply. It contained two pairs of mill-stones, which would have been quarried and fashioned locally in the Hook at Harrylock. A few yards from the mill was a separate mud-walled, thatched building which housed the kiln for drying the grain, preparatory to the manufacture of either flour or oatmeal. Local tradition relates that after the Battle of Ross, a party of military from Duncannon Fort sought two sons of Seán Rua at Dungulph, but not finding them, the soldiers burned the castle and also set fire to the mill before leaving. However, thanks to the convenient and plentiful supply of water in the mill-pond and the assistance of neighbours, the mill was saved, having suffered no serious damage. The windmill apparently was a substantial stone and mortar building and, being of a similar diameter, may have looked like the one still in existence at Tacumshane. The Dungulph windmill was razed at the turn of the present century and the stones utilised in the erection of farm buildings in 1904. Both mills near the castle were probably built in the second half of the eighteenth century and it was said locally that the water mill at one time served as a flax mill. The mill near Poulfur may be on the site of an older mill, as its mill race appears the more ancient of the two. There would have been little iron in any of those old mills; all the shafts, wheels, even the cogs, were usually fashioned from timber, likewise the water-wheels and the arms and sails of the windmills. They presented quite a fire hazard, more particularly if roofed with thatch, as many of them were.

Thomas Cloney and Eleanor Devereux had a family of nine children but not one grandchild. He died in 1869 aged 81, she in 1838 aged 40; both, together with some of their children, were buried with other branches of the Cloney family in Whitechurch graveyard, Glynn. None of their sons married; Thomas and Patrick died in their twenties, John, assisted by his sister Mary, was the proprietor of a general store or shop in New Ross, which was sold when their brother, Garrett, who had taken over the Dungulph farm on the death of their father, died in 1888, aged 56.

Plate xxxii: The thatched kiln at Dungulph mill c.1900

In 1872 Garrett was shown on an Ely (Loftus) estate map as holding 117 acres plus a windmill which was given a valuation figure of £2 (the 1987 acreage is reckoned to be 115 acres).[70] Some of the old ledgers from John's New Ross shop survive and they provide much information on the type of business carried on there. A wide range of merchandise was supplied, groceries, seeds, manures, (fertilisers), tobacco, spirits and beer, note paper, rope, wines, candles, soap, meal and flour, in fact, the general requirements of most country people. In addition to those from Shelbourne barony which lies between New Ross and the Hook, his customers came from localities where Cloneys or their relations were to be found, such as Castle Hayestown, Galbally (Glynn parish) Tominerly, Horetown, Tottenham Green, Browns Castle (these last three in Taghmon district where the Fortunes, Bolgers and Browners were all family connections), Courtnacuddy, Poulpeasty, Old Ross and a sizeable surrounding district but scarcely anyone was on the books from Kilkenny or Carlow and comparatively few from the town of New Ross.

On retiring from business in New Ross, John managed the farming and milling enterprises in Dungulph until his death in 1896 aged 77. Another brother, Martin, was a miller but the Dungulph windmill became disused after his death in 1878 aged 58. The only remaining brother, Nicholas, was the last of the family to die, in 1910, aged 73, having spent very many years a patient in an institution. Two sisters married; Margaret became O'Callaghan of Castle Hayestown (northeast of Camross) and Bridget became Murphy of Kilbride (east of Duncannon). Both their husbands died and, being childless, both sold their farms and retired to Dungulph with the proceeds of the sales. Margaret and Bridget might have been past child bearing age when they married. The premise that the husbands lacked the courage to take the necessary initial biological step to start a family is at least worthy of consideration. It would, however, be an understatement to say that the sisters were prudes; nevertheless, they were not too unusual for what were considered 'nice, respectable, ladies'. While outwardly pious, these ladies could show a vicious streak when considering illegitimate relations who lowered the family tone, in their opinion (appendix).[71] It is understandable that Michael Cloney did not bring a wife into Dungulph until his three formidable cousins died. Bridget died in 1900 aged 79 and Margaret in 1909 aged 84. Their spinster sister, Mary died in 1907, also aged 84.

Apart from the daughter already noted, another child of Martin's was Garrett, who was probably the eldest son, since he succeeded his father in Old Ross. He married his cousin, Johanna Cloney of Tominerly, about 1826 in what, it is almost certain, was an arranged match made by the respective fathers, Martin and John. Garrett took an interest and played some part in the local politics of the district, activities which caused him to be involved with the political fortunes of Lambert of Carnagh.[72] The present corn mill, now operated by John T. Browne in Old Ross, was largely rebuilt and modernised in 1848 by Garrett, as stated on an inscribed stone to that effect placed in the mill wall.

The Old Ross corn mill worked, as did most other mills like it, on a commission basis. At harvest time, farmers large and small from the district brought their grain in sacks to the mill to be weighed aad ground into meal or flour. After weighing, wheat was first of all dried on the kiln and was usually then stored until such time as the owner required a bag of it to be ground into wheaten meal. The fuel for the kiln was culm. Culm was a common term for anthracite as mined, that is, lumps, large and small as well as slack or fine dust not screened or graded in any way. Culm was also the fuel used to burn limestone in the lime-kilns. Grain for animal feed, oats, barley, beans, was usually stored on the farm and was brought to the mill as required, more especially during the winter months. It ground finer and had improved keeping qualities if dried first but that added to the cost which the miller charged and was calculated at a rate per barrel (1 barrel wheat = 20 st or 280 lbs or 127.27 Kg). Accounts were due for settlement yearly at harvest time and the miller might impound grain in overdue cases. One pair of mill stones was usually reserved for the grinding of wheat, another pair for grinding animal feed (called 'cattle stuff' in olden days) and possibly a third pair for 'shelling oats', which meant the making or manufacture of oatmeal. That was the milling arrangement from the time the Old Ross mill was modernised by Garrett in the 1840s. An overshot water-wheel supplied the power to operate one pair of mill-stones but in time of flood the machinery was capable of operating two pairs at the same time. As already stated, the customer was charged at a certain rate per barrel for the grinding of his own corn and that charge would vary, depending on whether or not the grain was dried. The miller would devote his full time to the milling enterprise because, even in the slack milling season in summer, mill-stones required 'dressing' (the roughening of the grinding surfaces and the cutting of depressions called 'furrows' which delivered the ground meal from between the stones to the outside) and there was considerable maintenance work on the mill race and especially on the mill machinery, much of which was of timber. In the busy season, immediately after the corn was threshed in the harvest and also through the winter, a total of three men or two men and a youth worked in the mill/kiln complex. In Old Ross, the additional hands employed in the corn mill in the winter would have been needed in the woollen factory in the summertime, which was the busy season for that enterprise, while occasionally throughout the year there was work in the smithy and separate well-equipped carpenter's workshop, both of which still functioned in living memory.

Garrett's wife, Johanna, was a beneficiary under the will of her father, John Cloney of Tominerly, made on the 13 July 1839 and which stated that the testator had the life of 'General' Thomas Cloney insured with the British Commercial Insurance Co 'for £100, late Irish currency'.[73] Garrett's own will was dated 10 April 1856 and the executors named were John Cloney, his son, Richard Neville, probably a cousin[74] and Benjamin William K. Whitney, who was one of his Protestant neighbours. It is indicative of the harmonious relations which existed between the Cloneys and their friends of another religious persuasion in Old Ross that, although being an apparently staunch Catholic with two sons in the priesthood, Garrett saw fit to name Benjamin as one worthy to perform such a duty of confidence and trust. Garrett died about 1860 and although no memorial stone has been found, it is very probable that both he and his wife, Johanna, were buried with their common ancestors in Rossdroit cemetery; if so, they were the last of the family to be interred there, as all of their nine children lie elsewhere.

Three of Garrett's daughters married Hickeys of the Meylerspark (New Ross) family. Catherine married Patrick Hickey of New Ross in 1857;[75] she died in 1904 aged 73. Margaret married Patrick Hickey of Park[76] in 1860 and lived in Misterin (Adamstown): she died leaving a small family in 1870. Anne in 1858 married John Hickey of Park;[77] she died in 1913 aged 71. A fourth daughter, Bridget, married a man named Doyle; they made their home in New Ross, but he must have died rather young as little is known about him. Bridget, however, was well known as 'Aunt Biddy' to the older New Ross Hickeys and Butlers, as well as to their rural kinsfolk in the various branches of the Hickey and Cloney families. She died in 1904 aged 76.

The Hickeys, according to their family tradition, came from south Tipperary and the first one of them to reside in Meylerspark (Park) was Cornelius, who was born in 1700 and died in 1779. One son, Michael, established the family in New Ross when he married a Mary Freaney in 1792. Their son Patrick, who married Catherine Cloney of Old Ross, first set up a small woollen factory and shop in Mary Street, near the junction with Brogue Lane, before later establishing an up-to-date woollen mill in Poulmounty; the shop was afterwards transferred to South Street. Farmers from west Wexford and from the neighbouring parts of two adjoining counties sold the wool fresh from the sheep to Hickey in New Ross. It was then weighed before being brought to Poulmounty, where it was washed, dried and put through a fulling mill which cleans and pounds it. (Fulling is a process which alters the texture of the wool fibres, resulting in a better cloth when the thread is woven). As well as spinning the wool into thread, it was also combed or carded and dyed to various colours before being woven into blankets and rugs to be sold in Hickey's shop in Ross and elsewhere in other shops all over the country. Poulmonty Mills also produced worsted cloth, which is a smooth product and in the manufacture of which only long wool fibres were used; it is the type of wool cloth used for suiting; in fact, men's suits of Hickey's blue serge were very popular for many years. Another son of Cornelius was Patrick, whose son again was Michael; he married a Catherine Barron (from Campile) in the early 1820s. They had eight children, three of whom, Patrick, John and Johanna married three Cloneys from Old Ross, Margaret, Anne and John, (a fourth Cloney, Catherine, a sister of the last three, was, as already stated, married to Patrick Hickey of Ross.) Little wonder that the Hickeys and Cloneys were said to be 'all the one'. The Hickey farm in Park was about 125 acres, so each family would consider the other as suitable when the time came to marry off children. These marriages would have obviously created very close kinship ties and was part of an elaborate marriage strategy which paired like with socio-economic like in careful 'matches'.

In its early days, Poulmounty woollen mill was powered by a waterwheel but in the twentieth century that was replaced by a water-turbine. An oil engine was also installed to provide power in summertime when water was scarce. The mill produced herring-bone twill and during the Emergency (World War II 1939-'45) cloth was produced for Irish Army uniforms. About thirty men were employed and the workforce absorbed many generations of numerous local families e.g. two of Irwin, three of Gladney, two of Roche and others represented were Murphy, Kehoe, Gahan, McCauley and Ralph. Due to the effects of foreign competition by large continental firms following on Irish entry into the E.E.C., Poulmounty Mills closed down about 1973. Before moving to Poulmounty, there was a Hickey woollen mill in the Maudlins, one mile east of New Ross.[78]

Two of Garrett's sons became priests; one, Sylvester, died P.P. of Castlebridge, the other, Thomas, died P.P. of Tagoat in 1895, aged 57.[79] In April 1886 he attended the last prisoner to be publicly hanged outside the old Wexford jail, now the county hall, when prison chaplain.[80] Two other sons died in the New World; one was Martin, who first of all went to the United States, where he frequently wrote to his father assuring him, among other things, of his conscientious attention to his prayers and other Christian practices. After some years, he returned home to Old Ross but then he again sought his fortune across the Atlantic, this time in Canada. Contact with him was later lost so it is not known if he ever married; it was thought most unlikely by the family. The other son to emigrate was Patrick, who in his early days worked the family woollen mill in Old Ross. His sister, Catherine was married to Patrick Hickey, the man who was making such a success of the Poulmounty woollen mills. It was decided to close down the enterprise in Old Ross and Patrick was employed by his brother-in-law in Poulmounty as he had the required expertise. Now living on the border of county Carlow, he made new friendships including one with a young lady named Eleanor Doyle of Ballyling,[81] whom he married in Glynn chapel in 1880. About a month later, the couple sailed for the U.S.A. and, having crossed the continent, they eventually settled on the west coast in the state of Washington where they reared a family of two boys, Gerald and Edward and three daughters Bridget, Mary and Anne. Patrick died in 1914 aged 70. Although both boys married, neither had any children, so the last American Cloney of the Old Ross family passed away when Edward died in 1975 aged 78.[82] Bridget (Bridie) who died a spinster in 1963 aged 72, came to Ireland in 1961 and staying at Dungulph with the writer; she visited the homes of both her parents at Old Ross and Ballyling, which were also visited a decade later by her sister, Mary, a nurse who married Stanley Macomber[83] and who died in 1979 aged 90. The remaining girl, Anne, married a John Jebb Law; she died in 1961 aged 80.

One of the executors of Garret's will was the already mentioned, John, his eldest son, who was also the principal beneficiary, by being granted Old Ross.[84] In 1861, he married Johanna Hickey of Park, two of whose brothers, Patrick and John, married her husband's sisters, Margaret and Anne. John Cloney of Old Ross was usually called 'Johnny' and seems to have been the only one of the clan to commonly spell his name with two 'O''s (Clooney). He was a big man with quite a personality but became rather deaf in later life, a factor which caused him to speak with an excessively loud voice. It was customary for him to walk the fourteen and a half miles from Old Ross to Mass in Poulfur chapel on many Sunday mornings throughout the year. Then he would visit to have a chat and a meal in Dungulph, before walking home again to Old Ross. On becoming a septuagenarian, he continued making this journey in similar fashion on a bicycle, until a few years before his death in 1920 aged 87. His wife predeceased him in 1917 aged 90. Although he lived during a period of considerable agrarian agitation, such as the Land League, John does not appear to have been very active in local politics. However he did pass on a quaint and rather whimsical sense of humour to some of his five children, a girl and four boys.

Mary, the youngest, was born in 1871. An early talent for painting was developed when attending a convent school in Wexford. Later she helped at home and nursed both her parents during their final illnesses, after which she entered the convent of Perpetual Adoration in Wexford, serving years later as mother superior on a number of occasions. Known as Mother Peter, she was a rather formidable lady who could be brutally direct and candid. Her decisions were clear-cut and in her opinions there were no shades of grey, only black and white. Her sense of humour and ability to smile were not noteworthy; nevertheless, she was highly regarded for her very obvious honesty and integrity. She died in 1961 aged 90. Two sons of John, Sylvester and Thomas, became priests of their own diocese of Ferns, like their two uncles; they even bore the same christian names.[85] Sylvester, the youngest boy, became P.P. of

Plate xxxiii: Michael Cloney and his son, Rev Thomas Cloney

Cloughbawn where he died in 1911 aged only 42. He seems to have been deeply religious and ascetically inclined. He is said to have refused the help of medical assistance in his last illness, preferring instead to accept 'The Will of God'. His brother, Thomas, was the second eldest and became one of the best known clerics in the diocese, as Canon, then Archdeacon and finally as Dean Cloney. He was classmate in Maynooth of the famous archbishop of Melbourne, Dr Mannix and after ordination, he served as curate in Kilmore Quay and spent some time on the teaching staff of St Peters College, Wexford before being appointed administrator of Wexford town in 1908.[86] Three years later, in 1911, he became P.P. of Templetown where he served for 44 years until his death in 1955 aged 91. 'Canon Cloney', as he was best known, was a very complex individual and he merits a separate biography. Like his father, John, he was a big man physically, over 17 stone when in his prime; his apparent size was further dramatically increased when he donned an enormous black tent-like cape, which he fastened around the neck by means of a gold coloured chain, which reached almost to the ground. Such a presence, coupled with a determined and serious mien often struck fear and dread into those who met him, so much so that many failed to notice the very humorous twinkle in the eyes behind the gold-rimmed spectacles. That humour and wit was a legend in his lifetime, particularly among the clergy of the diocese. A noted student of history, he became a Council Member of the Ui Ceinnsealaigh Society in 1921 and subsequently (1948) its President. He played, together with Canon Pat Murphy and Michael Kehoe, N.T., both of Glynn, a major role in the '98 commemoration ceremonies held in 1938 and again in 1948. He spoke from many platforms on those memorable occasions at places such as the Three Rocks and St Mullins, as well as unveiling memorials at other locations to those who fell on the rebel side in that rebellion. As a relative of 'General' Cloney, he was an appropriate choice. John's remaining two sons were the eldest, Garret, and the second youngest boy, Michael. Garret inherited Old Ross and married Margaret Browne of Bigbarn (Mayglass). Their union, however, was not blessed with any children, so that when he died in 1949, aged 87, Old Ross passed to his wife, who in turn, passed it to her nephew, John T. Browne, the present owner, shortly afterwards.

The meeting between Garrett and his future wife was arranged by Jo Hickey of Donanore. She was his first cousin, (her father Cornelius, had originally come from Park) and had a position under the Wexford County Committee of Agriculture, giving instruction classes in butter and cheese making, over a wide area of the county, around which she cycled from place to place. Two of her own four brothers, Aidan and Michael, were priests, so she would regard Margaret Browne, the niece of Bishop James Browne, to be a satisfactory partner for Garrett. Jo afterwards gave an account of that whirlwind courtship. She accompanied Garrett to Margaret Browne's house in Big Barn where the prearranged introduction to members of the host family took place. That was followed by social pleasantries and small talk until afternoon tea was served. With the meal over, it was suggested that the couple, Margaret and Garrett, might take a walk in the garden to view the shrubs and flowers, which they did. Having sat together for half an hour on a garden seat, they returned to the house, where the rest of the party had observed the proceedings from behind the lace curtains. The couple then announced their betrothal without any other preliminaries, not even a kiss; he was aged about 57 and she 42 and shortly afterwards began a happy marriage that lasted nearly thirty years.

A devout Catholic, Garrett counted among his closest friends the Protestant families in Old Ross who were his neighbours. Following an attack of rheumatic fever in early manhood, he was afflicted with a rather delicate constitution for most of his adult life but he was most careful with his health, as he was of all other things. This enabled him to live a long life in moderate comfort. In the late 1930s, he designed a small water-wheel to provide power to churn cream into butter for the household, as well as providing electricity for lighting and power to drive the kitchen fan or fire-bellows. Politically, he was a Parnellite, later a Redmondite, but he definitely was not a devotee of De Valera, nor Sinn Féin and he considered that however bad a British government might be for Ireland, a native one had been and would continue to be even worse for the country.[87] That he was a Blueshirt goes without saying and he might even have been a Black or Brown shirt as well, if that meant being anti-De Valera. However, he would have discarded these on the outbreak of World War II, since he was strongly pro-British during that conflict, possibly due to De Valera's advocacy of neutrality.

The remaining son, Michael, having attended Good Counsel College in New Ross, found a position as a clerk in a shop in Dublin but on reaching the age of 30 in 1896, a new future was opened to him. In that year his cousin, John Cloney of Dungulph died[88] leaving his spinster sister, Mary and widowed sisters, Margaret and Bridget, in need of someone to take his place. It was offered to Michael. He accepted the stewardship of Dungulph, probably with some trepidation, in view of the very severe and awe-inspiring countenance which those cousins displayed in an old photograph. However, they did have money,[89] a commodity which enabled him to embark on what was in those days a very extensive building and modernisation programme that continued for the next thirty years.[90] Being a man with modern ideas for his time, he was one of the first to use what is now called portland cement for construction purposes. He was ridiculed by local people when he built a wall on one side of the roadway from the public road to the mill with concrete. He was told that such a wall, composed of stones and gravel and with no lime/sand mixture to form mortar, would definitely collapse. Nearly ninety years later, that wall is still perfect. In 1897 he purchased the waterwheel at Tintern Abbey mill for £6 and from then until 1910 considerable amounts of money were spent completely modernising the Dungulph mill and corn-drying kiln. Both buildings had previously been separate but in 1908 the mill was enlarged in order to provide space for a third pair of mill-stones. At the same time, new buildings, one containing two kilns and the other a store and intake point, were added to the mill extension. In Davis's foundry at Enniscorthy, some large iron cog-wheels and brasses were cast to order and also shafting was supplied by two Dublin firms,

Plate xxxiv: The Cloney household at Dungulph c.1900. Back: Michael Cloney, Molly Hickey, Mary Cloney (mother Peter). Front: Mary Cloney, Bridget Callaghan

the Brunswick foundry and Woodham and Moore. These weighty goods were shipped by Grand Canal barge down the River Barrow, at least as far as New Ross but possibly to Arthurstown or Duncannon. An eight foot diameter iron spur wheel (spur wheel is a mechanical term which indicates that cogs are on the face of the wheel's edge) and a pair of millstones were purchased in Clogheen, county Tipperary and transported by rail to Ballycullane Station, then just opened. These items would have been good although second-hand and were taken out of another mill. Likewise, two other pairs of millstones, kiln tiles and shafting were acquired from Chilcomb Mills near New Ross. Around the turn of the century, the wages paid to a labourer working to modernise the mill was 9d per day (4/6 per week): the skilled stonemason got 2s. per day (12s. per week): the slater and carpenter each got 2/6 per day (15s. per week). The most highly skilled was, as is to be expected, the most highly paid; he was the millwright, who got 3s. per day (18s. per week). A millwright, who might have had little formal education, would have served very many years apprenticeship with a master millwright, travelling from mill to mill all over the county, carrying out repairs and installing new machinery. The necessary expertise often passed from father to son and generally they were highly skilled and intelligent men, unquestionably the elite of the milling profession.

The old windmill was demolished, the material of which was used to erect a lofted stable 40 feet long in 1904, and 1903 saw the erection of a new 3-span hayshed with lean-to, but it was during the early part of World War I that Michael undertook his major project, the restoration of Dungulph Castle as a residence. A bachelor contemplating marriage, he had the work completed by 1917, in time for the castle to be deemed a suitable home for his bride, Elizabeth Murphy of Kilmokea (Great Island).[91]

Much to his distress, she died a few months later but in 1925, he married Ellen Cavanagh of Templederry, near Clonevan, Gorey. Their only child, a son born in 1926, is the writer of this account of the family. These Kavanaghs usually spelled the name with a 'C' (Cavanagh) and they claimed descent from the royal line of Leinster. It was a clerical family; Ellen had two paternal uncles priests, Denis and Matthew Cavanagh and one maternal uncle, Canon D'Arcy, P.P. Kilrush. A granduncle was Canon Foley P.P. who died in Glynn. Michael's meeting with his wife-to-be was arranged by a fellow County Councillor, Myles Smyth of Glascarrig (near Cahore).[92]

Michael took a very active part in local politics where the interests of farmers and tenants were concerned but on the formation of the Free State and in the aftermath of the Civil War, he adopted a neutral position towards Republicans and Treatyites. A Justice of the Peace under the old regime, he was appointed a Peace Commissioner by the Free State, yet some of his dearest friends were well-known I.R.A. men.[93] He was one of the founders of the Shelbourne Co-Operative Society in Campile, becoming its first Chairman in 1919, a position he held until his death in 1934, aged 68. During his public life, he served the people of his native county by being a member of many councils and organisations, such as the County Council, County Committee of

Agriculture, County Library, County Health Board, New Ross Board of Guardians, New Ross District Council and the Fethard Lifeboat Disaster Fund Committee. Following his death, the Shelbourne Co-Operative Society erected a fine memorial to his memory in Templetown churchyard and in the course of an address at its unveiling ceremony in September 1935, Dr James Ryan, T.D., then Minister for Agriculture in De Valera's government, declared, 'We can only imagine what a glorious country we would have if we had in every parish one man with the public spirit, the tact, the ability and the breadth of vision of Michael Cloney'.[94] His second wife, Ellen, died aged 57, in 1943, having been an invalid suffering from rheumatoid arthritis for thirteen years before being laid to rest beside her husband on the hill of Templetown.

The Cloney families of Moneyhore, Old Ross and Dungulph provide a well documented example of a Catholic big farm and milling family over a period of three hundred years. Similar case studies will help to expand our knowledge of county Wexford and put a conceptual flesh on bare genealogical bones.[95] Without understanding the matrices of family, farm and class from which they evolved, the culture, politics and society of the county will remain elusive.

APPENDIX

A letter preserved in Dungulph Castle illustrates the mentality and especially the morality or more correctly the pseudo-morality so typical of the class in those times. The letter (written on St Stephen's Day 26 December probably about 1905) is a reply by Michael Cloney to his brother, Rev Thomas, who had requested information about a distant relative named Mrs Gallagher. It began:

'Dear Fr Tom, In reply to yours received yesterday, you would wish to know something about Mrs Gallagher. Mary here [Mary Cloney, one of the three elderly cousins with whom he had come to live] say the less you know about her the better [meaning Mrs Gallagher] but to give you something of her history. James Raynard was never married. This is one of the many illegitimate children of his and the only one that helps to keep his memory green, the others as they appeared were removed to some place so that they never turned up to claim a relationship. This one's mother was the daughter of a labourer the name of Furlong that lived on the Horse Fair of Taghmon. This child was sent to nurse out the way in Piercetown'.

The letter goes on to relate that years later,

'when all were dispersed and only Miss Raynor [sic] lived in the house in Taghmon, this one got in to live with her and I believe remained there till she [Miss Raynard] died, that may be close on twenty years ago. Here is a little personal experience of Mary's years after she left Taghmon. [It seems that Mary had once lived in Taghmon for a time]. She was returning from a visit to Hayestown, [where her sister, Margaret Callaghan, then lived] as she was passing Miss Raynors door she met Miss Raynor who invited her in to have a cup of tea, as it was on the table, she accepted, as she approached the parlour, she got a glimpse of this one presiding at the teapot, she (Mary) stopped and said it had not come to that with her to sit down and take tea with a bastard, then turned on her heel and walked out. This was the last time Mary saw her'.

The letter then went on to mention a few attempts made by the unfortunate girl to approach members of the Cloney family in Dungulph and Ross as well as the Fortunes of Taghmon but they all 'did not receive her very well'. She was harshly victimised for the actions of her father. Mary Cloney ardently claimed to be a committed Christian yet at the same time managed to be uncharitable and unforgiving, although presenting a portrayal of holiness by being photographed holding a large prayer book. One solution to the embarrassment of the arrival of a child out of wedlock is seen from the passage telling of James Raynard's other children

'as they appeared [were born] were removed to some place so that they never turned up to claim ...'

Another practice was to pay somebody, often a servant, to take the illegitimate child away and rear it as her own, but for the poorer classes, it was a case of the hapless girl going into the workhouse or rearing her baby at home to a life of shame.

Continuity and change in rural county Wexford in the nineteenth century

Some of Wexford's more distinctive qualities as a county and as a diocese may be attributed to its location in the southeastern extremity of the island of Ireland. For most of its long history it has acted as a cul-de-sac where older life-styles and values have persisted. On occasions it became a stepping stone, a threshold for the colonisation of Ireland from Welsh, English and continental bases. In particular its modern geography was transformed as a consequence of two major attempts at colonisation and settlement from Britain. The range of family names, as these were recorded in the valuation books for the mid nineteenth century, reveal the presence of the descendants of three main ethnic groups which we shall refer to as Irish, Old English and New English, respectively. This variety of peoples will be a primary consideration in our search for explanations of territorial patterns of human behaviour.[1] County Wexford is also rich in its physiographic diversity, and tillage has long played a distinguished role in its agricultural economy, especially on the extensive dry mineral soils of the acid brown earths. Like the other southern counties it has a substantial urban population, largely based on old and vigorous port towns. Commentators on the rural Ireland of the nineteenth century were especially concerned with 'improvements' in life-styles at a time of great technological and social changes. We shall attempt to identify the geographical nature of change in life in the Wexford countryside employing three main categories of data. These are the large-scale maps of the Ordnance Survey, the elaborate statistical information incorporated in the Griffith's valuation of rateable property and the surviving field evidence. Special attention will be given to conditions of landholding and land working, the estate system of land owner-ship and the impact of the new Catholicism.

In the search for factors with a territorial dimension and a statistical basis making for continuity and change in nineteenth century Ireland, the most reliable index would probably be the condition of the Irish language. According to the census of population, however, Irish had already ceased to be spoken in county Wexford by 1851. The surviving landscape evidence entails a consideration of vernacular style farmsteads, especially those in the southeastern baronies of the county — Ballaghkeen South, Shelmaliere, Bargy and Forth. The distribution of the hedge school might, in the early nineteenth century, locate communities where older values were most cherished. The hedge school, like the Sunday school in nonconformist Wales, was an attempt to provide rudimentary educational facilities outside the formal assignments now being offered by the state. The areas most prominently associated with the 1798 uprising would suggest to us the whereabouts of communities which reacted most violently against what was seen as oppression on the part of an alien landed oligarchy. In more recent times, a pertinent index to changing loyalties and obligations might be the distribution of parishes in county Wexford where the Gaelic Athletic Association has been successful.

In Ireland generally in the nineteenth century the differing historical experience of ethnic groups has influenced the forces making for continuity and change. Family names have been used as a crude means of identifying people of differing ethnic origins for county Wexford. Some 3,800 heads of household with Old English names (excluding Walsh and Redmond) were found among the dispersed rural population of the county in mid century. Half of this total was located in the three southern baronies of Shelburne, Forth and Bargy (fig. 13.1), where they accounted for one-fifth of all the family names. By contrast the three northern baronies — Scarawalsh, Gorey and Ballaghkeen North — contained only 15 per cent of the total number of Old English names within the county. Exceptionally high densities of names of Old English origin were found in Bargy, in the parishes of Kilmore, Bannow, Duncormick and Mulrankin, and in Forth, in Mayglass, Tacumshin, Kildavin, Rosslare and Rathaspick.[2] In Shelburne the highest aggregates were in the parishes of St James and Dunbrody, and Fethard. No other part of Ireland retained such a large number of Old English patronymics as these parishes in south county Wexford. The exclusive nature of the intermarrying English colony of medieval origin in Wexford was suggested by the presence of constantly repeating names in particular areas. One-third of all the Old English names in the county consisted of one of the following:— Furlong, Sinnott, Roche, Power, Stafford or Rossiter. Some of these names were rarely encountered among rural communities outside the county. This indicates an old-established and territorially stable society where traditional values would be likely to be upheld. Whilst the Sinnotts and the Roches were widely scattered, the Furlongs, Staffords and Rossiters were largely concentrated in the county's southern baronies. Over 80 percent of heads of household with the name Furlong were found in the baronies of Bargy, Bantry, Shelmaliere West and Forth. Furlong and Sinnott together formed the numerically dominant names in the substantial concentration of Old English patronymics aligned along the border between Bargy and Forth, extending north from Kilmore. The historic homeland of the Furlongs was located in the barony of Shelmaliere West and in 1850 it remained the principal name of Anglo-Norman origin in the contiguous belt of parishes which extended southwards from Adamstown in

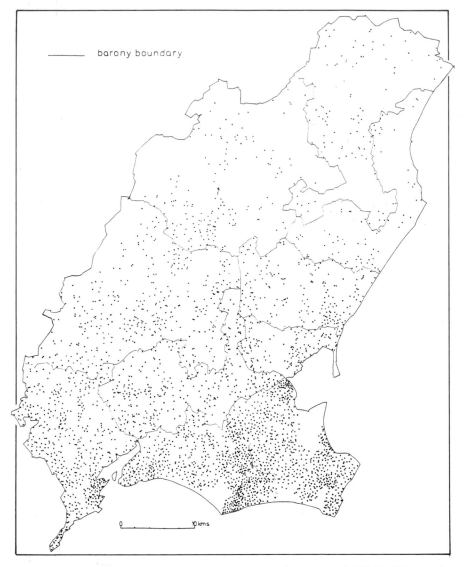

Fig. 13.1: Dispersed rural households with family names of Old English origin c.1850 (Walsh and Redmond excluded)

Bantry, through Clongeen and Kilgarvan in Shelmaliere, to the parishes of Duncormick, Bannow and Killag in Bargy. Similarly one-half of the total number of Power names in county Wexford were located in the barony of Shelburne, where they accounted for the large concentration of Old English names among the parishioners of St James and Dunbrody, Fethard, Tintern and Templetown. Their presence in such number may account for some of the Munster qualities exhibited in the geography of colonisation and settlement in Shelburne. The long-standing stability of the dispersed rural communities, where Anglo-Norman family names were numerous in south Wexford, may also be illustrated by the presence of rare non-Irish patronymics. Examples drawn from the mid nineteenth century list of names of heads of household included Meyler (the Welsh Meilyr)[3] in the parishes of Carn and Mayglass in Forth, Kent in St James and Dunbrody in Shelburne and Colfer in Bannow in Bargy. Discrete survivals of this kind from the medieval period were rare elsewhere among communities with Anglo-Norman names in nineteenth century Ireland.

As compared with some of the transit counties of the east midlands of Ireland, including Meath, nineteenth century Wexford possessed a very narrow range of Gaelic personal names. The numerically dominant Gaelic names in county Wexford included Murphy, Doyle, Byrne, Curran and Kavanagh. A total of about 2,600 of these five names were found among the dispersed rural heads of household in mid-century. Of these as many as 43 percent were Murphy and 30 percent Doyle. Despite the turbulent tenurial conditions of the colonial era, Irish rural society in county Wexford was relatively homogeneous and stable. In our search for forces making for continuity and change, it was therefore appropriate to attempt to locate resilient areas or communities, employing repeating family names as guidelines. Murphy was the one name that was ubiquitous in the county in 1850. The exception was the barony of Forth, where, in some six parishes, including Ballymore and Kilmacree, the name was entirely absent. Forty-five percent of the total number of heads of household named Murphy were found in a belt which straddled the county from the barony of Ballaghkeen South in the east to Scarawalsh and Bantry in the west. As many as 20 percent of the total number of Murphy families were located in the barony of Ballaghkeen South, with the highest aggregates in the parishes of Ballyhuskard, Castle-ellis, Ballyvaldon, Killisk, Edermine and Kilmallock. This was the country that was traditionally referred to as 'the murrowes'. High Murphy aggregates were also present in the parishes of Taghmon (Shelmaliere West), Rossdroit (Bantry), Templeshanbo, Clone and Kilrush (Scarawalsh) as well as Monamolin (Gorey). Unlike Murphy, half the Doyle patronymics were confined to the western baronies of Scarawalsh and Bantry. The highest Doyle aggregates occurred in the four Scarawalsh parishes of Templeshanbo, St Mary's Newtownbarry, Monart and Kilrush, followed by Rossdroit in Bantry and Kilcavan in Gorey. Half of the combined total number of Murphy and Doyle names were located in the three baronies of Scarawalsh, Bantry, and Ballaghkeen South. The highest combined Murphy and Doyle aggregates were found in the parishes of Templeshanbo, Monart and St Mary's Newtownbarry in Scarawalsh, Rossdroit in Bantry and Newbawn and Taghmon in Shelmaliere West. These data confirm the existence in nineteenth century county Wexford of a powerful stable Gaelic heartland, whose principal base was in the east, in the barony of Ballaghkeen South, but which extended westwards to incorporate the extensive baronies of Bantry and Scarawalsh. The presence of this distinctive heartland has to be constantly reckoned with in interpreting the county's geography in the nineteenth century.

Wexford is a county with an exceptionally high ratio of place-names which are of cultural origin, that is, they relate to human activity rather than to the physiographic character of an area. This feature is typical of areas in Ireland which have experienced long, varied histories of colonisation and settlement, especially during the Anglo-Norman period. In these circumstances place-name elements of physiographic origin often denote areas which were regarded as less desirable for settlement. Among the generic cultural elements in county Wexford, by far the most numerous is *baile* ('place, land, farm') which is present in about 20 percent of all townland names. The highest number of *baile* names, 35 percent of the total, occurs in Ballaghkeen South and this must be among the highest ratio of the element for any barony in the entire island. In this barony the following parishes have one-third or more of their townland names incorporating the element *baile*:— Ballyhuskard, Ballyvaldon, Ballyvalloo, Castle-ellis, Killila, Killisk, Kilmallock and Skreen. In county Wexford, therefore, *baile* is the most numerous in a barony which was the most profoundly Gaelic, in terms of its range of family names, in the nineteenth century. Other baronies where over one-quarter of the townland names contain *baile* were Ballaghkeen North, Gorey and Shelmaliere East. The lowest aggregate, 9 percent of the total townland names, occurs in Bargy. As in the adjoining county of Wicklow, *baile* in Wexford is most conspicuous in a broad band of east-facing coastlands.

The English equivalent to *baile* in Irish place-names is the suffix *town*. In county Wexford this in only found in 10 percent of the total number of townland names and, unlike *baile*, is severely restricted in its distribution. About 70 percent of the total number of *town* townlands are confined to the two southeastern baronies of Forth and Bargy, where it is present in a quarter of all townland names. Forth is quite exceptional in its nomenclature for Ireland as a whole, in that over 40 percent of its townland names contain either the *baile* or *town* element. Some 15 percent of the total number of townlands in county Wexford had English name elements other than the suffix *town*. The most numerous of these were *land*, *park* and *mount* and they too were largely confined to Forth and Bargy. In Bargy they accounted for a quarter of the townland names. When taken together with the suffix *town*, we find that in Forth and Bargy half the total number of townland names are English. In Ireland generally this high ratio of English place-names is likely to be exceeded only in parts of north county Dublin. It suggests that the anglicisation process in Forth and Bargy was well advanced by the late medieval period, when most of these names are likely to have been forged.

The dominance of *baile* along the coastlands of Wexford and Wicklow should clearly be considered in conjunction with a similar dominance of the suffix *town* in the coastlands of north Leinster.[4] In the seventeenth century ledger-books dealing with land transactions, the two elements were treated as if they were complementary. In north Leinster the *town* element combines most frequently with the commonest of Old English personal names. *Baile*, on the other hand, was a more flexible element and along the coastlands of Wicklow and Wexford it combines indiscriminately with a wide spectrum of name elements. In the seventeenth century when these place-names finally came to be recorded in their anglicised forms, the Norman impact prevailed in north Leinster, whilst Gaelic influences were supreme in south Leinster, north of the Wexford sloblands. In the coastlands of county Wexford we may be witnessing, in the place-names, surviving traces of two powerful cultures struggling for supremacy in threshold country. Furthermore, the evidence from east Leinster indicates that areas rich in name elements of cultural origin, especially *baile* and *town* compounds, were among the most favoured by both Gaelic and Norman peoples in the early colonisation processes. Ironically, if we are to judge from the distribution of non-Irish personal names in county Wexford in 1850, it was in the *baile* coastlands that the English also established their most durable plantations in the seventeenth century.

In the search for traditional areas in county Wexford in the nineteenth century, conditions of landholding are significant, for which detailed statistical evidence is available from the valuation books. Special attention will be paid to the whereabouts of unconsolidated farm holdings and their associated grouped settlements, as these are depicted on large-scale ordnance survey maps. Unconsolidated farm holdings revealed themselves in the nineteenth century landscape in the form of scattered parcels of land in openfields, which were occasionally linked to small groupings of farmsteads by a mesh of trackways. These features were at their maximum territorial extent in mid-century, and they were anathema to the agrarian reformer. They were more widespread in county Wexford than had been anticipated. About 80 small groups of farmsteads, each containing three or more households and holding land in a scatter of parcels, or alternatively sharing a communal lease within the one townland, were identified (fig. 13.2). Over two-thirds of these clusters were scattered across the southwestern baronies of Bantry and Shelburne. Seventeen distinctive groups of farmsteads were found in Forth but only four in the adjoining barony of Bargy. They were rarely encountered along the coastlands north from Wexford harbour. Only five were identified, for example, in the extensive barony of Ballaghkeen. They were therefore not necessarily typical of those areas which were the more Gaelic parts of county Wexford. By comparison with their Connacht or Ulster counterparts, or even the farm villages which were numerous at the time in Glencullen or the King's River valley in the Wicklow Mountains, the typical Wexford farm group was small, both in terms of the number of families it housed and the area of land which it worked. The nearest parallels in Leinster were probably to be found in the Collon hills in south county Louth.[4]

The most substantial groups of farmsteads in county Wexford in 1850 included Kellystown and Newtown in the parish of Adamstown in Bantry. In Kellystown eight families held a joint lease on 120 ha of land from a small absentee owner. The average valuation of the farmsteads was as low as thirty shillings. With one exception all the families possessed Gaelic names, including two Murphys and two Doyles. In this sense Kellystown belonged to the Gaelic heartland in county Wexford. The settlement also included four landless families, who occupied dwelling houses valued at only five shillings

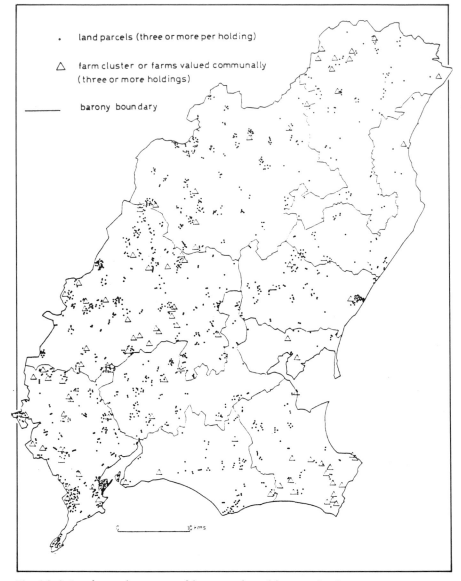

Fig. 13.2: Land parcels, groups of farmsteads and farms valued communally c.1850

each and these had female heads of household. Kellystown was a particularly fragile social as well as physical entity. It is not surprising therefore to find that, among the relatively affluent rural communities of county Wexford, farm groups of this kind were occasionally given derogatory English names.[5] In Owenduff parish in Shelburne, for example, there were clusters known as Thistletown and Rookery, giving the impression that their occupants were held in low esteem, as if they were interlopers, and interlopers are not usually upholders of traditional values.

In county Wexford, as in the Cooley peninsula in county Louth, farm groups were part of the heritage of both Gaelic and Anglo-Norman cultures.[6] In the barony of Forth families with Old English names sometimes dominated over groups of farmsteads. Ring, on Lady's Island Lake in Carn parish, for instance, contained six farmsteads, five of which were occupied by families called Furlong, Hayes, Codd, Harpur and Corish. As in Cooley the clusters in the Old English baronies differed from their counterparts in the county's Gaelic heartland. They were conspicuous landscape features in that they formed the dominant, if not the only, form of settlement within their townlands. The townland net and the settlement framework were closely related to each other and the farmers themselves rarely worked land beyond the townland boundaries. The townland in the hands of the farm group therefore acted as a social as well as an agrarian entity and contributed to the cellular nature of Irish rural life. The cluster at Ballygeary in the parish of Kilrane at one time contained the dwelling house of a landowner, which occupied the site of a late medieval tower-house. Unlike some of the ephemeral farm groups in the more Gaelic areas of county Wexford, the clusters in the Old English baronies often had deep roots. Moreover farm groups in Forth would occasionally possess windmills for grinding corn and would perform functions other than farming. Churchtown in Carne acted as the settlement centre of a parish and contained its church. These are among the characteristics which we have come to associate with the spectacular farm villages of the barony of Iverk, in south county Kilkenny.[7] The Iverk villages acted as the settlement underpinnings for both parish and townland networks in their most formative early years. In Iverk the majority of its pre-reformation parishes had such settlements at their centres. These included Fiddown, Ballytarsey, Portnascully and Pollrane. We may therefore be justified in regarding the clusters in the Old English baronies of south Wexford as representing the weak eastern edge of a powerful farm village culture focussed on south county Kilkenny. In general, the Wexford clusters were, both in their rudimentary composition and in their peripheral distribution, lowly and residual features in Ireland's settlement hierarchy. They had failed to acquire even the most basic of central-place functions, as part of the modernisation process that characterised the nineteenth century. As such they were probably good indicators of the whereabouts of communities where traditional values were upheld.

Around 1,300 farmers in county Wexford in 1850 worked land which was not consolidated into a single unit. Unconsolidated holdings, consisting of three or more parcels, were widely scattered throughout the county (fig. 13.2), but two-thirds of the total were located in the western baronies of Shelburne, Bantry and Scarawalsh. Five of the eastern baronies — Shelmaliere East, Ballaghkeen North, Gorey as well as Bargy and Forth — between them contained only about one-fifth of the total. By the mid nineteenth century, therefore, a dichotomy emerged in county Wexford between a culturally exposed east and a more sheltered and isolated west. Parishes which were particularly rich in traces of unconsolidated holdings included Templeshanbo and St Mary's Newtownbarry in Scarawalsh, Killann and Ballyanne in Bantry,

Clongeen in Shelmaliere West, Ballyhuskard in Ballaghkeen South, Kilmore in Bargy and Templetown, Fethard and Owenduff in Shelburne. Northern parishes which had endured plantation with English tenant farmers from the early seventeenth century, including Crosspatrick, Liskinfere, Kilgorman and Kilpipe in Gorey barony, and Killenagh and Kiltennell in Ballaghkeen North, contained few traces of openfield farming. The New English rarely participated in traditional Irish practices in any part of the island.

The largest and most intricate example of a farm village with unconsolidated holdings in county Wexford in 1850 was found in isolation on the east coast, among the sandhills of the parish of Ballyvaldon in Ballaghkeen South, a barony already identified as being outstandingly Gaelic in terms of its human content in the nineteenth century. The entire 120 ha townland of Ballyconnigar Upper was held in a complex scatter of land parcels, mostly from the Catholic Talbot family of Castle Talbot. The nineteen participating families included three Murphys and three Kehoes. One Murphy family held as many as eight separate parcels, the largest of which was 1.2 ha. With two exceptions the Ballyconnigar villagers were entirely of Irish stock. Extensive and complex unconsolidated holdings were particularly numerous in the south-western baronies of Bantry and Shelburne. In Bantry the more numerous were found in the townlands of Courtnacuddy in Rossdroit parish, Rathnure (Killann), Ballyveggin (Ballyanne) and Ballynahearne (St Mullins). As elsewhere in south Leinster, in the absence of extensive lowlying wetlands, unconsolidated farm holdings were best displayed strewn along the sunnier east-facing slopes of the uplands, including, in county Wexford, those of Mount Leinster and the Blackstairs Mountains. In Scarawalsh and Bantry land parcels were found dispersed within townlands at the head of the broad basins of the tributaries of the river Slaney, including the Clody, the Urrin and the Boro. Here, as in the glens of the upper Liffey and Bray river basins, at the northern end of the Leinster Mountains, isolated farming communities were the denizens of the fluctuating altitudinal edge of the occupied area, at the height of population pressure on land in the nineteenth century.[8] They held grazing rights on the unenclosed upland commonages. In these circumstances the joint farm groups, and their supporting scatter of land parcels, may not have represented residual survivals of traditional practices but, as along the western seaboard of the island, late and peculiar adaptations to exceptional demographic and physiographic conditions.

In the more accessible and physically more desirable locations, it is not easy to discern the relationships between the upholders of traditional life-styles and the reforming landlord system. In the southeastern baronies of Shelmaliere West and Forth, for instance, archaic conditions of landholding were more prevalent on small absentee estates, which were managed by middlemen of Irish or Old English stock. Tattered conditions of ownership seemed to offer shelter from the full force of landlordism. By contrast unconsolidated farm holdings in the strongly Gaelic barony of Bantry were widespread, cheek by jowl with well-cared-for core areas of substantial modern landlord estates, including those of Carew of Castleboro, Blacker of Woodbrook and Richards of Grange. On the Blacker estate in Killann parish, for example, in the 200 ha townland of Rathnure Lower, in the upper Boro river basin, 70 ha were held in 44 separate parcels between eight families called Clare, Kavanagh, Kelly, Forrestal, Heffernan and Moran, together with two Murphys. Similarly, in Shelburne, powerful estates, including those of Templemore of Dunbrody, Colclough of Tintern Abbey and Ely of Loftus Hall, which had emerged as a consequence of the re-distribution of confiscated monastic property, harboured some of the finest examples of archaic agrarian structures to be found anywhere in south Leinster. Unconsolidated holdings and their associated farm villages were profound features of the townlands of Grange in the parish of Fethard, Churchtown (Hook), Lewistown and Broomhall (Templetown) as well as Great Island (Kilmokea). On the extensive Ely lands in the townland of Grange, which included the estate town of Fethard as well as farm villages known as Wood Village and Newtown, eight families with the south Munster name of Foley worked 40 ha of land which was dispersed among as many as 45 distinct parcels. The presence of names such as Barden, Power, Devereux, Grace and Hurdus, among the other holders of parcels in Grange, indicated that traditional agrarian practices in the barony of Shelburne were not necessarily confined to families of Gaelic stock. Whilst English landlords could not be described as being the custodians of older life-styles and values anywhere in nineteenth century Ireland, in the Gaelic and Old English baronies of county Wexford, modern landlordism and archaic farming practices were not territorially mutually exclusive.

The modern landlord estate, as it emerged in Ireland from the sixteenth century, was on the one hand a territorial feature that made for cohesion, uniformity and continuity.[9] On the other hand, it was an element in the settlement system that was the most sensitive to the need for innovation and adaptation to the rapidly changing circumstances of the eighteenth and nineteenth centuries. Landowning units were particularly significant geographically in that their owners were among the principal decision makers locally. This was especially important in a county where most of the house-holders — urban as well as rural — were tenants to a small group of property owners, few of whom were of Irish stock. In this profound sense the landed estate in Ireland was in origin, composition and function an alien institution. Moreover, as was typical of colonial conditions elsewhere, property in nineteenth century Ireland was frequently not held directly from its owner, but through a complicated tier of middlemen whose names are laboriously recorded in the rateable valuation books. Their presence makes it difficult to identify the territorial extent of individual estates. It is necessary therefore to devise other means of analysing the nature of land-ownership structures in nineteenth century Ireland. In this respect a useful guide is the estate core, or that area that lay in the immediate vicinity of the landowner's residence.[10] The tillage counties of southern Ireland were rich in their numbers of small resident owners and the core areas of their estates could easily be identified, and their leading properties enumerated. The coming of the estate system of land management must have revolutionised territorial relationships in early

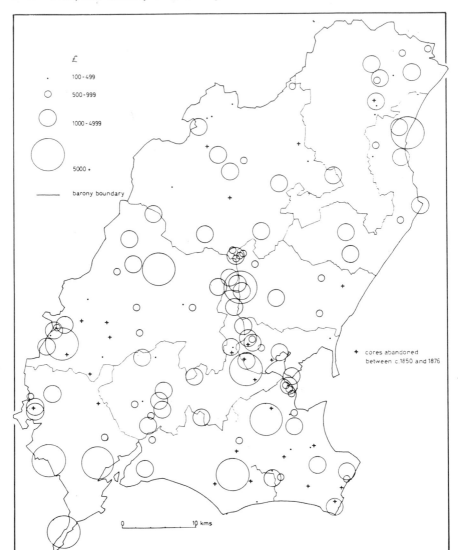

Fig. 13.3: The valuation of estates of resident landowners, 1876

modern Ireland and the distribution of estate cores, in the later nineteenth
century (fig. 13.3) should suggest the whereabouts of areas in county Wexford
which were intimately influenced by these changes.

In the planted baronies of north county Wexford, as in Ulster, estate cores
were generally modern creations. Examples from the barony of Ballaghkeen
North included those of Stopford of Courtown in Kiltennell parish, Richards
in Ardamine, Doyne in Wells (Killincooly) and Bolton in Island House
(Meelnagh). In Gorey barony, the Ram family resided in Ramsfort House in
Kilcavan parish. The systematic pillaging of these great houses in the 1798 insurrection was a reflection of how the presence of the New English was

resented in north Wexford; their late arrival was illustrated in the mid nineteenth century by the freshness and modernity of their estate landscapes, urban as well as rural. In the southern baronies on the other hand, the Old English had been manipulating property on a manorial basis for five hundred years; the core areas of southern estates frequently possessed extensive and ancient roots. Loftus Hall, the residence of the Marquess of Ely, in the Hook peninsula in the barony of Shelburne, for instance, was a modern successor to a Redmond dwelling house, whilst Rosegarland House, in Ballylannan parish in Bargy, was Sinnott property until the seventeenth century confiscations. The Old English territories of south county Wexford had in this way been long exposed to powerful and varied intrusive influence. The occasional incongruous presence of a late medieval tower-house alongside a sumptuous eighteenth century mansion, as, for example, at Mulrankin in Bargy, or Killiane in Forth, was a reminder of the easier marriage of the older and the newer traditions in the Old English baronies.[11]

A comprehensive *Civil Survey* enables us to plot the distribution of landownership patterns in county Wexford for the mid seventeenth century (fig. 13.4); family names may be used in an attempt to identify the ethnic or national origins of proprietors.[12] Our principal concern was with earmarking the lands that were still in Gaelic hands. In the southern half of the county, in the baronies of Shelmaliere, Shelburne, Bargy and Forth, the Old English were the leading owners of property in 1654. Over this extensive and strategically significant region, the Gaels had relinquished their lands to aliens long before the emergence of modern landlordism. In 1654 parishes which were shared between Gaelic and New English owners, on the other hand, were almost entirely confined to the northern baronies of Gorey, Ballaghkeen North and Scarawalsh. Examples included Kilnahue and Kiltrisk in Gorey, Killenagh and Kilmuckridge in Ballaghkeen North and Carnew in Scarawalsh. The parishes of Kilpipe, Crosspatrick, Kilmakilloge and Liskinfere in Gorey, Kiltennel in Ballaghkeen North, as well as Kilcomb and Toome in Scarawalsh, were already entirely in English hands in the mid seventeenth-century. They also provided examples of areas from the Wexford-Wicklow borderland which were systematically planted with communities of English farmers in the early modern period.[13] This process entailed the injection of alien influences and controls to rural life, on a scale and with a determination, and a degree of success, that was probably unparalleled in any other west European country at the time. In this respect the Irish experience may be significant in the understanding of Europe's general agrarian geography. It provides the opportunity to draw tentative comparisons and contrasts between the behaviour patterns of two peoples of differing historical experiences in territorial juxtaposition.

Unlike the Ulster province, no communities of exclusively planter stock were found in any one parish in the Wexford-Wicklow borderland in the mid nineteenth century. Nevertheless, no Gaelic names were found among the tenant occupiers of farms valued at £50 and over in the parish of Liskinfere in Gorey in 1850. In an area of great diversity in physiography and farming

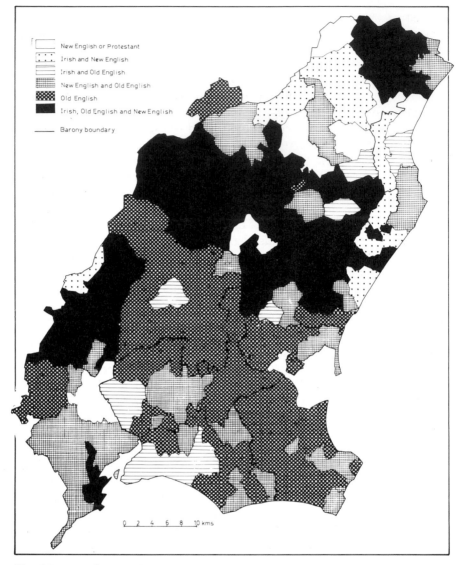

Fig. 13.4: Land ownership, 1654

potential, the planter baronies of the Wexford-Wicklow borderland produced evidence that families with Irish names tended to occupy subordinate and subservient positions within the agrarian hierarchy under colonial conditions. Within the townland framework, which appears to have governed the allocation of property among planter communities, the land of the Gael was of a lower valuation and his farmstead occupied a peripheral position in relation to a larger, centrally placed unit. In other words, if there was a displacement of the pre-existing population, it was highly localised in its impact. In a wider perspective, and employing family names as primary evidence, it was difficult to demonstrate within the baronies of Gorey and Scarawalsh generally that there was a systematic eviction of the pre-existing Irish population to less congenial environments in marginal locations. In the upper reaches of the Bann valley in the parishes of Kilnenor and Kilnahue in the barony of Gorey, for instance, no coherent Gaelic farm communities were identified upslope of planter settlements. On the east and southeast facing slopes of Croghan Mountain and on the Forde estate in Gorey, families of planter stock were in 1850 the tenants of large farms on the edge of the occupied area. At elevations of up to 250 metres, they provided examples of some of the highest altitudes ever attained by large-scale tillage farming in Ireland. Their presence confirmed that planter communities were not necessarily in occupation of the most desirable farmland in north county Wexford in the nineteenth century. Moreover, there were few indications in 1850 that this physically marginal planter world was collapsing. In this respect it is essential to recall that the revolutionary land legislation at the turn of the century was aimed at eliminating the great landowner and not the non-Irish planter tenant. In the Wicklow-Wexford borderland, as in Ormond in north county Tipperary, planter communities have proved to be remarkably resilient to the political traumas of twentieth century Ireland.

The *Civil Survey* of 1654 showed that many landowners with Gaelic names had retained a foothold in a broad band of country extending from the baronies of Bantry and Scarawalsh in the west to Ballaghkeen in the east (fig. 13.4). In Scarawalsh, Irish names were the more numerous among the proprietors in the upland parishes of Templeshanbo and St Mary's Newtownbarry, as well as in the *Dubh-Thir* or Duffry country lying between the river Slaney and its tributary, the Urrin, in the parishes of Ballycarney, Monart and Ferns. In Ballaghkeen there were owners with Gaelic names in the parishes of Templeshannon, Ballyhuskard, Kilcormick and Monamolin, whilst in the barony of Bantry they were present in piedmont country in Ballyann, Oldross and Templeludigan parishes. Judging by the numerical dominance here of the most common of Wexford Gaelic patronymics, as well as the widespread presence of unconsolidated farm holdings in the mid nineteenth century, these parishes in Ballaghkeen and Bantry formed the more representative sectors within the surviving Gaelic heartland in the county. In this respect Wexford may have been more Gaelic than any other Leinster county. The topographic heart of Gaelic Wexford was represented by a triangular area of low hills that had its base immediately north of the sloblands of Wexford harbour, and its apex in Ballycanew in the barony of Gorey. Judging by the proliferation of mementoes to the insurrection of 1798, located in both old and new parish centres, this region in the baronies of Ballaghkeen and Shelmaliere had experienced the bitterest expressions of the Irish backlash to the colonial presence at the time. Among these hills, tolerance of old-established practices found expression in a variety of ways, especially in the confused topography of the stoneless kame country of the coastal parishes of Kilmuckridge, Killincooly, Ballyvaldon, Skreen and Ballyvalloo in Ballaghkeen. Ballyvaldon, as we have seen, contained county Wexford's most substantial farm village.

Together these parishes harbour some of the finest examples of well-maintained, single-storey, mud-walled and thatched, central-hearth dwelling houses to have survived in late twentieth century Ireland.

By the closing decades of the nineteenth century the ethnic pattern of ownership in Wexford had changed utterly, as the forces making for modernisation of agricultural practices, in the form of New English landlordism, had overwhelmed the county. In 1876, out of a total of 238 owners, resident and non-resident, 153 had New English names.[14] Yet, unlike some other Leinster counties, the fundamental distinction to be drawn in this county, even in the closing decades of the nineteenth century, is between a clear majority of New English owners on the one hand and a substantial minority of owners of Old English and Gaelic stock on the other. This was a significant distinction because as the century progressed it became increasingly reinforced and emphasised by differing religious allegiancies. The Old English, like the Irish, had remained faithful to the pre-reformation church.

The great estate, of the kind encountered in the pastoral areas of north Leinster and east Connacht, or in the planted counties of Ulster, was rarely seen in southern Ireland in the closing decades of the nineteenth century. The only estate of a resident owner valued at £10,000 in county Wexford in 1876 was that of Tottenham of Talbot Hall, alongside the town of New Ross. Despite Wexford's long-standing relative affluence there were no more than thirteen estates in the county which were valued at £5,000 and over, and ten of these were in English hands. These latter included Forbes of Johnstown Castle in Forth, Morgan of Ardcandrisk House in Shelmaliere and Templemore (Chichester) of Dunbrody Park, Shelburne. Three of the New English owners of these larger estates — Foster, Hatton and Portsmouth — were absentees. Despite its thoroughly alien character in terms of its personnel, landlordism did not appear to be as powerful as an innovative force in Wexford as it was, for example, in county Meath.[15] The average rateable valuation of an estate worth £5,000 and over in county Meath in 1876 was £14,000; the comparative figure for Wexford was £7,500. The more subdued presence of the landlord locally in county Wexford found expression in the values attached to the principal components of estate cores. In county Meath out of a total of 121 home-farms, 51 were valued at £300 and over. Of the 82 home farms identified for county Wexford, only six were valued at £300 and over.

Unlike the Ulster province, few estates in the southern counties of Ireland were manned by New English tenants. Judging by their family names, a large proportion of the strong farmers of county Wexford had remained of Gaelic or of Old English stock. It was primarily for this reason that the larger estates of the southern counties were not necessarily centres of agrarian innovation. The capacity or willingness of an individual landlord to effect change locally could be estimated in terms of the ratio of townlands per parish which were held directly from their owners, as opposed to those in the charge of an agent or a middleman. In nineteenth century Leinster it was unusual for a townland to be shared between more than one owner. During the colonial era, it was the townland rather than the individual farm holding which had remained the

basic unit of ownership. In the absence of the owner-occupier, the townland
net was therefore of great consequence in unravelling the territorial nature of
tenurial relations. Nevertheless the fragmentation of the ownership of land
beyond the townland entity was such that in county Wexford it was most
unusual for an entire parish to be in the hands of a single landlord, even in the
immediate vicinity of the most substantial of estate cores. Rare exceptions in
1850 were the adjoining parishes of Chapel and Killegney in the barony of
Bantry, which were held by Carew of Castleboro, together with the large
parish of St James and Dunbrody in Shelburne, which was held by
Templemore. In sharp contrast was the parish of Killesk in Shelburne, where
six out of its seven townlands were each held by a different lessor and Kilcavan
in Bargy where there were seven different lessor names for a total of eight
townlands. In parishes of such intense fragmentation of interests, old styles of
living were often seen to be tolerated by default.

The superficial presence of modern landlordism in county Wexford was
perhaps best demonstrated by the general absence of estate inspired and
sponsored village and small-town life in their core areas. The estates of Carew
of Castleboro in Bantry, Rowe of Ballycross in Bargy, as well as Morgan of Ardcandrisk in Shelmaliere, each valued at over £5,000, for example, possessed
barren or non-village cores. In Ulster, by contrast, planned and disciplined
village and small-town communities, whose settlements were highly selective
in their content and function, provided the innovative landowner with a
powerful tool with which to make economic, social and cultural changes
locally. In Wexford, as in southern Ireland generally, village and small-town
life was usually of pre-landlord origin.[16] Landlord inspired settlements in
county Wexford included the late eighteenth century village of Arthurstown
on Waterford Harbour on the Templemore estate, and Fethard at the entrance
to Bannow Bay on the Ely estate, both in the barony of Shelburne. There was
also the town of Newtownbarry on the Maxwell estate in Scarawalsh. Few
counties in Ireland possessed such a small and undistinguished number of
landlord settlements. A further example of a subdued type of estate village was
provided by Coolgreany in the barony of Gorey. It had been conceived and
planned as the central item of settlement of a small, compact estate that was
typical of the planter areas of the Wexford-Wicklow borderland. In Coolgreany the entire village was held directly from Lambe, who was the sole
owner. Coolgreany however possessed no core of more substantial residences,
occupied by planter families, of the kind seen in the pastoral counties of north
Leinster and east Connacht. In 1850 its population was, on the contrary, overwhelmingly Gaelic, and in this way it was no more than a small, planned
service settlement caring for the growing needs of a relatively affluent and
ethnically mixed farming community. The more substantial dwelling houses,
each valued at £3 and over, were aligned along the sunnier east-facing side of
the street axis, whilst the opposite side consisted entirely of a terrace of single
storey labourers houses. Coolgreany possessed no distinctive pre-landlord
roots, and the absence of a church indicated that it was a rare example from
south Leinster of a village that was not attached to either of the parish systems.

The all-pervasive impact of the landowner in nineteenth century Ireland was not confined to the countryside but reached, however tenuously, deep into the island's town network, even in areas such as south Leinster, with their old, complex urban tradition. The absentee Earl of Portsmouth (Wallop), for example, acted as a patron for the town of Enniscorthy. Smaller property owners, such as the Devereux families in Wexford and Enniscorthy, were eager to provide the substantial capital that was required to provide facilities for the processing of agricultural produce, which was a primary function of port towns during their heyday in tillage country. The estate core towns of southern Ireland, like the villages, were, however, older than the landlords and, unlike their Ulster counterparts, they remained overwhelmingly Gaelic in disposition and content. The great Presentation and Mercy convents that tower over Enniscorthy, together with St Aidan's church elevated to cathedral status in the early nineteenth century, were striking indicators of the town's eagerness to serve the needs of the majority population. The town of Gorey, on the other hand, was essentially a by-product of the powerful role played by the Ram family in the seventeenth century plantation of the Wexford-Wicklow borderland. Its novel origins were reflected in the presence of a corporation acting as the town's administrative body. Unlike most urban centres of its size in south Leinster, Gorey's main street was domineered over by planter families living in substantial houses that were valued at £10 and over. Their names in 1850 included Richards, Flusk, Freeman, Bell, Hollingsworth and Lett. A dynamic and varied Irish sector was, however, emerging in mid century on the lands of the Catholic Esmonde of Ballynastragh family, in the vicinity of St Michael's church. By contrast, the planter extremity of the town, focussed on the Anglican Christchurch, exhibited the restraints and the aloofness associated with the coloniser in southern Ireland. The Gorey of the nineteenth century served to demonstrate the manner in which villages and towns had come to act as overt if peaceful battlegrounds between two traditions and the more truculent features in the struggle had found landscape expression. The renaming earlier in the present century, in the Irish language only, of the main streets of Gorey, as well as the erection of the great Anglican church, sponsored by the Earl of Carysfort, in the town of Arklow in 1900, may rank as such symbolic gestures. In general, as in Ulster, planter towns have provided a constant opportunity for a fusion of interests, and Gorey emerged as one of the most adaptable, daring and successful of Ireland's smaller urban centres in the difficult post-colonial years.

Between 1850 and 1876, during a period of great agrarian turbulence, only 60 percent of the estate cores of county Wexford had remained in the same hands. In this quarter of a century 28 out of a total of 120 cores had been abandoned by their owners (fig. 13.3). In the immediate post-famine decades, according to this evidence, the more stable areas, tenurially, were located in the planted north of the county. In the baronies of Gorey and Ballaghkeen only two cores had been abandoned, as compared with six in Forth. The abandoned cores in Forth included those of three estates of seventeenth century origin, namely Nunn of St Margaret's parish, Bush of Bushville, Ballybrennan, and

Lloyd of Thornville, Mayglass. Modern planter estates were vulnerable in the Old English baronies. The map locating the core areas in 1876, classified according to the total valuation of land held by each within the county, therefore represents a residual distribution of the survivors in the closing decades of the colonial period. Seven of the ten cores of estates valued at £5,000 and over in county Wexford were located either on the coast or on the lower reaches of navigable rivers. Access to arterial routeways, by sea as well as by land, was of growing consequence in the market-orientated landlord economy of the nineteenth century. Of these more substantial core areas, only one, that of the Earl of Courtown, was located in the planted northern baronies of Gorey, Ballaghkeen North and Scarawalsh. As in county Offaly, and its annexe in Ormond in north county Tipperary, great estates were not necessarily integral features of modern plantations in southern Ireland.[17] In county Wexford, as in Tipperary, the highest number of core areas were located in the former Old English baronies of Shelburne, Bargy and Forth, where they had struck deep roots. In Shelburne the more substantial old cores were represented by those of Templemore of Dunbrody, Colclough of Tintern Abbey and Ely of Loftus Hall. Counties, as long-standing administrative units, had acquired their own clusters of estate cores, at which could be seen as their major confluence areas. In Cavan, for instance, this type of cluster was focussed on the county town and the old diocesan centre of Kilmore.[18] In Wexford a more substantial gathering of cores had emerged from the seventeenth century along the attractive axis provided by the lower Slaney river basis, between Enniscorthy and the head of Wexford harbour. Judging by the freshness and variety of its landscape, this was the area in county Wexford which had been the most thoroughly exposed to the forces making for improvement and modernisation in the nineteenth century. The lower Slaney complex embraced 26 out of the total of 120 cores which have been identified for the county in 1876. The more distinguished included those of Power of Edermine and Morgan of Ardcandrisk, each representing estates valued at over £5,000. Among the thirteen others, whose estates were valued at over £1,000 each, were Alcock of Wilton Castle, Richards of Mackmine, Cliffe of Bellevue and Walker of Tikillin. Not one Irish name was found among the owners of estates valued at £1,000 and over, in this lower Slaney complex. Together with its urban population of 20,000 in 1851, it represented a concentration of intrusive interests placed in the geographical heart of the county.

In their mature condition, from the late eighteenth century, estate cores had transformed Ireland's countryside, especially by embellishing it for the first time with some of the refinements more commonly associated with the aristocratic landscapes of England and continental Europe. These included the exotic tastes displayed in the content of mansion and farmstead, as well as in the composition and layout of garden, orchard, avenue and parkland. In their simplest form features of this kind were best demonstrated among the smaller, newer estates perched in the attractive piedmont country along the eastern flanks of the south Leinster mountains. In the barony of Bantry, they included the core areas of the estates of Richards of Grange, Bruen of Coolbawn, Carew

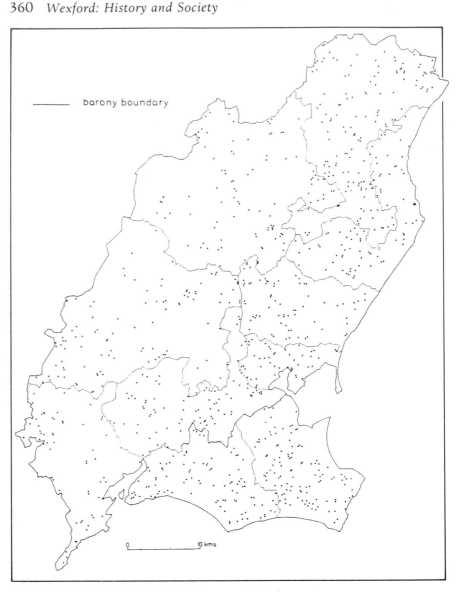

Fig. 13.5: Farms valued at £50 and over, c.1850

of Castleboro and Blacker of Woodbrook. These were the bases from which
the landowners became involved in the regimented extension of the farmed
area along the slopes of the Blackstairs Mountains and Mount Leinster. The
cores of estates of this kind, however, placed on the margins of the occupied
area in hill country, deteriorated rapidly with their enforced abandonment
from the early decades of the twentieth century. They now remain among the
m⸱ st conspicuous of the many scars left from the colonial era in Ireland's rural
landscape.

As with the great estate, the strong farmer was not an outstanding feature of county Wexford's tenurial structures in the nineteenth century.[19] In Ireland generally the fragmentation of property and holding had proceeded furthest in the mixed farming and the tillage areas. In Wexford there were some 930 farms which were valued at £50 and over in 1850 (fig. 13.5). This compared with 1,700 for the grazier county of Meath, where good quality pasture land still commanded the highest values. In Meath 540 of this total were valued at £200 and over, as compared with 235 farms in Wexford which were worth £100 and over. Forty-two percent of the latter were located in the northern baronies of Scarawalsh, Gorey and Ballaghkeen North. In the planted counties of south Ulster, the larger holdings were conspicuously associated with the physically better lands. In the physically better endowed counties of south Leinster, however, with their long and varied experiences of colonisation and settlement, the more highly valued holdings were widely dispersed. Only occasionally in county Wexford was there an obvious relationship between elementary physiographic circumstances and their location. In Scarawalsh, for instance, half the total number of holdings valued at £50 and over were found in the parishes of Kilrush, Ballycarney and Clone, within easy reach of the arterial routeways of the middle Slaney basin. As many as a quarter of the total number of farms valued at £50 and over in county Wexford were located in the baronies of Forth and Bargy. In Forth they were numerous even among the confused tenurial conditions that prevailed in the parishes of Ballymore, Mayglass and Kilrane. High aggregates of strong farmers were also encountered in the Old English baronies of Clanwilliam, Middlethird and Iffa and Offa East in south county Tipperary.[20] Ormond in Tipperary and Gorey in Wexford were also alike in that the presence of high ratios of strong farmers in both was largely a consequence of modern plantation. One-fifth of the total number of farms valued at £50 and over in county Wexford were located in Gorey, especially in the parishes of Kilnahue, Ballycanew, Inch, Liskinfere and Kilcavan. In Liskinfere in 1850, Webster of Ballinacur, Waring of Ballinclay and Warren of Ballygallen were typical of this type of planter farmer. Only occasionally was there a relationship between the presence of a large estate and high farming. Most of the strong farmers in Kilnahue in Gorey, for example, were found on Powerscourt land. Similarly in the south of the county, all ten large farms in the parish of St James and Dunbrody in Shelburne were tenants of Templemore, whilst 18 out of the 25 large farms in Bannow parish in Bargy were on the lands of Boyce of Bannow House. In Wexford, as elsewhere in nineteenth century Ireland, the large farm in planter hands acted locally as the backbone of the colonial enterprise.

If we are to judge from their family names, no more than about 40 percent of the strong farmers of county Wexford in 1850 were of New English stock. One-third had Old English names, whilst the remainder were of Gaelic stock. An ethnic spread of this dimension was rarely encountered among large farmers elsewhere in the island. In the grazier county of Meath 40 percent of holdings valued at £50 and over were occupied by families with Irish names. In the planted county of Cavan, on the other hand, as many as 80 percent of the large farms were occupied by persons with English or Scottish names. Unlike

Cavan, there was in county Wexford a considerable territorial variation in the ethnic composition of the large farm population. In Wexford the highest aggregate of New English, 60 percent of the total, was found in Scarawalsh, whilst the lowest aggregate, 25 per cent of the total, was in Bargy. In Bargy half the strong farmers had names of Old English origin, amongst the highest ratio in any part of Ireland in the mid nineteenth-century. In county Wexford, as in Tipperary, the Old and the New English as substantial tenant farmers tended to be territorially mutually exclusive. In both counties they were separated from each other by the presence of a central band of country where large farms occupied by families of Gaelic stock were most numerous. In Wexford the highest aggregate of large farmers with Gaelic names, 37 percent of the total, was found in Ballaghkeen South, and the lowest, 14 percent, in the barony of Forth. Thirty-five per cent of the strong farmers in Shelburne were also Gaelic. The presence of this middle tier of Gaelic farm population was confirmed when the family names of the occupiers of holdings valued between £20 and £50 were examined. Over half the total number of farms in this valuation category in the baronies of Ballaghkeen South, Bantry, Shelburne, Scarawalsh and Shelmaliere West, were in Gaelic hands. This compared with Bargy and Forth where less than 30 percent of farms valued at between £20 and £30 were occupied by families with Gaelic names. In Gorey and Ballaghkeen North the corresponding figure was 40 per cent. Overall, despite their tenant status and their varied ethnic origins, there was little evidence forthcoming from county Wexford in the mid nineteenth century that this class of strong farmer was disintegrating. Few individual farms were left vacant in 1850 and few were in the hands of agents and herds. County Wexford shared the resilience and adaptability of Ireland's principal tillage areas in the difficult post-famine years.

For evidence of the impact of the famine on rural Wexford, we need to identify the whereabouts of the poor in the community. Endemic poverty was an ubiquitous condition in rural and urban society in nineteenth century Ireland. In county Wexford the rural poor in 1850 have been identified as the landless population and householders whose land was valued at less than £5. No less than 57 percent of the total number of dispersed rural households fell into this category. The poor therefore numerically formed by far the largest single element in the population, and their distribution (fig. 13.6) serves as a guide to the density of population in rural areas in the immediate post-famine decade. In county Wexford, as elsewhere in tillage country in nineteenth century Ireland, a high ratio of the rural poor were landless labourers, who were sometimes attached to individual farms and were therefore widely scattered over the county in 1850. By contrast the majority of the rural poor in county Cavan were smallholders rather than landless labourers. Few distinctive communities of poor smallholders of the Ulster type were found in county Wexford. In Wexford the lowest aggregates of poor families, about half the total number of dispersed rural households, were located in the north and west of the county, in the baronies of Gorey, Scarawalsh and Shelburne. The rural poor were least in evidence in Gorey, in the planter parishes of

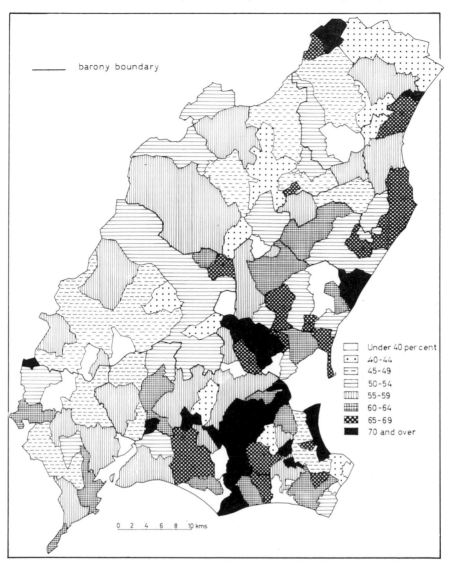

Fig. 13.6: The percentage of the total number of households in rural areas with land valued at less than £5, c.1850

Liskinfere, Kilnenor, Kilmakilloge, Inch and Kilgorman. In Shelmaliere East, Forth and Bargy, on the other hand, the dispersed poor always accounted for at least 65 percent of the rural population. In the parishes of Ballynaslaney, Kilpatrick and Artramon, at the head of Wexford harbour, in Shelmaliere, and among the most substantial concentration of estate cores in the county, the poor aggregate amounted to over 70 percent of the population; this is likely to have been among the highest for any rural community in Leinster. Territorially the rich and the poor co-existed parasitically everywhere in nineteenth century

Ireland. Exceptionally high aggregates of poverty were also encountered in the parishes of Kerloge, Rosslare, Killinick and Rathaspick in Forth, and in Kilmore, Mulrankin and Taghmon in Bargy. As in north county Dublin, the poor of Forth and Bargy incorporated the tiny fishing communities of the coastlands.

In the nineteenth century the rural poor in Wexford, as in Ireland generally, were what the Welsh referred to as *pobl yr ymylon*, the peoples of the extremities. They formed a surreptitious element in society for whose settlements the old-established townland network, for example, had the least relevance. Sometimes they are seen in the valuation books huddled together at major road intersections, including those that were in orbital positions in relation to the larger towns, such as Wexford and Enniscorthy. Roadside gatherings, especially if located at old fairs sites, would occasionally crystallise in tillage country into hamlets of labourers, which never acquired institutions or administrative functions. Examples would include Broadway in Forth, Bridgetown and Tullycanna in Bargy and The Harrow in Gorey. Their modern English names emphasised their recent origins. The confused condition of the ownership of glebe land sometimes prompted the infiltration of poor people on to the old parish centres. Taken together, for example, the parish centre townlands of Killenagh and Monamolin in Ballaghkeen North, Duncormick in Bargy and Fethard and Templetown in Shelburne contained 297 dwellings, of which 233 housed poor families in 1850. In Duncormick townland, which incorporated the parish centre village, 65 out of a total of 68 households fell into the poor category, as this has been defined for our purposes. Similar accretions of poor people were found alongside the new Catholic churches of the early nineteenth century, where they acted as a lowly incipient stage in the growth of what have come to be known as chapel villages.[21] In 1850 the villages of Monageer and Kiltealy in Scarawalsh, together with Carrick and Kilmore Quay in Bargy, contained 235 households, 185 of which fell into the poor category. In Monageer 37 out of a total of 45 families lived in houses which were valued at between five and fifteen shillings each. In nineteenth century Ireland the poor were the people of the extremities in the sense that, away from the old-settled areas, they were constantly associated with physically inferior land. In county Meath, for instance, the majority of the rural poor in 1850 were encountered on the bog edges. Lowlying wetlands were scarce in county Wexford. In the ill-drained basin of the river Sow, in the Gaelic barony of Ballaghkeen South, for example, the townlands of Ballymurry and Ballynamuddagh in the parish of Ballyhuskard together contained 80 out of a total of 100 householders who were either landless or who worked land that was valued at less than £5. Wexford was unusual among the Leinster counties in that the most substantial number of the rural poor were accommodated, not on the wetlands, but on free land available on baronial commonages, usually consisting of low value, unenclosed upland. Out of a total of 300 households found on the Forth Mountain commonages in Shelmaliere, Forth and Bargy, 280 were poor, as they have been defined for our purposes. Collectively the landless or near-landless peoples of nineteenth century Ireland acted as the jobbers that made possible the perpetuation of what was still largely a self-sufficient society.

As might be anticipated, it is in the religious world that we are best able to display cartographically for the nineteenth century the geographical implications of the interaction between an indigenous native culture, on the one hand, and an intrusive or colonial culture on the other. In county Wexford, as elsewhere in southern Ireland, the absence of religious non-conformity of the kind encountered in nineteenth century Wales or in Ulster helps to simplify and clarify the dichotomy. Territorial patterns of religious behaviour had an important bearing on the changing form and function of settlements, as well as on the nature of administrative frameworks.

The names that were bestowed on parishes of pre-reformation origin, as well as their complex territorial structures, remind us of the profound impact of early Celtic Christianity along the coastlands of south Leinster, and the Irish Sea littoral generally. What would have been the fate of this heritage had the religious reformation of the sixteenth century not been imposed upon Ireland as part of a colonial package? Ironically, in post-reformation Ireland, it was the colonial church which had become the custodian of the nation's rich and varied Christian heritage. By the mid nineteenth century, however, it had become abundantly clear that what had been acquired originally as part of a colonial booty had become an encumbrance and an embarrassment. Even the title which the Anglican church had given itself in Ireland appeared as an arrogant anachronism. In the mid nineteenth century the Church of Ireland in county Wexford appeared to be maintaining only a skeletal presence. Its diocesan town itself displayed in its composition and layout the dilemma that confronted an institution that was of rapidly decreasing significance. Ferns had old, powerful ecclesiastical and secular roots; its linear layout had been directed by the presence of a medieval castle at one end, and a medieval cathedral at the other end. Diocesan towns are of particular interest in the Irish urban hierarchy because they benefited the least from landlord patronage. Placed at the southern edge of the planted area in Scarawalsh, Ferns had emerged as a town of divided loyalties. During the nineteenth century it had become increasingly committed to the requirements of two cultures and two peoples, who appear to have had little to say to each other, and who rarely intermarried. This dual role revealed itself structurally in the polarisation of functions at the extremities of the main throughfare. Institutions which provided the more mundane requirements of daily life for the majority population were increasingly gathering in the vicinity of a Catholic chapel erected in 1826, at a point at the castle end of the settlement which was furthest removed from the cathedral which was now in Protestant hands. These included a fair's site, a memorial to the heroes of the 1798 insurrection, a court house, a constabulary barracks, local authority housing and a number of public houses, together with a primary school and a parochial hall. The consequent metamorphosis left the other extremity of the thoroughfare with an Anglican diocesan cathedral, dedicated to St Edan, to preside over the remains of a bishop's palace, the core area of the Irvine estate, as well as a multiplicity of ruins of earlier Christian institutiòns. Meanwhile, the centre of the modern Roman Catholic diocese of Ferns was translated to Enniscorthy. In Ferns the polarisation process has now ceased, and the once proscribed church is today represented by an attractive and costly structure erected at the centre of the town, domineering over its tired sinews.

The dilemma facing the Anglican church in Ireland in the mid nineteenth century may be demonstrated by an examination of the material content of its parish centres. The condition of the historic or Anglican parish centre in the nineteenth century serves as an important index to the sensitivity of areas and communities to the subsequent religious changes. Most of them withered away and ceased to have a secular or ecclesiastical meaning in the lives of the population. Some of the survivors, in common with other central-place elements that were commandeered by the colonial administration, withdrew from the general surge of modern Irish life. Examples of these included Delgany on the La Touche estate and Newcastle, on the Fitzwilliam estate in county Wicklow.[22] Others, for a variety of reasons, were thrust into the mainstream of village and small-town development. Unlike many other Irish dioceses, it appears that few attempts were made in Ferns in the early nineteenth century to resuscitate religious life by, for example, renovating the decaying fabric of the church with financial assistance from the Board of First Fruits. The typical rural church in the diocese of Ferns was rarely valued at more than £10, and its glebe house was less palatial than elsewhere in Leinster. In county Wexford the only major revision of the parish network, which was specifically designed to cater for the changing needs of the Protestant community, was carried out in the barony of Scarawalsh. Here the modern parishes of Ballycarney and Monart were carved out of the exceptionally large parish of Templeshanbo, which embraced most of the area of late settlement known as the Duffry. In the adjoining county of Wicklow, Aughrim, Tinahely and Shillelagh had been patronised by the Fitzwilliam of Coolattin estate, as parish centres for new and affluent Anglican communities. Similarly, on the lands of the Earl of Wicklow in the barony of Arklow on the Wexford-Wicklow border, the village of Redcross had been specifically created and designed to serve the needs of an estate and a new Church of Ireland parish which was formed as late as 1829. Typically the church at Redcross was dedicated, not to an early Celtic Christian leader, as were so many of the older foundations in south Leinster, but to the Holy Trinity. It was also typical of the nineteenth century for the village miller to be a planter, in this instance called Ruskell, and for the smith to be a Gael by the name of Duffy. The village community exhibited its alien origins in 1850 also in its wide display of family names of English origin. These included Hepenstal, Tyrrell, Winder, Tyndall, Arthur, Mates and Sherwood. Unlike most other settlements of its rank in south Leinster, Redcross has not responded to the demand for a more sophisticated range of services in the countryside in the late twentieth century. The collapse of the Earl of Wicklow's estate, together with the rationalisation of service functions in favour of the more accessible small towns, has led to Redcross's rapid contraction. It provides an unusual example from Leinster of a church village in decay, in the closing decades of the twentieth century. Within county Wexford, Hollyfort on the Powerscourt estate in Kilnahue parish in Gorey and Clonevan on the Cahore estate in Donaghmore parish in Ballaghkeen North are among the few church villages of the Redcross type that have been identified. Their absence may serve as an indication of the general weakness of both church and landlord in the Wexford of the nineteenth century.

There were other pointers in the settlement system which indicated that the Anglican communion presented itself more humbly in Wexford than in some other Leinster counties. The devastating impact of the sixteenth century religious reformation in the county becomes evident when it is realised that of the 140 historic parish centres in 1850, as many as 83 were without a church. In the northern baronies of Scarawalsh, Ballaghkeen North and Gorey. 60 percent of the old centres were still in use. Abandoned sites in the barony of Gorey included Kilnahue, Kiltrisk, Rosminoge, Kilcavan and Kilgorman. The highest ratio of abandoned sites, three-quarters of the total, was in the south-eastern baronies of Ballaghkeen South, Shelmaliere, Forth and Bargy. In Forth the aborted centres included Kildavin, Ishartmon, Kerloge, Killinick, Lady's Island, Mayglass and Killiane. Castle-ellis was the only centre to have survived in Ballaghkeen South. Ballylannan church in Shelmaliere West had survived only as a mausoleum for the Leigh family of Rosegarland, and the church at Kilpatrick in Shelmaliere East had become a domestic chapel for Arran of Saunderscourt. In county Wexford the destructive implication of the Reformation on the development of settlement was therefore the most keenly felt among the rich and varied Christian heritages of the Old English baronies.

Parish centre farms, which bore the parish name and on whose land was placed the modern Anglican church or its ruined precursor, were difficult to identify in the diocese of Ferns. Elsewhere in Ireland the association between parish centre and large farm or manorial unit was a fundamental feature of colonial and perhaps pre-colonial settlement structures. In the Old English baronies of Wexford, their former high status in the settlement hierarchy was indicated by the presence of a late medieval tower-house, as, for example, the Rossiter tower at Rathmacknee in Forth, and that of Browne at Mulrankin in Bargy. No more than 56 parish centre farms, excluding glebe holdings, have been identified, out of a total of 140 pre-reformation parishes in county Wexford, and only 22 of these were valued at £100 and over. Moreover, judging by the names of their occupiers in 1850, only 21 of the total were in New English hands. Among the more substantial parish centre farms occupied by tenants of non-Gaelic stock were Newbawn House (Sweetman) in Shelmaliere West, Kilmallock House (Peare) in Ballaghkeen South and Ballinclare House (Roe) in Toome parish in the barony of Gorey. Occasionally New English landowners, like their medieval counterparts, had sought old parish centres as sites for their home farms. When this marriage of the secular and the ecclesiastical took place, it served to strengthen the status and influence of the parish centre within the settlement hierarchy. In county Wexford, in 1850, a total of ten estate-core farms were located in pre-reformation parish centres, and seven of these were in the Old English baronies of Shelmaliere and Forth. In Shelmaliere East they included Le Hunte's home farm at Artramon and Walker's at Tikillin, and in Forth, Nunn of St Margaret's and Richards of Rathaspick House. In other Leinster counties, parishes which in this way had become directly embroiled in the estate system of land management had their standing further enhanced as they were deliberately allocated to the largest and most favoured of planter tenants. Thus the principal tenants of the Earl of Wicklow's estate in Kilbride parish in the barony of Arklow in 1850 included names such as Prestage, Stringer, Borbidge and Tuke. Parish centre patronage of this kind was rarely encountered even in the planted baronies in county Wexford. The fusion of estate core and parish centre was commonplace in the English homeland, where it contributed handsomely to the enrichment of village and small-town life, as it did in less convivial circumstances in the province of Ulster. In Ireland, the marriage of these two most prominent nodes in the rural settlement network enabled the church to turn to its principal lay patron for succour and shelter. In this way, Kiltennell church in Ballaghkeen North attached itself to the core area of the Courtown estate, Killegney church in Bantry became part of the Carew of Castleboro complex, whilst the modern church at Clone in Scarawalsh was placed on the demesne lands of Richards of Solsborough House. In turn, the lay councillors of the Anglican church were increasingly drawn from leading landlord families.[23] In the diocese of Ferns in the mid twentieth century, its councillors included Templemore of Dunbrody, Blacker of Woodbrook and Doyne of Wells.

The general malaise of the Anglican church in county Wexford in the nineteenth century was in sharp contrast to the militant attitude adopted by the new Roman Catholicism, as it became a principal force making for the modernisation of the native culture. The church which today towers over the former Anglican diocesan centre of Ferns owed its remarkable popularity in the nineteenth century partly to its concern for the secular as well as the religious experiences of its followers. In its stride it cultivated a religiosity which, as in non-conformist Wales, came to embrace the entire Irish population. In both countries vigorous new forces were unleashed, which forged a fresh national consciousness, which, in the case of Ireland, ensured its early political separation from the countries of Britain, and the dismantling of its colonial apparatus. As with Welsh non-conformity, the Catholic church in Ireland offered a creative outlet for the Gael, which had spiritual sanction, and in which the alien culture in their midst did not, or could not, partake. Consequently, from the early nineteenth century, institutionalised Catholicism became a significant cementing force in Irish life, in the countryside as well as in the towns. The geographical implications of the coming of the new Catholicism to county Wexford may be demonstrated in a variety of ways. In the circumstances which prevailed in late eighteenth and early nineteenth century Ireland, the renewed church, which drew its inspiration and direction from a vast and closely administered international network, appears to have had few qualms about dissociating itself from aspects of Ireland's older culture. In its endeavour to modernise Irish life, this urbane church was prepared to dispense, where necessary, with the nation's ancient language, to ignore its early Christian leaders in its selection of parochial dedications, and also to isolate itself from the usurped network of dioceses and parishes and their settlement complements. It was in these circumstances that the thriving river port of Enniscorthy replaced Ferns as the new diocesan centre.

How did the dynamic leaders of the revitalised church, with its enduring continental linkages, view the chaos and decay among the old Christian structures in Ireland? One reaction in Leinster was to proceed to construct fresh spatial orders, which were frequently incompatible with the pre-existing territorial and settlement frameworks. At a time of increasing mobility, and a widening of physical and cultural horizons, new parish structures were assembled in Ireland, and the geographer is particularly concerned with the selection of areas and communities which were to form the bases for the new frameworks[24]. No other west European country is likely to have experienced such a radical transformation of its ecclesiastical territorial arrangements during the nineteenth century. The vigorous and all-embracing character of the new Catholicism ensured that the rural parish once more became the secular as well as the ecclesiastical fulcrum of local life, as well as the most significant administrative entity below the county. For the first time, entire communities were marshalled which were not necessarily tied together by spatial propinquity, kin relationships or historical inertia. In the new Catholic parochial arrangements the Gael came to possess a precisely defined territorial net which embraced the entire island, and which was specifically designed for his own purposes. Hitherto he had not taken easily to the territorial regimentation of his country, which had been for so long initiated by colonial peoples for their own purposes. Although the modern parish has never been recognised by government as a secular administrative entity, it soon acquired a new and urgent meaning in the lives of the rural population.

In county Wexford 40 modern rural Catholic parishes came to replace 140 pre-existing historic parishes. Only 12 of these entities in 1850 had retained the names of their pre-Reformation precursors. These included Taghmon and Newbawn in Shelmaliere, Kilmore in Bargy and Lady's Island in Forth. There seems to have been an element of self-denial in the apparently casual manner in which nineteenth century Catholic parishes were named and where their principal churches were located. This may be illustrated from the former Cistercian monastic properties in the barony of Shelburne. The Tintern lands are today mainly found in a parish known as Ballycullane, whilst the Dunbrody monastic estate is partly within a Catholic parish which was initially named after an Old English family of Sutton, but which is today known as Horeswood, after the location of its principal church. Similarly, another modern parish, which incorporates part of the Dunbody lands, is focussed not on the garrison village of Duncannon, on Waterford Harbour, nor on the estate village of Arthurstown, nor on the river port of Ballyhack, but on the church of St James, located in a recently emerged chapel village of Ramsgrange. In this respect it is important to bear in mind that the location of a Catholic church in the early nineteenth century was frequently dependent on lay patronage especially as this was forthcoming from among the strong Catholic tenant farmers.[25] St Anne's church at Rathgarogue in the parish of Cushinstown in Bantry was located on the lands of Gobbinstown House, and a farm valued at £200, occupied by a family with the Old English name of Fitzhenry. Similarly, the church of St James and Ann at Tomhaggard, at the head of Tacumshin Lake in Bargy, was on the lands of a Devereux, whose farm was valued at £130 in 1850.[26] The chapel at Newbawn, in Shelmaliere West, was on the Sweetman farm of Newbawn House, alongside the site of the historic parish centre.[27] In the more Gaelic baronies, where central-place functions were traditionally less in evidence in the settlement net, the early nineteenth century chapels of a foot-loose church were conspicuously lonely ingredients in the open countryside. The three chapels at Cushinstown, Terrerath and Rathgarogue in Cushinstown parish on the Bantry and Shelmaliere border stood alone, as did the chapels of Davidstown and Courtnacuddy, in Davidstown parish, in the barony of Bantry. These early nineteenth century chapels appear also to have been fragile structures. The parish centre churches at Ballindaggin, Marshalstown and Davidstown, for example, were valued at no more than £5 each. Nevertheless, fledgling Catholic parishes and their chapels, in places such as Monaseed, Kiltealy, Castledockrell and Cloughbawn, were among the most dramatic components of the changing settlement structures, along the eastern flanks of the Leinster mountains in the famine years. In Arklow barony on the Wicklow-Wexford border, the chapel-of-ease at Barranisky, aloft at 200 metres, and overlooking the fat planter farms of the Earl of Wicklow's estate in Kilbride parish and dedicated to St Patrick, provided the stereotype. Humble and alone, it was a conspicuous and defiant portent of future development.

It is clear that in any attempt to compare the old and the new among the ecclesiastical territorial arrangements in county Wexford, a critical index is the choice of the location of the modern Catholic church. The spatial rift in Ireland between two peoples or cultures, as a consequence of the Reformation and its colonial ramifications, was most apparent in the planted counties of south Ulster. In Cavan, for example, only 5 out of a total of 63 modern Catholic chapels occupied the pre-Reformation sites. In county Meath the comparative totals were 38 and 86, and in Wexford they were 15 and 83 respectively. It appears that in county Wexford the early re-entry of the Catholic church onto the older sites was more in evidence in the areas which we have recognised as being Gaelic in sentiment. As many as 10 of the 14 Catholic churches occupying pre-reformation sites in county Wexford were located in the three baronies of Shelmaliere, Bantry and Ballaghkeen. In Shelmaliere the churches concerned were at Clongeen, Newbawn, Ballymitty and Taghmon, and in Bantry they were at Adamstown, Templeludigan and Clonmore. In the east in Ballaghkeen South, chapels were found alongside the historic parish centres at Glenbrien, Litter and Monamolin. No similar enthusiasm for the spatial fusion of religious institutions was found in the Old

English baronies. In the four baronies of Shelmaliere East, Shelburne, Forth and Bargy, only five modern Catholic churches were found in the old centres, and three of these were in Forth, at Kilrane, Lady's Island and Mayglass. As in Cavan, the rift between the two peoples was most keenly felt in the planter baronies of the north of the county. In 1850 no Catholic chapel was located alongside a historic parish centre in either Gorey or Scarawalsh.

Some of the consequences of the marriage of the old and the new in historic parish centres are seen in the nineteenth century in Rathnew in the barony of Newcastle in the adjoining county of Wicklow. Rathnew provided an example of a historic parish centre that had acquired fresh focal values, because it had early succumbed to the needs and the aspirations of the new Ireland, that was dramatically emerging in the nineteenth century. The litmus test for the transfer of allegiance in Rathnew was the appearance of the Catholic chapel-of-ease alongside the ruins of an early Christian church. Another was the rapid growth of a village community as part of a parish centre. In this respect, Rathnew, like Lusk in north county Dublin or Duleek in county Meath, was exceptional in that it possessed a parish commonage, and in 1850 as many as 160 households were accommodated on 2.5 ha of this free land, and in dwelling houses which were rarely valued at more than £1 each. Most of these poor villagers had Irish names, and among the most numerous were Byrne and Doyle. Of the 44 female heads of household, 20 were called Mary. Exceptional devotion to a faith and to a church that must have provided succour to their ancestors is still evident in Rathnew in the display of roadside shrines and grottoes, features which otherwise are rarely encountered in southeast Leinster. Ballycanew in Gorey and Taghmon in Shelmaliere were examples from county Wexford of old parish centres, like Rathnew, which had yielded to the new order, and had benefitted from being located on busy arterial roads.

Throughout Ireland Catholic churches which did not occupy pre-Reformation parochial sites stood to gain from the powerful forces which in the nineteenth century were making for the nucleation of an ever increasing range of service functions in village centres. Mid century was also the time when the spatial diffusion of these services was reaching its maximum. It was in this kind of atmosphere that the new Catholic Chapels were found emerging as the gaunt centrepieces of embryonic settlements, which are now being referred to as chapel villages, and these villages in turn were to become the settlement centres of new Catholic parishes. A national school alongside the chapel ensured that parish consciousness was cultivated early in these fresh nineteenth century settlements. The rounded character of life in a chapel village, focussed on its one church and venerated graveyard, must have contrasted strongly with the confused and divided loyalties generated among similar communities in nonconformist Wales, where the parish system and its churches had lost their meaning in the lives of the majority of the population. Nevertheless, like most of the trappings of the refurbished church, the typical chapel village was historically rootless. It was altogether modern in form, content and function and in this way collectively provided a rare example from the western Europe of the nineteenth century of a new village system that was not of industrial origin. Evidence is forthcoming that the density of chapel villages varied substantially from one part of the island to another. They seem to have emerged and flourished most in the mixed farming, tillage or dairying counties of the south, where the church of the renewal had itself established its most vigorous and innovative early foothold. Only two chapel villages have been identified for Cavan, and nine for Meath.[28] By contrast there were 21 in Tipperary[29] and 30 in Limerick.[30] The 34 which have been isolated for Wexford may provide the highest density for any one county in the entire island. Within Wexford only eleven of these villages were located in the five southern baronies of Shelmaliere West, Shelmaliere East, Shelburne, Forth and Bargy. Examples from Bargy included Kilmore Quay, Hilltown and Carrig-on-Bannow.[31] In county Wexford the chapel village came to fill a void in the central-place hierarchy left by the general absence of estate sponsored village settlement. They were therefore more numerous in baronies which hitherto had been largely deprived of village communities. In this way half the total in 1850 were located in Scarawalsh, Bantry and Ballaghkeen South. They were primarily features of the Gaelic heartland of the county. Among the most coherent examples drawn from the eastern sector of this heartland were Ballaghkeen, Ballygarrett, Glenbrien, Oylgate, Blackwater, Ballymurn and Oulart in the barony of Ballaghkeen, Boolavogue in Gorey and Monageer in Scarawalsh. Communities of this kind acquired fame as the generous nurseries of the growing number of clergy that were demanded, from the later nineteenth century, to man the rapidly expanding mission fields of the Irish church overseas, as well as in the homeland. It was among communities of this calibre that the battle between traditionalism and modernisation was most prolonged in county Wexford.

A Transatlantic Merchant fishery: Richard Welsh of New Ross and the Sweetmans of Newbawn in Newfoundland 1734-1862

So little has been written on the nature of Irish mercantile settlement overseas that students of the Irish past might conclude with some justification that such a phenomenon rarely occurred and, when it did, it was ephemeral and peripheral. The literature on Irish migration and settlement abroad understandably focuses on the poor and disadvantaged. Certainly the emigrants were poor, probably disproportionately so, but not all. Some were artisans with varying degrees of skill, others strong and middling farmers or more frequently their surplus sons. These people brought with them at least expertise, and sometimes capital, to continue careers in new settings. By contrast only a tiny fraction of the migrating Irish were merchants and traders or advanced to that status overseas. However, they had a considerable influence on the management of Irish commerce abroad, as the pioneering work of scholars such as Louis Cullen is beginning to reveal.[1] Waterford, the smaller port of New Ross, and their hinterlands emerged early as important sources of Irish Catholic merchants in the great seaports of France and Iberia. Drawing on a long tradition of intensive commercial farming in the physically favoured pockets of the southeast, particularly in the fertile basins of the Barrow, the Nore and the Suir, merchants in this region specialised in the export of salt provisions to the continent through the eighteenth century and in the importation of wines, brandy, fruit, and salt. Much of this trade was handled abroad by merchants who were not from Ireland. Irish mercantile participation was substantial, however, and probably increased as the century progressed.

While merchants from Waterford and other ports were engaged in southern Europe, a distinctive trade, also with strong southeast Irish connections, was emerging across the Atlantic, in distant Newfoundland. This commerce was similar in several ways to that practiced by Irish merchants on the continent but it also involved the migration of labour, seasonal at first, then permanent, to prosecute the cod fishery. These migrations were organised by merchants and their agents, many of whom belonged to the southeast. Wexford was important not only as a source of servants but also of merchants and agents to exploit the fishery. This chapter attempts to open up for discussion neglected aspects of Irish migrations and the character of Irish mercantile settlement overseas by probing the contribution of a single merchant house in Newfoundland with deep roots in south Wexford soil.

The firm founded by Richard Welsh of New Ross in Placentia, Newfoundland, continued by his son-in-law William Saunders of Bideford and later by Welsh's own likely descendants, the Sweetmans of Newbawn, lasted for more than a century. From modest beginnings the firm became a giant in the Newfoundland trade. At its peak this house owned a dozen ocean-going vessels, employed or supplied several hundred men and shipped over £25,000 of dried cod in a season to markets around the North Atlantic. After 1800 the company was responsible for the settlement of scores of Irish immigrants throughout its trading territory in Placentia Bay. They came mainly from Wexford and other counties of the southeast; their descendants dominate parts of the bay to this day.

Richard Welsh was born in New Ross in 1718 and moved to Placentia in 1734 at the age of sixteen.[2] Little is know of his social origins except that he came from a relatively modest background.[3] He probably began as an apprentice clerk or an assistant storekeeper to an English trader in Great Placentia harbour. Placentia was at that time the centre of a thriving migratory ship fishery based in north Devon. A cluster of ports in Bideford Bay were involved: Barnstaple on the river Torridge, Bideford on the Taw and their outports Northam and Appledore. Each spring the fishing ships would set sail from these small ports with fishermen and supplies for Placentia and other harbours in the southern half of the Avalon peninsula. Here they would anchor for the summer while crews were deployed in shallops to fish for cod inshore. When dried the cod was shipped to the major markets in southern Europe or the West Indies and in the fall these Devon fishermen returned home. Twenty such fishing ships docked at Placentia and nearby harbours in 1734, the year of Welsh's arrival, with some 600 fishermen who operated 100 shallops and caught over 30,000 quintals of cod.[4] There was at this time also a small fishery conducted by some fifty planters who lived at Placentia and nearby harbours year-round. These residents were mainly from the English West Country; some were married with family. The planters hired servants or 'passengers' who were brought out annually on the fishing ships to work for a summer or more on contract before returning home. Fewer than fifty passengers arrived at Placentia in the spring of 1734 and the resident fishery accounted for less than 1/5 of the season's catch.

From their inception the Irish migrations to Placentia were an integral part of the transient ship fishery and the resident operation that it spawned. Late in the seventeenth century some of the fishing ships departing Devon for Newfoundland in the spring began calling in regularly en route to the port or harbour of Waterford to collect provisions for the summer cod fishery. In March, 1697, for example, the merchants of Bideford and Barnstaple requested a convoy for the fishing ships bound for Newfoundland 'to stop with ye said ships in ye River of Waterford forty-eight hours only for taking on board their bread and provisions that are ready to be shipt ...'.[5] Early in the eighteenth century the fishing ships also began taking on passengers annually from the southeast to work as servants in the fishery. Following the Treaty of Utrecht in 1713 and the cession of Plaisance (Placentia), the regional capital of France's extensive fishery on Newfoundland's south coast, this splendid harbour became the focus of a fishery from north Devon and consequently an important centre for early Irish migrations and indeed settlement. 'There are not above ten French residents in St Peters, St Lawrence and Placentia who conform to the treaty of peace and are supplied with craft and servants from England' wrote a British naval commodore in 1720 'but here are brought over every year by the Bristol, Bideford and Barnstable ships great numbers of Irish Roman Catholic servants, who all settle to the southward in our plantations ...'.[6] The governor reported that the 'vast increase' in the amount of fish cured at Placentia was 'in part owing to the great quantity of Irish papists and non-jurors ... who yearly come out and settle here'.[7] The English authorities complained that several unlicensed Irish fishing ships were actually operating from Little Placentia and from other harbours across the bay formerly occupied by the French. 'They bring with them a number of Irish servants, some of whom they leave in the winter and by that means stake out the very best of the ancient fishing rooms'. The threat of an independent Irish fishery, of unemployed overwintering Irish servants and of Irish Catholic disloyalty worried the English officials on this remote fishing frontier. Should war resume with France they 'would join with the enemy' a commodore warned. and be 'a direct means of losing the country'. A large group of Irish servants rioted in St Mary's harbour in 1724, after the British man-of-war had left in the fall. Although uncertain about the legality of an independent Irish fishery and Irish settlement in Placentia the authorities moved to suppress them to 'make room for His Majesty's subjects, duly qualified'.

It is against this complex web of economic, ethnic, religious and political tensions that the role of a cultural broker like Richard Welsh must be examined. The English controlled the fishery as it expanded but depended increasingly on Irish servants to catch and especially to cure the fish. Welsh helped regulate Irish labour in Placentia, placing young servants with English planters and supervising the several specialised tasks undertaken by the Irish ashore. Each fall servants had to be paid on the expiry of their contracts and provision made for their passages home. In 1753, for example, five servants sued a Bideford captain for the 'cruel treatment they had received on their passage to Ireland'.[8] Apparently they had managed to get aboard without paying their passage money. Welsh and another Bideford captain testified that 'passage money is always by custom paid by the planters' and the court ordered Welsh to see to it that this be done.

Placentia was by now the centre of a flourishing fishery. The number of fishing ships and fishermen had almost doubled since Welsh's arrival but more striking was the growth in the resident fishery and associated Irish passenger trade. Between 600-900 servants arrived annually, there were 170 planters in the district and the residents catch accounted for 45% of the total. The passengers were predominantly southeastern Irish and a decade later overwhelmingly so. With the outbreak of war between Britain and France in 1756, the migratory ship fishery from north Devon collapsed, never to recover. During the war Placentia depended largely on a resident fishery conducted inshore. Poole in Dorset replaced the north Devon ports as the organisational centre and the importance of Waterford and its hinterland as a source of labour and provisions increased. It was under these changing conditions that Richard Welsh, twenty years a resident of Placentia, finally entered trade on his own account.

Few data survive on the details of Welsh's early trade. In 1753 he rented some ground on the Great Beach of Placentia from a long-established English planter and built a premises there. Over the next few years he acquired at least five more properties from English planters nearby.[9] These properties formed the core of Welsh's trading domain and continued as headquarters for more than a century.

Although overshadowed by Waterford, Ireland's third busiest port, New Ross was the pivot of Wexford's links with Newfoundland and the base for a small but independent trade from there in passengers and provisions through the eighteenth century. It was managed by a closely-knit Protestant merchant community at Ross, notably the Elmses, Nappers, Allens, Koughs, Glasscotts, Goffs and Lamphiers and was directed primarily to the port of St John's. This commerce had begun by the time Welsh moved to Newfoundland but there is no evidence that the Ross merchants were involved in trade with Placentia during his long stint as agent there. In the spring of 1759, however, 'Richard Welsh, late of this town, now of Placentia, merchant' was given the status of freeman of Ross for the purpose of trading.[10] Among the signatures of the town council were three of the leading merchants in the Newfoundland trade: James Napper, Highate Allen, and Thomas Kough. Three other 'Papists' were admitted with Welsh. One, William Furlong, recorded as a mariner with a house on Mary Street in 1750 and as a shopkeeper in 1759, was a relative.[11] The others, Dominick Farrell and Thomas Knowles, were established merchants and freemen of Waterford and already engaged in colonial commerce. These admissions almost certainly represent an attempt by Welsh to cultivate his home place as a source of labour and supplies for the fishery at Placentia, now that the north Devon ports had declined.

Welsh quickly emerged as the leading merchant in the harbour of Placentia where the Irish outnumbered the English two to one. Indeed the district of Placentia was the most Irish part of the island, accounting for ⅓ of the total Irish population in the summer of 1759 and over 40% of all Irish women and children. Welsh took advantage of his connections to build up an ethnic trade but also maintained commercial links with the local English planters. His drive to capture the commerce of the district was contested by the merchants of Poole and a bitter struggle ensued. In 1759 a new Poole house established in Little Placentia sent out one of their sea captains with a letter of recommendation to Welsh to act as their agent through the summer. Welsh 'pretended a great friendship' and promised the new firm supplies on reasonable terms if they ran short. This he failed to do and was accused by the agent 'of iniquitous and unreasonable proceedings', supplying the Poole company's planters and servants at low prices in exchange for fish, and even the company's own servants despite written contracts and the customs of trade.[12] Welsh did sell supplies to the company in winter, but at exorbitant prices, and appropriated their fish in exchange. 'In this condition we unfortunately labour'd from year to year . . .' the agent reported, causing 'the ruin of three gentlemen in England who have spent their fortunes here and become bankrupt. . . . If some speedy remedy don't take place it will be impossible for any English merchant to carry on any employ or trade here as Mr Welsh will throw every impediment and opposition in his way'. Six planters, two of them English, the rest Irish, protested that the Poole merchants never had adequate supplies and without Welsh they could not have continued their fishery.

Of the merchant families from Poole attempting to establish a branch at Little Placentia during the war, only the Quaker house of Neaves and Company, drawing on Quaker merchants in Waterford for passengers and provisions, succeeded and persisted as the main rivals to Welsh and his successors. Welsh dominated trade at Great Placentia but did not monopolise it. He apparently focused on local traffic, issuing supplies to planters and servants and collecting their fish. Data are thin but there is little evidence that Richard Welsh was an important shipowner with a network of correspondents overseas. In 1760 he purchased a 50 ton brig from Boston, likely for coastal trading, and evidently chartered a vessel that spring which sailed from Appledore to Placentia and took a cargo of cod to Bilbao.[13] This venture, under the management of Richard Kavanagh, a Wexford sea captain, ended when the vessel sank returning to Placentia with salt from Cadiz.

Welsh depended largely on other traders for supplies from overseas in exchange for fish.[14] He depended also on the honesty of planters and servants to whom he advanced provisions in the spring on the promise of fish in the fall. In 1762 a group of planters and servants supplied by him fled to Halifax with cod, oil and shallops. Five Irishmen hired to build boats through the winter also deserted. He petitioned the governor that all winter servants carry shipping papers to prevent their absconding in spring and taking up work in other harbours.[15] Like most merchants Welsh was harsh in his treatment of planters and servants alike, appropriating their properties and possessions when unable to pay their debts and withholding wages and supplies.

Trade at Placentia peaked after the seven years war as settlement expanded and the harbour continued to dominate the fishery of the bay. It was during this period that Richard Welsh laid the foundations for a merchant firm transatlantic in scope with respectable international connections. He hired William Saunders of Bideford as his principal agent and revived links with old shipowning families such as the Hoggs and Salmons of north Devon and Placentia, long engaged in the trade. More importantly, he forged closer ties with Waterford, Wexford and with Iberia.[16] These commercial connections were facilitated and consolidated by the marriages of his three daughters prior to his demise. In 1767 his daughter Bridget, with a dazzling dowry for the times of £10,000, married Paul Farrell, son of Dominick, one of the leading merchants in Waterford in the Irish-Newfoundland trade (fig. 14.1).[17] Dominick Farrell was engaged in a ship fishery at Trinity harbour, north of Placentia, but Paul apparently linked up with his father-in-law and focused on triangular trade between Waterford, Placentia and Cadiz where the Farrell dynasty operated a major branch house. He was admitted freeman of Waterford shortly after his marriage and owned or had shares in the 100 ton brig *Bridget*, built in Newfoundland probably by Welsh.[18] Another daughter, Ann, married William Saunders and, although the evidence remains circumstantial the third, Mary, most likely married Roger Sweetman, son of Michael of Newbawn, a big farmer.

Richard Welsh died at Placentia in the fall of 1770, still relatively young but one of Wexford's most successful merchants overseas. More than twenty years after his death Aaron Graham selected him as a prime example of a man from a modest background who made a fortune in the cod trade.[19] Welsh bequeathed over £15,000 and properties in Placentia to his immediate family and kin. His wife Mary, likely a Furlong from Ross, was awarded £100 a year from Welsh's 'capital stock of £5,000 in the New South Seas annuity'. He gave £2,000 to his three daughters, £1,000 to two Farrell grandsons in Waterford and £200 'to Mary Furlong, daughter of William Furlong of Ross'. Although long a resident in Newfoundland more than ⅓ of the money awarded by Richard Welsh was interest from investments in Ireland, mainly New Ross. This pattern of investment was typical of a colonial merchant in the eighteenth century fishery. One of his principal heirs was Paul Welsh Wibault, probably a nephew, who received £3,000; should he die this sum was to be transferred to the six sons of David Wibault. Deborah Wibault was given £1,300 with two dwelling houses and a store at Placentia. Little is known of this family in Newfoundland but James Wibault was a chief engineer, colonel and deputy governor with the garrison at St John's in 1741 and was subsequently with the garrison at Placentia.[20] Welsh's main heir was his son David to whom he bequeathed his wife's annuity after her death, £2,500 'in the hands of Charles Tottenham, Esquire', a leading landowner in New Ross, plus 'plantations, stock-in-trade ... all household goods, plate, china and furniture for the purpose of carrying on in Great Placentia or elsewhere in Newfoundland the business ... I now follow'. He appointed his son-in-law William Saunders agent in Placentia 'as long as my said trustees shall think proper and he appearing to be faithful'. His salary was not to exceed £150 a year 'sufficient maintenance for himself and his present wife, Ann Welsh, and for whatsoever children he might have by his said wife'. Welsh also directed his trustees, Thomas Hogg of Appledore, Edward Smith of Bideford, and Joshua Bowden of Northam, merchants, to make 'a true and just inventory' of all his 'goods, wares and merchandise that shall be in the store at Great Placentia' or elsewhere in Newfoundland six months after his death and again when his son reached the age of twenty-one. He showed the caution of a mature merchant when recommending that Saunders drop ⅓ of their planters in the event of war with France or Spain.

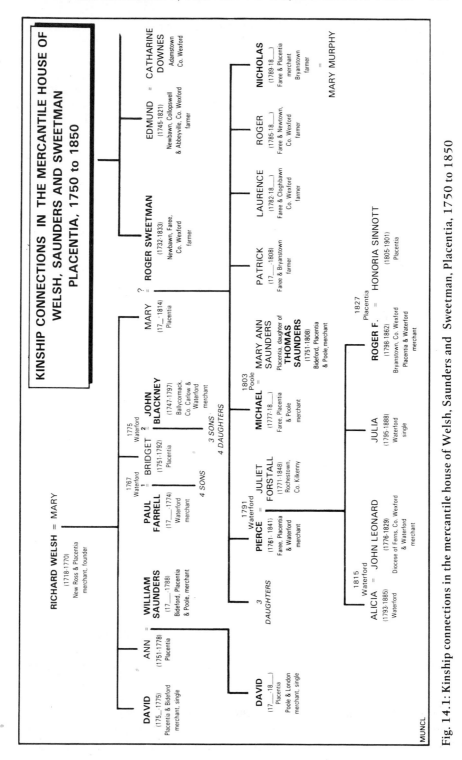

Fig. 14.1: Kinship connections in the mercantile house of Welsh, Saunders and Sweetman, Placentia, 1750 to 1850

The Welsh Succession

Welsh's demise did not alter significantly the firm's pattern of trade. William Saunders settled down with his family at Placentia, directing the business from there. He was assisted by his brother Thomas who alternated residence between his native Bideford and Placentia, and by David Welsh. Like their fathers before them, David Welsh and Paul Farrell were admitted together as freemen of Ross but there is no evidence of trade from there.[21] Farrell's Waterford and Spanish connections, however, were strategic. Ships engaged in the firm's freights usually departed Bristol, Bideford or Waterford in the spring with supplies and passengers for Placentia, proceeded to Iberia, principally Alicante and Cadiz, with cod, and returned to ports in southern England and particularly Waterford with salt, wine and fruit.[22] Paul Farrell built what was described as 'the best salt works in Ireland' on Catherine's Pill near his main premises in the east end of Waterford. He was a leading importer of Iberian and Newfoundland products. In 1772-1773, he exported £5,000 of salt provisions, mainly to Newfoundland with smaller shipments to Poole, Bristol and Bideford for the cod fishery. Little is known of his trading arrangements with David Welsh and the Saunders but Farrell did not engage exclusively in the Newfoundland trade and he probably operated on his own account. Close to half his exports went to Liverpool, Campveer, Bordeaux (where his older brother resided), Port Mahone and especially to London and Cadiz.

Paul Farrell died suddenly in 1774 and David Welsh shortly thereafter.[23] This essentially ended Farrell links with the Placentia cod trade. As a trustee to Paul's marriage in 1767 and executor of his will, Dominick Farrell was involved in the administration of the Welsh estate.[24] He received a bond of £6,000 from Bridget Farrell for the benefit of his four grandsons — also the grandsons of Richard Welsh — and in 1776 requested, jointly with Hogg, Bowden and Smith of Appledore, that all debtors and creditors of the late Richard Welsh submit their accounts. Bridget remarried in 1775, John Blackney, member of a long-established, landed Catholic family in county Carlow who had moved to Waterford and was engaged in the wine trade there.[25] Her dowry of £15,000, most of it her father's fortune, was rarely surpassed in merchant marriage settlements in eighteenth century Ireland. William Saunders of Placentia and Roger Sweetman of Faree were appointed trustees and most of the money was reserved for the development of the Placentia cod fishery.

John Blackney acquired one of Farrells' premises and replaced Paul Farrell as Waterford agent in this trade. He had close family ties with members of the Catholic sub-gentry in the southeast, including the Archbolds, the St Legers, the Wyses and the Anthonys of Waterford. Typical of this group, Blackney focused more on the local land market than on commerce overseas. In contrast to the Farrells, who were shipowners with a network of correspondents on the continent, Blackney did not invest in shipping and did not attempt to integrate the cod trade in Iberia with his Waterford trade as the Farrells had done.

Indeed there is no evidence that he ever established a formal partnership with his brother-in-law William Saunders in the Placentia fishery. Like the majority of Waterford merchants he worked for a commission, assembling provisions on Saunders' request, recruiting labourers for the season and arranging their passages, paying these servants on their return to Waterford in the fall and taking cod and cod oil from Placentia for sale locally.[26]

The enterprise expanded during the American War of Independence. New England's substantial supply trade to Placentia was disrupted and the Poole merchants turned to ports in Britain and Ireland, particularly Waterford and the southeast, for extra provisions. William Saunders finally moved his English base from his native Bideford down to Poole during the war. He had depended largely on North Devon shipowners and sea captains for freight to Placentia as Richard Welsh had done. Saunders now purchased some of these vessels but also began building ships at Placentia during the winters. By 1780 the firm had seven or eight ocean-going vessels engaged in the trade, one of the leading shipowners in the fishery. The fleet sailed from Poole and other ports on England's south coast and increasingly from Waterford.

Encouraged by a growing fishery in the 1770s, William Saunders consolidated and expanded the properties and trade bequeathed by Richard Welsh. Despite the intensification and spread of settlement, seasonal and permanent, along the southern coast the harbour of Great Placentia maintained its monopoly over trade in the region.[27] 'If Placentia were to fall' an official reported in 1772 'it would destroy the fishery of twenty harbours'. In a petition a decade later from seven Poole firms for better fortifications at Placentia, the town was described as 'the repository for all the coast between Cape Pine and Cape Ray' with cod exports amounting to nearly ⅓ of the island's total.[28] Like his father-in-law, Saunders was the principal merchant in this fishery and headed the only major house in the harbour. Early in the 1770s he conducted this trade 'for the trust of the late Richard Welsh' but following the death of David Welsh assumed control of the firm. He established close links with the military, particularly during the war, securing contracts to carry supplies from St John's and elsewhere to the garrison at Placentia.[29] Saunders also secured material from the military to defend the firm's premises in the outharbours, at Point Verde and at Marticott (fig. 14.2). Following the death of his wife in Placentia in 1778 Saunders moved to Poole, rotating residences on both sides of the Atlantic with his younger brother Thomas, now a partner in the trade. By 1783 the Saunders were one of the leading houses in Poole, a position they maintained until the end of the century. They had opened up trade on company account in a dozen ports in southern Europe, employed over fifty mariners and sea captains, carried hundreds of men annually to and from the fishery and supplied even more customers in Placentia Bay.

The Sweetman Connection

The Sweetmans of Newbawn entered this fishery as it neared its peak. An Anglo-Norman family, dislodged from their towerhouse and deprived of their

Fig. 14.2: Fishing premises and property held by Saunders and Sweetman c.1800

lands during the Cromwellian conquest, they managed to survive the upheavals of the seventeenth century to emerge as big farmers with considerable wealth. Family tradition holds that they cleared land in Newbawn, part of an extensive forest, following the Cromwellian confiscations. Pierce Sweetman is recorded there in 1700 with his wife, Elizabeth Downes, member of another important farming family in nearby Adamstown. He was likely responsible for the construction of the commodious two-storey farmhouse with five bays which still survives in Newbawn (fig 14.3). Such places provided the classic background for entry into eighteenth century mercantile trade or a career in the upper echelons of the re-emerging Irish Catholic church. Pierce Sweetman's son, Patrick, born in Newbawn in 1705, moved to Cadiz in 1730 as an agent and then merchant in the wine trade.[30] He married a Wexford women there and travelled extensively through southern Europe and to England in pursuit of commerce. Nicholas Sweetman (1696-1786), an older brother, was sent to the Irish college at Salamanca, returned to Wexford after ordination and in 1745 became Bishop of Ferns, an office he held longer than anyone else. In 1752 Michael Sweetman (1711-1776), possibly Pierce's youngest son, worked 347 Irish acres at Newbawn, leased from the Leighs of Rosegarland.[31] This was by far the largest farm in the area, its boundaries virtually coterminous with those of the townland. A pre-reformation church (in ruins) and a cemetery, the historic core of the old civil parish (also called Newbawn), were located within the farm. These large townland farms, bearing the same name as the parish, were characteristic locations for privileged families such as the Sweetmans in the normanised southeast.

Michael Sweetman divided the farm and other land he had acquired amongst his sons, initiating a gradual dispersal of Sweetmans across the south Wexford landscape (fig 14.4, table 1). One son, Edmund, was bequeathed Collopswell where, according to tradition he built a house similar to that at Newbawn. This house was burned in 1798 and Edmund moved to nearby Abbeyville (pl. xxxv).[32] Another son, Nicholas, rented a farm in Ballygalvert, well north of the Sweetman country, from the Byrnes and the Blackneys. It was one of several land transactions between Blackneys and Sweetmans after 1775, reflecting marriage and mercantile ties; Nicholas later returned to Newbawn to share the home farm with his brother Michael (1747-1833), the youngest son. The eldest son, Roger, was given a large farm in Faree, east of Newbawn, by his father where he built a substantial dwelling house in typical georgian style (pl. xxxvi). Although he was admitted a freeman of Ross in 1786 and recorded as a merchant there two years later, there is no evidence that Roger Sweetman was ever engaged directly in overseas trade.[33] He was, all his life, a big farmer. The precise details of his marriage settlement are not known but Richard Welsh left £500 to Mary Welsh in his will, or, should she die, to her children plus an equal share of the business at Placentia. Most likely in keeping with these agreements Pierce Sweetman, eldest son of Roger, was sent to William Saunders at Poole and to Placentia to learn the trade. Pierce Sweetman's early travels typify the considerable mobility of an apprentice merchant in the cod fishery. He was first recorded at Placentia in the fall of 1785 and 1786 and since he was there in the summer of 1786, he had likely overwintered there. In the fall of 1787 he witnessed the will of William Saunders at Poole, sailed for Placentia the following summer for a year and thence to Cadiz, journeying overland through Iberia and France to Poole to prepare for another trans-atlantic passage.[34]

The death of William Saunders in 1788 had important long-term impli-

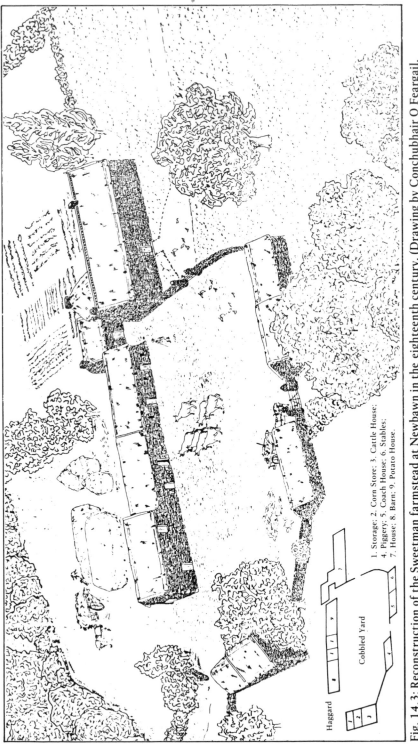

Fig. 14.3: Reconstruction of the Sweetman farmstead at Newbawn in the eighteenth century. (Drawing by Conchubhair O Feargail, reconstruction by Kevin Whelan)

1. Storage; 2. Corn Store; 3. Cattle House; 4. Piggery; 5. Coach House; 6. Stables; 7. House; 8. Barn; 9. Potato House.

Haggard

Cobbled Yard

cations for the Sweetmans' position within the company. David Welsh Saunders, only son of William, inherited the trade but he was still a minor and was apparently in poor health. William's brother Thomas was given £2,000, an annual salary of £100 and ⅓ of David's share in the profits to manage the business 'whilst there is a prospect of it turning out advantagous'. Although apparently he had only ¼ the amount of capital accumulated by Richard Welsh to bestow, Saunders gave small sums to a number of relatives and friends including his brother in Massachusetts, who was nominated heir with Thomas should David die, to James, 'born in adultery to my wife in Placentia' and 'to my sister [in-law] Mary Sweetman of Wexford'.

The death of William Saunders left space for the Sweetmans to assume a more active role in this fishery. In replying to a letter written by Roger Sweetman of Wexford in spring, 1788, Thomas Saunders acknowledged that his brother's death 'brings a large share of the burden of business' on him but assures Roger that he will pay strict attention to the trade', hoping to carry it on in an amicable way and 'profitable for the benefit of all parties'. Saunders goes on to comment on prospects for the fishery, expresses the hope that Pierce Sweetman will arrive soon in Placentia, sends regards to Roger's family and signs himself 'assured friend and honorable servant'. It is clear from this and subsequent correspondence that Sweetmans were major shareholders in the firm and formal partners by the fall of 1789 when the company's name was changed from Saunders and Company to Saunders and Sweetman.

The cod fishery at Placentia, 1788-1793

In 1788 the company had a dozen deep-sea vessels at its disposal and considerable data survive on their voyages. Eight of these vessels arrived at Placentia from ports in Europe between mid-April and mid-June: four directly from Poole, one each from Poole, Bristol, Alicante-Cadiz via Waterford and one with salt from France. Two of these ships made a second voyage to Placentia from Poole and France later in the summer. Saunders and Company were sole owners of all but one of these vessels, a brig chartered from Bird and Company of Poole. This firm was engaged in the fishery at Fortune Bay, west of Placentia. Its head was executor of William Saunders' will and agent at Poole for the company while David Welsh Saunders was in his minority. Every month between May and November one or more of the fleet departed Placentia for south European ports with dried cod. Three of the early vessels returned with salt in time to take on a second cargo and in the late fall most ships arriving at Iberian markets proceeded with salt to Poole. One of the vessels arriving Placentia early in spring was despatched to the Grand Banks and fished there through the summer, another was sent to Quebec for supplies and the firm reserved one brig for a shuttle trade with St John's. Construction was completed on two vessels during the year. One was sent to Iberia with cod, the other to Waterford in November with cod oil and passengers, and thence to Poole. Finally, a vessel sailed directly from Placentia home to Poole to complete the season's shipping.

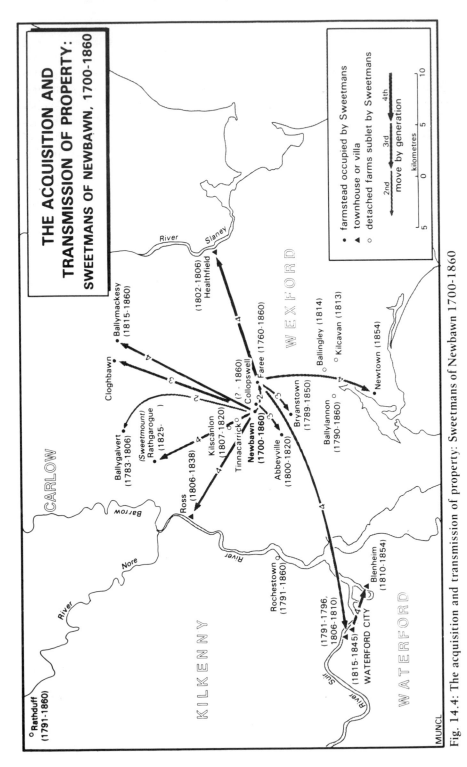

Fig. 14.4: The acquisition and transmission of property: Sweetmans of Newbawn 1700-1860

Table 1

	C	Acres			Generations		
● Newbawn	1700-1860	347	Pierce	Michael	Michael & Michael	Peter F.	(Cadigan)
● Collopswell	? -1860	240	?	Michael	Edmund		Roger F. Edward O'Farrell
● Faree	1760-1860	224		Michael	Roger	Roger Catherine Harriette (Farrell)	Edward O'Farrell
● Bryanstown	1789-1850	178			Roger	Pierce Patrick Nicholas Mary (Ryan)	
● Abbeyville	1800-1820				Edmund		
● Cloghbawn	1810-				Lawrence		
● Newtown	-(1854)					Roger	
● Ballymack-essey	1815-1860	160				Lawrence	Lawrence
● Rathgaroge (Sweetmount)	1825-	225				Edmund	Edmund Farrell
▲ Healthfield	1802-1806	80				Pierce	
▲ Waterford City	1791-1796, 1806-10					Pierce	
▲ Waterford City	1815-1850						Alicia (Leonard) Roger F
▲ Blenheim	1810-1854	52				Pierce	Roger F
▲ Ross	1806-1838					Nicholas	
° Ballygalvert	1783-1806	80			Nicholas		
° Ballylannon	1790-1860	200			Roger	Catherine	
° Ballingley	? (1814)	84			Roger		
° Kilcavan	(1813)	199			Edmund	Michael	
° Tinnacarrick	(1819)	107			Roger		
° Kilscanlon	1807-1820	101				Pierce	
° Rochestown	1791-1860	95				Pierce	Roger F Juliet
° Rathduff	1791-1860	350				Pierce	Juliet

● Farmsteads occupied by Sweetmans

▲ Townhouse or villa

° Detached farms sublet by Sweetmans.

This pattern of voyages, linking three disparate regions in the north Atlantic in a primarily triangular network of trade, typified the cod economy and persisted into the nineteenth century. Fig. 14.5 reveals the pattern at its peak. Departures from Poole and Waterford for Placentia outnumbered direct arrivals from there, three to one. By contrast, only a small proportion of the ships arriving at Iberia with cod sailed back directly to Placentia. Poole was the pivot of this trading network, the port where the vessels were owned and registered and where the final decisions on their deployment were usually made. Poole and its hinterland provided much of the technology and some provisions for this fishery. Early each spring the firm assembled a bewildering variety of commodities, many produced specially for this distinctive trade in the towns and villages of Dorset. Other goods were re-exported through Poole. Breadstuffs, dried peas, teas, beer, brandy, condiments, cooking oil, cooking utensils, cook-room or kitchenware, tobacco and pipes, fishermen's footwear and clothing, bedding, fishing tackle, construction material and tools, hunting and trapping gear, even agricultural implements and garden seeds were stored in Saunders' warehouse in Poole harbour and crammed into the vessels bound for Placentia. Probably the most valuable commodity loaded at Poole was salt, carried northwards from the Iberian ports in the cod ships through the winter and warehoused in Poole until the ships were ready to sail.

Food and drink were the most expensive commodities in the fishery and accounted for over 60% of the company's extensive supply trade. Waterford was an important source of food. 'I have drawn on Mr Blackney for the servants' wages' wrote Tom Saunders at Placentia in 1789' but a great deal of this will return to us again for [their] provisions'. Each fall Saunders and Sweetman sent their orders to John Blackney for Waterford pork, which was highly regarded, butter, and other supplies including porter casks for Dorset beer to be shipped from Poole in the spring.[35] Sometimes the provisions were put on the passenger vessel returning from Placentia and stored at Poole through the winter; more often they were warehoused in Waterford and shipped out directly in the spring. Despite his kinship with the company Blackney did not have a monopoly on the Irish traffic to Placentia, even in salt provisions. St John's had emerged by this time as an important source of supplies throughout the island. Saunders and Sweetman dealt extensively there (fig 14.5) procuring a wide range of goods, including Irish provisions, from their agents, the Poole house of Hart and Eppes. Prices for provisions were much higher than at Waterford but brokers like Hart and Eppes were willing to accept low quality fish for the West Indies market in exchange.[36] Blackney did not provide breadstuffs and the firm depended on a number of sources for this critical commodity including their Poole and Placentia neighbours, Neaves, who specialised in the bread trade, and St John's houses. During the War of Independence Quebec replaced America as an important source for bread and flour and William Saunders opened up direct trade there. In January 1788, for example, he placed an order in Poole through his London agents for £1,500 of breadstuffs from Quebec and his brother sent on one of their ships from Placentia that summer.[37]

Waterford's main contribution to the prosecution of this fishery was the provision of manpower. Three of the firm's fleet arrived in Waterford in March 1788, to take on passengers and provisions. Precise details on the numbers of servants boarding these vessels for Placentia, their places of origin or mode of recruitment do not survive. John Harries, an Anglican minister who came out to Placentia in 1788 with Pierce Sweetman and lodged at the company residence, claimed the firm brought out 700 Irish servants each

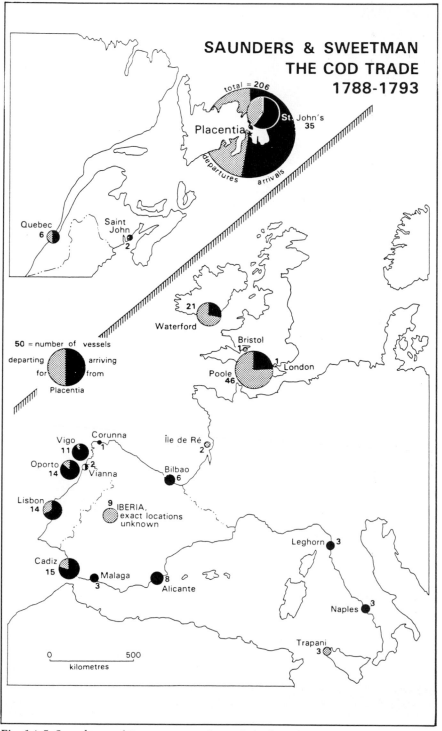

Fig. 14.5: Saunders and Sweetman — The Cod Trade 1788-1793

Plate xxxv: Abbeyville, home of Edmund Sweetman

Plate xxxvi: Faree, home of Roger Sweetman

Plate xxxvii: Bryanstown, home of Pierce Sweetman, then of his brother's Patrick and Nicholas

Plate xxxviii: Ballymackesy

season, an exaggeration.[38] Whatever the numbers it is certain that they came from southwest Wexford, south Kilkenny, southeast Tipperary and Waterford. John Blackney's principal task was the arrangement of labour contracts. Some were hired for a season only, others for two summers and a winter, still others for a longer spell. Details of their wages and terms of employment were confirmed and clothing suitable to the conditions of the fishery advanced, sometimes with food and accommodation while waiting to sail. Nothing is known of Blackney's network of contacts through the migration basin but it probably included Roger Sweetman of Faree, one of whose former servants was recorded this year at Placentia. Nothing is known either of the role of the firm's sea captains, still all English, in the recruiting process. They could hire men independently at Passage, where the vessels usually anchored prior to departure and the servants boarded. Alternatively, and more likely, they could liaise with Blackney in Waterford, regulating labour contracts and organising the shipping of provisions. The stopover at Waterford extended from four to six weeks between 1788-1793 but some ships cleared port more quickly, particularly if not taking on supplies. Vessels with passengers usually departed during the first two weeks of April, arriving at Placentia in late April and early May after 30-35 days passage.

Timing was crucial to the successful prosecution of an intensely seasonal fishery 2,000 miles from home. Labour was divided between fishermen and shoremen. The former were required early to get the boats to sea. 'Since your crew are all fishermen' wrote Tom Saunders to one of his captains bound for Italy in the fall of 1788 'come back in March and reach here by April for the start of the season'. Each spring the agents chafed over late arrivals. 'If the passengers had arrived earlier' noted Pierce Sweetman the following summer 'we would have had one of the best spring voyages since my coming to the country'. James Downes complained bitterly over a passenger vessel arriving on 10 June from Ireland 'for a spring fishery'. Delays were usually blamed on adverse physical conditions during the Atlantic crossing. 'The vessels in general had a long passage this spring' Saunders reported following the arrival of two of the fleet after 'disagreeable' voyages of 35 to 41 days against westerly winds. Pierce Sweetman's journey from Poole that summer took 52 days, 'a long, tedious passage'. Even after reaching the roadstead in Placentia vessels were sometimes hindered entering the harbour because of ice or southeasterly gales. One vessel from Waterford, loaded with passengers, listed off Gibraltar rock near the entrance to the harbour and was saved only when the passengers crowded into the forecastle and righted her.[39]

Close to one thousand men arrived in Placentia and neighbouring harbours in the spring of 1788, a peak not surpassed subsequently. More than ¾ of these were Irish, the remainder from Dorset and from Jersey. Most of the servants, fishermen or shoremen, were despatched on arrival to company planters and the firm was reimbursed for their passages in fish through the summer. All of the shoremen were Irish but some of the fishermen, particularly those belonging to the fishing ships, came from Dorset and fished for the company on the Banks. The preference for Irish labour, however, was clearly expressed by Thomas Saunders in a letter to his brother in Poole: 'I would advise you never to send out more English youngsters than will just clear the vessels. They run away in winter, they never stick to a place, have any attachment to it. and for hard labour one Irish youngster is worth a dozen of them'.

The fishery at Placentia commenced in April with a search for herring, the main spring bait. Herring migrations were unpredictable, the bait often difficult to procure but it was essential for a successful spring fishery. Both Saunders and Sweetman believed a northeasterly wind kept the herring out and waited anxiously each season for a southwesterly 'brush' to blow them deep into the bay. Here they were trapped in chosen grounds using skiffs and deep nets. Once sufficient bait was secured, crews of three to five men were deployed in shallops and jacks to jig the cod. Pierce Sweetman reported in 1789 that the company had 19 shallops at sea by 1 May under the management of Captain Salmon who had brought passengers from Waterford that spring. By the end of May they had caught an average of 50 quintals a boat. The fishery peaked in June with the arrival of millions of tiny capelin who drew the cod inshore. By late June the boats had averaged 220 quintals with 'the fish now coming in very fast'. Sweetman looked forward to a final haul of 350 quintals or £250 a boat, an excellent catch.

Hand in hand with this company fishery was the resident planter operation. Sweetman ordered Salmon at the beginning of June to 'back' 25 planters once the capelin struck ashore. These were the company's principal dealers, either the most productive and reliable among the planter community or bound to the firm through debts. Some had ties with the house back in the days of Richard Welsh, others were quite recent arrivals. Over one half were Irish, the remainder from England and Jersey or their offspring. Almost all had two to three boats and were concentrated in the four leading harbours of the district: Great and Little Placentia, Point Verde and Paradise, the locations also of the company's rooms (fig 14.2). These planters had been supplied by the firm with provisions and servants early in spring, had agreed to deal with Sweetman through the summer and deliver their fish and cod oil to him in the fall.

Following a successful spring venture by company and planters alike, conditions deteriorated early in July, foreshadowing the fickle nature of this fishery. Poor weather and a shortage of servants ashore hampered the curing process but Sweetman could still report a good voyage in mid-August. Then the weather worsened, destroying the fall fishery. An unprecedented amount of fish lay uncured on the planters' rooms by October, delaying the settling of accounts and requiring extra overwintering servants to help with the curing in the spring. They probably had adequate time to do so, since the subsequent spring fishery also failed due to lack of bait. By late May, Tom Saunders, who had replaced Pierce Sweetman as manager in Placentia, reported that the company's boats had not averaged five quintals, compared to fifty quintals the previous season. Herring was scarce and the capelin were late but when they did strike the cod fishery zoomed to 'fantastic' proportions. In September, Pierce Sweetman went to St John's to charter an extra vessel to freight this unexpected catch to market.

Management of an enterprise notorious for its unpredictability, with sudden bursts of activity followed by languid spells, with fluctuating seasonal yields and rapid price shifts for fish and for supplies in widely separated geographical areas, required a high degree of mercantile skill. Through the 1780s the fishery in Placentia grew considerably, attracting new planters, new boats, new merchants and interloping traders. Saunders and Sweetman's central objective was to protect their trading territory and planter clientele in the face of increased opposition. The difficulties of doing so were made clear in the copious correspondence of James Downes, likely a Wexford kinsmen of Pierce Sweetman who, like the latter, first appeared in Placentia in 1785 and was managing agent there in 1792. The season did not begin auspiciously. Herring were plentiful enough but the company did not have adequate nets to catch them. The second passenger vessel from Waterford did not arrive until 10 June, keeping ten company shallops ashore and forcing Downes to recruit some expert shoremen from the more expensive St John's labour market. He estimated that the company boats lost an average of 100 quintals in the spring fishery alone. A poor capelin season followed. By late July Downes was reporting 'the worst fishery in a decade' and that their company had fared worst of all. If Saunders and Sweetman did not send out adequate nets and other supplies next season, he warned, their boats 'will be the laughing stock of the bay'.

The inshore fishery was overcrowded. While Downes' claim that a thousand 'northern' boats had entered the bay was hyperbole, an unprecedented number had arrived, probably deflected from a rapidly declining banks fishery. By August the company's boats were dispersed from Placentia to Cape St Mary's, east to Cape Pine and all along the western shore of Placentia Bay in search of fish (fig 14.2). The company's difficulties were compounded by intense competition amongst traders for cod. An increasing number from St John's, the West Indies, even Quebec, were calling in at Placentia, attracted by the inflated numbers of fishermen inshore. They were willing to sell supplies at prices lower than those set by the company, in exchange for fish. 'Don't let those peddling Jews make their fortunes at our noses' James Downes howled in July but Placentia continued to be 'stocked with peddlers' through the summer and fall. All through the season Saunders and Sweetman were short of supplies. Downes was forced to purchase goods from neighbouring firms including Pennels of Trepassey, Spurriers of Oderin and a Jersey house in Placentia, but this did not ward off the loss of custom. The company's chief rival in 1792 was Fitzhenry, Doyle, Power and Company, a Bristol-based firm with Waterford and Wexford connections who had established a branch at Placentia a few years previously and were making serious inroads into Saunders and Sweetman's Irish trade. John Power took up residence in Placentia and his firm sent out vessels from Bristol and Waterford with passengers and provisions. He despatched two vessels to America for bread-stuffs and lumber in the summer of 1792 and another was loaded early for the market. In the fall three vessels arrived from Bristol with supplies. 'This business will never be as it was' lamented James Downes but his Irish rivals expanded too quickly and were forced to withdraw from Placentia a few years later.

Downes' complaints reveal in part an experienced firm refusing to be lured into supplying a surfeit of fishermen. He himself cautioned that their dealers would fall into debt. They had taken on too much supplies and were paying extravagant wages for labour. In the fall a few attempted to 'smuggle' fish and oil to interloping traders, forcing Downes to consider confiscating their possessions to pay servants' wages and recover credits extended by the company in the form of supplies that spring. He advised headquarters that the planter fishery was no longer viable and that the firm should focus in future on a merchant fishery. While the number of boats run by the company evidently did expand to 32 in 1793, this fishery accounted for only a small proportion of the cod shipped. The planter operation remained the backbone of the enterprise at Placentia.

Whether they worked directly for the company or for the planters, most of the servants' contracts expired in October and many went home, 'Our vessel going to Ireland will be thronged' Tom Saunders informed a fellow merchant in September 1788 'as I intend sending a great number of men out of the country. The vessel I go to Poole in will be packed also'. Early in November he instructed one of the company captains to proceed to the Passage of Waterford, land the passengers there and send their sea chests up to the quay in lighters together with cooking equipment and water casks. The latter items were to be stored in Blackney's warehouse until the first spring voyage. Unless there were orders from Poole to the contrary, the captain was directed to proceed to this port on the first fair wind, discharge the crew there and go to headquarters for further instructions. In a separate letter to John Blackney at Waterford, Saunders enclosed a list of bills drawn on him for the servants' wages which he was to honour. Blackney in turn drew on the company's London bankers for these amounts. No records survive of the number of servants paid but 162 printed company bills were sent from Placentia, the remainder written by hand. More than 200 bills were cashed by Pierce Sweetman in Waterford in 1793.

Shipping dried cod to Iberia and Italy was the nub of this fishery. Commercial success hinged on the quality of the cargoes to Europe. Considerable time and expertise were invested in ensuring that fish was properly culled and sorted to suit regional tastes abroad. Most vessels were loaded at company headquarters in Placentia under the supervision of Saunders, Sweetman, Downes and other trusted agents or by experienced company captains and masters of the voyage. 'Sweetman has seen the whole of it shipped so it must be good' Tom Saunders commented on a cargo to Alicante in 1798. Vessels arriving early in spring from England and Ireland were usually loaded directly with old fish. They departed Placentia through May and early June mainly for the Portuguese market (table 2). By 6 June 1791, for example, more than £10,000 of cod had been shipped by the firm to Iberia. A lull followed this transatlantic spring traffic while poorer quality fish, 'the sweepings of the rooms', was collected and shipped to Hart and Eppes in St

John's for the West Indies. By late August the first of the new fish was ready for Europe. Company vessels lying idle through the summer or engaged in local fishing or trade were now pressed into service in the scramble to markets. Saunders and Sweetman sent prime saleable cod to thirteen or more merchant houses in a dozen ports virtually encircling Iberia and east to Italy (fig 14.5). Each captain was issued written instructions to proceed to a particular port and deliver to the firm's agents there a bill of lading, notes on the quality of cargo, news from the fishery and the firm's expectations in the markets. The European agents usually received additional instructions on marketing strategies from Poole and sold the cod on company account, either in their home port or elsewhere, depending on prices. They were also entrusted with securing a cargo of salt or other freight for the subsequent outward voyage and remitted the balance from these transactions to the company's bank in London with a statement of account to headquarters in Poole.

Table 2: The Seasonal flow of Cod from Placentia, 1788-93

Vessels Departing Placentia:	St. John's	Total
May 9:		
Oporto 4　Lisbon 2　Bilbao 1　Cadiz 1　Alicante 1	1	10
June 5:		
Oporto 1　Lisbon 1　Vigo 1　Corunna 1 Cadiz 1	5	10
July 0:		
	5	5
August 6:		
Oporto 3　Viana 1　Bilbao 1　Malaga 1	0	6
September 15:		
Cadiz 4　Alicante 3 Bilbao 3　Lisbon 2　Vigo 1　Malaga 1　Naples 1	3	18
October 15:		
Cadiz 5　Alicante 3 Leghorn 2 Naples 1　Lisbon 1　Oporto 1　Vigo 1	1	15
November 14:		
Vigo 5　Oporto 5　Lisbon 2　Bilbao 1　Cadiz 1　Alicante 1 Malaga 1 Leghorn 1 0		14
December 3:		
Vigo 2　Lisbon 1	0	3
	15	82

The company's south European correspondents comprised an interesting mixture of English, Irish, and continental merchants. Some were known personally to the firm, some were recommended by Poole and other houses in the trade. Saunders and Sweetman sent the bulk of their shipments to agents with whom they had personal ties and could trust, notably the Harrisons of Poole at Lisbon, the Staffords in Oporto and the Stranges in Cadiz. More than 40% of all cod was shipped to two houses and a further 22% to two others (table 3). The long commercial and cultural links between southeast Ireland and Iberia facilitated Sweetman's relationship with members of the substantial Irish Catholic merchant community. They were on friendly terms with Stafford of Oporto, the firm's most active agent who may have had Wexford connections. Stafford sent luxury items including choice port to

Roger Sweetman in Wexford through Blackney and Portuguese table linen to Pierce. Sweetman's main contacts were the Stranges of Cadiz. Originally from Waterford, a branch settled in Aylwardstown in southeast Kilkenny late in the seventeenth century and in Cadiz before Patrick Sweetman of Newbawn established trade there.[40] They were one of a number of families from the big farmer class in this corner of Kilkenny who settled in southern Spain to prosecute the wine trade. Later in the eighteenth century the Stranges established a partnership with the Farrells of Waterford and became one of the leading merchant houses in Cadiz. Their main imports included salt provisions from Waterford and Newfoundland cod. In the 1780s the house was headed by Laurence Strange, who had moved to Cadiz in 1758, assisted by his kinsmen John and Peter, who settled later, and by Patrick. They were the leading agents for Saunders and Sweetman's extensive trade in southern Spain. Pierce Sweetman visited the family in Cadiz and later offered to act as their correspondent in Waterford. Stranges kept the firm informed on local prices, sold their cod in Cadiz or despatched the company's vessels throught he Streights to more profitable markets in the Mediterranean, procuring salt and other goods for the return voyage.

Table 3:

Cod sold by Saunders and Sweetman in Iberia and Italy, 1788-1793

	Quintals				%
1	33,909	Harris, Stafford & Co.	Oporto & Vigo	1788-89, 1791-93	22.5
2	27,246	Strange Bros., Doudall & Co.	Cadiz	1788-93	18
3	19,597	Hudson, Harrison & Gonne	Lisbon	1788-93	13
4	13,637	Douat, Labat & Plante	Bilbao	1788-93	9
5	10,466	George Moore	Alicante	1790-93	7
6	10,190	Pennell, Smith & Co.	Oporto & Viana	1788, 1790, 1792-3	6.8
7	8,219	Valine & Warrington	Naples & Trapani	1790-93	5.5
8	6,875	Greveney & Co.	Malaga	1790-92	4.6
9	6.621	Robert Porter	Leghorn	1788, 1790	4.4
10	6,026	Peter Arabet	Alicante	1788	4
11	3,061	Rodd & Comyn	Alicante	1789	2
12	2,945	Earle, Hodgson & Drake	Leghorn	1792	2
13	1,849	Patrick Morrough	Corunna	1788	1.2
	150,641				
14		De Lamard	Barcelona	No Sales	
15		McDonald & Co.	Cartagena	No Sales	

Saunders and Sweetman were among the giants of the Newfoundland trade. In 1788, the peak of the eighteenth century Newfoundland fishery, they shipped close to 38,000 quintals of cod from Placentia, 4% of the island's total. Few firms ever exceeded this amount. It required roughly 140 shallops, 500 fishermen and perhaps half that number ashore. Over the next two seasons the company's volume of exports dropped dramatically, consistent with the general Newfoundland pattern. But in 1792, James Downes' criticisms notwithstanding, the firm equalled the quantity exported in 1788, now an impressive 7% of the island's catch. Despite operating a fleet equal to the leading shipowners, Saunders and Sweetman sometimes had to charter an extra vessel or two to transport surplus fish in the fall. Some of their vessels carried 4,000 quintals of cod, worth £3,000. In the absence of a ledger it is impossible to estimate the value of their imports or the number of men they supplied. Another perplexing question is the extent to which Saunders and Sweetman could capture the trade of independent planters. James Downes despaired of any success in this sector because interloping traders and competing resident merchants offered better prices but such traders were transient and unreliable. Unless they were approaching bankruptcy, independent planters normally preferred a more stable trading arrangement with an established and expensive house. Although Saunders and Sweetman increased the volume of their trade as the fishery grew, they did not expand noticeably the territory they fished and traded in since the days of Richard Welsh. Firms from Poole continued to dominate St Mary's Bay, Little Placentia, Oderin, Mortier and Burin. Although there was competition and on occasion deceitful dealing, Saunders and Sweetman's relations with neighbouring Poole houses were generally harmonious and co-operative. They met annually in Poole or Placentia to fix the prices for provisions and fish, carried each others agents and passengers if space allowed, occasionally shared freight, exchanged trade information and delivered letters and messages for each other. There is little evidence of the alleged rapacity of Richard Welsh in the 1780s. Much of the company's ire was reserved for their upstart Irish rivals in Placentia harbour and for coasting hawkers.

Over 400 men remained in the harbours of Great and Little Placentia in the winter of 1788-1789. Fewer than 20% of these were planters, the remainder servants. Winter was spent cutting and hauling timber from the woods. Early each December Saunders and Sweetman despatched crews of around a dozen men in shallops and schooners across the bay to Mortier (fig 14.2) or to the densely forested river system in Bay D'Espoir, 200 kilometres west. Some of these crews were employed by the company, others worked on contract on their own account but were usually given winter provisions by the firm. 'Our crews are all in the woods' Pierce Sweetman recounted in December 1788 'I hope they make good returns for the vast quantity of provisions they consume'. In May he could report that these winter crews had done great work, one group procuring over 600 fine ships' timbers. These timbers were hauled over frozen rivers and streams, then shipped to Placentia and other company rooms in the spring. Almost all of this timber was used for ship and boat construction. It included fine plank and board for sheathing, spars, keels, 'knees' and top timber. A massive amount of timber was required for the construction of houses, stores and fishing installations onshore. This timber was usually cut locally in the arms east of Placentia harbour and along the cape shore.

The local Newfoundland forest could not provide sufficient timber for vessel construction. Like neighbouring firms, Saunders and Sweetman purchased special ship timber, notably oak, from St John's — where it was imported — St John, Quebec and America. Deep-sea vessels were built beside the company's main premises on the Great Beach at Placentia. While almost all the men working in the woods were Irish, the small group of specialised craftsmen engaged in shipbuilding, including the master shipwright, carpenters, the blacksmith, caulker and sailmaker, came from England. Poole provided most of the materials not available locally to finish and furnish the vessels: nails, anchors, cordage, canvas, tackle and cooking equipment. Once completed, the vessels were taken by their captains to St John's and registered, then readied for a transatlantic voyage. Two such ships were built in the winter of 1788, one with a carrying capacity of 2,500, the other 4,000 quintals.

Winter work implied year-round residence and encouraged the growth of permanent settlement. Between 1786 and 1788 close to 60% of the men engaged in the summer fishery in the bay had stayed the previous winter and this proportion grew steadily subsequently. Tom Saunders noted 'a great number of unshipped men' staying on in the fall of 1789 and 'a vast number' the following fall. Official statistics record 67% and 74% of the summer population of Placentia and adjoining harbours overwintering in these two years. Winter men found extra employment building or repairing wharves, stores and dwellings, mending nets and making wooden casks for shipping the staples of the trade. In the absence of contracts some Irish worked just for food and shelter. Gradually these 'dieters' and shipped servants acquired or built cabins of their own, cleared small parcels of land for potatoes, married, and started families. In 1790 the Irish accounted for over 60% of the winter population of Placentia. This population was greatly augmented over the next half-century, primarily under the direction of the Sweetman dynasty who finally came to dominate the fishery in eastern Placentia Bay.

The Sweetman succession and the Napoleonic Wars

In 1791 Pierce Sweetman married Juliet Forstall, daughter of a well-to-do Catholic farmer, middleman and occasional merchant from Rochestown, county Kilkenny (fig 14.1). The Forstalls, of Anglo-Norman stock, had been more successful than the Sweetmans in retaining part of their medieval patrimony in the upheavals of the seventeenth century. Several branches of this once influential family continued to operate substantial holdings beside ancestral castles in the southeastern corner of the county. Like the Sweetmans, the Forstalls also engaged in trade. Nicholas Forstall, for example, moved to Nantes early in the eighteenth century and thence to Martinique where he married the daughter of an Irish merchant. Their son settled in New Orleans and became governor of Louisiana. Another member of the 'sept' was a sea captain, trading out of New Ross and Waterford with southern Europe. Juliet Forstall's father was also involved in trade at Waterford but focused mainly on the management of his large farm at Rochestown and the properties sublet to tenants along the Barrow.[41] He allowed his daughter a dowry of

£2,000, the standard sum for offspring of her class. Sweetmans agreed to pay an annuity of £200 and £3,000 should Pierce pre-decease her. An elaborate marriage settlement involved Forstall properties in Rochestown and Rathduff Edmund Sweetman's farm in Collopswell and Blackney's interests in Traceystown, in the parish of Taghmon.[42] Blackney was appointed one of the trustees. Some of these lands passed eventually to Pierce Sweetman and his offspring (fig 14.1, table 1). The marriage did not recruit a Forstall to the Placentia partnership; even if this were desirable, there was no son to spare. It did, however, connect the Sweetmans with some important families, including the firm of Wyse and Quans, a major merchant house in Waterford.

Pierce Sweetman replaced John Blackney as director of the company's operations in Waterford in 1792 and began his long career as a resident Irish merchant. Blackney's wife, Bridget, had died, leaving a large family, none of whom was involved subsequently in the Placentia trade. He married a wealthy Waterford widow but apart from financial and property transactions related to Pierce Sweetman's marriage settlement for which he was executor, those of his own two marriages for which Roger Sweetman was executor, and the management of the Welsh fortune, Blackney had no further dealings with the Sweetman family or with the Newfoundland fishery. Roger Sweetman's second son, Michael, now entered the trade. He was sent to Poole as an apprentice, then to Placentia where he was joined by his youngest brother, Nicholas of Faree.[43]

The Napoleonic wars imposed new strains on the management of a trans-atlantic merchant fishery. Traditional provisions were increasingly redirected to feed the garrisons at home and abroad. Some company vessels were trans-ferred from the fishery to serve in this trade. Traditional cod markets were vulnerable under the fluctuating geopolitical conditions of war, established lanes of commerce were severely disrupted on the Atlantic, vessles were under continual threat from enemy shipping, their flexibility further hampered by tardy convoys. Finally, both fishermen and mariners were the targets of roving press gangs. Passengers returning home from Placentia in the fall attempted to avoid the press by landing in safer havens west of Waterford or Poole, sometimes with the collusion of company captains or agents, sometimes not. 'Get rid of the passengers before you reach Poole' James Downes advised a captain at the outset of the war. In the following fall Tom Saunders wrote Pierce Sweetman at Waterford: 'I have given [Captain] Shepard orders should [the passengers] force him into any port in southwestern Ireland not to go to Waterford with their chests. If the winds are favourable he should try to make land at the east of the cape [Cape Clear] and frustrate their scheme'.[44] Arrivals from Placentia at Dingle, Crookhaven, Baltimore, Kinsale, Cork and Youghal during the war attest to the disruption of company shipping. Some of these vessels did, however, call in at Waterford en route to Poole and the port was a focus for outbound traffic early in the war. At least six shipments of supplies were despatched from Waterford to Placentia in 1794 and there were four arrivals, making this the busiest year recorded for the firm's operations there in the eighteenth century. Pierce Sweetman was made freeman of the city in 1794 but his Newfoundland trade soon weakened. The flow of passengers to Placentia was reduced to a trickle and there were difficulties finding local mariners to man the company of ships. 'Our crew are Swades and Danes, but one who was with us last voyage', King Elmes, mate on a company vessel anchored at Portsmouth, informed his father in Old Ross.[45] Elmes feared impressment, claiming that his status as mate did not exempt him from service in the navy during war.

Pierce Sweetman moved from Waterford to Wexford in 1796, returning to the port only periodically over the next decade. The trade there was entrusted to Thomas Quan, husband of Juliet Forstall, Sweetman's sister and a leading merchant in the house of Wyse and Quans. The Sweetmans took up residence in Bryanstown (fig. 14.4 pl. xxxvii) a large farm leased by Roger Sweetman in 1789 for £150 a year. Whether Pierce's departure from Waterford was due less to the slump in company business than a desire to return to his home place, kin and presumably inheritance at a time when the big farm economy was expanding is difficult to say. Few merchants made such a move so early in their careers and Sweetman was back to active trading in 1798, going to Poole and then to Placentia. Over the next several years he was the epitome of the mobile merchant, journeying between Waterford, Poole and Placentia to co-ordinate the company's trade and to Wexford to care for his farm and growing family.[46] Some hint of the Sweetman's enhanced social status among Wexford's middle class is suggested in the family's move in 1802 to Healthfield, Killurin, a fashionable demesne pleasantly situated on the western bank of the Slaney. Although the property contained only 52 acres, some of it wood and parkland, it cost £130 a year.

The slump in Saunders and Sweetman's fortunes during the early stages of the war was evident in all their trading areas. In 1794 the firm still had nine vessels registered at Poole but only five by 1800.[47] During this short period, moreover, the value of the company's trade there was halved. Their Irish trade faced new pressures. Britain's burgeoning population, with its appetite for fresh food, stimulated the export of grains and bacon before the war, and livestock by the end of the century. The traditional Irish salt meat trade was being rapidly dislodged and the growing demands of the British army and navy for provisions drove up the price of food in the fishery. Waterford's merchants sought victualling contracts with the military, causing problems in Newfoundland's supply. Pierce Sweetman advised Tom Saunders in Poole to write to Cork and Limerick as well as Waterford for pork prices 'since our Waterford friends will up the price if they think we're dependent on them'.[48] He also advised against purchasing all company supplies in the spring. With three of their vessels in England they could afford to delay some transactions until mid-summer when demand dropped off and prices were lower. Problems with Poole and Waterford sources forced the firm to look increasingly to the more costly St John's supply market and to ports on the mainland. For the first time in company history Pierce Sweetman sent a vessel to Boston for pork in 1803 and the firm secured special licenses to import food from there in 1806 and 1807. However, British ports remained the principal sources of supply through the war. Michael Sweetman reported that English bread was better than Boston bread and pork was hard to find there. Apart from one or two seasons, imports from the mainland were modest. America closed its ports to Newfoundland traffic in 1807 and farming in the Maritimes was still relatively undeveloped. Almost all the pork and butter entering Placentia during the war was Irish. England supplied the bulk of the breadstuffs and other comestibles. Even West Indies produce such as rum, sugar, and tobacco was shipped mainly through English ports as was much of the company's Iberian salt.[49] Halifax controlled the trade in molasses. Small amounts of Canadian pork, butter, bread, flour, beer, soap, candles and coal were imported with timber, the mainstay of this trade. Despite disruptions, Poole and Waterford maintained their dominance over company supplies but new ports, notably Liverpool and Halifax, entered the trade after 1800.

The fishery in Placentia became almost totally sedentary during the war. Apart from Saunders and Sweetman in Great Placentia and Neaves and Company at Little Placentia, no other firm was involved in the transatlantic passenger trade to this part of the bay. Over 300 passengers had arrived in 1793, the first year of the war, a mere 21 were recorded two years later and none at all in 1797. There was a brief revival in passenger traffic with the cessation of hostilities in 1802 but the numbers arriving thereafter were trifling until the final years of the war. Interruptions in the regular flow of servants from Ireland caused problems in the fishery. A company vessel with passengers from Waterford was captured in 1804 leaving Michael Sweetman with a severe shortage of shoremen 'to split, salt and cure' the company catch and the catches of their dependent planters. 'Half the crewmen' he concluded 'will have to work ashore'.[50]

The slump in Irish passengers directly to Placentia was partly relieved by recruiting in St John's. This port was now the destination for the vast majority of spring servants from Ireland. It was also the centre for unshipped over-wintering men who flocked there from the outharbours in the hope of getting casual work or some government relief. Michael Sweetman went to St John's in spring 1804, for example, and shipped fifteen fishermen for the company boats. This fishery was much reduced. In 1803 the firm had nineteen boats at sea, compared to thirty-two in 1790, and now employed around 100 fishermen and shoremen. Only fourteen company boats were put to sea the subsequent season and Michael Sweetman planned to sell three or four in St John's the following spring. Both Pierce and Michael Sweetman were relatively satisfied however, with the company catch: 'A few of our boats have done well . . . they kill as much fish as most shallops . . . better than our neighbours . . . the best in the bay'.[51] There is no record of the magnitude of their planter fishery, but it was in difficulty. Planters' debts mounted and insolvencies increased during the war. Auspicious seasons in the late 1780s had boosted some Irish servants to substantial planter status but they lacked the capital and expertise to ride out hard times. John Farrell, for example, was an ordinary servant in the summer fishery of 1788. That winter he was appointed master of one of Saunders and Sweetman's timber crews, graduated to boatkeeper status the subsequent spring and was supplied by the company. By 1794 John Farrell operated six shallops in Freshwater, four supplied by Saunders and Sweetman, two by another merchant. His debts to Saunders and Sweetman were close to £600 at the end of the season. James Downes agreed informally to accept repayments in fish and oil at £100 a year but Farrell died unexpectedly after one payment leaving the firm to fight it out with competing creditors for possession of the insolvent estate.[52] Another of Saunders' and Sweetman's Irish planters departed with a debt of £740. The company's most reliable and most productive planters were mainly members of long-established British families, by now a small minority in an overwhelmingly Irish area. They included the Collins, Martins, Millers and Viguers, of English stock, St Croix of Jersey and the Greens, a Quaker family of American loyalist background centred in Point Verde.

The most precise measure of the company's fortunes during the war is the export of cod. This ranged from 10,000 to 12,000 quintals annually, ⅓ the volume exported in 1788. Over 80% of this cod was shipped to Iberia in the early years of the war. Spain closed its ports to Newfoundland traffic in 1796 and Portugal emerged as the principal market. Saunders and Sweetman focused on Lisbon, cultivating their connections with the Harrisons of Poole and the Cork Murroghs, formerly of Corunna. Murrogh and Co. was joined in 1806 by George Walsh and later by two partners from Poole to form a major cod importing house and the focus of Sweetman's south European trade until 1850. Oporto ranked next to Lisbon in the firm's foreign trade. Here the Dartmouth house of Hunt and Newman was foremost. It was part of an impressive network of family firms established in St John's, Ferryland, Renews, St Lawrence, just west of Placentia Bay, and in Waterford. Pierce Sweetman was artful enough to refer to Robert Hunt, head of the branch in Waterford, when sending instructions with a cargo of cod to Hunt and Newman at Oporto: 'Get the best freight you can, preferably for Waterford or Liverpool. If for Waterford, I ask that you ship a tun of best port to my friend Mr Hunt'.[53] Personal and family ties were more important than ever in the fragile market situation during the war and the Sweetmans at Placentia made every effort to cultivate connections in southern Europe. 'My brother Nicholas, goes passenger on the *Boadicea* to your care' Pierce Sweetman informed John Bushel of Dorset, correspondent for the company at Alicante. 'I commit him in full belief that you will be a Parent and Friend to him. If you can't make room for him at Alicante, or McDonnell can't take him, place him in some good situation to learn Spanish and give him whatever money is necessary. Charge it to our house, or better still, to me'.[54]

Disruptions in the south European markets resulted in a greater concentration of company shipping in the home ports. Waterford and particularly Poole were the traditional centres for the sale of cod oil, shipped with returning passengers each fall. In 1796, for example, the company sold £1,700 of cod and seal oil in Poole. Fish was also shipped to home ports through the war, particularly in difficult years. When Portugal closed her ports in 1808, for example, over 80% of the cod at Placentia was sent to Britain. Pierce

Sweetman moved permanently to Waterford around this time, causing a shift in company trade as Saunders' control at Poole weakened. All the cod, cod oil, fur and timber exported by the company in the fall of 1809 went to Waterford.[55] Some of the fish was re-exported to Iberia, but most was sold locally, cheap protein for the expanding Irish poor in Waterford, New Ross and their hinterlands.

Sweetmans gained sole control of the fishery during the war. Tom Saunders returned permanently to Poole after a brief spell in Placentia in 1793 and none of the family was subsequently in Placentia. In poor health, he made his will in 1797, leaving almost all his property to his illegitimate daughter, Mary Anne Ryan.[56] She married Michael Sweetman in Poole in 1803, reinforcing the ties between the two families and strengthening Sweetmans' position within the company. Although he became a formal partner in 1805, William Saunders' son, David, remained in London and was not active in company trade. Michael Sweetman took up permanent residence in Poole, assisting his father-in-law manage a diminishing trade. Although the company depended on a succession of agents, English and Irish, to direct the business in Placentia through most of war, the temporary presence of Pierce Sweetman and his brothers there, and at Poole, was important in securing the Sweetman succession.

Following the death of Tom Saunders in 1808 the company was finally dissolved and their 'extensive and desirable' premises at Placentia advertised for sale. Despite the decline in the firm's fortunes, the property accumulated represented one of the most substantial and specialised mercantile cod establishments recorded at this time. It comprised (1) a capital dwelling house with two extensive stores in front; an excellent kitchen garden; a new fish store and sail loft in front of the garden; a long fish store at the back; a beach (for drying fish) in front and at the rear of the house (2) a plantation adjoining with an extensive fish store, loft, a pork store, wine cellar, bread loft, an iron stove, a forge, a carpenter's shop, a cooper's shop, two cook rooms (pl. xxxix) (3) a plantation and beach beside lot 2 (4) two extensive stores, a wharf, the lower salt house and wharf, all at Mount Pleasant. (5) a very good fishing room with an extensive store, two smaller stores, stages, a wharf and appendages, called Le Caplin's room (6) an excellent fishing room at Point Verde, comprising a house, two stages with all utensils, a good fish store, a salt house, an oil house, two good cook rooms, and John Lambe's room (pl.xl) (7) Bruley farm, well fenced (pl. xli), with a dwelling house, cow house and fowl house (8) Point Roche room at Little Placentia, now vacant (9) a house, stage, beach and garden leased to Philip Power in Little Placentia (10) the island of Marticott, with houses, stores, stages, flakes and a farm (11) John Lambe's room and Long Tom's room, at Paradise. There were, in addition, thirteen houses in Great Placentia, most with gardens, leased to Irish servants for between £1 to £12 a year.[57]

Some of these properties had been acquired by Richard Welsh, others by William Saunders. No record of their precise value survives but Pierce Sweetman suggested in 1803 that the company headquarters alone was worth several thousand pounds. Part of the property in Point Verde had been sold that year for £700, and Bruley was valued at £500. Pierce Sweetman bought out Saunders' interest in the Placentia estate and became sole proprietor. He moved in 1810 from his town house in Waterford to Blenheim lodge (pl. xliv), a substantial villa on thirty acres on the south bank of the Suir.[58] Just a few miles downstream from the quay of Waterford, with a commanding view of the river and its traffic, Blenheim was an ideal location for a merchant shipowner and remained the chief residence of the Sweetmans until 1850.

Mercantile influences and the expansion of permanent Irish settlement

Despite the substantial Irish migration through the eighteenth century most families in Placentia are descended from immigrants arriving after 1800 and many attribute their origins in the area to Sweetman's transatlantic fishery. Seasonal migration was replaced by emigration from the southeast during the war. 'So few of our servants speak of going home', Pierce Sweetman noted in 1802, 'I'm not inclined to send our ship to Waterford ... If we get sixty passengers, which I doubt, I'll let her touch at either Cork or Waterford, if not, direct to Poole. She will make a very fine vessel for Irish passengers in the spring'.[59] Close to 600 passengers were recorded arriving directly from Ireland at the harbour of Great Placentia between 1811-1827.[60] The vast majority of these young men were recruited by Pierce Sweetman and transported on his vessels to serve out their terms of contract in a transatlantic merchant fishery. By this time, however, passengers from Ireland to Placentia accounted for no more than 5% of the manpower engaged there in a season. Whether they worked for the company or for planters most servants were now residents and living mainly in Placentia.

Details on the recruitment of labour locally are sparse for the decade following the war but some data survive from 1825. That fall Roger Sweetman, who was sent to Placentia by his father, Pierce, in 1813 when he was only fifteen to help revitalise a languishing trade, hired servants in Placentia and in St John's.[61] Labour was still specialised in the fishery and expertise was reflected in the spread of wages. Foreshipmen were paid £21, able midshipmen £23 and a boatmaster £24 to man the shallops. A youngster, hired to work as a general labourer ashore from May to October, agreed to do so for £14. But skilled shoremen were as well or better paid than fellow servants at sea. Able splitters were given £22 and three carpenters, two of whom could double as a splitter and a boatmaster, were allowed £26 for the season. One man was hired as master of a winter crew, master of a bait boat in the spring and as an able splitter of cod fish through the summer for £30. The highest seasonal wage, £32, was for the supervisor or master of the voyage. Almost all wage contracts were for the summer season only but some of these men were taken on as winter dieters and were given clothes and provisions and accommodation, but no wages. All were Irish and only a few could sign their names.

Plate xxxix: Placentia in 1786 (Logbook, *HMS Pegasus*). Company headquarters are indicated by a heavy black line

Plate xl: Fishing rooms at Point Verde, 1786 (Logbook)

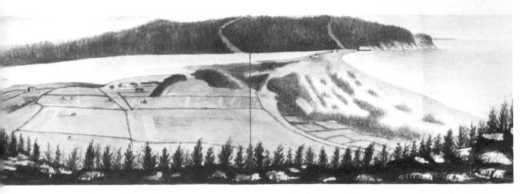

Plate xli: Bruley farm, Placentia, 1786. Acquired by Richard Welsh in 1756 (Logbook)

Plate xlii: Sweetmount (Rathgarogue)

Plate xliii: Fary (Clongeen)

This pool of labour was augmented from Waterford in the spring. Between 2-14 March, 1826, Sweetmans hired captains and youngsters at £8 and £6, respectively, for the season. Each servant signed a standard contract designed for the trade: 'I have this day hired with R. F. Sweetman to proceed on board the brig *Concord*, James Wagg, master, and there to serve R. F. Sweetman, his agents or assigns, in the capacity of an able captain or other employment for the good of the voyage, until November 1. The balance of wages to be paid in cash'. A shallop captain was below a foreshipman but the substantially lower contract wages for both captains and youngsters at Waterford probably reflected the costs of passage and supplies. The captains and even some of the youngsters had been to Newfoundland before; one captain had spent three summers there and his wages were raised to £10. Martin Walsh of Fethard, on the other hand, agreed to work as a youngster 'if unable to function as a captain'. Each servant had a guarantor from his home place who pledged to reimburse Sweetmans should the servant abscond.

This archaic mode of labour recruitment and indentured migration persisted to mid-century. Roger Sweetman shipped 44 servants in Placentia in November 1839, 25 for the boats, the remainder to work ashore. In addition to the specialised occupations listed in the fragmentary account of 1825, they included several headers, a salter, a cooper and a cook. Apart from the carpenter, who earned £36, wages had hardly changed in fifteen years. Unskilled shoremen were paid as little as £9 for the season, with a promise of £2 extra if proven satisfactory. A substantial number of these servants were born in Placentia, the sons of Irish immigrants, but others were recruited from Ireland.

One of the interesting unanswered questions on a migration managed by merchants is to what extent entrepreneurs used family, kin and traditional neighbourhood links to fetch labour from home places. The Sweetmans maintained close ties with their native Newbawn through the management of lands inherited there and with their farming kin scattered across southwest Wexford (fig 14.4). Although there were plenty of Wexfordmen on Sweetmans' vessels, there is no convincing evidence of a specifically Newbawn or indeed Wexford bias in the origins of Irish settlers in Placentia. Sweetman's residence at Blenheim, the chapel at nearby Ballygunner, the outport of Passage and particularly the family's premises in Waterford were more at the nub of their social or trading territory. The quay of Waterford was a magnet for labour migrations from at least three counties, Waterford, Kilkenny and Tipperary. Immigrants settling in Sweetman's trading territory in Placentia (fig 14.2) came from these places as well as from Wexford. We do not know how actively the Sweetmans were engaged directly in recruiting labourers in Ireland for their fishery or to what extent it was delegated to captains and clerks. Writing from Placentia in the fall of 1802 Pierce Sweetman noted that the captain of their passenger vessel, Dan Carroll, was 'very capable of shipping the servants' at Waterford in the spring 'in the case of my absence'. On the other hand William Doyle of Ballyruane, a nephew of Father Hearn of Placentia, came out through the Sweetman connection and worked at

Placentia prior to establishing a business in St John's. There are several other specific examples.

Homeland, county and local loyalties were evident in many spheres of Irish life in Placentia. In 1845, for example, Patrick Hogan, Sweetman's principal agent there, became embroiled in a conflict with the other leading resident power, the popular Father Walsh of Mooncoin, county Kilkenny. A fight between Hogan, some of his staff, and the priest's workman quickly spread to involve the servants and some local families and their servants. The civil authorities supported Hogan's men, arresting fifteen rivals. Despite opposition from the bench, all were acquitted by a local jury. Angered by both sides, Bishop Fleming, a native of Carrick-on-Suir, decided to transfer Father Walsh to Merasheen Island. This sparked a riot. Ten of the leading heads of household refused to be enrolled as special constables and government troops were requested from St John's. Hogan wrote despairingly on Sweetman in Waterford:

> All the county Wexford men are to be driven out. The gang on the street publicly singing "out now the Y.Bellys" ... Father Nowlan's influence here is nothing ... They call him a good for nothing old Yellow Belly ... I dare not stay. A storm has been raised against me. My life is sought in open day.[62]

Hogan changed his mind, however, and two weeks later wrote Sweetman from St John's for passengers and provisions.

> Send out 8 youngsters, County Wexford men. No Carrick men or County Kilkenny men ... The Wexford men ... from the same neighbourhood, if possible. This is more important than you may think for the preservation or order ... Your presence will be indispensible at Placentia the ensueing spring. Those whom you shipped there can only be brought to their senses by yourself ...

Sweetman's attitude to this thicket of conflict is not known but it was generally acknowledged that his presence in Placentia would have prevented such turbulence. The family were clearly respected by members of the community. A nostalgic letter to the St John's *Patriot* from a Placentia man, for example, noted that the people of Placentia, poor and struggling in recent years, had derived 'considerable advantage in past times from the establishment of the house of Sweetman, a house established here probably more than a century'. He goes on to describe their patronage and benevolence:

> 'ministering to God's poor ... At Christmas time all the people of the Shore, as far as Distress, were in the habit of coming to Placentia. In those days the cookroom was always open and abundant with excellent food and comfortable lodgings freely granted to all comers, there being accommodation for 40 persons there. On Christmas Eve several prime head of cattle were killed and cut up for Christmas presents for the poor ... decanters of spirits would be filled ... tea, molasses, flour, etc. ... distributed. In the days of the Sweetmans never was it thought of that application should be made to the government to relieve the poor. It is only under his representatives that the system is adopted of looking abroad for that which had always been

dispensed at home . . . Their love for Mr Sweetman gave him an influence over them that made his word law . . .'

Not everybody would agree with this rather romantic view of an outharbour merchant but a distinctive oral tradition persists pertaining to the Sweetman's role in transporting Irish immigrants from the homeland and fostering settlement in Placentia. Between 1800-1840, partly under their auspices, settlements were established or expanded along the northeast and southeast arms of Placentia, on some of the less favoured coves on the islands to the west, and particularly along the Cape Shore. In the eighteenth century these places had been used by the Sweetmans and others to procure timber in winter for vessel and other construction at Placentia and for herring and caplin in the spring.

The Irish who came to occupy these places permanently focused on farming; their settlements and material folk culture are described in some detail elsewhere.[63] Sweetmans promoted farming to feed their servants, particularly with the disruptions in the Irish provisions trade during the war. John Lambe, a company planter at Point Verde, began farming in Big Barrasway (fig 14.2) with his family as early as 1782. By 1800 he worked fifteen acres of intervale, probably the oldest farm on this shore.[64] It was subsequently acquired by Sweetmans who used their winter crews to extend the clearings. They placed one of their servants, Patrick Keefe, there as manager, sometimes with as many as ten young labourers. Fresh vegetables, particularly potatoes, and butter were sent in shallops to company headquarters and fatstock driven along the pathway to Placentia each fall. Keefes eventually acquired the farm. John Skerry of Mooncoin, county Kilkenny, first came to Placentia in 1768 as a migratory fisherman. He spent 34 years with Welsh, Saunders and Sweetman before he petitioned successfully to settle at Ship Cove with his family, recently transported from Kilkenny. Like his neighbour John Lambe, Skerry established a farm and was later joined by two other Mooncoin men, servants of Sweetmans, who married Skerry's daughters. By 1802 the Conways had established two stock farms further south in Distress Cove, under Sweetman auspices.

Over the next three decades some fifty Irish families established farms along the Cape Shore — the vast majority immigrants transported on Sweetman's vessels from Waterford, or their descendants. Several served for a period as shoremen in Placentia prior to taking up land and retained close commercial ties with company headquarters. Like planters in the fishery they were supplied by Sweetmans, on the promise of agricultural produce in the fall. A few farms were managed initially by Sweetman servants — Bruley, Point Verde, Barrasway, Point Lance, Marticott — but most were owned from inception by their occupiers, others purchased later as the Sweetman dynasty declined. This was in striking contrast to the pervasive tenant farms of the homeland. Despite the differences inherent on the frontier, however, society and settlement in Placentia came to resemble to some extent Sweetmans' native Newbawn. Although far more numerous, the young male servants in

Plate xliv: Blenheim, county Waterford, home of Pierce and Roger F. Sweetman

Plate xlv: Blenheim, Placentia, home of Roger F. Sweetman

the company cookrooms at Placentia, Point Verde and Marticott were the equivalent of the labourers who slept in farmstead lofts at Faree, Newbawn and Bryanstown. Servants' families living in houses, some with small potato gardens, leased from Sweetmans on the beach at Placentia, were similar to the cottier settlements around the edges of the big Wexford farms. Although they did not normally have to pay an annual rent for their properties, the planters and farmers scattered around Placentia Bay resembled the small tenant farmers around Newbawn. Some of them were Sweetman tenants on both sides of the Atlantic.

An Irish Cod Fishery, 1810-1850

These settlements at Placentia were spawned by a merchant cod fishery that endured to mid-century. Sweetmans continued to rely on sources overseas for food, despite the growth of local agriculture, and for technology on land and sea. With the demise of the Saunders's, Poole was replaced by Waterford as the organisational hub of the fishery and virtually vanished as a source of supplies. Twice as many company vessels entered Placentia from Waterford between 1811-1846 than from all other ports combined, excepting St John's. Almost all the food, drink, clothing, soap, candles and a range of lesser goods needed for this fishery were now produced in Waterford, New Ross and their hinterlands. Moreover, manufactured items were collected by Sweetman's vessels in Bristol and particularly Liverpool and were shipped mainly through Waterford with salt from Lisbon and Cadiz. When distant Hamburg emerged after 1827 as an alternative source of food for Newfoundland the company vessels went there, sometimes shipping the salt provisions and breadstuffs directly to Placentia. Halifax emerged briefly during the conflict with America and the final stages of the Napoleonic wars as an important source of supplies. The Irish community in this port had strong cultural ties with Placentia and the southern Avalon. Sweetmans linked up with two Irish cod merchants in Halifax, William Power and Hugh Cleary. In 1810 and 1811 they brought 43% of the bread and flour, 17% of the pork, some soap and candles and all the beer, rum, molasses, tobacco, pitch and tar and timber imported by the company from overseas.[65] These supplies were exchanged for fish. Apart from two shipments of salt from Iberia, all other goods from overseas in these two years came from Waterford.

The value of goods imported, while considerable, is difficult to determine. Pierce Sweetman's shipments of pork, butter and bread alone from Waterford amounted to almost £8,000 in 1810-1811. He was no giant, however, in the ranks of Waterford's extensive trading community, Smith credits him with only £1,300 exports of salt provisions and breadstuffs in the year 1813-1814, placing him 71st out of 83 exporting merchants.[66] Smith's lists, however, ignore several specialised commodities characteristic of the Newfoundland trade. Moreover, Sweetmans sent their ships to other places to collect produce for sale in Placentia and, in contrast to the majority of Waterford merchants, they traded on their own account. The firm sold close to £13,000 of supplies in

Placentia in 1816; this would place them in the middle ranks of the Waterford merchant community.

Some exporting merchants integrated the processing and packaging of provisions at Waterford into their general trade. Sweetmans did not. They relied instead on local processors and established exporting houses for Newfoundland produce: Wyse and Quans, Fogartys, Nevins, Penroses and Ridgways for pork and butter, Cherrys, Strangman and Davis for porter and beer, Hunts for bread and flour, the cordwainer John Farrell for boots and shoes, Grahams for iron, Whites for cordage and other ship material, Gatchells for Waterford glass. Half of these firms were Quaker and all of them long engaged in the Newfoundland trade. Sweetmans also shipped goods on the account of artisan producers like the Fennellys, butchers in Waterford, to small traders and even to planters; and they transported passengers and provisions to their Poole neighbours in Little Placentia.

Although the fishery in Newfoundland grew during the latter stages of the Napoleonic wars the quantity of cod produced or exported from Placentia did not. Governor Gower commented in 1805 on how much the once considerable trade of this harbour had declined. Only one merchant house continued there and no more than six to eight vessels arrived each season. Between 1810-1827 an average of only four to five vessels arrived at Great Placentia from Europe for cod. Across the bay, by contrast, Burin was booming.[67] Fewer than 200 fishermen and shoremen were based in the harbour of Placentia and coves nearby, producing 10,000-12,000 quintals of fish in a good season. Most of this fish, once cured, was delivered by the planters to Sweetman's premises, the Beach Stores at company headquarters beside Blenheim the family residence (pl. xlv) or the Jersey Stores, at the north end of the harbour.

Although there was as always competition from local and visiting traders, Sweetmans apparently still dominated the export of cod from Great Placentia. In 1810 and 1811, for example, 21,000 quintals of cod, worth around £15,000, were shipped overseas from there, 80% by the company. The remainder was taken to Halifax by three traders almost certainly operating through Sweetmans. Over 54% of the fish exported in these two seasons went to Waterford, 27% to Lisbon and 19% to Halifax. Waterford endured as possibly the principal market until the demise of the company's transatlantic trade after 1850. Each year two to four cargoes of cod and some herring arrived at Sweetman's premises on Quay Lane or later at their warehouse in the west end of the city. Cod and seal oil, seal pelts, a small amount of furs, hides for tanning, and timber were also imported. In 1846 close to 8,000 quintals of cod arrived at Waterford in four shipments and were sold for £4,700. Sweetmans also transported cod for neighbouring merchants such as the Koughs of New Ross and Merasheen and Nicholas Hayes of Waterford and Little Placentia.

Little is known of the details of distribution of Newfoundland cod in the growing Waterford market. Sweetmans were one of a score of firms engaged in this trade. They advertised cod for sale from their 'Newfoundland Fish Store' on Georges Street and also delivered fish directly to traders on the quay.

The widow Margaret Brownrigg, whose family had leased warehouses on Quay Lane to Pierce Sweetman in 1815, handled a cargo of 2,530 quintals of cod arriving from Placentia in October 1833 and a number of shipments subsequently. She supplied fresh food and other necessities to the ship's crew, paid whatever expenses were incurred unloading the cargo and settled sailor's accounts with wives and kin after the vessel departed. Through the winter the fish was sold in small amounts to local dealers, mainly women. Upon completion of sales Brownrigg sent a statement of account to Roger Sweetman at Placentia with comments on the Waterford market, charged a commission and remitted a balance of £1,300 to his father.

The emergence of Waterford as an important market for company cod in the nineteenth century reflected the spread of poverty there and the concomitant demand for cheap protein. Unlike the majority of Irish merchants now engaged in this trade, however, Sweetmans maintained their links with Iberia and it continued as a cornerstone for company traffic. Roger Sweetman visited there during the depression that followed the war to bolster sales and he was the only Irish merchant attending a meeting in London two decades later to discuss high duties on Newfoundland cod in south European markets.[68] According to official statistics, 70% of all cod shipped from Great Placentia overseas between 1810-1827 went to Iberia. Cod was sometimes shipped through Waterford and although the Sweetmans traded with a geographically diffuse range of ports, from Bilbao and Corunna to Madeira and Alicante, their principal markets were Lisbon and Cadiz. Roger Sweetman had close personal ties with the firm's main Iberian agents, Morrogh and Walsh of Lisbon, acting as an occasional agent for them both in Waterford and in Newfoundland where they were anxious to develop trade.

Sweetmans remained overwhelmingly committed to the cod fishery but did engage in some ancillary trading after the war. Vessels arriving at Placentia from Waterford in the spring were sent on to Quebec, sometimes in ballast, sometimes with fish and other produce, to take timber back to Waterford. Quebec pine and other lumber were advertised for sale off their vessels at anchor in Waterford quay.[69] Sweetmans also sent their ships from Waterford to English ports, notably to Bristol and Liverpool, with grain, flour and other commodities and brought back manufactured goods for the local market. They shipped provisions from Waterford and Cork to St John's and took fish from there on freight or on their own account, working through old agents like Hart and Robinson or Hunters and Company. The intensive shuttling of ships between Waterford and Newfoundland, with side voyages to England and Canada, was a popular pattern amongst Irish merchants engaged in the cod trade in the nineteenth century.

As the Newfoundland economy emerged from its post-war slump, Sweetmans rebuilt their fleet. In 1815 they owned a mere three vessels but by 1835 they had twelve, most of them ocean-going. No more than half a dozen Irish merchants in the trade operated a fleet of this magnitude. Almost all of these vessels were built at company headquarters or in Cape Breton, under the direction of a company shipwright. Sydney and Bras d'Or also became

Sweetman's main source of timber for local construction of coal and occasionally livestock. With an expanded fleet Sweetmans entered the seal fishery. In 1828 Pierce Sweetman sent detailed instructions from Waterford to one of his Irish captains to sail for the ice fields and follow the example of experienced sealers. Despite their locational disadvantage on the south coast, each winter thereafter the company sent two or more vessels with 50-60 local men to the front. The sealers were signed on at Placentia in March, were given supplies and charged 10/- each for a berth. Work on the ice was arduous but the season relatively brief. By mid April Sweetman's crews were home. The seal pelts were usually sold in St John's and the men rewarded with a share of the catch.

Pierce Sweetman died at Blenheim in Waterford in 1841, having prosecuted the cod trade for over half a century. 'No man better sustained, in distant countries or at home, the character of a British merchant' stated an obituary '... he was a deservedly adored husband, parent, friend, and a finished gentleman'.[70] His only surviving son moved with his family from Placentia to Blenheim and assumed sole management of the firm. No other Irish merchant could claim such deep roots in the Newfoundland trade. Roger Sweetman, born in county Wexford at the end of the eighteenth century, was likely the great-grandson of a Placentia merchant and he himself had spent close to thirty years managing the fishery by the time his father died. Sweetman maintained the traditional triangular pattern of cod trading through the 1840s, the only Waterford-based merchant to do so. He continued to send passengers and provisions to the fishery and to build vessels at Placentia; a 222 ton brig was launched there in 1843. Imports of cod to Waterford increased during the famine but so did company debts across the Atlantic. The economic and demographic impact of the famine, moreover, virtually ended the residual cod trade with Irish ports. The Sweetmans left Waterford permanently for Placentia in 1850. By now an economic backwater, Placentia had little traffic overseas. The firm's extensive premises were still intact, however, and Roger Sweetman endeavoured to preserve a diminished trade. He survived a bankruptcy in 1854 although he did not register any vessels subsequently. In 1860 after a wretched fishery, Sweetman had to let some of his servants go. Debts owed him exceeded £12,600, only £1,000 less than in 1847. Yet he ordered supplies from two of the family's agents in St John's in the following spring and wrote enthusiastically about the prospects for the fishery at Placentia that July. He requested a vessel of around 14,000 quintals capacity from Tobins of Halifax together with a comprehensive cargo of provisions. A year later he was dead and a family business that extended back over a century finally closed.

Culture and Class: The Merchant Society

The background and behaviour of the dozen or so merchants engaged with the house established by Richard Welsh raises several important issues regarding the nature of Irish mercantile society in the century after 1750. The firm's founder came from a small but active port with a venerable trading tradition and served a long apprenticeship overseas before attaining mercantile status.

This route was probably characteristic of many successful merchants from modest backgrounds in eighteenth century Ireland. Much work has yet to be done on the social origins of Irish merchants before the representativeness of Welsh's career can be assessed. Scholars suggest that the nascent Irish merchant needed £400 to £500 capital and connections to established houses. Welsh probably accumulated the requisite capital on his own but it is likely that most beginners were bequeathed some cash to launch mercantile careers. Braudel's suggestion that 'the best way to make a fortune was to have some money to begin with' generally holds true. All of Welsh's successors were middle class. Four were the sons of merchants, four the sons of big farmers, and John Blackney was sub gentry. All these men had access to credit, whether it came from Irish land, Waterford commerce or the profits of the Placentia cod fishery.

The importance of daughters in the absence of male heirs and the centrality of marriage and affinal kin in the perpetuation and to some extent vertical integration of a mercantile house is demonstrated in the Welsh succession. His three daughters married in their teens, two of them departing the rudimentary society of a maritime frontier for the relative social sophistication of the homeland. Apart from recruiting men from four strategic families to protect and continue the trade, these marriages gave the firm better access to critical source areas for labour, provisions and capital and to a lesser extent, access to markets or market information. Successful trading depended to a considerable degree on trust and this was best ensured through ties of kin. In contrast to some colonial staples like sugar and tobacco, the cod fishery did not spawn elaborate formal mercantile partnerships.

Apart from its high-water mark in the 1780s the Placentia firm was never much more than a loose association of two or three families operating under the direction of a single head, Braudel's *campagnia*.[71] There is no evidence that affinal relatives such as William Furlong, Roger Sweetman, Paul Farrell or John Blackney were ever active formal partners. When the Sweetmans began to gain control Pierce's two brothers were recruited, but they did not play a major role. Three other brothers remained on their Wexford farms and none of Pierce's brothers-in-law, nor his Wexford son-in-law, a Waterford merchant, were involved. After 1810 the enterprise was managed by Pierce Sweetman and his son and then by his son alone. The profits from the cod trade could be considerable, as Richard Welsh vividly revealed, but this fishery did not require an extensive investment of capital to mount a venture. A large group of individual firms, small in scale and centred on the nuclear family, dominated cod commerce for four centuries. Saunders and Sweetman in the 1780s were more the exception than the rule. The individualism pervading entrepreneurship in the cod fishery stands in contrast to the large extended family partnerships or syndicates that typified the business organisation of, for example, the tobacco lords of the Clyde.[72]

Despite the importance of daughters and their dowries in the formation of mercantile partnerships and the continuity of a firm, merchant society was strongly patriarchal. Women were rarely involved directly in trade. There is no record of wives or daughters engaged in clerical work in the counting houses of Welsh, Saunders and Sweetman. Indeed they are seldom mentioned outside marriage settlements, wills and associated property transactions. Richard Welsh's headstone inscription reflects the male ambience of the merchant's world in a colonial setting. In the socially more mature homeland, however, women had a more important role. The relatively commodious villas or town houses were the foci of merchant socialising and wives sometimes travelled with their husbands on business. The Waterford chronicle reported, for example, the arrival of 'John Blackney, Esq, and his lady' from Bristol on the *Tyrone* yacht, a vessel owned by Blackney's brother-in-law, John Wyse.[73] Pierce Sweetman's entourage for England in 1793 included his lady, his two sisters, his two sisters-in-law, some servants, attendants and their chaplain, Reverend Deane. At Blenheim they employed four servants, two labourers and a family in the gate lodge. Pierce's daughters were educated by the French Benedictine nuns at Winchester. When she 'entered society' his eldest daughter was reportedly fluent in French and 'one of Ireland's leading harpists.' After their mother's death, Pierce's two surviving daughters entered the Ursuline convent in Waterford and became reverend mothers, typical of middle class Catholics in the nineteenth century.

Marriage involving spouses from another country or even denomination were relatively rare in merchant society in the homeland. Less is known of Irish merchants abroad but the opportunity for mixed marriages was greater. The presence of Protestant English spouses like Wibault and the Saunders in the Welsh and Sweetman marriage field reflects the social and economic conditions of a fishing frontier: Marriageable women, especially English, were scarce in Placentia. Management of the fishery there required the close co-operation of a tiny trading class, composed of English and Irish. Inter-ethnic partnerships sometimes resulted and could be accompanied by a marriage as in the case of William Saunders and Ann Welsh. Such unions were rare but understandable in a frontier society where the church was indifferent and the middle class were few. Something of the indiscipline of eighteenth century mercantile society in Placentia is revealed in the birth to Anne Saunders of a son in adultery. Thomas Saunders, moreover, did not marry his Irish mistress but bequeathed his property to one of their children whom Michael Sweetman married in the Anglican church in Poole.

Both Saunders and Sweetman welcomed the establishment of a resident Catholic clergy in Placentia. It was probably the best guarantee of law and order among the servant class. They provided a house and land near company headquarters for Father Burke in 1785 and collected £20 from their servants to help build a chapel.[74] When Burke's jurisdiction was challenged by Father Lonergan, an unlicensed priest popular among the Irish servants, William Saunders used his influence with the governor in St John's to have him banished. Pierce Sweetman was the third most generous donor, after Prince William Henry, the future monarch, and Thomas Saunders, to the fund to build an Anglican church in 1786. On the insistence of the prince he also took the oath of allegiance, something his kinsman Bishop Sweetman in

Wexford would not have approved. Pierce Sweetman was a close friend of the Anglican ministers in Placentia. In order to attract a replacement in 1803, for example, he offered ½ an acre of company ground near the church and money to build a parsonage.[75] The amicable relationship was maintained by Roger Sweetman. In a speech to the Catholic Association of Waterford, attended by Daniel O'Connell, Patrick Morris, the St John's merchant, instanced the role of the Sweetmans in the maintenance of religious harmony in Newfoundland. When the Anglican Church had deteriorated there and was threatened with closure, Roger Sweetman and Father Cleary of Bannow organised the Irish congregation to help the small Protestant community have it repaired.[76] Placentia avoided much of the sectarian tension that split society in larger centres like St John's after 1830.

Sweetmans were among the mainstays of the Catholic church in Placentia from its inception. Most of the priests were from Wexford and Sweetman vessels were available to transport goods and materials for them. Bishop Fleming stayed at Blenheim on his tour of southern Newfoundland and Bishop Doyle (J.K.L.) visited Pierce Sweetman at Blenheim in Waterford. Sweetman's long association and kinship with Wexford bishops conferred social status at home and abroad. Relics of Bishop Nicholas Sweetman are still in the family's possession in Newbawn and, like most big farmers, the Sweetmans were a significant source of support for the local parish church as it emerged from the seclusion of the eighteenth century. There are few closer analogues in the evolution of society and settlement on both sides of the Atlantic than the Irish Catholic Church with its middle class nurture, exemplified here by the Sweetmans of Newbawn and Placentia.

Despite their status as leading residents in a small colonial community, neither Richard Welsh, Pierce Sweetman nor his brothers were ever appointed to administrative positions in Placentia. Catholics were not allowed to hold office and all surrogates, magistrates, justices of the peace, constables, jurors, customs officers and other officials were drawn from the Protestant class. Richard Welsh's only recorded public duty was to collect taxes from planters and servants for the upkeep of the Anglican cemetery, courthouse, gaol and for those in distress. This responsibility, traditionally assigned to the leading merchant in a harbour, was assumed by his successors. Fear of Irish Catholic disloyalty in Placentia continued among the authorities to 1750 but there is little reference to it there after. Certainly the Catholic merchants were loyal, as they were almost everywhere in the empire. Welsh and Sweetmans enjoyed the full confidence of the colonial authorities, to their mutual benefit. They co-operated closely to maintain social order and ensure economic control. In this they were usually supported by the church. When Michael Sweetman insulted the local court, the Anglican minister intervened on his behalf and the governor advised a light sentence since his presence at Placentia was essential for a successful fishery. This is not to say that mercantile loyalty and economic power meant total dominion over planters and servants. Richard Welsh was fined by the local court for assault, mistreatment of servants and on several occasions was ordered to pay them their wages or reimburse planters. So were his successors.

The military at Placentia, the strong arm of colonial authority, bolstered mercantile control and ensured total loyalty. It not only protected a merchant fishery but was a source of lucrative contracts to merchant houses, particularly during the war. Richard Welsh established healthy relations with the military through the Wibaults and the company was active thereafter in the local garrison trade. James Downes took advantage of his position as chief company agent to organise a local force of some ninety men for the protection of the harbour early in the Napoleonic campaign. He had problems, however, procuring funds from St John's. Pierce Sweetman had more than pure loyalism on his mind when he informed Colonel Skinner that he was always willing to aid the work of His Majesty in a communication on the parlous state of the town's fortifications. Sweetman had taken the oath, perhaps under pressure from the virulently anti-Catholic Prince William Henry, but was willing to serve on a committee over forty years later to pledge loyalty to William as king. His behaviour in 1798 illustrates the primacy of profits in the merchants' world. While his uncle plotted rebellion in Newbawn, Pierce Sweetman left his family at Bryanstown for Poole to organise the season's shipping and then proceeded to Placentia.[77]

A gradual liberalisation of laws proscribing Catholics from holding office allowed merchants to participate more in political life, first in Ireland, then in Newfoundland. Following the Catholic declaration of loyalty, signed by over 200 men in Waterford in 1793, two of the three Catholic merchants elected to the Grand Jury, John Blackney and Thomas Quan, had close company connections. Pierce Sweetman's social status was also enhanced when appointed justice of the peace for Wexford in 1806. Like most Catholic merchants he was a supporter of the Waterford Liberal Protestant M.P. Sir John Newport and was active in the struggle for Catholic emancipation.[78] While in Waterford Sweetman did not run for any political or administrative office. He focused instead on humanitarian causes, particularly the alleviation of local distress. His son belonged to a much more politicised generation of Irish-Newfoundland merchants, emboldened by the success of their idol, O'Connell. As the leading resident in Placentia, Roger Sweetman played an important part in the effort to improve local conditions through political representation in the 1830s, a critical decade in Newfoundland's evolution. He was elected foreman of the Grand Jury in 1830, justice of the peace shortly thereafter and represented Placentia in Newfoundland's first House of Assembly between 1832-1836. Sweetman served on several committees in the House, using his expert knowledge of the fishery, trade and agriculture to stimulate development in his district and to introduce social and institutional reform. On his return to Waterford he followed the example of other merchants formerly resident in Newfoundland, notably Patrick Morris, James Kent, Thomas Fogarty and Thomas Meagher (a relative by marriage and former neighbour in Blenheim) all of whom entered local politics. Sweetman was a member of Waterford Town Council from 1842-1850. He was active in the movement for Repeal and visited O'Connell in Richmond gaol. During the famine he was treasurer of the local relief committee. His final years as a public servant were spent in

Placentia, beseeching the government in St John's for funds to ameliorate the growing poverty in the bay.

Perhaps the most notable feature of the firm established by Richard Welsh was its longevity. Continuity was not a characteristic of merchant society. Most family firms lasted only a generation, few more than two. In the century after 1750 over 100 Irish firms entered the Newfoundland trade and although some, such as the Elmes' and Koughs of New Ross, were remarkably enduring, none matched Welsh and his successors. Indeed few English merchant houses in Newfoundland survived for more than a century. The durability at Placentia appears more striking when one considers that, over the four generations of merchants active in the company, only Pierce Sweetman produced a lasting male heir. However studies of durable merchant houses have revealed the importance of matrilineal descent in patterns of succession. Socolow, for example, found that over 40% of the merchants of Buenos Aires had no male heirs and brought in daughters to perpetuate family firms.[79]

The Sweetmans came from a traditional middle class Catholic society in Wexford with a strong sense of a distinguished past. Pierce Sweetman's father and grandfather lie buried with other members of their families beside Bishop Sweetman in Clongeen. They are commemorated in impressive tombstones similar to that for Richard Welsh in Placentia. They had survived the calamitous seventeenth century and with renewed vigour branched out from their heartland in Newbawn subsequently. The Sweetman family crest decorated the company's bills of exchange issued in Waterford and Placentia. Their tenacity in the volatile cod trade was mirrored in their retention of lands inherited or purchased in southeast Ireland (fig 14.4, table 1) and in Newfoundland. Richard Welsh established a pattern by investing some of the profits from Placentia in the New Ross land market through the Tottenhams. Roger Sweetman continued to collect rents from tenants on the ancestral farm at Collopswell up to the 1840s when it was passed on to his cousins, the Farrells of Fary. Sweetmans relied on their farming kin in Wexford to administer this and other holdings in their absence from the county. Although they departed Wexford for good in 1806, Pierce and his family are still remembered in family tradition there. They may not have had the cohesiveness of a Scottish clan but they maintained their links with their native place, even when overseas. Cod from Placentia was sent to the farm at Ballymackesey, for example, as late as the 1840s. Although permanently resident in Placentia by 1853 Roger Sweetman still had a farm of 70 acres in Faree, let to an undertenant, and he still retained the family interests in Blenheim. Lists of tenants, details of leases and maps of farms from Wexford and Kilkenny survive in Placentia. His sister Juliet leased 95 acres to six tenants in Rochestown and 350 acres to seven tenants in Rathduff. At least part of the latter property was still in her hands in 1868. Roger Sweetman died in 1862 leaving a widow and one child, a daughter, who was married to an English mining engineer. Although they inherited the premises and lived in Placentia, they did not continue the business into a fifth generation. Placentia's long tradition of overseas trading was over. Yet the property in Placentia, procured by Richard Welsh in the 1750s, remains in the family's possession to this day.

Acknowledgements

This paper is drawn from research begun in 1973 and is part of a larger project on the Irish migrations to Newfoundland. For research assistance, my thanks to Howard Brown, Edward Tompkins and Maura Mannion; to the Institute for Social and Economic research, Memorial University and the Social Sciences and Humanities Research Council, Ottawa, for funds; to Randall Verran and the Careens of Placentia, the Cadigans of Newbawn, the Sweetmans of Ballymackessey the Cullens of Adamstown and Danny Dowling of Glenmore for assistance in the field. Special thanks to Gary McManus, MUNCL, Department of Geography, St. John's, for the maps and figures and to Conchubhair Ó Fearghail for the Newbawn sketch.

15 *Bruce Elliott*

Emigration from South Leinster to Eastern Upper Canada

Emigrants from county Wexford to Newfoundland and Nova Scotia were largely Catholics from the southwestern parishes of the county, part of the hinterland of the port of Waterford. This movement was an extension of long-standing seasonal patterns of migration to the Newfoundland fisheries.[1] Movement from south Leinster to Upper Canada (now Ontario) in the first half of the nineteenth century was very different. This migration drew mostly upon the Protestants of north Wexford and south Wicklow and was not dependent upon pre-existing trading patterns with any one port. Rather it took the form of chain migration by farmers possessed of means to afford the passage, journeying to any south-eastern port to embark for a frontier agricultural region in the New World where relatives and friends had already settled.[2]

This wave of migration must be understood in the context of Protestant apprehensions following the disturbances of 1798.[3] Though the farmers of south Leinster were comparatively prosperous and many Protestants enjoyed a privileged position in the eyes of their landlords, their special status was less secure than it had been. In the parish of Killegney in which Protestants were few an observer noted in 1814 that 'the Protestant religion declines among the lower classes, as the people of that description are not encouraged, are apt to emigrate when opportunity serves, and to gain favour with the great majority, are apt to turn Roman Catholics'.[4] Initially such migration appears to have been directed to the United States more than to the British colonies in America. A small colony from the Arklow area began forming at Pratt's Hollow in Madison County, New York at least as early as 1806, and there is evidence of further settlement not far away in Utica.[5]

However, sectarian tensions in this period are not sufficient to explain the establishment of a large south Leinster (predominantly Wexford) population in eastern Ontario. Emigrants to Canada were few before the War of 1812 and the contemporaneous movement of Protestants from south-eastern Ireland to eastern Upper Canada was a mere trickle. The opening of the floodgates after the termination of hostilities in 1815 owed at least as much to the onset of the postwar depression and to the happy reports of emigrant friends as to the continuing insecurities of these Irish Protestants. A Wexford gentleman noted in 1817 that 'the very great over population of this part of Ireland so severely felt last spring, and the extremely gratifying letters that have been received from the families who have settled in upper Canada from these counties are the more immediate causes of the general and unprecedented desire to emigrate'.[6] Encouraged as well by false hopes of government assistance, many seized the opportunity to follow friends and relations to a frontier in the New World where hard work offered the small and middling farmer and tradesman the possibility of providing a secure future for his children.

From a North American perspective this south Leinster migration is significant because Canadian scholars have only recently begun to examine the stereotypes that have coloured our image of nineteenth century Irish immigrants. Discussion of Irish immigration and settlement formerly focussed upon the Famine migration of the late 1840s and the Peter Robinson parties of 1823 and 1825. Study of the former was largely uncritical and impressionistic, and the latter two groups, government-sponsored emigrations of poor Catholics from county Cork, were highly atypical of Irish movement into Canada.[7] Recent work has corrected some misimpressions by indicating that two-thirds of the Irish in nineteenth century Ontario were Protestants and that the vast majority of Irish of all faiths settled on farms and not in urban ghettoes.[8]

Our knowledge of the social and regional origins of the Irish population of Ontario remains very limited.[9] Historians have often assumed that Ontario's Irish Protestants were Ulstermen.[10] Cousens's delineations of the patterns of Irish emigration have been taken as proof of the accuracy of this generalisation.[11] However, because of the evident prevalence of regional chain migration, general patterns of emigration from one country seldom equate with specific patterns of settlement in another. The origins of Ontario's Irish immigrants is a question of some importance, for the Irish were not an un-differentiated group of people. Their religious, linguistic, social, and economic characteristics varied considerably from region to region and among social classes. If we are to understand the effects of the dominance of the Irish as the largest ethnic group in nineteenth century Ontario, we must study the immigrant Irish as they were and not as we presume them to have been.

Chain migration gave to the eastern part of Ontario a distinctive character, for the region became home to a much larger southern Protestant component than the existing historiography suggests. The false perception of the region's emigrant Protestants as Ulstermen is not new. The *Bytown Gazette* editorialised in 1849 to correct the assumptions o the *Montreal Herald*: 'The Herald is again at fault when he asserts that the real Settlers are Protestants, from the North of Ireland. There is a great majority in Carleton, whether Protestant or Catholic from the South of Ireland, and the Herald is, therefore, grossly mistaken when he supposes that they are 'Scotch Irishmen' generally

... You are not Irish ... oh! no; you are a sort of improved, Scotchified Irish'![12]
Even when correct origins have been remembered, ignorance born of later
historical circumstances has caused Canadian writers to assume that the
places mentioned are in Ulster, as occurred in 1934 when the *Perth Courier*
placed the headline 'Northern Irishmen As Hardy Pioneers' above an article
which noted that the early Irish of that vicinity hailed largely from county
Wexford.[13]

Cullen has pointed out that 'Wexford and Wicklow were the most
successful Protestant settlements outside Ulster'.[14] In 1831, 60,000 of the
400,000 residents of the three southeastern counties of Ireland were
Protestant, nearly 15 per cent of the total population. In county Wicklow 20
per cent of residents were Protestant, in Wexford 13 per cent, and in Carlow 9
per cent.[15] Protestants were concentrated most heavily in the coastal parishes
of county Wicklow and in south Wicklow and north Wexford along the base
of the Wicklow Mountains. The zone of Protestant occupation extended
westward across county Carlow in a less concentrated form as far as the
mining area near Castlecomer, county Kilkenny (fig. 15.1).

The first emigrants from this region arrived in the Johnstown District of
Upper Canada before the 1812 War. The earliest arrivals seem to have been
John and Nicholas Horton who bought land in Elizabethtown Township in the
spring of 1809.[17] The 1812 assessment roll lists also Adam Horton, John
Horton Jr., Benjamin Tackaberry, Frederick Moor, and Francis Jacob.[18]
Emigration effectively ceased during the war with the United States between
1812 and 1815, and even in the years before the war, boarding an emigrant
ship sometimes had unexpected consequences. Benjamin Tackaberry, who
settled in Elizabethtown in 1811, was almost certainly the Benjamin
Tukerbury who with his family sailed from Dublin for New York on the
Belisarius that year. The vessel was boarded on the high seas by the crew of the
Atlanta, a British sloop of war, and most of the passengers were carried away
to Halifax. Forty-three were sent to the island of St John's to settle on the
estate of Lord James Townshend and seventeen men were pressed into service
on the *Atlanta*. Benjamin Tukerbury and family were among those taken to
Halifax but they are listed neither among the party sent to the Townshend
estate nor among those impressed. Possibly Tackaberry was able to provide
evidence of his intention to settle in Upper Canada and for that reason was
allowed to go on his way.[19] Such incidents can have done little to encourage
emigration. Nonetheless, before the war another small cluster of Wexford
expatriates formed two townships to the west of Elizabethtown, in Leeds and
Lansdowne. William Johnson (c 1740/45-1825) from Wells, county Wexford
settled there in 1811. Only Peter and George Johnston appear in the 1812
assessment roll, but the 1815 listing shows also William, Richard, and John
Johnson, Samuel Copeland, and William Webster, all Wexford emigrants.[20]
Samuel Whaley from Kilcormick, who settled in nearby Yonge, also came in
1811.[21]

The emigrants from southeastern Ireland received no assistance from the
British government, but their attempts to obtain passages and provisions,

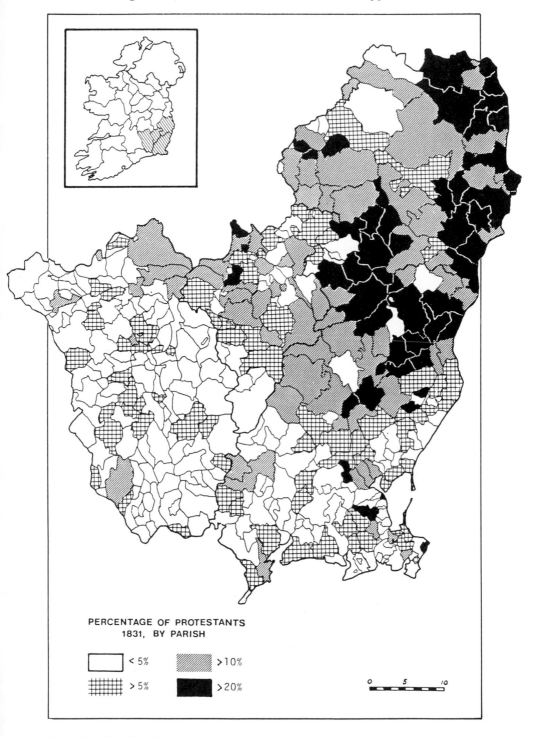

PERCENTAGE OF PROTESTANTS
1831, BY PARISH

< 5%		>10%
> 5%		>20%

0   5   10

Fig. 15.1: The distribution of Protestants in South Leinster in 1831

largely through the mediation of two gentlemen named Elly of New Ross, have left documentation of the beginnings of a massive movement of people to join their compatriots near Brockville, Upper Canada. The Ellys were brothers of a Quaker merchant who imported timber and staves from Quebec. Samuel Elly Jr. commonly shipped out passengers in the vessels he chartered to bring timber to Ireland, so it was natural for the residents of Wexford to seek advice and information from his family.[22] Joseph Elly wrote to the Colonial Office in 1815 that many people in his neighbourhood had seen newspaper articles about government encouragement for emigrants to Canada and were applying to him for advice. He wrote that his only motive in writing was to obtain correct information for these applicants and 'preventing an increase however small to the population of an enemy at the expense of our own', alluding to the movement of people from south Leinster to the United States.[23] Elly's brother Robert wrote to the Colonial Office in January 1817 that applications to go to Canada were 'numerous beyond measure'. Because no assisted passage had been offered the year before, Elly asserted, a great number from his neighbourhood had gone to the United States, which was 'holding out baits' to get settlers from his region. He pointed out that most of the emigrants were 'men of excellent character' whose loss to the British dominions was regrettable. On the strength of Lord Bathurst's letters recommending individual settlers for land grants, some had proceeded to Canada at their own expense and letters from them had induced others to ask Elly to secure similar recommendations for them. He estimated that from 100 to 300 more settlers who could not afford the conveyance would go if provisions were supplied, though inevitably without a 'political move' by government many would go to the United States since the passage was less expensive. Elly even stated that a gentleman friend would go along to Canada to establish a colony if desired. Lord Bathurst replied enclosing letters of recommendation, but impressed upon Elly that no assisted passages or provisions would be given.[24]

Virtually besieged by applicants, the Ellys decided to compile a list of those wanting to go to the Canadas (appendix I). As letters arrived from Canada and word spread about the Ellys' list the Colonial Office began to receive indications in letters from more distant towns in the region that interest in emigration was endemic among the Protestants of south Leinster. In September 1817 the Rev G. F. Vaughan, the curate of Enniscorthy, wrote that his parish clerk and sexton intended emigrating in the spring. 'To such an extent does *this spirit* prevail', he wrote, 'that upwards of two thousand individuals as I am informed are determined upon emigration from the Neighbourhoods (of) Newtown Barry and Carlow at the same time'.The clergyman wrote to offer his own services in the colonies. The Colonial Secretary was taken aback by Vaughan's information and instructed his clerk to reply as follows:

'Acquaint him that there never has been any intention on the part of Government of encouraging emigration to Canada in the manner or to the extent to which his letter refers and that so far from giving any further encouragement to persons proceeding thither, it is extremely doubtful whether that limited encouragement heretofore held out to them of a limited grant of land on their arrival will be continued during the next year'.[25]

By October word of the Ellys' activities had reached Rathdrum, county Wicklow, for Isaac Saul Jr. of that place wrote to the Colonial Office seeking information on behalf of many respectable families in and about the town who asked him what he knew about 'the encouragement': 'they tell me there is a Person taking down Such Families Names as wish to Emigrat [sic] in Carnew a small Town about 20 Miles from this, but they do not know his Name else I would have written to him to know the truth and not to have troubled Your Lordship'. Bathurst's reply was more positive than the response the Rev Mr Vaughan had received, for it stated that encouragement was not being offered at the moment merely because the season was too far advanced. However, the Colonial Secretary informed Saul that any person taking down names was altogether unauthorised by government.[26]

In December Joseph Elly forwarded the list, noting that if the government wished to form a 'particular settlement' they would not find 'a more loyal brave industrious and well regulated body of men' who, in return for free passages, would gladly form themselves into a fencible regiment willing to serve anywhere in the province. Elly requested immediate action as he had prevailed upon the eager emigrants only with difficulty not to dispose of their 'little property (insufficient to convey them to Canada)' before 1 January, 1818.[23]

The list more than supported the previous assertions about the numbers desirous of proceeding to Canada. It contained the names of 710 Protestant heads of family and 281 Roman Catholic families, a total of 5,502 individuals, including upwards of 1,100 able-bodied Protestants capable of bearing arms. Though the heading of the list indicated that the potential settlers were residents of Carlow and Wexford intending to emigrate in the ensuing spring, it also contained the names of many residents of counties Wicklow and Kilkenny (appendix 1).

The suspicions and distrust that had been the cause of the violence of the 1798 Rebellion, which in Wexford had degenerated from the republican ideals of its Ulster leadership to become a campaign of mutual atrocities, had been strengthened by the slaughter of hundreds of Protestants during the insurrection. The deteriorating economic climate further accelerated the fears of southern Protestants. The Protestants of Wexford assumed that the privilege of securing government assistance, to emigrate would be offered only to Irishmen of proven loyalty.[28] In common with most Irish applicants for emigration assistance before Peter Robinsons's first group of Roman Catholics left Cork in 1823, Mr Vaughan, the curate of Enniscorthy, assumed that the government meant to establish in Canada 'a Colony exclusively Protestant'. Though no official statement was made on the subject, this was apparently the common perception, for few Roman Catholics bothered to write to the Colonial Office in these early years. Even those Protestants who did not think that there was any ban on Catholic emigrants thought that membership in the Established Church gave them an additional qualification for favourable consideration.[29]

Joseph Elly's agents diligently collected names of Roman Catholics as well as of Protestants, but Elly questioned the loyalty of the Roman Catholics and submitted the names in two separate lists, with extensive editorialising:

The Protestant families of which this list is composed are remarkably sober, industrious and well educated, can procure the most satisfactory recommendations and have generally [in] some of their branches members of yeomanry corps, many of these families possess considerably more property than sufficient to remove them and all fixed in their determination of joining their relatives and families who have so happily settled in Upper Canada upon land granted by the British Government within these last two years. Many other Protestant families of most respectable character tho unable to bear the expenses of removal, are unsettling themselves under the idea of being assisted with a free passage to British America ... Most of the men of these families capable of bearing arms in the Rebellion of 1798 were actually employed in the defence of their country.

On the second list Elly wrote a more qualified recommendation:

The Roman Catholic families which compose this list are generally respectable Farmers, have procured tolerably good recommendations for sobriety, industry, and good conduct, but as Farmers and work men they possess the want of order, neatness, and economy which generally designates the religious persuasion to which they belong. The Protestant immigrants look on their being accompanied by these families with a dissatisfied and jealous eye. Most of the Catholic families are quite unable to bear the expenses of a passage to Quebec and providing for their subsistence on arriving at their destination and are unsettling themselves under the idea of the British Government furnishing a conveyance to the colonies.[30]

There is no question but that the horrors of 1798 weighed heavily upon the minds of the Protestant minority in Wexford and Wicklow. Their individual petitions echoed Elly's commentary with assertive, even aggressive expressions of loyalty to the Crown, couched in assumptions of favoured status. The more perceptive among them sensed that such a bluffly bellicose attitude might be read as an attempt to compensate for a profound sense of insecurity, and tempered their expression of loyalty with assurances of good behaviour.

The movement into eastern Upper Canada from south Leinster was predominantly Protestant, but it was also drawn largely from those who possessed the means to emigrate independently but were of no great wealth or social standing. Thomas Graham from Clondaw near Enniscorthy explained to his mother in letters from Brockville in the late 1820s that it was men like himself who profitted from emigration: 'Men must labour very hard here; but they are well fed and well paid; and what a man has is his own: there is no landlord or tyrant to reign over them. Men who came here some years ago, have large clearances now, and are taking their ease'. And again, 'Let any who can live without working at home, stay at home; but for him who can labour, this is the best country'.[31]

Much the same conclusions were reached by Samuel Elly's son-in-law, William Graves, a Lieutenant in the Enniscorthy yeomanry and formerly an Ensign in the 79th Foot. In 1820 he resolved to emigrate to Canada in the wake of many of his father-in-law's more humble correspondents. He sailed that spring from Ross on the *Maria*, armed with letters of introduction from Lord Carrick, Charles Tottenham of New Ross, and the local member of parliament. His trip was an exploratory journey, made to discover what advantages Canada offered the man of means, and so he left his wife and children at home. As a prospective emigrant of some wealth and standing, Graves displayed no interest in accompanying the farmers who sailed on the same ship to join their friends near Perth. Instead he waited upon the Governor General, Lord Dalhousie, at Quebec and obtained further letters of introduction before setting off to explore Upper Canada in search of the best location.

What he saw discouraged him. He visited three acquaintances from Wexford Quaker circles who had bought farms a year or two earlier in a settlement of American Friends in Prince Edward County to the west of Kingston. Mr S. Baker gave Graves favourable accounts of the Canadian winter and the generally salubrious climate, but Graves was less satisfied with the quality of Baker's land. Baker had been too short a time in the country to offer a firm opinion on what advantages farming there possessed but 'He said he would not have left Ireland had he got a farm he offered for near Taghmon ... his eldest daughter ... speaks with much regret at her Father leaving the "Old Country" and thinks he will not do better in "the New".' Waring and Taylor had purchased developed farms nearby, Waring 300 acres, 70 of it clear, with a small house, for £1,000, and Taylor 51 acres, partly cultivated and with a house, for £250. 'Were I to conclude from the manner Waring expressed himself', Graves noted in his diary, 'he would be as well pleased had he not made the change. He said he had formed an opinion of the country it did not deserve. S. B[aker] thinks Taylor is not likely to do well. His means and age are too much against him'.[32]

Graves visited several other Quaker settlements composed of families resident for generations in America, but was singularly unimpressed: 'Adolphustown is chiefly settled by Quakers who like their neighbours on the opposite side of the Bay are not likely to prepossess the stranger in their favour who has not been accustomed to associate with their sect in the Mother country. Their habitations — manners — and dress are of the lowest order'.[33] He proceeded on to York (Toronto), where he had an interview with the Lieutenant Governor. The latter tried to persuade him to examine the Lake Simcoe district, but he was recommended favourably to P. Lossing, a respectable Quaker of the Niagara area, and set off for Lossing's farm. To his horror, Graves found the dress and manners of these Quakers as offensive as he had those of Adolphustown. He confided to his diary: 'Since the day I parted from my beloved charge, my mind has not been so truly unhappy as on this. The idea of being able to realise fond hopes for their benefit I never relinquished till my visit to P. Lossing. Tho' many difficulties often appeared to me, I never allowed them to dwell on my mind supposing I would be enabled to surmount them.

The Idea of my Exertions for their welfare proving fruitless is truly discouraging'. Graves concluded that 'having a delicate partner with three young children' and 'not being able or accustomed to go thro' much manual labour' he might best postpone thought of emigration till his children were of an age to help in the fields.[34] Upon his return home he entered the mercantile business, in which he prospered. His son eventually moved their interests to Liverpool, where he became member of parliament and Lord Mayor.[35]

Very few of the families named in Elly's list came to Upper Canada when they learned that the British government would not provide a free passage for them. Nonetheless, a great many of the people named did turn up in various townships in the eastern part of the province by the mid-1820s, making the journey without government assistance.

Even by the time the precursors of this movement had arrived in Elizabethtown in 1809 most of the surveyed lands in the townships fronting on the Saint Lawrence River (fig. 15.2) had been granted to Loyalists and Americans. The existing population lived for the most part within a few miles of the river but held title to lands in the rear. New Irish settlers followed the Hortons' example in purchasing these rear lots, and as friends and relatives arrived they built up a solidly Irish neighbourhood in the vicinity of Lamb's Pond, later christened New Dublin. In Lansdowne, too, relatives arrived to join the early Wexford emigrants. George Johnston, one of the settlers of 1811, wrote in 1819 that 'during the last two years, ten Families, and Relations to Your Petitioner, have arrived from Ireland and Settled in Lansdowne and its Vicinity', including his aged mother.[36] However, the survey of new townships north of the Rideau River and the establishment of the Perth Military Settlement there in 1815 opened up a new front of settlement to the north in which free grants on land were available to civilian arrivals as well as to discharged soldiers. When emigration resumed after the termination of the wars, the post-1815 emigrants from south Leinster continued to buy lands in the rear of the St Lawrence townships but they also journeyed north to Perth to take up free grants there.

From 1816 to 1820 the Superintendent of the Perth Military Settlement was responsible for settling discharged soldiers and emigrants in the old settled townships of the Johnstown District as well as in the townships that had been newly surveyed in the neighbourhood of the military establishment at Perth. The Settlement Register therefore permits analysis of the arrival and settlement of the Irish in the whole district in the immediate postwar years, although it excludes those who purchased lands privately.[37] From 1818 and 1820 respectively one must also supplement the information in the Settlement Register with the returns submitted by the Superintendents of the Richmond and Lanark Military Settlements which were carved out of Perth's territory in those years.[38] The records of the Perth Settlement provide the most detailed information of the three, for the Superintendent noted not only the date he located the settlers and the lot and concession number of the location, but also the names of the vessels which had conveyed the settlers to Canada and the dates the ships had reached Quebec. By cross-checking this information with

Fig. 15.2: Johnstown District, 1822

the lists of ship arrivals in the *Quebec Gazette* one can determine the ports from which the vessels sailed and the number of passengers each had carried. One can therefore discover who arrived together and estimate the concentration of south Leinster people among the early Irish settlers of the district (table 1).

Table 1

Irish immigrants located for land grants in the Rideau Military Settlements, 1816-1822

	Individuals			Locatees*			
Year	Arr. Quebec	Perth	Lanark	Perth	Richmond	Lanark	Total
1816	(211)	199	—	69	—	—	69
1817	2,285	496	—	150	—	—	150
1818	4,703	121	—	40	37	—	77
1819	6,996	307	—	129	79	—	208
1820	5,421	93	249	38	62	129	229
1821	3,707	64	69	27	75	26	128
1822		93	28	38	99	163	145
		1,373	346	491	352	163	1,006

Sources: 'Quebec Gazette', Perth Settlement Register.

* 49 South Leinster

Table 2

Irish passengers arriving at Quebec, 1817, and preceeding to Perth Military Settlement, by port of sailing.

Port	Irish arrivals		To Perth M.S.		% from port to Perth
	n	%	n	%	
Coleraine	155	7	0	0	0
Belfast	772	34	49	12	6
Cork	226	10	12	3	5
Dublin	567	25	106**	25	19
Limerick	15	1	11	3	73
Sligo	175	8	6	1	3
Waterford	78	13	19	5	24
Wexford	287	13	216	52	73
Total	2285		419		18%
Unlisted vessels	?		67		
			486		

Sources: Quebec Gazette, Perth Settlement Register.

** at least 26 from South Leinster

Three major Irish parties totalling 199 individuals reached the Perth Settlement in 1819. Fifty-four people came out from northern Ireland, half of them passengers of the *Alexander* out of Belfast. These settlers were located mostly in Bathurst Township. The remaining two parties were composed of emigrants from south Leinster, 33 people coming on the *John* and another 37 on the *Betty & Mary*. The Superintendent settled these families mostly in Drummond, though he located a few in Beckwith. Several arrived in other ships that year, and three James' families were located in Drummond after being sent north from New York by James Buchanan, the British Consul there: thus 87 of the 199 Irish who came to Perth in its first year of existence were from south Leinster, just under half the total.

Such families made up a much larger proportion of the greater numbers who came out in the 1817 season. The Johnstown District received 486 Irish immigrants that year, 343 of whom were from Wexford or adjoining counties, more than 70 per cent of the total. Seven ships accounted for most of these. Three sailed from Wexford itself, two from Dublin, one from Waterford, and one from an undetermined port. In most cases the settlers who reached Perth were not a majority of the passengers who landed from these ships, though 123 of the 126 passengers on the *Mary Ann* came to eastern Upper Canada, as did 68 of the 96 on the *General Moore*. Most of the south Leinster people who arrived in 1817 were located on reserves and other vacant lots in the old settled townships of Yonge, Lansdowne, South Crosby, and South Gower, near the families who had settled in Elizabethtown and Leeds and Landsowne before the War. County Wexford born residents of Johnstown county in 1821 are listed in appendix II.

One may judge the regionalisation of settlement another way by listing the eastern Upper Canada arrivals of 1817 by port of departure and comparing their numbers with the statistics of total Irish arrivals from the various ports published in the Quebec newspaper, as in table 2. Just under one-fifth of the Irish who landed at Quebec that season came to the Johnstown District. The northern Irish port of Belfast accounted for a third of the immigrants but for less than a tenth of those who went to eastern Upper Canada. Perth, on the other hand, received three-quarters of those who sailed from Wexford, a quarter of those leaving Waterford, and a fifth of those sailing from Dublin, half at least of the latter identifiable as people from south Leinster.

In 1818 the number of Irish arriving at Quebec more than doubled but a much smaller proportion arrived in the Military Settlements than heretofore. The British government's negative response to Elly's petition may have deflated expectations. However, many may have remained hopeful (that some assistance might be forthcoming at a later date) in the light of government sponsorship that year of Richard Talbot's Tipperary group and several other experiments in England and Scotland. Only 121 Irish reached Perth in 1818 of whom 43, just over a third, were from Wexford. The 43 came in two parties which were settled where the settlers of 1816 had been: the 28 on the *Henry* out of Dublin in Beckwith Township and the 15 on the *Maria* from Waterford in Drummond. In that year another 37 Irish families settled in the townships east of Perth in the new Richmond Military Settlement. Nineteen of these families were from Tipperary, part of Talbot's sponsored party that had sailed from Cork on the *Brunswick*. Most of the remainder (thirteen) were from south Leinster.

Interest was renewed in 1819 when 307 Irish were settled from Perth of whom 184, or sixty per cent, were from south Leinster. At least eight ships brought these emigrants from the south-east of Ireland, three sailing from Waterford, one from Wexford, one from Ross, two from Dublin, and one from an undetermined port. Almost all the arrivals were located by the Superintendent in Beckwith, Drummond, and Bathurst. Another 59 Irish families came to Richmond in 1819, six of them from Tipperary and 19 from south Leinster.

From 1820 to 1822, when the Perth Military Superintendency was abolished and the area returned to civilian administration, no large parties were recorded in the Settlement Book. Indeed, only 93 Irish came to Perth in 1820, 64 in 1821, and 93 in 1822, mostly to take up locations in Bathurst and Sherbrooke where land still remained unallocated. However, these statistics take no account of immigration to the old surveyed townships of the present counties of Leeds and Grenville, where the power of location was returned to the civil government in 1820 and where the Superintendent had not located settlers in any case since 1817, nor of those settling in the townships administered from Richmond or, after 1820, from Lanark.

For example, *Maria*, which brought settlers from Ross in most seasons, is not listed in the Settlement Book as having brought any locatees to Perth in 1820. However, the diary kept by William Graves indicates that passengers did come to the Perth area, if not to the townships administered from there.[39] These people were probably among the fifty or so south Leinster families located in the Lanark Military Settlement before the start of the 1821 shipping season. Most were located in Lanark Township and a few in Ramsay. A few more such families continued to settle in these townships in 1821 and 1822. Captain Burke, the Superintendent at Richmond, continued to receive south Leinster families too, allocating lands to 22 such families in 1819, 16 in 1820, 14 in 1821, and 22 in 1822, mostly in south-eastern Beckwith and western Goulbourn. Burke, an Irish half-pay officer from county Tipperary, appears to have deliberately placed Wexford emigrants in south-eastern Beckwith, away from a Perthshire Scots party in the north-eastern quarter of the township.

Immigrants continued to arrive after the military jurisdiction was terminated. Relatives of settlers already in the colony wrote to the Colonial Office in hope of securing passages to join their kin in Canada. They were encouraged to write by promises of passages made by Colonel Cockburn, the Deputy Quarter-Master General. Nine Goulbourn residents managed to get their families on the one list Cockburn sent to England before new policy statements shattered hopes of further requests being honoured, and the number of individual inquiries to the Colonial Department diminished.[40] However, settlers continued to come out without aid. A number of those who importuned the Colonial Office in the early 1820s were relatives of the parties that had settled in Beckwith beginning in 1816. William James petitioned in 1822 from Rosdelig, county Carlow for passage for himself, with wife and four children to join his parents and brother in Beckwith.[41] George Kidd of Knockabranar, Old Leighlin, county Carlow wrote the same year asking passages for himself, wife, and three children to join his parents and siblings who went to Beckwith in 1821.[42] William Leech of Clonjordan, parish of Templeshanbo, near Enniscorthy wrote that his three sons and two daughters and their families were resident in Upper Canada and solicited passages for the rest of the family.[43] Samuel Sutton of the same place wrote mentioning his 'many relatives in Canada' and stated that he had received a letter from his brother-in-law Robert Davis.[44] George Wilson of Bilboa, county Carlow wished to join his stepfather, William Kerfoot, his four brothers, and his mother in Beckwith.[45]

Immigrants from south-eastern Ireland continued to come into eastern Ontario for some decades, and one can trace a gradual expansion of the settlement patterns (fig. 15.3). The very heavy clustering in the New Dublin neighbourhood in the rear of Elizabethtown, for example, spilled over into the northwestern corner of Augusta some time after 1822, and late arrivals often remained only briefly in the Franktown area of Beckwith before moving south into northern Montague. An initial cluster in north-eastern Goulbourn, near the site of Hazeldean, spread north in scattered numbers into the townships of March and Huntley after they were surveyed in 1820, and onto adjoining lots in Nepean to the east. The south Leinster names which can be identified on late-nineteenth century property ownership maps in Marlborough and North Gower were largely those of second-generation migrants from Beckwith and Goulbourn. The residential locations of identified families of south Leinster descent in eastern Upper Canada in 1863 are indicated in fig. 15.3.

As new generations came of age the search for land recommenced, and examples of chain migration to more distant points may also be cited. In the 1860s the Beckwith colony spawned at least two secondary settlements at some remove, one near Micksburg in Stafford Township, Renfrew County, up the Ottawa River,[46] and the other hundreds of miles to the west in Brooke Township, Lambton County.[47] A number of families came from Wexford in the 1840s and 1850s settled in Renfrew County soon after arriving, as uncleared Crown land was then still available for purchase in that rough, northern county.[48]

That the south Leinster immigrants to eastern Ontario were largely Protestant is apparent from a brief glance at census statistics. Nearly three-quarters of the Irish inhabitants of Leeds and Grenville counties in 1871 were Protestant.[49] A quarter of the Irish Catholics there, but less than ten per cent of the Protestants, then lived in the three towns of Brockville, Prescott, and Gananoque. In the rural parts, Irish Catholics were most strongly concentrated in North Crosby (63 per cent of the Irish), south Elmsley (51 per cent) and South Crosby (34 per cent), but in the townships where Wexford Protestants settled in the greatest numbers, Elizabethtown and the Rear of Yonge and Escott, nearly 90 per cent of the Irish were Protestant and in Leeds and Lansdowne Rear the Irish were fully 97 per cent Protestant. Similarly the Irish population of Beckwith in Lanark County, the vast majority of whom, like the Irish of Elizabethtown and North Augusta, were from Wexford, was more than four-fifths Protestant. Though the Irish Catholic population of this region was not numerous, some of the Catholics at least were from the same part of Ireland as their Protestant compatriots. Several gravestones in the Roman Catholic cemetery at Trevelyan in Yonge Township give evidence of Wexford origins.[50]

Though the south Leinster population appears to have been the largest Irish group created by the process of chain migration in eastern Ontario, the movement to Canada appears to have gone largely unremarked at home after the heady days of the 1810s. The local clergy and gentry in their replies to the Poor Law Commissioners in the mid-1830s seldom alluded to emigration to the Canadas. A few parishes reported such departures, but none in great numbers. Witnesses spoke more often of emigration to 'America', which is an ambiguous designation. Because informants in Tipperary said 'the Americas' when they meant 'the Canadas', the Wexford informants at the very least are likely to have meant the United States as much as the colonies to the north. In any case the scale of the movement appears not to have impressed the informants. A few parishes in the south of county Wexford reported some poor people emigrating to Newfoundland,[51] contributors to the emigration from the port of Waterford to Newfoundland and Halifax.[52]

It is possible that the volume of departures from south Leinster to the Canadas declined significantly after the 1820s. Certainly the improving economic picture there and the comparatively settled social condition of county Wexford in later decades gave the Protestant population less cause to leave. When the Poor Law Commissioners in the 1830s asked witnesses in various parts of Ireland whether the condition of the poor had improved since 1815, it was only in Wexford and Wicklow that the balance of responses was affirmative. The larger size of farms reduced dependence on the potato and during the Famine of the 1840s Wexford and Carlow experienced the lowest excess death rates outside Dublin, with Wicklow and Kilkenny not far behind.[53] This contrasted with overpopulation and increasing violence in Tipperary. Statements to the Poor Law Commissioners from north Tipperary parishes with a considerable Protestant population noted that movement from that region was motivated partly by these causes and was directed overwhelmingly toward Upper Canada.[54] Tipperary Protestants emigrated mostly to the Ottawa and London areas of Upper Canada until the tide of emigration turned to Australia and New Zealand in the mid-1850s, and very few seem to have gone to the United States.[55] We do not know the full story of the Wexford migrations. Even in the early years of the movement to Canada more people disembarked at Quebec from the ships bringing south Leinster people from Wexford, New Ross, Waterford, and Dublin than came to eastern Ontario. It is certain that south Leinster people were going to other places as well. Many probably continued to follow the well-established migration channels to the United States. If the Poor Law witnesses can be believed, the movement to

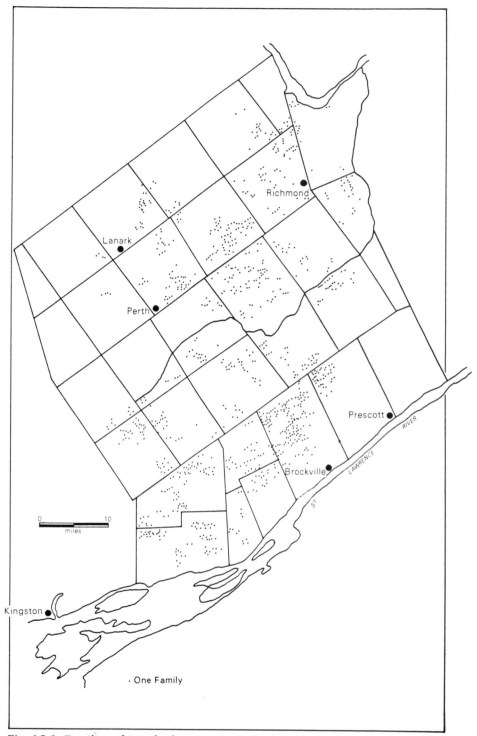

Fig. 15.3: Families of Wexford area origin in Eastern Ontario 1862-3

Canada by the 1830s was insignificant compared with the numbers going to the American republic.

The effect of this population movement on Upper Canada was not insignificant, however. The Irish immigrants came to outnumber the existing population and the Irish assumed the mantle of control from the old Loyalist population and redefined Upper Canadian Toryism in largely Irish terms.[56] Yet the Irish of the Johnstown District have remained historiographically an anonymous band of undefined 'Irish' whose interests were personified by their leader and candidate Ogle Gowan. Viewed in the context of the pattern of migration and settlement I have outlined, however, is it any wonder that Gowan, who emigrated from Mount Nebo to Brockville in 1829 and founded the Grand Orange Lodge of British America there the following year, was able to exercise such strong political influence among the Irish Protestants of eastern Upper Canada? He was himself a Wexford man, the illegitimate son of Hunter Gowan, well-known for his opposition to the rebels of 1798. In championing the interests of the Irish settlers in the rear of the St Lawrence townships against the Loyalists of the front, Gowan was campaigning for the eager support of his fellow countrymen.[57]

Acknowledgement

Research for this paper was in part supported by the Social Sciences and Humanities Research Council of Canada.

Appendix I

'A return of Protestant families preparing to Emigrate from the counties of Carlow & Wexford in the ensuing Spring, Ross, November, 1817.'

PRO, CO.384/1, Public Archives of Canada reel B-876.

blank — farmer   M — farmer & mechanic

Name	No. in Family		Name	No. in Family		Name	No. in Family	
(f 178RR)			Wm Elliott	2		Willm Devett	8	
Mathew Connor	13	M	John Elliott	3		Thos Ruddock	5	
Thos Jiff	7		Joseph Shaw	5		Ben Dockrel	8	
Jas Cant	3	M	John Ferrar	1		Geo Graham	3	
Wm Hazelwood	7	M	James Keys	2		Arnold Bookere	8	
Richd Hazelwood	5	M	Edwd Bayley	11		Saml Wellwood	2	
Wm Dunn	10		Robert Power	5		Man Hughes	10	
Eben Ferns	5		George Dixon	4		Lanct Griffith	8	
Abm Ruddock	7		Benjamin Bayley	5		Jno Scott	10	
Jno Foley			Henry Bayley	5		Jacob Bradley	5	
Richd Wilson	5		John Bayley	9		Jacob Deacon	7	
Wm Cuthbert	12		Thos Bayley	2		Jno Acres	8	
Martin Kearns	7		Christopher Young	5		Wm Ralph	8	
Robert Dormer	8	M	Thos Dagg	7		Thos Smith	4	
Jno Dormer	2	M	Geo Heyney	8		Wm Swain	3	M
Thos Jacob	7	M	Richd Green	5		Henry West	7	Shop-keeper
Joseph Molton	5	M	George Berry	2				
Jno Molton	7		Thos Webster	3	M	Alex Kinch	7	
Jno Warren	7	M	Willm McCutcheon	5		Jno Kinch	8	M
Thos Clampit	9		Richd Whitney	6		Jno James	6	
Wm Wilkinson	9		Wm Leveston	5		Job Deacon	6	
Jno Atkinson	6		James Heyney	4		Thos Wood	6	
Robt Blake	8		James Quire	9		Josh. Birr	8	
Edwd Swain	9		Geo Keys	5		James Abram	8	
Wm Kavenagh	5	M	Heny Kenchela	2		Peter Sumner	5	
Wm Bradley	10	M	Henry Bradley	6	M	Geo Derment	10	M
Jno Rathwell	11		Thos Keys	6		Gar't Sutton	9	
Saml Power	7		James Nurse	3		Wm Gregory	6	
Francis Perrin	3		Willm Molten	10	M	Geo Molton	8	
George Perrin	3		Jno Haughton	7		Jno Langford	8	
James Humphreys	5	M	Jno Shortley	7		James Waters	6	
Thos Perrin	8		Joseph Roberts	4		Issac Bucky	4	M
Wm Thornton	5	M	John Jiff	6		Burch Humphreys	4	
Henry Lee	4		Thos Codd	6		Issac Bookey	5	M
Jno Roberts	9		Jno Bayley Jr	2		(179V)		
Mark Molton	8		(179R)			Jo. Thornton	8	
Jno Power	4		Jno Bayley	6		Widow Saunders	7	
(178V)			Wm Bayley	5		Thos Kidd	5	
James Cannon	5		Thos Bayley	5		James Bierney	11	
Alex Henderson	4		James Codd	4		Wm Willis	8	
James Warner (?)	6		Wm Shene	5		Edwd Dornby	7	
Edward Fitzgerald	10		Wm Roberts	2	M	Wm Pierce	7	
Joseph Ellard	7	M	Geo Hudsoner	5		Wm Nicholson	7	
James Rath	6		James Smith	8		James Barrington	2	M
Matt Sargeant	3		James Connor	6	M	Francis Sherlock	7	
Willm Sargeant	2		Henry Connor	6		Jno Sterne	9	M
Spencer Elliott	5		Jno Rose	4		James Sherlock	4	M

Name	No. in Family		Name	No. in Family		Name	No. in Family
Danl Ryan	7	M	Jos'h Dockrell	2		Peter Connors	6
Fosse Sterne	3		Jno Steacey	2		John Pool	11
James Leeson	3		Jno Miller			Wm Pool	9
Jno Monergan	9		Saml Walker	2		Mattw Pool	9
Ben Dockgrell	2		Wm Clarke	5		Elizth Pool	8
Jno Williams	2		Jno Driver	1		Richd Errat	6
Daniel Foster	9		Michl Fox	1		Thomas Brannon	4
Richd Woodriffe	6	M	Jas Somerton	2		Maurice Ward	4
Robt Hopkins	2		Thos Reed	8		James Butler	12
Wm Lee	7		Robt Weymouth	3		James Griffin	4
Wm Humphreys	9		(180V)			Wm Lumsden	6
Jno Humphreys	6		Jno Somerton	8		Jas Bryan	4
Willm Smith	6		Elizth Wear	8		John Willaby	1
Wm Williams	2		Nathl Stedman	1		Richd Murph	8
Edwd Foster	2		Thos Dowdell	12		Isaac Murphy	4
Edwd Foster	1		Thos Steward	10		Robt Moorhouse	5
Michl Richmond	2		Dennis Doyle	4		Thos Moorhouse	1
Jno Rooke	6		Wm Harper	5		Richd Annes	1
Edwd Farrell	7		John Williams	7		Thos Oughten	3
Edwd Stiles	9	M	Richd Murphy	9		Jas Lumsden	3
Pat Stiles	4	M	Hannah Bates	12		John Earl	5
James Maurice	7		Jas Fitzsimmons	7		Thos Lumsden	8
Peter Moore	9	M	Abm Miller	6		Jas McClean	8
Wm Restrick	4		Richard Woodroff	14		Luke Byrne	8
Robert Taylor	2		John Taylor	1		Thos Evans	11
Richd Keys	3		John Saul	10		John Ayres	1
Edwd Tully	7		Jas Neil	4		Geo Weymouth	2
Robert Pepper	10		Christy Neill	4		John Thornton	1
Wm McEvoy	5		Anthy Sheridan	1		(181V)	
Tim Kavanagh	4		Thos Fitzhenry	7		Jas Giffin	7
Saml Kendrick	5		Mary Carr	2		Hen'y Percival	7
Jno Quinsey	9		Francis Rickaby	2		James Johnson	2
(180R)			Michl Dowsard	2		Jno Anderson	3
John Martin	6		Thomas Bell	3		Issac Blorg(?)	
Wm Basset	7		Thomas Elliot	4		Edwd Cook	5
Wm Walker	2		Wm Walker	11		Jno McGuire	3
Thos Weir	8		Saml Pierce	8		Nichs Horton	7
Wm Harding	4		Jno Jacob	7		Benjn Godkin	6
Wm Davis	6		Jas Murphy	3		Chas Vaney	3
John Coubyrne	9		Han Free	5		Mary Bolger	2
Ally Rynehart	7		Jas Warbrook	4		Richd Stedman	4
Wm Asselforth	6		Jos'h Gilbert	6		Anne Traynor	8
Wm Jacob	3		Saml Bogs	7		Jno Bennet	6
Patt Davis	9		Geo Warbrook	7		Cathne Dezel	1
Robt Harding	6		Rice Free	9		Benjn Francis	5
Thos Harding	9		James Johns	1		Jno Rickaby	3
Peter Davis	8		Thomas Sharp	4		Barnaby Bannon	3
Edwd Davis	6		Jno Hopkins	1		Thomas Bates	1
Thos Kavanagh	9		Saml Smith	3		Joseph Bates	7
John Ford	3		(181R)			Joseph Banester	8
Neil Quinsey	3		John Smith	8		Joseph Needham	8
John Ireton	7		John Styles	1		Thos Conyers	8
Jno Handstock	2		Jno Hendrick	8		Michl Hes [?]	8
Natt Thomson	9		Ralph Stone	2		Nathl Burgess	10
Saml Boyce	8		Wm Warren	10 yeoman		Saml Seel	7
Jas Summers	9		Peter Summers	6 yeoman		Wm Fox	3
Wm Atkinson	10		Thomas Davis	5 yeoman		Luke James	5
Jas Patsel	4		Bernard O Brien	3 Pensioner		Roger Hawkins	9
Bridget Patsel	6					Issac Whitby	3
Heny Duncan	6		Thomas Davis	8	M	Thomas Watts	5
Edwd Mand	2		Hen'y Connors	6		Henry Watts	7

Name	No. in Family		Name	No. in Family		Name	No. in Family
Thomas Earl	5		Jno Walker	9		Jas Floyd	2
Saml Taylor	6		Jas Edwd	11		Richd Grivelle	9
Wm Taylor	5		Peter Bond	1		Wm James	11
John James	3		Ralph Davis	11 M		Richd Tackaberry	4
Wm Burgess	7		Thos Foxton	5		(183V)	
(182R)			Martha Devit	6		Robt Tackaberry	4
Wm Burgess Jr	6		Edwd Young	4		Jno Thorp	7
Andrew Bagnell	4		Wm Edwards	5		Richd Hanton	2
Thos Saunders	4		Alexr Bolton	8		Geo Atkins	9
James Saunders	4		Wm Green	8		Thos Chase	9
Edwd Keatin	4		Jno Green	10		Wm Hoply	5
John May	7		Wm Lord	8		Thos Breen	4
Hennesy May	6		James Sheal	8		Richd Dixy	8
Robt Daly	4		Robt Humphreys	5		Wm Fannen	2
Chas Kavenagh	7		Charles Blunt	7		Henry Shaw	4
Thos Stone	1		Jas Hawkins	4		Geo Oakes	6
Jno Love	7		James Wade	7		Thos Stanford	8
James Love	6		John Rathwell	11		Pat Plumer	3
Simon Regan	4		Wm Rathwell	7		Jno Hinley	6
Jno Shaw	9		Jas Rathwell	10		Luke Molton	7
Jno Barber	3		Thos Rathwell	8		Jno Marr	4
Henry Lancaster	9		Saml Rathwell	8		Jas Jordon	10
Jno Rowsome	11		Jno Rathwell Jnr.	5		Moague Leech	8
James Doyle	9		Geo Crumpton	7		James Ward	5
Francis Richard	6		James Morris	5		Wm Leech	3
Michl Murphy	9		(183R)			Jno Clampet	5
Cath Scully	8		Saml Jacob	5		Wm Plumer	6
Jno Davis	7		Jas Scott	4		Mary Clampet	3
Thos Woods	9		Wm Scott	2		Wm Thompson	5
Jno Rowsome	5		Robt Davis	3		Jacob Green	5
Benj Steacey	10		Wm Davis	4 M		Richd Pigeon	7
Edwd Graves	8		Wm Sutton	2		James Coleman	1
Wm Taylor	8		Danl Wigmore	6 M		Edwd Jordon	2
Darby McCarthy	20		Wm Woods	2		Stephn Mullet	1
Francis Butler	5		Luke Stephens	8		James Lucas	7
Wm Spencer	9		Phil Nevill	4		Henry Lucas	9
Jno Dunn	7		Thos Pierce	3		Edwd Lucas	1
Richd Sterne	7		Wm Pierce	4		Robt Leech	4
George Steacy	5		Jas Cockrell	7		Jno Giff	5
Elizabeth Parkinson	4		Wm Hall	3 M		Con Kavenagh	7
Henry Chalburn	3		Robt Hall	4 M		Dan Damond	9
Richd Derenzy	6 M		Henry Williams	4		Wm Sparrow	3
Richd Dixy	8		James Morris	8		Jno Willis	10
Saml Needham	5		Edwd Rathwell	4		Edwd Hanton	8
Alexander Long [?]	5		Saml Rathwell	5		Edwd Earl	10
(182V)			John Rathwell	3		Anthy Rudd	8
Joseph Quincey	7		Wm Rathwell	7		Christopher Marten	8
Joseph Davis	4		Chas Rathwell	6		Nehem Wright	8
hos Cartain	6 M		Benj Rathwell	6		John Wright	1
Thos Francis	6		Geo Leacock	4		Jas Rynehart	11
James Downey	18		Jno Fannen	5		Jno Williams	10
James Woods	4		Jno Fannen Jun	7		Edwd Hanton	8
Wm Harding	5		Wm Percival	9		Edwd Pepper	8
Jacob Abraham	8		James Fielding	3		Luke Dunne	1
Jno Armstrong	5		Thos Hayes	6		Jas Green	1
Jno Webster	4		Natl Hayes	4		Joseph Leary	2
Geo Love	5		Edwd Dowcar [?]	2		Jas Doyle	1
Miles Keegan	9		Saml Sutton	4		John Sinnot	1
James Longstaff	7		Robert Molton	7		John Sheehan	7
Robt Shaw	7		Jno Hannen	3		Edwd Dunn	8
Charles Wilby	2		Wm Tackaberry	8		Patk Brown	4

Name	No. in Family	
Patk Doyle	8	
Patk Furlong	1	
John Howard	5	
Robert English	6	M
Nat Fennel	8	M
John Bradly	7	
Jacob Little	3	
Robt Kerr	3	M
Thos Sutton	10	
Jas Kerr	3	M
Geo Borris	2	
Geo Johnson	9	M
Hen'y Tackaberry	1	
John Ward	1	
John Bolton	8	
(184V)		
John Keys	3	
Law'e Mead	5	
John Kelly	4	
John Dillon	1	
Thos McMurry	8	
John McKeon	7	
James Voss	6	
Patk Voss	4	
Wm Voss	4	
Edwd Voss	2	
Con Shepley	1	
Zebediah Milton	6	
Chas Hill	1	
Joseph Williams	9	
John Jacob	9	
John Nutter	9	
Thos Burrows	4	
John Wilson	1	
Henry Bolton	1	
Steph Tomlinson	1	
Edwd Basset	5	
John Ward	1	
Saml Waters	1	
Tos Sutton	1	
Steph Murphy	5	
Hen'y Bolton	1	
Mattw Evoy	6	
John Evoy	2	
Darby Evoy	2	
John Sutton	1	
Robt Foster	1	
Joseph Williams	6	
Jas Moran	2	
Robt Thomson	7	
John Smith	4	
Geo Kerford	3	
John Warner	3	
Jas McDowel	1	
Patk Lawler	1	
Henry Marten	7	
Robt Shepley	3	
Jno Lummocks	2	
Peter Bagnel	5	
John Whealan	3	
Danl Buckall	6	

Name	No. in Family	
(185R)		
Patk Dowling	7	
Jas Altimas	11	
Richd Dixon	5	
Jacob James	1	
Edwd Johnson	1	
Jas Toole	9	
John Killin	6	
Wm Kerfoot	5	
John Garland	14	
Richd Garland	4	
Lau'ce Cunnigan	6	
Wm May	10	
Thos Downy	2	
James Dagg	13	
Abm Wynne	10	
John Bowles	9	
Hugh Gahan	7	
Thos Burris	7	
Ellen Ellward	5	
James Breen	3	M
Steph James	8	
Laughlin Moran	9	
Ben Whitaker	11	
T[?] Gainer	8	
Philip Butler	7	
Dennis Conrahy	6	
John Griffin	6	
Richd Walsh	11	
John Budd	7	
Thos Budd	6	M
Steph Budd	5	M
John Budd	2	
Richd Budd	7	
Wm Westerman	3	
John Griffith	4	
Edwd Holmes	6	
John Chapman	6	
(185V)		
Sylvy Magrath	1	
Edwd. Hana	3	
John Knight	7	
John Moran	10	
Patt Stapleton	3	
Joseph Willwood	3	
Thos Fenton	4	
James Stapleton	4	
Pierce Tennant	3	
Robt Tennant	3	
Thos Tennant	13	
John Magee	2	
James Newman	3	
John Rynard	5	
James Bradley	5	
Geo Leckey	4	
Thos McCormick	11	
Geo Willoby	9	
Joseph Bugbear	4	
Thos Taylor	2	
Thomas Kenny	7	
Richd Bradley	3	

Name	No. in Family	
Robt Shore	5	M
John Ryan	4	
John Taylor	8	
John Boyle	4	
John Lynch	7	
Thos Hand	8	
Saml Bagnel	3	
Geo Roberts	4	
Edwd Keating	3	
Wm Shore	6	
John Anderson	8	
Thos Scarf	5	
Andrew Delany	2	
Michl Madden	2	
Saml Bradley	2	
Robt Boyle	7	
John Brennan	9	
John Foley	2	
(186R)		
Thos Ward	7	
Thos Tomlinson	7	
Wm Tomlinson	5	
Jno Bradley	2	
Jno Leacock	7	
Danl Fitzpatrick	6	
Saml Jones	4	
Robt Kennel	8	
Stephen Hill	3	
Jas Fitzgerald	1	
Thos Mathews	5	
Richd Burrows	8	M
Pat Graham	10	
Jno Kennedy	5	
Geo Kidd	1	
Wm Kidd	1	
Jno Tindall	2	
Jno Griffith	1	
Tim'y Corrigan	4	
Stephen Wright	8	M
Thos Murphy	5	
Thos Norman	5	
James Foley	3	
Robt Booth	8	M
Geo Wilson	4	
Jno Nowland	6	
Mark Wilson	9	
Alex Kinch	4	
Michl Deevey	4	
Jno Redmond	4	M
Stephen Hill	3	
Tom Tunstadt	5	
Henry James	9	
Jno Sameways	5	
Jos Scarf	1	
Henry Duck	4	
Thos Saunders	6	
Edwd Washington	5	
Wm James	7	
(186V)		
Wm Harris	6	
Wm Coomes	5	M

Name	No. in Family		Name	No. in Family		Name	No. in Family	
Richd Upton	9		Saml Waters	12		Wm James	2	
Thos Darcy	6		Arnold Sutton	9		James Dinnal	7	
Pat Walsh	7	M	Francis Toole	6		Jno English	6	
Wm Bradley	6	M	Garr't Shea	9		Thos Jones	1	
Richd Budd	4	M	Thos Tobin	7		Thos Neale	2	
Wm Alcock	2	M	Hen'y Jenkinson	3		James White	1	
Wm Howe	4	M	James Butridge	3	M	Michl Grout	1	
Wm Tackaberry	6		Geo Rynard	5	M	(187R)		
Robt Phillips	2	M	And Betz	2		Thos'Hansen	1	
Wm McNally	4		Thos Peelo	8		Jno Rynard	5	
Jos'h Condell	3		Thos Mills	9		Pat Hackett	8	
Wm Walkin	10		Abm Bradley	4				
Lau Dagdon	6		Saml Bradley	5				
Geo Wilson	8		Wm Steacey	8		4,027		

Total of Protestant families preparing to emigrate from the Counties of Carlow & Wexford to this date 710 families containing 4,027 individuals of whom upwards of eleven hundred are able bodied men. Ross, 29 Novemb. 1817.

'A Return of Roman Catholic families preparing to emigrate from the Counties of Carlow & Wexford in the ensuing Spring. Ross, Novem. 1817'

blank — farmer   M — farmer & Mechanic

Name	No. in Family		Name	No. in Family		Name	No. in Family	
Thos McKean	5		Batt Goff	7		Robert Foley	2	
Henry Shea	6		Wm Cormick	4		Moses Clear	11	
Alex Kinch	3	M	Richd Rudd	3		Martin Clark	2	
Wm Hawkings	9	M	Thos Rudd	3		Patt Byrne	8	
Thos Keon	4	M	James Wain	3		Jno Kelly	3	
Barry Pierce	9	M	Robt Leviston	8		Arthur Cricton	1	
Robt McGlaughlin	6	M	Saml Watkins	4		Peter Killfoil	8	
Lott Holmes	5		Geo Watkins	6		Jno Kelly Jur	3	
Wm Holmes	4		Joseph Crofts	6		James Linen	2	
Saml Swain	9		(188V)			And Clear	8	
Joseph Swain	8		Jno Bayley	9		Edwd Doyle	7	M
John Swain	6		Thos Chapman	3		Patt Doyle	5	
Elizh Swain	8		Jno Chapman	5		James Connoly	1	
Geo Moody	4		James Langford	2		Owen Connor	9	
Jno Webster	3		Thos Jordan	6		James Congrove	3	
Henry Peltus	7		James Boyce	3		James Gregan	1	
Jno Crowley	7		James Rynshart	11		Lau Greegan	1	
Saml Oakes	6		James Pepper	3		Hen Roberts	3	
Joseph Love	2		Edwd Pepper	5		Wm Farrel	4	
Wm Henders	8		Edwd Sutton	10		Patt Hoar	7	
Thos Smith	7		James Boyce Jun	4		Widow Dunn	8	
Goe Grey	8		Caleb Stameford	2		Patt Doyle	7	
Richd Tindaile	3		Richd Byrne	11		James Doran		
Nat Tackabe'y	4		Jas Doyle	4		(189R)		
Jose'h Fennel	7		Matt Roberts	9		Pat Colclough	9	

Name	No. in Family	Name	No. in Family	Name	No. in Family
Neil Tunny	7	Jacob Hess	8	James Shiel	3
Pat Cain	7	Nat Tobin	5	Martin Brown	6
Charles McCarney	7	Michl Kavenagh	11	Jno Clowry	4
Nichs Foley	14	Jno Holding	2	Philip Gorman	8
Wm Waddick	5	Pat Reagan	3	Robert Walker	5
Patt Kavenagh	4	Danl Murphy	12	Pat Cormick	6
Danl Kavenagh	1	Thos Butler	1	Miles Doyle	3
Lau Nowlan	5	Michl Whelan	7	Jno Ayres	4 M
Richd Laurriston	2	Bartel Mishall	3	James Walsh	8
Francis Farrel	3	Thos Redmond	12	Jno Ryane	3
James Jordan	2	Michl Dun	6	Ml Connors	9
Bryan Leonard	1	Michl Carter	4	Jno Murphy	4
James Doyle	4	James Downey	18	James Farrel	4
James Maher	1	Richd Rock	5	Tiney Ward	10
Patt Whelan	1	Miles Keegan	9	Ml Nowlan	9
Patt Fenlan	2	Pat Doyle	4	Phil Dinen	4
Jno Roach	4	(190R)		Thos Mooney	10
Geo Smith	6	Pat Flinn	8	Thos Fitzpatrick	2
Edwd Ryan	7	Miles Kelly	5	Ml Pondon	3
Matt Foley	3	James Dealy	5	Jno Pondon	3
Patt Scully	5	Pat Redmond	6	Pat Collins	5
James Bryan	8	Lewis Wedlock	9	Simon Nowlan	8
James Hart	2	John Duff	2	Wm Farrel	4
Jno Curran	4	Morris Doyle	3	Ml Smith	1
Patt Jordan	4	Thos Connoly	3	Henry Donahoe	6
Patt Hughes	9	James Sunderland	7 M	Charles Fitzpatrick	4
Thos Colclough	8	Anty Waddock	6	Pat Byrne	4
Richd Nowlan	1	Edwd Brennan	2	James Byrone	4
James Fitzsims	7	Wm Murphy	6	Jno Hare	3
Amr Miller	6	Francis Dooling	4	Wm Curran	12
James Bell	10	Wm Murphy Jun	6	Pat Murray	12
Jno Reddy	6	Bryan Walsh	5	Wm Byrne	2
Owen Donahoe	2	Wm Cullin	7	Ml Tracy	4
Wm Nowlan	8	Pat Bruges	10	Jno Nowlan	1
Danl Kehoe	9	Darby Lawler	6	Thos Farrel	7
Peter Doyle	1	Jno Lamb	6	Pat Conron	4
Michl Kitty	2	Luke Molton	7	Jno Conron	3
Jno Kennedy	6	Jno Maher	4	(191R)	
(189V)		James Jordon	10	Richd Tobin	3
James Dempsy	2	Mogue Kehoe	9	Dennis Moran	1
Jno Redmond	6	Wm Kelly	5	Arthur King	5
Jno Kean	4	Patt Hacket	8	Wm Fannen	4
Thos Carter	4	Jno Murphy	2	Pat Fannen	3
Garratt Kavenagh	7	Patt Dowling	4	Thos Fannen	3
Michl Doyle	7	Patt Heynes	6	James Laler	7
Wm Casey	2	Jno Whelan	8	Pat Comerford	2 M
Phelan Lacy	5	Edwd Byrne	5	Patt Dormer	2
Ml Byrne	7	Patt Purcell	5	Thos Walsh	9
Chas Delany	6	Richd Runy	11	Jno Brennan	8
James Smith	1	Pat Lynop	1	Jno Nowlan	6
Ben Doyle	4	Wm Byrne	5	James Nowlan	1
Jno Toole	4	Hugh Bulger	4	Danl Kenny	3
Thos Traverse	2	Pat Brophy	5	Moses Doyle	6
Patt Whelan	8	Ml Shore	5	Michl Conran	6
Morgan Redmd	7	Henry Shore	6	Wm Conran	1
Jno Fitzsimmons	1	Thos Ryan	3	Wm Barry	9
Andw Mullet	1	Thos Hooper	11	James Harris	7
Walter Keegan	11	(190V)		Patt Grumley	2
Hannah Keys	3	Malachy Clark	6	Michl Mealy	3
Thos Fortune	1	James Brennan	4	James Murphy	9
Thos Lawler	3	Edwd Kelly	7	Jno Doyle	3

Name	No. in Family	Name	No. in Family	Name	No. in Family
James Doyel	2	Thos Kinchela	1	Wm Ryan	1
Peter Shaughanessy	5	Michl Shean	4	Pat Byrne	8
Michl Byrne	5	Michl McDaniel	8	Michl Moore	5
Thos Hennesy	2	(191V)			
Jno Burke	8	Michl Burk	5		1,475
Edwd Burke	2	Jno Heyden	1		
Cathr Whelan	3	Pat Rourke	5		
Thos Coughlin	4	Jno Moran	1	Families 281	
Edwd Purcell	6	Wm Kennedy	3	Individuals 1,475	
Thos Kelly	11	Pat Kennedy	1		
Jno Kelly	5	Laurence Lennan	6		
Jno Kelly	10	Jno Cantwell	8	New Ross,	
Jno Kinchela	5	Edwd Moore	7	Novemb. 29, 1817.	

Appendix 2

Extracts from 'Return of Locations of the Johnstown District Land Board to Persons applying through them to 17 December 1821'. Archives of Ontario, RG1 C-1-4, vol. 47; microfilm, ms. 693, reel 163, or LDS film 1376211.

q — quarter lot   h — half lot   bnk — broken lot   Lot/Concession, township

Date	Name	Location	Acres	Where born	Age	Period of arrival in the province
20 March 1820	RYAN Matthew	nw q 1/7	Lansdown	Town of Gowrie, Co Wexford	21	Jul 1818
	HORTON Henry	ne q 1/7	Lansdown	Clough, Co. Wexford	33	Nov 1816
	JOHNSON Richd	nw q A/8	Lansdown	Killincoolay, Co. Wexford	36	1810
	EDWARDS Edward	se q 7/10	Yonge	Kilcormick, Co. Wexford	28	1817
	ERRET Isaac	sw q 7/10	Yonge	Askintenny, Co. Wexford	24	June 1819
	REDMON Jas	bkn 5/2	Yonge	Monomolin, Co. Wexford	28	1916
	DOCKERILL Benj	w h 16/6	Yonge	Clonagill, Co. Wexford	36	Aug 1818
	RICHARDS Edw	e h 16/6	Yonge	Ardamine, Co. Wexford	28	Aug 1816
27 March 1820	FOLAY Thos	ne q 7/10	Yonge	Killtresk, Co. Wexford	31	Jun 1818
	EARL William	e h B/13	Lansdown	Gowrie, Co. Wexford	28	Jun 1819
	GODKIN Joseph	w h B/13	Lansdown	Ballicanew, Co. Wexford	21	Jun 1819
	AYRES Henry	se q 23/6	Yonge	Killincoolay, Co. Wexford	22	Jun 1819
	WHALEY Samuel	sw q 23/6	Yonge	Kilcormuck, Co. Wexford	47	1811
	SHAW William	se q 2/4	Leeds	Town of Barrey Gowrie, Co. Wexford	30	Aug 1818
	HAZELWOOD Wm	sw q 3/5	Leeds	St. Mary's, Co. Wexford	57	1918
3 April 1820	QUINSEY John	sw 1 15/5	Yonge	Ballincanew, Co. Wexford	23	Oct. 1819
	GREEN Mark	ne q 3/6	Leeds	Bree, Co. Wexford	31	1818
12 June 1820	JORDAN Thos	20/7	Yonge	Newtown Barry, Co. Wexford	30	May 1820
3 July 1820	GREEN Richard	ne q A/8	Lansdown	Kilcormuck, Co. Wexford	23	Jun 1820
14 August 1820	ROWSON Henry	nw q A/7	Lansdown	Monomoline, Co. Wexford	23	Jun 1819
	BOULTON John	ne q A/7	Lansdown	Monomoline, Co. Wexford	26	Jun 1819
23 October 1820	TOWNSEND Thos	sw end of w h 4/8	Lansdown	Clowmulsk, Co Carlow	33	Jun 1820
6 Nov. 1820	LEARY Alexr	se h 12/5	Yonge	Ferns, Co. Wexford	44	August 1820
	QUINSEY Thos	sw h 12/5	Yonge	Monomoline, Co. Wexford	27	August 1820
17 Sept. 1821	BOWDEN Jas	nw q 13/5	Leeds	Carlow, Co. Carlow	34	1818
17 Dec. 1821	POOLE Benj	ne q 6/8	Lansdown	Co. Wexford	23	1817
	POOLE Abel	nw q 6/8	Lansdown	Co. Wexford	21	1817

Certified by Solomon Jones, Chairman, Land Board, District of Johnstown. Brockville, 1st January 1822.

16 *J. H. Andrews*

Landmarks in early Wexford Cartography

It may be useful to begin by distinguishing cartographic history from regional history. The cartographic historian deals with maps as artifacts, with the processes of creating them, with the structure of the map-making profession, and with the role of maps in past societies. For the regional historian the perception of his chosen area by early map-makers and map-users is only one of many aspects of that area that may legitimately interest him, and in studying most of those aspects his main use for maps is simply as realistic portraits of the earth's surface. The present essay, while written from the carto-historical viewpoint, is nevertheless addressed to the historians of one particular region — to readers who habitually seek out maps in guides and catalogues without regard to the 'structuring principles' of the cartographic philosopher.[1] My thesis is that even the most empirical researcher can benefit from a little theorising or 'modelling', for these activities may draw attention to previously disregarded source materials as well as throwing light on those that are already familiar. It is true that cartographic scholars would prefer their models to be universal, whereas the practical user of early maps is often bound by a single county or parish.[2] The remedy may be to limit the scope of the proposed model, while at the same time making it capable of extension by readers of a more theoretical temper. It is with such a possibility in mind that the following essay has been deliberately pitched to fall between two thematic stools: one of them is maps of county Wexford earlier than *c.* 1900, the other is the abstract notion of a landmark in cartographic history.

A 'map history' may be defined as the aggregated histories of all maps which take a given area as their subject and which specify the name of that area in their titles, if any. For the student of regional perception, the character of such title-areas is a matter of some interest, though in landscape history it may be better to ignore labels and remember how fluidly a unit of this kind can emerge from, or be absorbed into, a title-area larger than itself. In general a legally constituted territory of any size tends to generate its own map history (territorial

447

entities without legal status were slow to do so until the rise of modern geo-graphical science) and in Ireland the most important of these territories is the county. Because of its marginal position Wexford has been somewhat backward in cartographic enterprise compared with counties nearer Dublin and Belfast, but it still has several attractions for the map historian. It is of above average size and well defined by natural boundaries, among them the cartographically challenging boundary between land and sea. Its physical and human landscape make a colourful patchwork, its settlement pattern a blend of farmsteads, hamlets, villages and boroughs, including a county capital that once ranked fourteenth among the towns of Ireland. It also combines two con-trasting historical theatres: a southern 'pale' of intensive Anglo-Norman settlement and a northern Gaelic heartland not effectively anglicised until the seventeenth century. Both north and south, together with the transition zone between them, have suffered most of the vagaries of modern Irish history.

Historians, however well endowed with 'period sense' in their own field, will generally prefer an early map to give the same kind of information, with the same degree of reliability, that they would expect from a modern map. In deference to this view, and without prejudice to broader philosophical issues, a 'good' map for the present purpose is one that would be judged good, in 1987, by everyone except map historians and map philosophers. On such a definition it is hardly surprising that in general maps improve as they become more recent — allowing for a middle-aged user's attachment to the maps of his youth. But it is not just egocentricity that justifies a 'Darwinian' approach to cartographic improvement, for early map-makers were often spurred on by the complaints of their own contemporaries, many of whom would almost certainly have accepted the standards of more modern generations and might even have agreed that some kinds of cartographic progress are open to objective measurement. Nor are the causes of improvement since the medieval period far to seek, though there is no need to extrapolate them into pre-renaissance times — or into the future, for that matter. On the demand side, there are the cartographic needs created by modern revolutions in government, industry, agriculture, transport, education and the rest. On the supply side there is scientific and technical progress affecting the actual production of maps in field and office.

Faced with a continuous loss of cartographic quality as he works backwards, the intelligent landscape historian will seek to eliminate one kind of error and omission by selecting the small minority of maps that embody first-hand information, ignoring the large majority that are merely copies of other maps. Yet in practice originality may be an unattainable ideal. Many surveys exist only as redrawn by non-surveyors. Even a surveyor's own handiwork may be a 'fair draught' copied for the benefit of posterity from a 'foul plot', itself no longer extant, embodying his original observations; and the errors he makes in transcribing fair from foul, though perhaps not very numerous, are no different in kind from those of less careful copyists. 'Original' must therefore be interpreted as 'less unoriginal than any available alternatives'. Even then it is a quality with no claim to be predicated of complete maps. The ultimate unit of cartography is not the map itself, but the triad of identifiable features within the map, and it is normal rather than exceptional for good and bad, new and old, to appear side by side within the same frame. In short, the following classification must be regarded as something less than watertight.

Original Surveys

'Survey' in the present context means any process of cartographic data-gathering that involves direct acquaintance with the objects represented on a map. The merit of a survey depends on both its accuracy (in all legitimate senses of a much-abused word) and its comprehensiveness. It will be convenient to treat these two variables together, but in practice they cannot be expected to keep strictly in step, for even the most slapdash cartographer may hit on some interesting feature that his successors choose to ignore. At this point the idea of cartographic merit may be extended to include consistency, or the application of regular principles in the choice of map detail; and (to antici-pate a theme developed below) it is with the cultivation of consistency that the difference between general and thematic maps becomes increasingly clear. If these various properties were measurable in any large group of European maps covering the same area, they would show an overall upward trend between the middle ages and the twentieth century. There are also several secondary map characteristics exhibiting the same kind of directional change, with scale ratios becoming larger, line-work finer, and the representation of material objects more planiform. Of course all these attributes are matters of degree: the only discrete advances immediately visible to the map reader are the intro-duction of explicit scale-statements (whether of linear distances or geo-graphical coordinates) and north-points, and since such marginalia were sometimes added by a later hand without forming part of the main production process they are far from infallible as a guide to accuracy.

As the cartographer's product improved his work became slower, more liberally capitalised, technologically more complex, and more dependent on both skill and training. Progress in field and workshop may be equated with new measuring appliances or new survey designs, but unfortunately such inno-vations can seldom be given a date and they were in any case almost invariably combined with older methods. Thus sketching was retained in an instrumental survey to fill the spaces between measured points; in difficult terrain triangu-lation might give way to the less reliable method of traversing; even hearsay, crudest of all techniques, survives in a scientific age as the cartographer's source of evidence for placenames and for the function and ownership of buildings. In practice, earlier and later procedures have been combined in such varying ratios as to leave the continuity of cartographic progress unbroken. The same applies to the growth of a professional identity among map-makers, for the emergence of the modern surveyor-cartographer was preceded by a long period of occupational overlap and confusion.

In spite of everything the best determinants of periodisation for the landscape historian are probably the means by which map-data were collected.

Each technical advance can then be seen as part consequence and part cause of society's rising demand for cartographic value, a rise that levels off when maps finally become as good as most people want them to be. In a cradle of innovation like the Low Countries or later France, supply and demand are kept more or less in balance. With increasing distance from this core, demand rises more slowly and technological innovations may be correspondingly delayed, perhaps failing to materialise altogether. Evolutionary stages may also be occluded by a vertical jump in demand under the influence of, for example, a colonial incursion. For these reasons the sequence suggested below is not necessarily of very wide application.

COUNTY SURVEYS

Like many other kinds of title-area, counties began and in a sense have almost ended by being mapped as parts of some larger unit. In what follows, any survey that includes a whole county will be treated as a county survey.

(1) In the most primitive stage of cartographic evolution the existence of a county or its territorial equivalent may be asserted by a map, but no single feature within it is shown by both words and symbols, and no spatial significance attaches to the placement of these marks within the area concerned, whose internal geography thus remains unrepresented. An Irish example, from the Gough map of *c.* 1360, is the name 'Develyn', unaccompanied by either symbols or boundaries and with no other information about the county in question.[3] There seems to be no case of this not-very-interesting phenomenon in county Wexford.

(2) Next comes the mapping of elementary spatial relationships such as contiguity, enclosure, connectivity and linear order, without reference to numerical bearings or distances. Such purely topological representation requires some familiarity with the study area but need make no use of actual measurement or any other *ad hoc* research. Sub-stages within this category are distinguished by quantity rather than by character of information. Thus in the map of western Europe attributed to Giraldus Cambrensis the only details for Wexford are the county town and the River Slaney, and it seems unlikely that any other medieval cartographers in the same monkish tradition did any better.[4] Only in the sixteenth century, apparently, was Giraldus's achievement matched by placing not one but two Wexford towns on their respective rivers, the second being New Ross on the Barrow.[5] Connecting towns and rivers comes under the same topological head as simply listing capes and bays in order along a coastline, a common form of geographical statement before maps had become widely current.[6] The appearance of Glascarrig and Fethard on mid-sixteenth-century maps of Ireland, along with unnamed islands presumably representing Tuskar and the Saltees, may be an importation from this non-cartographic genre.[7]

(3) Estimates of distance between Irish towns were often quoted in the early sixteenth century, and it must have been a significant breakthrough when these were adopted as a basis for map-making.[8] Not all such 'itinerary' maps gave distances, or even roads; indeed in Irish examples from this era the use of

mileages can only be conjectured from superior locational accuracy, a more complete record of inland towns, and the presence of a linear scale. The gradualness of improvement makes it hard to date the onset of this stage, but there are two scaled maps — those of Laurence Nowell (*c.* 1562) and Gerard Mercator (1564) — that depict the comparatively peaceful parts of Leinster and east Munster in far more detail than anything earlier (fig. 16.1),[9] including settlements, rivers, hills and forests,together with a modicum of new maritime detail and a number of Irish family and territorial names. It is not known whether maps like Nowell's and Mercator's were based on a special programme of data collection for the whole kingdom, or put together 'anecdotally' from the facts that one or more compilers happened to have become aware of. In either case their authors met a problem which is especially acute in Irish cartography and which has never been solved, that of making a meaningful selection from a stock of placenames, all more or less equally important, which is too large to be mapped in its entirety.

(4) The next distinction is between the itinerary map and an expert's measured survey. A realistic model must postulate a succession of such surveys, each more accurate and technically complex than the last, occupying the greater part of the period between the sixteenth century and the present day.

(*a*) The first map of any large part of Ireland likely to have been based on terrestrial measurement was made for the government by the English military engineer Roberty Lythe, who visited Wexford in 1569 between surveying in Kilkenny and Carlow.[10] Like his British counterparts Christopher Saxton and Timothy Pont, Lythe is thought to have taken angular observations between one viewpoint and another, and like them he did little or nothing to map the roads he travelled. But apart from records of his journeys and the sums paid to him the only positive evidence for Lythe's methods is his high level of accuracy, and this is more apparent in other counties than in Wexford, where he must have depended heavily on sketching and on name-lists supplied by local residents. Regrettably, his survey is now known only through small-scale derivatives, some in his own hand, others by not very faithful copyists. This makes it hard to judge the degree of randomness with which he chose his detail, but in Wexford, as would be expected in the sixteenth century, he seems to be most informative on the 'English baronies' of the south. As was also to be expected, it is along the fluctuating margins of the Englishry that his place-names are now hardest to identify (fig. 16.2).

(*b*) In European cartography at large the next sub-stage was a network of road traverses measured by chain or wheel and by azimuthal sight-lines, with off-road detail added by intersections or by sketching. Only later would surveyors make chain surveys along the minor territorial boundaries dividing any large tract of country. An unusual feature of Irish map history is the way in which the sixteenth and seventeenth-century confiscations threw this sequence into reverse, so that the leading survey technique in Wexford and other territories planted between 1580 and 1700 was the admeasurement of townlands and other small denominations by detailed boundary traverses. The

N

Clohamon

Ferns

Glascarrig

Moneyhore

Enniscorthy

Ross

Old Ross

Deeps

Wexford

Dunbrody

Rosegarland

St Leonards

Clonmines

Ballybrennan

Ballyhack

"Balemagh"

Tintern

Duncannon

Bannow

Carn

Ballyteige

Ballyhealy

Hook

0   5 km

Fig. 16.1: Settlements and settlement-names according to Laurence Nowell, c.1562, and Gerard Mercator, 1564 (see note 9). Base map and orthography are from the Ordnance Survey. Regional and physical names are omitted.

Fig. 16.2: Settlement and settlement-names according to Robert Lythe, 1569. No single map shows the whole of Lythe's survey. This is a conflation, on the Ordnance Survey base, of the Lythe map at Petworth House, Sussex (see note 10) with those derived from the same survey by Gerard Mercator (1595), Baptista Boazio (1599) and John Speed (1610). Lythe generally preferred the prefix 'Bally' to the suffix 'town' and this preference has been respected. Otherwise most of his names have been converted where possible to Ordnance Survey spelling. Unidentified names are underlined and spelt as in the original. Regional and physical names are omitted. The rivers are those of the Petworth map. This map must be regarded as provisional, and certain of its identifications are likely to be corrected by further research.

north Wexford plantation surveys of 1611 and 1617 do not survive,[11] but Dr William Petty's Down Survey of 1655 is available as both barony maps and (less completely) parish maps.[12] Although Petty's resources were immensely greater than Lythe's, his men worked at high speed under difficult post-war conditions and many of their townland acreages were too small, while their mapping of roads and buildings was seriously incomplete, as can be seen by comparing the graphic and written sections of the survey.[13] As a record of names and boundaries the Down Survey was extraordinarily comprehensive, and although its coverage of townlands was confined to the area of Cromwellian forfeiture, the county and barony boundaries were complete even on unconfiscated land, providing the basis for outline county, provincial and national maps that were all eventually published in Petty's *Hiberniae delineatio* (1685).

(*c*) Road traversing came to Wexford with a military survey undertaken by Lt-Col Charles Vallancey in 1776.[14] Vallancey's subject matter was quite different from Petty's, excluding all territorial divisions smaller than a county and concentrating instead on hills, water, bogs, settlement (especially gentlemen's seats) and roads. But the results are hard to classify. Some of them are sub-county maps, confined to those roads in northern Wexford that were likely to bring a French invasion force from Waterford Harbour to Dublin. There was also a general military map of Ireland, the basis of Aaron Arrowsmith's *Ireland* published in 1811; for this Vallancey seems to have combined his own surveys with those of other cartographers such as George Taylor and Andrew Skinner.

(*d*) The civilian equivalent of Vallancey's surveys was a more accurate and detailed topographical coverage of communications, physical features and major settlement units, with the addition of barony and perhaps parish boundaries. These are the typical contents of the grand jury maps that marked the apogee of Irish county cartography in the narrow sense between the mid eighteenth century and the advent of the Ordnance Survey in 1824. The Wexford survey was made by Valentine Gill and published in 1811, making Wexford the last section of Ireland's eastern seaboard to appear in this form.[15] In some go-ahead counties the sequence of instrumental surveys was continued by a second grand jury map in which the road traverses were tied to a scientifically rigorous trigonometrical control network. Gill's map fell manifestly short of the highest contemporary standards, but its second (1816) edition showed no substantial difference from the first and the Wexford authorities apparently made no attempt to commission a new survey. Since the main purpose of a grand jury map was to facilitate road planning, their lack of dynamism may have been a tribute to the existing county Wexford road network; or perhaps a sign that in this county the kind of traffic that suffered most from bad roads was able to travel by water.

Gill's scale was one inch to one statute mile, and his principal subject-matter was that of contemporary English Ordnance Survey maps: latitudes and longitudes; coasts, rivers, hills, bogs, woods, mines and quarries; country houses and demesnes; towns and villages in simplified ground plan; large farmhouses (though not cabins), churches, chapels, mills and barracks. To these he added hydrographic data, the names of resident gentry, and barony boundaries. It was a regional map in the fullest sense; and although such maps are sometimes less exact than their national counterparts they usually have more to say about local idiosyncrasies — as witness Gill's nine references to Wexford military history ranging from the time of Strongbow to the 1798 rebellion.

(*e*) In a modern state the succession of instrumental surveys will culminate in a single government map of the whole country and the re-submergence of more localised cartographic identities. In Ireland the government map in question was that of the Ordnance Survey, whose coverage of county Wexford, published in 1841, included baronies, parishes, townlands, rivers, roads, buildings, enclosures and several kinds of land cover, all in a style that was almost uniform throughout the thirty-two counties and with a precision and clarity never previously approached for any area of comparable size.[16]

(5) The Ordnance maps are too well known for further discussion apart from one last theoretical point. Once maps have finally overtaken the public's expectations, they will be revised to keep pace with changes in the landscape, but no longer replaced by new original surveys. For several decades after 1846 the six-inch Irish Ordnance Survey maps exemplified this last and most perfect stage of cartographic evolution. Then in 1887 it was decided for reasons of national agrarian policy to switch from revision to resurveying (except in the kind of large mountain or moorland area that is unrepresented in county Wexford) at the monster scale of 1:2,500. But there is one sense in which the 1:2,500 scale can be said to illustrate our fifth stage, for although the landscape was remeasured after 1887 the mathematical foundations of the new maps were inherited from the original Ordnance survey.

PARTIAL SURVEYS

If Wexford map history is pictured as a vertical column, each of the afore-mentioned maps and map-groups would be a horizontal line across the full extent of the county. But if such lines are to be identified with new survey techniques they must be fretted with upward and downward projections of varying lengths and widths. Apart from differences within the same survey, many small areas were precociously mapped by superior methods not yet feasible for a whole county; conversely, cartographers working within narrow limits sometimes made do with procedures that would no longer have been tolerable on a wider canvas. Two kinds of partial survey are firstly those wholly confined within one county and secondly those of linear features, such as roads, coasts, inland waterways and railways, that continue from one county to another. A third, not further discussed here, is the kind of county map that spreads some way across its own boundary, in this case from Wicklow, Carlow, Kilkenny or Waterford.

Linear surveys

From 1327 onwards the names of Irish coastal features began to appear on the portolan charts produced as navigational aids by Italian and Catalan ship masters. In southern Europe the portolans are so accurate that they are generally attributed to some kind of compass survey,[17] but this accuracy does not extend to Ireland, where the portolan coastlines are too distorted for minor features to be recognisable, and where most modern readers rely on the ingenuity displayed in the writings of T. J. Westropp for the interpretation of obsolete names (table 1).[18] In the sixteenth century, charts (other than large-scale charts of single harbours) were superseded by land maps as records of terrestrial information such as placenames, and it became rare for marine surveyors to achieve priority in this field: a Wexford example is Broomhill overlooking Waterford Harbour, recorded as 'Bumhill' by Dutch chartmakers many years before its first appearance on any Anglo-Irish map.[19]

By contrast strip road maps, as exemplified by George Taylor and Andrew Skinner's *Roads of Ireland* (1778), are a major source for regional history, and

Table 1

Coastal names in south-east Ireland from portolan charts and related maps
(For source see note 18)

Rois, 1339, 1351, 1375, 1552; roxi and rofin, 1360; roxin, 1384; roi, 1450, 1544; roxa, 1373; rox, 1426; roye, 1513; aros, 1593 (Ross).

Ardart, 1436; ardamna, 1367 (unidentified, between Waterford and Hook Head).

Donduban, 1327; dondub, 1339, 1436; dondiab, 1351; dondab, 1373; dōdab, 1426; donibab, 1384; condali, 1467; conciab, 1497; dontal, 1513; candab, 1552 (Dun Dubhain, Hook Head).

Frith, 1327; fredit, 1339, 1360, 1367, 1375, 1384, 1426; fredid, 1373; fedis, 1436; indit, 1467; frerit, 1497; fredit, 1513; ffredit, 1552; freda, 1551, 1593 (Fethard).

Elleibano, 1327; clelane, 1351; leban, 1360; elebano, 1367; ellebano, 1384, 1426, 1436, 1467, 1552; elebani, 1513 (Bannow).

Carn, 1384 (Carn).

Saltis, 1327, 1339; ganf (salis), 1367; saliez, 1426; saltei, 1450, 1544, 1552; y de sallos, 1500 (Saltee Islands).

Tisalt, or risalt, 1327, 1339, 1375, 1552; tasal, 1384; rasal, 1373; rixalt, 1360, 1593; risal, 1367; tasart, 1436; risata, 1497; tissalt, 1426; risati, 1513; ussalt (risalt), 1467 (Tuscar, 'or perhaps even Rosslare').

Riosia (?), 1384 (perhaps Rosslare).

Oxfordo, 1351; Ocordo, 1360; ocfordo, 1367, 1467, 1552; Osforde, 1373; ocsorda, 1375, 1497; auforit, 1384; cossard, 1426; casorda, 1436; arforda, 1450; orfordo, 1513; ariforda, 1544; achefort, 1559 (Wexford).

Rexna, 1360; rexnas, 1367; resnax, 1375; resnas, 1426; ressnas, 1436; renal, 1497, 1552; remes, 1593; teynos, 1339; tenab, 1513 (unidentified: either Rosslare or Courtown Harbour).

may be seen as a stage in the evolution of new-style topographical maps like Gill's, showing not only roads but also many villages and country houses previously unrecorded (fig. 16.3), such as Snugboro near Artramon, Rookley Lodge near Ballycarney and 'Erskinville' near Scullogue Gap. Other strip maps were drawn as proposals for roads not yet constructed, but these generally included a number of existing routes. The best Wexford example is William Duncan's mail coach road survey of 1814 which shows roadside houses, gentlemen's seats, quarries, the names of occupiers along the intended new line, and sketch plans of Coolgreany, Gorey, Clough, Camolin, Ferns, Enniscorthy, Oilgate and Wexford.[20]

Local surveys

Despite their varied subject-matter, surveys of areas smaller than a county have several features in common. Like most kinds of map they increase in number as well as in value, the exact rate of increase being related to the development of county surveying. The older the most recent general survey, the more necessary is the next local survey. On the other hand, the better the county survey, the more local purposes it can serve. Whatever the theoretical import of these axioms, in practice Irish local cartography reached a peak immediately before the arrival of the Ordnance Survey. The diffusion of surveying activity also included a 'hierarchical' element, for in any system of territories or central places, some units are quicker to claim attention than others, cartographically as in other ways. It was the larger towns, the busier harbours, the more strategically important fortifications, and the more professionally managed estates, that were first to acquire their own maps. A critical point on the upward curve of local surveying activity is the emergence of resident map-makers who could undertake small commissions for which it would not have been worthwhile to import a surveyor from outside the county. In most parts of Ireland the dates of the first truly local full-time surveyor and of any resulting quantum leap in cartographic progress are impossible to fix with precision, though in the present state of knowledge an average of around 1720 seems fairly probable. A likely Wexford candidate for priority is William Jones, address unknown, who appears at three widely separated places in the county between the 1720s and 1740s without yet having been recorded anywhere else in Ireland.[21] Thenceforth Wexford always had its own surveying community, though it would be premature to offer a list that distinguished inhabitants from visitors.[22] Some claims to residential status would rest, like Jones's, on nothing more than the absence of a record in any other county. Examples are Isaac Jackson (1735), Walsingham Bolton (1764-8), William Day (1800) and William F. Jackson (1819); and some members of this group, like James Urner (1735) and Robert Shaw (1801), are known only for a single map. A more interesting though still by no means conclusive hint is when a Wexford map carries a distinctive Wexford surname, like those of the surveyors John Stafford (1755), James Nuzum (1779), Edward White (1792), John Nuzum (1801), Thomas Connick (1809) and Walter Keating (1835). Surveyors with authenticated county Wexford addresses are few indeed:

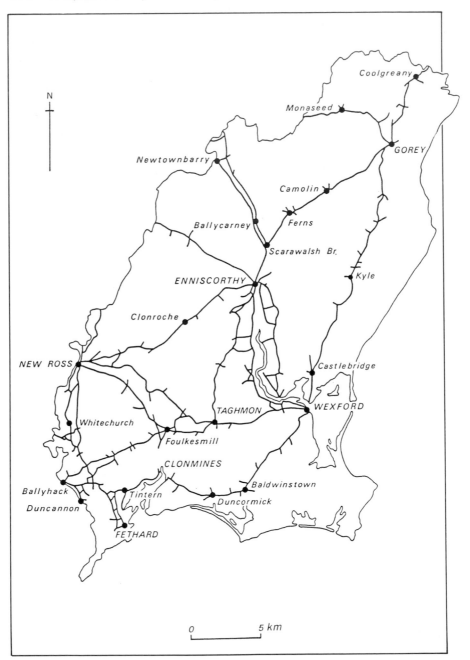

Fig. 16.3: Towns, villages, main roads, and junctions of main roads with minor roads, 1777 (George Taylor and Andrew Skinner, *Maps of the roads of Ireland* (London and Dublin, 1778), 134, 142-6, 149-54). Taylor and Skinner show nucleated settlements on the main roads by clusters of generalised building blocks and use capital letters for the names of parliamentary boroughs; otherwise towns and villages are not distinguished.

Charles and Richard Frizell from Mountfin near Enniscorthy and later from Askamore near Gorey (1761);[23] Valentine Gill (1811) and Andrew Henrick (1821-2) from Enniscorthy;[24] and James Carty (1835) from Wexford[25] — not much of a basis for claiming that the local profession was more active in north than in south county Wexford, though there might well be convincing agrarian explanations for such a state of affairs. None of these surveyors founded a recognisable 'school' of Wexford cartography — not even the energetic Frizells — and Dublin surveyors could always find work in the county on projects of special importance, a traffic that was continued and increased by the coming of the Ordnance Survey.

The main varieties of local survey will now be enumerated. Local charts begin with Waterford Harbour (including the Hook peninsula) in *c.* 1601[26] and first become topographically informative in 1737, when William Doyle's harvest of south-west Wexford placenames included a St Brecan's Bridge on the foreshore near Slade to go with the better-known St Patrick's Bridge further east.[27] Wexford Harbour, never much frequented by large ships, had to wait until 1764 for a chart of its own[28] and did not become a focus of cartographic activity until the early nineteenth century, when the issue of harbour improvement became linked with the equally map-worthy theme of land reclamation.[29] In the field of military mapping, terrain surveys like Vallancey's had been preceded by plans of individual fortifications, but the only surviving early examples from county Wexford are those of Duncannon Fort, repeatedly surveyed on a quasi-architectural scale from 1587 onwards[30] and first mapped in relation to the other forts of Waterford Harbour in 1591.[31] Apart from Duncannon, which is best regarded as a cartographic extension of Munster, county Wexford was too remote from Ireland's strategic trouble-spots to play a major part in pre-eighteenth-century map-making. Only in 1798 did it produce its own cartographic explosion, much of it fuelled from second-hand sources though with some original coverage of Wexford town, New Ross and Vinegar Hill.[32]

Estate surveys, thanks to their large scales and high level of originality, are among the most useful of all maps in landscape history, though they are also the hardest to find. A few served some public purpose, like the surveys of Bantry Commons and other crown lands in the 1820s[33] and the tithe maps of a few years later,[34] but most were commissioned by individual private proprietors acting in isolation from every other map-making agency, and many must remain in the possession of former landowning families or their solicitors. Nevertheless the map-histories of many landed estates have paralleled those of counties, with a succession of general surveys interrupted by local (in this case farm) surveys, the former often prompted by a change of owner, the latter by a change of tenant. The earliest examples, including those of the Frizell family, were in the outline style made familiar by the Down Survey:[35] one may search hard among the names, acreages and boundaries of townlands on these maps before finding such non-territorial nuggets as the site of the old silver mines at Clonmines[36] or 'Bloody Gap' in the parish of Whitechurchglynn.[37] It was not until 1803, on Lord Stanley Spencer

Chichester's estate at Dunbrody, that Wexford landscapes began to be mapped in something more like the 'topographical' style that had been current among the most progressive Anglo-Irish landowners for several decades. Then, in an area of over 10,000 statute acres, the Dublin firm of Sherrard and Brassington mapped roads, houses, farm boundaries, land quality, mills, churches, chapels, limekilns, milestones, a fair green, a ball alley and a 'boiling well', with a view of Dunbrody Abbey thrown in on the title page.[38] Such wealth of detail is disappointingly rare. Indeed, surviving or recorded estate maps of any kind seem less abundant in Wexford than in many other counties.[39] This may be an illusion with purely archival causes, or it may reflect an unusually stable pattern of land-holding.

Urban life in all its aspects has impinged upon cartography at innumerable points and town plans are correspondingly difficult to categorise. A plausible distinction in the present context might be between independent town surveys justified in their own right and those that would count as parts of more extensive surveys except that they happen to need plotting on a larger scale than rural areas. In Ireland the latter definition applies to both the Ordnance Survey and the associated Griffith valuation. The Ordnance surveyors drew a separate manuscript plan of Wexford town in 1841; the valuation office mapped no less than thirty-one of the county's towns and villages at various times after 1830 on scales of either 1:1,056 or 1:2,122.[40] These plans were for official use, but in 1872 the government agreed to publish towns with populations exceeding 4,000, and Wexford, New Ross and Enniscorthy all appeared at 1:500 in the course of the next decade. It would be interesting to project such population thresholds backwards (and upwards) into the world of private commercial publishing as it existed before 1824 and so construct a model for the independent town plan, but in Wexford no such plans exist:[41] the only surviving specimens are by-products of military history,[42] estate management,[43] or official boundary delimitation.[44]

EARLY THEMATIC MAPS

'Thematic' cartography, where matter of specialised interest is made to stand out visually against a recessive 'base map', is often seen as part of a nineteenth-century intellectual revolution.[45] But it might also be modelled with a slowly rising curvature like that of cartographic evolution in general, progress being measured not only by the range of subject-matter treated in such maps but also by the clarity of the separation between base map and 'foreground'. Neglect of this latter distinction may cause trouble when early thematic maps are treated as if they were topographical surveys; for base maps, despite the novelty of what is superimposed on them, have a habit of reverting to an earlier evolutionary phase. They may be no more than diagrammatic sketches, for example, at a time when non-thematic maps had graduated to the instrumental survey, an example from county Wexford being the revival of topology in 1677 to show how surviving woodland was related to the River Slaney and its tributaries.[46] From this it follows that early base maps may achieve a perhaps unexpected originality, for it is easier to be original in a sketch than in a map aspiring to planimetric correctness. A case in point is the rough map of proposed new counties south of Dublin drawn in 1579, which was clearly independent of Lythe's recent survey and which included several features not seen on any other sixteenth-century map.[47]

Derivative Maps

Derivative maps as such have nothing to offer the landscape historian, but when a second-hand source is deputising for a lost original some knowledge of how map contents are transmitted will clearly be of use to him. This subject may be approached by arranging a map's possible destinies as a continuum. At one extreme it may be lost or forgotten without ever being used; at the other, it may enter the cartographic equivalent of a perfect market, remainingly effortlessly and eternally available to every consumer. Cartographic progress has meant not only making original surveys more accurate but bringing maps in general further from the first of these situations and nearer to the second. Availability may involve a physical transfer from one user to another, as has happened to many estate maps when a property changes hands, but the normal way of connecting producer and consumer has been for maps to be copied and at the same time editorially processed.

Not all transmission systems can be ranked on a scale of efficiency or placed in an evolutionary sequence. For instance, some of the necessary links could develop within a single organisation such as the state (though neither the London nor the Dublin government ever did much to coordinate their cartographic holdings), while in the private sector there were manuscript copyists who reached their sources and clients along the branches of an informal 'grapevine', which is how much Anglo-Irish map-making became known in the late sixteenth and early seventeenth centuries. By that time, however, geographical information was generally being communicated to greater effect among European map-users by means of engraving, printing, publishing and retailing — developments which in the main centres of innovation may be assumed (in the interests of tidy model-building) to coincide with the advent of instrumental surveys out of doors. Thenceforth progress in map-use brought the publisher into an ever-widening range of cartographic endeavour, adopting successively smaller territorial units as title-areas and printing them at successively larger map-scales, until in Ireland the mid-nineteenth-century encumbered estates court carried even the estate map for all practical purposes into the public domain.

The cartographic market embraces many levels of commitment. The weaker the public's interest in any region, the less detailed, accurate and up-to-date are the facts needed to satisfy that interest, and the smaller the map-scale on which these facts can be displayed. Surveys of different qualities and different ages have their own markets, which may coexist in space as well as time; thus the map of Ireland in a world atlas would probably be based on an earlier source than the best sheet map of the country available from the same printseller. But the markets may also be pictured as geographical areas with a value-gradient falling across them. The theorist will visualise such areas as concentric rings with the survey in the middle, each zone expanding outwards over the next as new information is diffused. More realistically, the 'rings' can be characterised by their political and cultural affiliations, so that the innermost zone, in the present case, consisted of Anglo-Irish government officials, engineers and other professional men, followed successively by Ireland in general, Britain, continental Europe, and perhaps the rest of the world. An unwelcome fate for the modern historian is to find himself consigned by accidents of survival to a less central zone than the one appropriate to his own level of interest.

Market areas as thus conceived differ not only in the age, scale and accuracy of their chief model for the country in question, but also in the extent to which that model was augmented with additional facts. At the theoretical centre of the system, never encountered in real life, the only acceptable map is a perfect synthesis of all previous cartography, national, regional or local. Outwards from this centre are ranged compilers using both printed and manuscript maps, those using two or more printed maps and finally those making reduced copies of a single printed map. The nearer to the centre, the more ability and effort are needed to strike the right balance between supply and demand. At an early stage of cartographic history an 'insider' may even find it less difficult to make a new map by collating readily available non-graphic information than to seek out existing maps and assess their relative merits. This explains (reverting to the subject of original surveys) why so many different map-images survive from the 'topological' and 'itinerary' periods.

As market frictions are smoothed out, contradictory maps may start provoking sales resistance and publishers will seek to maximise consumer satisfaction by tacitly agreeing on a single outline. Not necessarily the best outline: George Lily's *Britanniae insulae* (1546) soon became the standard version of Ireland, but it was by no means the most accurate or comprehensive in existence — certainly not for Wexford, which it completely ignored. But our Darwinian assumption implies that better maps should eventually win the struggle for survival, and in the European cartography of Ireland the first clear victory for merit went to Mercator's map of 1564, which was still being reproduced by minor foreign publishers as late as 1627.[48] Once the historian has identified a popular source map, a comparison of source with derivatives may throw some light on contemporary editorial behaviour, giving a useful basis for analogy in cases where no such source is available. For instance, when an early cartographer reduced his model for republication on a smaller scale, did he maintain the original balance between sparse and crowded areas or did he meet some quasi-aesthetic standard by evening out the density of detail? And in selecting placenames, did he choose at random or did he prefer names that were short, intelligible, linguistically congenial, and prominently placed on his model? Unfortunately, such questions have as yet received very little study.

A case where analogy might prove helpful is that of Robert Lythe, who has left a numerous cartographic progeny but no ancestor. Each surviving version of his work is in some way peculiar: thus among Wexford names Innersgarat occurs only in Mercator (1595), Slewbor only in Boazio (1599) and B. Done only in Speed (1610). On what grounds are Boazio and his contemporaries classed here as derivatives of Lythe and not left for the next section of this essay as maps of dual origin? Mainly because the details unique to them are so trivial. Any other original survey that picked up such minutiae would probably leave some documentary trace of the money spent on it, but in south-east Ireland Lythe's is the only Elizabethan instrumental survey on record. In any case, even if there was another, non-Irish cartographers would have been lucky to obtain a copy of it: getting a sight of Lythe's was improbable enough. And if they had done so, the resulting mixture would presumably have included some disagreements with Lythe's far-from-perfect model instead of just a series of apparent additions to it — additions which doubtless originated with his huge master map, now no longer available. Despite these complications, Darwinism prevailed in so far as it was Speed's *Ireland*, the fullest version of Lythe to reach print, that became most popular in Britain and later on the continent, where it was still being copied with no substantial improvements at the end of the seventeenth century.[49]

By that time Petty had replaced Speed as trend-setting British cartographer of Ireland, and Petty was not to be finally ousted until the publication of the Ordnance Survey. *Hiberniae delineatio* brought more than a change of archetype: while Speed's imitators had accepted his Ireland as they found it, the *Delineatio* in a more competitive and sophisticated age was subject to drastic modification from the start.

Maps of Dual Origin

This section introduces the cartographer who, having weighed the available map sources and found them wanting, reverts to more original methods for part but not all of his own composition. Such combinations of map and non-map belong naturally to the innermost circles of a post-medieval market area, but otherwise have no particular theoretical interest. Their importance to the landscape historian lies in introducing elements of factual originality that can easily pass unnoticed.

Three motives for synthesis may be adduced. Firstly a map may have its errors corrected or its content updated without losing its own identity. In pre-eighteenth-century Ireland, where consumer feedback hardly existed, such changes appear to have been unusual. In fact it was only with the Ordnance Survey that revision became established as a routine, a county Wexford example being the roads built since 1841 that were surveyed for inclusion in the Survey's new one-inch map of Ireland published for this area in 1856.

Secondly, the balance between general and thematic cartography could be deliberately altered by incorporating new material. Perhaps the most familiar change of this kind in modern times has been the addition of geology to a topographical base, but in the present context it is the opposite process that requires attention. Petty's Down Survey, though made by conventional methods, might almost be described as a thematic map of territorial boundaries, and much subsequent Irish cartography was an attempt to turn it into a general map. An early example, from 1657, was Thomas Hunt's addition of woods, roads and buildings, as well as new proprietorial data, to his own Down Survey barony map of Scarawalsh.[50] On a broader scale, and several decades later, Petty's published maps of Ireland were to receive much the same treatment.

As a general atlas *Hiberniae delineatio* shared all the faults of the Down Survey. Besides omitting much essential topography it showed more territorial boundaries than most readers would consider necessary, and its dearth of information in unforfeited country was matched elsewhere by a dense clutter of apparently meaningless names. In particular it was only in his small one-page map of Ireland that Petty chose to publish any roads, just two of which (Arklow to Ferrycarrick and Wexford to New Ross) passed through the county of Wexford. But with the outbreak of war in 1689 the *Delineatio* quickly assumed importance as a source for general maps of Ireland, first in London and later in Amsterdam and other foreign publishing centres. The earliest adaptations, of which the best was by Philip Lea and Herman Moll in 1690, had few new facts or ideas to offer apart from preferring Petty's parish names to his townland names — a well-meant gesture that failed to recognise the diminishing importance of parish centres in the Irish settlement pattern.[51]

The first major advance came in 1708 with Henry Pratt's *Tabula Hiberniae novissima et emendatissima*. Pratt had worked for several years in Ireland as a land surveyor[52] and the *Tabula* was said to have been corrected for him by another Irish surveyor, Thomas Moland.[53] Its main novelty was a much extended road network featuring a rather improbable five-line junction at Mocurry near Kiltealy (fig. 16.4). Even when Pratt's minor names came from the *Delineatio* they were almost all different from those selected by the Petty imitators of the 1690s, for his main reason for choosing them was to help define the courses of roads and barony boundaries. His original contributions were more evident in north Wexford than in the south, a sign that the information-gradient of the sixteenth century had now been corrected and reversed. They included several physical features, like Tara Hill and the Blackstairs Mountains, and a number of the non-Gaelic settlement names (Prospect, Wells, Foulkesmill, Loftus Hall etc.) whose role in Irish cartography was now steadily increasing. Pratt also modernised some of Petty's spellings, among them Enniscorthy, Ros[s]lare and Templeshannon, though at the same time he made enough mistakes, such as 'Ballyback' instead of Ballyhack, for a Pratt 'family' to show itself among cartographers who followed suit, including Henry Overton, John Senex, Herman Moll, Thomas Jeffreys, John Rocque and Bernard Scalé.

The first compiler publicly to disown this family was the Revd Daniel Augustus Beaufort in his *Memoir of a map of Ireland* (1792). The map that accompanied the *Memoir* was to a large extent thematic, identifying Church of Ireland parishes and dioceses, distinguishing rectories, vicarages, curacies and chapelries, and locating glebes and parsonage houses as well as actual churches both ruined and intact. Beaufort broke with the new general cartography by showing no roads except those between post towns. But he did introduce a few commendably Irish-looking physical names and a light scatter of villages, some of which, like Broadway and Ramsgrange, had not yet been mapped as such in print. In fact, contrary to thematic tradition, Beaufort's base map was a remarkable feat of scholarship, exemplifying the third and most general reason for mixing original and derivative cartography, which is simply to give a more truthful account of geographical realities. Later all-Ireland maps must be

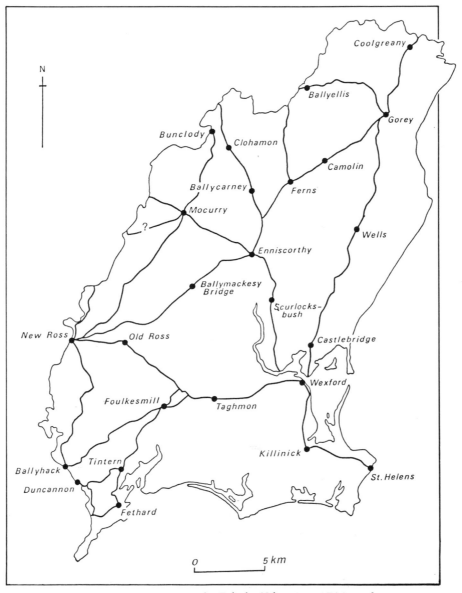

Fig. 16.4: Roads from Henry Pratt's *Tabula Hiberniae,* **1708, redrawn on an Ordnance Survey base, with a selection of Pratt's placenames in Ordnance Survey spelling.**

left for future research. On theoretical grounds they seem unlikely to yield any large accession of original detail; but no theory can eliminate surprises altogether and it is to underline this simple truth that we may end with one of the less predictable chapters in the Wexford cartographic story.

The rebellion of 1798 brought an urgent demand for maps of county Wexford without allowing time for an extensive new survey. The first response was a catchpenny production by the Dublin land surveyor Arthur R. Neville, who simply added a number of battlefield-symbols and recently notorious placenames to a base map of the Pratt variety.[54] Two years later, Sir Richard Musgrave's ultra-loyalist and anti-catholic *Memoirs of the different rebellions in Ireland* adopted a more strictly topographical approach in its maps of north and south Wexford, with relief, rivers, numerous roads, principal settlements and gentlemen's seats, all somewhat in the manner of Vallancey (though with many differences of detail from Valancey's surviving maps) and with an extensive overlap into neighbouring counties which in itself suggests a military rather than a civil origin. Musgrave's maps were closely followed in Robert Frazer's *Statistical survey of County Wexford*, published by the Dublin Society in 1807. By this time, however, a new map had appeared in Edward Hay's *History of the insurrection of the county of Wexford* (1803). Unlike Musgrave, Hay was a Wexford man, a member of the Royal Irish Academy, the proposer of a national population census and a Catholic — all in their way sound reasons for publishing a better map than his rival's. He was indeed right to offer it as the best map of the county that had yet appeared, though admitting it to be based on 'a variety of materials' rather than an original survey. One of the materials was presumably Musgrave's recent book, for in many places their maps are identical. But Hay also added roads, rivers and bogs (especially near his family's home at Ballinkeel), corrected the county boundary, made considerable changes to the coastline, and added a touch of regional consciousness with the names 'Mackomores' and 'Duffry'. With hindsight the rebellion maps are easily explained. War accelerates the process of cartographic evolution, and the Wexford of 1798 was in any case overdue for a new published map. But the cartographic roots of the Musgrave-Hay efflorescence remain invisible. Among them there may have been an otherwise unknown military map and, in Hay's case, an unknown county map of local origin, conceivably a prototype of the one later published by Gill. It is one of the many problems in Wexford map history that await the attention of the county's own scholars.

The Browne Families of County Wexford

The durable Norman imprint in the south of the county is one of Wexford's more striking features. Continuity in family names is only one of a range of conservative features in the area, especially in Forth and Bargy. Only rarely in Ireland is it possible to link families across the cataclysmic break of the mid-seventeenth century fracture in land ownership; in south Wexford, it is possible to do this with a number of families, who can be accurately traced from their Norman forebears down to their present representatives. One such family is the Brownes of Mulrankin, who can be taken as a prototype.

The first representative of the Browne family in Wexford was Philip Browne, who came to Ireland in 1169 with the initial band of Norman adventurers.[1] Philip and his brother William apparently volunteered for this invasion because of the ill odour in which they were held in Britain, as a result of their support for the unsuccessful claims of King Stephen against the Empress Maud and her son, Henry II. Their father, Hugh, was a Welsh marcher lord whose family, Le Brun, had originated from Poictou in Normandy. Hugh had four sons, of whom Philip and William were the two youngest: they therefore had the slightest prospects. It was common for younger sons to become involved in expeditions, in the hope of securing a patrimony for themselves by force of arms. While Philip settled in Mulrankin, his brother William settled at Clondalkin in Dublin. The Browne families of Galway and Mayo are said to derive from this William. Philip Le Brun was governor of Wexford in 1178 and was subsequently granted the manor of Mulrankin, which consisted of half a knight's fee, according to inquisitions of 1247 and 1307[2].

The Brownes welded themselves securely to the colonial power in Ireland and became prominent in the feudal administration of county Wexford. In 1365, for example, Nicholas Le Brun was high sheriff of Wexford. In 1376 Laurence Browne was one of the members for the borough of Wexford who attended King Edward's parliament at Westminster. In 1410, **Reginald**

Browne was chief sergeant of Wexford and in 1521, Walter Browne was seneschal of the Palatinate Liberty of Wexford.[3] For generation after generation, the Brownes were a mainstay of the Anglo-Norman colony in south Wexford, administering law and order, serving on juries, providing military service and generally backboning the continuation of English rule in the area. Similarly they were responsible for the local support of the church — with the advowson of St David's church in Mulrankin whose dedication recalled their Welsh origin. They also supplied many clergy: in 1409, for example, Nicholas Browne was treasurer of the cathedral of Ferns and in 1537 Richard Browne was parson of Our Lady's Island.[4] However, like other influential families in the area, they did not scruple to benefit from the dissolution of the monasteries: Walter Browne obtained a twenty-one year lease of the suppressed monastery of Selskar in 1540, presumably because of his loyal service to the English crown, not least as seneschal of the county in 1521.[5]

At Mulrankin, the Brownes operated within the framework of the manorial system. Even to the present day, the typical trilogy of castle, church and mill is evident. Indeed, the present mill at Bridgetown is probably on the same site and is a direct descendant of the original medieval mill, which is frequently referred to in early documents. The original stone castle (which replaced the initial motte at Oldhall) was extended in 1422 to become 'Mulrankin Hall' when an oblong 'great hall' was built onto the tower.[6] Nothing now survives of this hall and its extensive bawn, although the tower is still excellently preserved (pl. xlvi). It measures thirty by eighteen feet, with four and a half feet

Plate xlvi: Mulrankin Castle and farmhouse, 1890

thick walls and is primarily built of granite with some sandstone facings. An unusual feature is the staircase, which is not spiral in shape but runs straight from the top of the vault to the battlements. The seventeenth century documents suggest that the castle was surrounded by a cluster of thatched cabins, presumably the dwelling places of the Browne's labourers and servants. The manor of Mulrankin and the medieval parish of Mulrankin were probably co-extensive. The Brownes, as well as nominating the clergy of the local parish church, would have convened and staffed the local manor court and so would have held unrivalled legal and ecclesiastical sway over the Mulrankin area until the mid seventeenth century. Their power was consolidated by their marriages with other similarly placed landed families. In the close-knit world of the Old English gentry of Forth and Bargy, the Brownes were one of the main pillars of the establishment. The Brownes extended their holdings and held Oldtown, Bridgetown and Rathronan castles as residences for junior family members.

The Brownes — known in the barony of Forth rhyme as 'Gentleman Browne' because of their pride and high notions — had only one fly in their ointment — the increasing threat of attack from the Kavanaghs and other Gaelic families from the north of the county. Especially in the sixteenth century, the colony was being whittled back and even the 'English baronies' of Forth and Bargy were not impregnable from attack. The Brownes, with their kinsmen the Devereuxs of Ballymagir, played a leading role in defending the colony; in so doing, Robert Browne of Mulrankin enraged and insulted Brian M'Cahir Kavanagh of Ballyanne in 1572. Kavanagh sought the ultimate remedy, by attacking Mulrankin castle on 6 May 1572 and killing Robert Browne.[7] In this, he was aided by Fiach McHugh M'Shane O'Byrne. Curiously, the killing became a *cause celèbre*, engaging the personal attention of Queen Elizabeth, who wrote a strongly worded letter on the subject to Nicholas White, seneschal of the county (whose daughter was married to Browne). In her letter, the queen described Browne as a 'young gentleman of great valour, wholly given to our service against the disobedient Irishry.' She also advised the seneschal 'to look to the safety of the poor young gentlewoman his wife and her children' and also 'to have good regard to the defence of the said Browne's castle and towns ... against the said murderers and their followers'. the whole episode had a curious sequel, when Walter, the younger brother of Robert, married Isabella, the sister of Brian Kavanagh, who himself married the sister of the man he had killed. This ended the Browne/Kavanagh feud and it also paved the way for the growing sense of solidarity between the Catholic Old English and the Catholic Gaels against the encroachments of the New English Protestants.

The Brownes remained loyal to the Catholic religion after the Reformation. Indeed, there is a tradition that the unsuccessful rebel, Viscount Baltinglass, had been hidden in Mulrankin castle, following his abortive pro-Catholic rising in 1580.[8] Their attempts to reconcile their Catholicism with loyalty to the English crown were fraught with difficulties. The 1630s were not auspicious years for the family, as they made numerous mortgages of their lands to Wexford town merchants — William Keating, Patrick French Thomas Stafford and Walter Wadding.[9] Even more disturbingly, they mortgaged a large part of their estate to Nicholas Rowe, a protestant clergyman, who settled in Bridgetown. The money gained in these transactions was used in making preparations for the forthcoming struggle. In 1641, the Confederate Catholics rose in a powerful rebellion, which was only terminated by Cromwell's brutal campaign. For the first time since their arrival in Wexford, the Brownes found themselves in open rebellion. William Browne financed the raising of a regiment of foot, whose colonel he became, to fight on the side of the confederates in 1641. Two depositions relating to the 1641 rebellion — by William Stafford and Ursula Rowe (wife of his mortgagee, Nicholas Rowe) — clarify his activities during the war.[10] According to Stafford, Browne remained on at Mulrankin after the area had fallen to the Irish and 'did not remove as divers Protestants neere him did, into the English quarters.' Browne also contributed men and arms to the Irish cause, was a member of the county militia, and later colonel of a regiment which took part in the attack on Duncannon. Ursula Rowe reported that Browne's servants (Barnaby Reilly, David Hore, John Rourke), his uncle, Richard, his brother Walter and several of his undertenants had taken up arms. Browne had also reported to Lord Roche in Munster that in the Mulrankin area 'ye English did fly away from their dwellings as fast as bees on a rainy day hasten to their hives'. Browne had sent his uncle and six of his servants to Bridgetown 'who came in a hostyll and violent manner and threatened with pickaxes and irons to break down ye gates' of the castle if they were not immediately admitted. They had seized five stacks of corn in the haggard, one ox and three plough horses. They also threshed the Rowes' corn and carried it away, despite Ursula's protests. When she asked for a small portion of it for her own use, William Browne told her 'she was not well in her wits to demand any such thing'.

William Browne was aged thirty-four in 1641. He fought throughout the campaign until his capture at the Battle of Dungan's Hill in 1647. By breaking his parole, he escaped to France. There are conflicting reports of his subsequent fate, but it seems most likely that he continued to serve Charles II abroad. However, in his absence, the Browne estates were forfeited; his relative, Margaret, was ordered to vacate Mulrankin castle and transplant to Connacht in 1653.[11] Male members of the family had obviously gone into hiding. There is no evidence that any of the Brownes made the long trek to Connacht but the transplantation certificate of 19 December 1653 provides detailed information, which illustrates the large household composition of a mid seventeenth century castle. At this time there were twenty-eight people in the household; the Brownes also had 26 pigs, 23 cows, 22 yearlings, 20 sheep and 8 goats plus 26 acres of winter wheat and 21 acres of summer wheat. The Bridgetown area is still renowned as good fattening land.

According to tradition, John Browne, brother of William, was killed on the stone stairs of Mulrankin castle in 1649, by a party of Cromwellian troops, sent out from Wexford town after the massacre there. His wife, Anne Devereux, give birth to a son, William, in the same year, who was destined to carry on the Browne line, when all other male Brownes had been scattered. The Brownes lost about 2,000 acres by confiscation, including the townlands of Harpoonstown and Mulrankin which were to return later to the family. The bulk of their land was in Mulrankin parish, with a substantial portion in Newbawn (the manor of Colpe) and smaller properties in the Bannow, Taghmon and Kilmore areas dispersed among the different branches.[12] The confiscated lands were parcelled out to Cromwellian soldiers in lieu of wages — William Ivory, John Cliffe and John Ansloe. The astute John Cliffe was Henry Ireton's secretary and bought the debentures of his fellow grantees to ensure his sole ownership of the property. The Cliffes were landlords of Rathronan and Mulrankin until 1903, when they sold it back to the tenants, including Michael Browne, the direct descendant of the pre-Cromwellian occupier. Family tradition held that the Cromwellian families of Grogan and Ivory intermarried with the Browne daughters, to increase their local prestige and acceptability.[13]

When it was taken over by Cliffe, Mulrankin faded into insignificance. The medieval church crumbled and a Protestant church was built on its site in 1777. This was only a token gesture as Protestants were thin on the ground in south Wexford. At the same time, the old Browne vault in which generations of the family had been deposited was demolished, perhaps deliberately.[14] Subsequently, the Brownes were buried in Mayglass cemetery, where an early Catholic chapel had been built.[15] While landowners who converted to Protestantism (like the Codds of Castletown) retained their lands, the Brownes remained steadfastly Catholic.[16] They also assumed a strong sense of their own importance — even in the twentieth century. Local opinion had it that 'the Brownes considered themselves two steps above buttermilk'. No wonder then that Cromwell should feature as a *bête noire* in the family tradition. In a letter written in 1832 by Michael Browne, he is described as 'that monster'.[17] Even two and a half centuries after his visitation, Kathleen Browne bore him and the families associated with him an inveterate, malignant hatred, bordering on bigotry. Under Cromwellian occupancy, Mulrankin faded like many of its neighbours into picturesque insignificance. There were too few planters on the miniscule estates of south Wexford to allow for wholesale remodelling of villages. The Mulrankin area and the barony of Bargy generally, became host to a litany of decayed medieval settlements — Killinick, Bridgetown, Baldwinstown, Mulrankin, Mayglass and Tomhaggard.

The exiled William Browne, despite his allegiance to Charles II, never regained his old property. A 1666 list of dispossessed landowners included him as a person who had continued to serve the king abroad and who was therefore to be restored to 600 acres in Mulrankin.[18] Only two other landowners in Wexford (James Devereux of Ballymagir and Dudley Colclough of Monart) were to be assigned such large estates. William's nephew, also called William, escaped the Cromwellians because of his extreme youth: he was only born in 1649, the year his thirty year old father was killed in Mulrankin castle. His mother died in giving birth to him, and the youngster was reared unmolested among his relatives. As a young man, he was able to obtain a lease of a farm at

Loughgunnan (Mayglass), perhaps as a result of assistance from his mother's family, the Devereuxs of Ballymagir. A Devereux aunt had married into the Neales of Rea house, who survived as small Catholic landowners. William Browne died in 1721 but he was the crucial link across the mid seventeenth century divide, and he was the progenitor of a long line of Browne families in south Wexford. He had five sons and two daughters (who died unmarried). Two sons died young (as was typical in an age of high mortality); his eldest son, William, married and stayed in Loughgunnan; his second son Michael (known as *Mickale* in the yola dialect) settled as a tenant in Harpoonstown ('The Moor'), on land which had been owned by his grandfather. He married Eleanor Cullen of Doonooney (Adamstown) whom family tradition cited as the first person of small stature in the Browne family. William's third son, Patrick, married and settled in Johnstown townland on the Grogan estate. It is possible that there had been an earlier Browne-Grogan marriage and that this accounts for the Brownes getting this lease. Preferential treatment is suggested in the next generation when the Grogans decided to build a demesne in Johnstown; they moved the Brownes to a new farm at Mayglass.[18]

Michael Browne (1690-1767) of Harpoonstown (also called the moor of Mulrankin) subdivided his farm between his two sons, Patrick and James. Their houses, in a typical arrangement, were adjacent, separated only by a garden. Another son John married Catherine Molloy and lived at Bridgetown, again adjacent to Mulrankin castle. John became a shopkeeper and general dealer as well as a farmer. Michael's two daughters married two Rossiter brothers of Ramstown (Fethard), a strategy which was to surface frequently with the Brownes and which cemented strong kinship ties. Similarly his two sons, Patrick and James, both married girls from the townland of Battlestown near Fethard — Anne Devereux and Catherine Barron. Patrick Browne and Anne Devereux had a family of five boys and one girl, which was dispersed in typical fashion. The girl, Anne, was married off to a neighbouring farmer, Murphy of Gibberpatrick. Two of the sons, James (New Ross) and Thomas (Wexford) moved into trade. Two other sons were placed on other farms — Laurence at Ballyell (Lady's Island) and John at Bigbarn (Mayglass). John Browne took over Bigbarn from the Nolan family. In 1803, he was leasing sixty acres (a substantial farm in Bargy terms) at a rent of ninety pounds per annum for twenty years from Rev Edmund Ferrers.[19] In an arranged match, the Bigbarn farm reverted to the Nolans who had moved to Quitchery in the interim.

John Browne was doing well in his general shop in Bridgetown and amassed sufficient money to place his family well. His daughter Mary, was married to Patrick Kelly, a miller at Rathmacknee. An unusual china wedding jug, made in the Chamberlain works at Drinagh, to mark their marriage survives. As well as their names, it bears the inscription 'Long may they live, happy may they be, blest with content and from misfortunes free, and all the family'. Their son, Denis, was to become a Catholic priest, a Newfoundland missioner, and ultimately achieved a reputation as a living saint, 'the hermit of Kilmachree'.[20] The two sons of John Browne, Michael and John, stayed at home in Bridgetown.

John married and had a family of daughters. Michael married Eleanor Whitty and had a son, John (called after his uncle) who inherited the now thriving store in Bridgetown. With money generated from this enterprise. John was able to lease back the family's ancestral property at Rathronan castle, the old *fortalicé* of Mulrankin. This townland had been in the hands of the Protestant Jeffares family as tenants of the Cliffes in the eighteenth century.[21] They had roofed down the castle to align it with the adjacent thatched farmhouse (pl. xlviii).

The final member of Michael of Harpoonstown's family was James (1734-1809), who had inherited half of his father's farm. However, in the next generation the Harpoonstown farm reverted back into single ownership. This had been the only example of subdivision indulged in by the family. James' two sons, Richard and Peter, followed in the family footsteps by marrying the two Kehoe sisters, Ann and Mary, of Fardystown. Richard (1767-1835) the eldest son in this way acquired the Fardystown farm. Peter moved into trade, initially to Wexford as a malster and then Liverpool, which had close links with the Wexford grain trade in the pre-famine period. He was to successfully oversee the transplanting of several nephews into Liverpool, finding them jobs and lodgings, and smoothing their passages.

Plate xlvii: The old farmhouse at Bigbarn c.1940 (now demolished)

The success of the Brownes in placing sons on farms in the eighteenth century was due to a number of factors. One was their tightly controlled marriage strategy, which saw them making astute matches, perhaps aided by the prestige associated with their name. 'Gentleman Browne' of Mulrankin still counted for something in the conservative, localistic world of eighteenth century Forth and Bargy, where status was ascribed rather than achieved. A second factor was the willingness of the Brownes to move into trade and use money generated from it (as at Bridgetown) to finance the acquisition of further advantageous leases. The Brownes, with the short lived exception of Harpoonstown, did not sub-divide their farms, preferring instead to place surplus sons elsewhere. Finally, the eighteenth century was a generally expansive period, in which it was feasible to place sons and daughters in a number of readily accessible niches. All of this was conducive to the spread and consequent consolidation of Browne families in the immediate vicinity of their ancestral heartland at Mulrankin.

Reflecting their cultural conservatism, the Browne houses were mainstream vernacular farmsteads of the south Wexford type — mudwalled, hipped thatched, whitewashed houses, one room deep, with cobbled, courtyard farmyards. In some cases, as at Rathronan, Mulrankin and Fardystown, physical continuity was signalled in the addition of the farmhouse to an older castle (pls. xlv, xlvii). An 1841 description catches the flavour of these Browne houses:

'Their habitations, though built with clay, are neat, cleanly and commodious, plastered with a finer preparation of clay and whitened with lime. It in general consists of two stories, the upper storey lighted by a well-sized casement in the end. Every house has a porch with one or two good windows at each side ... The gables are uniformly hipped, a little higher than is usual to admit a sufficient window in the second floor. To gain the proper headroom, the roof is at a steep pitch, thatched in general with wheaten straw and with as much attention to the neat appearance as to the durable execution of the work. The eaves are made to project considerably and are secured from the ruffling of the wind (as the ridges and hips are also) by scollops forming a fancy border, which gives to the whole a character of skillful workmanship: at the extremities of the roof are placed pinnacles compactly formed of straw, securely roped, of 18 inches high and 12 inches at the base which ... constitute much of the characteristic peculiarity of these buildings[22] (pls. xlvi, xxlvii, xvi, xvii).

The Brownes maintained close ties to the Catholic church as, for example, in the erection of the Catholic chapel on the moor of Mulrankin, on the edge of their farm at Harpoonstown. A portion of the moor, which had been used as a hurling green, was sold off and the proceeds used to erect a small chapel. This association of Catholic big farm (especially one associated with a family who had been seventeenth century landowners) and the location of chapels was highly characteristic of county Wexford.[23] In neighbouring Tomhaggard, an exactly analogous situation existed with the Devereux family and the chapel there.[24] The Brownes were closely connected with the chapel on the moor:

indeed Richard Browne (of Fardystown) who was born there, expressed a death bed wish that his son James (1796-1886) should attend every funeral there — a wish which was fulfilled. Richard's wife, Anne, was a pious woman, with especial devotion to the Franciscan church in Wexford. She joined the Confraternity of the Third Order of Saint Francis there in 1773 — one of twenty-four Browne women to do so in the period 1763-1825. Only two of the menfolk, the brothers Thomas (of Harpoonstown and Wexford) in 1772 and John (of Bigbarn) in 1800 joined but almost all the women did.[25]

As well as piety, the Brownes were noted for their attachment to education. Payments to teachers figure in their farm account books: for example, in 1822, Richard (of Fardystown) paid four shillings and two pence per quarter for the education of his son Patrick by a schoolmaster called Wallace.[26] In the early 1800s the future bishop, James Browne, was sent to the Franciscan academy at Peter Street in Wexford, to be educated at a cost of half a guinea a quarter.[27] While in town, he lodged with his uncle Thomas, the malster. His good education there was to pave the way for a distinguished Maynooth career. Again in the 1820s the young male Brownes of the Fardystown family were sent to Hayes, a surveyor-cum-school teacher for education. When they subsequently emigrated to Liverpool and Buenos Aires, their sound literary skills stood them in good stead.

In the 1798 rebellion, some of the Browne families became involved.[28] Richard Browne of Fardystown was an active rebel, believed to have been one of the captains in the Mulrankin corps. This corps was recruited from the Mulrankin hurling team which played on the green on the Moor, adjacent to the Browne's Harpoonstown farm.[29] Richard fought throughout the campaign, armed with a fowling gun. After the defeat at Bunclody, he was returning to Fardystown, when he was pursued by soldiers, one of whom he shot. While fighting at Horetown, two men were loading his gun, while he was firing it. He was allowed to return to his farm because he was well regarded by the local gentry due to his prowess as a horseman and huntsman. Browne's motivation to fight was that he was only three generations removed from the Browne of Mulrankin who was killed by the Cromwellians on the stairs of his castle. The Brownes would have been regarded as the local heads of the Catholic community. Bishop Browne (of Kilmore) used to relate that his father when young remembered seeing the then representative of the Brownes of Mulrankin 'riding on a grey pony around the parish . . . he was then an old man and much respected by the people' (this would have been Patrick Browne of Harpoonstown).[30] That vestigial respect for the Brownes was still evident in 1798. When the Mulrankin corps were defeated at the battle of Horetown, they returned to the moor and consulted with James Browne (1734-1809), father of Richard, one of their captains.[31] He advised them to give up the fight and disband, which they did. The women of Fardystown made a magnificent patchwork quilt during the rebellion, which was extant until the 1930s.[32] For some of the period, they had to camp out, as their house was being continually raided. Indeed, one son, John, was born in the open air in the orchard at Fardystown as a result.

Meanwhile, Thomas Browne (1757-1838), who had settled at Old Pound House in Wexford town, was also implicated in the rebellion. He owned two malt houses and was affected, like so many others involved in the rebellion, by the changes in malt legislation and the disastrous slump in prices in 1796 and 1797.[33] Browne would have maintained close rural links as a result of his trade in barley and would have shared the resentment building up in Catholic Wexford in the 1790s.[34] He was married to Alice Stafford of Baldwinstown castle, whose family were the eighteenth century representatives of the Staffords of Ballymacane, a family with whom the Brownes had previous marriage links.[35] The forty-one year old Browne was associated with the rebel occupation of Wexford town and especially with Cornelius Grogan, the popular liberal landlord of Johnstown Castle; there had been a number of previous Browne-Grogan linkages. When Grogan and Browne were marched past Browne's house in Main Street on the evening prior to their scheduled execution, his wife Alice held up his daughter Ellen in her arms to have a last look at her father before he was hanged. Browne was reprieved the next morning but Grogan was hanged. His hair turned snow-white the night before he was executed.[36] Thomas Browne was a prominent figure in the re-emerging Catholic community of the town; he was a subscriber to Catholic devotional books, a member of the Third Order of Saint Francis Confraternity, a subscriber to several Catholic charities and executor to Rev Edan Murphy, parish priest of Kilrush (whose mother was a Stafford of Baldwinstown).[37]

The early nineteenth century generations of the Brownes continued to multiply. Michael Browne of the Moor (Harpoonstown) married twice before his death on 2 September 1844. His executor was his brother James, who then lived in Liverpool and later in New Ross. He left his property to his spinster sister Johanna, who lived with him at the Moor, with reversion to his daughter Alice 'and her heirs as long as the generations hold'.[38] Michael had extended his leasehold interests to Lattimerstown, Woodtown and Ballycoppage, as well as his 'lease on the common of the moor of Mulrankin'. Alice married Peter ffrench, later M.P. for south Wexford, who acquired the Harpoonstown farm as a dowry; it thus passed out of the hands of the Brownes after four generations. Thomas, the Wexford town merchant, had a large family. His two sons, Edmund and Patrick, died unmarried, although Patrick, a feckless rake, who was 'encouraged' to leave the country in 1831, had at least three illegitimate children. Edmund became a successful business man in Dublin in partnership with Andrew Carton. He lived at 109, Abbey Street and left £1,081 sterling at his death in 1831.[39] This money went to his uncle, Rev William Stafford, parish priest of Rathmines and builder of the imposing Catholic Church there.[40] Edmund also bequeathed money to look after his illegitimate nephews and left legacies to his sisters as well. As was common in Browne wills, he appointed his priest relatives, Rev William Stafford (uncle) and Rev James Browne (cousin) as executors. His two sisters, Ellen and Alice, married the Synnott brothers, Peter (Pierce) and Walter. The Synnotts were the descendants of yet another family analogous to the Brownes, in that they were descended from the Synnotts of Rosegarland, who had been initially displaced to Clongeen and subsequently to Wexford, where they became involved in the grain and malt trade.[41] Obviously, the double marriage suited both fathers, who were involved in the same trade. Peter (Pierce) Synnott of Summerhill had an extensive corn and malt business, which was wrecked by the Hessian cavalry in 1798.[42] His wife, Catherine Nolan of Bigbarn, was aunt to John Nolan who subsequently married into the Brownes of Bigbarn, cousins of the girls who married her two sons. Peter and Catherine Synnott's son, Pierce, founded the corn business now known as W. J. O'Keefe and Son. His son, William Synnott (1833-1911), was parish priest of Templetown.[43] The second Synnott-Browne couple, Walter and Alice, lived at Baldwinstown castle, inherited through Alice's mother, but died without issue. There were four other girls in Thomas Browne's family: one married a brother (R. Carton) of her brother Edmund's business partner, one became a nun and two others married into Wexford families (Barry and Stafford).

The Ballyell (Broadway) branch of the Brownes lasted three generations. Laurence (1797-1868) was succeeded by his son James (1828-1984), the last of the family. The Bigbarn branch was represented by John (1749-1836) who married Eleanor Rochfort (1758-1802). Their son, Thomas (1788-1792), died at the age of twelve. His only brother, James (1786-1865), became a Catholic clergyman, very surprisingly, as it was usual for an only surviving son to take over the farm.[44] He was educated by the Franciscans in Wexford (with whom the Brownes maintained close ties) before moving to Maynooth College in 1806. After his ordination in 1813, he was appointed curate in Bunclody for two years, before being recalled to Maynooth as junior dean in 1814. He subsequently held the chair of Sacred Scripture (1816) and Hebrew (1818). On 10 June 1827, he was appointed coadjutor bishop to Farrell O'Reilly in Kilmore, with rights of succession. He became bishop on 30 April 1829 and tackled the job with great determination. A big man, weighing seventeen stone, he was well able for the taxing physical demands of administering and visiting a sprawling diocese. When he took over the diocese, it was in disarray, largely due to the inability of the previous bishop to control a clique of O'Reilly priests who informally ran the diocese. Browne, accustomed to the tighter ecclesiastical discipline of Fern's diocese and Maynooth, moved decisively to curtail unruly clerics, put down endemic clerical quarrels, suspended recalcitrant clergy and revitalised the infrastructure of chapels and schools. Simultaneously, he tried to curb the major lay abuses — wake games and membership of illegal societies. He increased the number of priests in Kilmore diocese from 54 in 1822 to 92 in 1865, the year of his death. While applying his episcopal new broom, Browne adroitly avoided controversy, displaying considerable qualities of tact, kindness, firmness and diplomacy. Equally cautiously, he refused to embroil himself in public issues, maintaining a political profile so low as to be practically invisible. He refused to be drawn into, for example, the bitter polemics of the 'New Reformation' period, and won the good opinion of even the heavily evangelical Lord Farnham.

Browne's sense of duty and commitment was remarkable and helped him to successfully apply 'Leinster' standards of church organisation in the *laissez faire* ecclesiastical world of Cavan. Browne was also responsible for switching the diocesan centre of Kilmore from Cootehill to Cavan. In a piece of earlier Wexford chauvinism, he had described Cavan town as 'not much larger than Taghmon'. The acquisition of a permanent episcopal residence, the building of a new cathedral and the founding of Kilmore Academy in 1839 all cemented Cavan's role as a diocesan centre.

Although based in Maynooth and Cavan, James Browne maintained close links with his Wexford family. In 1820 he was appointed sole executor or the will of his father, John Browne, for whom he had already invested eight hundred and seventy nine pounds in Government stock.[45] He was also given exclusive control over arranging the marriages of his sisters, whose dowries of £258 were to be cut to one shilling 'if they should transgress before marriage or marry contrary to the consult of Revd James Browne.' His son was also given sixty pounds to look after his funeral expenses.

John Browne's farm at Bigbarn, in the absence of a farming son to whom to transfer it, passed to John Nolan of Quitchery via an elaborate marriage settlement of 1814.[46] Browne, on foot of the intended marriage of his daughter Alice to John Nolan, agreed to pass the lease of Bigbarn to his future son-in-law for a sum of £200, while retaining half of the land (60 acres) during the rest of his life, with reversion to Nolan. He also agreed to pass over all stock, furniture and chattels to him. If Alice died childless within two years, Nolan was to give up the lease and receive a gratuity of £300. Alice's sisters, Ann, Judith and Margaret, were to have rights of residence at Bigbarn and were also 'to be dieted, clothed, educated and supported' until their marriage. All three did subsequently marry — Judith to a Busher of neighbouring Couzenstown,

Plate xlviii: Rathronan Castle

Margaret to Ellard of Carne and Anne to a Michael Furlong. John Nolan (1784-1848) by virtue of his marriage to Alice Browne (1794-1840) took over the Bigbarn farm, which thus reverted to the Nolan family who had previously held it. However, John and Alice experienced severe financial problems in managing the property, more especially as a result of a financial guarantee to local builders, the Days of Gollough, which was lost when that firm went broke. The Days were an influential local family who built the Catholic chapel in Kilmore in 1801.[47] However, a financial rescue package was put together by Bishop James Browne of Kilmore, who stayed in Bigbarn for two weeks every summer because Alice was his favourite niece.

On foot of this package, the Bigbarn property eventually reverted back to Browne control. Alice and John's two daughters, Eleanor and Kate, both died young in 1848. Bigbarn passed through the hands of the other Browne bishop (James of Ferns, 1846-1917), from him to his unmarried brother Richard (*ob.* 1904) and sister Mary (*ob.* 1925), from them to their unmarried nieces Teresa (*ob.* 1966) and Jack (*ob.* 1963), and from them to their brother Bernard. His son, Michael Browne, now farms the property, which consists of about 240 acres. The current slated dwelling house of Bigbarn was built c. 1850 by the Bishop of Kilmore: the older thatched farmhouse was demolished in recent times, although photographs of it survive (pl. xlvii) Relics of Bishop Browne preserved in the house include a fine portrait in oils, correspondence, his chalice and pix, and a small oratory.[48]

The Bridgetown branch of the family were represented in the nineteenth century by Michael (*ob.* 1830) who married Eleanor Whitty (*ob.* 1877). In what was obviously an arranged match, John married a distant cousin, Catherine Browne (*ob.* 1880) daughter of Richard Browne of Fardystown. John's grocery and hardware shop in Bridgetown was a thriving concern and in 1851 he was able to lease 227 acres of the Browne's ancestral land at Rathronan (held by them in the seventeenth century and earlier) from the Cliffes, the family who had displaced them. However, the Cliffes did not stay long at Rathronan moving first to Dungulph Castle (pl. xxxi) and then to Bellevue, the old Ogle property. It would appear that John Browne was very deliberately reclaiming what he would have perceived as the Browne patrimony. He was an enterprising man and Rev William Hickey provides a detailed account of his activities at Rathronan:

> In 1851, Mr Browne became tenant to Mr Cliffe of 227 acres at Rathronan, near Bridgetown. This farm was then in a very bad condition, the greater part being very wet and productive only of bad harbages, rushes and abundance of furze. Of this, 148 acres were drained by the landlord under the provision of the drainage act and subsequently 68 acres by the tenant, of which a great part was redraining, the first operation having partially failed. Mr Browne, by constant attention, outlay of capital and the application of lime in the proportions of about sixty barrels to an acre has rendered this land very productive, though much yet remains to be done in draining. His rotations are (i) wheat on lea, limed; (ii) oats; (iii) green crops; (iv) barley; (v)

meadow; (vi) pasture. His stock consists of 9 horses, 14 milch cows, 15 two year olds, 12 yearlings, 68 sheep and 25 pigs. He employs 13 male labourers constantly (most of them receiving diet in his farmhouse) and 5 women and is considered a very kind and satisfactory employer, neither changing his labourers nor captiously finding faults with them. The progressive, improving quality of his farm is very obvious. Mr Browne has, in addition, a small farm (at Bridgetown) of better quality and more easily cultivated.[49]

In 1903, under the provisions of the Wyndham Land Act, John's son, Michael, bought the fee simple of Rathronan from the Cliffes. His daughter, Margaret, married Michael Hassett, son of a doctor in Bridgetown, who eventually acquired Rathronan. Their son Daniel Hassett sold Rathronan in 1985 to his cousin Hyacinth Browne, a well known Dublin surgeon, and a grandson of Michael Browne. The atmospheric house at Rathronan (pl. xlvii) therefore still remains in the possession of the Browne family, as it has done for centuries.

Like other mixed farms in south Wexford with a high tillage component, the Browne farms absorbed a good deal of local labour in pre-mechanical days. The close relationship between the farmer and his labourers tantalisingly recalls earlier arrangements. One wonders if many of the characteristics of the farmer/labourer relationship in the arable southeast were directly inherited from the medieval world. The pattern, for example, whereby labourers were 'dieted' in the house and slept in the byres and barns may recall the pattern in the towerhouse, where the labourers probably lived in the bawn.[50] The paternalistic, autocratic side of the relationship may also mirror an earlier form of social organisation. An example is Judy Sinnott (née Redmond) of Ballysheen who went to work for Richard Browne in Fardystown at the age of 27 in 1809, where she remained until her death in 1889 at the age of 107. She was a woman of massive strength who could lift an eighteen stone sack from the ground and place it on her shoulder without assistance. Richard and Anne Browne were parents of 14 children, many of whom she nursed. Her account for 1815 with the Brownes survives. She was illiterate and depended totally on her employers for money.

'Agreed with Judy Redmond from May 1st 1815 for £3.6.8
Sept. 2nd for a pair of soles, 10d.
Oct. 2nd for to go to the ball at Lynches, 10d [probably a mummer's ball]
Nov 1 going to the fair, 10 shillings.
Nov. 23 going to the barony of Forth, 6d.
   to buy a rack [comb], 5d.
   to pay a weaver, 5 shillings.
   for brogues and tacks, 3 shillings and eight pence.
   to buy a coat, £1.

The large family of the Fardystown branch of the Brownes was dispersed all over the globe. One of the seven sons, Peter (the last born, when his mother was close to fifty years old) died at the age of three. When the others were in their teens, they were allocated all over the globe, with the exception of Martin, the eldest, who was to inherit Fardystown. A later letter of his explains the situation. 'We were six young boys then. Two of us went to Buenos Aires, two to Liverpool, one to New York and I stopped at home, working the farm and they all assisted me in paying off the arrears'.[51] These arrears had accumulated in the bad years after the post-Napoleonic collapse in agricultural prices. The first of the young Brownes to go to Liverpool was Michael, who was sent to the care of his uncle Peter. On 17 May 1819, he wrote back to his mother:

'We left the first place we went to and went to another which happened to be Catholic and we like this pretty well. We pay 4 shillings a week for our lodging and about 1 shilling and 2 pence for washing. We mostly have bread and milk for our breakfast and bacon or a bit of fresh beef for our dinner and bread and milk for our supper which is common diet here and we must do as they do here or we would be taken notice of as the Irish are watched so closely'.[52]

Michael got a job in a warehouse due to his uncle's contacts; here he worked from 6 a.m. to 9 p.m. six days a week, supervising the movement of material, mostly cotton, in and out of the warehouse. His employers were involved in the Dublin and Brazil trade. He was soon joined by his brother John, who got a similar warehouse job, with less responsibility, less pay and less hours (7 a.m. — 7 p.m.). In 1828, Michael's wages were 16 shillings a week.[53]

In Liverpool, the Brownes were part of a well established Wexford colony, which even had its own public house in which to socialise. They also maintained close ties to Wexford via the shipping which passed frequently between the two ports; regular news was sent back to Fardystown of the price of cattle, grain and beans. When a Wexford ship was lost at the harbour mouth in 1820, the four drowned men '(Philip Walsh of Knockrooth, Walsh the cooper of Slippery Green, Pierse of Rathaspeck and Old Leary, the butcher)' were waked and buried from the Wexford public house at its owner's expense.[54] Wexford sea captains, in particular, were the vehicles of contacts. However, the Brownes found that a bustling colonial port of Liverpool's stature was a tough challenge. Michael Browne wrote to his mother on 31 March 1823:

It takes nearly a man's lifetime to be up to the villainy of this place. I often heard it said that certain persons would take the coat off your back but here they would take the shirt and skin too if possible'.[55]

A third son, Patrick, went to Liverpool in 1822 at the age of sixteen. His uncle Peter (whose wife Mary was a sister of Patrick's mother) got him a job in the firm of Dickson, Montgomery and Company, import and export merchants, who had branches in Valparaiso and Buenos Aires. In 1824 he and his brother, Laurence, decided to join the substantial Forth and Bargy colony in Buenos Aires, sailing in the brig *Cossack* of Whitehaven. According to their brother, Michael, in a letter to their parents, 'on board the ship they had about 2 gallons of spirits, 2 or 3 bottles of port wine, a dozen bottles of ale, and a dozen large bottles of preserved fruits'. They had also 'taken a famous stock of books

especially religious and my aunt has loaded Patrick with Religious books'.[56]
The ship foundered just at the entrance to Monte Video harbour and Patrick
Browne arrived eventually in Buenos Aires aged eighteen and with only 'the
clothes that he stood in' as possessions. However, Laurence and Patrick both
did well in Argentina, married Irish girls, and had large families (in Patrick's
case, thirteen). Their cousin, John, later joined them in Argentina and also
married an Irish girl, Anne Salmon from Mullingar.

The Brownes developed their own *estancia* mainly for sheep farming. John,
however, also became a banker, a director of the Primitiva Bag Company, a
director of the Buenos Aires railway and the Lacroza Tramway Company, as
well as several other enterprises. While some of the Brownes did intermarry
with Argentinians, most of the first generation settlers had Irish wives, thus
maintaining the cohesiveness of the Irish colony there. However, by the third
generation, the balance switched in favour of Argentinian wives. Yet, contact
is even still maintained with Ireland. Argentinian Brownes are well known at
the Curragh and Goff's bloodstock sales; many of their children were sent to
school at Mount St Mary's College near Chesterfield and some were also
educated at the Convent of the Faithful Companions of Jesus in Bunclody.

Meanwhile, the Fardystown farm encountered difficulties in the post-
famine period. By 1858, its landlord, Walter Redmond, was trying to raise the
rent, with the aid of his agent, a solicitor from Wexford called Hogan. The
farm then consisted of 86 acres and Redmond wanted to increase the rent from
14 shillings to one pound an acre, and give a new lease of only 21 years.[57] James
Browne (who was then running it) thought that 'a pound an acre is a high
rent', because the land still required massive improvement, and that a lease of
31 years at least was necessary to justify the expenditure on reclamation. At
the same time, he felt that 'to walk out on it would be hard after spending a
century making improvements on it without ever getting one shilling out of
it'.[58] James wished to borrow money to pay his arrears and regretted the death
of his clerical relative Fr Patrick Keating 'who would have assisted me if he had
lived'.[59] In a fervent plea to Redmond, he argued that :

> 'We always thought it hard to go out of it after doing so much work on it,
> making all the ditches of every kind and making shores in the greater part
> of it. There is upwards of £1,500 worth of our own labour in it. When my
> grandfather commenced it was a commons and my father and myself
> brought it to a farm of land from land covered with bushes, heath, bogs and
> rocks'.[60]

However, on James' death in 1886, Fardystown passed out of the possession
of the Brownes.

As well as the seven Fardystown boys, there were seven girls: Margaret, like
her brother Peter, died as an infant in 1810; Catherine married her cousin John
Browne of Bridgetown; Mary (1803-1888), Anne (1807-1886) and a second
Margaret (1812-1886) all died unmarried, perhaps reflecting the difficulty of
settling such a large family. Mary, however, had a shop bought for her in 1840
in Murntown, which had belonged to Nicholas Harris, at a cost of £107.[61] The

money was borrowed from John of Bridgetown (his son had married Mary's sister), 'as we have no money ourselves to manage the affair'.[62] There was a slated dwelling house, a thatched bake house and a small yard involved. Mary ran a busy shop here. She also lodged the local priest. Eventually tongues began to wag in the area and Mary found herself forced to defend herself. She wrote a letter to her relative, Bishop James Browne, asking him to quell the rumours being propagated by some priests of the diocese, or she would be forced to take action:

'When Fr John Keating was curate in this parish, he lived in my house. When he left to go to Mt. Melleray — retiring from the mission — people said he had been suspended and according to rumour "I was the cause of it". I must deny this. I never knew he was suspended'.[63]

Her sister Ellen had married James Keating of Dennstown, the priest's brother. The Keatings of Dennstown were the descendants of the seventeenth century Keatings of Kilcowan and so this marriage represented yet another careful matching of like with like in the Browne marriage strategy. In Mary's old age, she received a letter (20 November, 1886) from Rev Laurence Cosgrove, a Franciscan friar in Wexford:

'My dear Mary, I hope you will not consider me taking too much liberty in requesting you to make your will and to leave whatever you will die possessed of to your good sister's children, Thomas and Peter Keating. It is the very best charity you can give and I would say you are bound in justice to leave it to them and I think you could not receive the last sacraments if you gave it away from them'.[64]

Mary heeded the friar's advice and the shop passed to Thomas Keating of Dennstown.[65] Her sister's marriage produced fourteen children, of whom two (Patrick and George) became priests and two (Anne and Margaret) became nuns — perhaps representing a handy solution to the problems of disposing of a large family of sons and daughters in the constricted circumstances of the nineteenth century. While Rev George died aged only 27, Rev Patrick Keating became a Franciscan. His uncle Patrick Keating had been a parish priest in Murntown, where he had been very helpful to the Browne families.

The final member of the Moor (Mulrankin) family was Peter (*ob.* 1829) who had married a sister of his brother's wife. While his elder brother, Richard, acquired the leasehold of Fardystown by this arrangement, Peter moved to Wexford town. By so doing, he allowed the Moor farm (which had been split in the previous generation between his father James and his uncle Patrick) to be re-assembled as one unit in the hands of his cousin, Michael. In Wexford town, Peter was initially involved in the then thriving malting barley trade, owning a malt house.[66] Subsequently, he moved to Liverpool where he became involved in shipping and the port's trade to the Americas. He looked after his young cousins when they came to Liverpool. He had himself a family of five: his grandson, George, became a Catholic priest on the English mission, thus maintaining the Browne's traditionally close ties to the Catholic Church. The

Liverpool Brownes maintained their interest in Wexford; Richard's son, John, and Peter's son (another John) both subscribed to Thomas Cloney's *Personal Narrative*.[67]

The Moor families who descended from Michael Browne (1698-1747) were those of Harpoonstown, Wexford, Ballyell, Bigbarn, Bridgetown, Rathronan, Fardystown, Buenos Aires and Liverpool. A collateral branch descended from Michael's brother, Patrick, who settled in Johnstown Deerpark, possibly as a result of his marriage with Anastasia Codd. He is buried in Rathaspeck. When Johnstown Castle demesne was being created in the mid eighteenth century by the Grogans, the family was relocated to Mayglass, where his son John (who married a Pettit) received a farm. John was succeeded by Michael Browne who married Anne Cardiff; their son, another Patrick, married Margaret Barry (of the Poulrane family). They had a large family of nine children. Of these James Browne (1842-1917) was the most famous, becoming bishop of Ferns diocese from 1884 to 1917. He was ordained in Maynooth in 1865 and appointed to St Peter's College.[68] He subsequently was moved to Barntown as curate, then to Wexford town and finally elevated to parish priest of Piercetown in 1880. As a bishop, he kept a low profile. Ecclesiastically, he was a typical Cullenite bishop, strong on organisation and discipline. For example, in a series of letters to the administrator of Rowe Street parish in 1909, he set out a punishing daily programme. They were to rise at 6.15 a.m., to be followed by one hour's meditation. They were then to be available to hear confession. At 9 a.m. the clergy were to meet and recite the Rosary. At 2 p.m. the office was to be said in common.[69]

Three of the bishop's sisters, Margaret, Mary and Agnes, did not marry; neither did his brother Richard. His brothers George and John and his sister, Anne Marie married. His brother Michael married Margaret Codd of Mulrankin Castle[70] and had a large family of six sons and four daughters (pl. xlv). Two sons, Patrick and Bernard, shared Ballysheen farm, before it was sold by Patrick. Bernard then moved to Bigbarn. In a made match, a sister, Margaret, married Garrett Cloney of Old Ross, whose family had also extensive clerical connections. There was no issue from this marriage and Garrett died in 1949, leaving the Old Ross mill and farm to his widow. When Patrick sold Ballysheen in the 1940s, he went to live with his sister in Old Ross, where he died in 1956. Because there was no issue from the Old Ross marriage, and no available Cloney nephew, John T. Browne, a Bigbarn nephew, went to live with the couple in the 1940s. In 1956, when Patrick died, Margaret signed over the property in Millquarter to her nephew and retired to Bigbarn (where she died in 1973 aged 94). John T. married his Old Ross neighbour, Eithne Rochford in the same year. His son, Bernard is co-author of this article.

Bernard Browne (1886-1976), the senior member of the Bigbarn family, was politicised through his early involvement in the Gaelic revival, being a founder member of St Fintan's football club, a member of the Gaelic League in Wexford town, and finally of the Irish Republican Brotherhood (I.R.B.) in 1903. He and his brother Jim were involved in a business in North Main Street, Wexford (where Joyce's hardware shop is now), before he went to farm at

Ballysheen and later Bigbarn (which he acquired from his unmarried brother and sister, Teresa and Jack). Bernard took part in the occupation of Enniscorthy in May, 1916 and was subsequently active in flying columns in Munster during the period up to 1921. After the treaty was signed in 1921, he would involve himself in no further political groups, on the grounds that he would not fight other Irishmen. He and his well known relative, Kathleen A. Browne, never spoke again after this decision, as she took a strong pro-treaty line. He believed that when negotiations began in London in 1921 the ideal for which he fought, a United Republican Ireland, was gone. He felt that the Irish delegation was tricked in the negotiations and that Britain deliberately fomented the Civil War. He had strong views on de-anglicising Ireland and felt that the country lost its national identity when nothing was done to restore the Irish language. While some felt that the G.P.O. in 1916 was the cradle of the new Republic, Bernard Browne felt that after the execution in May 1916 it was our coffin, in which was placed the flower of the new Ireland.[71]

The Bridgetown/Rathronan branch of the family were represented in the later nineteenth century by Michael Browne (*ob.* 1912) son of John and Catherine. He married his cousin Mary Stafford of Baldwinstown castle (just as his parents has been cousins). The Brownes had a previous connection with Baldwinstown castle through the marriage of Alice Stafford to Thomas Browne (of Harpoonstown and Wexford). Their daughter Alice Browne had married Walter Synnott and occupied Baldwinstown castle; as there was no issue from this marriage, the castle and farm reverted back to the Staffords. The Staffords were the nineteenth century representatives of the Staffords of Ballymacane, a family exactly equivalent in status and history to the Brownes of Mulrankin castle. Michael Browne of Bridgetown was an active and capable politician at local level in the post famine years. He was an early member of the county Wexford Independent Club; he was involved in the Tenant League, and later the Land League; he was an active Redmondite.[72] In 1898, he was elected to the first ever Wexford county council, thus emulating the role of his ancestors as political representative of his area and people. He had earlier been a Poor Law Guardian for Wexford Union. Michael Browne was especially prominent in promoting the welfare of the numerous agricultural labourers of Wexford county. He ensured that the provisions of the labourer's acts were fully implemented and he was one of the main reasons why so many labourers cottages were built in the Wexford Union area to a high quality design and finish.[73] The respect in which he was held by the agricultural labourers was demonstrated at his funeral in 1912. 'A large body of labourers attended the funeral and were insistent that they should carry the remains of the lamented deceased to the church, he being the warmest friend of that class'.[74] Michael Browne's status in the community was reflected by the presence of two hundred carriages and twenty-eight priests at his funeral. His grave was one of the first in Wexford to have a gaelic inscription, reflecting his involvement in the cultural revival of the early twentieth century.

The most famous of Michael's children was the redoubtable termagant Kathleen A. Browne (1878-1963), although it also included Richard, a priest

who died as chaplain to the nuns in Loftus Hall in 1950. His sister Kathleen
was educated locally and at convent school in Wexford. She joined Sinn Féin
and became prominently associated with the work of Arthur Griffith for
fifteen years. She was secretary of the Gaelic League in Wexford and became
involved with the Irish Volunteers in the 1914-1922 period. After flying a
tricolour from the roof of Rathronan Castle at Easter 1916, she was arrested
and jailed in Mountjoy, along with her close friend Nell Ryan of Tomcoole.
However, she joined the Free State side during the Civil War and Nell and
herself never spoke again. Kathleen Browne became a member of the Senate
from 1929 to 1938, making many contributions on cultural and agricultural
issues. At this stage, she was a prominent member of Cumann na nGaedhal.

Plate xlix: Kathleen A. Browne

Later, she joined the Blueshirts and gained notoriety for wearing her own blue blouse in the Senate. A hard, uncompromising, dogged individual, she had tunnel vision and refused to acknowledge any merit in her opponent's views. She was self opinionated and self righteous and alienated many of her family, her neighbours and her erstwhile friends, especially after the Civil War.

However, she did have an abiding interest in history and became an acknowledged expert on Wexford in particular and her family also. Indeed, it is her transcripts of documents since destroyed in the Record Office fire, and her diligence in assembling a family archive which allow the Mulrankin Brownes to be thoroughly documented. She was committed to the romantic nationalism of the early twentieth century, liking to be photographed with an Irish wolf-hound while wearing her 'Celtic' dress, (pl. xlix). Her committee work in historical circles included the Uí Cinnsealaigh Historical Society, the Royal Society of Antiquaries of Ireland, and the Society for the Preservation of the Memorials of the Dead. She was the prime mover in having the Great Saltee island created a bird sanctuary in 1938. Kathleen Browne also wrote numerous newspaper articles (including a fine series on the castles of county Wexford and their associated families) on Wexford history. She was an expert on the Yola dialect and wrote what must be the last ever letter to be written in it (appendix 1).

The Browne family illustrates a number of key points in Wexford history. Their rapid expansion in the four or five generations after the Cromwellian dislocation illustrate how a sense of grievance and of historic resentment could be diffused widely in a short period of time (fig. 17.1). This sense of belonging to an old landholding elite was a key component of the ideology of the farming class of south Wexford in the eighteenth and nineteenth centuries; it was one of the main sources of their cultural cohesiveness and fostered a sense of pride which allowed them to take on and ultimately dismantle the newer land-owning regime in the area. The Brownes were not unique in their ability to maintain position and power in their own area in the eighteenth century, despite the loss of landownership status; indeed a perusal of their marriage strategy shows that they married into other families in a similar position — the Keatings of Dennstown, the Staffords of Baldwinstown, the Synnotts of Summerhill, the Devereuxs of Battlestown.[75] Their ability to disperse family members by marriage, emigration or movement into trade was consistent and helped to maintain their farms at a competitive size. Astute use of the kinship network strengthened and consolidated the family's economic, social and cultural position. Their stress on the value of education and of close allegiance to the Catholic Church were also noteworthy and dovetailed neatly with family strategy.[76] In this way, the Brownes were a quintessential Catholic big farm family of a type which proliferated in south Wexford in the post-Cromwellian period; their committment to Catholicism was no doubt accentuated by their opposition to the new, almost uniformly Protestant, landowners of the area. Ultimately, the Brownes were to regain control and ownership of at least some of their ancestral lands — one of the most remarkable achievements in Wexford in the three centuries following the Cromwellian upheaval.

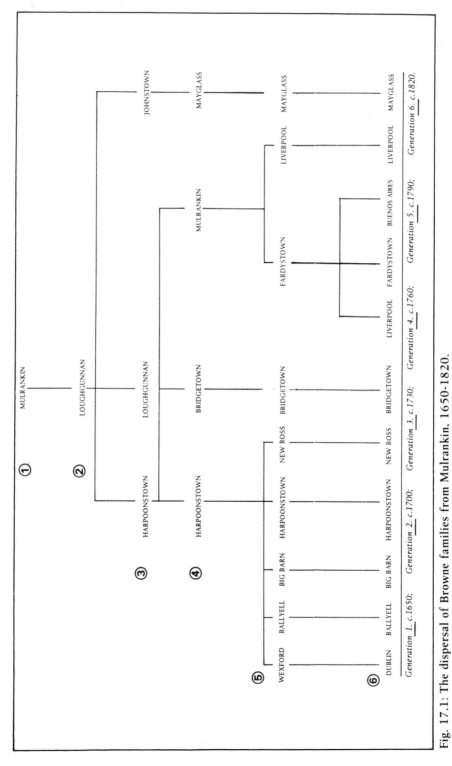

Fig. 17.1: The dispersal of Browne families from Mulrankin, 1650-1820.

Appendix 1

Letter in Yola dialect from Kathleen Browne (1893)
Burstheoune, Avril 10, 1893
Vourneen Joan,
    'cham goan hend a sparkeen wough theezil, ing oure yola talk o' Baronie Forthe. Fan yartha goane t'yie ons hyme zwae?. Gee o gooude riesph to ee ball an Vreedie nyeght an zend up ee score ower varty an than drink a heall ing yooure usquebaugh to ercha vriend o' livertie. Fan thyme yurae be coome w'oul maake a teoune yn Ballygeary an hoave oure Parliament houze thaare. 'cham glaude t'zee ee Redmondites epealtheen aan-anooree yn Dublin. Thommeen Healy beeth a quiel-laaune, mot av hea goe maake gaaume o' thee Chaungher ee lugges an hollybulkaane 'em. 'Cham youreen baarich an dicke arraugh curthere be zo thyne. Ich well no leiangh aany valler. Zo heoll, grien an kin apaa thee,
An chan,
Yer vriende,
Kealeen Browne.

Translation
Bridgetown, April 20, 1893

Dear Joan [female personification of Ireland]
    I am going to speak with you in our old Barony Forth dialect. When are you going to come home to us? Give a good stroke to the ball on Friday night and send up the score [of pro-nationalists M.P.s] over forty and then drink a health in your own whiskey to every friend of liberty. When that time will come, we'll make a town in Ballygeary and have our Parliament House there. I am glad to see the Redmondites fighting with one another in Dublin. Tim Healy is a smart lad, asking if they are going to make a laugh of you, pulling their ears and ridiculing themselves. I am sowing barley this spring season: as it is fine, I will not idle any further, so health, good weather and regards to you.

I am, your friend,
Kathleen Browne.

Acknowledgement

We would like to thank John T. Browne, Michael Browne, Tomás Hayes, Pat Sills and Seán Cloney for their assistance.

18 *John De Courcy Ireland*

County Wexford in Maritime History

Wexford's long coastline, off which two important seas meet, has decisively shaped its history and the county's agriculture has always been influenced by proximity to the sea. Similarly, the county's rich and diverse maritime past has played a major role in the unfolding of its history.

Since Ireland has been an island since the closing stage of the last Ice Age, it is evident that all the varied strains that make up the Irish people must have come here over the sea. While it is true that the present state of our arch-aeological knowledge does not suggest that the country's very first inhabitalts settled in Wexford, and also that a few of the first dwellers might have come from elsewhere in Ireland overland — but much more likely in skin-boats or dugout canoes along the coast — it is certain that very early in the country's pre-history people came to Wexford county across the sea. These were the first to sow the seeds in this corner of Ireland that was to flower into the great tradition that has produced Ambrose Sutton of Clonard, a hero of the greatest French voyage of discovery of the eighteenth century; his contemporary Bates (of Kilmore) who piloted the corsair Thurot up the Irish Sea; John Barry of Ballysampson considered to be the 'father' of the navy of the United States; John O'Neill, first marine superintendent of the sadly defunct Irish Shipping Limited, under whom it prospered; the astonishing *M.V. Kerlogue* episode of December 1943, and the career of that prince among the unsurpassedly brave and skilful county Wexford lifeboatmen, Dick Walsh of Rosslare Lifeboat Station.

Bowen argues that even in Mesolithic times there was maritime contact between the Irish Sea and the west coast of what is now France. If so, the daring seamen making these occasional voyages to and fro can hardly have failed to touch county Wexford. In Neolithic times, 'the grey waters of the Irish Sea were as bright with Neolithic argonauts as the Western Pacific is today'.[1] The Wexford coast unquestionably provided landfalls and departure points for frequent voyages. Settlements were made in the Saltees despite the navi-

490

gational problems in reaching them. In the Bronze Age, the Wexford coast continued to be the point of arrival of influences, artefacts, seafaring families and individuals from Britain and the Continent; some at least of the local coastal dwellers must have crossed the sea themselves in these exchanges.[2]

By the time Celtic speaking people were established here, the coastal areas of the county were evidently well populated and known on the Continent, as is clear from the survey of the Greek geographer Ptolemy in the second century A.D. He identified Carnsore Point as 'the Sacred Cape' and the inhabitants of this corner of Ireland as the *Brigantes* a much travelled and undoubtedly seafaring people, known also in the coastal region of Britain between the Humber and the Firth of Forth, and in the Netherlands. By now, possibly as a direct consequence of communication with the seagoing *Veneti* more or less due south in what is now southern Brittany, quite sophisticated wooden ships were being built in Ireland (still very widely and thickly forested). Maps suggest the participation of the Wexford coast in the voyages of 'saintly scholars' in the period called the Irish 'Golden Age', which was certainly a golden age of Irish navigation.[3]

By the tenth century Scandinavian seafarers were well established in the one-time land of the Hibernian *Brigantes* and were introducing a powerful new maritime element into the local population. It was these seafarers who, noting the shelter offered by the lower reaches of the Slaney for raiders by sea, developed earlier plundering expeditions into later sophisticated commercial operations and founded a permanent settlement on the southern bank of the estuary. Although the estuary is not technically a fjord, it resembled one sufficiently for them to give it a name that has survived — *Waesfjord*, the fjord of the mudflats. There was clearly an economic transformation when unprotected monastic establishments whose inmates drew their boats ashore alongside their buildings were transformed into walled towns with quays for the loading and discharging of shipping.

Scandinavian Wexford developed into an independent maritime statelet whose ships and seafarers initiated innumerable voyages, partly commercial, partly aggressive, particularly in the direction of Wales, and participated in very many others, some of which went across the Bay of Biscay and along the coast of Iberia. By the second half of the twelfth century, Wexford was a flourishing seaport town now engaged almost wholly in maritime trade, and also as a port of embarkation or disembarkation for travellers, especially on the age-old routes between southeast Ireland and south Wales.

At this stage yet another maritime element was injected into the area that was soon to be designated as the county of Wexford. Five Gallo-Norman expeditions sailed in 1169-70 over the 135-odd kilometres from Pembroke to land twice in Bannow Bay and once each near Baginbun Point, at Wexford and near Duncannon. The Hiberno-Norse had long abandoned the warlike *drakkar* or 'longship' for the *knorr*, the standard North European cargo ship of the early Middle Ages. The possibility of keeping a fleet of twelfth century warships on constant patrol against the hazard of an invasion did not exist.

It is clear that the locations chosen by the newcomers for their landings were well selected, on the advice of experienced seamen. Evidently, too, the mariners in charge of the expeditions were at least as expert as those who just over a century before had guided William the Conqueror's incursions across the narrower stretch of sea that divides the mouth of the Somme from Pevensey Beach. Only two ships of William's big armada were lost (from overloading). None was lost in 1169, and there is no mention of losses in the 1170 expeditions either.

Gallo-Norman ship types evolved from Norse prototypes. Fitzstephen's and Prendergast's ships were without doubt beached quite easily once the right place and conditions were secured, as they were of shallow draught and comparatively flat-bottomed. Their warriors, horses and stores were then discharged. The real achievement of this new generation of Wexford seafarers lay in their sound choice of locations and times to land, dependent on their observation of tidal and meteorological conditions, and in their skilful manoeuvering of their ships past perilous hazards to safe sands. We shall never know if, when or how often these seamen had visited Bannow or Baginbun before.

The Gallo-Normans of 1169 and 1170 had no charts, no written navigational aids, no compasses, buoys, lightships or lighthouses (though it seems that before long monks were to keep a nightly beacon burning on Hook Head); charts were four and a half centuries ahead, written sailing instructions for the Irish Sea three centuries off, and, though the Chinese had long known the compass, it reached the Mediterranean only in the mid-twelfth century, and North Europe not for perhaps another hundred years. These sailors would have been lucky if they sighted the Hook Peninsula in under 24 hours and would have spent hours at sea, even in May, in darkness in ships steered by clumsy steering oars over the starboard (steerboard) quarter. The sandy south Wexford coast is not as it was then (heavy coastal erosion is a constant factor in Wexford maritime history) but the sand shifted in the same treacherous way, and the Keeragh Islands, the rocky ledges near them, Selskar Rock and Brecaun Bridge were hazards. Those twelfth century pilots certainly kept their eyes skinned, as Neolithic, Bronze Age and Celtic speaking Irish mariners had previously done, for shoal water and other dangers. They had confidence in the structure and the manoeuverability of their vessels and in their own ability to choose the right stretch of sand to beach on and the right moment of wind and tide for the beaching.

Their arrival accelerated the progress of the county's maritime economy, already lively through the *knorrs* of the Hiberno-Norse of Wexford town. Fish was being exported from Wexford to the Bristol Channel in 1171. From then on throughout the Middle Ages, an unfolding story is revealed of constant maritime activity, both in shipbuilding, merchant seafaring and sea fishing, by the people of Wexford town, now a chartered borough. Late in the thirteenth century, New Ross also obtained a charter and developed quickly to challenge Waterford, then the country's leading port, for supremacy. As early as 1301 Ross was able to provide King Edward I with a 70 ton ship, *Sancte Dieu*, the eighth largest of twenty seven hired or requisitioned for participation in an expedition to Scotland.[4] The rivalry between Ross and Waterford became so intense that in 1318 the Mayor of Waterford 'with many Spaniards, Frenchmen, Bretons and Irish came riotously with a fleet of boats and ships' on a piratical raid to assault the leading maritime town of Wexford county.[5] Ross exported hides, tallow, woolfells, rugs, friezes, barrel-staves, grain and salmon among other commodities. As early as 1265 it had strong town walls and a network of active craft guilds engaged in manufacture (including ship-building) as indeed had also Wexford. According to Burke, 'at the dawn of the fifteenth century Ross was regarded as the most important of the Irish ports being twice as important as Waterford which was second to it'.[6] Ships from Ross regularly visited Bordeaux for wine in the fourteenth century.

Well into the sixteenth century, exports of fish from Wexford town and New Ross became more and more important. Above all it was for herrings that the Wexford sea fishermen went out. In January 1566, Patrick Furlong of Wexford unloaded herring at Chester, and in February the *George* of Wexford discharged there eighteen barrels of white herring and 10,000 red herring. Two weeks later the *John* of Wexford brought to Chester thirty barrels of white herring and 10,000 red herring.[7] As late as 1588, Bristol imported fifty haddock (for 1/8d) from Ross and in 1591 'two burdens of codfish' from Wexford.[8]

In the middle of the sixteenth century Ireland began to import coal on a large scale and for a time the Welsh coal trade to Ireland was principally in Wexford vessels, which have been surmised to be specimens of the famous Wexford cot, one of the longest lived and most seaworthy of all the traditional craft of north-west Europe. It is virtually certain that the thirty-five (of only fifty-five) Irish ships that brought Irish exports to the distant and not easily accessible Somerset port of Bridgewater in 1560-1 were cots. Their cargoes were fish, hides, cloths, boards and re-exported French salt and 'corrupt' wine. Of fifty-eight ships carrying imports to Ireland from Bridgewater in the same period, thirty-six were Wexford ships and four Ross-owned. It is interesting that of 731 wolf skins imported from Ireland to Bristol in 1558, 101 were shipped out of New Ross.[9]

Timber was another commodity exported up to the early part of the seventeenth century for shipbuilding from Wexford ports. In 1586 timber cargoes including boards, laths, hopstaves, poles and twelve oar-blades at 6/8d each were shipped from Ross and Wexford to the Welsh ports of Cardiff and Milford. Longfield cited as typical of this trade the arrival on 11 June 1586 at Milford of the *Saviour*, master, Richard Mossoer, a Wexford ship with boards and other timber, 'burthen 6 tonnes' — probably a cot.[10]

The sixteenth century was accompanied by much destruction, social upheaval and fighting. Wexford town was accused of shipping out much of the timber used by Scots to build the war galleys which intermittently were able to deliver supplies and reinforcements for Hugh O'Neill during his nine years' war of resistance to the English invasion of Ulster. By the beginning of the seventeenth century with its new political order, much had changed. Dublin, in spite of the notorious navigational hazards of its bay, was becoming Ireland's major port, New Ross was in decline, forests were being rapidly eliminated and prosperous sea fisheries were facing intimidating difficulties. The medieval pilgrim traffic from Wexford had also died. Wexford port, however, despite complaints about the silting and erosion problems, was still an active centre of trade. Waterford and Wexford in 1598 were operating more ships than all the other ports of Ireland. Robert Cogan, King James I's Inspector of Customs, reported that Wexford still exported timber, barrel staves, hides, tallow, wool-fells and herrings, and imported wines, iron, and salt. He valued the exports and imports at £4,000 annually, much more than at Youghal, Kinsale and Dungarvan and twice those at once supreme New Ross — 'a poor ruined town, out of trade, but one of the best harbours for shipping in the Kingdom'. Cogan also said 'a ship of 500 tons may ride afloat fast by the quay'.[11] Now 500 ton ships were in the big ship category in 1611, some four times the size of the biggest ship in Columbus's little squadron that crossed the Atlantic in 1492. Cogan clearly understood what a commanding situation for the country's economy New Ross had. As late as 1848, Doyle reported that 500 ton ships could lie at the upper end of the quay at high water, but only 200 ton ones at low water.[12]

The changed circumstances after the Flight of the Earls in 1607 altered some things for the Wexford maritime community, but in no way killed its enterprise or reduced the importance of Wexford port itself. Moreover, it was early in the new era that a Wexford seaman made history by being the first Irishman and one of the first men anywhere to be involved in the new science of hydrography, the development of which was an inevitable consequence of the opening up of the oceans of the world through the great Renaissance voyages of discovery initiated by the Portuguese. Mariners sailing between Britain, Ireland, South West Europe, the Mediterranean and the newly discovered transatlantic lands needed navigational references to supplement their instincts and experience. Since the late fifteenth century *rutters* or sailing instructions, for the perilous Irish Sea and above all its southern gateway between Wexford Tuskar and Welsh Smalls, had been compiled by Genoese and Venetian seamen. They were however, rough and ready. The Dutch, emerging as the outstanding seamen of northern Europe, improved the type of *rutter* in circulation, making the new type of sea-centred map showing sand-banks, submerged rocks, seamarks, which we call charts. The first chart of part of the Irish coast was printed in the 1596/7 edition of Waghenaer's *Nieuwen Spieghel der Zeevaert*, first published in London in 1583. It was probably compiled by the great explorer Barendts. It shows with considerable accuracy the coast of Wexford as it then was, with features like sandbanks and the Saltees, and this was the revolutionary new aid to navigation supplied by a chart with soundings right up to *Wachtfaert*.[13]

In the next few years Dutch seafarers began to worry also about pirates (soon also to be joined by North African privateers) who were haunting the creeks and inlets of southern Ireland and attacking shipping in the 'Western Approaches'. The Dutch Admiral Houltain was determined to have accurate *rutters* and charts of the area. He enlisted the help of pioneer English hydrographer, John Hunte of Plymouth, who depended greatly on a Wexford mariner, Levy, in doing the work that had given him the reputation that brought his name to Houltain's attention. Very little has so far come to light about Levy's background other than that he originated and worked in Wexford.

A noteworthy proof that times had changed (by which date, evidently, previous exploitation of the once extensive native forests had been compounded by the greed of new settlers) is that in 1626 for the first time there is a record of importation of Norwegian timber at Wexford. The very first importation of timber from that source to Ireland was only in 1625.[14] Such imports continued intermittently during the century: in 1678 New Ross imported some Norwegian timber, ranking eleventh out of twelve Irish ports making such imports from the point of view of quantity landed.

Essentially during the seventeenth century Wexford port imported coal and exported fish. It is not impossible that south-west Wexford fishermen had been fishing on the Newfoundland Banks in the sixteenth century. Certainly they went there in the late seventeenth century when West of England fishing craft regularly called in south-east Ireland to pick up extra crewmen and it is well known that one fifth of Newfoundland's Irish population is of Wexford descent.[15] Roberts suggests that the 'bateaux' employed on the River St Lawrence from 1680 on probably derived from the Wexford cot.[16] Convincing evidence of this possibility has yet to surface. The seagoing version of the cot was probably the vessel most used, both for fishing and for cargo carrying, and was ideal for the waters around the entrance to Wexford estuary where there 'was variety and abundance of bass, mullet, flukes, eels, hake, herrings: oysters, cockles, mussels, roe and herring have been sold at 3d per ... 612'.[17] Egerton's diary of 1634 describes the great prosperity of the Wexford herring industry, 'the town boats bring up to £40 worth in one night', a vast quantity for a time when beer cost less than a shilling a gallon.[18] In the 1630s, Wexford dealt with an estimated 100,000 barrels of fish annually for export; a complaint was made that at times up to 200 English, French and Dutch vessels were to be seen loading Wexford-caught herrings.[19] In 1698, English ports round the Dover Straits were seriously worried at the competition of Wexford-caught herrings in those parts.

Seventeenth century Wexford did not escape the war-like upheavals of the time. The port was the principal supply base for the Kilkenny Confederation's army frigates — a new ship type in north European waters destined to survive and develop down the centuries — arrived there under Irish commanders from the Spanish Dunkirk. Wexford-owned and manned ships, notably under remarkable freebooters Rossitter and Synnott, hung around the Saltees to drive off any English attempt to blockade. There were actions in the estuary and up the Suir connected with the Cromwellian attacks on Wexford and New Ross. It was from Duncannon in a Wexford ship that James II, himself an old seaman, fled to France after his defeat at the Boyne.[20]

Victims of resistance to the Cromwellian conquest were transported to the West Indies from Kaat's Strand in Wexford town, named for the Dutch captain of the ship that took them.[21] Whatever the obstacles to the development of Irish seaborne trade and fisheries, Wexford men continued to carry cargoes and to fish in and out of Irish ports in the eighteenth century. Wexford seamen continued to make names for themselves. One such was Bates from a still thriving and still maritime Kilmore Quay family.[22] When the French commercial adventurer François Thurot made a spectacular raiding voyage in the Irish Sea in 1759, Bates was his pilot, to the consternation of the British Admiralty who considered him about the most knowledgeable seafarer of the time concerning these waters. There was also the remarkable Sutton family of Clonard, a sea-connected branch of which also flourishes still at Kilmore Quay. One of these became a director of the great French East India Company and a man of political might not only in France but in Britain and in her then rebelling North American colonies.[23] A brother of his became a captain in the French navy; so did his celebrated oldest son who, after an exciting earlier career, was the specially selected second-in-command to the great French explorer La Pérouse in the *Boussole* on the ambitious Pacific exploration expedition of 1785-8. A cape in Korea was named after him. This Sutton's younger brother was killed in Admiral d'Estaing's attack on St Lucia in the West Indies in the War of American Independence. A cousin was assistant navigator of the battleship *César* at the decisive French victory in that war off the Virginia Capes in 1781, while a possible great-uncle commanded small French warships in the War of Austrian Succession, 1742-8.

To this same period belongs John Barry, born at Ballysampson, the superb seaman chosen to command the first custom-built commissioned warship of the US Navy, *USS United States*. After many years at sea, first commanding a Philadelphia trading schooner, *Barbados*, then as captain of a number of ships, Barry carried out a series of audacious enterprises in the American War of Independence. His death in 1803 at the early age of 58 was a bitter loss to the infant United States Navy, whose senior officer he was.[24].

During 1798, four Wexford oyster boats, each with a crew of twenty-five, patrolled the county's coast, carried out reconnaissances and captured English merchant ships and a ship carrying English military officers.[25]

Grattan's Parliament enacted that the port of registry, tonnage and crew-size of all Irish ships must be declared. In 1788 of 26 ports (and 1034 ships) where such declarations were made, Wexford owned the sixth largest number of ships (44, against, for example, Waterford's 41, Dublin's 240 and Cork's 99). At the same date Ross owned 18 ships, two of them larger than 100 tons. The number of seamen registered at Wexford was 187 and 115 at Ross. However, Wexford's ships were all under 100 tons, while Waterford had 10, Dublin 50 and Cork 37 larger than that.[26] Wexford's small ships were due to the notoriously shallow and heavily silted waters of its harbours, a factor which loomed ever greater as ship sizes (and therefore their draughts) increased. Ultimately, these shallow waters were to choke Wexford as a port. The first ship registration had been taken as early as 1762, but applied only to 'boats, except gabbards and ferry-boats', on the stretch of coast from Wexford by way of Rush to Derry. It was chiefly concerned with fishing craft and was linked to the shortening of the season for herring fishing to the period from 1 July to 1 November.[26] Arthur Young was soon afterwards (1776-9) in Ireland and reported abundance of herring off the Wexford coast.[27]

It is in the eighteenth century that wrecks, a constant feature of the Wexford coast since time immemorial, began to be fairly regularly recorded. One such wreck occurred on 18 December 1768 when the *Cavavaille*, celebrated like many another wreck in the *Songs of the Wexford Coast* (appendix 1), foundered on the Blackwater Bank, scene of numerous such dis-

Plate 1: A threemaster of the type which traded into New Ross in the eighteenth and nineteenth centuries. The drawing is a cartouche from a map of Ida barony 1812.

asters.[28] Incidentally, the current version of this song contains passages that have accrued since, for instance, a line referring to 'Tuskar's revolving light', but the language and terminology of the ballad are indisputably of the eighteenth century.[29] Three years before the *Cavavaille* wreck a notable maritime event off the Wexford coast was the barratry (sinking by its own crew) of the *Earl of Sandwich*, carrying a large number of bags of Maria Theresa dollars. The ship's master was drowned but the dollars were got ashore. However, rash talk led to the culprits' apprehension and the recovery of 250 dollar bags — the rest are supposed to lie hidden still somewhere between Carnsore Point and Hook Head. Two of the miscreants were hanged in chains at the Muglins off the south Dublin coast in 1765, the last people so executed at this 'pirates' execution place.

It was a combination of the spreading influence of humanitarian ideas in this Age of Enlightenment and of the rapid growth of the quantity and value of seaborne trade that led to serious steps at last being contemplated to prevent shipwreck. A beacon is believed to have been kept intermittently lit for the guidance of seafarers on dangerous Hook Head from the fifth century on, first by Celtic church monks, then by monks of the Augustinian Order, who, after the Normans came, used Raymond le Gros's tower for the purpose. Various attempts were made to resume and improve this primitive service, notably in 1657, and in 1671 a coal fire light was established at the Hook, one of six run under licence (and for profit) by a Sir Robert Reading[30]. Since then, first the Barracks Board, then the Customs Board, then Dublin Port Authority, and finally (from 1867) the Commissioners of Irish Lights have been charged with the lighting of our coast. The second of these bodies built the present Hook Lighthouse in 1791.[31]

The high point in the battle to provide proper lighting for the dangerous coast of Wexford was the decision to build a lighthouse on Tuskar Rock. A survey in 1807 of the county's coast had mentioned 'the terrible list of ship-wrecks caused through lack of a lighthouse'. The erection of three fixed light on the Saltees was suggested but Dublin Port Authority decided in 1810 to build a 113 foot light tower on the Tuskar. In May that year a Whitehaven collier *Hamond* had been lost there with all hands. In October 1812, a storm struck the Tuskar, where twenty-four workmen spent their nights in wooden huts. The huts were swept away, fourteen were drowned, the rest left hanging to the uneven rock surface, without shelter or food, for three days. Help at last came and the survivors volunteered to continue work. The tower was com-pleted at last, a revolutionary new aid to navigation on the Wexford coast, on 4 June 1815. It was said with its oil wick lamp to give a light as powerful as the totality of lights around the Irish coast forty years before, and as good as any lighthouse anywhere. Progressive improvements have been made to Tuskar Lighthouse ever since and it is one of Ireland's most powerful, with explosive fog signal, radio beacon and radio telephone. Other ameliorations to navi-gation guides off the Wexford coast, mostly achieved since 1867, have included the strengthening of the Hook Light, the positioning of a lightship by the Coningbeg Rock on the south coast and of others later replaced by powerful buoys at the Barrels Rocks south of Carnsore Point and off Black-water Head and the careful buoyage of the approaches to Rosslare, of the Blackwater Bank and the Suir Estuary. This has changed beyond recognition the conditions of navigation endured by navigators for so many long centuries along this hazardous coast.

A coastguard system was established for Ireland in the 1790s but was concerned chiefly with the prevention of smuggling. From the 1830s until 1922, a very efficient coastguard operated, housed in formidable barracks close to the sea, some of which survive. Though it was inevitably associated with government authority, and though some members (notably those indicted in a Cahore ballad partially preserved by Ranson referring to wrecks there in 1850 and 1856 robbed by coastguards) got up to no good, many, particularly on the Wexford coast, performed deeds of great heroism saving life from shipwrecks.[32] A lifeboat service was started around Dublin Bay in 1801 but it was not until 1838 that the Lifeboat Institution (founded in 1824) opened, at Wexford town, the county's first lifeboat station, whose early records have disappeared, and which lapsed between 1851 and 1858, when a lifeboat was stationed at Rosslare Fort.

In 1859 one of the worst of all Wexford wrecks happened, that of the Liverpool — New York emigrant sailing ship *Pomona*. The Irish third mate saved 21 of the 409 passengers and crew. The rest perished. Rosslare lifeboat located the wreck next day. The lifeboat at recently opened Cahore station could not be launched owing to the fury of the storm. Relics of this disaster are at Enniscorthy Museum. It resulted in a new lifeboat being placed at Wexford. The Rosslare Fort station was closed in 1897, reopened at a different spot in 1921, and washed away in 1924. From 1925-7 the boat was kept at Wexford, the station at which had been closed in 1921 and from 1927 the station has been at Rosslare Harbour. Between them, these stations had from 1858 to 1982 a record of 508 lives saved, mostly in appalling conditions. Few lifeboat stations in the world and none in Ireland have such a history. The conduct of coxwains Marcus Boyle, Edward Wickham, James Wickham and Dick Walsh and their crews, in situations requiring exceptional skills and courage — the *SS Montagu* wreck in 1878, the *SV Mexico* disaster in 1914, the *SV Mountblairy* rescue in 1929 and the astonishing service, the only one in the Irish Sea known to have occurred in an officially recorded force 12 hurricane, to the tanker *World Concord* in 1954 — was beyond praise.

In addition to the Cahore station mentioned, which stayed open till 1916, launched its boat 58 times and saved 105 lives, lifeboat stations have operated at Carnsore from 1859-97 (crews here had an outstanding record) — 34 launches, 130 rescued — Kilmore Quay (still in existence) 169 launches, 106 rescued, the last Irish lifeboat station where a crew member lost his life in service (on 24 December 1977), and Fethard (replacing Duncannon 1869-86, 8 launches, 43 rescued) 1886-1914, 8 launches, 4 rescued, this last station celebrated for the gallantry of the crew of its boat *Helen Blake III*, nine of whom perished in a dramatic service to the wrecked Norwegian *SV Mexico* on the Keeragh Rocks in February 1914.[33]

Other notable casualties at sea off the Wexford coast among so many include the stranding in 1920 of the big battleship *Barham* on the hitherto uncharted sandbank near the Tuskar that now bears its name; the loss of the last Irish sailing schooner, the *Brooklands* (1954) and of the senior ship of the Marine (now Naval) Service *Muirchú* (ex *HMS Helga*) on the way to the scrapyard (1947) off the Saltees, and the sinking of the Irish Lights tender *Isolda* by German aircraft in 1940 south of Carnsore Point, with six killed and seven injured.

As early as 1822 a wooden paddle steamer was engaged in carrying passengers to and from Wexford, the 70 feet long *Abbey*. Other paddle steamers in the next few years developed a regular service to Liverpool, which was triumphantly joined in 1837 by the larger Wexford-built *Town of Wexford* which carried on this service for the next sixteen years. The usual fare was 12/6 saloon, 6/- steerage. Occasionally competition from outsiders forced these fares down. Local control of the service passed in the last quarter of the century to J. Bacon of Liverpool, the company that eventually originated the powerful Coast Lines concern that absorbed, among other ferry companies, the B&I line. Intermittently also services were run, but not by Wexford interests, to Milford Haven, Bristol (1857-1911), Dublin (this last took five hours, charge, 6/- saloon, 4/- deck), Ayr and Glasgow. The problem with all these services was that as large ships were necessarily brought into use, the passage over Wexford bar became more and more difficult.

At length in 1896, Rosslare Harbour was opened, and after a somewhat chequered career is now one of the chief ports in the State, harbouring not only a regular service to South Wales, for which it was originally intended, but for twenty years a ferry service to France for which the country had been crying out ever since a separate Irish state was established.[34] In addition, car-carrying cargo ships, Irish Lights' tenders and a few other vessels use the port. Two companies, one Irish, one English, experimented in 1832 with paddle steamer passenger services between New Ross, Bristol and Liverpool, but quickly gave up. A Scottish firm revived the project with weekly sailings in 1878 but withdrew in 1879.

The enterprising Stafford family of Wexford, successful owners of sailing cargo ships, bought their first steamer *Elsie Annie* in 1919, employing her in the cross-channel cargo trade, and in 1930 set up the Wexford Steamship Company. The vessels of this company played a vital role in keeping this country supplied, thus also ensuring preservation of its neutrality, during the 1939-45 war. The head of the company took a notable part also in the founding in 1941 and the early success of the now defunct state shipping company, Irish Shipping Limited, which also owed a great debt to Wexfordman Captain John O'Neill, its first marine superintendent and from 1948 to 1961 its joint general manager. Born in 1892, he had gone to sea in ocean sailing ships as an ordinary seaman, transferred to steamers, passed for first mate in 1914, survived the trials of the 1914-18 war at sea, and commanded ships for the now defunct Reardon Smith Line of Cardiff for ten years.

Staffords had owned eleven schooners between 1892 and 1919, two of them sunk by submarines in the 1914 war. After the *Elsie Anne* they acquired the SS *JFV, SS Wexfordian* and *SS Menapia* (ex *Inniscarra* of Cork). These had been replaced by the end of 1939 by three modern motorships: *MV Edenvale, Kerlogue* and *Menapia II.*

These were largely involved at first in importing essential coal supplies from Britain. During this period the *Kerlogue* under Captain Owens of Carrick-fergus saved a badly damaged British collier and beached her on Rosslare Strand. Then, with the supply situation rapidly worsening, the three ships were one by one transferred to the run to neutral Lisbon, whence urgently needed supplies, shipped there from North America, could be brought here. *Edenvale,* under Captain Jones was attacked by German aircraft and slightly damaged in August 1941. She had three Wexfordmen in her crew at the time. In October 1943, the *Kerlogue,* under Captain Desmond Fortune, from a Wexford family settled in Dublin, was attacked by RAF planes and her captain and three other crew badly injured. In December that year the repaired *Kerlogue* under Captain Donohue of Dungarvan, carried out the epic rescue in the stormy Bay of Biscay, of 168 German naval survivors from ships recently sunk by a British squadron. The little ship, with barely room aboard for those rescued even to stand, disregarded standing allied orders, to report at Fishguard before proceeding to an Irish port, as she had the survivors' request to be landed in occupied France. The German seamen, apart from four who died on passage, were put ashore at Cork and interned.[35]

The *Menapia* made history by a voyage across the Atlantic to Boston in 1942 and another in 1944 to São Jomé in West Africa (to load crude oil). Each time her commander was Captain John Poole, of Killinick, county Wexford, later master in Irish Shipping ships. The last wartime master of the *Kerlogue* was Richard O'Neill of the Faythe, Wexford. Thirteen Wexfordmen were among the 156 seamen in Irish ships whose lives were lost as a result of the Second World War, a high proportion from a single county.

Regrettably, in 1949, 1954 and 1965, first *Edenvale,* then *Kerlogue,* then *Menapia* were sold and merchant ships are no longer owned in county Wexford, thus breaking a tradition that had been continuous since Wexford town was founded. Certainly the last three were worthy successors of the *knorrs,* cogs, cots, barques, brigs and schooners which had made Wexford's name known for so long in ports on so many seas. They were worthy successors of ships like those of the Devereux fleet of Wexford engaged in the Black Sea grain trade in the 1840s, of the Devereux *Hantoon* of 1864 lost off Portugal and subject of a haunting ballad, of Codd's ocean-sailing barques involved in the emigrant trade to North America, returning with raw cotton, of the famous *Antelope,* the last Wexford-built sailing schooner, once in the Canadian timber trade and survivor of two world wars, and of the mid nine-teenth century New Ross sailing ships that sailed even as far as Australia.

Shipowning and shipbuilding may have passed away from county Wexford, but seafishing certainly has not. The authorities in Ireland did little, if anything, to encourage our seafisheries until the end of the nineteenth century. They were little encouraged even in the early days of the new state, when the annual catch fell to a mere 10,000 tons (now around 200,000).[36] Yet, Wexfordmen obstinately went on employing their skills as sea fishermen, and Kilmore Quay grew in importance as a fishing port (despite setbacks like the destruction of twenty fishing craft in a single storm). Courtown harbour was built in the 1830s and by 1846 thirty fishing craft were using it.[37] In 1932 Wexford ports were third after only those of Donegal and Wicklow in the register of herring caught.

When, from 1962 onward, with the development of government interest in the industry, it began to thrive, Wexford was to the fore. In 1964, the county's ports were reporting rising herring catches and Kilmore Quay's fishing fleet acquired its twenty-fourth vessel with the arrival of the 72-foot *Alliance*. The fishermen's co-operative began there in 1955 (Ireland's first) raised its turnover from £90,000 in 1969 to £155,000 in 1970 and it was reckoned that this village of 225 souls was earning £240,000 annually from seafishing. The fishermen there were opening up new possibilities with concentration on catching crabs and by 1971 Kilmore Quay owned twenty eight vessels and export outlets had been found as far away as Italy and Czechoslovakia. If expansion of the Wexford fishing fleet has been stopped in the 1980s, in all probability only temporarily, remarkable and pioneer progress has been made in fish-farming, one of the great hopes for the country's economic future. As *An Bord Iascaigh Mhara* reported in 1981, 'Mussel culture on the sea bottom as in Wexford, produced large meaty mussels, ideal for processing, pickling or canning. Wexford mussels in a number of forms are now exported to most EEC markets'.[38]

If recent history has seen the demise of shipowning and shipbuilding in Wexford (shipbuilding was temporarily and successfully revived in the 1960s and 1970s in New Ross), so also unhappily has it seen the demise of Wexford as a commercial harbour. Short lived Courtown Harbour, from which forty vessels traded in the century of its commercial existence, had preceded it, and for the same reason on the proportionately smaller scale — it silted up for want of funds to dredge it.[39]

Seven hundred and eighteen vessels discharged cargo in Wexford in 1856, chiefly maize, barley, coal and wheat; 697 in 1866. In 1856, 728 ships shipped out exports, chiefly sheep, oats and malt, and in 1866, 421. The average size of these ships was about 105 tons. A century later, according to an answer given in Dáil Éireann on 26 March 1958, in 1957, two Dutch ships of 292 tons altogether and four Irish ships of 577 tons in all used Wexford. Commercially speaking, the port had ceased to count since the mid 1950s, for want of the £600,000 that, it was reckoned, would then have sufficed to clear the channel into the harbour. Many plans were discussed, even the possibility of making Wexford a hoverport, many experts were consulted, but in 1970 the government of the day finally turned down all suggestion of the port's revival. Fishing craft, however, still use it, and, again like Courtown but on a grander scale, it is developing as a port for leisure craft. Meanwhile, public money has been spent on improving Kilmore Quay and Rosslare, and the evergreen palm of Wexford maritime resilience has passed to New Ross.

As far back as 1954, it became evident that New Ross was one of only three minor Irish ports handling more shipping than before the war. The enterprising and far-seeing Arklow ship owners were pointing out how ideally situated this inland port was for handling many commodities. The number of ships sailing from New Ross in 1957 was nine (7 Dutch, 1 British, 1 Irish) of 1,721 tons in all. In 1963, a scale model was put into use at Trinity College, Dublin of tidal portions of the Barrow to help solve the port's dredging problems. The swing bridge on the Barrow was removed. By 1971, 496 ships were handled at New Ross; in 1972, 524; in 1973, 613. In 1972 a Ro-Ro terminal for continental traffic, costing £80,000, was opened, the first in Ireland. In 1984, despite the recession, New Ross was the seventh of the 15 leading Irish ports for quantity of goods handled, importing 669,000 tons and exporting 28,000. In the first half of 1985, more than 9,000 Toyota cars were discharged at New Ross from car-carriers out of Cherbourg, Toyota's north European distribution centre.

Plate li: A Slaney gabbard at Castlebridge (late nineteenth century)

Cots and gabbards were built throughout the last century on the Slaney. The gabbard era, described by Hadden, is over, but as late as 1979, there were ten cots at Rosslare Harbour, five at Carne including one double-ended one, and three at Wexford.[40] The famous Wickham lifeboat family built cots.[41] These vessels remain part of the unique county maritime tradition which has produced numerous fine vessels and even more first-class seamen. Carroll's boat-yard at Ballyhack continues to produce fine vessels. The *Topographical Dictionary* of 1837 called Wexford 'a nursery of seamen'[42] The *Irish Times* of 29 July 1941 recorded the hundreds of Wexfordmen then at sea, and declared that 'for every Wexfordman who had seen Bundoran, a hundred had seen the Baltic.'

Wexford seamen have served under many flags, thus underlining Thomas Aquinas's famous dictum that the sea unites people whereas the land divides them. Several of the county's many expert seamen have been named. It would be unjust to omit the names of two who rose to Admiral rank in the British navy, in which Wexford seamen were particularly valued as capable and reliable petty officers. These were Robert McClure, a stern disciplinarian who was nevertheless one of the greatest Arctic explorers of all time, after whom the key stretch of water is called, discovery of which at last proved the existence, for centuries disputed, of the North-West Passage from the Atlantic to the Pacific, and the rash but dashing David Beatty of Borodale, who rose to be Commander-in-Chief of Britain's Grand Fleet in the first World War.[43]

Happily, in the lightship *Guillemot*, moored in Wexford harbour, there has been for twenty years now a maritime museum to recall the varied facets of the county's remarkable maritime past. It is to be hoped that money will be found to preserve, improve and extend the fine collection there.

APPENDIX I:

Songs of the Wexford Sea Coast

THE LOFTY 'CAVAVAILLE'

You feeling hearted Christians of high and low degree,
I hope you pay attention and listen unto me,
A loss of life and property upon Blackwater shore,
Leaves orphans wives and mothers a sad tale to deplore.

The eighteenth of December, it was the fateful date,
The sky had a gloomy aspect, pregnated with sad fate;
O'er the celestial orbs of light great sable clouds were drew,
As in the east horizon a ship appeared in view.

She proved to be a Frenchman, the lofty *Cavavaille*;
Jehovah seemed to favour her with a sweet and pleasant gale.
Her noble captain, Ormsby, no danger e'er betook,
Until Blackwater sand-bank that fateful night he struck.

When the gallant vessel struck the bank her every sail did jibe.
"Come, lower your boats, make no delay," the noble captain cried.
But Boreas blew in fury, and so without delay,
The repeated roaring billows washed all their boats away.

But Providence ordained it so, Whom we should ever thank
For on the flow of water she drifted from the bank.
Her cable and best bower were instantly hove out,
Besides her strongest hawser, to bring the ship about.

Yet their case was now no better for her steerage tore away,
And Boreas blew with vengeance until the break of day.
And at the glimpse of daylight Blackwater Tower they see,
And Tuskar's grand revolving light they had it on their lee.

The steady crew worked hard, indeed, their precious lives to save,
Contending with the foaming flood and mountains high each wave.
But Boreas and rude Neptune together did agree,
And threatening rose up from the deep in dir'st calamity.

Her anchorage and her moorage they quickly did give way;
On Blackwater beach their barque was cast by the repeated sea.
Their fine new ship to pieces split, which caused each soul to weep;
And twenty-seven fine young men lay slumbering in the deep.

Her bills of lading they were filled with precious merchandise:
The produce of Asia Minor, and Zanzibar likewise,
The Cape of Ottahetta, and far Honduras Bay,
Jahoga's Sound where wealth abounds in rich Amerikay.

Now to conclude and finish my sad and tragic tale:
For those that were the victims God's mercy we appeal;
And may those noble French tars from every crime be free,
And may their souls in glory shine and forever happy be.

Words taken down from Margaret Mitten, Morriscastle, Nov. 1937. The air was taken down by Miss K. G. Flood, from the singing of John Codd, Blessington, Tagoat. 'Ottahetta' (Otaheite) is Tahiti of the 'Bounty' fame. I think 'Jahoga' is for Chacao on the Island of Chiloe, off the coast of Chile, S. America. I do not know when the wreck of this vessel took place. [Editorial note by Fr Joseph Ranson, *Songs of the Wexford Coast* (Wexford, 1948).]

References

1   G. Stout

1. M. Gardiner and A. Ryan, *Soils of county Wexford* (Dublin, 1964), pp 1-19
2. J. Jackson, 'Metallic ores in Irish prehistory: copper and tin' in *Origins of metallurgy in Atlantic Europe* (Dublin, 1978)
3. E. Culleton, *Early man in county Wexford* (Dublin, 1984), pp 2-4
4. P. Woodman, 'The chronological position of the latest phase of the Larnian' in *R.I.A. Proc.*, C, LXXXIV (1974), pp 237-65
5. P. Woodman, *The mesolithic in Ireland* (Oxford, 1978), p. 190
6. A. Went, 'Irish salmon — a review of investigations up to 1963' in *Sci. Pro., R.D.S.*, I, pp 365-412
7. T. Butler, *A parish and its people (History of the parish of Carrig-On-Bannow)* (Wellington Bridge, 1985), pp. 8-9
8. E. Brunicardi, 'The shore-dwellings of ancient Ireland' in *R.S.A.I. Jn.*, XLIV (1914), p. 189
9. Butler, *Carrig-On-Bannow*, pp 8-9
10. J. Ffrench, 'Group of bone and ivory objects from the Hook Peninsula' in *R.S.A.I. Jn.*, XLII (1912), pp 67-8
11. P. Woodman, 'The post-glacial colonisation of Ireland: The human factor' in D. Ó Corráin (ed.), *Irish Antiquity: essays and studies presented to Professor M. J. O'Kelly* (Cork 1981), p. 96 (henceforth '*Irish Antiquity*')
12. P. Woodman, 'Seeing is believing — problems in archaeological visibility' (Cork, 1983), pp 16-17.
13. Woodman, 'Post-glacial colonisation', p. 96
14. Culleton, *Early man*, p. 7
15. C. Cotter, 'MacMurroughs' in *Excavations* 1985 (Dublin, 1986) p. 41
16. G. Cooney, 'Stone axeheads of county Louth: a first report' in *Louth Arch. Soc. Jn.*, XXI (1985), pp 78-99; G. Thornton, A survey of earthen enclosures of the Boyne valley and related sites, unpublished M.A. thesis, U.C.D. (1980), pp 24-7
17. Culleton, *Early man*, p. 10
18. A. Sheridan, 'Porcellanite artifacts: A new survey', in *U.J.A.*, XLIX (1986), pp 19-32
19. I. Smith, 'The chronology of British stone implements' in *C.B.A. research report*, XXIII (1979), p. 20
20. J. Corcoran, 'An adze and axehead from county Wexford' in *R.S.A.I. Jn.*, XCVI (1966), pp. 93-5
21. G. Cooney, 'Stone axeheads'
22. T. Hayes, personal communication
23. Culleton, *Early man*, p. 10
24. A. Collins, 'The flint javelin-heads of Ireland' in *Irish Antiquity*, pp 111-33
25. W. Grattan Flood, 'County Wexford dolmens' in *R.S.A.I. Jn.*, XLII (1912), pp 13-17; T.

Powell, 'Megalithic tombs in south-eastern Ireland' in *R.S.A.I. Jn.*, LXXI 1941), pp 9-23
26. M. Herity, 'The finds from Irish portal dolmens' in *R.S.A.I. Jn.*, XCIV (1964), pp 123-44
27. S. Ó'Nualláin, 'Irish portal tombs: topography, siting and distribution' in *R.S.A.I. Jn.*, CXIII (1983), p. 103
28. W. Borlase, *The Dolmens of Ireland* (Dublin, 1897), II, pp 416-7
29. A. Lucas, 'Neolithic burial at Norrismount, county Wexford' in *R.S.A.I. Jn.*, LXXX (1950), pp 155-7
30. M. Herity, 'Irish decorated neolithic pottery' in *R.I.A. Proc.*, C, LXXXII (1982), pp 255-6
31. G. Kinahan, 'Sepulchral and other prehistoric relics, counties Wexford and Wicklow' in *R.I.A. Proc.*, C, XVI (1879-88), p. 156; M. Ryan, 'Poulawack, county Clare: the affinities of the central burial structure' in *Irish Antiquity*, p. 144
32. C. Manning, 'A Neolithic burial mound at Ashleypark, county Tipperary' in *R.I.A. Proc.*, C, LXXXV (1985), pp 76-9
33. J. Taylor, 'The relationship of British early Bronze Age goldwork to Atlantic Europe' in M. Ryan (ed.), *The origin of metallurgy in Atlantic Europe* (Dublin, 1978), p. 230
34. J. Taylor, 'Early Bronze Age technology and trade' in *Expeditions* (1979), p. 25; M. Herity and G. Eogan, *Ireland in prehistory* (London, 1977)
35. J. Jackson, 'Metallic ores in Irish prehistory: copper and tin' in Ryan, *Metallurgy*, pp 107-25
36. L. Flanagan, 'The Irish earlier Bronze Age industry in perspective' in *R.S.A.I. Jn.*, CXII (1982), pp 93-101
37. P. Harbison, *The axes of the early Bronze Age in Ireland* (Munich, 1969)
38. *Ibid*, p. 25
39. N.M.I., 1959:62; N.M.I., 1968:292; A. Lucas, 'Archaeological acquisitions in the year 1969' in *R.S.A.I. Jn.*, CI (1971), p. 209
40. N.M.I. 1959:62: A. Lucas, 'Archaeological acquisitions in the year 1959 in *R.S.A.I. Jn.*, XCI (1961), pp 74-5
41. Harbison, 'Axes', p. 62
42. W. Bremer, 'A founder's hoard of the Copper Age at Carrickshedoge, Nash, county Wexford' in *R.S.A.I. Jn.*, LVI (1926), pp 88-91
43. P. Harbison, 'Mining and metallurgy in early Bronze Age Ireland' in *N. Munster Antiq. Jn.*, X (1966), p. 9
44. Harbison, 'Axes'
45. J. Waddell, 'Irish Bronze Age cists: a survey' in *R.S.A.I. Jn.*, C (1970), pp 91-139
46. P. Hartnett and E. Prendergast, 'Bronze Age burials in county Wexford' in *R.S.A.I. Jn.*, LXXXIII (1953), pp 46-9; 'Proceedings and papers' in *R.S.A.I. Jn.*, VII (1860-1863), pp 144-5; E. Prendergast, 'Cist burial at Bolinready in *R.S.A.I. Jn*, XCVIII (1968), PP 161-2; R. Kavanagh, 'The encrusted urn in Ireland' in *R.I.A. Proc.*, C, LXXIII (1973), p. 567; Waddell, 'Cists' N.M.I., Topographical Files
47. J. Raftery, 'A prehistoric burial in county Wexford' in *Old Wexford Soc. Jn.*, I (1968), p. 51
48. Anon., 'Proceedings' in *R.S.A.I. Jn.*, XVIII (1878-88), p. 348
49. J. Waddell, 'Cists', p. 137; J. Ffrench, 'Cinerary urn discovered at Adamstown, county Wexford' in *R.S.A.I. Jn.*, XIX (1889), pp 19-20
50. E. Rynne, 'Bronze Age cemetery at Scarawalsh, county Wexford' in *R.S.A.I. Jn.*, XCVI (1966), pp 34-46
51. R. Kavanagh, 'Pygmy cups in Ireland' in *R.S.A.I. Jn.*, CVII (1977), pp 61-95
52. T. Westropp, 'On Irish motes and early Norman castles' in *R.S.A.I. Jn.*, XXXIV (1904), p. 321
53. Rynne, 'Scarawalsh', pp 39-4
54. Kinahan, 'Sepulchral relics', p. 154
55. Westropp, 'Motes', p. 321
56. Culleton, *Early man*, p. 51
57. Kavanagh, 'Encrusted urn', pp 508-11
58. Rynne, 'Scarawalsh', pp 39-46
59. N.M.I., 1984:112
60. Anon., 'Donations to the Museum' in *P.S.A.S.*, XII (1876-78), pp 61-2
61. Kavanagh, 'Encrusted urn', p. 567
62. S. Ó'Riordáin, 'Two Bronze Age burials from county Wexford' in *R.S.A.I. Jn.*, LXVI (1936), p. 187; N.M.I., 1984:IA/184/84
63. J. Waddell, 'Cultural interaction in the insular Bronze Age: some ceramic evidence' in J. de Laet (ed.), *Acculturation and continuity in Atlantic Europe (Ghent, 1978)*, pp 284-94
64. M. Ryan, 'Urn burial at Ballintubrid, Blackwater, county Wexford' in *R.S.A.I. Jn.*, CV

(1978), p. 135. A fragment of another battleaxe has also been recovered from Tomacurry, Wexford.

65. G. Orpen, 'Mottes and Norman castles in Ireland' in *R.S.A.I. Jn.*, XXXVII (1937), p. 136
66. R. MacAlister, 'A Circular stone fort in county Wexford' in *R.S.A.I. Jn.*, LXXVII (1907), p. 311
67. Harbison, 'Axes', p. 43
68. T. Westropp, 'Five large earthworks in the barony of Shelbourne, county Wexford' in *R.S.A.I. Jn.*, XLVIII (1918), pp 13-14
69. Culleton, *Early man*, p. 31
70. R. Fitzhenry, 'The Cross of the Shad' in *St Peter's annual*, II (1917), pp 25-33
71. S. Ó'Nualláin, 'The stone circle complex of Cork and Kerry' in *R.S.A.I. Jn.*, CV (1975), pp 83-131
72. E. MacWhite, 'A new view on Irish Bronze Age rock-scribings' in *R.S.A.I. Jn.*, LXXVI (1946), pp 59-80
73. G. Kinahan, 'Sepulchral and other prehistoric relics, counties Wexford and Wicklow' in *R.I.A. Proc.*, C, XVI 1879-88), pp 157-258; O. Davies, *Irish tourist association survey*, C, (1940) unpublished, N.M.I.; G. Kinahan, 'Notes and queries' in *R.S.A.I. Jn.*, XVI (1883-. 84), pp 40-1; G. Kinahan, 'Proceedings' in *idem*, pp 224-5; Butler, *Carrig-On-Bannow*, p. 239; MacAlister, *Corpus Inscriptionum*, pp 47-8
74. Herity and Eogan, *Prehistory*, p. 137
75. Kinahan, 'Notes and queries', p.40
76. Davies, 'Survey'.
77. S. Ó'Nualláin, 'Grouped standing stones, radial stone cairns and enclosures in the south of Ireland' in *R.S.A.I. Jn.*, CXIV (1984), pp 63-5, 68, 71
78. M. Kelly, 'Excavations and experiments in ancient Irish cooking places' in *R.S.A.I. Jn.*, LXXXIV (1954), p. 138
79. A. Brindley, personal communication
80. J. Ranson, 'Some unrecorded Wexford antiquities' in *R.S.A.I. Jn.*, LXXV (1945), pp 53-5; His site at Knockbrandon Lower was not discovered until 1942 so it was not included in the 1940 revision.
81. N.M.I., Teacher's survey, (1974-76)
82. R. Cleary, 'Excavation of a Fulacht Fiadh at Dromnea, near Kilcrohane, county Cork' in *Cork Hist. Soc. Jn.*, XCI (1986), pp 52-3
83. G. Eogan, *Hoards of the Irish Bronze Age* (Dublin, 1983), p. 7
84. F. Aalen, *Man and the Landscape in Ireland* (Dublin, 1978), pp 72-3
85. N.M.I. 1943:55; Culleton, *Early man*, p. 21
86. G. Eogan, *Catalogue of Irish bronze swords* (Dublin, 1965), p. 161; Culleton, *Early man*, p. 21
87. B. Raftery, 'Dowris, Halstatt and La Tène in Ireland: problems of the transition from Bronze to Iron' in S. J. de Laet (ed.), *Acculturation*
88. Eogan, *Hoards*, p. 7
89. Herity and Eogan, *Prehistory*, pp 212-6
90. W. Frazer and E. Johnson, 'Gold fibulae discovered in Ireland' in *R.I.A. Proc.*, C, XIX (1883-86), pp 776-83; Culleton, *Early man*, pp 25-6
91. W. Armstrong, 'An ancient earthen ware vessel and certain bronze antiquities found in it, at Kilmuckridge, county Wexford' in *R.I.A. Proc.*, C, IV (1850), pp 369-70; Eogan, *Hoards*, pp 170-1; W. Wilde *Catalogue of the antiquities ... in the museum of the R.I.A.* (Dublin, 1857), p. 158; Culleton, *Early man*, pp 24-5; N.M.I., 1929:3; W. Frazer and E. Johnson, 'Gold fibulae discovered in Ireland' in *R.I.A. Proc.*, C, XIX (1883-96), pp 776-83
92. Eogan, *Hoards*, p. 10
93. Herity and Eogan, *Prehistory*, p. 193
94. 'Miscellanea' in *R.S.A.I. Jn.*, XX (1891), p. 486
95. N.M.I. ,1959:126
96. Herity and Eogan, *Prehistory*, pp 194-5; N.M.I., 1968:259
97. A. Lucas, 'Archaeological acquisitions in 1968' in *R.S.A.I. Jn.*, CI (1971), p. 219
98. Herity and Eogan, *Prehistory*, p. 195
99. Eogan, *Hoards*, pp 170-1
100. *Ibid.*, pp 172-3
101. *Ibid.*, p. 7
102. G. Eogan, 'The associated finds of gold bar torcs' in *R.S.A.I. Jn.*, XCVII (1967), p. 132
103. *Ibid.*, pp 161-2

104. Eogan, *Hoards*, pp 45-6
105. T. Grattan Esmonde, 'Some further finds in north Wexford' in *R.S.A.I. Jn.*, XXXII (1902), pp 68-70; Culleton, *Early man*, p. 23; H. Maryon, 'The technical methods of the Irish smiths in the Bronze and early Iron Age' in *R.I.A. Proc.*, C, XLIV (1938), p. 206
106. Eogan, 'Gold bar torcs', p. 131
107. Eogan, *Hoards*, pp 171-2; Culleton, *Early man*, pp 24-5
108. G. Eogan, 'Gold discs of the Irish Bronze Age', in *Irish Antiquity*, pp 148-50
109. G. Eogan, 'The gold vessels of the Bronze Age in Ireland and beyond' in *R.I.A. Proc.*, C, LXXXI (1981), pp 345-82
110. Eogan, 'Gold discs', p. 156
111. *Ibid.*, p. 151
112. *Ibid.*, p. 149
113. Anon., 'Miscellanea' in *R.S.A.I. Jn.*, V (1895), p. 386
114. Frazer and Johnson, 'Fibulae', pp 776-83
115. Herity and Eogan, *Prehistory*, pp 213-14
116. *Ibid.*, p. 212
117. Herity and Eogan, *Prehistory*, p. 223
118. B. Raftery, 'Dowris, Halstatt and La Tène'
119. B. Raftery, *La Tène in Ireland* (Marburg, 1984), p. 14
120. T. Grattan Esmonde, 'Notes on crannóg and other finds in north county Wexford' in *R.S.A.I. Jn.*, XXIX (1899), p. 405; W. Wood-Martin, *The Lake Dwellings of Ireland* (Dublin, 1886), p. 44
121. *Ibid.*, p. 48
122. R. Macalister, 'A circular fort in county Wexford' in *R.S.A.I. Jn.*, LXVII (1937), p. 311
123. St Joseph aerial photographs, Cambridge University College Aerial Photographs (CUCAP)(AYK 23); (AYK B); (AIC 35); (BDJ 65)
124. Westropp, 'Earthworks' pp 12-15; T. Westropp, 'Notes on certain promontory forts in counties Waterford and Wexford' in *R.S.A.I. Jn.*, XXXVI (1906), p. 241; Westropp, 'Promontory forts', p. 241; P. Sinnott, 'Duncannon' in *Old Wexford Soc. Jn.*, III (1970), pp 3-12; Westropp, 'Earthworks', p. 15; R. Roche and O. Merne, *Saltees: island of birds and legends* (Dublin, 1977), p. 23
125. B. Raftery, 'Iron Age burials' in *Irish Antiquity*, pp 173-204
126. B. Colfer, personal communication
127. CUCAP (BOE 4); GSI T 194/193
128. *O.S. Letters, Wexford*, I, p. 3; *Ibid.*, p. 14; L. Harte, 'List of ancient churches, graveyards, castles, wells etc.' in *Past*, III, p. 90
129. T. Knox, 'Miscellanae: Croghans and Norman motes' in *R.S.A.I. Jn.*, XLI (1911), pp 270-1
130. Raftery, *La Tène*, pp 308-9
131. E. Rynne, 'Celtic stone idols in Ireland' in *C.B.A. Research Report*, IX (1976), pp 79-93
132. R. Roche, 'Two decorated stone heads from Gibberwell' in *Kilmore Parish Journal*, XIV (1985-6), p. 33
133. N.M.I. 1959:216; N.M.I. 1959:214
134. G. Dunning, 'The swan's neck pin and ringheaded pins of the early Iron Age in Britain' in *Archaeological Journal*, XCI (1934), pp 269-95
135. T. Graham and E. Jope, 'A Bronze brooch and ibex-headed pin from the sandhills of Dunfanaghy, county Donegal' in *U.J.A.* XIII (1950), pp 54-6

2

1. S. Tóibín, *Cúig Cuigí Éireann* (Dublin, 1963), p. 3
2. Luaite i Tóibín, *op.cit.*, p. 27
3. Keating, *Foras feasa*, III p. 306 'Fairche Fhearna nó Locha Garman ó BheigÉirinn go Míleadhach don leith thiar don Bhearbha, is ó Shliabh Uidhe Laighean budh dheas go muir'
4. C. L. Falkiner, 'The counties of Ireland' in *R.I.A. Proc.*, C, XXIV (1903), p. 172
5. A.L.C., II, p. 96; A.F.M., IV, p. 784
6. Keating, *Foras feasa*, III, p. 300
7. BK. *Rights*, ed. O'Donovan, p. 211

8. Ó Dubhagáin and Ó Huidhrin, *Topog. poems*, línte 1085-8
9. *Cal. Carew MSS 1515-74*, p. 6
10. Ó Dubhagáin and Ó Huidhrin, *Topog. poems*, línte 1097-1100
11. *O.S. namebooks, Wexford*
12. Ó Dubhagáin and Ó Huidhrin, *Topog. poems*, línte 1081-2
13. *BK Rights*, ed. O'Donovan, p. 208
14. *Ibid.*, p. 209
15. *Cal. pat rolls Ire.*, *Jas I* 'Kinshealagh's country'
16. *O.S. namebooks, Wexford*
17. *Cal. pat. rolls Ire.*, Jas I
18. *Knights' fees*, p. 16
19. *Cal. pat. rolls Ire.*, *Hen. VII-Eliz*, p. 308
20. Hore, VI, p. 456
21. *BK. Rights*, ed. O'Donovan, p. 209
22. A. P. Smyth, *Celtic Leinster: towards an historical geography of early Irish civilisation AD 500-1600* (Dublin, 1982), pp 61-2
23. P. Power, 'The bounds and extents of Irish parishes' in S. Pender (ed.), *Féilscríbhinn Torna* (Cork, 1947), p. 218 *et. seq.*
24. E. de hÓir, 'Nóta faoi dhá logainmneacha i gco. Loch Garman' in *Past* VIII (1970), pp 75-9
25. Hogan, *Onomasticon*
26. Hore, IV, p. 266
27. *Fiants Ire.*, *Hen. VIII*, no. 343
28. *Cal. pat rolls Ire.*, *Eliz*, p. 459
29. Flood, *Ferns*, p. 206
30. *Registry of Deeds, abstract of wills* I, p. 245
31. *Cal. pat. rolls Ire.*, Jas I, 1618
32. D'éag Solomon Richards i 1684 (Hore MSS, St Peter's College, Wexford)
33. *O.S. namebooks, Wexford*, Clone parish
34. *Cal. pat. rolls Ire.*, Chas I, 19 Jan 1630
35. A map of the barony of Scarawalsh in 1657, Clayton MSS, P.R.O.I. (henceforth 'Scarawalsh, 1657')
36. Herman Moll, *A new map of Ireland* (London, 1714)
37. R. Fraser, *Statistical Survey of county Wexford* (Dublin, 1807), map
38. *Knights' fees*, pp 6-7
39. *Ibid.*, p. 12
40. *Ibid.*, p. 12
41. *Cal. pat rolls Ire.*, Chas I, 19 Oct. 1630
42. *Knights' fees*, p. 39
43. *Cal. pat. rolls Ire.*, Jas I
44. *Cal. pat. rolls Ire.*, Chas I, 19 Oct. 1630
45. 'Scarawalsh 1657'
46. Hore, IV, p. 400
47. *Fiants Ire.*, *Hen. VIII*, no. 529.
48. Hore, IV, p. 398
49. *Cal. pat. rolls Ire.*, *Eliz.*, p. 307
50. *Cal. pat. rolls Ire.*, Chas I, 20 Sept. 1626
51. *Ibid.*, 4 Oct 1633
52. *Census Ire.*, 1659
53. *Cal. pat. rolls Ire.*, Jas I, 17 Jan 1611
54. *Ibid.*, 20 Feb 1611
55. *ibid.*, 17-Apr.-1611
56. G. Hatchell, *Abstracts of grants of land under the Commission of Grace, 1684-88* (Dublin, 1839), p. 44 (henceforth *Commission of Grace)*
57. Ballydaw nó Davidstown (Monart), Ballydawmore Clone), Ballymartin (Ardcavan), Ballymacshoneen (Kilpatrick), Ballygarrett (Donaghmore), Ballymurragh (Killincooly) Ballyshane (Artramon), Ballyhamilton (Templeshanbo).
58. Ballynabola (Kilscanlan).
59. Bolabaun (Killurin), Boleybaun (Kilcavan), Bolaboybeg agus Bolaboymore (Meelnagh), Bolacreen (Kilnahue), Bolobeg, Boladurragh, Bolamore (Templeshanbo).
60. *Cal. pat. rolls Ire.*, Chas I, 17-4-1629
61. Hatchell, *Commission of Grace*, p. 42

62. W. H. Grattan Flood (ed.), 'Bishop Nicholas Sweetman's visitation of the diocese of Ferns in 1753' in *Archiv. Hib.*, II (1913), p. 104

63. Tá an nóta seo ag J. F. Shearman, *Loca Patriciana* (Dublin, 1879), p. 87: 'There is on the side of Tara Hill a small chapel called Kill Diarmid. It was dedicated to Diarmid, abbot of Inishlothran in Loch Ree. He died 10 Jan. c. 540'.

64. *Cal. pat. rolls Ire.*, *Hen. VIII-Eliz*, p. 146

65. *Cal. pat. rolls Ire.*, *Eliz*, p. 459

66. *Census Ire.*, *1659*

67. Down Survey maps for county Wexford, N.L.I., MS 970

68. *O.S. namebooks*, *Wexford*, Kilmallock parish

69. *Cal. pat. rolls Ire.*, *Jas 1*

70. *Cal. pat. rolls Ire.*, *Hen VIII-Eliz*, p. 68

71. V. Gill, *A new map of the County of Wexford from an actual survey* (London, 1811)

72. *Census Ire.*, *1659*

73. *Cal pat. rolls Ire.*, *Chas. 1*, 21 July 1629

74. *Cal. pat. rolls Ire.*, *Eliz*, p. 267

75. J. B. Leslie, *Ferns clergy and parishes* (Dublin, 1936), p. 243

76. *O.S. namebooks*, *Wexford*, Clonleigh parish

77. *Grand Jury Presentments, county Wexford, 1801* (Wexford, 1801)

78. *Cal. pat. rolls Ire.*, *Jas I*, 9 June 1623

79. *Census Ire.*, *1659*

80. Tuairim an Athair Joseph Ranson, nach maireann

81. *Cal. pat. rolls Ire.*, *Jas I*, 3 Apr. 1606

82. *Fiants Ire.*, *Ed. VI*, No. 1061

83. *Cal. pat. rolls Ire.*, *Jas I*, 17 July 1610

84. *Registry of Deeds, abstract of wills*, II, p. 51

85. *Freemans Journal*, 20 Nov. 1830 'Moneygeer'

86. J. G. Simms (ed.), 'Irish Jacobites' in *Anal. Hib.*, XXII (1960), PP 11-187

87. *O.S. namebooks*, *Wexford*, Kilnahue parish

88. *Cal pat. rolls Ire.*, *Chas I*, no. 5

89. *Ibid.*, no. 48

90. *Ibid.*, no. 91

91. Simms, 'Irish Jacobites'

92. Moll, 'Map, 1714'

93. Fraser, *Statistical survey*

94. *Fiants Ire.*, *Ed VI*, no. 397

95. Moll, 'Map, 1714'

96. *Cal. pat. rolls Ire.*, *Jas I*, 20 Mar. 1604

97. *Ibid.*, 20 Feb. 1618

98. *Cal. pat. rolls Ire.*, *Chas I*, no. 53

99. *Fiants Ire.*, *Ed VI*, no. 369

100. *Grand Jury Presentments, county Wexford* (Wexford, 1844)

101. *Knights' fees*, p. 19

102. *Fiants Ire.*, *Ed VI*, no. 1061

103. *Cal. pat. rolls Ire.*, *Jas I*, 19 Oct. 1615

104. *Cal. pat. rolls Ire.*, *Chas I*, 26 Nov. 1630

105. *Cal. pat. rolls Ire.*, *Chas I*, 19 Oct. 1630

106. Moll, 'Map, 1714'

107. Fraser, *Statistical Survey*

108. *Shapland Carew papers, passim*

109. *O.S. namebooks*, *Wexford*, Ballybrennan parish

110. J. H. Todd and W. Reeves (ed.), *Félire na Naomh nErennach* (Dublin, 1864)

111. R. I. Best and H. Lawlor (ed.), *Féilire Thamlachta* (London, 1931)

112. *Cal. pat. rolls Ire.*, *Jas I*, 7 Sept. 1604

113. *Ibid.*, 14 Mar. 1619

114. *Cal. pat. rolls Ire.*, *Chas I*, 6 Sept. 1625

115. *Grand Jury Presentments, county Wexford* (Wexford, 1827)

116. *Cal. pat. rolls Ire.*, *Chas I*, 6 Sept. 1625

117. *Ibid.*, 14 Mar 1619

118. *Census Ire.*, *1659*

119. Hatchell, *Commission of Grace*, p. 42

120. *Grand Jury Presentments, county Wexford* (Wexford, 1827)
121. *Cal. pat. rolls Ire., Jas I*, 18 Feb. 1612
122. *Ibid.*, 17 Jan 1618
123. *O.S. namebooks, Wexford*, Monart parish
124. *Cal. pat. rolls Ire., Jas I*, 9 Feb. 1618
125. Hore, IV, *passim*
126. *Knights' fees*, p. 17
127. Hatchell, *Commission of Grace*, p. 42
128. *Cal. pat. rolls Ire., Jas I*, 10 Jan. 1611
129. *Ibid.*, no. 55, 1625
130. *Ibid.*, 21 Feb. 1611
131. R. D., 55-472-37864
132. P. W. Joyce, *Irish names of places* (Dublin, 1895) I, p. 261
133. Fraser, *Statistical Survey*
134. Gill, *op. cit.*
135. *O.S. namebooks, Wexford*, Templescoby parish
136. *Grand Jury Presentments county Wexford* (Wexford, 1831)
137. Joyce, *op.cit.*, II, p. 427
138. *Cal. pat. rolls Ire., Chas I*, 19 Oct. 1630
139. *Cal. pat. rolls Ire., Jas I*, no. 45
140. *Shapland Carew papers*
141. Gill, *op.cit.*
142. *Cal. pat. rolls Ire., Chas I*, 8 Apr. 1630
143. *Ibid.*, 28 July 1632
144. 'Scarawalsh, 1657'
145. Hore MSS, XLVIII, p. 239
146. Simms, 'Irish Jacobites'
147. *Wexford People*, 26 Apr. 1890
148. *Cal. pat. rolls Ire., Chas I*, 19 Oct. 1618
149. *Cal. pat. rolls Ire., Jas I*, 21 Feb. 1630
150. *Ibid.*, 19 Oct. 1630
151. *Cal. pat. rolls Ire., Jas I*, 17 July 1610
152. *Ibid.*, 1 Oct. 1619
153. *Ibid*, 17 Jan. 1618
154. *Cal. pat. rolls Ire., Chas I*, 19 Oct 1630
155. *Col. pat. rolls Ire., Jas I*, 28 Feb 1604
156. *Cal. pat. rolls Ire., Chas 1*, 6 Sept 1625
157. *Ibid.*, 24 Oct 1634. Ba le 'Taddy Jordan' é san am sin.
158. *Cal. pat. rolls Ire., Eliz*, p. 185
159. *Cal. pat. rolls Ire., Jas I*, 3 Apr. 1606
160. *Cal. pat. rolls Ire., Chas I*, 14 Apr. 1634
161. *Cal. pat. rolls Ire., Jas I*, 1 Oct. 1612
162. *Cal. pat. rolls Ire., Chas I*, 28 Apr. 1627
163. *Cal. pat. rolls Ire., Jas I*, 21 Feb. 1612
164. *Ibid.*, 28 Feb. 1604
165. *Ibid.*, 7 Sept. 1605
166. Hatchell, *Commission of Grace*, p. 47
167. R. D., 3-37-562
168. *Registry of Deeds, abstract of Wills*, II, p. 719
169. *O.S. namebooks, Wexford*, Killurin parish
170. 'Scarawalsh, 1657'
171. *Cal. pat. rolls Ire., Chas I*, 29 Aug. 1633
172. Hatchell, *Commission of Grace*, p. 47
173. *Cal. pat. rolls Ire., Chas I*, 8 Oct. 1629
174. *Shapland Carew papers, passim*
175. *Cal. pat. rolls Ire., Jas I*, 5 Oct. 1608
176. *Ibid.*, 27 July 1610
177. 'Scarawalsh 1657'
178. Knights' fees, p. 19
179. *Cal. pat. rolls Ire., Chas I*, 28 July 1632
180. *Census Ire., 1659*

181. *Cal. pat. rolls Ire.*, *Jas I*, 18 Jan. 1612
182. Deonú do 'Will. Parsons of Dublin esq.', *Cal. pat. rolls Ire.*, *Jas I*, 17 Jan 1618
183. *Cal. pat. rolls Ire.*, *Chas I*, 21 July 1629
184. *Ibid.*, 19 Oct. 1630
185. Gill, *op.cit.*
186. *O.S. namebooks, Wexford*, Ardcolm parish
187. *Ibid.*, Clone parish
188. *Cal. pat. rolls Ire.*, *Chas I*, 19 Oct. 1630
189. *Fiants Ire.*, *Ed VI*, no. 959
190. *Cal. pat. rolls Ire.*, *Chas I*, 21 July 1629
191. *Cal. pat. rolls Ire.*, *Jas I*, 1 Sept. 1605
192. 'Scarawalsh 1657'
193. *Cal. pat. rolls Ire.*, *Jas I*, 17 Jan 1618
194. *Knights' fees*, p. 16
195. R. D., 5-40-1248
196. *Cal. pat. rolls Ire.*, *Jas I*, 23 Feb. 1605
197. *Cal. pat. rolls Ire.*, *Chas I*, 28 Mar 1626
198. *Grand Jury Presentments county Wexford* (Wexford, 1827)
199. *Knights' fees*, p. 19
200. *Census Ire.*, 1659
201. *Grand Jury Presentments county Wexford* (Wexford, 1826)
202. *O.S. namebooks, Wexford*, Templeshannon parish
203. Keating, *Foras feasa*, III, p. 328
204. *Knights' fees*, p. 94
205. Fraser, *Statistical survey*
206. *Knights' fees*, p. 100
207. *Cal. pat. rolls Ire.*, *Jas I*, 14 Mar. 1619
208. Flood, *Ferns*, p. 206
209. *Grand Jury Presentments county Wexford* (Wexford, 1826)
210. *O.S. namebooks, Wexford*, Kilmakilloge parish
211. *Fiants Ire.*, *Hen VIII*, no. 342
212. *Cal. pat. rolls Ire.*, *Eliz*, p. 459
213. *Cal. pat. rolls Ire.*, *Jas I*, 27 Aug. 1610
214. J. Ranson, 'St. Maelruan' in *Past*, V (1949), p. 166
215. *Cal. pat. rolls Ire.*, *Eliz*, p. 490
216. Cal. pat. rolls Ire., Jas I, no. 33
217. *Wexford Herald*, 25 Aug. 1830
218. *Grand Jury Presentments county Wexford* (Wexford, 1831)
219. Ranson, *op.cit.*, pp 161-7

3　*Billy Colfer*

1. Orpen, *Normans*; Otway-Ruthven, *Med. Ire.*; R. Roche, *The Norman invasion of Ireland* (Tralee, 1970)
2. A. Otway-Ruthven, 'Knight service in Ireland' in *R.S.A.I. Jn.*, LXXXIX (1959), pp 1-15
3. A. Otway-Ruthven, 'The character of Norman settlement in Ireland' in *Hist. Studies*, V (1965), p. 76
4. A. Scott and F. Martin (ed.), *Expugnatio Hibernica; the conquest of Ireland, by Giraldus Cambrensis* (Dublin, 1978), p. 35
5. Orpen, *Normans*, I, p. 393
6. G. H. Orpen (ed.), *The song of Dermot and the Earl* (Dublin, 1892), lines 3070-1
7. Scott and Martin, *Expugnatio Hibernica*, p. 95
8. *Ibid.*, p. 121
9. Orpen, *Normans*, I, p. 373
10. E. Curtis, *A history of medieval Ireland* (London, 1936; 2nd. ed., 1938), p. 76
11. C. Empey, 'Medieval Knocktopher; a study in manorial settlement' part one in *Old Kilkenny Rev.* II, no. 5, (1982), p. 333

12. Hore, VI, pp 266-74
13. Orpen, *Normans*, III, p. 59
14. C. Empey, 'The Norman period: 1185-1500' in W. Nolan (ed.), *Tipperary: history and society* (Dublin, 1985), p. 91
15. Orpen, *Normans*, I, pp. 367-93; Brooks, *Knights' fees*
16. Orpen, *Song of Dermot*, lines 2769-816
17. Brooks, *Knights' fees*, p. 134
18. Orpen, *Normans*, I, p. 238
19. *Ibid.*, p. 393, n. 2
20. *Chartul. St Mary's, Dublin*, II, p. 154
21. Hore, VI, p. 9
22. *Ibid.*, V, p. 40
23. Brooks, *Knights' Fees*, p. 146
24. *Ibid.*, p. 134
25. *Ibid.*, p. 130
26. Orpen, *Normans*, I, p. 387
27. Brooks, *Knights' fees*, p. 98
28. C. Empey, 'A case-study of the primary phase of Anglo-Norman settlement: the Lordship of Kells' in *Old Kilkenny Rev.*, III, no. 1 (1984), pp 32-40
29. Otway-Ruthven 'Knight Service', pp 1-15
30. Empey, 'Knocktopher', p. 331
31. Otway-Ruthven, *Med. Ire.*, p. 109
32. *Chartul. St Mary's, Dublin*, I, p. 355
33. Orpen, *Normans*, III, ch. 26
34. *Cal. pat. rolls, 1364-7*, p. 271
35. Brooks, *Knights' fees*, p. viii
36. Hore, V, p. 106
37. B. Graham, 'Anglo-Norman settlement in county Meath' in *R.I.A. Proc.*, C, LXXV (1975), p. 224
38. *Civil Survey*, Wexford
39. B. Graham, *Anglo-Norman settlement in Ireland* (Athlone, 1985), p. 19
40. A. Otway-Ruthven, 'Parochial development in the rural deanery of Skreen' in *R.S.A.I. Jn.*, XCIV (1964), pp. 111-22
41. Otway-Ruthven, *Med Ire.*, p. 126
42. A. Simms, 'Rural settlement in medieval Ireland: the example of the royal manors of Newcastle Lyons and Esker in south county Dublin' in B. Roberts and R. Glasscock (ed.), *Villages, farms and frontiers* (Oxford, 1983), p. 146
43. For an account of the various types of manorial tenant see A. Otway-Ruthven, 'The organisation of Anglo-Norman agriculture in the Middle Ages' in *R.S.A.I. Jn.*, LXXXI (1951), p. 11
44. Brooks, *Knights' fees*, p. 32
45. Otway-Ruthven, 'Anglo-Norman agriculture', p. 10, n. 51
46. Otway-Ruthven, 'Knight service', p. 10
47. *Ibid.*, p. 11
48. Brooks, *Knights' fees*, p. 106
49. Hore, VI, pp 189-91
50. *Ibid.*, pp 342-3
51. Empey, 'Tipperary', pp 84-5
52. Hore, VI, p. 185
53. *Ibid.*, p. 191
54. Otway-Ruthven, 'Norman settlement', p. 76
55. B. Graham, 'The mottes of the Norman liberty of Meath' in H. Murtagh (ed.), *Irish Midland Studies* (Athlone, 1980)
56. T. McNeill, *Anglo-Norman Ulster* (Edinburgh, 1980), p. 65
57. R. Glasscock, 'Mottes in Ireland' in *Château-Gaillard*, VII (1975), p. 110
58. *Ibid.*, p. 96
59. *R.S.A.I. Jn.*, XVI (1886), p. 39
60. T. Westropp, 'On Irish motes and early Norman castles' in *R.S.A.I. Jn.*, XXXIV (1904), p. 321
61. G. Orpen, 'Mottes and Norman castles in Ireland' in *R.S.A.I. Jn.*, XXXVII (1907), p. 136
62. *Cal. inq. post mortem*, III, no. 1912, p. 222
63. Brooks, *Knights' fees*, p. 137

64. *Ibid.*, p. 24
65. Jeffrey, *Castles*, p. 205
66. D. King and L. Alcock, 'Ringworks of England and Wales' in *Chateau Gaillard* III (1969), pp 90-107
67. Scott and Martin, *Expugnatio Hibernica*, pp 53, 81
68. *Ibid.*, p. 57
69. I. Bennett, 'Preliminary archaeological excavations at Ferrycarrig ringwork, Newtown, county Wexford' in *Wexford Hist. Soc. Jn.*, X (1984-5), pp 25-43
70. Claire Cotter, personal communication
71. First edition ordnance survey maps, county Wexford, sheet 32
72. Brooks, *Knights' fees*, p. 147
73. W. Colfer, Anglo-Norman settlement in medieval Shelburne 1169-1307, unpublished M.Litt. thesis, T.C.D. (1986)
74. G. Hadden, 'Some earthworks in county Wexford' in *Cork. Hist. Soc. Jn.*, LXIX (1964), p. 120
75. Graham, *Mottes*
76. Orpen, *Normans*, II, p. 343
77. R. Glasscock, 'Moated sites and deserted boroughs and villages: two neglected aspects of Anglo-Norman settlement in Ireland' in N. Stephens and R. Glasscock (ed.), *Irish Geographical Studies* (Belfast, 1970), p. 164
78. T. Barry, *Medieval moated sites of south-east Ireland* (Oxford, 1977)
79. *Ibid.*, p. 103
80. *Ibid.*
81. Terry Barry, personal communication
82. C. Empey, 'Knocktopher', pp 334-5
83. *Chart. St Mary's, Dublin*, II, p. 154
84. G. Orpen (ed.), 'Charters of Earl Richard Marshal of the forests of Ross and Taghmon', in *R.S.A.I. Jn.*, LXVI (1934), pp 54-63; Brooks, *Knights' fees*, p. 110
85. T. Barry, 'The medieval moated sites of county Wexford' in *Old Wexford Soc. Jn.*, VI (1976-7), pp 5-17
86. G. Stout et al., 'Sites and monuments record of county Wexford' in *Wexford Hist. Soc. Jn.*, XI (1987), pp 4-13
87. Graham, 'Meath', p. 225
88. Glasscock, 'Moated sites', pp 173-4
89. Colfer, 'Shelburne'
90. J. Bradley, 'Planned Anglo-Norman towns in Ireland' in H. Clarke and A. Simms (ed.), *The comparative history of urban origins in non-Roman Europe* (Oxford, 1985), pp 414-21
91. *Cal. doc. Ire.*, *1171-1251*, no. 39
92. B. Graham, 'The towns of medieval Ireland' in R. Butlin (ed.), *The development of the Irish town* (London, 1977), pp 28-60
93. Bradley, 'Anglo-Norman towns'
94. R. Glasscock, 'The study of deserted medieval settlement in Ireland (to 1968))' in M. Beresford and J. Hurst (ed.), *Deserted medieval villages studies* (London, 1971), p. 288
95. Hore, VI, p. 609
96. *Ibid*, p. 185
97. Graham, 'Towns', p. 33
98. *Ibid.*, p. 32
99. Otway-Ruthven, 'Norman settlement', p. 79
100. *Cal. doc. Ire.*, 1252-1284, no. 1330
101. Graham, 'Towns', p. 37
102. Bradley, 'Anglo-Norman towns', p. 419
103. Orpen, *Normans*, II, p. 230
104. Hore, II, p. 19
105. W. Colfer, 'The tower of Hook' in *Wexford Hist. Soc. Jn.*, X (1984-5), pp 69-78
106. Graham, 'Towns', p. 41
107. Bradley, 'Anglo-Norman towns', p. 425
108. Glasscock, 'Moated sites', p. 170
109. Otway-Ruthven, *Med. Ire.*, pp 37-9
110. N. Furlong, *Dermot King of Leinster and the foreigners* (Tralee, 1973), p. 92
111. A. Gwynn and R. Hadcock, *Medieval religious houses: Ireland* (London, 1970), p. 117
112. Otway-Ruthven, *Med. Ire.*, p. 127

113. Orpen, *Normans*, II, p. 324
114. *Chart. St Mary's, Dublin*, I, p. 357
115. For a full account of the history of Dunbrody Abbey see J. Ffrench, 'Dunbrody and its history' in *R.S.A.I. Jn.*, XXVI (1896), pp 336-48
116. *Chartul. St Mary's, Dublin*, II, pp 307-8
117. J. Bernard, 'The foundation of Tintern Abbey, county Wexford' in *R.I.A. Proc.*, C, XXXIII, (1917), pp 527-9
118. Orpen, *Normans*, II, p. 207
119. *Chart. St Mary's, Dublin*, II, p. 151
120. Hore, II, p. 16
121. *Extents of mon. possessions*, pp 353-8
122. H. Wood, 'The Templars in Ireland' in *R.I.A. Proc.*, C, XXVI (1907), pp 327-371; C. Falkiner, 'The Hospital of St John of Jerusalem in Ireland' in *Ibid.*, pp 275-317
123. Orpen, *Normans*, I, p. 274
124. *Cal. doc. Ire.*, 1171-1251, no. 85
125. Hore, IV, p. 261
126. Gwynn and Hadcock, *Religious houses*, p. 329
127. *Ibid.*, p. 339
128. *Extents of Ir. mon. possessions*, pp 100-103
129. H. Shields, 'The walling of New Ross: A thirteenth century poem' in *Long Room*, XXII-XVI (1976), pp 24-33
130. J. F. Lydon, *The Lordship of Ireland in the middle ages* (Dublin, 1972), p. 169
131. Hore, I, p. 142
132. *Cal. doc. Ire.*, 1252-1284, no. 1873
133. R. Frame, 'The Justiciar and the murder of the MacMurroughs in 1282' in *I.H.S.*, XVIII, (1972-3), pp 223-30
134. *Cal. inq. post mortem*, III, no. 1912, p. 222
135. P.R.I. rep. D.K. 26
136. Memorandum rolls, P.R.O.I., Cal. Ex. 2/Z, p. 251
137. Brooks, *Knights' fees*
138. Otway-Ruthven, *Med. Ire.*, pp 224-76
139. Hore, VI, p. 18
140. H. Leask, *Irish castles and castellated houses* (Dublin, 1941), p. 75
141. C. Cairns, *Irish tower houses: a county Tipperary case study* (Athlone, 1987)
142. Leask, *op.cit.*, p. 76
143. Hore, V, p. 412
144. Jeffrey, *Castles*
145. Hore, V, p. 413
146. M. Gardiner and P. Ryan, *Soils of county Wexford* (Dublin, 1964)
147. Otway-Ruthven, *Med. Ire.*, p. 286

4   *Richard Roche*

1. For the formation of baronies, see W. Nolan, *Tracing the past* (Dublin, 1984), pp 13-15.
2. The southern coast of Ireland has traditionally been regarded as one of the most dangerous in Europe. R. Frazer, *Statistical survey of county Wexford* (Dublin, 1807), pp 20-36
3. M. Gardiner and P. Ryan, *Soils of county Wexford* (Dublin, 1964)
4. The full Irish name for Forth is Fotharta an Chairn, to distinguish it from Fotharta Fea or Fothartha Uí Nualláin, now the barony of Forth in county Carlow.
5. E. Culleton, *The south Wexford landscape* (Dublin, 1980)
6. J. Dalton, 'Loch Garman' in *Past*, I (1920), pp 15-61
7. E. Culleton, *Early man in county Wexford* (Dublin, 1984)
8. J. Lymbery, 'A silver groat of Mary, before her marriage to Philip of Spain' in *Royal Hist. and Arch. Assoc. Ire. Jn.*, II (1873), p. 328
9. The Carnsore dolmen apparently stood in what is now known as 'Kemp's Park'.
10. The standing stone at Cotts, near Broadway, was excavated in 1921 by R. A. S. MacAlister, but nothing substantive was discovered.

11. *Lr Gabála*, I
12. Ptolemy named the Menapii among the Celtic tribes who colonised the coast of Leinster; it is suggested that Menapia, an old name for Wexford, was derived from this.
13. The inscription on the Saltee ogham stone has been deciphered as *Lonamni avi Bari*, which may mean Lonam Ui Bairr, or Lonam of Bargy. Lonam may have been a hermit. MacAlister, *Corpus Inscriptionem*, I, p. 48.
14. G. O'Brien, 'The holy wells of Wexford' in *Wex. Hist. Soc. Jn.*, IX (1983-4), pp 27-35
15. M. O'Kelly, *Archaeological survey and excavation of St Vogue's church enclosure and other monuments at Carnsore, county Wexford* (Cork, 1975)
16. T. C. Butler, O.S.A., personal communication
17. It was probably these Norse who were referred to as 'the foreign people' occupying the area in the ninth century.
18. In 1283, a group of Ostmen still survived on the Wexford coast, according to an inquisition of William de Valence. Curtis, *Med. Ire.*, pp 406-7.
19. R. Roche, *The Norman invasion of Ireland* (Tralee, 1970) pp 65-6
20. *Gir. Camb. op.*, V
21. G. Orpen, *Song of Dermot and the Earl* (Oxford, 1892)
22. [R. Holinshed,] *Holinshed's Irish chronicle* (reprint, Dublin, 1979 of orig. ed. London 1579)
23. Orpen, *Normans*, I, pp 396-7
24. M. Gwinell, Some aspects of the historical geography of county Wexford 1770-1870 unpublished Ph.D. thesis, University of London, 1983
25. H. Hore (ed.), 'An account of the barony of Forth in the county of Wexford' in *Kilk. and south east of Ire., Arch. Soc. Jn.*, IV (1862), pp 53-84
26. Brooks, *Knights' fees*
27. 'List of dispossessed landowners in 1664' in *Ir. Geneal.* IV, no. 4 (1971), pp 275-302.
28. Hore, 'Account'
29. Orpen, *Song*, pp 254-5
30. Orpen, *Normans*, I, p. 324
31. H. Leask, *Irish castles and castellated houses* (Dundalk, 1941)
32. *Ibid;* B. Colfer, *The county of Wexford* (Wexford, 1981), refers to a total of 365 castles; K. Browne, *Wexford* (Dublin, 1927), refers to 77 in Forth and Bargy.
33. There was a convent of Franciscan friars near Wexford and a convent for Knights Templar at Kerlogue (Forth). The Augustinians were at Our Lady's Island and subsequently at Grantstown, having been ejected from neighbouring Clonmines.
34. P.R.O.I. Cal. Plea Roll, 10 June 1305
35. As early as 1339, John Le Botiller, constable of the King's Castle of Ballytrent (Forth) was granted one hundred shillings for his labours and expenses in repelling the Kavanaghs. P. Hore, 'The Barony of Forth' in *Past*, I (1920), pp 62-106
36. H. Hore, 'The Clan Kavanagh, temp. Henry VIII' in *Kilk and south-east of Ire. Arch. Soc. Jn.*, II (1858), pp 73-92
37. *Cal. Carew MSS*, V, p. 342
38. *Ibid*
39. *Cal. S.P.I.*, XXXIII
40. H. Hore, 'Account', *passim*
41. About 60 per cent of Wexford land was confiscated after the rebellion of 1641.
42. Browne, *Wexford*
43. In 1613-14, the landowning class in county Wexford numbered a little over 3,000 people, out of a total population of 15,000. W. Butler, 'Confiscations in Irish history IV — the plantation of Wexford' in *Studies*, IV (1915), pp 411-27.
44. H. Hore, 'Account'
45. [R. Stanyhurst] *Richardi Stanihursti Dubliniensis de rebus in Hibernia gestes* (Antwerp, 1584)
46. H. Wallop to Walsingham, 8 June 1581, *Cal. S.P.I.*, *1574-1585*, p. 322
47. D. O'Muirithe and T. Dolan, 'Pooles Glossary' in *Past*, XIII (1979), pp 1-69
48. There appears to have been a strong Flemish element among the first colonists of the twelfth century. Names of Flemish origin still found in Forth and Bargy include Prendergast, Roche, Fleming, Cheevers and Siggins. Orpen, *Normans*, I, pp 396-8
49. Under the Grand Jury system, each barony was responsible for the upkeep of its own roads.
50. H. Hore, 'Account'
51. C. de la Tocnaye, *A Frenchman's walks through Ireland 1796-7* (reprint, Belfast, 1984 of orig. ed. Dublin, 1797), pp 54-5.

52. K. Whelan (ed.), 'An account of the baronies of Forth and Bargy in 1814' in *Wex. Hist. Soc. Jn.*, XI (1986-7), pp 14-32
53. A. Griffith, letters to *Dublin Magazine*, Sept. 1764
54. S. Hall, *Ireland, its scenery, characters, etc.*, (London, 1841-3), II, pp 183-4
55. Browne, *Wexford*, pp 87-8
56. The water mill of medieval origin at Mulrankin is still (1987) in operation. Another, the 'Mill o' Rags' in Johnstown, closed only in the 1970s.
57. The windmill at Tacumshane, still in working order, is preserved as a national monument and is perfectly typical of the mills that once proliferated in the barony.
58. *People*, 6 May 1887
59. *People*, 8 Apr 1899
60. *People*, 19 Sept 1908

5   *Henry Goff*

1. B. Colfer, *The county of Wexford* (Wexford, 1981)
2. *Ordnance Survey*, table of areas, county Wexford
3. *Inq. cancell. Hib. repert.*, 1, Jas I, no. 3
4. *Ibid*.
5. *Ibid*.
6. *Ibid*.
7. The descent of the lordship of Wexford from the time of Henry II is given in full in Hore, V, pp 41-5. Details of knights' fees for Scarawalsh barony from the thirteenth to the fifteenth century are in Brooks *Knights' fees*, pp 5-9, 92-5, 129-41, 143-4.
8. See below p. 136
9. See below p. 148
10. See below p. 149
11. A. Gwynn and R. Hadcock, *Medieval religious houses in Ireland* (London, 1970), pp 250, 175, 169.
12. Kavanaghs in 1543 acknowledged that Enniscorthy and Ferns were crown manors and also agreed that the king hold Clohamon and Clonmullen.
13. *Cal. pat. rolls Ire., Hen VIII-Eliz.*, pp 43-5. The agreement is incorrectly placed under the year 1538 in the calendar. It was signed in Sept. of the thirty fifth year of the reign of Henry VIII.
14. *Cal. pat. rolls Ire., Hen VIII-Eliz.*, p. 43
15. For examples of these preliminary surrender and regrant submissions see *Cal. Carew MSS, 1515-74*, nos 116, 159, 160, 163, 164, 165, 167, 171.
16. *Cal. pat. rolls Ire., Hen VIII-Eliz.*, pp 43-4
17. H. Hore, 'The clan Kavanagh, temp. Henry VIII' in *R.S.A.I. Jn.*, V (1858-9), pp 87-8.
18. *Fiants Ire., Philip and Mary*, no. 6809
19. *Ibid*.
20. See below p. 144
21. See below p. 146
22. 'Abstract of the Kavanaghs and their lands as it has been delivered in times past', (1572) P.R.O., S.P., 63/38/65
23. Nicholas Heron was probably a member of the Heron family from Northumberland, who came to Ireland and settled in the Pale during the reign of Henry VIII. He made himself useful to the government and was appointed constable of Leighlin, sheriff of Carlow, justice of the peace, seneschal of Wexford in 1562, constable of Wexford castle in 1563 and constable of Fern's castle in 1565. P.R.O., S.P. 63/106/70-1; *Fiants Ire., Eliz*, nos 34, 182, 218, 381, 545, 1118, 2285; Hughes, *Patentee officers*, p. 65.
24. Memorial on the state of Ireland by lord lieutenant Sussex, 1562, *Cal. Carew MSS, 1515-74*, p. 345
25. *Fiants Ire., Philip and Mary*, no. 251; *Fiants Ire., Eliz.*, nos 232, 958
26. For a fuller discussion of Sidney's policies see N. Canny, *The Elizabethan conquest of Ireland* (Hassocks, 1976), pp 48-51.
27. Sidney's directives to seneschals, (1566) P.R.O., S.P. 63/17/13
28. Nicholas White to Cecil, 10 June 1569 P.R.O., S.P. 63/28/24

29. *Fiants Ire., Eliz.*, no. 1196
30. Pedigree of Masterson of Wichmalbank, Cheshire, Ferns, Rosseminock, Clone and Monaseed, *c.* 1370-1815, G.O. MS 168, pp 334-41.
31. *Fiants Ire., Eliz.*, no. 1285
32. Sidney and Irish council to the English privy council, 27 Dec. 1569 P.R.O., S.P. 63/29/86.
33. *Fiants Ire., Eliz.*, nos 6789, 6790
34. *Ibid.*, no. 2446
35. White was yet another Englishman anxious to acquire lands and offices in Ireland. He was appointed seneschal of Wexford and constable of Wexford castle in 1569 on Elizabeth's instructions. Three years later, he received a further appointment as master of the rolls and the following year became a commissioner of the courts of wards. One of his daughters married Robert Browne of Mulrankin, a member of the long established family in the barony of Bargy, county Wexford. White died in England in 1590 and after his death the property descended to his son Andrew, who held title until his death in 1599. Andrew's successor was a boy of sixteen also called Nicholas. Hughes, *Patentee officers*, p. 138. Inquisition *p.m.* taken at Wexford on 6 Nov. 1600 after Andrew White's death is printed in full in Hore, VI, p. 558 but no source is quoted. *Inq. cancell. Hib. repert.*, I, Wexford, Chas I, no. 76.
36. *Inq. cancell. Hib. repert.*, I, Wexford, Jas I, no. 16
37. Hore MS 31, Pedigrees of Anglo-Irish families
38. *Fiants Ire., Eliz.*, no. 2214
39. *Ibid.*, nos 1577, 2121-2
40. *Ibid.*, no. 2663
41. Thomas Masterson to Sir Francis Knelleys, treasurer of her majesty's household, 23 May 1580 P.R.O., S.P. 63/73/66, I; *Cal. S.P. Ire., 1574-85*, p. 229; Masterson to Irish privy council, 10 Apr. 1580 P.R.O., S.P. 63/72/42.
42. Wallop to Walsingham, 1 Mar. 1581 P.R.O., S.P. 63/81/2; *Cal. S.P. Ire., 1574-85*, p. 290
43. Russell was appointed lord deputy and a commissioner of the court of wards in 1594; Hughes, *Patentee officers*, p. 114; Grey to Elizabeth, Sept. 1582 P.R.O., S.P. 63/95/82
44. Extensive list of persons pardoned in *Fiants Ire., Eliz.*, no. 3904
45. *Ibid.*, nos 4091, 4092
46. *Ibid.*, nos 3786, 4245
47. *Ibid.*, nos 4242, 4244, 4245
48. Burke, *Landed gentry of Ireland* (1911), pp 119-20
49. *Fiants Ire., Eliz.*, no. 2890
50. Wallop to Burghley, 12 Aug. 1586 P.R.O., S.P. 63/109/48; *Cal. S.P. Ire.*, 1586-8, p. 134 [*D.N.B.*, XX, p. 608, states that the abbey lands were estimated to contain 12,464 acres. This is a ridiculous figure. Wallop's own estimate of 360 acres probably underestimates the actual acreage.
51. *D.N.B.*, XX, pp 607-9
52. Wallop to Walsingham, 6 Jan. 1586 P.R.O., S.P. 63/122/15; *Cal. S.P. Ire., 1586-8*, p. 5
53. Wallop to Walsingham, 8 June 1581 P.R.O., S.P. 63/75/83; *Cal. S.P. Ire., 1574-85*, p. 306
54. Wallop to Walsingham, 28 July 1581 P.R.O., S.P. 63/85/27; *Cal. S.P. Ire., 1574-85*, p. 317
55. Wallop to Walsingham, 6 Jan. 1586 P.R.O., S.P. 63/122/15; *Cal. S.P. Ire., 1586-8*, p. 5
56. See above p. 146
57. *Inq. cancell. Hib. repert*, I, Wexford, Jas I, nos 7, 21
58. See fig. 5.4
59. *Fiants Ire., Eliz.*, nos 5964, 6043. For additional information on Norris, see M. MacCarthy-Morrogh, *The Munster Plantation* (Oxford, 1986), *passim.*
60. Ground rents are collected by the Wallop heirs' local agent, Huggard and Brennan, solicitors, Wexford.
61. *Inq. cancell. Hib. repert.*, I, Wexford, Jas I, no. 21
62. See fig. 8.1
63. *Fiants Ire., Eliz.*, nos 5596, 5731
64. *Ibid.*, no. 5596
65. *Ibid.*, no. 5731
66. The admission papers to the King's Inns in London contain names of a number of Wexford Anglo-Irish including William Sinnott later to be appointed justice of the liberties of Wexford and Edward Sinnott also of Wexford, both of whom were admitted to the Inner Temple. D. Cregan, 'Irish Catholic admissions to the English inns of court, 1558-1625' in *Ir. Jurist*, V (1970), p. 111
67. Hore MS 31

68. *Description of Ire., 1598*, p. 63
69. *Cal. S.P., 1599-160*, p. 52
70. *Ibid.*, p. 52; *Inq. cancell. Hib. repert.*, I, Wexford, Jas I, no. 7
71. *Cal. S.P. Ire., 1596-7*, p. 71
72. *Ibid.*, pp 169-71, 184-5
73. An overthrow of the English soldiers in the county of Wexford, Chronicles of Ireland, 25 May 1598, B.M., Harl MS 3544.
74. Davys to Cecil, Feb. 1604 *Cal. S.P. Ire., 1603-6*, p. 146
75. *Inq. cancell. Hib. repert.*, I, Wexford, Jas I, nos 1, 5; *Cal. exchequer. inq.*, Wexford, Jas I, nos 2, 5, 7, 21, 26
76. *Ibid.*, no. 7; *Cal. pat. rolls Ire., Jas I* pp 64-5
77. *Inq. cancell. Hib. repert.*, I, Wexford, Jas I, no. 1
78. *Cal. pat. rolls Ire., Jas I*, pp 55-8; J. Ainsworth and E. Mac Lysaght, 'Report on Colclough papers' in *Anal. Hib.*, XX (1958), pp 9-16
79. *Cal. pat. rolls Ire., Jas I, p. 64; Civil Survey*, pp 278,287; Hughes, *Patentee officers*, p. 61; The name is consistently spelled 'O'Breine' in the *Civil Survey*, 'O'Bryan' in the Down Survey and 'O'Brien' in the inquisitions.
80. *Cal. pat. rolls Ire., Jas I*, p. 130; Hughes, *Patentee officers*, p. 61; *Civil Survey* p. 263
81. Petition of Teig O'Brien to English privy council, July 1609 (Philadelphia papers, in Hore MS 62, pp 63-4)
82. *Cal. pat. rolls Ire., Jas I*, p. 64
83. *Cal. pat. rolls Ire., Jas I*, p. 64; Petition of Dermot Kavanagh on behalf of his father Dowling macBrien to Sir Ralph Winwood, *Cal. S.P. Ire., 1647-60*, p. 41
84. *Cal. pat. rolls Ire., Jas I*, pp 74, 500
85. Petition of Eleanor Kavanagh on behalf of her husband Donal Spainneach, the freeholders and inhabitants of Templeshambo, *Cal. S.P. Ire., 1647-60*, p. 42; Petition of Morgan Kavanagh to Sir Ralph Winwood, *ibid.*, p. 42; *Cal. pat. rolls Ire., Jas I*, p. 500
86. *Ibid.*, p. 74
87. English privy council to Chichester, 21 Jan. 1608 *Cal. S.P. Ire., 1606-8*, pp 396-7
88. *Cal. pat. rolls Ire., Jas I*, p. 141
89. *Ibid.*, p. 141
90. *Ibid.*
91. *Cal. S.P. Ire., 1611-14*, pp 451-2; *Carew MSS, 1603-24*, pp 251-2
92. *Idem*
93. *Cal. S.P. Ire., 1611-14*, p. 218
94. *Cal. pat. rolls Ire., Jas I*, p. 208
95. *Cal. pat. rolls Ire., Jas I*, pp 450-1
96. Court of castle chamber records, in Egmont MSS, *H.M.C., rep. 17*, pp 1-60
97. Cal. S.P. Ire., 1615-25, pp 124-6, incorrectly placed under May 1616.
98. I have prepared a paper on the plantation for publication in a forthcoming issue of *I.H.S.*
99. Scheme is not set down in any one place but is based on various sources: *Acts privy council, 1616-17*, pp 334, 243, 310, 333-4, 352; *Cal. pat. rolls Ire., Jas I*, pp 357-9, 404, 422-3, 482; Council to St John, 18 July 1617, *Acts privy council 1616-17*, p. 310.
100. O.S. acreage for the area is 106,659 acres.
101. Servitor Henry Murphy was son of John Murphy, a member of the jury which had found the king's title to the area. *Cal. pat. rolls Ire., Jas I*, p. 366
102. Figures are abstracted from *Cal. pat. rolls Ire., Jas I*.
103. Docwra to [ ], 3 Mar. 1618 *Cal. S.P. Ire., 1615-25*, p. 187; Hughes, *patentee officers*, p. 42
104. Blundell to the English privy council, 20 July 1620, P.R.O., S.P. 63/235/22; St John and Irish council to English privy council, 6 Dec. 1620 *Cal. S.P. Ire., 1615-25*, p. 303.
105. St John to the English privy council, 29 Sept. 1619 *Cal. S.P. Ire., 1615-25* p. 262-3; *ibid.*, 9 Nov. 1619, p. 267.
106. St John and the Irish privy council to the English privy council 6 Dec. 1620 *Cal. S.P. Ire., 1615-25*, p. 304.
107. *Ibid.*, p. 306; A. Gwynn, 'Irish emigration to the West Indies, 1612-43' in *Studies*, XVIII, no. 71 (1929), pp 375-93
108. *Cal. pat. rolls Ire., Jas I*, p. 255
109. *Acts privy council, 1617-18*, pp 12-13
110. *Cal. pat. rolls Ire., Jas I*, pp 412, 445
111. Falkland, report on the state of Ireland, 1625 P.R.O. S.P., 63/241/190; *Cal. S.P. Ire., 1615-25*, pp 71-6)

112. See below.
113. Falkland, report on the state of Ireland, 1625 *Cal. S.P. Ire., 1625-32*, p. 72
114. *D.N.B.*, I, pp 475-6
115. *Cal. pat. rolls Ire., Jas I.*, p. 358. Acreage figures abstracted from *Civil Survey*. He was son of Thomas Annesley, high constable of Newport, Buckinghamshire. Born in 1585 he came to Dublin in 1606 and was particularly friendly with Chichester, the lord deputy from 1604 to 1615, who secured a number of small offices of state for him. In May 1612 he was granted a reversion of the clerkship of the check of the armies and garrisons and in 1614 he became M.P. for county Armagh in the Irish parliament. From then on his career advanced quickly. He was knighted in July 1616, became principal secretary of state for Ireland in 1618 and was appointed an Irish baronet in 1620. In 1628 he was appointed Baron Mountnorris and in 1632 became treasurer at wars.
116. He was elder son of Sir Richard Wingfield, governor of Portsmouth and was nephew of William Fitzwilliam, Lord Deputy of Ireland. Unlike Annesley, who was by training and inclination an administrator, Wingfield trained as a soldier and was deputy to the vice-treasurer of Ireland, Henry Wallop, from 1580 to 1586.
117. *Cal. pat. rolls Ire., Jas I*, p. 404
118. *Civil Survey*, pp 7, 8, 9, 264
119. *Ibid.*, pp 12, 16, 18, 19, 20, 59
120. *Ibid.*, p. 18
121. *Cal. pat. rolls Ire., Jas I*, pp 221-2
122. *Inq. cancell. Hib. repert.*, I Wexford, Chas I, no. 53
123. *Cal. pat. rolls Ire., Jas I*, p. 404
124. T.C.D., Deposition of Jonas Rushworth, F2, 12, 165, printed in Hore, VI, p. 479
125. *Civil Survey*, pp 266-8, 271, 293-4
126. Wallop to Walsingham, 1 Mar 1581 P.R.O., S.P. 63/81/2
127. *Civil Survey*, p. 260. Edward Masterson of Ferns and Richard Shorthall married the other two heiresses and as a result also acquired lands in the area.
128. Down Survey, pp 63, 65a, 65b
129. *Cal. pat. rolls. Ire., Jas I*, p. 58; Down Survey, p. 65b
130. *Inq. cancell. Hib. repert.*, I, Wexford, Chas I, no. 90; P. O Mórdha, 'The MacMahons of Monaghan (1603-1640)' in *Clogher Rec*, II, no. 1 (1957), pp 148-69; II, no. 2 (1958), pp 311-27; P. Ó Gallachóir, 'The 1641 war in Clogher' in *ibid*, IV, no. 3 (1962), pp 135-47; B. Ó Bric, Galway townsmen as the owners of land in Connacht, 1585-1641, unpublished M.A. thesis, U.C.G., 1974
131. *Inq. cancell. Hib. repert.*, I, Wexford, Jas I, no. 91; details of Mullineux's lands given in the course of a grant to Sir James Craig on 21 Mar 1622, *Cal. pat. rolls. Ire., Jas I*, p. 531.
132. William Brereton's travels in Ireland, 1635, in Falkiner, *Illustrations*, p. 390; *Inq. cancell. Hib. repert.*, I, Wexford, Jas I, no. 16; *Civil Survey*, p. 266
133. *Inq. cancell. Hib. repert.*, I, Wexford, Chas I, nos 90, 91, 97, 108; *Civil Survey*, pp 279-80, 287
134. Grand panel of the county of Wexford, 25 July 1608, *Cal. Carew MSS, 1603-24*, p. 35
135. P.R.O.I., Memoranda rolls of the exchequer, 12 Chas I, m. 126, calendared in Hore, VI, pp 572-81
136. *Civil Survey*, p. 273; Down Survey, p. 65b. Aughrim is the modern townland of Killoughrim.
137. *Civil Survey*, pp 268-9, 280
138. *Cal. pat. rolls. Ire., Jas I*, p. 500
139. Down Survey, pp 63, 64, 65b
140. Ten O'Briens are listed as owning 5,950 acres in the *Civil Survey*, pp 262, 273-4, 276-80, 283-4, 286; Down Survey, pp 63, 65b
141. P.R.O.I., common pleas fines entry book, 1A/52/171, pp 116, 123
142. O.S., Wexford, nos 4, 5, 9, 10, 14, 15
143. Return of Thomas Ram, bishop of Ferns, regal visitation, 1615, printed in Hore, VI, pp 257-74
144. B.M., Harl. MS 4297, p. 54
145. *Civil Survey*, p. 267; Down Survey, p. 63
146. All these figures should be treated with caution as 5 D.S. Acres = 4 C.S. acres. The Ordnance Survey acreage for the barony is 106,659 acres, a figure which demonstrates the extent of the under-measurement of the Down and Civil Surveys.
147. See fig. 5.4. For purposes of ascertaining individual owners, the size of the holding was computed by dividing the total acreage by the number of owners unless otherwise indicated.

148. The first five are catholics, the remainder are protestants.
149. The origin of Hire and Turner is uncertain; possibly they were Old English.
150. The lands of Thornton and Wale are also included in Bart. O'Brien's holding.

6   *Nicholas Furlong*

1. E. Gwynn (ed. and transl.) *The metrical Dindshenchas*, 5 vols. (Dublin, 1900-35)
2. P. Corish, 'Reformation and Counter-Reformation' in M. Berney (ed.), *Centenary history of Wexford's twin churches* (Wexford, 1958), pp 35-49
3. Hore, V, pp 200-1
4. *Idem*
5. *Ibid.*, p. 230
6. *Ibid.*, pp 229-30
7. H. Murphy, *Families of county Wexford* (Dublin, 1986), pp 246-9
8. Hore, V, pp 236-7
9. F. Martin, 'The Rossetters of Rathmacknee castle' in *Past*, V (1949), pp 103-116; VI (1950), pp 13-44
10. F. Grannell, *The Franciscans in Wexford* (Wexford, 1980), pp 17-19
11. *Idem*.; Corish, 'Reformation'
12. Hore, V, p. 240
13. *Ibid.*, pp 247-9
14. Corish, 'Reformation', pp 44-5
15. Flood, *Ferns*, pp xvi, 215-7; N. French, *The bleeding Iphigenia* (Louvain, 1674)
16. Hore, V, p. 257
17. *Ibid.*, p. 253 *et. seq.*
18. *Ibid.*, p. 247
19. *Ibid.*, pp 256-7
20. Martin, 'Rossetters'
21. Hore, V, p. 303
22. Corish, 'Reformation', p. 48
23. Hore, V, p. 298
24. *Ibid.*, p. 298 *et. seq.*
25. *Ibid.*, p. 296
26. *Ibid.*, p. 312
27. *Ibid.*, p. 320
28. *Ibid.*, p. 321
29. R. Simington (ed.), *The transplantation to Connaught 1654-1658* (Dublin, 1970)
30. Grannell, *Franciscans*, p. 31
31. K. Browne, *Wexford* (Dublin, 1927), p. 82
32. H. Hore (ed.), 'Particulars relative to Wexford and the barony of Forth by Colonel Solomon Richards, 1682' in *R.S.A.I. Jn.*, VII (1862-3), pp 84-92
33. S. Cloney, 'The Colclough family' in *Wex. Hist. Soc. Jn.*, X (1984-5), pp 44-54
34. For the Earl of Tyrconnell, see D. Dickson, *New foundations: Ireland 1660-1800* (Dublin, 1987), pp 29-40.
35. P. Corish, *The Catholic community in the seventeenth and eighteenth centuries* (Dublin, 1981)
36. C. Murphy, 'The evolution of the Catholic community in Wexford town', unpublished lecture to Wexford Historical Society, 1985
37. The 1704 list of registered clergy is printed in Flood, *Ferns* pp 206-8.
38. Corish, *Catholic community*, p. 78
39. W. Burke, *The Irish priests in the penal times* (Waterford, 1914) pp. 312-14
40. Flood, *Ferns*, p. xviii
41. H. Fenning 'Some problems of the Irish mission 1733-1744' in *Collect. Hib.*, VIII (1965), pp 58-109
42. For his Newbawn background, see K. Whelan (ed.), *A history of Newbawn* (Newbawn, 1986).
43. N. Furlong, 'The times and life of Nicholas Sweetman 1744-1786' in *Wex. Hist. Soc. Jn.*, IX (1983-4), pp 1-19

44. P. Ó Suilleabháin, 'Documents relating to Wexford friary and parish 1733-1798' in *Collect. Hib.*, VIII (1965), pp 110-28
45. N. Furlong and J. Hayes, *Wexford in the rare oul' times* (Wexford, 1986)
46. See photographs in Berney, *Centenary record*, pp 55-7
47. Hore, V, pp 398-400
48. *Ibid.*, p. 400
49. A. Griffith, letters to *Dublin Magazine*, Sept. 1764
50. Furlong, 'Sweetman'
51. *Wexford Chronicle*, 14 Oct. 1784
53. *Idem*
53. Hore, V, pp 56-7. For a very good description of the Protestant families of late eighteenth century Wexford town, see D. Goodall, 'The freemen of Wexford in 1776' in *Ir. Geneal.*, V, no. 1 (1974), pp 103-21; V, no. 3 (1976) pp 314-34; V, no. 4 (1977), pp 448-63.
54. R. Hayes, *Biographical dictionary of Irishmen in France* (Dublin, 1949), p. 38
55. T. Powell, 'An economic factor in the Wexford rebellion of 1798', in *Studia Hib.*, XVI (1976), pp 140-58.
56. T. Bartlett, 'The Irish militia disturbances of 1793' in *Past and Present* XCIX (1983), p. 43
57. P. Kavanagh, *A popular history of 1798* (Dublin, 1916)
58. T. Pakenham, *The year of liberty* (London, 1969); C. Dickson, *The Wexford Rising in 1798* (Tralee, 1955)
59. Powell, 'Economic factor', p. 147
60. T. Handcock, Narrative of the battle of Enniscorthy 30 May 1798, NLI MS 16,230
61. D. Goodall, 'Dixon of Castlebridge, county Wexford' in *Ir. Geneal.*, VI, no. 5 (1984), pp 629-41
62. N. Furlong, *Fr John Murphy of Boolevogue* (forthcoming)
63. This was a well known phrase of T. D. Sinnott's.

7   *Rolf Loeber and Magda Stouthamer-Loeber*

1. The plantation has not been studied extensively, considering the large body of available documentation, but see W. Butler, 'The plantation of Wexford' in *Studies*, IV (1915), pp 412-27; *Anal. Hib.*, VIII (1938), p. 37; Bodl. Laud MS, 611, ff. 51, 54; A. Smyth, *Celtic Leinster: towards an historical geography of early Irish civilisation* (Dublin, 1982), p. 150.
2. Arthur Chichester credited Richard Masterson, who owned a vast tract of land in the area before the plantation, with the discovery of the King's title (Hore, VI, p. 458). The shading on the map indicates the townlands mentioned in the letters patent for the plantations (*Cal. pat. rolls, Ire., Jas I, passim*). However, as the identification of townlands often was difficult or impossible to accomplish, the shaded areas can best be considered approximations of the extent of the plantation estates. Bodl. Laud MS 611, f. 45; *Civil Survey passim*.
3. Hore, VI, pp 410-1, 451, 453
4. B. Bradshaw, *The dissolution of the religious orders in Ireland under Henry VIII* (London, 1974), p. 43; *HMC rep 15, app. III*, p. 281; Smyth, *Celtic Leinster*, p. 63; *Civil Survey*, p. xvii; *Cal. pat. roll Ire., Jas I*, p. 403; For example, when the Lord Deputy Strafford travelled in 1637 to his Fairwood park in Cosha, county Wicklow, he took the coastal road into Wexford, and then turned west at Limerick castle (*Ormonde MSS*, I, p. 40).
5. A. Grosart (ed.), *Lismore papers* (London, 1886-8), ser. 2, II, p. 164; *Anal. Hib.* VIII (1938), p. 37
6. *Cal. Carew MSS. 1603-1624*, p. 321
7. Grosart, *Lismore*, I, p. 142; The northern section of the coastal land, which is shown as a blank on fig 7.1, was granted to James Ware, Auditor-General, in 1618, but without plantation conditions (*Cal. pat. roll Ire., Jas I*, p. 361). It is possible that this was a reward for his assistance in proving the King's title, given Ware's familiarity with ancient records. Another grant went to Nicholas Kenney, the escheator for Leinster, who had helped in the initial phases of the plantation (Bodl. Laud MS 611, f. 46; *Cal. pat. roll Ire., Jas I*, pp 219, 357, 517). In each case, there is no evidence that these grantees were bound to build, or that they actually erected plantation structures.
8. *E.H.R.*, XXII (1907), pp 111-2. *Cal. S.P. Ire., 1663-5*, p. 60; Leighlin Castle and Duncannon

Fort, respectively; Hughes, *Patentee officers*. Fortescue was initially listed as a grantee, but his name does not recur in later records; *R.S.A.I. Jn.*, IV (1862-63), p. 77.

9. *Cal. S.P. Ire.*, *1611-4*, p. 80

10. *R.I.A. Proc.*, C, LXXIX (1979); For Richard Wingfield, William Parsons, and Francis Annesley, see P. Robinson, *The plantation of Ulster* (Dublin, 1984), pp 198-9

11. *R.I.A. Proc.*, C, XLVIII (1942) p. 131; *Cal. pat. rolls Ire.*, *Jas I*; p. 532; R. Gillespie, *Colonial Ulster* (Cork, 1985), pp 124, 185; T. Rabb, *Enterprise and empire . . .*, (Cambridge, 1967), p. 248.

12. The only grantee from England was an Irish expatriate Conway Brady, who does not seem to have come over. J. Gleeson, *History of the Ely O'Carroll territory* (Dublin, 1915) pp 13, 30; *Cal. pat. roll Ire.*, *Jas I*, pp 247, 268, 338-9, 578; J. Gilbert (ed.), *Calendar of ancient records of Dublin* (Dublin, 1889-1944), II, pp 530-1; *H.M.C.*, *rep 12*, app. V., p. 114; app. VI, p. 212; *Cal. S.P. Ire.*, *1647-60*, pp 41-2; Public Library, Pearse Street, Dublin, Gilbert MS 169, ff 120, 122, 213; *E.H.R.*, LXXX (1965), p. 1032; T.C.D., MS MUN/P/25/4, P/24/48 ff.; J. Stubbs, *The history of the university of Dublin . . .*, (Dublin, 1889), p. 34; J. Gilbert, *A history of the city of Dublin* (Dublin, 1854-9), I, pp 163-4; J. Crawford, *A bibliography of royal proclamations . . .*, (Oxford, 1910), II, p. 20; *Cal. S.P. Ire.*, *1615-1625*, p. 176.

13. For Annesley, see Lodge, *Peerage Ire.*, (Dublin, 1789) IV, pp 109-17; R. Loeber, *A biographical dictionary of architects in Ireland, 1600-1720* (London, 1981), pp 13-4; *Census Ire., 1659*, *passim*

14. Edward Fisher had five daughters: Mary married Walshingham Cooke, Alice married William Marwood, Lettice married William Cooke, second brother of Walshingham, and Elizabeth married Edward Chichester, grandson of Arthur Chichester. [C. T. Lamacraft], *Some funeral entries of Ireland*, (Dublin, n.d. p. 157); *Cal. pat. rolls, Ire.*, III, pp 356-7.

15. *Cal. S.P. Ire.*, *1611-14*, pp 492-4; *Anal. Hib.* XXXI (1984), p. 126. I have not found a copy of the plantation conditions that was actually signed by one of the grantees; *Anal. Hib.*, XXXII (1984), p. 126.

16. *Acts privy council Ire.*, *1616-7*, p. 237; *Cal. Carew MSS 1603-1624*, pp 211-3; Bagwell, *Stuarts*, I, p. 161

17. Exeter College, Oxford, MS 95, f 21-3; *Cal. pat. roll Ire.*, *Jas I*, p. 243; B. M. Harl. MSS 3292, f 42-42v

18. He did not include the small plantation estate of Conway Brady; Hore, VI, pp 470-1; B. M. Add. MSS 4756, f 124v; Kent county record office, Maidstone, ON 8462.

19. These castles were slightly smaller than a surviving plantation castle of this plan in Roscommon. M. Craig, *The architecture of Ireland* (London, 1982, p. 131).

20. For Annesley and Molyneux see Loeber, *Dictionary*, pp 13-4, 73-5. Letters patent of the period make frequent mention of Mountfin, also called Ballyturner, and surrounding lands, which had been confiscated after the Tyrone war (*Cal. pat. rolls Ire.*, *Jas I*, pp 64, 135, 242, 266, 531). Documents indicate that Molyneux held woods closeby as early as 1611, that he 'was in . . . occupation' of these lands in 1614, acted as a Justice of the Peace in the county in 1618, and was active in the area at least as late as 1624 (Hore, VI, pp 456, 548; *Cal. pat. rolls Ire.*, *Jas I*, p. 266; *Cal. S.P. Ire.*, *1615-25*, p. 478). A contemporary source mentions that he died at St John's, south of Enniscorthy, a property acquired by his brother Daniel in 1615 (P.R. O.I., MS 1A.53.67, f. 133; *Cal. pat. rolls Ire.*, *Jas I*, p. 320; W. Smith (ed.), *Calendar of Salisbury correspondence* (Cardiff, 1954) p. 69; Hore, VI, p. 558. This house was described in the *Civil Survey* of 1654 as 'a faire stone house', but has since been replaced (*Civil Survey*, p. 224).

21. Contrary to Hore, VI, p. 560, contemporary documents show that the largest part of the property of Mountfin and the nearby Tomgarrow were owned by two members of the Breine family; *Civil Survey* p. 278; *Inq. cancell. Hib. repert.*, *Chas II* nos 9, 11, 30; the ownership in the early seventeenth century is less clear; it is possible that Molyneux was only a tenant. Additional information and a photograph was kindly supplied by the late R. Eustace, who lived at Mountfin as a youth. His recollections were that an asymmetrically placed hall faced the front with a drawing room on the right hand side. A large dining room and the kitchen occupied the back portion of the main floor. Smaller rooms were in the towers. It should be made clear that contemporary records do not reveal when Mountfin was built. It is not clearly mentioned in the *Civil Survey*, while the map of the barony of Scarawalsh in 1657 possibly shows a small building at this site. P.R.O.I., Clayton MS no. 27.

22. *Cal. pat. roll Ire.*, *Jas I.*, pp 412, 445; *Census Ire., 1659*, p. 552. I am indebted to David Dickson for his interpretation that the poll tax account refers to adult males. Whether all adults, however poor, were included is not clear. Hore, VI, pp 615-6.

23. In comparison, a contemporary estimate of the number of houses in Ferns in 1645 was 50 or 60 *(Father Luke Wadding* (Dublin 1957), pp 569), which compares well to the 76 inhabitants noted in *Census Ire., 1659*, p. 555; *Cal. S.P. Ire., 1615-25*, p. 305; T. Barry, *Medieval moated sites of south-east Ireland*, (Oxford, 1977)p. 153; T.C.D., MS 818, f. 16; *Civil Survey passim*; B.M. Add. MSS 4756, f 137; *H.M.C. rep. 15* app. III, p. 294; Kent county record office, Maidstone, ON 8732; *Cal. pat. rolls Ire., Jas I*, p. 403

24. J. O'Callaghan, 'Fortified houses of the sixteenth century in south Wexford' in *Old Wex. Soc. Jn.*, VIII (1980-1), pp 1-51

25. For Enniscorthy castle, see Hore, VI, *passim*; for Ferns, see *Cal. S:P. Ire., 1625-32*, p. 95; *N.H.I.*, IX, figs. 36-7; Barry, *Moated sites*, pp 140, 143; for the sparse surviving medieval sculpture in this area of this period, see J. Hunt *Irish medieval figure sculpture, 1200-1600* (Dublin, 1974), I, pp 236-240; Smyth, *Celtic Leinster*, p. 150

26. K. Nicholls, *Gaelic and Gaelicised Ireland in the middle ages* (London, 1972), p. 172; Bodl. Laud MS 611, f. 48v-49v; J. Hughes, 'The fall of the clan Kavanagh' in *R.S.A.I. Jn.*, II (1872-3), pp 282-305; K. Nicholls, 'The Kavanaghs, 1400-1700' in *Ir. Geneal* V (1974-9), pp 435-47, 573-80, 730-4. J. Lodge, *Desiderata curiosa Hibernica* (Dublin, 1772), I, p. 372; *Cal. pat. roll Ire., Jas I*, p. 91 shows, for example, that the Synnotts of Ballybrennan had been granted lands in the late sixteenth century, forfeited by the attainder of some of the O'Morchoes.

27. Judging from P. Harbison *Guide to the national monuments . . .* (London, 2nd ed., 1975), and the *Civil Survey*. The latter source mentions a few castles, (probably tower houses), owned by native inhabitants, as at Brownswood, on the Slaney, at Ballymore near Ferns (survey of 1657 at Ballymore House), Cooladine, Garrynisk, Oulart, Borris, and Tomenmaghtiry. *Civil Survey*, pp 1, 61, 261; *Cal. pat. roll Ire., Jas I*, p. 361. Stone houses stood at Tomgarrow and Tombrick (both on the Slaney) and Clondaw. *Civil Survey*, pp 58, 278; *Cal. pat. roll Ire., Jas I*, *passim*; Barry, *Moated sites*, pp 149, 151, 213-31. Examples of moats are Oulartwick where Henry Synnott FitzPierce lived, Ballinhask the residence of Edmund Synnott, Edmund Synnott at Garrynisk, Jasper Synnott at Ballymore, Stephen Synnott at Corbally. *Cal. pat. roll Ire., Jas I*, p. 361; E. Hawkins (ed.), *Sir William Brereton. Travels in Holland, the United Provinces, England, Scotland, and Ireland, 1634-5* (London, 1844), p. 148

28. Many of these woods survived until at least 1657, judging from the Scarawalsh barony map of that date.

29. *N.H.I.*, IX, fig. 52; Hawkins, *Travels*, pp 149-50; *Salisbury*, IV, p. 217; Nicholls, 'Kavanaghs' pp 575-6. Tincurry was originally included in the letters patent to the settler James Carroll in 1617, leading to the forcible ejection of Derby's father Dowling McBrian to Tomacurry across the river. However, vigorous protests by the son Dermot (also called Derby) Cavanagh led to the omission of Tincurry in a subsequent regrant to Carroll in 1618, and a grant to Dowling MacBrian Cavanagh in that year. This seems to explain Derby's probable residence at Tincurry in 1635, when it already was mortgaged to the Dublin apothecary Turner (*Cal. pat. rolls Ire., Jas I*, pp 206, 218, 358, 366; *Cal. S.P., Ire., 1647-60*, p. 41). The property was no longer in the hands of the Kavanaghs at the time of the *Civil Survey* p. 266, when Turner was the owner.

30. *Cal. S.P. Ire., 1611-14*, pp 134-6; Bodl. Laud MS 611, f. 55; B.M. Add. MSS 4756, f. 123; Bodl. Laud MS 611, f. 49v-50; M. Hickson, *Ireland in the seventeenth century* (London, 1884) II, p. 272-4; *Cal. S.P. Ire., 1647-60*, p. 41; Hore, VI, pp 463-4; Butler, 'Confiscation', p. 426; Smyth, *Celtic Leinster*, p. 70; *Cal. pat. rolls Ire., Jas I*, p. 403; Lodge, *Peerage Ire.*, I, pp 384-7. These are imperfect transcripts; a more complete copy, indicating the family names of most of the native inhabitants, can be found in Bodl. Laud MS 611, f. 48v-49v. Both Gaelic Irish and Old English were among those to be removed. Note, however, that ultimately, more native inhabitants were able to retain their lands than mentioned here (see *Cal. pat. rolls Ire., Jas I*, *passim*).

31. Hickson, *Ireland*, II, p. 77

32. *Ormonde MSS*, III, p. 22; *Cal. pat. rolls Ire., Jas I*, p. 403; Hore, VI, p. 654; *Cal. S.P. Ire., 1633-47*, p. 350; 1647-60, p. 82. It was ruined in 1654. *Civil Survey*, p. 10

33. Richard Stafford at Rahale, George Cheevers at Ballynaclash, Piers Synnott at Middleton, all of whom had purchased the plantation estates; Thomas Esmond at Limerick by descent; James Carroll's daughter and heir had married the Catholic Bartholomew Breine or Bryan.

34. *Cal. pat. rolls Ire., Jas I*, pp 218, 358; *Cal. S.P., Ire., 1647-60*, pp 41-2; Hawkins, *Travels*, p. 149; Gilbert, *Ir. confed.*, II, p. 251; *Civil Survey*, p. 265; Hore, VI, 116; *Census Ire., 1659*, p. 555. Brereton placed the house at Ballyeskerne, which Hore stated is at Ballycarney. According to the *Bks Survey and Dist., Wexford*, the lands of Ballycarney were assigned to James Carroll and Thomas Geoghegan in 1663. Jeffrey *Castles*, p. 93.

35. *Cal. pat. rolls Ire., Jas I*, pp 260, 404; *Civil Survey*, p. 8. A manor of Wingfield was granted in 1613 to John Wingfield a relative of Richard, but this property was in a different location. *Cal. pat. rolls Ire., Jas I*, p. 260; *Inq. cancell. Hib. repert.*, Chas I, no. 140

36. *Cal. pat. rolls Ire., Jas I*, pp 257, 349, 422-3; Hore, VI, pp 498-9; *Civil Survey*, p. 57; *Inq. cancell. Hib. repert.*, Chas I, no. 3 and Chas II, no. 15

37. *Cal. pat. rolls Ire., Jas I*, pp 260, 359, 407; *Camden Society*, ser. 1, 1872, pp 105, 116; *Cal. Carew MSS*, I, pp 325, 327; *Camden Society*, 1872, III, pp 161, 291; Smyth, *Celtic Leinster*, p. 65; *Civil Survey*, pp 47, 78; Jeffrey, *Castles*, p. 178

38. *Cal. pat. rolls Ire., Jas I*, p. 358; *Civil Survey*, p. 43. The Castle Murrough estate was later claimed by the descendants of Capt. George Trevelyan (see Ballyvoodock), but it is not clear how this was possible since Castle Murrough appears to have been part of the Annesley estate (*Camden Society*, 1872, III, p. 291).

39. *Cal. pat. rolls Ire., Jas I*, pp 260, 461, 482; *Cal. S.P. Ire., 1615-25*, pp 293, 323; Smyth, *Celtic Leinster*, p. 69; *Civil Survey*, p. 72

40. *Cal. pat. rolls Ire., Jas I*, pp 222, 358; *Acts Privy Council, 1616-7*, p. 237; *Cal. S.P. Ire., 1615-25*, pp 396, 577, 609; *1669-70*, p. 556; H.M.C., *Egmont*, I, p. 121; *Ormonde MSS*, I, p. 40; *Civil Survey*, p. 15; Huntington Library, San Marino, California, HAM Box 78; A drawing of the ruins was made in 1840, but is difficult to interpret (Hore, VI, p. 650, see also pp 491, 652); *Census Ire., 1659*, p. 553; Jeffrey, *Castles*, p. 97; *O.S. letters, Wexford; Bks. Survey and Dist. Wexford; R.S.A.I. Jn.*, IV (1862-3), p. 77.

41. *Cal. pat. rolls Ire., Jas I*, pp 260, 482; B.M. Add. MSS 4756, f. 125; N.L. Wales, MS 1595, f. 192; Exeter College, Oxford, MS 95, f. 23; T.C.D., MS 818; *Civil Survey*, pp 272, 292; Hore, VI, p. 124; Estate map of Ballymore demesne, 1672, Ballymore house; Richard Donovan of Ballymore house, personal communication, 1983. An early photograph of Camolin house shows a 7-bay, two-storey building with a dormer roof; its pedimented front door resembled that formerly at Platten hall, Meath.

42. *Cal. pat. rolls Ire., Jas I*, p. 359; Bodl. Rawl. MS 439, f. 100v; *Census Ire., 1659*, p. 550 *Civil Survey*, p. 36

43. *Cal. pat. rolls Ire., Jas I*, pp 258, 299, 349, 560; *Cal. S.P. Ire., 1615-25*, p. 304; T.C.D., MS 818, f. 29v; *Civil Survey*, p. 7; *Census Ire., 1659*, p. 553

44. *Cal. pat. rolls Ire., Jas I*, pp 260, 448; *Civil Survey*, p. 271; Nicholls, 'Kavanaghs', p. 440

45. *Cal. pat. rolls Ire., Jas I*, pp 359, 573; Hickson, *Ireland*, II, p. 271; *Civil Survey*, p. 11; *Census Ire., 1659*, p. 553

46. *Cal. pat. rolls Ire., Jas I*, pp 218, 358; *Acts Privy Council, 1616-7*, p. 237; Gilbert MSS 169, f. 116; *Cal. S.P. Ire., 1647-60*, p. 344; Hore, VI, p. 645; *Civil Survey*, pp 35-6; Jeffrey, *Castles*, p. 190

47. *Cal. pat. rolls Ire., Jas I*, pp 260, 358; *Civil Survey*, pp 65-6; *Census Ire., 1659*, p. 552; Barry, *Moated sites*, p. 223; Jeffrey, *Castles*, p. 191

48. *Cal. pat. rolls Ire., Jas I*, pp 218-9, 357; *Anal. Hib.* XXXI (1984), p. 126; Bodl. Carte MS 118, f. 139; T.C.D., MS 818, ff. 21v, 82; *H.M.C. Rep. 12 app II*, p. 180; *Civil Survey*, p. 38; Hore, VI, p. 571; Birr Castle, MS A 25/13, 16; W. Philimore and G. Thrift, *Indexes to Irish wills* (Baltimore, 1970), p. 110; Jeffrey, *Castles*, p. 187

49. *Cal. pat. rolls Ire., Jas I*, p. 366; T.C.D., MS 818, f. 21; Hore, VI, p. 568

50. T.C.D., MS 809, f. 336; MS 810, f. 78v; MS 811, ff. 79, 309, 336-7; *Civil Survey*, p. 10

51. Hore, VI, pp xiv, 280, 614, 630; Lord Killanin and M. Duignan, *The Shell guide to Ireland* (London, 1967), p. 298; Gilbert MS 169, f. 213; *Civil Survey*, p. 17

52. *Cal. pat. rolls Ire., Jas I*, pp 141, 295-6; B. M. Laud MS 611, f. 59v; R. Haslam, 'Kiplin Hall, North Yorkshire', in *Country Life*, 28 July (1983), pp 202-205 (its building was in progress in 1622, see Sheffield City library, Wentworth MS 2, f. 86-9); *Cal. S.P. Ire., 1611-14*, pp 492-4; *Ibid.*, 1625-32, pp 95, 177, 305, 321, 388; Gilbert, *Ir. Confed.*, II, p. 251; [P. Luckombe], *A tour through Ireland* (Dublin, 1780), p. 64; *Census Ire., 1659*, p. 555

8   *Daniel Gahan*

1. T. Barry, *Medieval moated sites of south-eastern Ireland* (Oxford, 1977), pp 101-3

2. This was especially true of parishes in Normanised areas. See Otway-Ruthven, *Med. Ire.*, pp 119-120; C. Empey, 'The Norman Period, 1185-1500', and M. Hennessey, 'Parochial organ-

isation in medieval Tipperary' in W. Nolan (ed.), *Tipperary: history and society* (Dublin, 1985), pp 62-3, 85.

3. A similar pattern has emerged from studies of Tipperary. See W. Smyth, 'Land Values, land ownership and population patterns in county Tipperary for 1641-60 and 1841-50: some comparisons' in L. M. Cullen and F. Furet (ed.), *Towards a comparative study of rural history* (Paris, 1980), pp 68-71 and 'Property, patronage and population-reconstructing the human geography of mid-seventeenth century county Tipperary' in Nolan, *Tipperary*, pp 104-39.

4. Composite Down Survey/O.S. six inch maps drawn by R. Johnston, N.L.I., D.20

5. For a parallel pattern see Smyth, 'Land values', pp 69-74 and 'Property', pp 118-22.

6. T. S. McErlean, 'The Irish townland system of landscape organisation' in T. Reeves-Smyth and F. Hamond (ed.), *Landscape archaeology in Ireland* (Oxford, 1983), pp 315-40.

7. The importance of rundale in Gaelic areas of eastern Ireland remains a subject of debate. Earlier research implied that rundale was the dominant land use pattern in such areas. More recent work suggests that such a communal model may not have been so widespread. Smyth 'Land values', pp. 81-2.

8. W. Nolan, *Fassadinin: Land, settlement and society in south-east Ireland, c. 1600-1850* (Dublin, 1979), p. 21

9. *Bks. Survey and Dist., Wexford*

10. For descriptions of similar patterns T. Hughes, 'Society and settlement in nineteenth century Ireland' in *Ir. Geog.*, V (1965), pp 79-96.

11. The plantation or Irish acre is utilised in this section of the discussion.

12. Church lands accounted for an insignificant proportion of Wexford land in 1641.

13. For a case in favour of the view that monetarisation was advanced in Ireland by the eighteenth century see L. M. Cullen 'Hidden Ireland: The Reassessment of a concept' in *Stud. Hib.*, IX, (1969), pp 45-6.

14. For an insight into agrarian development in a colonial situation similar to that of seventeenth century Ireland and a discussion of the notion of 'neo-manorialism' see F. Chevalier, *Land and society in colonial Mexico* (Berkley, 1963), pp 207-20.

15. T. C. Bernard, 'The Enniscorthy ironworks' in *R.I.A. Proc.*, C, LXXXV (1985), pp 101-44

16. Hore, I, p. 90

17. Close to ninety percent of the land of Wexford was confiscated in the Cromwellian/Williamite settlements.

18. For further comments on the importance of such fragmentation see J. H. Andrews, 'Land and People' in *N.H.I.*, IV, pp 463-4.

19. J. Blum, *End of the old order in rural Europe* (Princeton, 1961), pp 95-7

20. The use of surnames as well as christian names as an indicator of religious affiliation is a well-established convention in Irish agrarian studies. See Smyth 'Patronage', pp 130-1; T. J. Hughes 'The large farm in nineteenth century Ireland' in A. Gailey and D. Ó h-Ógáin (ed.), *Gold Under the Furze* (Dublin, 1982), pp 93-100.

21. Blum, *Old Order*, pp 18-19

22. The south-eastern baronies were firmly within the 'Liberal' camp in terms of eighteenth century Wexford politics.

23. Further information on the extent and management of this property can be garnered from R. D. 20-330-10811.

24. The Esmondes mortgaged large amounts of land in the early eighteenth century. Some of these mortgages are summarised in R.D. 19-267-10130, 47-444-31388, 47-4444-31389, 64-143-44434, 74-426-5189.

25. Hore, I, pp 249-50

26. *Shapland Carew Papers*

27. Jones Hughes has noted similar resilience of ecclesiastical boundaries. See 'Society and settlement' pp 80-6 and 'Landholding and settlement in the Cooley Peninsula of Louth' in *Ir. Geog.*, IV (1964), p. 152.

28. It is assumed here that smaller landowners did not possess the resources to support second residences and that most of these small properties were owned by individuals who did not have another estate elsewhere.

29. For similar methods of mapping estate boundaries see Smyth 'Land Values', pp 72-5 and J. Burtchaell, 'Nineteenth century society in county Waterford' in *Decies*, XXX (1985), p. 16.

30. For discussion of similar findings on Waterford and Tipperary see Burtchaell, 'Waterford', pp 16-17; T. Hughes 'Landholding and settlement in county Tipperary in the nineteenth century' in Nolan, *Tipperary*, pp 339-66.

31. Research on county Wexford would suggest that few middlemen survived until the 1850s.

See D. Gahan, The middleman tenant in south-eastern Ireland, 1700-1820, Unpublished Ph.D. dissertation, University of Kansas, 1985.
32. Discussion of 1850 and 1876 data is based on statute rather than plantation acres.
33. Nolan has revealed a similar pattern in Kilkenny; see *Fassadinin*, p. 84.
34. The Whites of Peppard's Castle had been the largest tenants and main agents of the Angleseys in Wexford since 1692; *Report on Private Collections, N.L.I.*, No. 3, p. 859.
35. *Return of Landowners in Ireland, 1876 (county Wexford)*
36. Despite their small size many of these catholic estates may have been rented. *Griffith's Valuation* reveals that at least in 1850 Wexford landowners, large and small, almost all rented their property.
37. North Wexford was chosen for this exercise because of the relatively simple pattern of land-ownership there.

9 *Patrick J. Corish*

1. J. Glynn, 'The Catholic Church in Wexford town 1800-1858' in *Past*, XV (1984), pp 5-54
2. See the references in notes 36, 39, 40 below. The text of the papal grant (undated, but probably 1607) is in *Archiv. Hib.*, III (1914), pp 260-4.
3. J. Scarisbrick, *The Reformation and the English people* (Oxford, 1984); P. Williams, *The Tudor regime* (Oxford, 1981), especially pp 253-92, 351-406
4. B. Bradshaw, 'Sword, word and strategy in the Reformation in Ireland' in *Hist. Jn.*, XXI (1978), pp 475-502; N. Canny, 'Why the Reformation failed in Ireland: *une question mal posée*' in *Jn. Ecc. Hist.*, XXX (1979), pp 423-50; C. Brady, 'Conservative subversives: the community of the Pale and the Dublin administration, 1556-86' in P. Corish (ed.), *Radicals, rebels and establishments* (Belfast, 1985), pp 11-32.
5. P.R.O., S.P. 63/58/2 (*Cal. S.P. Ire. 1574-85*, p. 112); Hore, V, p. 178
6. P.R.O., S.P. 63/84/12 (*Cal. S.P. Ire. 1574-85*, p. 310)
7. For Roche see A. Bruodin, *Propugnaculum Catholicae Veritatis* (Prague, 1669), p. 457. Howlin's account is in Moran, *Spicil. Ossor.*, I, pp 94-5, 103-4. The original is in the Salamanca papers, *legajo* xi, no. 4. It is in a very clear italic hand. Moran's edition may have been made from a hasty transcript, for it contains a few serious errors. The transcription of 'Cavanagh' as 'Canavan' is excusable, but it is hard to see how the clearly-written 'Wexfordia' in every case appears in print as 'Waterfordia'.
8. E. Hogan, *Distinguished Irishmen of the sixteenth century* (London, 1894), pp 29-47, supplemented by information from Francis Finegan, S. J.
9. His letter is printed in Hore, V, pp 203-4.
10. Ram's Report in 1612 is in Hore, VI, pp 258-65; for the Royal Visitation of 1615 see *ibid.*, pp 266-74.
11. *Archiv. Hib.*, II (1913), 1-36
12. He lists thirteen in his Report of 1612 (Hore, X, p. 260).
13. There are accounts of Candidus Furlong in a number of Catholic seventeenth-century writers. See in particular J. Hartry, *De Cisterciensium Hibernorum viris illustribus* (written 1649, ed. D. Murphy, Dublin, 1895), pp 270-73.
14. His brief of appointment is in the Vatican Archives, *Sec. Brev.* 425, ff 310 ff.
15. *Archiv. Hib.*, IV (1915), pp 127-8
16. See 'A note of Archbusshoppes and Busshoppes, etc., of Ireland consecrated and authorised by the Pope' (T.C.D. MS E.3.15), printed in W. Carrigan, *The history and antiquities of the diocese of Ossory*, I (Dublin, 1905), pp 90-91.
17. *Wadding papers*, pp 24, 27, 61; *Archiv. Hib.*, xviii (1955), p. 122 — the brief calendared entry of this letter (Vatican Library, MSS Barberini Latini 8626, f. 23rv) does not mention the reference to him.
18. Two copies in archives of the Congregation of Propaganda, Rome (calendared in *Collect. Hib.*, X (1967), pp 17, 50).
19. P. Corish, 'An Irish Counter-reformation bishop: John Roche' in *Ir. Theol. Quart.*, xxv (1958), pp 14-32, 101-23, XVI (1959), pp 101-16, 313-30
20. P. Corish, 'The beginnings of the Irish College, Rome' in *Father Luke Wadding* (Dublin, 1957), pp 284-94

21. Contemporaries anglicise (or latinise) his name as 'O'Brien'.
22. In Hore, VI, pp 281-2
23. B. Jennings, 'Irish students in the University of Louvain' in S. O'Brien (ed.), *Measgra i gchuimhne Mhichíl Uí Chléirigh* (Dublin, 1944), p. 78
24. *Comment. Rinucc.*, II, pp 652-3
25. I have summarised this from contemporary sources in *N.H.I.*, III (Oxford, 1976), pp 340-42. See also the account in A. Fraser, *Cromwell our chief of men* (London, 1973), pp 343-7.
26. P.R.O., S.P. 63/307/65 (*Cal. S.P. Ire.*, 1660-62), pp 335-7, and see the comment in Fraser, *op.cit.*, p. 346
27. For his guardianship see C. Giblin (ed.), *Liber Lovaniensis* (Dublin, 1956), pp 17, 23, 356. His account is in a MS in Stonyhurst. It has been several times printed, e.g., by D. Murphy in *Our Martyrs* (Dublin, 1896), pp 314-17 and in *Cromwell in Ireland* (Dublin, 1897), pp 164-6. Francis Stafford was later captured and imprisoned in Inishboffin and was working in Ireland in 1661 (*Liber Lovaniensis*, pp 40, 68).
28. These are: (i) '*Apologia pro se et aliis Catholicis*', the only copy of which appears to be in T.C.D. MS F.4.20 (652), no. 2; and (ii) a letter from him to the internuncio in Flanders, dated Antwerp 2 Jan. 1673: the original is in the archives of the Congregation of Propaganda, Rome, *Congressi, Irlanda* 3, ff 383r-384v, printed in Moran, *Spicil. Ossor.*, I, pp 510-11; for an English summary see *Collect. Hib.*, XXI-XXII (1979-80), pp 42-3; and for the relevant sections of both documents in English translation see Murphy, *Cromwell*, pp 162-4.
29. *Comment. Rinucc.*, IV, p. 627
30. Note 26 above.
31. Material printed by Hore, I, pp 335-46; V, pp 311-27; *Ibid.*, 'The Barony of Forth' in *Past*, II (1921), pp 38-44 gives some indication of the great social upheaval. There is much local detail still to be extracted from what records remain.
32. *Shapland Carew papers*, pp 1-10
33. Lynch, *De praesulibus*, I, pp 358-60
34. Hore, II, pp 188-91
35. *Archiv. Hib.*, XXIX (1970), pp 50-1
36. P. Corish (ed.), 'Bishop Wadding's notebook' in *Archiv. Hib.*, XXIX (1970), pp 49-114
37. Archives of the Congregation of Propaganda, Rome, *Congressi, Irlanda* 3, ff 106r-107v. For an English summary see *Collect. Hib.*, XVIII-XIX (1976-7), pp 54-5.
38. P. Power, *A bishop of the penal times* (Cork, 1932)
39. H. Hore (ed.), 'A chorographic account of the southern part of county Wexford, written anno 1684, by Robert Leigh, esq., of Rosegarland in that county' in *R.S.A.I. Jn.*, V (1858-9), pp 17-21, 451-67; 'Particulars relative to Wexford and the barony of Forth, by Colonel Solomon Richards, 1682' in *ibid.*, vii (1862-6), pp 84-92
40. 'An account of the barony of Forth in the county of Wexford written at the close of the seventeenth century' in *R.S.A.I. Jn.*, VII (1862-3), pp 53-83
41. Hore, I, pp 359-71; V, pp 365-86
42. 'The diocese of Ferns and the penal days' in *Past*, VIII (1970), pp 5-17
43. Extracts in Hore, I, pp 371-3
44. For references see *Past*, VIII (1970). A few names from an enumeration made in 1744 have survived — see W. Burke, *Irish priests in the penal times* (Waterford, 1914), pp 312-14. I have edited the list for 1772 in *Past*, IX (1972), pp 77-8.
45. See J. Mannion's article in this volume. N. Furlong, 'The times and life of Nicholas Sweetman, bishop of Ferns (1744-1786)' in *Wex. Hist. Soc. Jn.*, IX (1983-4), pp 1-19
46. P. Corish (ed.), 'Ferns diocesan statutes 1722' in *Archiv. Hib.*, XXVII (1964), pp 76-84
47. H. Fenning, 'A guide to eighteenth-century reports on Irish dioceses in the archives of Propaganda Fide' in *Collect. Hib.*, XI (1968), p. 26
48. In *Archiv. Hib.*, IV (1915), pp 166-71
49. Note 44 above.
50. His replies to his interrogation are printed in Burke, *Irish Priests*, pp 316-19.
51. *Freeman's Journal*, 10 Apr. 1779 in J. Brady, *Catholics and catholicism in the eighteenth-century press* (Maynooth, 1965), pp 197-8
52. Sweetman's anger is obvious from Carpenter's reply, dated 23 Feb 1774: M. Curran (ed.), 'Correspondence of Archbishop Carpenter with Bishop Sweetman of Ferns' in *Rep. Nov.*, I, no. 2 (1956), p. 400.
53. W. Grattan Flood (ed.), 'The diocesan manuscripts of Ferns during the rule of Bishop Sweetman (1745-1786)' in *Archiv. Hib.*, II (1913), pp 100-5
54. G. Fitzgerald, 'Estimates for baronies of minimum level of Irish-speaking among successive

decennial cohorts' in *R.I.A. Proc.*, C, LXXXIV (1984), p. 132 and map 7
55. P. Corish (ed.), 'Bishop Caulfield's *Relatio Status, 1796*' in *Archiv. Hib.*, XXVIII (1966), pp 103-13
56. Burke *Irish priests*, p. 317
57. Flood, 'Diocesan manuscripts', pp 113-23
58. *Archiv. Hib.*, IV (1915), pp 168-9; Burke, *Irish priests*, p. 313
59. *Archiv. Hib.*, III (1914), p. 118; Burke, *Irish priests*, p. 315
60. *Archiv. Hib.*, III (1914), pp 116-19
61. See, for example, the remarks by J. Bossy, *The English catholic community 1570-1850* (London, 1975), pp 108-48.
62. C. O'Dwyer (ed.), 'Archbishop Butler's visitation book' in *Archiv. Hib.*, XXXIII (1975), pp 1-90, XXXIV (1976-7), pp 1-49
63. *Freeman's Journal*, 14 Sept. 1777 in Brady, *Press*, p. 186
64. Burke, *Irish priests*, pp 312-13
65. P. Ó Súilleabháin (ed.), 'Documents relating to Wexford friary and parish, 1733-98' in *Collect. Hib.*, VIII (1965), pp 110-28
66. P. Ó Súilleabháin (ed.), 'The library of a parish priest of the penal days' in *Collect. Hib.*, VI-VIII (1963-4), pp 234-44
67. Hay, *History*, p. xi
68. P. Ó Snodaigh, 'Notes on the volunteers, militia, yeomanry and orangemen of county Wexford' in *Past*, XIV (1983), pp 5-48
69. L. Cullen, *The emergence of modern Ireland 1600-1900* (London, 1981), pp 210-33; 'The 1798 rebellion in its eighteenth-century context' in Corish, *Radicals*, pp 91-113
70. J. Donnelly, 'Irish agrarian rebellion: the Whiteboys of 1769-76' in *R.I.A. Proc.*, C, LXXXIII (1983), pp 293-331

10   *L. M. Cullen*

1. C. Dickson, *The Wexford Rising in 1798* (Tralee, 1955), p. 40
2. *Ibid.*, p. 203
3. *Ibid.*, pp 21-2, 181
4. *Ibid.*, p. 23
5. T. Pakenham, *The year of liberty* (London, 1969), pp 141, 143
6. T. Powell, The background to the Wexford rebellion 1790-1798 unpublished M.A. thesis, U.C.D., 1970, pp 145, 147, 148, 158
7. T. Powell, 'An economic factor in the Wexford rebellion of 1798' in *Studia Hib.*, XVI (1976), p. 156
8. T. Powell, thesis abstract in *Ir. econ. soc. hist.*, II (1975), p. 63
9. *Commons Jn. Ire.*, XVII, pt ii, app., dccclxx, dcclxxii, dccclxxiii
10. Powell, 'Background', pp 140-1
11. *Commons Jn. Ire.*, XVII, pt ii, app., dccclxxxvii
12. Lecky, *Ire.*, IV, p. 402
13. Gordon, *History*, p. 105
14. Hay, *History*, pp 51-2
15. Byrne, *Memoirs* I, p. 13
16. T.C.D., Luke Cullen MS f. 132
17. S.P.O., R.P., 620/40/20
18. Gordon, *History*, p. 258
19. H. Wheeler and A. Broadley, *The war in Wexford* (London, 1910). Some of Mountnorris's letters are reproduced in this volume.
20. Luke Cullen MS f. 168
21. Hay, *History*, p. 55
22. *Ibid.*, pp 56, 60
23. Cloney, *Narrative*, pp 10, 192
24. Gordon, *History*, p. 106
25. Hay, *History*, p. 78
26. Luke Cullen MS f. 13

27. P. Kavanagh, *A popular history of the insurrection of 1798* (Dublin, 1916), p. 88
28. Cloney, *Narrative*, p. 6
29. *Ibid.*, pp 192-4
30. Gordon, *History*, p. 103
31. *Ibid.*, p. 105
32. Kavanagh, *History*, p. 299
33. C. Dickson, 'A note on 1798' in *Ir. Sword*, IX (1969), p. 109
34. Dickson, *Wexford rising*, pp 10, 24, 24n
35. *Ibid.*, pp 35, 181
36. Lecky, *Ire.*, IV, p. 344
37. *Ibid.*, p. 345
38. Powell, 'Economic factor', p. 144
39. Powell, 'Background', pp 143, 149, 150
40. Dickson, *Wexford rising*, p. 10
41. S.P.O., R.P. 620/36/142
42. S.P.O., R.P. 620/36/92, 28 Mar. 1798
43. Luke Cullen MS f. 175
44. Powell, 'Economic factor', p. 156
45. Dickson, *Wexford rising*, p. 188
46. Hay, *History*, p. 100
47. *Ibid.*, p. 219
48. *Ibid.*, p. 222
49. Gordon, *History*, p. 178
50. J. Holt, *Memoirs of Joseph Holt* ... (London, 1838), I, pp 15-20. See also introduction, pp ix, xi-xii, xv.
51. Cloney, *Narrative*, pp 195, 212-3
52. *Ibid.*, pp 206, 211
53. *Ibid.*, p. 16
54. *Ibid.*, p. 119
55. Dickson, *Wexford rising*, p. 201
56. Cloney, *Narrative*, pp 1, 16, 215
57. Dickson, *Wexford rising*, p. 199
58. Cloney, *Narrative*, pp 145-6
59. *Ibid.*, p. 242
60. *Ibid.*, p. 215
61. *Ibid.*, p. 105
62. *Ibid.*, p. 10
63. *Ibid.*, pp 78, 142
64. *Ibid.*, p. 20
65. *Ibid.*, p. 208
66. Dickson, *Wexford rising*, p. 205
67. J. Barrington, *Personal sketches of his own times* (London, 1827), I, p. 270
68. Cloney, *Narrative*, p. 208
69. Memorial of 1 Apr. 1797 to deed of 13 Sept. 1795. R.D. 508/242/330088. Edward Roche was a witness on both occasions.
70. Case of Edward Roche, enclosed with letter of 25 Aug. 1798, S.P.O., R.P. 620/39/206
71. S.P.O., R.P. 620/39/109, 24 July 1798
72. R. Hayes, *The last invasion of Ireland* (Dublin, 1937)
73. Kavanagh, *History*, p. 84
74. *Ibid.*, p. 280
75. *Ibid.*, pp 100n, 100, 291n
76. *Ibid.*, p. 295
77. *Ibid.*, p. 292
78. *Ibid.*, p. 88
79. *Ibid.*, pp 238-9
80. *Ibid.*, p. vi
81. *Ibid.*, p. 225
82. *Ibid.*, p. 241
83. Dickson, *Wexford rising*, p. 219
84. Irish College, Paris, Fanny Byrne to the Rector of the Irish College, 13 Apr. 1868. I am indebted to the *proviseur* of the college, Rev Liam Swords, for bringing this letter to my attention.

85. Byrne, *Memoir*, I, pp 6, 14, 15, 24, 243, 279; iii, pp 82-3
86. *Ibid.*, I, pp 24, 29
87. *Ibid.*, I, p. 189
88. *Ibid.*, I, p. 57
89. *Ibid.*, III, p. 243
90. *Ibid.*, I, pp 181, 186. Elsewhere the only references to him are in pp 55-6 where Hay has the sarcastic epithet 'honest Edward Hay', and where Hay is stated to be 'one of the Catholic aristocracy, who had his brother executed in Wexford, as an united Irish man'.
91. Dickson, *Wexford rising*, p. 219
92. Byrne, I, p. 65
93. *Idem*
94. *Ibid.*, I, pp 348-358
95. *Ibid.*, I, pp 186-7
96. Dickson, *Wexford rising*, pp 206-7
97. Musgrave, *Memoirs* (3rd ed.), II, p. 516. See also Caesar Colclough, 7 Apr. 1798, S.P.O., R.P. 620/36/142. Musgrave had observed in the context of Irish food exports (and hence of Munster more centrally than any other region) that 'the complaint in many parts of Ireland is scarcity of milk'.
98. S.P.O., R.P. 620/32/152, 5 Oct. 1797
99. Elliot to Pelham, 3 June 1798 in Gilbert, *Doc. Ire., 1795-1805*, pp 125-6
100. *Faulkner's Dublin Journal* 13 Jan. 1798 quoted in Pakenham, *op cit.*, p. 379
101. S.P.O., R.P. 620/35/28, 9 Jan. 1798
102. S.P.O., R.P. 620/36/1, 14 Mar. 1798. On the Montgomery and Keating links, see M. Duggan, County Carlow 1791-1801: a study in an era of revolution, unpublished M.A. thesis, U.C.D., 1969, pp 129-30, 132-3
103. A. McClelland, *The formation of the orange order* (n.d.), p. 14
104. Duggan, 'Carlow', p. 136
105. McClelland, *Orange Order*, p. 14. Captain Robert Rochfort was the county grand master and is sometimes confused with Colonel J. S. Rochfort, founder of the Order in the county. See Duggan,'Carlow', pp 129-130, 136.
106. McClelland, *Orange Order*, p. 13. On the Carlow lodges, see also Duggan, 'Carlow', p. 136, which identifies nine lodges.
107. Pakenham, *Liberty*, p. 379, note 24
108. *Commons Jn. Ire.*, XVII, pt. ii, app. dccclxix, dccccxiii, dccccxiv
109. Pakenham, *Liberty*, p. 34
110. *Ibid.*, p. 65
111. S.P.O., R.P. 620/36/61, 24 Mar. 1798
112. N.L.I., MS 5398
113. McClelland, *Orange Order*, p. 13
114. Powell, 'Background', p. 169
115. S.P.O., R.P. 620/34/27, Robert Cornwall, 9 Nov. 1797; 620/33/44, Stephen Ram, 12 Nov. 1797; 620/33/124, Lord Ely, 6 Dec. 1797
116. McClelland, *Orange Order*, p. 14
117. S.P.O., R.P. 620/30/103, 30 May 1797; 620/32/163, 4 Oct. 1797
118. Musgrave, *Memoir*, II, p. 324
119. S.P.O., R.P. 620/33/124
120. S.P.O., R.P. 620/35/109
121. S.P.O., R.P. 620/36/92
122. S.P.O., R.P. 620/36/149, John de Renzy, 8 Apr. 1798; 620/36/202, John James 23 Apr. 1798
123. [T. Handcock], 'Reminiscences of a fugitive loyalist in 1798' in *E.H.R.*, I (1886), p. 537
124. Cloney, *Narrative*, p. 74
125. N.L.I., Ms 5398
126. S.P.O., R.P. 620/33/93. A less partial magistrate in the northern half of the country at Moynalty had drawn a similar conclusion. S.P.O., R.P. 620/31/55, Norman Steel, 8 Jun. 1796
127. Musgrave, *Memoirs*, I, pp 397-8, 401
128. L. M. Cullen, 'The 1798 rebellion in its eighteenth-century context' in P. Corish (ed.), *Rebels, radicals, establishments* (Belfast, 1985), pp 107-8
129. S.P.O., R.P. 620/36/201
130. S.P.O.S.O.C.P. 30/191, quoted in Powell, 'Background', pp 185-7, 192

131. Cloney, *Narrative*, p. 111
132. Luke Cullen MS f. 216
133. Musgrave, *Memoir*, II, p. 386
134. *Ibid.*, II pp 379, 384, 386
135. *Ibid.*, II, p. 386
136. *Ibid.*, II, p. 450
137. Luke Cullen MS f. 126
138. Byrne, *Memoirs*, I, p. 127
139. *Commons Jn. Ire.*, XVII pt. ii, app. dccclxxxix
140. Byrne, *Memoirs*, I, p. 15
141. Luke Cullen MS f. 68
142. Gordon, *History*, p. 125
143. Hay, *History*, p. 89, 136
144. *Ibid.*, p. 220
145. S.P.O., R.P. 620/36/92, 28 Mar. 1798
146. Byrne, *Memoir*, I, pp 192-3
147. D. Goodall, 'Dixon of Castlebridge, county Wexford' in *Ir. Geneal.*, VI (1985), pp 632-3, 635
148. Perry's confession is reproduced in Dickson, *Wexford rising*, pp 45-7
149. *Ibid.*, pp 225-6
150. *Commons Jn. Ire.*, XVII, pt. ii app. dcccxxxix, dccclxxix
151. *Ibid.*, XVII, pt. i, app. dccclxix
152. Dickson, *Wexford rising*, p. 21
153. Powell, 'Background', pp 141-2
154. Byrne, *Memoir*, I, pp 128-9
155. *Ibid*, pp 12, 54-5
156. Powell, 'Background', pp 150-151
157. S.P.O., R.P. 620/30/103
158. S.P.O., R.P. 620/30/226, 29 May 1797
159. Powell, 'Background', pp 154-8
160. Enclosed in S.P.O., R.P. 620/33/124, 6 Dec. 1797
161. S.P.O., R.P. 620/32/163
162. Mountnorris letters of 5 Oct. 1797 quoted in Dickson, *Wexford rising*, pp 22-3
163. Powell, 'Background', p. 164; R.P. 620/33/44, 12 Nov. 1797
164. Luke Cullen MS ff 224-5
165. Kavanagh, *History*, p. 299
166. C. Coote, *Statistical survey of the county of Armagh* (Dublin, 1804), p. 365
167. Gordon, *History*, p. 69
168. Powell, 'Background', p. 136
169. R. McDowell, 'The personnel of the Dublin society of United Irishmen' in *I.H.S.*, II (1940-1), p. 33. He is stated as of county Carlow. Clonegal is in Carlow.
170. Flood, *Ferns*, p. 16
171. S.P.O., R.P. 620/30/232
172. S.P.O., R.P. 620/31/39, 5 Jun. 1797
173. S.P.O., R.P. 620/31/101, 15 Jun. 1797. The name is incorrectly identified as Ferns in the MS calendar.
174. Cloney, *Narrative*, p. 6
175. *Ibid.*, p. 7
176. S.P.O., R.P. 620/34/20, Alex Durdin, Huntingdon, 20 Sept. 1797
177. S.P.O., R.P. 620/36/149
178. S.P.O., R.P. 620/36/202, John James, 23 Apr. 1798
179. J. Alexander, *Some account of the first apparent symptoms of the late rebellion* ... (Dublin, 1800), p. 30
180. F. Plowden, *An historical review of the state of Ireland* ... (London, 1803), II, pt. 2, pp 717-8
181. Cloney, *Narrative*, p. 13. Synnott is described as 'a rich farmer' in the Luke Cullen MS f. 34 v.
182. Handcock, 'Reminiscences', p. 538. For Cloney's version of their meeting, see *Narrative*, p. 5.
183. *Ibid.*, pp 35, 36
184. Luke Cullen MS f. 84
185. *Ibid.*, f. 204
186. Cloney, *Narrative*, p. 22. Furlong's and Cloney's townlands, Moneyhore and Templescoby, were adjoining.

187. Byrne, *Memoirs*, I p. 75
188. Cloney, *Narrative*, pp 35-6
189. Byrne, *Memoirs*, I, p. 71
190. Cloney, *Narrative*, p. 13
191. Byrne, *Memoirs*, I, p. 127
192. Luke Cullen Ms f. 34v. See also f. 231v
193. Cloney, *Narrative*, pp 41, 155. On Nicholas Grey, see also J. Ranson, 'A '98 diary by Mrs Barbara Newton Lett' in *Past*, VI (1948), pp 132, 148-9
194. S.P.O., R.P. 620/33/124
195. Elizabeth Richards' diary. I am indebted to Mr Desmond FitzGerald, Knight of Glin, for access to a typescript copy of the diary.
196. *Commons Jn. Ire.*, XVII, pt. ii, app. dccclxx
197. Dickson, *Wexford rising*, p. 46
198. Barrington, *Sketches*, III (London, 1832), p. 294
199. G. Taylor, *An history of the rise, progress and suppression of the rebellion in the county of Wexford …* (Dublin, 1864), p. 48
200. *Ibid.*, p. 165; Wheeler and Broadley, *War*, pp 195-7; Keugh was superseded as a justice of the peace in 1792, not 1796 as often suggested. *Commons Jn. Ire.*, XVII, pt. 2, app. dcclxvii.
201. Quoted in Wheeler and Broadley, *War*, p. 197
202. Dickson, *Wexford rising*, p. 24
203. F. Plowden, *An historical review of the state of Ireland* (London, 1803); op.cit., II, pt. ii, p. 717
204. Quoted in Goodall, 'Dixon', p. 635
205. Luke Cullen MS f. 11
206. Kavanagh, *History*, p. 94
207. *Ibid.*, p. 103
208. Hay, *Insurrection*, pp 87-8
209. Kavanagh, *Ibid.*, p. 242
210. *Ibid.*, p. 296
211. *Ibid.*, p. 247n
212. *Ibid.*, p. 295
213. Powell, 'Background', p. 176
214. *Ibid.*, p. 182
215. Powell, 'Background', pp 182-3
216. Byrne, *Memoir*, I, p. 30
217. Kavanagh, *History*, p. 89
218. *Ibid.*, p. 87
219. See Taylor, *History*, p. 33; Wheeler and Broadley, *War*, p. 81
220. Luke Cullen MS ff 10-11
221. *Ibid.*, f. 11
222. *Ibid.*, f. 12
223. Hay, *History*, p. 77-80. See also *Authentic detail of the extravagant and inconsistent conduct of Sir Richard Musgrave*, pp 5-6
224. Handcock, 'Reminiscences', p. 538; Richards diary, Saturday, 26 May; Wheeler and Broadley, *War*, p. 163
225. Taylor, *History*, p. 25
226. Luke Cullen MS f. 18
227. *Ibid.*, f. 13
228. Handcock, 'Reminiscences', p. 538. Mrs Brownrigg notes in her diary that Lyster, lieutenant of Ogle's yeomen cavalry, received orders in Wexford at 6 p.m. to join his corps at Bellvue (Wheeler and Broadley, *War*, p. 163.)
229. Kavanagh, *History*, pp 94-5
230. Musgrave, *Memoirs*, II p. 333
231. Kavanagh, *History*, pp 98-9
232. Luke Cullen MS ff 18-9
233. *Ibid.*, f. 206
234. *Ibid.*, f. 22
235. Taylor, *History*, p. 37
236. Kavanagh, *History*, p. 100
237. *Ibid.*, p. 291
238. Taylor, *History*, p. 38

239. Luke Cullen MS f. 23
240. *Ibid.*, f. 33
241. *Ibid.*, f. 215
242. Taylor, *History*, p. 125; Handcock, 'Reminiscences', p. 538
243. Luke Cullen MS f. 173a
244. Hay, *History*, p. 213
245. Luke Cullen MS f. 26
246. Kavanagh, *History*, p. 100
247. Luke Cullen MS f. 33
248. Wheeler and Broadley, *War*, p. 197
249. Byrne, *Memoirs*, I, p. 74
250. *Ibid.*, I, pp 163, 168
251. Kavanagh, *History*, p. 101
252. Luke Cullen MS f. 214
253. *Ibid.*, f. 23
254. *Ibid.*, ff. 31-4
255. Byrne, *Memoirs*, I, p. 95
256. Kavanagh, *History*, p. 109

11 *Kevin Whelan*

1. There is as yet no satisfactory account of the 1798 Rebellion in Wexford. The standard account by T. Pakenham, *The year of liberty* (London, 1969), is fatally flawed by its lack of understanding of eighteenth century Wexford. C. Dickson, *The Wexford rising in 1798* (Tralee, 1955) is still the most balanced published account. T. Powell, The background to the Wexford rebellion 1790-1798, unpublished M.A. thesis, U.C.D. (1970) is very useful, even though its overemphasises economic factors. Recent studies, especially by L. Cullen, have begun to radically revise the orthodox accounts. L. Cullen, *The emergence of modern Ireland 1600-1900* (London, 1981), pp 210-33; L. Cullen, 'The 1798 Rebellion in its eighteenth century context' in P. Corish (ed.), *Radicals, rebels and establishments* (Belfast, 1985), pp 91-113; K. Whelan, 'The religious factor in the 1798 rebellion in county Wexford' in P. O'Flanagan, P. Ferguson and K. Whelan (ed.), *Rural Ireland 1600-1900* (Cork, 1987), pp 62-85.
2. The documentation includes all the standard histories of the rebellion, contemporary apologetic pamphlets, the archives of the State Paper Office and the Dublin Diocesan Archive, local histories and newspapers and the extensive folklore of the period.
3. Bishop James Caulfield of Ferns to Bishop John Troy of Dublin, 22 Apr. 1792, Troy papers, Dublin Diocesan Archives (D.D.A.). The Caulfield-Troy correspondence is henceforth cited as *C.T.C.*
4. *C.T.C.* 31 Mar. 1792
5. S.P.O., R.P. 620/36/9
6. *C.T.C.* 6 Aug. 1799
7. *Ibid.*, 3 July 1798
8. *Ibid.*, 10 Sept. 1799
9. *Ibid.*, 23 Sept. 1799; 2 Sept. 1798
10. *Ibid.*, 23 Sept. 1799
11. Byrne, *Memoirs*, I, p. 86. The well informed Plowden specifically states that 'only Roach (sic) had entered as a priest into United Irish politics prior to the Rebellion'; F. Plowden, *An historical review of the state of Ireland* (London, 1803), II, p. 716.
12. Veritas, *The state of His Majesty's subjects in Ireland professing the Catholic religion* (Dublin, 1799), p. 48 (henceforth cited as *Veritas*); Plowden, *State*, II, pp 717-9
13. Shallow's affidavit is in J. Caulfield, *The reply of Right Rev Dr Caulfield Roman Catholic bishop and of the Roman Catholic clergy of Wexford to the misrepresentations of Sir Richard Musgrave, bart.*, (Dublin, 1801), pp 47-50, (henceforth cited as *Reply*). For Shallow, see K. Whelan (ed.), *A history of Newbawn* (Newbawn, 1986), p. 16, pp 45-9.
14. Kavanagh's affidavit is in *Reply*, pp 51-5.
15. Byrne, *Memoirs*, I, p. 121; T. Handcock, 'Narrative of the battle of Enniscorthy on 28 May

1798, with a detail of the circumstances antecedent and subsequent thereto', N.L.I. MS 16,232, p. 106 (henceforth 'Narrative').

16. Evidence of John Boxwell, 24 Aug. 1798; Quit Rent papers, *P.R.I. rep. D.K.* 57, p. 47.

17. Handcock, 'Narrative', pp 2-3; P. Moran (ed.), *Spicilegium Ossoriense: being a collection of original letters and papers illustrative of the history of the Irish church* (Dublin, 1874), (henceforth *Spicil. Ossor.*)

18. *Reply*, p. 51

19. *Veritas*, p. 59

20. *Freeman's Journal*, 10 Feb. 1798; P. MacSuibhne, *A history of Clonegal parish* (Carlow, 1970), pp 81-2, 169-70; C. Topham Bowden, *A tour in Ireland* (Dublin, 1791), pp 60-4

21. *Veritas*, p. 26

22. *Freeman's Journal*, 10 Feb. 1798

23. *Veritas*, p. 18

24. *Spicil. Ossor.*, III, pp 573-4

25. S.P.O., R.P. 620/34/20

26. S.P.O., R.P. 620/36/202; S.P.O., R.P. 620/36/149

27. *Freeman's Journal*, 13 Jan. 1798

28. Musgrave, *Memoirs*, app. pp. 79-80

29. J. Brady, *Catholics and Catholicism in the eighteenth century press* (Maynooth, 1965), pp 321-2

30. Cullen, '1798 Rebellion'; Musgrave, *Memoirs*, pp 321-2, app. pp. 81-2

31. *Freeman's Journal*, 1 Mar. 1798. Murphy was from the barony of Bargy and was related to the Staffords of Baldwinstown castle and the Brownes of Harpoonstown. His will (dated 13 June 1796, proved 24 June 1803) is abstracted by the Commissioners for Charitable Donations and Bequests, P.R.O.I.

32. J. Alexander, *Some account of the first apparent symptoms of the late rebellion* (Dublin, 1800), p. 30

33. G. Taylor, *An historical account of the rise, progress and suppression of the rebellion in the county of Wexford* (Dublin, 1800), p. 25; *People*, 17 May 1913 (letter signed by 'Ballyharty')

34. D. Goodall, 'Dixon of Castlebridge, county Wexford' in *Ir. Geneal.*, VI, no. 5 (1984), pp 629-41

35. Goodall, 'Dixon', pp 630, 633; will of Michael Furlong (Templescoby) in N.L.I., *Reports on private collections*, no. 43, (Furlong papers)

36. C.T.C., 7 Sept. 1798

37. *Ibid.*, 23 Sept. 1799; 6 Dec. 1798 (cited in P. Moran, *History of the Catholic church in Australasia* (Sydney, 1894), pp 35-6; Hay, *History*, p. 72; for Sparks see L. Cullen, *Personal recollections of Wexford and Wicklow insurgents of 1798* (Enniscorthy, 1959), pp 100-1. See also L. Cullen's article in this volume.

38. Diary of Elizabeth Richards of Rathaspeck, 26 May-22 June 1798, N.L.I. mic. 6486, p. 1.

39. Hay, *History*, pp 145-6; Taylor, *Historical account*, pp 98-9

40. C.T.C., 6 Dec. 1798 in Moran, *Australasia*, pp 35-6

41. Musgrave, *Memoirs*, app. p. 62

42. C.T.C., 21 May 1799; 23 Sept. 1799

43. Cloney, *Narrative*, pp 13-14 for Doran/Synnott connection. For Roices of Tinnacross, see *People*, 25 Feb. 1911 and will of Peter Roice, abstracted by Commissioners for Charitable Donations and Bequests P.R.O.I., 1814.

44. The Murphy family moved soon after Michael's birth at Kilnew to Ballinoulart. Murphy/Stafford links are shown in the bequest by Nicholas Murphy (Ballinoulart) to Rev Nicholas Stafford in his will dated 23 July 1806 (Charitable Donations and Bequests, P.R.O.I., 1806). Stafford's gravestone is in Ballyvalloo. My thanks to Larry and Molly Mythen (Ballingowan) for details of the life of their relation and for showing me various artefacts which belonged to him, including a table and rosary beads.

45. 'The dispossessed landowners of Ireland in 1664' in *Ir. Geneal.*, IV, no. 4 (1971), pp 275-302

46. Musgrave, *Memoirs*, app. p. 62

47. [R. Musgrave] *A concise account of the material events and atrocities which occurred in the present rebellion, by Veridicius* (Dublin, 1799), p. 47

48. *Spicil. Ossor.*, III, p. 577

49. *Veritas*, p. 63. Similarly, after another priest called to administer the sacraments to a condemned informer, had attempted to dissuade the rebels from executing him, he was told

that 'he had done what he had been called to do and that if he did not get away, they would make short work of him', *Veritas*, p. 50.

50. Flood, *Ferns*, p. 16
51. For the Hay-O'Connor connection, see *People*, 21 Dec. 1912.
52. *People*, 31 Aug. 1912
53. Richards, 'Diary', p. 37
54. P. Kavanagh, *A popular history of the insurrection of 1798* (Dublin, 1918), pp 296, 302
55. 'Notes on the Clinch family by Anthony Ryan' in *People*, 2 Dec. 1950
56. Letter from G. O'C Redmond, *People*, 29 Feb. 1908; Taylor, *Historical account*, p. 54
57. Luke Cullen, *Personal recollections*, p. 95
58. Downes family history, *People*, 22 Mar. 1913; will of Bernard Downes in *Ir. Ancestor*, I, (1976), p. 49; H. Murphy, *Families of county Wexford* (Dublin, 1986), p. 79.
59. N. Furlong, *Fr John Murphy of Boolevogue* (forthcoming).
60. I am grateful to T. C. Butler, O.S.A. for specifying Keane's birthplace.
61. J. Stock, *A narrative of what passed at Killalla* [sic] (London, 1800), p. 82
62. *Veritas*, p. 47. For Murphy's earlier career, see Taylor, *Historical account*, pp 25-32
63. J. Jones, *An impartial narrative of the most important engagements* (Dublin, 1799), pp 31-3
64. W. Grattan Flood (ed.),'An account of the visitations made by Nicholas Sweetman in 1753' in *Archiv. Hib.*, II (1913), pp 101-5
65. *C.T.C.*, 5 Sept. 1798
66. K. Whelan, 'County Wexford priests in Newfoundland' in *Wex. Hist. Soc. Jn.*, X (1984-5), pp 55-68
67. *People*, 2 Dec. 1950
68. Hay, *History*, p. 165
69. Kearn's life is well described by L. MacShane in *People*, 24 Dec. 1898. For Kelly, see Cloney, *Narrative*, pp 211-12. For his family background, see I.F.C. schools MS 900, 901 (Rathnure N.S.).
70. Kavanagh, *Popular history*, pp 304-5
71. S. Heyden, 'A list of the Protestants in the parishes of Clone, Kilbride and Ferns in 1776', (MS in possession of Dean David Earle, Ferns). For a discussion of this document, see Whelan 'Religious factor', pp 63-5.
72. P. MacSuibhne, *'98 in Carlow* (Carlow, 1974), pp 11-20. The old Whitty farmstead still stands in excellent condition in Tomgarrow. James Whitty is buried in Templeshanbo.
73. There is an account of Michael Murphy by his relative T. Sinnott in *Echo*, 21 Aug. 1948.
74. For a detailed traditional account see the letters to *People*, 30 Apr. 1898 and 7 May 1898, signed by 'Oulart Hill'. This was the pen-name of Pierce Rowe, Ballinoulart, grandnephew of Michael Murphy (*People*, 1 June 1898).
75. *Echo*, 21 Aug. 1948
76. Camolin Yeomanry detail book, 1 June 1798 cited in H. Wheeler and A. Broadley, *The war in Wexford* (London, 1919), p. 104; Hay, *History*, p. 138, pp 87-8.
77. For Kearns see *People*, 24 Dec. 1898. According to Caulfield, 'he had been employed by Doctor Delaney for some time but latterly dismissed. He was notorious for drinking and fighting, joined the rebels amongst whom he made a gigantic figure and was hanged at Edenderry', *C.T.C.*, 2 Sept. 1798. Kearns may have imbibed his radicalism in France, where he was a student of the Irish College in Paris in 1778. Michael Murphy may have been similarly influenced during his stay in Bordeaux. *People*, 12 Nov. 1910
78. Musgrave, *Memoirs*, p. 478
79. Caulfield states that he was 'under censures the greater part of his life for drunkeness and other irregularities', *C.T.C.*, 2 Sept. 1798.
80. *Veritas*, p. 47; Musgrave, *Memoirs*, pp 482-3; *C.T.C.*, 21 May 1799; T. Butler, *A parish and its people: history of Carrig-on-Bannow* (Wellington Bridge, 1985), p 245
81. *C.T.C.*, 2 Sept. 1798; *Ibid.*, 17 Dec. 1799. Veritas states that he was 'a very zealous, active rebel' who was suspended by Caulfield. *Veritas*, p. 47; Musgrave, *Memoirs*, p. 483.
82. *C.T.C.*, 2 Sept. 1798; Musgrave, *Memoirs*, app. p. 148; He was 'deprived and suspended'. Veritas describes him as 'superceded *ab officio*' some years before the rebellion'; *Veritas*, p. 47; *C.T.C.*, 19 Oct. 1799.
83. Cloney, *Narrative*, p. 225
84. 'An account of the 1798 Rebellion in the Enniscorthy area', N.L.I., MS 25,004, p. 7; Musgrave, *Memoirs*, pp 384-5;'Mrs Brownrigg's journal of Wexford, 26 May-21 June 1798' in Wheeler and Broadley, *War*, pp 112-99; Gordon, *History*, p. 157
85. Taylor, *Historical account*, p. 92; C. Jackson, *A narrative of the sufferings and escape of C. Jackson* (London, 1798), p. 67

86. Hay, *History*, pp 183-4
87. Cloney, *Narrative*, p. 223
88. Handcock, 'Narrative', p. 124; 'Mrs Pounden's experiences during the 1798 rebellion in county Wexford' in *Ir. Ancestor*, VIII, no. 1 (1976), p. 6
89. Gordon, *History*, pp 217-8
90. *Ibid.*, p. 169
91. Hay, *History*, p. 144. The 'grand gallery' was so-called because it contained pews subscribed for by the wealthy Catholic merchants of the town, while the ground floor had standing room only.
92. Alexander, *Account*, p. 108
93. Whelan, 'Religious factor', *passim*
94. *C.T.C.*, 3 Nov. 1799; *Reply*, pp 30-2; Jackson, *Sufferings*, p. 58
95. *People*, 24 June 1911 (citing Mrs. S. C. Hall)
96. Butler, *Bannow*, pp 83-4
97. Brownrigg, 'Journal', p. 182
98. Pounden, 'Experience', p. 6; See also 'Declaration of Rev John Sutton' in *Reply*, pp 36-9.
99. Gordon, *History*, pp 185-6. See also *ibid.*, 2nd ed., (Dublin, 1804) p. 227. 'Fr John Redmond stood absolutely aloof from the rebels who called him an 'orange priest'. G. O'C, Redmond letter to *People*, 29 Feb. 1908
100. *Reply*, p. 51
101. *Ibid.*, pp 33-4
102. *Ibid.*, pp 31, 43; *Veritas*, p. 5; *Freeman's Journal*, 1 Mar. 1798
103. *Veritas*, p. 18
104. *Reply*, p. 32
105. *Ibid.*, p. 6
106. *Ibid.*, p. 35
107. *Ibid.*, p. 42
108. *Ibid.*, p. 51
109. S.P.O., R.P. 620/6/70/28
110. Family tradition as recited by Mrs Sean T. O'Kelly. My thanks to Hilary Murphy for providing me with a copy of his work on the Ryans of Tomcoole, which contains the piece on the Suttons.
111. Gordon, *History*, pp 185-6; Gordon, 2nd ed., p. 227; Cloney, *Narrative* p. 224; Fr John Redmond was a native of Ballinakill (Marshalstown).
112. Byrne, *Memoirs*, p. 7. For Mountnorris's equally violent assault on the dead Fr Michael Murphy, see Gordon, *History*, pp 258-9.
113. *C.T.C.*, 19 Oct. 1799
114. Goodall, 'Dixon'; Hay, *History*, pp 286-7; S.P.O., R.P. 620/39/184; S.P.O., R.P. 620/41/62
115. *C.T.C.*, 26 Apr. 1799; 19 Oct. 1799; 27 Oct. 1799
116. *Ibid.*, 17 Dec. 1799. For Lacy's brother, William, see Handcock, 'Narrative', p. 17 and Musgrave, *Memoirs*, app. p. 116.
117. *Ibid.*, p. 434; Handcock, 'Narrative', p. 125
118. Brady, *Press*, p. 307. For a detailed traditional account of this murder, see *People* 19 Nov. 1898. A copy of Ryan's will dated 1794 survives in the Troy papers, D.D.A.
119. *C.T.C.*, 27 June 1799; 12 July 1799; 28 July 1799
120. *Ibid.*, 19 Oct. 1799; 27 Oct. 1799; 19 Nov. 1799
121. 'Letter of John Etchingham to G. O'C. Redmond', 2 June 1910. My thanks to Bernard Browne for locating this letter.
122. *C.T.C.*, 30 July 1799
123. *People*, 4 July 1920
124. Whelan, 'Religious factor', *passim*
125. There is a detailed calendar of this material in the Troy papers in both D.D.A. and N.L.I..
126. C. Vane (ed.), *Memoirs and correspondence of Viscount Castlereagh*, IV (London, 1848)
127. *Spicil. Ossor.*, III, p. 577
128. Kavanagh, *Popular history*, pp 312-3. Murphy was a native of Garryhack (Ballymore). His family later moved to Churchtown. My thanks to Fr Lory Kehoe for this information.
129. Brady, *Press*, pp 309-10; *C.T.C.*, 17 Dec. 1799; *People*, 26 Apr. 1900; 9 Sept. 1916
130. *People*, 5 Feb. 1908; Butler, *Bannow*, p. 239
131. *C.T.C.*, 17 Dec. 1799
132. *Ibid.*, 26 Apr. 1799
133. *Reply*, p. 47

12   *Sean Cloney*

1. E. McLysaght, *Surnames of Ireland* (Dublin, 1979) p. 47. He fails to advert to the strong presence of the Cloney name in Kilkenny and Carlow. *Census Ire., 1659*, pp 414, 417, 549.
2. B. Cantwell, *Memorials of the dead: gravestone inscriptions of county Wexford* V and IX (Greystones, 1984-6)
3. Tombstone, Rossdroit cemetery. Unless otherwise stated, all subsequent dates of birth and death are taken from tombstone inscriptions. Cantwell, *Memorials*
4. Cloney papers, Dungulph castle
5. *Shapland Carew papers*, pp 19, 48
6. Will abstract in Charitable Donations and Bequests *P.R.O.I.*, 1844. A copy of his will survives in the Cloney papers (Old Ross) in possession of John Browne.
7. Cloney papers, Old Ross
8. Elizabeth's maiden name was probably Wadding. Cloney states that his family had lived at Moneyhore for upwards of a century; *Narrative*, p. 154
9. Cloney, *Narrative*, pp 13, 127
10. Flood, *Ferns*, p. 49
11. *Ibid.*, p. 50
12. Cloney, *Narrative*, p. 13
13. *Ibid.*, p. 127
14. Hore, VI, p. 536. 'Mat' could be a clerical error for Martin. Hore (footnote, p. 543) incorrectly identifies 'Curnecody' as Coolycarney.
15. S. Cloney, 'The Colclough family' in *Wex. Hist. Soc. Jn.*, X (1984-5), pp 44-54
16. Cloney, *Narrative*, pp 101, 152
17. Hore, VI, p. 538. Thomas Cloney was admitted freeman at the age of eight in 1782; *ibid.*, p. 544.
18. P. Hennessy, *Davidstown-Courtnacuddy, a Wexford parish* (Davidstown, 1982), pp 112-3
19. Cloney, *Narrative*, p. 36
20. *Ibid.*, pp 269, 274
21. *Ibid.*, p. 15
22. *Ibid.*, p. 36
23. Tombstone of Thomas Cloney in St Mullins. Catherine Kavanagh *neé* Furlong, who died in 1805 aged 80 would have been the grandmother to whom Cloney refers in his *Narrative*, p. 9. The Cloneys held tracts of land in county Carlow from Kavanagh of Borris for generations; Cloney, *Narrative*, p. 156.
24. *Ibid.*, p. 9
25. Encumbered estates court rental, lands of Mangan, 1855 (N.L.I.).
26. The Cloney papers (Old Ross) contain a letter signed by Catherine and Helen.
27. Cloney, *Narrative*, p. 92
28. *Ibid.*, p. 100. He was then aged 60 and is buried with his daughters, Helen and Catherine in Rossdroit.
29. Cloney, *Narrative*, p. 8
30. *Ibid.*, p. 50
31. *Ibid.*, p. 157
32. *Ibid.*, pp 157, 160, 161; P. O'Leary, *memoir of Thomas Cloney* (Wexford, 1898), pp 14-16
33. Byrne, *Memoirs*
34. *Ibid.*, p. 70
35. Cloney, *Narrative*; pp 154-5
36. Byrne, *Memoirs*, p. 72
37. This is the strong family tradition. The old dresser (now disintegrating) is still at Old Ross.
38. Cloney, *Narrative*, pp 124-5
39. The Keatings displayed strong O'Connellite leanings, as well as supplying Dr James Keating as bishop of the diocese of Ferns, 1849-56. Later on, the Dorans replaced the Keatings and this family still holds the old Cloney property. There is a photograph of their house in Hennessy, *Davidstown*, p. 35.
40. Cloney, *Narrative*, pp 148-9
41. *Ibid* p. 178
42. *Ibid.*, pp 168-70, 173-4, 183-4
43. *Ibid.*, p. 171
44. *Ibid.*, pp 173-4

45. *Ibid.*, p. 183. Also see the inscription on his tombstone at St Mullins. The General was one of the platform party at an O'Connell Repeal meeting at Tomduff, near Enniscorthy on July 1843, having arrived there at the head of many thousands from counties Carlow and Kilkenny; Hennessy, *Davidstown*, p. 47. There was an autographed portrait of O'Connell which he gave to Cloney hanging in Dungulph castle for many years.

46. A. Griffith, *Meagher of the sword* (Dublin, 1917), p. 207

47. *Idem.*

48. Cloney papers, Old Ross

49. The earliest mention of a mill in Old Ross is in 1281-2; Hore, I, pp 19, 20, 35. The still functioning mill is therefore a direct link to the Norman manorial mill.

50. Family tradition, as related to the present writer by his uncle's Thomas and Garrett.

51. H. Jones, *The Palatine families of Ireland* (San Leandro, 1965)

52. Observations on the Old Ross estate, 1818, Ram papers, N.L.I., MS 8238/10

53. The Cloney family papers (Old Ross) contain an undated letter by Martin's son Garrett, who wrote to Thomas Smith, Surveyor of Taxes, c. 1840: 'Sir, According to the directions in your notice to me, I filled in to the best of my knowledge and belief. I am surprised that any man in my station in life would be served with such a notice. I will give the particulars of my standing. I hold a lease of thirty-two acres (Irish) of land from Lord Carew for thirty-five pounds seven shillings and four pence, which half of it is wet land with a mill for carding wool which would not pay a man to attend it these six years past, the other mill, a common corn mill with two pair of stones for shelling and grinding oats and barley which would not make a hundred (pounds) for me in five years from the competition in this neighbourhood with grinding is reduced to nearly half. Three shillings in the pound Poor Rates with a heavy County cess, there is the whole of my property explained to you to the best of my knowledge and belief. G. Cloney'. It should be noted that before the modernisation of the mill, there is only reference to a shelling stone and a grinding stone (for oats and barley, i.e. animal feed), but no mention of wheat, so it is evident that oatmeal rather than wheaten meal formed the staple bread of the people in the years leading up to the Famine.

54. K. Whelan, 'The religious factor in the 1798 rebellion in county Wexford' in P. O'Flanagan, P. Ferguson and K. Whelan (ed.), *Rural Ireland 1600-1900* (Cork, 1987), pp 62-85

55. Family tradition as imparted by the writer's uncle's, Thomas and Garrett.

56. Cushinstown R.C. registers begin in 1750 but there are *lacunae* from 1759-'78 and from 1797-1801.

57. The property subsequently became the inheritance of a Miss Neville, who married a Nowlan of Maudlins (near New Ross). Another Neville girl married a Brennan of the licensed premises, later sold to Suttons, which is now known as the Horse and Hounds; John Doyle, retired miller, Old Ross, personal communication.

58. Cloney, *Narrative*, p. 43

59. *Ibid.*, pp 44, 220

60. Whelan, 'Religious factor', p. 68

61. It is the writer's belief that the Browners were from Taghmon. Although definite proof is lacking, it is probable that Matthew and Maria were the ancestors of the present Cloneys of the Caim/Killoughrim area. Matthew and John both subscribed to Cloney's *Narrative* in 1832.

62. Their marriage settlement is in the Cloney papers (Old Ross).

63. Musgrave, *Memoirs*, app. xx, p. 139: 'David Neville swore an information ... that John Devereux of Dungulph ... (was) busy in promoting the rebellion'.

64. Kinnagh had been settled on James Devereux by his brother, the extraordinary Alexander Devereux, first reformation bishop of Ferns and last abbot of Dunbrody. When the lease of Kinnagh fell due, Colclough's agent, Thomas McCord, demanded a stiff increase in rent, so Devereux refused to renew the lease. It then passed into the hands of Fr Peter Doyle (half-brother of the great J. K. L.) who built St Martin's Villa on it, just beside Kinnagh graveyard. Kevin Whelan, personal communication

65. Ballinruane later came into the hands of the Elmes's, a notable Old Ross family, of possible Palatine origin.

66. Hore, II, P. 115

67. The Devereuxs were burned out of their castle in 1642, when it was attacked by a military force from Duncannon Fort; Jeffreys, *Castles*, pp 137-8. The Devereuxs maintained a presence in the area. In 1798, Michael Devereux of Battlestown was a United Irish captain; Musgrave, *Memoirs*, app., p. 139. There have been Devereux families in Battlestown and Kilbride, an adjoining townland, until recent times. The current Kilbride family, Thomas and

Aidan Devereux and their sister, Mary Anne Connolly (Harrylock) are the nearest relatives. Their brother Fr James Devereux was parish priest of Piercetown; obituary, *New Ross Standard.*, 18 July 1986.

68. Cloney, *Narrative*, p. 43
69. Hore, IV, pp 332, 372
70. Ely estate maps, 1872.. N.L.I.
71. See appendix at end of this article.
72. Cloney family papers, Old Ross
73. *Ibid.*
74. Garrett's mother was Bridget Neville of Ballinaboola.
75. Patrick Hickey of Meylerspark (son of Michael of Meylers Park) was the founder of Patrick Hickey and Co. Ltd., New Ross and Poulmounty woolen mills.
76. This Patrick Hickey was a cousin of Patrick of New Ross.
77. John's brother, Michael, became the first Hickey in Garryrichard (Foulkesmills) and his brother, Cornelius, the first Hickey in Dononore (Cushinstown).
78. The Hickey family history has been supplied by Dr Garrett Hickey, grandson of the first Patrick Hickey of Poulmounty Mills.
79. Flood, *Ferns*, pp 154, 187
80. The prisoner, Patrick Power of Bunclody, had been found guilty of murdering his own father; *Past*, IX, p. 39.
81. The Doyle Ballyling farm is now occupied by their descendants, the Joyces.
82. Captain Cloney served in the U.S. navy all through the Second World War, having joined the merchant marines in 1929. He was mayor of Longview (Washington) 1949-53, where he and his wife ran a hardware store, after his retirement from the navy.
83. Stanley Macomber was a very wealthy steel mill owner in Canton, Ohio.
84. The will stipulated that if John had no male issue, 'then my property shall be given to the next male heir to my family of the name of Cloney; Cloney papers, Old Ross.
85. The two Sylvesters, uncle and nephew, were educated in Salamanca, Spain. Likewise the two Thomas's, also uncle and nephew, went to St Peters and then Maynooth.
86. Flood, *Ferns*, p. 129
87. The writer remembers countless strident political arguments in Old Ross between 'the Canon' and Garrett on Irish, Anglo-Irish, European and world issues especially those concerning Britain and Germany during World War II and on the Blueshirts and Volunteers in the 30s. The Canon seemed to gratify his own sense of humour by rising his brother, whose humour was of a quite different kind.
88. As already stated, John had sold his shop in New Ross in early 1890 to manage the farm and mill in Dungulph for his sisters.
89. This money would have come from the proceeds of the sales of their farms.
90. The detailed costings of these reconstructions are in the Cloney papers, Dungulph.
91. The Murphys of Kilmokea had previously lived at Ralph (Fethard).
92. Ellen Cavanagh had two brothers; Patrick married but died without issue in New Zealand; Arthur died unmarried in England. A sister, Elizabeth, married Myles O'Donoghue, Castle Talbot (Blackwater) and had five children.
93. Among his closest I.R.A. friends were the Ryans of Tomcoole, particularly Dr James and Fr Martin, who died curate of Poulfur in 1929; Pat O'Brien, Dungulph, an I.R.A. die-hard, was probably his closest friend of all. To counterbalance those men were some close Protestant comrades, such as William Hornick, Johnshill and Walter Bassett, Fethard. For the Ryans of Tomcoole, see H. Murphy, *Families of county Wexford* (Dublin, 1986), pp 219-21.
94. *New Ross Standard*, 13 Sept. 1935
95. D. Goodall, 'Dixon of Castlebridge, county Wexford' in *Ir. Geneal.*, VI (1984), pp 629-41; K. Whelan, 'The Devereux family of Tomhaggard' in *Kilmore parish Journal*, XV (1986-7), pp 23-6; K. Whelan, 'The Rossitters of Newbawn' in K. Whelan (ed.), *A history of Newbawn* (Newbawn, 1986), pp 60-68.

13   *T. Jones Hughes*

1. H. Murphy, *Families of county Wexford* (Dublin, 1986)
2. The parishes employed for reference purposes here are the civil or anglican parishes, as these

were recognised in the nineteenth century. These are referred to as the historic parishes to distinguish them from their modern Catholic counterparts.
3. T. Morgan and P. Morgan, *Welsh surnames* (Cardiff, 1985), p. 164
4. T. Jones Hughes, 'Town and baile in Irish place-names' in N. Stephens and R. Glasscock (ed.), *Irish geographical studies* (Belfast, 1970), pp 248-54
5. W. Nolan, 'Patterns of living in Tipperary 1750-1850' in Nolan, *Tipperary*, pp 308-16
6. T. Jones Hughes, 'Landholding and settlement in the Cooley peninsula of Louth' in *Ir. Geog.*, IV (1961), pp 149-74; *Ibid.*, 'A traverse of north Leinster' in *Baile* (1981), pp 2-7
7. T. Jones Hughes, 'A traverse of south Leinster' in *Baile* (1982), pp 3-10; L. Cullen, 'The social and economic evolution of south Kilkenny in the seventeenth and eighteenth centuries' in *Decies* XIII (1980), pp 28-51
8. T. Jones Hughes, 'A traverse of the western foothills of the Wicklow mountains' in *Baile* (1980), pp 3-7
9. T. Jones Hughes, 'Historical geography of Ireland from circa 1700' in G. Davies (ed.), *Irish geography: the geographical society of Ireland golden jubilee 1934-1984* (Dublin, 1984), pp 149-66
10. T. Jones Hughes, 'The estate system of landholding in nineteenth century Ireland' in W. Nolan (ed.), *The shaping of Ireland* (Cork, 1986), pp 137-50
11. J. O'Callaghan, 'Fortified houses of the sixteenth century in south Wexford' in *Old Wex. Soc. Jn.*, VIII (1980-1), pp 9-14
12. *Civil Survey, passim*
13. L. Cullen, *The emergence of modern Ireland* (London, 1981)
14. *List of landowners in Ireland in 1876* (Dublin, 1876)
15. T. Jones Hughes, 'Landholding and settlement in the counties of Meath and Cavan in the nineteenth century' in P. O'Flanagan, P. Ferguson, and K. Whelan (ed.), *Rural Ireland 1600-1900* (Cork, 1987) pp 104-41
16. L. Cullen, *Irish towns and villages* (Dublin, 1979); T. Jones Hughes, 'Village and town in mid-nineteenth century Ireland' in *Ir. Geog.*, XIV (1981), pp 99-106
17. T. Jones Hughes, 'Landholding and settlement in county Tipperary in the nineteenth century' in Nolan, *Tipperary*, pp 339-66
18. Jones Hughes, 'Meath and Cavan'.
19. T. Jones Hughes, 'The large farm in nineteenth century Ireland' in D. Ó h-Ógáin and A. Gailey (ed.), *Gold under the furze* (Dublin, 1982), pp 93-100
20. Jones Hughes, 'Tipperary'
21. K. Whelan, 'The Catholic parish, the Catholic chapel and village development in Ireland' in *Ir. Geog.*, XVI (1983), pp 1-15
22. T. Jones Hughes, 'A traverse of the coastlands of county Wicklow and east county Wexford' in *Baile* (1986), pp 2-12.
23. J. Leslie, *Fern's clergy and diocese* (Dublin, 1936)
24. K. Whelan, 'Catholic parish'
25. K. Whelan, 'The Catholic church in county Tipperary 1700-1900' in Nolan, *Tipperary*, pp 215-55; Hennessy, *Davidstown*, p. 10
26. K. Whelan, 'The Devereux family of Tomhaggard — a case study' in *Kilmore Parish Journal*, XV (1986-7), pp 23-26
27. K. Whelan (ed.), *A history of Newbawn* (Newbawn, 1986), p. 56
28. Jones Hughes, 'Meath and Cavan'
29. Jones Hughes, 'Tipperary', p. 361
30. P. O'Connor, *Exploring Limerick's past* (Newcastle West, 1987), p. 117
31. T. Butler, *A parish and its people: history of the parish of Carrig-on-Bannow* (Wellington Bridge, 1985), pp 157-66

14   *John Mannion*

1. There are now several studies of Irish merchants at home and their trade overseas but few scholars have yet examined Irish merchants abroad. W. Griffen, 'The Irish on the continent in the eighteenth century' in R. Rosbottom (ed.), *Studies in eighteenth-century culture*, V (Madison, 1976), pp 453-73; L. Cullen, 'Merchant communities overseas, the navigation acts and Irish and Scottish responses' in L. Cullen and T. Smout (ed.), *Comparative aspects of*

Scottish and Irish economic and social history, 1600-1900 (Edinburgh, 1977), pp 165-76; *Ibid.*, 'The Irish merchant communities of Bordeaux, La Rochelle and Cognac in the eighteenth century' in L. Cullen and P. Butel (ed.), *Négoce et industrie en France et en Irlande aux XVIIIe et XIXe siècles* (Paris, 1980), pp 54-4; *Ibid.*, *The emergence of modern Ireland 1600-1900* (New York, 1981), pp 117-20; E. Green 'The Irish in American business and professions' in D. Doyle and O. Edwards (ed.), *America and Ireland, 1776-1976* (Connecticut, 1980), pp 193-204; J. Mannion, 'The Waterford Merchants and the Irish-Newfoundland provisions trade 1770-1820' in Cullen and Butel, *Négoce* pp 51-63; *Ibid.*, 'Archibald Nevins' in *Dictionary of Canadian Biography*, V (Toronto, 1983), pp 623-5; *Ibid.*, 'Patrick Morris and Newfoundland Irish immigration' in C. Byrne and M. Harry (ed.), *Talamh an Éisc: Canadian and Irish Essays* (Halifax, 1986), pp 180-202; D. Doyle, *Ireland, Irishmen and revolutionary America, 1760-1820* (Cork, 1981);A. Ravina, *Burguesia extranjera y commercio Atlantico: la empresa commercial Irlandesa en Canarias (1703-1771)* (Santa Cruz, 1985)

2. Minutes, New Ross corporation, 16 Apr. 1759, Tholsel, New Ross; Headstone inscription, Anglican cemetery, Placentia

3. Testimony of Aaron Graham (17 June 1793) pp 433-63, Report from the committee on the state of trade to Newfoundland (1793), Great Britain House of Commons Journal, X, 1785-1810; Provincial archives of Newfoundland and Labrador (hereafter P.A.N.L.), GB/5

4. C.O. 194/9 (1734), pp 261-63; Governor's returns, scheme of the fishery, P.A.N.L.

5. C.O. 194/1 (1697), p. 107

6. C.O. 194/7 (1720), p. 48

7. C.O. 194/8 (1725), p. 52; /9 (1732), p. 212

8. GN2/1/A/2 (1753), p. 80 petition of John Bryan, William Bryan, Daniel Kennedy, Edward King and Michael Sullivan of Little Placentia servants, against captain Alexander Ley, Placentia, 14 Sept. 1753. P.A.N.L. C.O., 194/13 (1753), pp 113-4

9. Placentia court records, (hereafter P.C.R.) 15 Sept. 1757, 2 Sept. 1758, 6 May 1762, 16 Oct. 1764 in P.A.N.L.

10. Minutes, New Ross Corporation, 16 Apr. 1759

11. R.D., 187540 (1750); will of Richard Welsh, Placentia, 27 Sept. 1770 in P.R.O., London, Chancery court of Canterbury, 137, 6 Mar. 1771. I am grateful to my colleague Gordon Handcock for this latter document and for the wills of William and Thomas Saunders.

12. P.C.R., 6 Oct. 1767. In 1763 the court of Placentia had placed Welsh under a bond of £500 not to supply these planters and servants but was granted permission to do so when the Poole house ran short of provisions.

13. C.O., 194/15 (1760), p. 14; *Lloyd's list of voyages* (hereafter L.V.) 24 Aug. 1760; Admiralty (hereafter ADM.), Class 7 Misc./90 (1760), p. 90; Register, Mediterranean passes (hereafter M.P.) Admiralty, 23 May 1765. Data on shipping are located in the Maritime history archive (MHA), Memorial University..

14. P.C.R., 20 Sept. 1763

15. P.C.R., 13 Sept., 15 Sept. 1757, 29 Aug. 1758, 3 Mar., 28 July 1762, 3 Oct. 1763, 14 Jul., 24 Sept. 1764, 7 Oct., 14 Oct. 1765, 3 Oct. 1768, 28 Sept. 1770; GN2/1/A/3 (1764): 232-233.

16. ADM. 7/91 (1765), /92 (1766), /94 (1769): (L.V.) 12 Jan., 20 Jan., 17 Apr., 25 Apr., 26 Apr., 19 Nov., 26 Dec. 1768, 3 Nov., 15 Nov. 1769, 29 Jan., 22 Mar., 1770

17. *Faulkner's Dublin Journal*, 8 Sept. 1767; Mannion, 'Waterford merchants'.

18. L.V. 23 Aug. 1767; M.P., 4 Sept. 1767, 2 Dec. 1768; List of freemen, Waterford, 26 Jan. 1768; P.C.R., 6, 21 Sept., 1 Oct. 1768, 6 Sept. 1769, 1 Oct. 1770

19. Third report, committee on trade, 17 June 1793, pp 433-63. Welsh's obituary is published in *Finn's Leinster Journal* (hereafter F.L.J.) 1771 'Died, some time ago, Richard Welsh, Esq. Placentia, a gentleman universally and deservedly lamented by all degrees and ranks of people. Reported he died worth £100,000. Some time ago, married, at the same place, William Saunders to Miss Welsh, daughter of Richard, with an immense fortune'.

20. G. Nicholson, *The fighting Newfoundlander* (London, 1964), p. 5; J. Proulx, *Placentia: 1713-1811* (Ottawa, 1979), p. 137; C.O. 194/12 (1745) pp 33-36; G.N. 2/1/A/2 (1753), p. 83. A Paul Wibault was recorded at Placentia in 1753 and Paul Welsh Wilbault may be his son. The latter was nominated co-heir with Welsh's three daughters should David Welsh die. Paul Welsh Wibault, gent, was recorded living at Mount Prospect, a villa on the north bank of the Suir, outside Waterford, between 1778 and 1787. He is not mentioned in any subsequent administration of the Welsh fortune. F.L.J., 26 Dec. 1778; R.D., 390-298 (1787). He is mentioned as a sponsor in the R.C. registers of St Patrick's, Waterford, 13 Oct. 1772, 4 Feb. and 9 Sept. 1774.

21. Minutes, New Ross Corporation, 2 Oct. 1771. Records of shipping from New Ross were usually subsumed under Waterford in the eighteenth century.
22. *F.L.J.*, 18 Nov. 1768; L.V. 29 Jan., 15 Mar. 1770, 1 Jan., 10 Feb., 6 Apr., 19 Apr., 30 Aug., 9, 19, 29 Dec. 1771, 3 Jan., 27 Jan., 3 Mar, 13 Apr., 27 Nov., 3 Dec. 1772, 18 Jan., 23 Apr., 2 May, 23 May, 13 July 1773, 12 Feb., 26 Feb., 13 Mar., 7 Apr., 4 July, 8 Aug., 17 Oct. 6 Nov., 23 Nov. 1774, 4 Apr., 16 Oct. 16 Nov. 1775; ADM, 2 May 1772, 1 July 1773; *F.L.J.*, 15 Feb., 8 Sept., 25 Nov., 5 Dec. 1772, 27 Jan., 17 Apr., 19 May, 24 Dec. 1773, 1 Mar., 23 Mar. 1774, 1 Mar. 1775; *Waterford Chronicle* 16 Jan. 1771
23. *F.L.J.*, 18 Mar. 1775
24. *F.L.J.*, 15 Apr., 13 Dec. 1775; 31 Jan. 1776; L.V., 22 Dec. 1775
25. R.C. marriage register, Cathedral parish, Waterford, 11 Apr. 1775; *F.L.J.*, 27 Feb. 1773, 19 Jan., 28 May, 1774, 15 Apr. 1775, 4 Feb., 31 May, 20 Sept. 1775; minutes, Waterford corporation, 26 Sept. 1772
26. *F.L.J.*, 20 Sept. 1775, 7 Feb., 16 Oct. 1776, 3 Oct., 19 Dec. 1777, 14 Mar. 1780, 10 Dec. 1783; *Waterford Chronicle*, 23 July 1776
27. C.O., 194/30 (1772), p. 120. The town had attained 'the superiority of a capital over so many small harbours and coves in the extensive bay ... and of others situated further to the west-ward'.
28. C.O., 194/35 (1781), pp 139-42
29. GN 2/1/A/5 (1773), p. 97; /8 (1779), p. 12; GB 2/1 14,25 Sept. 1775, 26 Sept., 6 Oct. 1776, correspondence, Royal engineers, St John's, P.A.N.L.
30. My thanks to Julian Walton for this reference and the details on the Strange family from the notarial records in Cadiz. See footnote 40 below.
31. Leigh estate papers, Rosegarland House. Wexford. The lease was renewed in 1767 at £153 a year. My thanks to the Leigh family for allowing me to inspect these documents and an excellent eighteenth century map of the farms of Newbawn.
32. Will of Edmund Sweetman, Abbeyville, 1821. Sweetman papers, now at P.A.N.L. My thanks to the late Randall Verran of Placentia for access to these papers. R.D. 207262 (1760), 350184 (1782), 44246 (1791), 488154 (1794), 579573 (1806), 2215 (1839)
33. Minutes, New Ross corporation, 7 Oct. 1786, admission of Roger Sweetman, papist, gentle-man; R. Lucas, *A general directory of the Kingdom of Ireland*, (Dublin, 1788)
34. P.C.R., 29 Oct. 1785, 22 Aug., 24 Aug. 1786; will of William Saunders, Poole, 8 Nov. 1787, London, P.R.O.; Calvert 210, 1788; Letter book of Saunders and Sweetman (hereafter L.B.K.), 1788-1803, 24 June, 18 Sept., 25, 26 Sept. 1788, 20, 26 May, 26 Oct. 1789, 15 June, 13 Aug. 1790; P.A.N.L., P7/A/22; diary of Benjamin Lester, merchant, Poole, 8 Dec. 1789, 9 Feb., 21 Mar. 1790, P.A.N.L., P3/B/4
35. L.B.K. 24 June 1788
36. L.B.K., 4 Nov. 1788, 3 Nov., 6 Dec. 1789, 1 June, 27 Oct. 1793. Tom Saunders, Placentia, to John Blackney, 1 Nov. 1790: 'If you have 50 barrels of good pork made up when [captain] Warn arrives put it on board as we will need it at Poole for the fitting out of our ships in the spring'.
37. L.B.K., 11 June, 11 Aug., 6 Sept. 1788, 2 June, 22 Sept., 3 Nov. 1798, 20 May, 13 Sept., 15 Nov. 1791, 21 Sept. 1792, 1 Apr., 23 July 1793. Saunders complained that a poor harvest in Quebec in 1788 forced bread prices upwards in Newfoundland.
38. Society for the propagation of the gospel to foreign parts, 28 Oct. 1788, P.A.N.L. Box 1A/17 series C
39. L.B.K., 6, 11, 16 May, 3 June, 26 Sept., 20 Oct. 1788, 29 May, 3 June, 26 June 1789, 7 May, 1790, 1 June, 23 July 1793
40. J. Walton, 'Census Records of the Irish in eighteenth century Cadiz' in *Ir. Geneal.*, VI (1985) pp748-56. Pedro Doudall, in Cadiz since 1733, lived beside Lorenzo Strange who settled there ten years later, in 1743. Both were merchants and unmarried. Two of the Shiels family from Glenmore, one a cashier, one a clerk, apparently lived with Strange.
41. Waterford corporation, admissions of Freemen, 26 Nov. 1740, 5 Jan. 1778;,ADM 7/86 (1750) p. 1672; R.D. 188584 (1741), 330552 (1766); *Waterford Chronicle*, 12 Dec. 1771; R.C. register, marriages, St Patrick's parish, Waterford, 8 Apr. 1791
42. R.D. 44246 (1781), 465580 (1793), 492226 (1796), 497381 (1796), 512112 (1797), 586211 (1806)
43. R.D. 389129 (1785); Diary of Benjamin Lester, Poole, 6 Sept. 1791; Saunders, Sweetman Ledger, Placentia, 1799; Newman Ledger, 1 June 1799, P.A.N.L.; P.C.R. 18 Aug., 2 Nov., 7 Nov. 1800, 2 Sept. 1802; L.B.K. 2 Oct., 21 Oct. 1802, 20 Sept. 1803
44. L.B.K., 7 Dec. 1792, 7 Oct., 4 Nov. 1793, 24 Dec. 1803

45. Elmes Papers, 19 June 1794 (in possession of King Milne, Ballymorgan, Ferns). Elmes had been a crewman on one of Thomas Kough and Co. vessels in the New Ross-St John's trade and though offered a captaincy, moved to Sweetmans in 1791.

46. C.O. 194/40 (1798) p. 179; Lester Diary, Poole, 6 July 1798; Saunders and Sweetman Ledger, 1799; *Waterford Mirror*, 24 Sept., 21 Dec. 1801, 24 June 1807; R.D. 460330 (1789), 574129 (1802), 689287 (1804), 576181 (1805), 583105 (1806), L.B.K., 9 Sept., 6, 7, 9, 21 Oct. 1802, 2 Mar., 17 Apr., 8 July, 20 Aug., 14, 20 Sept., 6 Oct. 1803.

47. Name files, Saunders, M.H.A.

48. L.B.K., 6 Oct., 21 Oct. 1802; 20 Aug., 6 Oct., 7 Oct. 1803, 22 May, 15 June, 4 July, 20 Aug. 1804; GN 2/1/A/19 (1806), p. 61, (1807), p. 169-70

49. Imports to Placentia GN 2/1/A/19 (1805) pp 434-5, /20 (1809), pp 60-1, 100-1, /24 (1813), pp 91-2, /25 (1814), pp 105-6, /26 (1815), pp 89-90

50. L.B.K., 15 June, 1804. Only seven passengers are recorded from Ireland this spring, compared to 147 the previous season.

51. L.B.K., 6 Oct. 1802, 20 Aug. 1803, 4 July 1804

52. P.C.R., 3 Sept. 21 Oct. (1799); Duckworth Papers 3/9 (1811) P.A.N.L., PY5 Pleas, supreme court, St John's, 6 Nov. 1798, 11 Dec. 1799, P.A.N.L.

53. L.B.K., 20 Aug., 5 Sept., 20 Sept. 1803

54. L.B.K., 29 Sept., 6 Oct. 1802

55. Exports from Placentia GN 2/1/A/18 (1805), pp 432-3; /20 (1809), pp 58-9. 98-9; /24 (1813), pp 93-4; /25 (1813), pp 107-8; /26 (1815), pp 91-2; Duckworth Papers, Oct. 1809-Sept. 1811 *passim*

56. 2 June 1797 will of Thomas Saunders, Poole, Collingwood 215/1810 Dorset archives, Dorchester. Her brother, Francis Ryan, was given £500 but is not mentioned subsequently in connection with the firm. 5 Feb. 1803 Hants. Chronicle; P.C.R. 7 Nov. 1805; GN 2/1/A/19 (1809), pp 169-70; Name files, Saunders, M.H.A.

57. Data on the acquisition of property in Placentia Bay by the company are extensive and extend back to the 1750s. This list comes from the L.B.K., 13 Feb., 6 Mar. 1803, the Sweetman papers, 1810 and the *Royal Gazette* and *Newfoundland Advertizer*, St John's, 30 Aug. 1810. It was noted in the latter source that most of the properties were originally granted in the reign of Louis XIV of France.

58. R.D., 665552 (1810), 735231 (1818). The property of Blenheim was leased in 1791 by the Marquis of Waterford to Samuel Roberts, a Waterford architect and banker. He improved and sublet the demesne to Robert Porter in 1805 for £184 a year. Porter sold his interest to Sweetman for £1,000 five years later.

59. L.B.K. 6, 9 Oct. 1802

60. GN 2/1/A, 1811-1827. Passengers are rarely mentioned in newspaper reports of vessels arriving at Waterford from Placentia during this period.

61. Sweetman papers, indentures, 1825-6

62. Incoming correspondence, Colonial Secretary's office, LIII (1845), pp 53, 585-7, *The Patriot*, St John's, 12 Nov., 24 Dec. 1845, 7 Jan. 1846, P.A.N.L.; Sweetman papers, 2, 5, 16 Jan. 1846. Rev Pelagius Nowlan (1784-1871) came from Kilrush, Wexford and was priest at Little Placentia.

63. J. Mannion, *Irish settlements in eastern Canada: a study of cultural transfer and adaptation* (Toronto, 1974); Ibid., *Point Lance in transition: the transformation of a Newfoundland outport* (Toronto, 1976)

64. P.C.R., 11 Aug. 1800, 24 Sept., 16 Dec. 1802, 16 Feb. 1803; Sweetman papers, 9 July 1825

65. Duckworth papers 1810-1811. Later the Tobins, Halifax's leading Irish-Newfoundland firm, with branches in St. John's and Cork, were important Sweetman agents. GN 2/1/A, 1811-27, imports, Placentia

66. Smith's annual list of exports from Waterford, 1 May 1813-30 Apr. 1814, B.L. MS FF 240-243

67. GN 2/1/A/18 (1805), 28 Nov

68. Sweetman papers, 14 Mar. 1817; *Public Ledger*, 27 Mar. 1838.

69. L.V., 20 Aug. 1816, 12 Aug. 1817; *Waterford Chronicle*, 4, 9, 14 Aug. 1819; 21 July 1821; *Waterford Mirror*, 11 July 1828, 11 Aug., 21 Dec. 1830, 9 July, 9 Dec., 1831

70. *Waterford Mail*, 21 Apr. 1841

71. F. Braudel, *The wheels of commerce: civilisation and capitalism fifteenth to eighteenth century* (New York, 1982)

72. T. Devine, *The tobacco lords: a study of the tobacco merchants of Glasgow* (Edinburgh, 1975)

73. *Waterford Chronicle*, 23 July 1776; *Waterford Herald*, 22 June 1793
74. P.C.R., 10 Sept., 27 Oct., 29 Oct. 1785, 20 July, 1 Aug. 22, 24 Aug. 4 Sept. 1786; GN 2/1/A/10 (1785), p. 197
75. L.B.K., 6 Oct. 1802, 14 Sept. 1803
76. *Waterford Mirror*, 15 Jan. 1829; *The Newfoundlander*, 9 Apr. 1840
77. GN 2/1/A/12 (1794), pp 263; (1795), pp 351-352; L.B.K., 8 July 1803
78. *Waterford Herald*, 25 Apr. 1793; GN 2/1/A/12 (1794), p 263; (1795) pp 351-2; L.B.K., 8 July 1803; Sweetman papers, 9 July, 9 Aug. 1806; *Waterford Mirror*, 26 May 1807, 26 Apr. 1829; *Waterford Chronicle*, 13 Jan. 1819
79. S. Socolow, *The merchants of Buenos Aires 1778-1810* (Cambridge, 1978)

15   *Bruce Elliott*

1. J. Mannion, *Irish settlements in eastern Canada: a study of cultural transfer and adaptation* (Toronto, 1974), p. 13; W. Handcock, 'Spatial patterns in a trans-Atlantic migration field: the British Isles and Newfoundland during the eighteenth and nineteenth centuries' in B. Osborne (ed.), *Proceedings of the 1975 British-Canadian symposium on historical geography* (Kingston, 1976), pp 22-24, 29; T. Punch, *Irish Halifax: the immigrant generation, 1815-1859* (Halifax, 1981), pp 9-13
2. The register of the Perth military settlement, 1816-23, indicates that south Leinster emigrants arriving in the settlement had sailed on vessels out of New Ross, Waterford, Dublin, and Wexford. A few even came via New York, but none are listed on ships from Liverpool. Public Archives of Canada, (hereafter P.A.C., MG D8-27)
3. See K. Whelan, 'The religious factor in the 1798 Rebellion in county Wexford' in P. O'Flanagan, P. Ferguson and K. Whelan (ed.), *Rural Ireland 1600-1900* (Cork, 1987), pp 62-85
4. Rev J. Gordon's account of Killegny in William Shaw Mason, *A statistical account or parochial survey of Ireland* (Dublin, 1814), I, p. 458
5. The Pratt's Hollow settlement continued to draw immigrants from south-eastern Ireland after the War. In time land in the American colony became scarce and many of the second generation moved to south Leinster communities in Canada. A few went to Lanark township in eastern Upper Canada but greater numbers formed a small Wexford/Wicklow colony in London township, four hundred miles to the west. Gravestones in Fairview and Hillcrest cemeteries, Pratt's Hollow, N.Y.; information from Mrs Betty Taylor, Pratt's Hollow; Wm. Tuttle, 'Names and sketches of the pioneer settlers of Madison county', typescript, 1941, at hall of records, Madison county court house, Wampsvill, N.Y.; D. Beers, *Atlas of Madison county, N.Y.* (Philadelphia, 1875); *Grove cemetery ... city of London* (London branch, Ontario genealogical society, no. 143, 1982); obituaries in the Canadian Wesleyan weekly, the *Christian Guardian* of former Pratt's Hollow residents Rev M. Tuke, 10 May 1871; Elizabeth (Bilton) Tackabury, 29 Mar. 1876; John Tackabury, 11 July 1877; Mary Ann (Richards) Tennant, 23 May 1877; inscriptions in Tennant cemetery, Lanark township, Ontario; T. Leavitt, *History of Leeds and Grenville*, p. 83; B. Elliott, The north Tipperary Protestants in the Canadas: a study of migration, 1815-1880, unpublished Ph.D. thesis Carleton University (1984), pp 237-8
6. P.R.O., C.O. 384/1, ff. 170-171, P.A.C. reel B-876, Joseph Elly, Ross, 4 December 1817
7. E. Guillet, *The valley of the Trent* (Toronto, 1957), pp 84-130; A. Brunger, 'Geographical propinquity among pre-famine Catholic Irish settlers in Upper Canada' in *Jn. Hist. Geog.*, VII (1982), pp 265-282; H. Pammett, 'The Irish immigrant settler in the pioneer Kawarthas' in *Families*, XVII (1978), pp 154-74; W. Cameron, 'Selecting Peter Robinson's Irish migrants' in *Histoire sociale*, IX (1976) pp 29-46; Akenson reviews the literature on the Famine Irish in 'Ontario: whatever happened to the Irish?' in D. Akenson (ed.), *Canadian papers in rural history III* (1982), pp 222-5
8. Akenson, 'Ontario', pp 204-56; C. Houston and W. Smyth, 'The Irish abroad: better questions through a better source, the Canadian census', *Ir. Geog.*, XIII (1980), pp 1-19
9. B. Elliott, *Irish migrants in the Canadas: a new approach* (Kingston and Belfast, 1987)
10. C. Houston and W. Smyth, *The sash Canada wore: historical geography of the orange order in Canada* (Toronto, 1980), pp viii, 40; E. Mills, *Early settlement in Ontario*, Parks Canada research paper (Ottawa, 1971/2), *passim*

11. Akenson, 'Ontario', pp 254, 237, 73; p. 237
12. *Montreal Herald*, 8 Oct. 1849 quoted in M. Newton, *Lower Town Ottawa*, National capital commission manuscript report 104 (Ottawa, 1979), I, p. 288.
13. *Perth Courier*, centenary edition, 3 Aug. 1934, p. 6. I am grateful to G. Lockwood for this reference.
14. L. Cullen, *The emergence of modern Ireland* (London, 1981), p. 210
15. H.C. (1835) XXXIII, *First report of the commissioners of public instruction, Ireland*. By contrast, Protestants made up 17,000 of the 200,000 inhabitants of the north Tipperary region.
16. See fig. 15.1 drawn from data in H.C. (1835) XXXIII; on Protestant settlement in the Castlecomer area see W. Nolan, *Fassadinin: land, settlement and society in southeast Ireland, 1600-1850* (Dublin, 1979).
17. The Hortons purchased lot 24, con. 7, Elizabethtown from Daniel Shipman for £100 on 8 May 1809. Ontario Archives (hereafter O.A.), Elizabethtown abstract index to deeds (A.I.D.).
18. O.A. municipal records, assessment rolls, Elizabethtown, 1810, 1812. Adam Horton arrived in 1810; he had seen nine years' service in the Yeomanry. O.A. township papers, RG1 C-IV, Elizabethtown, pp 1361-7
19. D. Schlegel (ed.), *Passengers from Ireland - lists of passengers arriving at American ports between 1811 and 1817* (Baltimore, 1980), pp 35-6
20. William Johnson's gravestone gives his date of emigration and states that he was from Wells, county Wexford. Leeds and Grenville branch, Ontario genealogical society, *The abandoned Johnson cemetery* ([Brockville], 1976); O.A. assessment roll, Leeds and Lansdowne, 1812.
21. A return of locations made by the Johnstown district and board in 1820-21 notes Whaley's origin and year of arrival, and states, too, that Richard Johnson of Lansdowne arrived from Killincooley in 1810. Of the 28 south Leinster emigrants recorded in this document, 26 were from north Wexford and two from county Carlow. The return excludes the many immigrants who purchased land from existing residents and speculators. O.A. RG 1 C-I-4, XLVII (MS 693, r. 163). John Johnston, who arrived in 1812, had seen active service in the Yeomanry cavalry; his father was killed in the Rebellion. O.A. township papers, R.G. 1. C-IV, Yonge, p. 1671
22. C.O. 384/4, f. 163, P.A.C. reel B-877, Samuel Elly Junr. to Bathurst, New Ross, 13 Nov. 1819
23. C.O. 42/165, f. 197, P.A.C. reel B-134, Joseph Elly, New Ross, county Wexford, n.d. [1815]
24. C.O. 384/1, f. 162, P.A.C. reel B-876, Robert Elly, Elly's Walks, New Ross, 12 Jan. 1816 [recté 1817]
25. C.O. 42/177, f. 393-394, P.A.C. reel B-140, G. F. Vaughan, Enniscorthy. 26 Sept. 1817
26. C.O. 384/1, ff 445-446, P.A.C. reel B-876, Isaac Saul, Junr., Rathdrum, county Wicklow, 6 Oct. 1817
27. C.O. 384/1, ff. 170-171, P.A.C., reel B-876, Joseph Elly, Ross, 4 Dec. 1817
28. Petitions for 'clergy reserve lands' from Wexford settlers in the New Dublin area of Elizabethtown reveal that almost all the petitioners had served in yeomanry corps in Ireland, and some had been wounded or had lost property in the 1798 Rebellion. The petitions were submitted in 1828 through the Anglican clergyman, Rossington Elms. O.A., R.G.1 C-IV, Crown lands township papers, Elizabethtown; J. Godkin, 'The Yeomanry veterans of Elizabethtown' in *Ontario History*, LXIII (Dec. 1971), pp 243-64
29. C.O. 384/1, f. 378, P.A.C. reel B-876, Peter Roe, New Ross, 27 Apr. 1817
30. C.O. 384/1, ff. 178-187, P.A.C. reel B-876, Return of families preparing to emigrate from Carlow and Wexford in the ensuing spring, New Ross, Nov. 1817 (see Appendix I). I am grateful to Mrs William Tupper of Kars, Ontario for a transcript of this lengthy document.
31. M. Doyle [W. Hickey], *Hints on emigration to Upper Canada* (Dublin, 1834), pp 72-3
32. P.A.C. MG 24 H7, Diary of William Graves of New Ross: visit to Canada in 1820 [typescript], p. 13. See also C.O. 384/6, ff. 296-300, P.A.C. reel B-879, memorial of William Graves to Lord Bathurst, New Ross, 7 Apr. 1820 and P.A.C., Upper Canada sundries, RG5 A1, XLVII, pp 23425-6 and 23148, P.A.C. reel C-4605, recommendations of Lord Dalhousie and Lord Carrick of William Graves, 1820. Only the Warings were still in Hallowell township in 1852: P.A.C., 1852 census of Hallowell, div. 1, p. 3, reel C-11750.
33. Graves diary, p. 13
34. *Ibid.*, pp 18-21
35. B. Browne, *County Wexford connections* (Wexford, 1985), p. 9; P. Vigors, 'Alphabetical list of the free burgesses of New Ross, Wexford, from 1658 to 30 Sept. 1839' in *R.S.A.I. Jn.*, XXI (1890-1), p. 302

36. P.A.C. Upper Canada sundries, RG5 A1, Vol. 43, pp 20892-3 (reel C-4603), petition of George Johnston, Lansdowne, 25 Feb. 1819
37. The statistics given hereafter for the older townships are therefore minimums. P.A.C. MG9 D8-27. I am grateful to Howard Morton Brown of Ottawa for a copy of this document.
38. Records of locations for the Richmond military settlement, 1820-22, are to be found in O.A., RG1, Rideau military settlements, microfilm, MS 154, r. 1, copy at P.A.C. reel M-5505, item 2, last 18 pages. No record of the location dates in Goulbourn and Beckwith in 1818-19 appears to survive, but comparison of P.A.C., RG1 L3, pp 48d-k, reel C-2739, with a list of locations in the 'old surveyed townships', 1818-19, in P.A.C., RG1 L3, CDXX (Perth military settlement), p. 23, reel C-2739, suggests that the dates of completion of settlement duties given in the former are three years to the day from the dates of location. Locations in the Lanark military settlement, 1820-22, are in O.A., MS 154, r. 1, Pt. 2, pp 45 ff
39. P.A.C., MG24 H7, p. 9; C.O. 384/6, f. 296, P.A.C., reel B-879, Graves to Bathurst, Wellington, New Ross, 7 Apr. 1820
40. P.A.C., RG, DCXXV, p. 129, reel C-3159
41. C.O. 384/8, f. 186, P.A.C., reel B-881
42. *Ibid.*, f. 197, P.A.C. reel B-881
43. *Ibid.*, f. 204, P.A.C. reel B-881
44. *Ibid.*, f. 367, P.A.C. reel B-882
45. *Ibid.*, f 403, P.A.C. reel B-882
46. Gravestone inscriptions, St Stephen's Anglican cemetery, Micksburg, Micksburg United (Methodist) cemetery, abandoned Methodist cemetery, Wilberforce, Greenwood cemetery, Westmeath. Cf. Anglican Diocese of Ottawa archives, registers of Perth, Richmond, and Franktown; H. M. Brown (ed.), *Nominal rolls and state papers: north Lanark data.* I (1973), a collection of Beckwith and Ramsay census, assessment, and militia records given to me by the compiler.
47. P.A.C. census returns for Adelaide, Brooke, and Warwick, 1852, 1861; gravestone inscriptions, St James Anglican cemetery, Brooke; correspondence with Mrs Elizabeth Cahill, Montreal
48. E. Lloyd Lake, *Pioneer reminiscences of the Upper Ottawa valley: the church of St John the Evangelist,* (Eganville, 1964)
49. Akenson, *Ontario,* pp 27-28 for the method of calculation; *Census of Canada, 1870-71* (Ottawa, 1873), I
50. Leeds & Grenville branch, O.G.S., *The Ballycanoe and Trevelyan cemeteries* ([Brockville], 1982). Ballycanoe is a version of the Wexford placename Ballycanew.
51. *H.C.* (1836) XXXI-XXXIII
52. Mannion, *Irish settlements,* p. 13; Punch, *Irish Halifax,* pp 9-13
53. S. Cousens, 'The regional pattern of migration during the great Irish Famine, 1846-51 in T.I.B.G. XXVIII (1960), p. 130; J. Mokyr, *Why Ireland starved: a quantitative and analytical history of the Irish economy, 1800-1850* (London, 1983) pp 12, 267
54. Elliott, *North Tipperary,* pp 171-81
55. *Ibid.*, pp 181-95
56. On Gowan see D. Akenson, *The orangeman* (Toronto, 1986)
57. That Wexfordmen made up most of Gowan's political support is apparent from the poll list for the 1844 election: Brockville Recorder, 21 Nov. 1844, 28 Nov. 1844. I am grateful to G. Lockwood for a copy of this poll list.

16   *J. H. Andrews*

1. Guides to early Irish maps and their interpretation are listed in P. Ferguson, *Irish map history, a select bibliography of secondary works, 1850-1983, on the history of cartography in Ireland* (Dublin, 1983)
2. See especially M. Blakemore and J. Harley, 'Concepts in the history of cartography, a review and perspective' in *Cartographica,* XVII (1980), p. 27
3. E. Parsons, *The map of Great Britain circa 1360 known as the Gough map* (Oxford, 1958), p. 31
4. N.L.I., MS 700, reproduced in J. O'Meara (ed.), *The first version of the topography of Ireland by Giraldus Cambrensis* (Dundalk, 1951), frontispiece

5. 'Anglia figura . . .', n.d., *c.* 1534, British Library, Cotton MS Aug. 1, i, 9, reproduced in *Early maps of the British Isles*, Royal Geographical Society reproductions of early maps, VII (London, 1961), 12. Also untitled map of Ireland, n.d., *c.* 1558, P.R.O., London, M.P.F. 72.

6. An Irish example of such a list, attributed to the reign of Henry VIII, is in BL, Cotton MS, Dom.A.18.

7. *Hybernia nunc Irlant* (Rome, *c.* 1560), reproduced in P. Fox (ed.), *Treasures of the Library, Trinity College, Dublin* (Dublin, 1986), p. 180. Other maps of this family show Fethard but not Glascarrig.

8. Examples covering the period 1534-6 are in *State Papers, Ireland, Henry VIII*, II, pp 190, 203, 220, 299, 304, 326-7, 332, 345, 346, 365, 372, 413, 440.

9. Laurence Nowell, untitled map of Ireland, BL, Cotton MS, Dom.A.18, ff. 97, 101, 103. Ireland also appears in less detail with England on a map described in P. Barber, 'A Tudor mystery: Laurence Nowell's map of England and Ireland' in *The Map Collector*, XXII (1983), pp 16-21. G. Mercator, *Angliae, Scotiae et Hiberniae nova descriptio* (Duisburg, 1564), the Irish portion reproduced in N.L.I. *Ireland from maps* (Dublin, 1980). A third map of this period, 'Hibernia: insula non procul ab Anglia . . .', by John Goghe, 1567 (PRO, M.P.F. 68), has little information on Wexford, though useful for other parts of the country.

10. J. Andrews, 'The Irish surveys of Robert Lythe' in *Imago Mundi*, XIX (1965), pp 22-31, and 'Robert Lythe's petitions, 1571' in *Anal. Hib.*, XXIV (1967), pp 232-41

11. *Cal. S.P. Ire., 1611-14*, p. 134; Hist. MSS Com., *Buccleugh*, I, p. 190; *Acts of the Privy Council, 1616-17*, p. 243

12. Barony maps of Ballaghkeene, Bargy, Forth and Shelburne at 1:40,320, and of Bantry, Gorey, Scarawalsh and Shelmalier at 1:80,640, in the Bibliothèque Nationale, Paris, have been published in photographic facsimile by the Ordnance Survey (Southampton, 1908). Parish maps of all these baronies except Shelburne, as copied in 1786-7, are in N.L.I., MS 725, mostly on scales of 1:10,080 or 1:20,160. Copies of 34 parish maps made in 1778 are in the library of the King's Inns, Dublin. There are slight differences between these two sets of parish maps: in Adamstown parish, for example, the King's Inns maps show four cabins missing from the N.L.I.maps. A reconstruction of the Wexford Down Survey on an Ordnance Survey 1:10,560 base by Robert Johnston is in N.L.I., 20.D.

13. At Whitechurch in Bantry and at Kildavin in Forth, for example, the Down Survey terriers mention several buildings that do not appear on the maps.

14. J. Andrews, 'Charles Vallancey and the map of Ireland' in *Geogr. Jour.*, CXXXII (1966), pp 48-61. Vallancey's strip maps of 1776 are on a scale of 1:20,160, his general maps of Ireland, dated 1785 and 1795, on a scale of 1:161,280.

15. The treasurer of county Wexford reported in 1824 that Gill's map had been made in 1808 at a cost of £400. He added that the map had no scale (though this is not true of the published version) and that it was 'considered very incorrect' (*Report from the select committee on the survey and valuation of Ireland* 373, H.C. 1824 (445), viii). Nothing seems to have come of Alexander Taylor's offer to make a new survey of county Wexford for the grand jury in 1793 (P.R.O.I: 1096/18/22, a reference kindly supplied by Kevin Whelan).

16. J. Andrews, *History in the ordnance map* (Dublin, 1974) and *A paper landscape, the Ordnance Survey in nineteenth century Ireland* (Oxford, 1975)

17. Many portolan charts were copied from earlier charts. The various prototypes for Ireland are discussed in M. Andrews, 'The map of Ireland' in *Proc. Belfast Nat. Hist. and Phil. Soc.*, 1922-3, pp 16-23.

18. T. Westropp, 'Early Italian maps of Ireland from 1300 to 1600, with notes on foreign settlers and trade' in *R.I.A. Proc.*, C XXX (1913), pp 420-1

19. H. Doncker, *Yrlandt van Dubling tot Corkbeg* (Amsterdam, n.d., *c.* 1650). No important new Wexford placenames appeared on later general charts of the Irish coast until the publication of M. Mackenzie's *A maritim survey of Ireland and west coast of Great Britain* in 1776. Among the Wexford names introduced by Mackenzie were St Patrick's Bridge joining the mainland with the Saltee Islands, and Holden's Bed and the Dogger east of Wexford Harbour.

20. N.L.I., Irish Road Maps, 15.A.8

21. N.L.I., 16.J.14 (8, 9, 22-4), 21.F.104 (2); *Shapland Carew papers*, p. 5

22. The names listed below are derived mainly from N.L.I., 16.J.13, 16.J.14, 21.F. 104, and 21.F.161.

23. For the Frizell family see J. Andrews, *Plantation acres, an historical study of the Irish land surveyor and his maps* (Belfast, 1985), *passim*.

24. Gill and Henrick are both represented in N.L.I., 14.A.23.

25. N.L.I., 21.F.161 (4)

26. G. Hayes-McCoy, *Ulster and other Irish maps, c. 1600* (Dublin, 1964), p. 24, including references to later charts.

27. W. Doyle, *A new chart being an actual survey of the harbour of Rineshark and Waterford to the confluence of the Rivers Sure and Barrow and sea coast to them adjacent* (Dublin, 1738). Doyle's nomenclature for Wexford was closely followed by Robert Laurie and John Whittle's chart of the harbour published in 1794 and reprinted in 1808. For a rather pessimistic reference to the use of early maps in the study of changing coastal configurations see J. Orford and R. Carter, 'Geomorphological changes on the barrier coasts of south Wexford' in *Ir. Geog.*, XV (1982), p. 79

28. B. Scalé and W. Richards, *A map of the town and harbour of Wexford* (Dublin, 1764)

29. *Second report of the tidal harbours commission*, appendix B, pp 46-78, H.C. 1846 [692], xviii; *Copy (with plans annexed) of the report of Captain Vetch to Admiral Beaufort, on the improvement of the harbour of Wexford*, including a copy of Captain G. A. Frazer's admiralty chart (also separately published in 1845), H.C. 1856 (300), li; *Papers relating to the improvement of Wexford Harbour*, H.C. 1867 (468), lxiv. Other local charts include those by Alexander Nimmo of Crossfarnogue pier in 1819 (MS. N.L.I., 16.J.13 (3)) and of Courttown harbour in 1822 (printed).

30. R. Skelton and J. Summerson, *A description of the maps and architectural drawings in the collection made by William Cecil . . .* (Oxford, 1971), p. 61. For other early plans of Duncannon see Hayes-McCoy, *Maps.*

31. T.C.D., MS 1209, 64, reproduced in R. Butlin (ed.), *The development of the Irish town* (London and Totowa, 1977), p. 68

32. Musgrave, *Memoirs* includes maps of north and south county Wexford and the New Ross area with more detailed plans of Wexford town, New Ross, and Enniscorthy with Vinegar Hill.

33. Surveys of Bantry Commons, 1821, and Mollgannon, 1823, by Sherrard, Brassington and Greene, P.R.O.I, QRO 7/3/21 and 22. Local opposition made it impossible to produce a similar survey of Forth Mountain.

34. Tithe applotment books containing maps (a small proportion of all the books) are specified in a typescript list in P.R.O.I. A better than average example, showing houses and roads in *c.* 1834, is that of Davidstown and Rahard in the parish of Whitechurchglynn (P.R.O.I., TAB 31/56.)

35. Examples of Frizell estate atlases are those of the Nun estate in 1759 (N.L.I., mic. P. 7630) and of the Loftus estate in 1771 (N.L.I., MS 4153).

36. N.L.I., 21.F. 161 (Charles and Richard Frizell).

37. N.L.I., 16.J.14 (28) (William Thornton of Burton Hall, county Carlow)

38. N.L.I., 21.F.20. An atlas of the Hughes estate in 1823 by the same firm is in the possession of Messrs Kirwan and Kirwan, solicitors, Wexford.

39. Hints to this effect are the small number of Wexford maps in the Longfield collection (N.L.I., 21.F.48: the most interesting is not an estate map, but a survey for the canalisation of the River Slaney by John Brownrigg in 1794); the small number of tithe maps for the county (see above, note 34); and the absence of Wexford maps in William Shaw Mason's *Parochial survey or statistical account of Ireland* (3 vols, Dublin, 1816-19).

40. P. Ferguson, The valuation office maps and records, B.A. dissertation, U.C.D. 1977, pp 71-2.

41. 'A large and ancient folio manuscript, containing a full description and survey of the town and liberties of Wexford', was said to have been in the possession of Arthur Houghton of Burmount near Enniscorthy in 1737 (*Dublin Journal*, 3 Dec. 1748) but this did not necessarily include any maps.

42. See above, note 32. There is a manuscript plan of New Ross illustrating the rebellion in N.L.I., 16.J.13(11).

43. Plans of Enniscorthy in 1726 (by William Munday, a surveyor not otherwise recorded) and *c.* 1785 are in the Portsmouth papers at the Hampshire County Record Office, Winchester. The latter map is probably a later copy; its content has been dated from internal evidence by Kevin Whelan. Plans of New Ross in the early eighteenth century and in 1827 (the latter by Sherrard, Brassington and Gale) are in the Tottenham estate office, New Ross; A. Roche, New Ross: an historical study, B.A. dissertation, T.C.D. 1974, p. 37, pp 41-2).

44. Plans showing the proposed municipal boundaries of Wexford and New Ross at 1:10,560 were printed in 1831 (H.C. 1831-2 (519), xliii). Built-up areas are in block plan, distinguishing 'mud cabins and houses of inferior value'.

45. A. Robinson, *Early thematic mapping in the history of cartography* (Chicago, 1982). The most famous Irish thematic maps, those of population and traffic flow made for the Drummond commission, are described in the same author's 'The 1837 maps of Henry Drury Harness' in *Geogr. Journ.*, CXXI (1955), pp 440-50. See also A. Horner, 'Planning the Irish transport

network:parallels in nineteenth and twentieth century proposals' in *Ir. Geogr.*, x 61977), pp 44-57.

46. A. Yarranton, *England's improvement by sea and land* (London, 1677), opposite p. 40.
47. P.R.O., M.P.F. 69 (photostat, N.L.I. 16.L.5). Apart from maps of Waterford Harbour and Duncannon already cited (above, notes 26, 30, 31) this is the only sixteenth or early seventeenth-century regional map to include part of county Wexford.
48. Among foreign cartographers adopting Mercators's outline of 1564 were Abraham Ortelius (1570), Giovanni Magini (1596), Pieter van den Keere (1604), Baptista Doetecum (1605) and David Custodis (1627). For details see R. Shirley, *Early printed maps of the British Isles 1477-1650* (London, 1973).
49. H. Scherer, *Anglia Scotia Hibernia* (Munich, 1699)
50. P.R.O.I., Clayton MSS, 27 (1A.41.40)
51. For this and other Petty-based maps see S. Tyacke, *London map sellers, 1660-1720* (Tring, 1978), pp 42-50; and T. Stafford, A study of twelve eighteenth century maps of Ireland, B.A. dissertation, T.C.D. 1980.
52. J. Andrews, 'Henry Pratt, surveyor of Kerry estates' in *Jour. Kerry Arch. and Hist. Soc.*, XIII (1980), pp 5-38
53. Marmaduke Coghill to Edward Southwell, 4 January 1727, BL, Add. MS 21122, f. 40
54. *Map of the county of Wexford drawn from the best authorities* (Dublin, 1798)

17   *Bernard Browne and Kevin Whelan*

1. The following account is based (for the early period) on notes by Kathleen Browne of the Brownes of Mulrankin, derived from documents in the Public Record Office, since destroyed. These papers are now in Rathronan castle (typescript copy in possession of Bernard Browne). They contain a series of transcripts by P. H. Hore of documents from the Exchequer and Memoranda Rolls, relating to the Brownes. For a pedigree of the family, see *Jn. Assoc. Pres. Memorials Dead*, IX (1915), facing p. 403 and p. 404. For brief histories of the family, see H. Murphy, *Families of county Wexford* (Dublin, 1986) pp 20-3 and [Edward Hore] 'A history of Mulrankin castle and the Browne family, *People* 31 Aug. 1889.
2. Brooks, *Knights' fees*, pp 34-5, 118
3. Hore, V, p. 146
4. Hore transcripts, Browne papers
5. *Extents Ir. Mon. possessions*, pp 362-71
6. Jeffreys, *Castles*, pp 180-3
7. Hore, V, *passim*; Murphy, *Families*, p. 20
8. Note in Kathleen Browne's hand, Browne papers.
9. Hore transcripts, *ibid*
10. Hore, IV, p. 66; transcripts of 1641 depositions in Browne papers.
11. R. Simington, *The Transplantation to Connaught 1654-1658* (Dublin, 1970), p. 192. The transplantation certificate is summarised in Hore, VI, pp 503-4.
12. *Civil Survey*, Wexford, pp 72, 76, 84, 87-8
13. Murphy, *Families*, p. 21
14. W. Fitzgerald, 'Mayglass graveyard' in *Jn. Assoc. Pres. Memorials Dead*, IX pp 385-94
15. N. Synnott, 'Concerning the Browne family' in *ibid*, pp 403-8
16. W. Cavanagh, 'Castletown Carne and its owners' in *R.S.A.I. Jn.*, I (1911), pp 246-58; 2 (1912), pp 34-45
17. Letter of Michael Browne to John Browne, 2 Mar. 1832, Browne papers
18. 'The dispossessed landowners of Ireland in 1664' in *Ir. Geneal.*, IV, no. 4 (1971), p. 289
19. Lease from Rev Edmund Ferrers to John Browne, Bigbarn, 20 Apr. 1803. Browne papers
20. K. Whelan, 'County Wexford priests in Newfoundland' in *Wex. Hist. Soc. Jn.*, X (1984), pp 55-68
21. Jeffrey, *Castles*, p. 182
22. K. Whelan (ed.), 'An account of the barony of Forth and Bargy in 1814' in *Wex. Hist. Soc. Jn.*, XI (1986-7), pp 20-21
23. K. Whelan, 'The Catholic parish, the Catholic chapel and village development in Ireland' in *Ir. Geog.*, XVI (1983), pp 1-15.
24. K. Whelan, 'The Devereux family of Tomhaggard, a case study' in *Kilmore Parish Journal*, XV (1986-7), pp 23-6

25. List of members of the Third Order of St Francis, Wexford 1763-1824, MS C 342, Franciscan Archives, Killiney.
26. Letter of Richard Browne (Fardystown) to Martin Browne (Liverpool), 21 June 1823, Browne papers. See also account book of Richard Browne, 1822.
27. D. Kerr, 'James Browne, Bishop of Kilmore 1829-1865' in *Breifne*, VI (1983-84), pp 109-54
28. K. Whelan, 'The religious factor in the 1798 rebellion in county Wexford' in P. O'Flanagan, P. Ferguson and K. Whelan (ed.), *Rural Ireland 1600-1900* (Cork, 1987), pp 62-85.
29. *People* 15 June 1898
30. Synnott, 'Brownes', p. 406
31. *People* 15 June 1898
32. *Souvenir programme. Historical exhibition of '98 relics in The Athenaeum, Enniscorthy* (Enniscorthy, 1938). Item 88
33. T. Powell, 'An economic factor in the Wexford rebellion of 1798' in *Studia Hib.*, XVI (1976), pp 140-57.
34. Whelan, 'Religious factor'
35. N. Synnott, Miscellaneous notes and draft pedigree of the Brownes of Mulrankin, N.L.I. Mic. 7166
36. *Ibid*
37. Will of Rev Edan Murphy (1806), abstracted by Commissioners for Charitable Donations and Bequests, P.R.O.I.
38. Will of Michael Browne (Harpoonstown) 1844, *ibid*
39. Will of Edmund Browne (Dublin) 1831, N.L.I. Mic. 7166
40. Murphy, *Families*, p. 233
41. *Burke's Irish Family Records* (London, 1976) 'Synnott of Furness, county Kildare'
42. *Ibid*
43. Flood, *Ferns*, p. 131
44. Kerr, 'Bishop Browne'
45. Will of John Browne (1820), Browne papers
46. Marriage settlement of John Nolan and Alice Browne, 12 Sept. 1814, Browne papers.
47. Hilary Murphy, personal communication.
48. We are grateful to Michael Browne for showing us around Bigbarn.
49. Martin Doyle [William Hickey] *Notes and gleanings relative to the County of Wexford* (Dublin, 1868), pp 81-2.
50. C. Cairns, *Irish Tower Houses* (Athlone, 1987), pp 21-6
51. Letter of James Browne to — Hogan, 16 June 1858, N.L.I. MS 8561.
52. Letter of Michael Browne to Anne Browne, 17 May 1819, *ibid*.
53. Letters of Michael and John Browne 1819-20. *Ibid*
54. Letter of Michael Browne to Richard Browne, 12 Apr. 1820. *Ibid*.
55. Letter of Michael Browne to Anne Browne, 31 Mar. 1823. *Ibid*
56. Letter of Michael Browne to Anne and Richard Browne, 19 Feb. 1824. *Ibid*. For the Browne's subsequent career in Argentina, see E. Coghlan, *Los Irlandeses en la Argentina* (Buenos Aires, 1987) pp 78-81,
57. Letters of James Browne to Walter Redmond, 1888. N.L.I. MS 8561
58. Letter of James Browne to — Hogan, 16 June 1858. *Ibid*.
59. *Idem*
60. *Idem*
61. Letter of Richard Browne to Michael Browne, 19 Mar. 1840. *Ibid*.
62. *Idem*
63. Draft letter from Mary Browne to Bishop James Browne, n.d. *Ibid*.
64. Letter of Rev Laurence Cosgrove to Mary Browne, 20 Nov. 1886. *Ibid*.
65. Pat Sills, personal communication
66. An account of the number of malthouses located in Ireland, *Commons Jn. Ire.*, XVI (1796), *app.* ccccxix-ccccxlii
67. Subscription list, Cloney, *Narrative*
68. Flood, *Ferns*, p. xxii
69. Letter of Bishop James Browne to the clergy of Wexford town n.d. [1909], Rowe Street Church.
70. Family tree of Brownes of Mulrankin, in possession of Bernard Browne.
71. Transcript of interviews with Bernard Browne in the 1970s.
72. Obituary of Michael Browne, *People*, 7 Aug. 1912
73. H. Murphy, 'First labourers' cottages built in Ireland' in *Kilmore Parish Journal* XII (1984-5),

pp 14-16. John Francis Browne, eight year old son of Michael Browne, was asked to lay the foundation stone of the first cottage (because of his father's prominent role in getting them erected).
74. Obituary, *loc. cit.*
75. Murphy, *Families, passim*
76. For a wider perspective, see K. Whelan, 'The evolution of Catholic Society in County Wexford 1700-1850' (forthcoming).

18 *John De Courcy Ireland*

1. E. Bowen, *Britain and the western seaways* (London, 1972), p. 34
2. A good map illustrating Wexford's position in the sea traffic of those times is in W. Fitzgerald, *The historical geography of Ireland* (London, 1925), p. 72.
3. Bowen, *Seaways*, figs. 31 and 35; Fitzgerald, *Historical Geography*, p. 86
4. J. Lydon, 'An Irish army in Scotland 1296' in *Ir. Sword*, V (1962), pp 184-90
5. A. Green, *The making of Ireland and its undoing 1200-1600* (Dublin, 1920), p. 542
6. J. Burke, *Outline of the industrial history of Ireland* (Dublin, 1920)
7. D. Woodward, *The trade of Elizabethan Chester* (Hull, 1970)
8. E. Corus-Wilson, *The overseas trade of Bristol in the later middle ages* (Bristol, 1937)
9. G. Power and M. Postam, *Studies in English trade in the fifteenth century* (London, 1933)
10. A. Longfield, *Anglo-Irish trade in the sixteenth century* (Dublin, 1929)
11. *Ibid*
12. M. Doyle, [W. Hickey] *Notes and gleanings relative to the county of Wexford* (Dublin, 1868)
13. D. Waters, *The art of navigation in England in Elizabethan and early Stuart times* (London, 1958)
14. S. Tueite, *Engelsk-Norsk trelasthandel 1640-1710* (Kristiansand, 1961), app. A, pp 522-31
15. J. Mannion, 'The Waterford merchants and the Irish-Newfoundland provisions trade 1770-1820' in L. Cullen and P. Butel (ed.), *Négoce et industrie en France et en Irlande aux XVIIIe et XIXe siècles* (Paris, 1980), pp 51-63
16. P. Roberts, 'The cots of county Wexford' in *Mariner's Mirror* LXXI (1985), pp 13-34
17. Doyle, *Notes and gleanings*
18. Longfield, *Trade*, p. 65
19. Doyle, *Notes and gleanings*
20. A Lawlor, *Irish maritime survey* (Dublin, 1945)
21. Hore, V, pp 200-300
22. M. Beresford, 'François Thurot and the French attack on Carrickfergus 1757-1760' in *Ir. Sword.*, X (1972), p. 272
23. *La revue du tarn* (Spring, 1984)
24. J. de Courcy Ireland, *Ireland and the Irish in maritime history* (Dublin, 1986), p. 231
25. *Ibid.*, pp 50-1; P. Kerrigan 'The naval attack on Wexford in June 1798' in *Ir. Sword.*, XV (1983), p. 198
26. All figures are taken from the 'Abstract of the total number of ships with their tonnage, of 30 Sept. 1788' in P.R.O.N.I.
27. A. Young, *A tour in Ireland* (London, 1780)
28. J. Ranson, *Songs of the Wexford coast* (Enniscorthy, 1948)
29. J. de Courcy Ireland, *Wreck and rescue on the east coast of Ireland* (Dublin, 1983)
30. B. Colfer, *The promontory of Hook* (Wexford, 1978)
31. T. Wilson, *The Irish lighthouse service* (Dublin, 1968), pp 5-8
32. The two Cahore wrecks were noted in de Courcy Ireland, *Wreck and rescue*, p. 50. A number of five rescues by the county Wexford coast guards is listed in *Ibid.*, p. 252. Ballygarrett's chapel pews are made of timber saved from the wreck of the *Irrewaddy* in 1856.
33. J. Doyle, *The Helen Blake* (Wexford, 1979)
34. J. Maddock, *Rosslare harbour past and present* (Rosslare, 1986)
35. F. Forde, *The long watch* (Dublin, 1981)
36. J. de Courcy Ireland, *Ireland's sea fisheries, a history* (Dublin, 1981)
37. A. Kinsella, *The windswept shore: a history of the Courtown district* (Dublin, 1982), pp 70-1

38. Bord Iascaigh Mhara, Annual Report, (1981)
39. Kinsella, *Windswept shore*
40. G. Hadden, 'The Slaney gabard' in *Old Wex. Soc. Jn.*, IX (1983-4), pp 74-7
41. Roberts, 'Cot'
42. Lewis, *Topog. dict. Ire.*
43. W. Chalmers, *The life and letters of David, Earl Beatty* (London, 1951); S. Osborn (ed.), *The discovery of the North-West Passage by H.M.S. Investigator, captain R. McClure 1850-1854* (London, 1856)

Index to Persons

Murphy, 42, 138, 141, 160, 163, 345-7, 350-1, 472
Murphy, Fr. Bryan, 304-6, 309, 313, 315
Murphy, Fr. Edan, 301-2, 311, 476
Murphy, Fr. Edward, 241, 310, 313
Murphy, Francis, 303
Murphy, James, 322
Murphy, Fr. John, 131-2, 259, 261, 281, 281, 285, 287-9, 241-4, 248, 301-2, 304-8, 315
Murphy, Fr. Michael, 250, 269, 279, 285, 287, 297, 301-3, 305-9, 305-9
Murphy Mogue, 307
Murphy, Nicholas, 200, 270-4, 304, 307
Murphy, Fr. Patrick, 302, 336
Murphy, Philip, 270
Murphy, Thomas, 118
Murray, Paul, 294
Musgrave, Richard, 254-5, 261-2, 264-8, 285, 303, 466

Napper, James, 376
Neville, 99, 107, 110
Neville, A.R., 466
Neville, Bridget, 327
Neville, Nicholas, 242
Newport, Fr. Edward, 312
Nolan, 91, 472
Nolan, Catherine, 477
Nolan, John, 477-9
Nowlan, Charles, 275
Nowlan, Fr. Pelagius, 409
Nowlan, Timothy, 275
Nunn, 113, 168, 213, 217, 358, 368
Nunn, Rev. Joshua, 309
Nuzum, James, 457

O'Brien, 134, 137, 144-7
O'Brien, Patrick, 304
O'Byrne, 91, 133
O'Callaghan, Bishop Ambrose, 162
O'Connor, Fr. Miles, 277, 304, 310-11
O'Donovan, John, 42-3, 49, 52, 55-9
Ogle, George, 256, 258, 276, 312, 479
O'Hanlon-Walshe, Nicholas, 118
O'Morrow, D., 129-30
O'Neill, John, 490, 500
O'Toole, 91, 113

Palliser, 113, 167
Parle, Mathew, 118
Parsons, William, 175-81, 197-8
Paye, Fr. Walter, 163
Peppard, 137, 185
Perry, Anthony, 245, 269, 270-83, 304
Pettitt, 118, 184
Phayre, 278, 318, 321, 323
Piers, Henry 175, 177, 192
Pierce, 481
Plunkett, 141, 161, 212
Poole, Jacob, 117
Poole, John, 501

Power, 107, 217, 343-4, 351
Prendergast, 67-9, 76, 84, 98, 107, 110, 161, 304
Prendergast, John, 259, 285
Prendergast, Maurice de, 67, 160, 492
Prendergast, Patrick, 256
Purcell, Fr. James, 300-1

de Quency, Robert, 67, 69, 87
Quigley, Michael, 321-3
Quin, Martin, 270
Quinn, 216-7

Rack, 167
Ram, 113, 212, 214, 325, 352
Ram, Abel, 199
Ram, Stephen, 265, 276
Ram, Thomas, 145, 199, 225-6
Ranson, Fr. Joseph, 21, 22, 499
Raynard, James, 341
Redmond, 343, 353
Redmond, Fr. Edward, 301, 304, 311, 313
Redmond, Fr. John, 250, 266, 292, 296, 298, 301, 310-11, 315
Redmond, Fr. Michael, 292, 301
Redmond, Fr Nicholas 301, 312-3
Redmond, Patrick, 270, 304
Redmond, Walter, 482
Reilly, Barnaby, 470
Richards, 113, 350-2, 359, 368
Richards, Elizabeth, 282, 289, 303
Richards, Solomon, 45, 161, 223, 235-6
Ricroft, Thomas, 197
Ridgeway, Thomas, 180
Rinnucinni, Cardinal, 158, 229-30
Roberts 168
Robinson, 321
Roche, 68-9, 76-7, 97, 107, 161, 168, 307, 343
Roche, Christopher, 151, 224
Roche, David, 235
Roche, Edward, 172, 250, 257-8, 269-72, 250-1, 240-41, 304
Roche, Joan, 226
Roche, Bishop John, 119, 156, 226-9
Roche, Nicholas, 118
Roche, Nicholas, 118
Roche, Philip, 256, 279, 285, 292, 298, 304-10, 312, 315
Roche, Fr. Redmond, 301, 304
Roche, Thomas, 111
Rochford, 107, 263, 268, 454
Rochford, Eleanor, 477
Rochford, Paul, 231
Rochford, Robert, 224
Rogers, Fr. Thomas, 279, 310, 315
Roice, 303
Rossiter, 161, 343, 367, 472, 495
Rossiter, Christina, 224
Rossiter, Gregory, 118
Rossiter, Bishop Michael, 102, 328
Rothe, 228-9
Rotherham, Thomas, 181-2

Rotherham, Lady, 193
Rourke, John, 470
Rowe, 168, 357
Rowe, Nicholas, 470
Rowe, Ursula, 470
Royle, John, 164
Ryan, James, 340
Ryan, Nell, 486
Ryan, Fr. William, 296, 312

St. John, John de, 74
Sachaverell, William, 199
Saunders, 213
Scallan, 165, 168
Scallan, Bishop Thomas, 310
Scurlock, 206
Shallow, Fr. John, 298, 310-11, 313
Shapland, Ellen, 234
Shaw, Robert, 457
Shea, Mathew, 226
Shearer, John, 170, 255
Sheppard, 113
Sinnott, 74, 77, 98, 107, 124, 131, 133, 138, 146-7, 161, 165, 185, 235, 343, 353, 487, 495
Sinnott, David, 144
Sinnott, Edward, 138, 144
Sinnott, Fr. Edward, 270, 280, 302-3, 305-7
Sinnott, Fames, 318
Sinnott, Fr. John, 301, 312, 315
Sinnott, Judy, 480
Sinnott, Marcus, 233
Sinnott, Patrick, 242
Sinnott, Michael, 118, 301
Sinnott, Fr. Nicholas, 251, 304, 309, 312, 318
Sinnott, Piers, 193, 476-7
Sinnott, Richard, 129, 155, 224, 231
Sinnott, Thomas, 165, 277, 279-81, 294, 302, 304, 318-21
Sinnott, Walter, 129, 133, 144, 476, 485
Sinnott, Fr. William, 237, 313, 477
Sparks, George, 282, 290-4, 302
Stafford, 98, 107, 118, 161, 231, 343, 470, 476, 485, 485, 487, 500-1
Stafford, Catherine, 226
Stafford, Francis, 231
Stafford, James, 230
Stafford, John, 457
Stafford, Margaret, 153
Stafford, Colonel Nicholas, 156
Stafford, Fr. Nicholas, 269-70, 286, 301-3, 304-5, 310-3
Stafford, Peter, 155, 231
Stafford, Thomas, 470
Stafford, Rev. William, 476
Stannard, 113
Strongbow, 65-8, 84, 106, 455
Sutton, 95, 369, 496
Sutton, Ambrose, 490
Sutton, Edward, 297
Sutton, Fr. John, 310-11
Sutton, Mathew, 297
Sutton, Patrick, 297
Sutton, Samuel, 435
Sutton, Thomas, 238, 245

Index to Places

561